Tajikistan

A Political and Social History

Tajikistan

A Political and Social History

**Kirill Nourzhanov and
Christian Bleuer**

Australian
National
University

E PRESS

Published by ANU E Press
The Australian National University
Canberra ACT 0200, Australia
Email: anuepress@anu.edu.au
This title is also available online at http://epress.anu.edu.au

National Library of Australia Cataloguing-in-Publication entry

Author: Nourzhanov, Kirill, author.

Title: Tajikistan : a political and social history / Kirill Nourzhanov ; Christian Bleuer.

ISBN: 9781925021158 (paperback) 9781925021165 (ebook)

Subjects: Tajikistan--Politics and government--1991-
           Tajikistan--Social conditions.
           Tajikistan--Social life and customs.

Other Authors/Contributors:
           Bleuer, Christian, author.

Dewey Number: 958.6086

Cover design and layout by ANU E Press

Cover image: *A statue of Lenin in eastern Tajikistan rises in front of a portrait of Tajik President
Emomali Rahmon* by Theodore Kaye: www.theodorekaye.com

Printed by Griffin Press

Contents

List of Maps, Figures and Tables

Maps

Figures

Tables

Acknowledgments

The authors would like to acknowledge The Australian National University and especially its Centre for Arab and Islamic Studies (CAIS), which nurtured this project intellectually, administratively and financially. We could not have had a better environment in which to complete the book. Many people in Australia and beyond helped us with inspirational ideas, sources of information, by reading draft chapters and correcting errors and infelicities; we name but a few of them below and hasten to add that the mistakes that remain are wholly our responsibility.

Kirill Nourzhanov would like to thank Dr Christian Bleuer—that the book has been completed at all is due to his tireless energy, enormous expertise, and impeccable work ethic. Professor Amin Saikal, the CAIS Director, took personal interest in the project and gave me valuable support. I owe a debt of gratitude to Associate Professor Matthew Gray, Dr Doug Sturkey and Ms Leila Kouatly at CAIS for their friendship and sage advice. Professor Reuel Hanks at Oklahoma State University read the entire manuscript and offered criticism while seriously ill—you are a true champion! My thanks go to Professor Craig Reynolds, who had faith in the project despite Tajikistan's low profile on the Australian research agenda. I am forever in debt to Iskandar Asadulloev, Safar Haqdod and Zafar Saidi, who helped and sheltered me during the civil war in Tajikistan, and who have contributed to my research immensely over the past two decades.

Christian Bleuer would like to acknowledge the people who were instrumental in helping him complete his PhD dissertation, much of which made up his contribution to this book. First of all, I thank my dissertation committee: Professor Amin Saikal, Dr Kirill Nourzhanov and Dr Robert L. Canfield. I am extremely grateful to have had the benefit of this high level of expertise on Central Asia while a PhD candidate at CAIS. Professor Saikal provided the firm guidance that kept me on track and reasonably on time with my work. His knowledge of Central Asian culture, history and politics was invaluable. Dr Nourzhanov's deep understanding of Tajikistan and Central Asia is what allowed me to produce my dissertation. He never failed to guide me towards the best sources, and the feedback he provided on my numerous drafts enabled me to vastly improve on the work that I had produced. I am also very grateful to Dr Canfield, who, despite being far away at Washington University in St Louis, graciously agreed to be on my dissertation committee. His comments and criticism were valuable in refining my work into the state that it is now in.

Additionally, I would like to thank Professor Saikal and Dr Nourzhanov for working to secure a scholarship that allowed me to come to The Australian National University for my studies. I am indebted to the government and taxpayers of Australia for funding my scholarships (the ANU PhD scholarship and the Endeavour International Postgraduate Research Scholarship). And for helping me through the bureaucratic and administrative processes here at the ANU I would also like to express my gratitude to Carol Laslett, Anita Mack and Leila Kouatly. Outside the university, I would like to thank my parents for supporting my education. I would also like to thank my numerous friends who encouraged me at every step of my time in university. As for those many people in Tajikistan who helped me in so many ways, I will, due to the current social and political situation there, thank them personally—and privately.

List of Abbreviations

APC	armoured personnel carrier
ASSR	Autonomous Soviet Socialist Republic
BCP	Bukharan Communist Party
CC	Central Committee
CIS	Commonwealth of Independent States
CPCO	Committee for Protection of Constitutional Order
CPSU	Communist Party of the Soviet Union
CPT	Communist Party of Tajikistan
CPUz	Communist Party of Uzbekistan
DPT	Democratic Party of Tajikistan
GBAO	Gorno-Badakhshan Autonomous Oblast
GGT	General-Governorship of Turkestan
GNR	Government of National Reconciliation
GOSPLAN	Soviet State Planning Authority
IMU	Islamic Movement of Uzbekistan
IRP	Islamic Revival Party (of Tajikistan)
IRPU	Islamic Revival Party of the USSR
MRD	Motorised Rifle Division
NEP	New Economic Policy
NKVD	People's Commissariat of Internal Affairs
OGPU	Joint State Political Directorate
OMON	special police unit within the Interior Ministry
OSCE	Organisation for Security and Cooperation in Europe
PEEPFT	Permanent Expedition for Exploring Productive Forces of Tajikistan
RFE/RL	Radio Free Europe/Radio Liberty
SADUM	Spiritual Directorate of the Muslims of Central Asia and Kazakhstan
SSR	Soviet Socialist Republic
STB	Special Tasks Battalion
STTMC	South Tajik Territorial Manufacturing Complex
STTPC	South Tajik Territorial Production Complex
SWB SU	*Summary of World Broadcasts—Soviet Union* (BBC)
Tajik SSR	Tajik Soviet Socialist Republic

TASSR	Turkestan Autonomous Soviet Socialist Republic
TCCR	Temporary Committee for Crisis Resolution
TCP	Turkestan Communist Party
UTO	United Tajik Opposition
VKP	All-Union Communist Party
VKP(b)	All-Union Communist Party (Bolsheviks)
YDC	Youths of Dushanbe City

Note on Transliteration

The basic purpose for choosing the transliteration system that we have is to avoid any special characters that are not on a standard keyboard (with some further simplifications). For transliterating/Romanising Tajik names, places and concepts from the Tajik Cyrillic alphabet, we will avoid all systems of transliteration that use special characters or diacritics. Instead, we will use the unnamed system that has become the standard commonly used in Tajikistan. Basically, it is the BGN/PCGN system with some small alterations. The alterations: 'И' and 'Ӣ' will both be transliterated as 'i' (for example, the first and second 'i' in *Hisori* are different letters in Tajik Cyrillic); 'ъ' will be omitted (for example, *tarikh*, not *ta'rikh*) in the main text (with a few exceptions, such as for the *La'li Badakhshan* movement), but not in the bibliography and footnotes; both 'ӯ' and 'у' will be transliterated as 'u'; while 'э' and 'е' will both be rendered as 'e'. This system may be jarring for those familiar with common transliterations of Dari, Farsi, Urdu and Arabic due to name transliterations such as Abdullo and Rahmon instead of Abdullah and Rahman. Variants on place and people names from Tajikistan that have become commonly accepted in English will not be put through the same strict transliteration (for example, Tajikistan, Uzbek and Pamir; not Tojikiston, Uzbak and Pomir). What will be completely avoided in the main text is transliterating Tajik via Russian (for example, Kulob, Qurghonteppa and Rahmon; not Kulyab, Kurgan-Tyube and Rakhmon). An exception will be made when we directly quote an author.

Bibliographic entries and citations in Russian that include Tajik places or people will be transliterated using a Russian Romanisation system. The system of Russian transliteration for Slavic and Russian names, titles and concepts in the main text will not strictly follow one single system. The bibliography and footnote references for all Russian titles will follow a transliteration system closest to the BGN/PCGN standard, with an exception when another author's citation appears in the footnotes.

Map 1 Tajikistan's Neighbours and Major Cities

Source: National Library of Australia.

Introduction

At the very beginning of Perestroika an old dusty Tajik in Dushanbe said: 'If a single man dies of Perestroika, then what is this Perestroika for?' But thousands have died, and millions will die if this bloody dark mute Cart of Death roaming across the smashed Russian Empire is not stopped. O Allah! Where is that old Tajik? Perhaps, killed in the civil war, or died of starvation? Who listened to this old man and other old men of our land? What is happening in our destroyed bleeding country? This is a revolt of children against fathers and grandfathers … And this is the most horrid revolt! The most bloody and horrific primordial troglodyte sin in the land of men!

— Timur Zulfikarov

Pain and bitterness permeate these words of one of the foremost contemporary Tajik writers.[1] And bewilderment as well—bewilderment at the outburst of violence and destruction that in the early 1990s swept through Tajikistan, hitherto quiescent for so many years. Why did the bloodshed occur in Tajikistan and not in the neighbouring republics of the former Soviet Union? What were the origins of the conflict? Who was on the winning and losing sides? What factors shaped the composition of the opposing parties to the conflict? These are but a few questions, the answers for which can only be provided by a systematic exploration of the Tajiks' history, politics and society.

Until the break-up of the Soviet Union, Western scholars neglected Tajikistan for a number of reasons. Its remote geographic location made physical access to the republic almost impossible for foreigners. The fact that Tajikistan bordered Afghanistan and China and had a large network of strategic installations on its territory, including uranium mines and missile bases, had made Soviet security services extremely vigilant and alert in the republic, so the trickle of information emanating to the outside world from Tajikistan, and about Tajikistan, was heavily censored and scant. Finally, Tajikistan was always viewed, and not without grounds, as a bastion of Soviet power, invariably loyal to the Kremlin, and was always treated as a dull political backwater of the USSR even in comparison with other Central Asian republics. Not surprisingly, in seven decades of Soviet rule, only one monograph devoted to the history and politics of Tajikistan was published in the West, and that was in 1970.[2] Many important trends, events

---

1   Quoted from Timur Zulfikarov, 'Khodzha Nasreddin i perestroika', *Literaturnaia gazeta* (13 March 1996), p. 7.
2   Teresa Rakowska-Harmstone, *Russia and Nationalism in Central Asia: The Case of Tadzhikistan* (Baltimore and London: The Johns Hopkins Press, 1970). A truly unique study, in terms of scope and insightful generalisations, it has retained relevance until today, although the methodology employed in Rakowska-Harmstone's book, based chiefly on the notion of 'Russification' of Tajikistan, is discarded in the thesis.

and patterns of continuity and change in Tajikistan, especially in the crucial period between 1965 and 1992, have so far remained ignored, overlooked or misinterpreted by the scholarly community. In recent years there has been some excellent work done on the very late 1980s and early 1990s, but in only a narrow or fragmented manner. In the meantime, this country represents an important aspect of Central Asian politics, with all its inherent modalities and controversies unprecedentedly amplified and exposed in the post-communist era. Thus, analysing issues of political development in Tajikistan may facilitate a better and more nuanced understanding of the entire region.

The Tajiks and the Tajik State

Descended primarily from the original sedentary population of Central Asia, Tajiks followed a peculiar cycle of civilisational adaptation in the wake of numerous dislocations brought about by outside forces, usually in the form of military conquest: political subjugation, adjustment, cultural synthesis, the rise of a new social order and its decay, once again, due to external influences. The invasions of Alexander the Great, the Turks, the Arabs, the Mongols and the Uzbeks were the major landmarks in these processes. The latest cultural dislocation in Tajikistan was associated with the establishment of communist rule after 1917. It initiated a new adaptation cycle, which formed the broader historical context for political occurrences in modern Tajikistan. The state remains the major focus of analysis in this monograph, but only as one of a multitude of social institutions in Tajikistan that compete for the ability to prescribe rules of behaviour for the populace.[3] Even if the state in Tajikistan cannot challenge the lasting influence of people's loyalties to kinship, religious and ethnic groups, it is certainly capable of acting as a mediator and incorporator in relation to these communities. Henceforth, the political system in Tajikistan is analysed from positions of instrumentalism—that is, its efficiency in regulating the competition for resources amongst elites representing various communities.

From the 1930s until the mid 1980s the regime in Tajikistan did not face any legitimation crises, having attained a high degree of stability based on broad elite consensus, with formal and informal rules of political behaviour accepted, if not grudgingly, by all players involved. As part of the process of state consolidation in Tajikistan during the Soviet era, state structures did indeed penetrate local society; however, the process was only partially successful. The government had no choice at times but to accommodate local strongmen and traditional patterns

---

3   This approach, detailed by Joel S. Migdal, provides for a better understanding of autonomous political actors and their vibrancy and adaptability to crisis conditions. See Joel S. Migdal, *Strong Societies and Weak States: State–Society Relations and State Capabilities in the Third World* (Princeton, NJ: Princeton University Press, 1988).

of social organisation, religious belief, identities and loyalties.[4] The result at the level of centre–periphery relations was the central (Soviet Union) and republic-level (Tajik Soviet Socialist Republic) governments' use of local cleavages as a power-balancing and patronage tool—thereby sustaining the cleavages, even if in a transformed state. The alliance of local networks and actors with the central government gave regional actors a stake in the success or failure of the political arrangements in the national government—thereby tying highly localised issues to national political issues. In Tajikistan, such cleavages were present in the increasingly contentious politics of the late Soviet era and, strongly linked to Gorbachev's reforms, reached a critical situation in the second half of the 1980s.

The Civil War in Tajikistan

Generally referred to as the 'Tajik Civil War', the violent conflict in southern Tajikistan lasted from late spring 1992 until its official end in June 1997 with the signing of a peace agreement and power-sharing arrangement. In regards to the analysis of the war, the main focus in this work will be on the first phase of conflict that finished at the end of 1992. During this early period the majority of fatalities occurred—including both civilians and armed combatants. Early guesstimates (which went almost entirely unchallenged)[5] for the conflict as a whole cited the number of deaths as high as 100 000; however, a later study put the number at 23 500, with 20 000 of these deaths occurring in 1992.[6] This should in no way lessen the emphasis on the level of suffering during the war. Aside from the deaths of combatants and numerous unarmed civilians, the conflict generated a massive number of refugees and internally displaced persons, led to large-scale destruction and looting of property, resulted in the rape and torture of many, and further harmed the already fragile economy while devastating the livelihoods of many in Tajikistan.

At the end of 1992 the armed opposition suffered a heavy defeat and fled to mountainous areas of eastern Tajikistan and, importantly, to a safe haven in

---

4   Again, this phenomenon is referred to in Migdal's analysis of Third-World states. See, for example, Migdal, *Strong Societies and Weak States*, pp. 263–4.

5   This general assessment of problematic estimates for war fatalities matches Tajikistan quite well: 'For many conflicts, commonly cited estimates employed in media and NGO reports are repeated so frequently as to become unquestioningly accepted as truth … In many cases, the origin of these estimates is unknown or … even where this information is available, the methodology and definitional guidelines used in generating the estimates are rarely transparent.' See: Kristine Eck and Lisa Hultman, 'One-Sided Violence against Civilians in War: Insights from New Fatality Data', *Journal of Peace Research*, Vol. 44, No. 2 (2007), p. 237.

6   Vladimir Mukomel', 'Demograficheskie Posledstviia etnicheskikh i religional'nykh konfliktov v SNG', *Naselenie & Obshchestvo*, No. 27 (April 1997), Table 1, <http://demoscope.ru/acrobat/ps27.pdf>; 'Demographic Consequences of Ethnic and Regional Conflicts in the CIS', *Russian Social Science Review*, Vol. 42, No. 3 (2001), pp. 23–4, Table 1. Mukomel has a longer format study that includes full references: 'Vooruzhennye mezhnatsional'nye i regional'nye konflikti: lyudskie poteri, ekonomicheskii ushcherb i sotsial'nye posledstviia', in *Identichnost' i konfliki v postsovetskikh gosudarstvakh* (Moscow: Karnegi, 1997).

Afghanistan, where the 'Islamic' opposition attempted to regroup. The character of the war from this point was more that of a counterinsurgency with sporadic guerrilla warfare, as well as smaller operations against opposition strongholds in the mountains of the peripheral areas of the east, rather than what was seen during the first year: a complete collapse of the state and a fight that was roughly equal until October 1992. The first phase of the civil war went beyond ethnic Tajiks fighting each other, and included ethnic Uzbeks and Pamiris on opposite sides allied to their Kulobi and Gharmi Tajik allies, respectively. And even this is too simple a description, as it is not possible to neatly classify the main combatants into monolithic blocs based on ethnicity and, for Tajiks, region of origin. Nevertheless, factors such as ideology and religion will be de-emphasised, in line with much of the later scholarship on the civil war.

The relevance of social and political divisions necessitates an in-depth historical and social analysis of ethnicity, religion, social organisation, migration, state-building, politics and economics in Tajikistan (especially during the Soviet era). All of these factors played a role in shaping the loyalties and actions of individuals and groups during the prewar era through to the outbreak of conflict. When the power struggles in Dushanbe led to civil unrest and violent conflict, national-level elites and local powerbrokers mobilised support from the local level, drawing on and appealing to ties of identity, shared economic concerns and common security dilemmas. Language, ethnicity, sub-ethnic identity, religious sect, region of origin, collective farm affiliation, family ties, professional relationships, political party membership, employer–employee ties and government patron–client networks have all been cited as factors in determining individual and group participation or non-participation in the conflict. Each one of these categories played a role in determining behaviour during the civil war—of course some of them to a far lesser degree than others.

Analysis in this work will go beyond the national level in the capital and focus also on the main zone of violent conflict: the economically significant Vakhsh Valley of southern Tajikistan, a few hours' drive south of the capital, Dushanbe.

At the beginning of the Soviet era, the Vakhsh Valley was a sparsely populated river valley inhabited mostly by semi-nomadic Uzbeks.[7] It would soon become a grand project of Soviet agricultural and social engineering. After suppressing the *Basmachi* rebellion and securing the Afghan border during the 1930s, the Soviet authorities began their transformation of the Vakhsh Valley. The meandering Vakhsh River was soon controlled and diverted into a system of irrigation canals as part of a plan to boost agriculture in the Tajik Republic. Food production had limited economic significance for Soviet industrialisation plans, so agricultural production was focused mainly on cotton—a crop that required significant amounts of irrigation in the arid region.

---

7   This includes Uzbek speakers who claim a tribal affiliation as their primary identity (for example, Loqay).

Map 2 Satellite View of Tajikistan with the Vakhsh Valley Circled

Source: NASA public domain licence image. Upload credit: <http://commons.wikimedia.org/wiki/ User:Poulpy> Modification by authors: circle added.

One of the main requirements for the labour-intensive projects of building irrigation canals and farming cotton was a large pool of workers. This necessitated the massive in-migration of people from throughout Tajikistan and beyond. Since the economic potential of the mountains and foothills of Tajikistan was quite limited, people from these areas were selected as the primary core of migrants. The main groups of settlers were drawn, often forcefully, from the mountain valleys of Qarotegin (now known as 'Rasht') and Darvoz, as well as from the foothills of the Kulob region. Here in the valley they, and other outsiders (for example, Pamiris, Russians and others), were settled into the Soviet collective farms that were a common feature throughout the rural areas of the Tajik Soviet Socialist Republic (hereinafter Tajik SSR) and the rest of the USSR. At independence, more than half a century later, the Vakhsh Valley was part of Qurghonteppa Province—an administrative region with a high degree of social and political-bureaucratic fragmentation where competition for resources occurred increasingly along lines of ethnicity and, most significantly, mainly along lines of region of origin: the Gharmi Tajiks from the mountainous area of Gharm (Qarotegin and Darvoz) and the Kulobi Tajiks from the foothills of the neighbouring Kulob Province. Again, as mentioned above, the blocs in the conflict were not monolithic and should be seen as the end result of not just long-term historical and cultural factors, but also more recent political and economic competition, as well as a result of the initial tactics and strategies of mobilising for political struggles and war.

The Soviet authorities attempted to shape ethnic identities throughout the USSR, and in Central Asia there were particular difficulties as most people here did not see their primary identities at the ethnic or national level. As part of the Soviet process, languages were standardised, traditions codified, pre-existing sub-ethnic identities (for example, tribe or city) were suppressed (for instance, by being removed as an option in the official census), privileges were granted or denied based on ethnic identity, and many people found that they were outside the borders of their titular republic (for example, ethnic Uzbeks inside Tajikistan). Despite the continuing rhetoric that the divisions between nationalities (that is, ethnic groups) would eventually disappear and give way to a unified people, ethnic identities continued to be strongly promoted in the Soviet republics, and Tajikistan was no exception. There were, however, also divisions within the ethnic groups. For Tajiks, there was the reality that ethnic Tajiks from different regions had obvious differences in dialect and in many other aspects of their culture.

Regional differences are a common feature of many countries, but they held—and still hold—a particular social, economic and political significance in Tajikistan. During the post–World War II period, Tajiks from the northern province of Leninobod (now Sughd)—particularly from the city of Khujand—dominated the upper echelons of the Tajik SSR's government and they cultivated patronage networks that were dominated by co-regionals. Besides competition within northern Tajikistan, these northern Tajiks then had to contend with their less privileged southern counterparts, whose elites also organised intricate patronage networks that came to be identified with regions such as Kulob and Gharm. Of course, the people in these networks were not completely averse to cooperating with outsiders in mutually beneficial arrangements, especially at the higher levels. And the networks did not benefit all people in a particular region, so it should be considered that they were dominated by people from a single region and mostly based there (and in the capital) rather than entire regions and their populations competing against each other.

Nevertheless, the end result was the 'politicisation' of regional identities—elites and those within their regional networks would benefit or suffer based on government appointments and bureaucratic decisions. For example, when a Kulobi held the post of minister of the interior, Kulobi Tajiks dominated the ranks of that ministry. The police force continued to be dominated by Kulobis throughout most of the 1980s. But when a Pamiri was appointed to that post during the late 1980s, ethnic Pamiris moved into the ministry in large numbers and displaced Kulobis from their positions—creating a pool of unemployed (and presumably angry) Kulobi former police officers.[8] Concerning Tajiks from Gharm, they had a more modest level of access to national-level positions in the late Soviet era, and many turned instead to entrepreneurship and 'grey market' activities such as selling agricultural products to markets not just in Tajikistan, but in other republics as well. This activity was especially significant in the Vakhsh Valley, which was now home to many Gharmi and Kulobi Tajiks. At a more official level, the competition for government posts at the district and provincial levels, as well as for the top positions in the collective and state farms of Qurghonteppa Province (at times subsumed within Khatlon Province), was particularly fierce. An official position gave a person access to resources and jobs that they could then distribute. Losing one's position meant far more than one disappointed Communist Party cadre; an entire network would then be at risk of losing benefits such as jobs, university acceptance, equipment, fertilisers, and other political and economic goods.

The authorities in Dushanbe and Moscow were generally able to control this process within the authoritarian system of the Soviet Union; however, this 'control' was only in the sense that cadres did not challenge the arrangements at the highest levels. In Tajikistan, corruption was pervasive and local apparatchiks competed to replace each other—but within the system. Eventually, in the mid 1980s, this system began to break down in the Tajik SSR. Anticorruption campaigns and *perestroika* reforms resulted in the removal and replacement of many apparatchiks in the republic. By the end of this process, Gharmis and Pamiris were able to obtain positions that were previously out of reach. In the Vakhsh Valley the turnover of leadership at the district and provincial levels, as well as in the collective and state farms, was unprecedented. Kulobis and Gharmis, often living in mixed settlements, competed against each other for these positions as they were all-important in securing economic and social benefits locally. The local positions were tied into the political wrangling at the republic level, giving locals a strong stake in national politics.

Around the same time (the late 1980s and the beginning of the 1990s), the political and social atmosphere became less restrictive. Civil society groups and political parties began to form and agitate for further changes. After some time the political foes settled into two opposing coalitions: the incumbent leadership dominated by elites from Leninobod along with their primary junior partners from Kulob and Hisor, and the opposition coalition that included new political parties such as the mostly urban Democratic Party of Tajikistan, the Gharmi Tajik-dominated Islamic Revival Party, and the Pamiri party La'li Badakhshon. The first post-independence presidential election of November 1991, after some difficulty and the replacement of the top government candidate, was won by the

---

8   This anecdote is fully analysed later in this book.

incumbent forces' candidate, Rahmon Nabiev, at the expense of the opposition coalition and their cinematographer-turned-politician candidate, Davlat Khudonazarov—a man supported by anti-conservative politicians, journalists and cultural elites at the Union/Commonwealth of Independent States (CIS) level. This was followed by a period of government crackdowns and harassment of the opposition, resulting in large anti-government street demonstrations in the capital starting in early spring 1992. The largest contribution to the opposition's demonstrations was by the Islamic Revival Party (IRP). Meanwhile, the incumbents, geographically isolated in the capital from their home base in northern Tajikistan and unable to easily summon their supporters to the streets, relied instead on their junior Kulobi partners whose province was adjacent to the capital. The IRP's mobilisation effort also had a regional aspect. The leadership of the IRP, despite their pretentions to being a party for all (Sunni) Muslims, was heavily staffed by Tajiks with roots in one particular region. The IRP was more accurately a party for Muslims that was overwhelmingly dominated by Gharmi Tajiks.

As the demonstrations intensified and eventually turned to violence, political and social authorities who could not quickly mobilise manpower for violent conflict became powerless. The skilled technocrats increasingly lost power to savvy rural strongmen and religious leaders (for example, mullahs) who could call on the support of men willing to fight. The urban intellectuals and reformists of groups such as the Democratic Party were helpless in the face of military mobilisation. Soon it was clear that the real players in the conflict were the Kulobi Tajik militias allied to local Uzbeks and militias from Hisor on one side against the IRP's mullahs and their Gharmi Tajik followers allied to Gharmi-dominated Dushanbe street gangs and Pamiri police officers and militias on the other.

* * *

The violent civil conflict that erupted in 1992 was a striking watershed in Tajikistan's history. People in that country are now accustomed to view politics, social events, and often their daily lives—what they did, where they went, how they grieved and celebrated, even what they ate and drank—in terms of 'before' and 'after' this catastrophe. We, too, follow such bifurcation in narrating the past of Tajikistan by focusing on key trends and events that culminated in large-scale fratricide and national tragedy. Quite another story needs to be told about the subsequent process of healing and reconciliation, as well as that of state-building and the consolidation of power.

While there is no single authoritative scholarly examination of the civil war in Tajikistan,[9] there are many sources that provide a strong analysis of certain aspects of the conflict. The only problem here is that the analysis in this literature is focused mainly in two areas: variables that caused the conflict[10] and post-conflict state-building.[11] This is understandable as people, institutions and governments want to know what triggers conflicts, and, once they have commenced, how they may be resolved; however, a more comprehensive historical and social analysis is required in order to fully explain the processes that led to the Tajik civil war. And this necessitates a full historical background to the modern state of Tajikistan, to the social structure of the country, and to the shaping and formation of identities and loyalties in Tajikistan. Additionally, a special focus on the period immediately preceding the civil war will be provided. This requires a full narrative and analysis of the transition from political competition to violent conflict (late 1980s to May 1992) and a similar, but shorter, treatment for the mobilisation of forces and the first phase of the war (May 1992 to the end of that year). Other accounts give far too little information about these two periods as a whole, or provide great analysis of only a narrow aspect of the political competition and conflict. This book will demonstrate the logic behind the outbreak and continuation of conflict, and will show that the cultural and political factors shaping the opposing sides into regional and ethnic blocs are steeped in history.

---

9   The best, though still incomplete, candidate for this would be a Russian book: V. I. Bushkov and D. V. Mikulskii, *Anatomiia grazhdanskoi voiny v Tadzhikistane (etno-sotsial'nye protsessi i politicheskaia bor'ba, 1992–1995)* (Moscow: Rossiiskaia Akademiia Nauk, 1996).

10   Idil Tuncer Kilavuz, *Understanding Violent Conflict: A Comparative Study of Tajikistan and Uzbekistan*. Unpublished PhD dissertation, Indiana University, 2007; Lawrence Markowitz, *Collapsed and Prebendal States in Post-Soviet Eurasia: Cross-Regional Determinants of State Formation in Tajikistan and Uzbekistan*. Unpublished PhD dissertation, University of Wisconsin, 2005; Jonathan K. Zartman, *Political Transition in Central Asian Republics: Authoritarianism Versus Power-Sharing*. Unpublished PhD dissertation, University of Denver, 2004.

11   See, for example: M. Olimov, ed. *Mezhtadzhikskiy konflikt: put' k miru* (Moscow: Rossiiskaia Akademiia Nauk, 1998); John Heathershaw, *Post-Conflict Tajikistan: The Politics of Peacebuilding and the Emergence of Legitimate Order* (London: Routledge, 2009); Luigi De Martino, ed. *Tajikistan at a Crossroads: The Politics of Decentralization* (Geneva: Cimera, 2004).

1. Tajiks on the Crossroads of History, from Antiquity to the Age of Colonialism

It is impossible to study the process of change in any society in the modern era without exploring its historical setting. Establishing a multidisciplinary framework that first combines elements of ethnic history, social anthropology and comparative political development has obvious advantages when it comes to analysing such a complex and ancient society as Tajikistan's. Tajikistan has a rich and varied history that connects far beyond the area of present-day Tajikistan and Central Asia to the broader Eurasian landmass. It is notable that the caravan routes of what has come to be referred to as the 'Silk Road'[1] crossed the territory of what now is Tajikistan.[2] The road's northern trail went through Khujand and the Zarafshon Valley and the southern one traversed the Pamir Mountains of Badakhshan. This land had become the meeting point of Mediterranean, Indian and Chinese civilisations; people who lived here used this opportunity to adopt technologies, state concepts and religious teachings and to develop them further using vast local resources. There were, however, communities thriving here long before. Urban settlements that served as centres of commerce and craftsmanship were present in Central Asia in the early Bronze Age, circa 3000 BC.[3] The influence of ancient civilisations in the region was complemented by the constant interaction between sedentary and nomadic cultures. In the beginning of the second millennium BC the Indo-Iranian tribes penetrated Central Asia. The onslaught of these steppe herdsmen was a lengthy process and it was not until five centuries later that they succeeded in assimilating the local peoples, adopting the latter's achievements and giving up to a considerable extent their pastoral way of life. As a result, a number of mixed-type cultures emerged in the territory of Tajikistan, which combined highly developed arable farming with cattle-breeding and extensive use of the horse for military purposes and transportation.[4] The Aryans had laid the foundation for the formation of the Iranian ethnos and culture in the region; language continuity became a decisive factor in this process.

---

1   'Silk Road' is a term that was never used locally, but rather was coined in the nineteenth century by the German geographer Ferdinand von Richthofen.
2   The establishment of effective long-distance trade between China and the Mediterranean dates back to the late second millennium BC, whilst irregular trade and migratory contacts along the Silk Road might be far older. See: Andre Gunder Frank, *The Centrality of Central Asia* (Amsterdam: VU University Press, 1992), p. 30.
3   Frank I. Holt, *Alexander the Great and Bactria: The Formation of A Greek Frontier in Central Asia* (Leiden: Brill, 1988), p. 27.
4   V. M. Masson, 'The Decline of the Bronze Age Civilization and Movements of the Tribes', in *History of Civilizations of Central Asia*, Vol. I (Paris: UNESCO, 1992), pp. 350–1.

Prior to the rise of the Achaemenid Empire, centres such as Khorezm, Soghd and Bactria dominated in the region, while a number of lesser principalities such as Khuttal (contemporary Kulob) retained independence and ruling dynasties of their own; however, despite the ethnic homogeneity of the population and close cultural and economic bonds, these territories had not merged into a centralised state with a complex government machine. There still remained localised autonomies that once in a while recognised the supremacy of one over the others, for a short time only. In the wake of the military expeditions of Cyrus II in the middle of the sixth century BC, the central and southern regions of Central Asia became part of the Achaemenid Empire. Eventually, military defeats sustained by Darius III at the hands of Alexander the Great quickly led to the disintegration of the Achaemenid Empire. Alexander subjugated most of its eastern territories from 330 to 327 BC. In the centuries that followed Alexander's death in 323 BC, Transoxiana once again found itself a border zone, torn apart by different centres of power, such as Parthia, Graeco-Bactria and the Kushan and Sasanian empires. In the late fourth and early fifth centuries AD, a new force appeared in the steppes adjacent to Khujand—the north-eastern outposts of the Iranian civilisation—namely, the Turkic tribes of the Ephthalites[5] and the Huns. Like all their nomadic predecessors, they quickly settled down, mostly in urban centres. The Turks would come to exert a great influence over the formation of ethnic groups in Central Asia before the Arab conquest, and long after it.

V. V. Barthold expressed the view that a period of more than 1000 years from Alexander the Great to the advent of Islam passed almost unnoticed in terms of state formation and political organisation in Transoxiana.[6] By the time of the Arab invasion, the Central Asian lands were divided among as many as 27 petty princedoms.[7] Their rulers did not enjoy absolute authority, as the real power lay with the traditional landed aristocracy (the *dihqans*), who had fortified castles and small private armies at their disposal. In times of trouble, princes had literally to grovel to their supposed vassals for help.[8] The whole picture bore a striking resemblance to the post-Achaemenid period, when the political map of Central Asia was changing kaleidoscopically.[9] The Central Asian principalities never formed a viable confederacy. On top of mutual mistrust and hostility, there had emerged more fundamental divisions between the communities in

---

5   The assumption that the Ephthalites were Turkic prevails, but some authors trace Iranian (B. G. Ghafurov, *Tojikon: Ta'rikhi qadimtarin, qadim va asri miyona*, Vol. 1 [Dushanbe: Irfon, 1983], p. 278) or even Mongol (Rene Grousset, *The Empire of the Steppes* [New Brunswick, NJ: Rutgers University Press, 1970], p. 67) features in their making.

6   V. V. Barthold, *Sochineniia*, Vol. II, Part 1 (Moscow: Izdatelstvo vostochnoi literatury, 1963), p. 117.

7   H. A. R. Gibb, *The Arab Conquests in Central Asia* (New York: AMS Press, 1970), p. 8.

8   Iu. Yakubov, *Pargar v VII–VIII vekakh nashei ery* (Dushanbe: Donish, 1979), p. 41.

9   Some of the local oligarchs traced their roots down to the Kushan times. See: *Istoriia Tadzhikskogo naroda*, Vol. II, kn. 1 (Moscow: Izdatelstvo vostochnoi literatury, 1964), p. 45.

the Zarafshon and Oxus valleys by the seventh century AD. The populace to the north of the Hisor mountain range had become Turkicised to a considerable extent due to the endless immigration from the steppes.[10] By the seventh century AD, religious affiliations also varied considerably: people in the north of what is today Tajikistan professed Mazdaism, Nestorian Christianity and Manichaeism, while the bulk of the inhabitants of Tokharistan and Khuttal in the south still adhered to Buddhism.

Such conditions of disunion favoured the piecemeal conquest of Transoxiana (Central Asia) by the Arabs. Beginning in 651 AD, they organised periodic marauding raids deep into the territory of what they called 'Mavarannahr', but it was not until 705 AD that the caliphate adopted the policy of annexing the lands beyond the Oxus River (Amu Darya). Ten years later the task was accomplished.[11] By the mid eighth century, the Arabs had managed to solidify their hold over Transoxiana. They checked the advancement of the Turgesh Turks at Isfijab and defeated a strong Chinese army at Talas in 751, thus putting an end, once and for all, to Chinese claims for dominance in Mavarannahr. In regards to religion, Islam had spread rapidly in Mavarannahr; as early as 728 the authorities of Bukhara trumpeted the complete conversion of Soghdiana to the Muslim faith.[12] The new religion was mostly received with popular acclaim, for it promised greater social mobility and created favourable conditions for trade. Islam provided the peoples of Central Asia with spiritual and cultural bonds and brought them closer to each other as nothing had before. With Islam there came Arabic—not only the language of the holy Quran and the Abbasid court, but also the language of science and poetry and the lingua franca of trade and diplomacy. It also, with the massive influx of loan words, stimulated the emergence of the modern Persian language (Dari).[13] Based on the general economic rise in the region and the coexistence and fruitful interaction of Arabic and Persian literatures, the newly emerged Islamic culture reached its zenith during the rule of the Samanid dynasty (875–999). The Samanids, who originated from an old *dihqan* family, created a kingdom of their own that stretched from the

---

10 The migrants 'had swollen to such a mass as already to crush the original Iranian inhabitants under the exclusive dominion of the Turks'. See: Arminius Vambery, *History of Bokhara* (London: Henry S. King & Co., 1873), p. 18.

11 As Gibb noted, 'the existing dynastic houses were everywhere maintained, as the representatives of the conquered peoples and vehicle of the civil administration. The actual administrative authority in their territories, however, passed to the Wali, or agent of the Arab governor of Khorasan.' See: Gibb, *The Arab Conquests in Central Asia*, pp. 56–7.

12 Barthold, *Sochineniia*, Vol. II, Part 1, p. 456. Of course, the process of Islamisation in Transoxiana was somewhat more protracted, especially in its easternmost lands (Rushan, Shughnan and Vakhan in what is now Tajikistan); however, there is no doubt that the cultural reconciliation of Islam and Iranian tradition was accomplished in Transoxiana earlier than in the Iranian Plateau proper, where Zoroastrianism had become deeply entrenched, especially in the rural areas, under the Sasanian rule.

13 'The volume of Arabic lexicon, its share in the vocabulary of the Dari language remained exceptionally high until the first quarter of the nineteenth century.' L. N. Kiseleva, *Iazyk Dari Afganistana* (Moscow: Nauka, 1985), p. 40.

Persian Gulf to India. The relatively stable domestic and international situation allowed them to encourage learning and the arts. Intellectuals from all over the Islamic world came to Bukhara, the Samanid capital.[14]

The reign of the Samanids was brought to an end in 999 by the invasion of the Qarakhanid Turks, and power in Central Asia passed to Turkic rulers for the next nine centuries. One of the determining factors for the prosperity of culture and trades in Mavarannahr was that the new Turkic dynasties completed the process of liquidating the class of the old Iranian landed aristocracy, the *dihqans*, which had begun under the Samanids.[15] As a result, the highly stratified elite culture so characteristic of the Achaemenids and the Sasanians became more diffused amongst much of the population. Iranian urban-based strata—merchants, artisans, tradesmen—rose to eminence, and often had a say in political affairs under the Turkic rulers of Mavarannahr, who used them as a counterbalance to the nomadic nobility. This transition away from an aristocratic community made an important contribution to the formation of a single Tajik ethnic culture.

Mavarannahr fell as easy prey to the invasion of Chengiz Khan during 1219–21. The consequences of the attack of the Mongol hordes were truly horrible. Arminius Vambery has observed, in regards to the territory of what is now Central Asia, that 'no part of all Asia suffered so severely from the incursions of the Mongolian hordes as the countries bordering on the Oxus and the Yaxartes'.[16] On top of the immediate consequences of the invasion, such as depopulation, interruption of trade links and decay of cities, which were overcome to an extent in time, was that it had dramatic, long-term ramifications for Mavarannahr. The military expeditions of the Mongols were not accompanied by large-scale resettlement and sedentarisation of nomadic peoples from Mongolia. Transoxiana was treated as a source of booty to be procured during periodic raids and as a grazing ground for herds. In the absence of state-sponsored maintenance, the irrigation systems declined gradually, and vast spaces of arable land turned to pastures or even desert. In the thirteenth and the fourteenth centuries, whole clusters of villages and small towns disappeared from the map of Mavarannahr, especially in the basin of Syr-Darya.

After the death of Chengiz Khan in 1227, the Mongol Empire was divided amongst his four sons. While the Mongol rulers in Persia quickly converted to Islam, adopted all major elements of Iranian culture, language in particular, and readily employed local *ulamas* (Muslim scholars) to staff their relatively

---

14   Such was 'the influx of scholars that Bukhara won the epithet "the dome of Islam in the East", equal to Baghdad, because it was such a great meeting place for distinguished men of letters'. See: Richard N. Frye, *Bukhara: The Medieval Achievement* (Norman: University of Oklahoma Press, 1965), p. 43.

15   As Barthold has put it, 'in the beginning of the 13th century … the dihqans did not play any role and the word itself was used only in the meaning of "peasant"'. See: Barthold, *Sochineniia*, Vol. II, Part 2 (Moscow: Izdatelstvo vostochnoi literatury, 1964), p. 332.

16   Vambery, *History of Bokhara*, p. 137.

complex bureaucratic machine, the situation in Central Asia was quite different. It has been mentioned already that the Mongols themselves did not move in great numbers from their inner Asian heartland. The main force of the Mongolian explosion under Chengiz Khan actually consisted of a number of eastern Turkic tribes. They played an ever-increasing role in the Mongol army and were incorporated into the Mongol *oboghs* (clans).[17] By the beginning of the fourteenth century, the Chaghatai Mongol nobles in Central Asia had been thoroughly Turkicised and, as Samuel Adshead has pointed out, 'it was Turkish therefore that the collaborators learnt, and Turkish that they passed to the people of the oases generally'.[18] From that time on, the word 'Turkestan' gained currency in reference to Mavarannahr (the Arab term for Central Asia).[19]

All political entities based on the tribal system proved highly unstable in Central Asia. Even the impressive structure created by Timur (Tamerlane) from the Barlas tribe (1370–1405) did not survive its founder. There was an evident dichotomy, even antagonism, between the Turks who clung to the old nomadic way of life and the Turks who had become sedentarised. Their coexistence within a unified state was problematic. It was not unusual for whole groups of tribes to secede from the parent polity and return to the nomadic way of life, creating state entities of their own and ravaging their former kin. That was definitely the case in the Chaghatai Khanate, the Golden Horde and the Timurid Empire. From the end of the fourteenth century, all nomadic clans of different extraction who lived on the steppes between the Ural and the Irtysh rivers were known under the collective name of the Uzbeks.[20] In the fifteenth century they formed an autarchic community with the beginnings of state organisation, of which the Chengiz-inspired 'decimal' military machine was the most notable feature.[21] Like any other nomadic polity, it was bedevilled by the absence of legitimacy and clear rules of succession, and the central political authority remained viable only as long as it could wage successful wars, which provided clan aristocracy with plunder and status.

---

17 *Obogh*, or *unagan bogol*, is a tribal entity in which 'a single powerful clan subordinated completely some neighbouring groups of nomads, regardless of whether they were kinsmen or strangers'. See: L. P. Lashuk, 'Opyt tipologii etnicheskikh obschnostei srednevekovykh tiurok i mongolov', *Sovetskaia Etnografiia*, No. 1 (1968), p. 99.

18 S. A. M. Adshead, *Central Asia in World History* (New York: St Martin's Press, 1993), p. 80.

19 In fact, there are three Turkestans to be found in historical and geographic literature: Eastern, Western and Afghan. The second, however, was always recognised as superior culturally and politically, henceforth the general designation was conferred upon it.

20 B. A. Ahmedov, *Gosudarstvo kochevykh uzbekov* (Moscow: Nauka, 1965), p. 15.

21 The division of the army into units comprising 100, 1000 and 10 000 warriors was routine practice for steppe rulers long before Chengiz Khan; however, he applied this system as a centrepiece of the government machine: combat units became administrative units as well, and military commanders served as civil officials. See: Sh. Sandag, 'Obrazovanie edinogo mongolskogo gosudarstva i Chingiskhan', in *Tataro-mongoly v Azii i Evrope* (Moscow: Nauka, 1977), p. 35. In the Emirate of Bukhara each *vilayet* (province) consisted of several *tumans* (districts)—a word with the original meaning of a 10 000-strong army detachment.

By 1512, the Uzbeks had gradually conquered Mavarannahr and pushed vast masses of the sedentary population out of the fertile river valleys. This was the last large-scale influx of nomads into Turkestan. Afterwards, a distinctive demographic pattern emerged in what now is Tajikistan: mountainous regions were inhabited almost exclusively by the Tajiks; the broad river valleys and steppes were dominated by the Kipchak Uzbeks; while the expansive transitional areas between the two ethnic and geographic zones were characterised by a mixture of the indigenous sedentary population (Tajik and Turkic) and semi-nomadic Uzbeks.

Once the Uzbeks captured Mavarannahr, each clan was quartered around a certain city from which it collected taxes. In such circumstances the demise of the state of the nomadic Uzbeks was inevitable, but permanent warfare against the Safavids put it off until the mid 1580s. The Khans tried to find alternative means to create unity amongst the clans and sponsored Sufi orders, especially Naqshbandiya, to this end. This policy backfired, however, for the dervish brotherhoods failed to engender strong bonds in the society, and at the same time these orders became substantial economic and political forces themselves, due to lavish endowments made by the rulers. At the end of the sixteenth century, 'the Uzbek polity demilitarised itself and became a kind of Polish commonwealth: weak king, irresponsible aristocracy and dominant clericalism. The dervish orders became the leading institution in state, society and culture.'[22] The period of feudal sedition that ensued had disastrous results for Turkestan, comparable with those produced by the Mongol invasion. The endless fighting amongst Uzbek clans, exacerbated by the dramatic decline of the transcontinental caravan trade in the seventeenth century, led to economic devastation, which reached its nadir in the first half of the eighteenth century, when 'there were no citizens left in Samarkand' and 'Bukhara had only two inhabited *mahallas*'.[23] Even the rise of relatively centralised states—the khanates of Bukhara and Khiva and later Kokand—could not reverse the trend. The history of the principality of Uroteppa is illustrative of this process. In the period 1800–66, Uroteppa (Istaravshon) suffered some 50 attacks; as a result, it lost two-thirds of its population and turned into 'one of the most devastated areas of Central Asia'.[24]

---

22   Adshead, *Central Asia in World History*, p. 156.
23   A *mahalla* is a traditional neighbourhood community in a city, usually with a mosque as a centre of communal life. O. A. Sukhareva, 'Ocherki po istorii sredneaziatskikh gorodov', in *Istoriia i kultura narodov Srednei Azii (Drevnost i srednie veka)*, eds B. G. Gafurov and B. A. Litvinsky (Moscow: Nauka, 1976), pp. 133, 138.
24   A. Mukhtarov, *Materialy po istorii Ura-Tiube* (Moscow: Izdatelstvo vostochnoi literatury, 1963), p. 5.

Russia's Entry into Central Asia

In the mid nineteenth century the territory of present-day Tajikistan was divided between the emirs of Bukhara and the khans of Kokand, while Khujand, Uroteppa (Istaravshon) and Qarotegin (Rasht) remained disputed territories where dominance constantly shifted from one side to another. A number of eastern mountain *vilayets* (provinces), such as Bukhara's Darvoz and Kokand's Shughnan, Vakhan and Rushan, were virtually independent (they sent only occasional gifts to the emir or khan) and unpredictable in their political alignments, thus often presenting a liability rather than an asset for Bukhara and Kokand. In addition, Bukhara was engaged in permanent squabbles with Afghanistan over Balkh, Hisor, Kulob and the Pamir districts, and both Bukhara and Kokand had aspirations in Chinese Turkestan. On top of internal rivalries amongst constituent units and ongoing external conflicts, the khanates were cursed by a precarious dichotomy between the ancient oasis sites with their intensive agriculture, trade and urban life, on the one hand, and on the other autonomous groups of nomads who did not acknowledge the government's authority and exploited (or robbed) nearby towns at their discretion. The entry of Russia would eventually sweep aside these patterns of conflict.

In the eighteenth century, as Russia became a rapidly growing centralised land empire, it began to take an interest in expansion to the south, and took the bulk of the Kazakhs and Karakalpaks under its suzerainty between 1731 and 1742. The khanates of Turkestan, however, remained for the time being beyond the scope of Russia's imperial ambitions. The situation changed dramatically in the mid nineteenth century after Russia had suffered a number of setbacks in its European policy and, more importantly, lost its role as a major supplier of manufactured goods to world markets in competition with the United Kingdom, Germany and the United States. The share of grain and other primary produce in Russian exports to Europe reached 96 per cent, while textiles, machinery, metals and other processed goods made up 60 per cent of its sales to Central Asia.[25] In addition, Russia's nascent modern industry desperately needed raw materials, cotton in particular, which Turkestan could provide in large quantities. Such considerations induced the Russian authorities to conduct a more aggressive foreign policy in regards to the khanates of Bukhara, Khiva and Kokand. Russian expansion into Turkestan in the nineteenth century was 'a process apparently planned, logical and inexorable'[26] and so differed in this sense from the rather spontaneous mastering of Siberia. Adventurous expeditions, such

---

25   N. A. Khalfin, *Prisoedinenie Srednei Azii k Rossii* (Moscow: Nauka, 1965), p. 68.
26   Mary Holdsworth, *Turkestan in the Nineteenth Century* (Oxford: Central Asian Research Centre, 1959), p. 46.

as the Cossacks' raid on Urgench in 1603 and Bekovich-Cherkassky's mission to Khiva in 1717, gave way to a methodical advancement, based on thorough planning, which could be divided into three stages.

Between 1856 and 1864, the Russians strengthened their military presence in border areas and carried out three major reconnaissance missions in the region. While dismissing any large-scale aggressive actions, the imperial government sought to encourage Russian trade in Turkestan, to prevent the United Kingdom from inserting itself into Central Asian affairs and to foster closer ties with the Emir of Bukhara—'the most reliable and strong ruler in Central Asia'[27]—in order to exploit the animosity among the khanates.

Between 1864 and 1884, systematic conquest was launched and successfully completed. Even facing the threat of ultimate annihilation, the rulers of Bukhara and Kokand could not overcome mutual antagonism.[28] In 1867, the General-Governorship of Turkestan (GGT) was established, with its centre in Tashkent. It embodied all the territories of Kokand and Bukhara occupied until then by the Russian Army. In 1868, Kokand became a vassal of the Russian Empire and Bukhara ceded its northern cities of Khujand, Uroteppa, Panjakent, Samarkand and Qatta-Qurghon to the GGT and acknowledged its status as a Russian protectorate. Khiva followed suit in 1873 and the majority of petty principalities in eastern Bukhara (roughly corresponding with contemporary southern Tajikistan) were subjugated between 1870 and 1875. In 1876, Alexander II formally abolished the Khanate of Kokand, and in 1884, when the Turkmen city of Mary (Merv) surrendered, the whole of Turkestan was included in the Russian realm. In Hélène Carrère d'Encausse's adroit phrasing, 'despite initial anxieties as to the supposed strength of existing Muslim states and English opposition, the conquest of Central Asia had been, in the final analysis, rapid, and, on the whole, not very bloody, at least for Russia'.[29]

In the period 1866–99, the Russian authorities were preoccupied with organising efficient government and development of the subjugated territories. By the end of the century Russian Turkestan comprised the GGT with five *oblasts* (administrative regions) and two protectorates: Bukhara and Khiva. Once again the Tajiks found themselves divided by administrative borders. The northern and eastern parts of present-day Tajikistan with the cities of Panjakent, Uroteppa (Istaravshon), Nau, Khujand, Isfara and Tashqurghon were included in the

27   N. A. Khalfin, *Politika Rossii v Srednei Azii: 1857–1868* (Moscow: Izdatelstvo vostochnoi literatury, 1960) p. 123.

28   Russian General Romanovsky reported in 1866 that 'they don't conceal hatred towards each other ... and more than once expressed to me their readiness to assist us in our advancement: the Kokandis—if Bukhara is to be attacked, the Bukharans—if Kokand is to be attacked'. See: Z. D. Kastelskaia, *Iz istorii Turkestanskogo kraia* (Moscow: Nauka, 1980), p. 16.

29   Hélène Carrère d'Encausse, 'Systematic Conquest, 1865 to 1884', in *Central Asia: A Century of Russian Rule*, ed. Edward Allworth (New York and London: Columbia University Press, 1967), p. 149.

Samarkand and Ferghana *oblasts*, while the central and southern areas remained within the fold of Bukhara. In 1895, firm borders were established between Russian Turkestan and Afghanistan, which have survived until today. Rushan, Shughnan and part of Vakhan were acquired by Emir Abd al-Ahad of Bukhara in return for lands along the Panj River, which became part of Afghanistan. Russia retained garrisons in the Pamir *vilayets* of Bukhara and subsequently annexed them in 1905.[30]

The Russian Government deemed it feasible to preserve the Emirate of Bukhara intact for a number of reasons. First, it served as a buffer state covering a 1500 km border with Afghanistan. Second, the introduction of Russian administration to a country with a population of two million plus with centuries-long traditions of feudal unrest would be a costly affair with unclear results. Finally, Bukhara was a religious centre, renowned not only in Turkestan but also throughout the world Islamic community. At the end of the nineteenth century, its capital city of 80 000 people had 80 *madrasas* with up to 10 000 pupils, including students from India, Kashgar, Afghanistan, China and Russia, some 260 mosques and dozens of sacred places (*mazors*) associated with various Sufi saints.[31] The religious establishment played an important role in local politics, and the appointment of Russian officials there would have alienated Muslims far beyond the borders of Turkestan.

The relative isolation of Bukhara from the GGT led to a different pace of economic development in what is now Tajikistan. As Barthold has noted, the mining and manufacturing industries were in worse shape in the Khanates of Bukhara and Kokand in the beginning of the nineteenth century than under the Samanids in the tenth.[32] The Russian conquest paved the way for the penetration of a capitalist market economy, which was facilitated by the construction of the trans-Caspian railway between 1881 and 1886 and the creation of a unified monetary and customs zone in Turkestan between 1892 and 1895. The area of what is today northern Tajikistan, however, found itself in a privileged position compared with the territories of southern Tajikistan belonging to Bukhara. The Russian industrialists and merchants treated the south predominantly as a commodity market and source of raw materials until the beginning of the twentieth century. The feudal land-tenure and taxation systems did not undergo any changes there; as a result, in the words of a Russian geographer, 'the economic management of Bukhara is carried out in a predatory way and has deplorable consequences …

---

30   Governor-General Vrevsky remarked in 1895 that the reason for the annexation was that 'the Tajiks treat the Bukharans with animosity and we should value sympathies on the part of the Tajiks since all countries bordering the Pamirs—Badakhshan, Chitral, Gilgit, Kanjut, Tagarma—are inhabited by Tajiks who are related to the populace of Shughnan, Rushan and Vakhan'. See: *Istoriia Tadzhikskogo naroda*, Vol. II, p. 178.

31   O. A. Sukhareva, *Bukhara: XIX – nachalo XXv. (Pozdnefeodalnyi gorod i ego naselenie)* (Moscow: Nauka, 1966), pp. 288, 290, 308.

32   V. V. Barthold, *Sochineniia*, Vol. III (Moscow: Izdatelstvo vostochnoi literatury, 1965), p. 111.

The government sucks the blood of poor Bukharans and if some time Bukhara is attached to Russia, we will literally acquire a bunch of mendicant people.'[33] The cause of promoting Russian economic interests in Bukhara was largely left to private enterprise. It is symptomatic that the Russian Political Agency was not established there until 1885. On the contrary, the development of the Samarkand and Ferghana *oblasts* of the GGT was largely inspired by the Russian Government, and the construction of railroads and irrigation systems there was financed from the state budget or through government-owned banks. In 1886, new landmark legislation on the GGT was approved, providing for private landownership in Turkestan. The Russian authorities encouraged cotton-growing in Turkestan, and during 1883–89, introduced high-yield American varieties of cotton. Soon it became the main source of capital accumulation for Russian and local entrepreneurs: 'hundreds of clerks, officers, other government employees and merchants rushed to grow cotton … The fathoms of raining gold, the dream of American wealth in Turkestan eclipsed everything else. They planted cotton everywhere a piece of irrigated land could be found.'[34] By 1915, cotton plantations had occupied 60 to 95 per cent of arable lands in the Ferghana *oblast*;[35] thenceforth, cotton monoculture prevailed in this area.

While northern Tajikistan was gradually being included in the all-Russian market and division of labour, Bukhara, especially its eastern parts, stood aloof. The number of factories in the whole Emirate of Bukhara in 1917–28[36] was less than the corresponding figure for the single Khujand *uezd* (administrative subdivision) of the Samarkand *oblast* in the 1890s.[37] Though the emir joined the 'cotton rush' in Central Asia, and even though by the end of the nineteenth century cotton accounted for 40 per cent of his country's exports,[38] it was not until 1916 that a cohesive program was devised with the participation of the Russian Stakheev Concern to rationalise production and sales of cotton and to irrigate new, vast lands for cotton-growing.[39] Eastern Bukhara remained completely devoid of railroads, and pack animals were its main means of transportation.

The territory of Eastern Bukhara is of particular interest in this study, as this corresponds with the modern-day area that would see the worst of the civil war

---

33   L. A. Perepelitsyna, *Rol russkoi kultury v razvitii kultur narodov Srednei Azii* (Moscow: Nauka, 1976), p. 8.

34   A. Aminov and A. Babakhodzhaev, *Ekonomicheskie i politicheskie posledstviia prisoedineniia Srednei Azii k Rossii* (Tashkent: Uzbekistan, 1966), pp. 71–2.

35   A. M. Aminov, *Ekonomicheskoe razvitie Srednei Azii (kolonialnyi period)* (Tashkent: Gosudarstvennoe izdatelstvo Uzbekskoi SSR, 1959), p. 143.

36   *Istoriia Bukhary s drevneishykh vremen do nashikh dnei* (Tashkent: Fan, 1976), pp. 172–3.

37   *Istoriia Tadzhikskogo naroda*, Vol. II, p. 146.

38   Hélène Carrère d'Encausse, *Islam and the Russian Empire: Reform and Revolution in Central Asia* (London: I. B. Tauris & Co., 1988), p. 42.

39   T. M. Kitanina, 'Iz istorii obrazovaniia kontserna Stakheeva', in *Iz istorii imperializma v Rossii* (Moscow and Leningrad: Izdatelstvo AN SSSR, 1959), pp. 123–4.

in Tajikistan, specifically Qurghonteppa, the Vakhsh River region and Kulob. These lands were, throughout all historical periods, the isolated periphery of empires or under the control of various autonomous local powers, but never home to any strong entity that could project power outside the region.[40] After the collapse of the Timurids, the region was under fluctuating levels of influence of the Shaybanid, Janid and Manghit Uzbek dynasties. In the first half of the eighteenth century, as the Bukhara Emirate started to lose authority in the area, the Yuz Uzbeks took control of the Vakhsh Valley and Qubodiyon from their base in Hisor. And at times during the eighteenth century the Vakhsh would come under the control of Kunduz to the south, or Kulob and Baljuvon in the east.[41]

In 1870 the Bukharan Emirate, now under a certain level of tsarist control that would last two years, expanded its control over Qurghonteppa and Qubodiyon with Russian assistance. Qurghonteppa, along with other eastern areas, became a sub-province of Hisor, and the wider region of modern-day southern Tajikistan came to be referred to as Eastern Bukhara.[42] The Bukharan Emirate, allowed by the Russians to keep its bureaucratic structures and emir, *attempted* to create a bureaucratic structure that would incorporate local political, financial, judicial and religious structures at three levels of government, from top to bottom.[43] This is in line with the tsarist enactment in 1867 of an administrative and territorial reorganisation whereby civil and military powers were exclusively the domain of the military administration while 'all local affairs were relinquished to the traditional hierarchies';[44] however, the reality of Bukharan power was not quite so orderly. Hélène Carrère d'Encausse describes a state where many regions were 'living in a situation of almost total independence or constant

---

40   The lower Vakhsh and Kofarnihon valleys were 'under the orbit' of ancient Bactria and Balkh, which is shown in the numerous archaeological sites there. The town of Qurghonteppa was first mentioned in historical sources in the seventeenth century as it began to prosper. See: Habib Borjian, 'Kurgantepe', *Encyclopedia Iranica*, n.p. (2005), online: <http://www.iranica.com/articles/kurgan-tepe> Borjian notes that Khottalon (Kulob) 'remained a vassal of successive empires, but often with substantial degrees of autonomy due to its relative isolation'. Habib Borjian, 'Kulab', *Encyclopedia Iranica*, n.p. (2005), online: <http://www.iranica.com/articles/kulab>
41   Borjian, 'Kurgantepe', n.p. Borjian writes that Kulob, on the trade route from Hisor to Afghanistan, was an area of competition for surrounding Uzbek states, including the Janids in Balkh, the Loqay and the Qataghan Uzbeks in Kunduz (Beg Murad Khan appointed his son as ruler of Kulob). Influence from south of the Amu Darya lasted until the Durrani Empire took control of northern Afghanistan. After this point Kulob came under the expanding influence of Hisor. Then, for much of the nineteenth century, the area was a buffer zone between Bukhara, Kokand and Afghanistan. See: Borjian, 'Kulab', n.p.
42   Borjian, 'Kurgantepe', n.p. Shirin Akiner, *Tajikistan: Disintegration or Reconciliation?* (London: Royal Institute of International Affairs, 2001), p. 11.
43   Carrère d'Encausse, *Islam and the Russian Empire*, p. 26; Anita Sengupta, 'Imperatives of National Territorial Delimitation and the Fate of Bukhara', *Central Asian Survey*, Vol. 19, Nos 3–4 (2000), pp. 399–401, 407.
44   Sengupta, 'Imperatives of National Territorial Delimitation and the Fate of Bukhara', p. 401. For a discussion of Russian administrative policy and local autonomy in Central Asia and Turkestan, see: Daniel Brower, 'Islam and Ethnicity: Russian Colonial Policy in Turkestan', in *Russia's Orient: Imperial Borderlands and Peoples, 1700–1917*, eds Daniel R. Brower and Edward J. Lazzerini (Bloomington: Indiana University Press, 1997).

rebellion'.[45] The Bukharan Emirate had little semblance of territorial integrity. Geographic factors of distance, isolation and mountainous terrain gave the Eastern Bukharan lands a high level of autonomy. Anita Sengupta notes that 'complete control almost entirely eluded the Emirs and people preserved their family community structures'.[46] She goes on to note the lack of stability, with 'a constant process of flux where assimilation of certain parts was constantly accompanied by the threat of secession by others'.[47] B. I. Iskandarov similarly argues that Bukhara's failure to unite its eastern domains under centralised rule allowed small, autonomous local social units to prosper.[48] Especially relevant to Tajiks from the mountainous regions, the people here were able, thanks to their geographic location, to sidestep the emirs' attempts at centralised rule.[49] In Eastern Bukhara, in the eyes of the traditional communities and their leaders, any centralising agent constituted a potential menace. The non-Uzbek peasants and *beks* treated the emir as an alien ruler and oppressor.[50]

The period of tsarist rule in Turkestan ushered in a number of significant social and demographic changes. In the territories of the GGT, usage of the Uzbek language progressively increased from its already dominant position as the language of the majority. In 1868, people in Samarkand spoke Tajik almost exclusively; by 1904 it had given way to mostly Uzbek.[51] This dramatic shift was caused by the fact that the Russian administration utilised Turkic Kazakhs, Tatars and Bashkirs as interpreters and sometimes staff members. The improvement in communications and education was conducive to the wider circulation of a normative Uzbek literary language rather than a handful of Uzbek dialects. Interestingly, of 415 students who completed their studies at the Tashkent Teachers' Seminary in the 25 years from 1879 to 1904 there were only 65 natives; of these, 54 were Kazakhs or Kyrgyzs and not one was a Tajik.[52] Given that Tajiks accounted for 9 per cent of the population of Turkestan in 1897[53] and were settled compactly in the Samarkand and Ferghana *oblasts*, there was a deliberate policy of Turkicisation

---

45   Carrère d'Encausse, *Islam and the Russian Empire*, p. 25.

46   Sengupta, 'Imperatives of National Territorial Delimitation and the Fate of Bukhara', p. 399.

47   Sengupta, 'Imperatives of National Territorial Delimitation and the Fate of Bukhara', p. 399.

48   B. I. Iskandarov, *Vostochnaia Bukhara i Pamir v Pereod Prisoedineniya Srednei Azii k Rossi* (Tadzhikskoe Gosudarstvo, 1960), as cited in Sengupta, 'Imperatives of National Territorial Delimitation and the Fate of Bukhara', p. 399.

49   Olimova and Olimov state that 'hill valleys and their inhabitants with small pieces of cultivated land and no hope for irrigation came together in small groups and preserved their self-sufficient complex and independence from the central government'. See: S. K. Olimova and M. A. Olimov, 'Nezavisimi Tajikistan— trydni puch peremen', *Vostok*, No. 1 (1995), n.p., as translated and cited in Sengupta, 'Imperatives of National Territorial Delimitation and the Fate of Bukhara', p. 399. For example: while *hakims* had the responsibility of collecting taxes on behalf of the emir, areas outside effective central control such as Darvoz, Qarotegin and Karshi gave only occasional tribute to Bukhara. See: ibid., p. 400.

50   Kirill Nourzhanov, 'Reassessing the Basmachi: Warlords without Ideology?' *Journal of South Asia and Middle East Studies*, Vol. XXXI, No. 3 (Spring 2008), p. 61.

51   Barthold, *Sochineniia*, Vol. II, Part 1, p. 168.

52   Gavin Hambly, *Central Asia* (London: Weidenfeld & Nicolson, 1969), p. 223.

53   Rahim Masov, *Tadzhiki: istoriia s grifom 'Sovershenno sekretno'* (Dushanbe: Paivand, 1995), p. 52.

on the part of the Russian administration, which was later complemented by Russification. In 1891, the governor-general instructed *oblast* governors that *volost* chairmen, *qozis*, village headmen and other native administrative officials use the Russian language in the course of their duties, and that a good command of Russian should be a criterion for selecting candidates to fill vacancies.[54] After 1876, the Russian administration tried to introduce modern Russian-type schools with a single, officially proclaimed purpose: to train indigenous personnel devoted to the tsarist regime who subsequently 'will be given the task of handling all issues pertaining to [the] local population that are not of political essence'.[55]

In the beginning of the twentieth century there existed three types of educational institutions in Turkestan: 1) the traditional *maktab* and *madrasa*; 2) the so-called 'new method' (*usuli jadid*) schools, which combined Islamic education with modern European elements; and 3) Russian-type schools. The tsarist government grew more and more suspicious of the pan Turkic and pan-Islamic activities of the Jadid schools, run mostly by well-educated Tatars, but encouraged their spread in Bukhara where they could undermine the influence of the conservative clergy. On the whole, the achievements in the field of public education both in Bukhara and in Russian Turkestan were very modest; in 1917 literacy varied from 1 to 2 per cent—'considerably worse than India at that time';[56] however, a small stratum of middle-class intellectuals came into being in Turkestan, whose views were not confined either to Islamic dogma or to the geographic boundaries of the Russian Empire. They formed the nuclei of future Tajik and Uzbek national intelligentsias who, decades later, would 'invite [the] masses into history'.[57]

The struggle against Russian imperial domination had its own peculiarities in Bukhara and the Tajik-populated territories of the GGT. First, they did not suffer from the influx of Russian peasant migrants who had seized 49.2 million ha of the best land from Kazakhs and Kyrgyzs by 1907.[58] There were only 14 Russian settlements in northern Tajikistan (the Khujand *uezd*) in 1914; of these, 13 were located in the sparsely populated Hungry Steppe.[59] Consequently, popular revolts there were caused by excessive taxation and exploitation rather than by land confiscations. When Kokand was subjugated, the tax burden upon local peasants was somewhat lightened, but by the early 1880s it had increased

54 Perepelitsyna, *Rol russkoi kultury v razvitii kultur narodov Srednei Azii*, pp. 102–3.

55 Kastelskaia, *Iz istorii Turkestanskogo kraia*, p. 16.

56 W. P. Coates and Zelda K. Coates, *Soviets in Central Asia* (London: Lawrence & Wishart, 1951), p. 54.

57 Anthony D. Smith, *The Ethnic Origins of Nations* (New York: Basil Blackwell, 1987), p. 137.

58 G. F. Dakhshleiger, *Sotsialno-ekonomicheskie preobrazovaniia v aule i derevne Kazakhstana (1921–1929gg.)* (Alma-Ata: Zhazushy, 1965), p. 49.

59 A. Ia. Vishnevsky, *Leninskaia natsionalnaia politika v deistvii* (Dushanbe: Donish, 1982), p. 23.

two to threefold[60] and had become 'between 50 and 150 percent higher than those levelled upon the none-too-liberally treated people of European Russia'.[61] Russian industrial workers in Turkestan received wages almost twice as high as their native colleagues.[62] These grievances underlay peasant riots in Khujand (1872, 1889 and 1906) and in Uroteppa (1875, 1907) and tumult amongst native coalminers in Panjakent (1885). Periodic anti-feudal riots in Eastern Bukhara also gradually acquired an anti-Russian colouring, since Russian garrisons unfailingly helped government forces to suppress insurgencies. Interestingly, a huge peasant revolt headed by Abdul Vose that swept Baljuvon, Khovaling, Sary-Khosor and Kulob in 1885 and shattered the power of the emir[63] was one of the reasons for the establishment of the Russian Political Agency in Bukhara, which could advise local authorities how to avoid such calamities in future. At first, rebellious peasants of Eastern Bukhara constantly asked the Russian representatives to save them from the arbitrariness of the Uzbek *beks* and the emir officials,[64] but to no avail. Eventually Russian officers and travellers became the targets of a widespread form of spontaneous protest in Eastern Bukhara as well as in Turkestan: bandit attacks, assault and robbery. In the period 1899–1917, the number of such attacks registered more than a tenfold growth in Turkestan (from 50 to 547 annually).[65]

The native population of Central Asia rose up, protesting against poverty, infringement upon customs and religious feelings (the 1892 cholera riots in Tashkent), and forced conscription to labour battalions (the 1916 rebellion, which began in Khujand and then spread throughout Central Asia).[66] All these uprisings, however, were 'sporadic and limited in scope … and had no broader

---

60   Aminov and Babakhodzhaev, *Ekonomicheskie i politicheskie posledstviia prisoedineniia Srednei Azii k Rossii*, p. 99.

61   Coates and Coates, *Soviets in Central Asia*, p. 56.

62   Kastelskaia, *Iz istorii Turkestanskogo kraia*, p. 63.

63   The revolt began after several years of drought and locust invasions from Afghanistan had placed local farmers on the brink of complete ruin. It could not be pacified quickly because the emir's army at the time comprised just 'five or six units of soldiers, the majority of whom are thiefs, gamblers, drunkards, some of them are mad and insane, others are lame and blind, who have never heard a gunshot'. See: Mirza 'Abdal 'Azim Sami, *Tarikh-i Salatin-i Manghitiya* (Moscow: Izdatelstvo Vostochnoi Literatury, 1962), p. 119. The uprising was crushed by the irregular Uzbek cavalry from Hisor and Qarotegin. In the Soviet period a district in Tajikistan was named after Vose, who was being depicted as a fervent fighter against the emir's feudal oppression.

64   *Istoriia Tadzhikskogo naroda*, Vol. II, kn. 2, p. 191.

65   Carrère d'Encausse, *Islam and the Russian Empire*, p. 74.

66   Interestingly, for the first time indigenous women took an active part in anti-government demonstrations in Khujand and Uroteppa. See: Sh. Iusupov and D. Berdiev, 'Vosstanie 1916g. v gorode Ura-Tiube i Ganchinskoi volosti', *Izvestiia AN RT. Seriia: vostokovedenie, istoriia, filologiia*, No. 4 (28) (1992), p. 77.

revolutionary significance for the Moslem masses or the Moslem leaders'.[67] By no means were they inspired by an organised nationalist and/or anti-colonialist ideology. The tsarist regime fully succeeded in at least two important elements of its imperial policy in Central Asia: it managed to divide local peoples by artificial administrative and cultural boundaries, and it sealed off the whole region from the world outside. Even one of the severest critics of Russia, Lord Curzon, had to acknowledge ultimately the impregnable position of the Tsarist Empire in the region: 'I admit that Russia has in her career of Central Asiatic conquest by devious, and often dishonourable, means achieved a successful and salutary end.'[68] Despite its position of power, the Russian tsarist administration did not attempt to introduce truly radical changes to Central Asian societies. The Soviet authorities, however, would have different plans, creating 'socialist nations' by applying an awesome arsenal of communist-style modernisation to the mosaic of traditional local identities.

---

67   Teresa Rakowska-Harmstone, *Russia and Nationalism in Central Asia: The Case of Tadzhikistan* (Baltimore and London: The Johns Hopkins Press, 1970), p. 17.
68   Alexis Krausse, *Russia in Asia: A Record and A Study* (London: Curzon Press, 1973), p. 138.

2. Forging Tajik Identity: Ethnic Origins, National–Territorial Delimitation and Nationalism

Who are the Tajiks? The Problem of Tajik Ethnogenesis

Contemporary usage of 'Tajik' generally narrows to sedentary, Persian-speaking Sunni Muslims in Central Asia and Afghanistan (with a few exceptions such as Dari-speakers who claim Pashtun lineage). Beyond this simple categorisation, many scholars stress that 'Tajik' refers to Persian-speakers of diverse origins.[1] As for the language of the Tajiks—variously referred to as Persian, Farsi, Dari or Tajik—the historical linguistic changes in Central Asia within the Iranian-language family should be noted. The Eastern Iranian languages in Central Asia were superseded by a mutually unintelligible Western Iranian language (Persian)[2] several hundred years after the Arab conquests in a process that began well before the Arabs entered the region.[3] According to the Tajik historian Bobojon Ghafurov, the appeal and power of religious, cultural, political and economic factors all contributed to the spread of Western Iranian.[4]

While the claims of some Tajik writers that their direct ancestors include Noah's son Shem or Biblical Adam himself[5] should be attributed more to poetic imagination than to plausible historical fact, Tajik society demonstrates a surprising continuity over centuries. Official Tajik histories trace the completion of the Tajik's 'ethnogenesis' and the beginning of their 'statehood' to the era of the Samanid Empire (ninth–tenth centuries).[6] Contemporary Tajik scholars

---

1   Pierre Centlivres and Micheline Centlivres-Demont, 'Tajikistan and Afghanistan: The Ethnic Groups on Either Side of the Border', in *Tajikistan: The Trials of Independence*, eds Mohammad-Reza Djalili, Frederic Grare and Shirin Akiner (New York: St Martin's Press, 1997), p. 4; Akiner, *Tajikistan*, p. 9; Saodat Olimova, 'Regionalism and its Perception by Major Political and Social Powers of Tajikistan', in *Tajikistan at a Crossroads: The Politics of Decentralization*, ed. Luigi de Martino (Geneva: Cimera, 2004), p. 144.
2   That is, Farsi, Dari, Tajik.
3   Muriel Atkin, 'Tajiks and the Persian World', in *Central Asia in Historical Perspective*, ed. Beatrice F. Manz (Oxford: Westview Press, 1994), p. 127.
4   Ghafurov, *Tojikon*, p. 107. Ghafurov writes further: 'The Persian language spread from Marv, Balkh and other administrative, economic and cultural centres of Northern Khuroson into Movarounnahr [Central Asia], gradually taking the place of Eastern Iranian languages such as Soghdian and Tokharian (Bactrian).'
5   Orifjon Yahyozodi Khujandi, *Khujandnoma, yo qissaho az ta'rikhi Khujand va khujandiyon* (Khujand: Nashriyoti davlatii ba nomi R. Jalil, 1994), pp. 7–8.
6   Ghafurov, *Tojikon*, pp. 494–501; Kirill Nourzhanov, 'The Politics of History in Tajikistan: Reinventing the Samanids', *Harvard Asia Quarterly*, Vol. 5, No. 1 (2001); Marlene Laruelle, 'The Return of the Aryan Myth: Tajikistan in Search of a Secularized National Ideology', *Nationalities Papers*, Vol. 35, No. 1 (2007).

claim that 'the formation of the Tajik nation was completed during the rule of the Samanids'.[7] Ghafurov, an influential historian who was the first secretary of the Communist Party of Tajikistan from 1946 to 1956 and thereafter the director of the Moscow-based Institute of Oriental Studies of the Academy of Sciences of the Soviet Union, writes of the Tajiks as a clearly defined group from the Samanid era.[8] Ghafurov, commenting on the 'process of consolidation of the Tajik people', uses contradictory language: 'Although the formation of the Tajik people had already been completed by the 9th–10th centuries, in the following centuries it [that is, Tajik identity] did not remain unchanged.'[9] This phrasing allows Tajik scholars to claim all populations that preceded this era be included as ancestors of Tajiks and all cultural, linguistic and population changes after this era as not lessening the importance of the final 'consolidation' of Tajik identity. The Tajik archaeologist and historian N. N. Negmatov makes a similar claim of Tajik antiquity, albeit in somewhat more neutral terms, when he identifies all the Iranian-speaking populations of Central Asia during and before the Samanid era and argues that '[a]ll these people were ethnically related and spoke languages and dialects of the Middle Iranian and New Persian language groups; they were the basis for the emergence and gradual consolidation of what became an Eastern Persian-Tajik ethnic identity'.[10] Tajikistan's President, Emomali Rahmon, while extolling Ghafurov's works in the most flattering terms, dispenses with any academic caution and writes:

> I have had to stress again and again that it would be wrong to think that the first page in the history of Tajik statehood was written with the founding of the Samanid state. Long before the Samanid epoch, the Tajiks had already established a number of states. Little wonder that the Tajiks are recognised as one of the oldest peoples of Central Asia who laid down the very foundations of civilisation in these ancient lands … The Tajiks have a history stretching back many thousand years.[11]

---

7   Ghafurov, *Tojikon*, p. 494. There is a terminological confusion present in recent Tajik and Russian studies: the Tajik words *melleyat* and *mellat* (nationality and nation) as well as their Russian equivalents, *narodnost* and *natsiia*, are often used as synonyms.
8   Ghafurov, *Tojikon*, pp. 494–501.
9   Ghafurov, *Tojikon*, p. 500.
10   N. N. Negmatov, 'The Samanid State', in *The History of Civilizations of Central Asia*, Vol. IV, ed. M. S. Asimov and C. E. Bosworth (Paris: UNESCO, 1998), p. 94. Also: N. Negmatov, 'The Phenomenon of the Material Culture of Central Asia in the Samanid's Epoch', in *The Contribution of the Samanid Epoch to the Cultural Heritage of Central Asia*, UNESCO Colloquium, Dushanbe 1998 (Dushanbe: Adib, 1999), pp. 157–64.
11   Emomali Rahmonov, *The Tajiks in the Mirror of History, Volume I: From the Aryans to the Samanids* (Guernsey, UK: London River Editions, n.d.), pp. 5–6. Rahmon also traces the Tajiks to the mythological Peshdodids (who Rahmon notes ruled in the fifth, fourth and third millennia BCE): ibid., pp. 64–5. Rahmon seems to be also framing a response in his writing. For example: 'When Tajikistan finally gained independence and the process of state disintegration was progressing rapidly, we observed that there were some forces in our society which tended to belittle the historical role played by Tajiks, and to exaggerate the influence from other nations.' Ibid., p. 10.

It would not be correct to call the Samanid Empire the first Tajik state.[12] Rather, it was the last time the bulk of Iranian lands were under the domain of an Iranian ruler. Within the Samanid administration there was a discernible ethno-religious division: an Iranian chancery, staffed with recent converts, coexisted with the predominantly Arab *ulama*, while the core of the army consisted of Turkic slaves or mercenaries. Eventually, the attack of the Qarakhanid Turks ended its reign in 999, and dominance in Central Asia passed on to Turkic rulers. The contemporary social and political relevance of Tajik historiography and ethnogenesis, in particular their relation to post–Soviet state/nation-building, to the Government of Tajikistan, and to the various Tajik intellectuals (with a particular stress on the Samanids—all-important due to their status as the last 'Iranian' dynasty before the domination of Turkic dynasties),[13] are further explained later in this chapter.

The presence of a Tajik nation (or more precisely, a distinctive ethnicity, since the concept of 'nation' is a relatively recent phenomenon, which dates from the late eighteenth century) in the tenth century finds little corroborative evidence. It would be interesting, however, to speculate about the emergence of the primary form of ethnic community in Central Asia—the *ethnie*, in Anthony Smith's parlance. An *ethnie* is a given population, a social group 'whose members share a sense of common origins, claim a common and distinctive history and destiny, possess one or more distinctive characteristics, and feel a sense of collective uniqueness and solidarity'.[14] In the case of Tajiks, the problem of collective cultural individuality put in historical perspective is twofold: a) their distinctness from non-Iranian peoples of Central Asia, and b) their dissociation from the populace of Iran proper. The question of association with a specific territory in the tenth century is an easy one. The indigenous Iranian population constituted an absolute majority throughout Mavarannahr (Central Asia), both in cities and in villages. More importantly, this association had commemorative overtones: Ferdowsi's epic poem *Shahnama* includes Transoxiana (Central Asia) in Iranshahr,[15] and stresses this region's opposition to Turan (lands under the domain of Turkic peoples). On other counts, however, tracing a Tajik identity is much more complicated.

Certain elements are indispensable for the formation of a viable *ethnie*. The use of a collective, identifying name is one of the most important. Usage of the word 'Tajik' as a mode of self-definition, however, was not registered before the second quarter of the eleventh century.[16] Attempting to determine the origin of the term 'Tajik' and its social use throughout history is an exercise in

---

12 Masov, *Tadzhiki*, p. 125.

13 Nourzhanov, 'The Politics of History in Tajikistan'; Laruelle, 'The Return of the Aryan Myth'.

14 Anthony D. Smith, *The Ethnic Revival* (Cambridge: Cambridge University Press, 1981), p. 66.

15 Iranshahr was used to denote the entire realm of the Persian Sassanid Empire.

16 Abu al-Fazl Baihaki, *Istoriia Mas'uda 1030–1041* (Tashkent: Izdatelstvo AN Uzbekskoi SSR, 1962), p. 725.

speculation. Folk etymologies, single historical references, scholarly guessing, various shifting social usages and highly politicised attempts to find ancient origins all must be navigated when attempting to find the origin and historical usage of 'Tajik'.[17] It has been generally accepted amongst scholars that the term was initially used in Mavarannahr to refer to the Arabs (probably, it was derived from the Arab *Tai* tribal name). Afterwards it became a collective name for both Arabs and local converts to Islam (predominantly Iranians) and only much later was this term transformed into the ethnonym of an entity amongst Central Asian Iranians.[18]

Language and religion are considered the most basic traits of an *ethnie*'s shared culture. Under the Samanids, ordinary people continued to speak local dialects (Soghdian, Khorezmian, and so on), while Dari was primarily the language of official documents and court life, only beginning to spread en masse in Bukhara, Samarkand and Ferghana.[19] Literary modern Persian remained uniform in Western Iran and Central Asia until the fifteenth or even sixteenth century.[20] Similarly, behavioural patterns, legal procedures and educational systems based on *shari'a* stayed almost identical in both regions. Under the Samanids, the bulk of Turkic tribes beyond the Syr-Darya converted to Islam; it was a severe blow to the image of the Turk as a perennial enemy of the Iranian. The Sunni–Shi'a dichotomy was yet to become a watershed among different ethnic communities.[21]

Anthony Smith argues that 'a strong sense of belonging and an active solidarity, which in time of stress and danger can override class, factional or religious divisions within the community',[22] are the decisive factors for a durable ethnic community. This was not the case amongst Iranians in Mavarannahr before, during and after Samanid rule. Internal divisions in principalities, valley communities or other territorial subunits were more potent sources

---

17   For example, see: Ghafurov, *Tojikon*, p. 501, n. 83; Maria Eva Subtelny, 'The Symbiosis of Turk and Tajik', pp. 48–9; John Schoeberlein-Engel, *Identity in Central Asia: Construction and Contention in the Conceptions of 'Uzbek', 'Tajik', 'Muslim', 'Samarqandi' and Other Groups*, PhD Dissertation, Harvard University (1994), pp. 137–42, 144; C. E. Bosworth and B. G. Fragner, 'Tādjīk', *Encyclopaedia of Islam*, 2nd edn, eds P. Bearman et al. (Brill, 2009), Brill Online: <http://brillonline.nl/> As for the Tajik President, he says that '[t]he word "Tajik" is identical to "Aryan" (meaning "noble, highborn"). From the viewpoint of modern Tajik language the word "Tajik" is interpreted as "crowned" or "of noble origins".' See: Rahmonov, *The Tajiks in the Mirror of History*, p. 94. A prominent example of a single historical usage is Ghafurov, citing an eleventh-century quote wherein a man in a sultan's court said 'We, who are Tozik'. See: Ghafurov, *Tojikon*, p. 501. For a criticism of Ghafurov's reference, see: Schoeberlein-Engel, *Identity in Central Asia*, pp. 129–30, esp. n. 30.

18   A number of Tajik experts adhere to a different theory, which implies that the word 'Tajik' originated from the Persian '*Taj*' (meaning 'crown') and that as early as the eighth century Iranians of Mavarannahr, especially in the mountainous areas, called themselves Tajiks—that is, the 'Crown Headed'. Thus, these Iranians emphasised their supposed superior genealogy over all other local peoples. See: N. N. Negmatov, *Gosudarstvo Samanidov* (Dushanbe: Donish, 1977), p. 219.

19   *Istoriia Tadzhikskogo naroda*, Vol. II, kn. 1, p. 222.

20   Sadriddin Aini, *Vospominaniia* (Moscow and Leningrad: Izdatelstvo AN SSSR, 1960), p. 963.

21   It would later find its reflection in *Gurugli* through the mediation of the Turkic text. See: G. M. H. Shoolbraid, *The Oral Epic of Siberia and Central Asia* (Bloomington: Indiana University Publications, 1975), p. 103.

22   Smith, *The Ethnic Origins of Nations*, p. 137.

of identity than affiliation to an *ethnie*. Khuttal, Chaganian, Isfijab, Khorezm and princedoms of Badakhshan nominally acknowledged the supremacy of the Samanids, yet in practice they 'were ruled by local dynasties according to their old traditions'.[23] Four distinct regions had formed by the twelfth century on the present-day territory of Tajikistan that were characterised by political and cultural autonomy: 1) Northern Tokharistan and Khuttal (that is, southern Tajikistan); 2) the Zarafshon Valley; 3) the basin of Upper and Middle Syr-Darya, including Ustrushana, Khujand and Western Ferghana; and 4) the Pamirs. With some variations, these specific geographic-cultural areas have survived until today. Prior to the Mongol invasion, their populations *never* acted in unison to repel aggressors; moreover, cases of mass resistance to aggression were almost unheard of in Mavarannahr.

In summary, it is impossible to single out a distinct Tajik *ethnie* in the tenth century. Central Asian Iranians remained an integral part of a wide Iranian ethnic community that came into being in the Achaemenid era, and from which they drew their name, history, inspiration and shared culture. The Samanid period, however, can be regarded as a landmark in the process of the ethnogenesis of the Tajiks. It produced an encoded fund of myths, memories, values and symbols— the core of the future *ethnie* in Tajikistan. Eventually, the Samanids themselves moved into the realm of the legendary tradition of contemporary Tajiks.[24] As the future showed, the centuries-long absence of economic unity and a common polity did not lead to the dissolution of the Tajiks. The sense of shared origins and cultural markers allowed them to survive in the ocean of Turkic tribes, and later gave them a chance to reconstruct (or forge) their history, pedigree and ethnicity.

Tajiks and Turks

Tajiks have had a close historical and cultural relationship with the Turkic peoples. In Central Asia there is much shared culture and it is impossible to neatly divide two distinct Tajik or Uzbek cultures thanks to linguistic, cultural and genetic mixing that resulted from the massive in-migration of Turkic peoples into Iranian-populated lands;[25] however, the process of Turkicisation

---

23 Negmatov, *Gosudarstvo Samanidov*, p. 30.

24 For example, the main green bazaar in Dushanbe has been named after Shah Mansur (961–76), who is viewed as the epitome of a fair and caring ruler.

25 John Schoeberlein-Engel, 'Conflicts in Tajikistan and Central Asia: The Myth of Ethnic Animosity', *Harvard Middle Eastern and Islamic Review*, Vol. 1, No. 2 (1994), pp. 7–9; Schoeberlein-Engel, *Identity in Central Asia*, pp. 21, 23; Sergei Abashin, 'The Transformation of Ethnic Identity in Central Asia: A Case Study of the Uzbeks and Tajiks', *Russian Regional Perspectives Journal*, Vol. 1, No. 2 (2003), p. 32. Abashin uses 'Turkic' and 'Iranian' rather than 'Uzbek' and 'Tajik' in reference to the historical process of language, population and culture mixing.

was not accompanied by serious depredations or genocide. Statements to the effect that 'from the tenth to the thirteenth centuries the Turks ... advanced into Turkestan increasing the Turkic population there and destroying the Iranian culture[26] should be treated with extreme caution. This period witnessed the further growth of cities[27] and the important role of Persian language and culture. As John Armstrong has noted, before the rise of the Ottomans, 'all Turkic regimes used Persian as their Court language'.[28]

In the tenth century the ethnic boundary between Iranians and Turks and the cultural boundary between sedentarism and nomadism were roughly the same. The whole medieval history of Mavarannahr can be written in terms of the relationship between steppe pastoralism and oasis agriculture. These contacts went far beyond warfare and the exchange of goods. Samuel Adshead, while describing the symbiosis between the two modes, applies the words 'complementarity' and 'compenetration', and gives a lucid picture of political interaction:

> On the one hand, the sedentarist found the best defence against one set of nomads was another set of nomads. On the other hand, if the nomad wanted to organise an empire out of his conquests, it was best done from an oasis with its granaries, money, literacy and unifying religion. The oasis needed government and protection: the steppe could provide both. The steppe lacked administration and education: the oasis could provide both.[29]

Prior to the tenth century, sedentarist Transoxiana had demonstrated an almost infinite ability to accommodate nomadic tribes invading its territory. Within two or three generations the steppe-dwellers usually gave up their habitual way of life and language. Some experts believe that only 'the vast, sudden incursion by pagan Mongols in the mid-thirteenth century' (and their Turkic allies) broke the routine;[30] however, archaeological and anthropological data point to the fact that already in the eleventh century the situation in Mavarannahr was undergoing a radical transformation. There was a far greater influx of nomadic Turkic peoples during the earlier Qarakhanid era.[31]

---

26   Marie Czaplicka, *The Turks of Central Asia in History and at the Present Day* (Amsterdam: Philo, 1973), p. 72.
27   For example, the populations of Samarkand, Bukhara and Termez in the eleventh century stood at 100 000, 70 000 and 50 000 people respectively. See: *Istoriia Tadzhikskogo naroda*, Vol. II, kn. 1, p. 222.
28   John A. Armstrong, *Nations before Nationalism* (Chapel Hill: University of North Carolina Press, 1982), p. 248.
29   Adshead, *Central Asia in World History*, p. 25.
30   Armstrong, *Nations before Nationalism*, p. 40.
31   As T. K. Khojaiov writes, '[t]he greatest influx of anthropologically Mongoloid tribes to the territory of Central Asia dates from the Qarakhanid epoch. It is even more perceivable than in the period of Mongol invasion.' See: T. K. Khojaiov, *Etnicheskie protsessy v Srednei Azii v epokhu srednevekovia* (Tashkent: Fan, 1987), p. 59.

The historically close relations between Turkic and Iranian-speakers did not have just political and socioeconomic consequences, but ethnic and linguistic ones as well. This time the newcomers settled in rural areas as well as in towns; they not only retained their tongue but also eventually gave it to lands with ancient Iranian traditions. In Richard Frye's words, the spread of the Turkic languages in Transoxiana was 'nothing short of amazing'.[32] On top of the numerical strength of the Turks, the Qarakhanids' conversion to Islam, which supposedly took place under Satuq Bughra-khan (died about 955),[33] must have facilitated the infixion of the Turkic element in Mavarannahr enormously. Even before the Mongols, many Turkic toponyms had appeared in the Zarafshon Valley.[34] The interaction among Tajiks, sedentarised Turks and nomadic Uzbeks remained a highly complex process. Culturally, only language clearly demarcates the Tajik and Uzbek categories, and the prevalence of bilingualism lessens the importance of this division.[35] In Eastern Bukhara, where Tajiks constituted the majority of the population, large numbers of Uzbeks ultimately lost their native tongue and clan divisions, and adopted the way of life of the indigenous sedentary population.

The stereotypes of the 'ideal' appearance of Turkic peoples (including Uzbeks) and Iranian peoples (including Tajiks) are very different; however, the population of sedentary Central Asia has been intermixed for so long that it is impossible to accurately distinguish Tajiks from Uzbeks on physical appearance (phenotype) alone, particularly those who live on the plains and in the lower valleys.[36] The lowland Tajiks share more physical characteristics that are stereotyped as Turkic while mountain-dwellers share fewer linguistic and physical features with Turkic peoples.[37] A large number of the Uzbeks in Central Asia have Iranian ancestry while Tajiks who live outside the isolated mountain communities have

32   Richard N. Frye, *Islamic Iran and Central Asia (7th–12th Centuries)* (London: Variorum Reprints, 1979), p. 308.

33   Grousset, *The Empire of the Steppes*, p. 145.

34   Barthold, *Sochineniia*, Vol. II, Part 1, p. 253.

35   Olivier Roy, 'Is the Conflict in Tajikistan a Model for Conflicts throughout Central Asia?' in *Tajikistan: The Trials of Independence*, eds Mohammad-Reza Djalili, Frederic Grare and Shirin Akiner (New York: St Martin's Press, 1998), pp. 136, 144; Payam Foroughi, 'Tajikistan: Nationalism, Ethnicity, Conflict, and Socio-Economic Disparities—Sources and Solutions', *Journal of Muslim Minority Affairs*, Vol. 22, No. 1 (2002), pp. 45; Muriel Atkin, 'Religious, National and Other Identities in Central Asia', in *Muslims in Central Asia: Expressions of Identity and Change*, ed. Jo-Ann Gross (Durham, NC: Duke University Press, 1992), p. 50; Eden Naby, 'The Emerging Central Asia: Ethnic and Religious Factions', in *Central Asia and the Caucasus after the Soviet Union*, ed. Mohiadin Mesbahi (Gainesville: University Press of Florida, 1994), pp. 36, 38, 44; Schoeberlein-Engel, 'Conflicts in Tajikistan and Central Asia', p. 8.

36   Schoeberlein-Engel, 'Conflicts in Tajikistan and Central Asia', p. 8; Schoeberlein-Engel, *Identity in Central Asia*, pp. 21, 54–5, 294. See also Donald S. Carlisle, 'Geopolitics and Ethnic Problems of Uzbekistan and its Neighbours', in *Muslim Eurasia: Conflicting Legacies*, ed. Yaacov Ro'i (London: Frank Cass, 1995), pp. 75–6.

37   Schoeberlein-Engel, *Identity in Central Asia*, p. 148.

some Turkic ancestry.[38] In line with this description, it is noted that mixed marriages are common in Tajikistan,[39] with the Ferghana Valley the area where mixed marriages are most common.[40]

On the whole, the ethnic composition of the inhabitants of Tajikistan in the nineteenth century was characterised by extraordinary heterogeneity: apart from Tajiks and Tajik-speaking Turks (called Chaghatai in southern *vilayets*), there were also various Uzbek tribes,[41] Kyrgyz, Turkmen, Jews, Iranians, Afghans, Arabs, Lesgins, Armenians and Indians.[42] The Tajiks were subdivided according to their affiliation with ancient cultural and historical regions: Kulob (medieval Khuttal), Panjakent (in Zarafshon Valley), Asht (Upper Syr-Darya) and Qarotegin (foothills of the Pamirs); the Kulobis may have accounted for more than 60 per cent of the Tajik *ethnie* in Eastern Bukhara.[43]

In terms of genealogical memory, the oral tradition of the Asht Tajiks is illustrative of the tendencies in the Tajik ethnic community in the late nineteenth century. Asht was a locality in North-Western Ferghana that consisted of a number of *qishloqs* (villages)—with very different histories and ethnic composition—that could be divided into three groups. First, the titular *qishloq* of Asht allegedly had an uninterrupted cultural tradition since the Achaemenid period and its inhabitants readily referred to *Shahnama*'s Rustam, Alexander the Great and Qutaiba as contributors to their original Soghdian genealogy. Second, the citizens of Ponghoz claimed that their *qishloq* was established by migrants from the south, Darvoz in particular, whom they called 'real Tajiks', as opposed to the local mixture of Soghdians and Turks ('also Tajiks'). Third, 'real Tajiks' and 'also Tajiks' were very persistent in stressing their dissimilarity with the predominantly Uzbek-dwellers of Kamysh-Qurghon in terms of 'customs, outlook and especially consciousness', though they admitted that Uzbeks had been living in the region 'for a long time, too'.[44]

---

38   Schoeberlein-Engel, 'Conflicts in Tajikistan and Central Asia', p. 8.
39   Foroughi, 'Tajikistan', p. 45; Roy, 'Is the Conflict in Tajikistan a Model for Conflicts throughout Central Asia', pp. 136, 144; Naby, 'The Emerging Central Asia', pp. 36, 38, 44; Schoeberlein-Engel, 'Conflicts in Tajikistan and Central Asia', p. 8.
40   Naby, 'The Emerging Central Asia', pp. 36, 38, 44.
41   The number of Uzbek tribal names varies from 32 to 92. See: P. P. Ivanov, *Ocherki po istorii Srednei Azii. (XVI – seredina XIXv)* (Moscow: Izdatelstvo vostochnoi literatury, 1958), p. 128. Actually, the collective name 'Uzbeks' was used in Bukhara only in juxtaposition with other ethnic groups, such as Tajiks or Karakalpaks; the clan identification was far more important for these nomads.
42   *Istoriia Tadzhikskogo naroda*, Vol. II, kn. 2, pp. 67–8.
43   B. Kh. Karmysheva, *Ocherki etnicheskoi istorii iuzhnykh raionov Tadzhikistana i Uzbekistana* (Moscow: Nauka, 1976), p. 45.
44   The full paragraph is based on the study of a Soviet ethnographer: L. A. Chvyr, 'Ob istoricheskikh predaniiakh ashtskikh tadzhikov', in *Kavkaz i Sredniaia Aziia v drevnosti i srednevekovie* (Moscow: Nauka, 1981), pp. 163–76.

The Evolution of Tajik Statehood

The Tajik ethnicity has emerged as a result of cultural meiosis, through a succession of archetypal civilisation complexes: Aryan, Hellenistic, Greater Iranian, Perso-Islamic and Turkestani. Each stage of this process left an imprint on the collective knowledge systems of the Tajiks, characterised by a specific 'politics of memory'. By the beginning of the twentieth century, the Tajiks had retained the notion of sameness by maintaining cultural boundaries that kept them separate from Turkic ethnic groups in Central Asia—with some localised exceptions as in the case of the Uzbeks. The weak *solidarity* component of their *ethnie*, however, the inability to overcome dissonances *within* those boundaries, reflected in competing cultural elements on the sub-ethnic level, diminished their chances to seek national status in the modern era.

The policies pursued by the latest in the series of invaders, the Russian Empire, were conducive to the preservation of sub-ethnic consciousness amongst Tajiks. Cultural differences between people living to the north and to the south of the Hisor Range, or Valley Tajiks and Mountain Tajiks, were aggravated by administrative borders established by tsarist officials. In addition to this major dichotomy, smaller communities defined by geographic and historical features, although subject to ethnic awareness, remained remarkably passive in furthering it; this was the situation where 'an individual knows (s)he possesses a certain ethnic trait(s) which is no more meaningful than his or her other cultural, physical, social or territorial characteristics'.[45] The 1917 revolution in Russia brought the promise of change to this stalemated pattern.

In Central Asia the Bolsheviks at first had to rely heavily on local 'national communists'—essentially radical reformist intellectuals. In 1920, there were four communist parties in the region: the Russian Communist Party, the Turkestan Communist Party, the Bukharan Communist Party, and the Khorezmian Communist Party. The relationship amongst them was not without problems. At times national communists directly confronted the centre, as in January 1920, when Turar Ryskulov, the chairman of the Regional Muslim Bureau of the Russian Communist Party, put forward the ideas of forming a Turkic Republic that would embody not only Turkestan but Bukhara and Khiva as well, and a united Turkic Communist Party to govern it.[46] Even more blatant manifestations of dissent occurred in Bukhara, where a number of high-ranking party and state officials, including the chairman of the Central Executive Committee of the Bukharan People's Republic, Usman Khojaev, defected to forces of the rebel

---

45 James McKay and Frank Lewins, 'Ethnicity and the Ethnic Group: A Conceptual Analysis and Reformulation', *Ethnic and Racial Studies*, Vol. 1, No. 4 (1978), p. 415.

46 A. Ishanov, *Rol Kompartii i Sovetskogo pravitelstva v sozdanii natsionalnoi gosudarstvennosti uzbekskogo naroda* (Tashkent: Uzbekistan, 1978), pp. 80–1.

commander Enver Pasha in late 1921. Moscow applied a three-pronged policy to tighten its grip over Central Asian communist organisations: it dispatched experienced Bolshevik cadres to the region;[47] it recruited new indigenous personnel from circles other than the traditional intelligentsia;[48] and finally, by recurrent purges, it removed 'class alien' elements from the party structures.[49] In May 1922, the Central Asian Bureau of the Russian Communist Party was organised and assumed control over all existing communist structures. From that time, decisions made in Moscow could not be altered by local party organisations, which in fact were gradually transformed into mere executants of directives from the Russian Communist Party Central Committee.

National–Territorial Delimitation

The establishment of a uniform territorial administrative system based on centralised control from Moscow was another important step on Central Asia's way to 'USSR, Inc.'. Known as the national–territorial delimitation of 1924, this process of drawing borders remains a highly controversial issue in terms of its motivation and far-reaching results.[50] In Rakowska-Harmstone's words:

> [T]he process of delimitation was designed to grant political autonomy to major ethnic groups, in line with the stated policy of the right to national self-determination; the degree of formal autonomy granted depended on the degree of political development. Other reasons for

47   From February to December 1921, 869 party officials from Russia were posted to Turkestan. See: A. I. Khon, *Deiatelnost Kommunisticheskoi partii po osushestvleniiu novoi ekonomicheskoi politiki v Turkestane* (Tashkent: Fan, 1986), p. 163.

48   One of the most important sources of the formation of the new native elite was the Red Army, when Central Asian recruits underwent illiteracy liquidation courses and massive communist indoctrination. In the 1920s military service was viewed by local poverty-stricken peasants as a potent means to increase their social status and receive material benefits: the draft of volunteers to the Red Army in Tajikistan in 1927 was over-fulfilled by 20 per cent. Many Tajik soldiers were assigned to administrative positions in their republic immediately upon demobilisation. See: O. Khudoiberdyev, *Boevaia druzhba, rozhdennaia Oktiabrem* (Moscow: Nauka, 1984), pp. 102–5.

49   In 1922, 14 000 members were expelled from the BCP, leaving a total membership of 1560. See: Alexandre A. Bennigsen and S. Enders Wimbush, *Muslim National Communism in the Soviet Union: A Revolutionary Strategy for the Colonial World* (Chicago: University of Chicago Press, 1979), p. 82. The TCP lost 32 705 members of the original 49 206 from October 1921 to January 1923. See: Khon, *Deiatelnost Kommunisticheskoi partii po osushestvleniiu novoi ekonomicheskoi politiki v Turkestane*, p. 52.

50   A lucid generalisation made by Victor Zaslavsky can be fully applied to Tajikistan: 'Soviet nationality policy ... was one of the most successful policies of the Soviet regime, enabling it to reconcile a strong unitary state with a federal structure, and maintain internal stability in a country harbouring deep ethnic divisions. Ruthless suppression of nationalist movements, institutionalisation of ethnicity, large-scale affirmative action and transfer payment policies, institutional isomorphism of ethnoterritorial units—all these major planks of Soviet nationality policy must be taken into account if both its successful functioning and its eventual disastrous outcome are to be explained.' See: Victor Zaslavsky, 'Nationalism and Democratic Transition in Postcommunist Societies', *Daedalus*, Vol. 121, No. 2 (Spring 1992), p. 98.

the delimitation, equally important if not explicitly stated, were the Russian desires to facilitate All-Union (federal) control and to keep local nationalities apart by application of a 'divide and rule' policy.[51]

While it may be true that Tajikistan is 'the most artificial and flawed of all the Soviet territorial creations',[52] was this 'artificiality' a deliberate strategy of 'divide and rule' on the part of the Soviets? This assessment for Central Asia as a whole is shared by many scholars and appears time and time again in the literature.[53] Some make short references to the strategy. Muriel Atkin, for example, refers to national delimitation as *'divide et impera'* (divide and rule).[54] Others, such as John Schoeberlein-Engel and Olivier Roy, provide similar explanations;[55] however, the last two scholars qualify their remarks. Schoeberlein-Engel notes that the 'conventional wisdom' that portrays national delimitation as part of a 'divide and conquer' strategy has not been 'adequately documented',[56] while Roy questions whether national delimitation was a 'Machiavellian calculation', 'bureaucratic incompetence', or 'the power interests of local factions at work'.[57]

Certainly, it would be misleading to regard the process of setting internal Soviet republic borders as a scheme conceived and implemented exclusively by Bolshevik masterminds in Moscow. In reality, the delimitation was greatly influenced by nationalist forces in Central Asia. In regards to English-language literature on the subject, an alternative view was presented by Isabelle Kreindler, who argued that the apparently 'illogical' Central Asian administrative divisions are a result of the 'complexity of the task—intermingled, illiterate populations, unstudied dialects—rather than a deliberate policy to weaken Muslim peoples'.[58] When more significant attempts to adequately document national delimitation based on primary sources were eventually made (in English), it became clear that the 'divide and rule' theory is quite weak, most prominently as illustrated

51   Rakowska-Harmstone, *Russia and Nationalism in Central Asia*, p. 27.

52   Shirin Akiner, 'Melting Pot, Salad Bowl—Cauldron? Manipulation and Mobilization of Ethnic and Religious Identities in Central Asia', *Ethnic and Racial Studies*, Vol. 20, No. 2 (1997), pp. 386–7.

53   A good example is Svante E. Cornell, 'The Devaluation of the Concept of Autonomy: National Minorities in the Former Soviet Union', *Central Asian Survey*, Vol. 18, No. 2 (1999). Francine Hirsch, who researched national delimitation in Central Asia cites other authors who provide the same 'divide and rule' argument for Central Asian borders: Olaf Caroe, *Soviet Empire: The Turks of Central Asia and Stalinism* (London, 1953); Hélène Carrère d'Encausse, *The End of the Soviet Empire: The Triumph of Nations* (New York, 1993); Robert Conquest, *The Last Empire* (London, 1962), p. 29; Ahmed Rashid, *Jihad: The Rise of Militant Islam in Central Asia* (New Haven, Conn., 2002), p. 88; and S. Sabol, 'The Creation of Soviet Central Asia: The 1924 National Delimitation', *Central Asian Survey*, Vol. 14, No. 2 (1995), pp. 225–41. All as listed in Francine Hirsch, *Empire of Nations: Ethnographic Knowledge and the Making of the Soviet Union* (Ithaca, NY: Cornell University Press, 2005), pp. 160–1, ns 59, 61.

54   Atkin, 'Religious, National and Other Identities in Central Asia', p. 48.

55   Olivier Roy, *The New Central Asia: The Creation of Nations* (New York: NYU Press, 2000), p. 68; Schoeberlein-Engel, *Identity in Central Asia*, p. 25.

56   Schoeberlein-Engel, *Identity in Central Asia*, p. 23.

57   Roy, *The New Central Asia*, p. 69.

58   Isabelle T. Kreindler, 'Soviet Muslims: Gains and Losses as a Result of Soviet Language Planning', in *Muslim Eurasia: Conflicting Legacies*, ed. Yaacov Ro'i (London: Frank Cass, 1995), p. 36.

by Francine Hirsch.[59] Olimov and Olimova argue that the borders of Tajikistan were not created on the basis of 'ethnic lines', which were 'never a reality', but on the 'administrative realities' of geography, land usage, economics and communication.[60] At the same time, writing specifically about Tajikistan, the Tajik historian Rahim Masov noted that national delimitation was a complex process in which native Central Asian cadres presented different proposals and argued their cases before the Soviet authorities.[61] In summary, the presumably 'divide and rule'-motivated policy of national–territorial delimitation proved to be in line with the aspirations of ethnic elites in Central Asia. It is rather the way this policy was conducted that echoes today in numerous inter-ethnic disputes in the former Soviet Union. These tensions are caused either by unclearly defined borders or by the perception that these borders were drawn wrongfully in the first place. As Masov has written, 'it is still not clear what criterion was decisive for the incorporation of this or that settlement into the newly created republics, how other factors were treated, and whether economic, historical, national and other peculiarities were considered objectively, and whether interests of every nationality were taken into account'.[62] And in Masov's view, the main villains of national delimitation are not the Soviet central authorities, but rather the Uzbek leaders allied to the Bolsheviks who manipulated the process of national delimitation to create an unfairly large Uzbek Republic at the expense of ethnic Tajik-dominated areas.[63]

In October 1919, the Russian Government stated that 'self-determination of the peoples of Turkestan and elimination of all kinds of national inequality and privileges of one national group at the expense of another constitute the backbone of the entire policy of the Soviet government of Russia'.[64] Ostensibly this declaration was aimed at overcoming the image of Russians as a domineering force in Central Asia. In January 1920, the *Turkkomissiia* published the draft document entitled 'On the Dismemberment of Turkestan for Three Separate Republics According to National Features'—that is, Uzbekistan, Kyrgyzstan and Turkmenistan.[65] Why was it decided to create these particular national units instead of devising plain administrative divisions according to

---

59   Hirsch, *Empire of Nations*, esp. pp. 160–86. On Tajikistan in particular, see: Paul Bergne, *The Birth of Tajikistan: National Identity and the Origins of the Republic* (London: I. B. Tauris, 2007).
60   M. A. Olimov and Saodat Olimova, 'Ethnic Factors and Local Self-Government in Tajikistan', in *Local Governance and Minority Empowerment in the CIS*, eds Valery Tishkov and Elena Filippova (Budapest: LGI Books/Open Society Institute, 2002), p. 248.
61   Masov, *Tadzhiki*, pp. 158–93. As cited in Akiner, 'Melting Pot, Salad Bowl—Cauldron', pp. 373–4.
62   R. M. Masov, *Istoriia istoricheskoi nauki i istoriografiia sotsialisticheskogo stroitelstva v Tadzhikistane* (Dushanbe: Irfon, 1988), p. 185.
63   Rakhim Masov, *Istoriia topornogo razdeleniia* (Dushanbe: Irfon, 1991), esp. pp. 103–5. Throughout the book, Masov also hurls abuse at ethnic Tajiks who did not resist the process strongly enough. For a more neutral assessment, see: Bergne, *The Birth of Tajikistan*, pp. 105–10.
64   *Dekrety Sovetskoi vlasti*, Vol. VI (Moscow: Izdatelstvo politicheskoi literatury, 1973), p. 457.
65   A. I. Zevelev, *Iz istorii grazhdanskoi voiny v Uzbekistane* (Tashkent: Gosudarstvennoe izdatelstvo USSR, 1959), p. 452.

territory and population, or simply retaining existing borders, as some Russian orientalists advised? It appears that the leadership of the Russian Communist Party believed the fledgling sense of national identity a force to be countered. As Stalin emphasised at the Twelfth Congress of the Russian Communist Party in April 1923, apart from the danger of Great Russian chauvinism, 'there is local chauvinism, especially in those republics that have several nationalities. I allude to Georgia, Azerbaijan, Bukhara, and partly Turkestan, where we have several nationalities whose progressive elements may soon begin to compete with one another for primacy.'[66] Indeed, the fact that Bukhara and Khiva had become People's Socialist Republics by no means alleviated any historical animosity between Tajiks and Uzbeks, or Turkmen and Uzbeks. If anything, the turbulent years of revolution and civil war had politicised previously dormant ethnic elites, so that in the 1920s traditional raiding, plundering and blood feuds were compounded by confrontation along ethnic lines in local party committees. The creation of national entities under Moscow's strict supervision appeared to be the best way to placate nascent nationalist sentiments, avert a serious conflict in the already ravaged region, and in the long run utilise Central Asian elites in building communism.

There is little doubt that Islamic, tribal and local affiliations remained potent sources of identification for indigenous people in Central Asia at the beginning of the twentieth century. Still, this region was not immune to the general rise of nationalism in Asian countries, such as in Turkey, Iran or Afghanistan, where it had successfully ousted ideas of pan-Turkism and pan-Islamism. In Central Asia, too, 'the development of a capitalist economic order, the spread of literacy, written communication and modern education culminated in the rise of local and regional elites which … identified themselves consciously with a particular region and ethno-linguistic group and language. These elites were the architects of the forthcoming nation.'[67]

Arguably, the Tajiks suffered most from the arbitrariness of new administrative borders. Prior to 1924, 47.7 per cent of some 1.2 million Tajiks of Central Asia lived in what was to become the Tajik Autonomous Soviet Socialist Republic and 52.3 per cent lived in the Bukharan People's Soviet Republic (31 per cent of the total population of the Bukharan Republic);[68] however, Tajik participation in Central Asian political life was negligible. As of September 1924, 49 per cent of Bukharan Communist Party (BCP) members were Uzbeks, 22 per cent Russians, 8 per cent Turkmen, 5 per cent Tatars and only 0.7 per cent Tajiks.[69] There were no Tajiks in the BCP Central Committee or in any other important

---

66 I. V. Stalin, *Sochineniia*, Vol. V (Moscow: Gospolitizdat, 1947), p. 239.
67 Kemal Karpat, 'The Old and New Central Asia', *Central Asian Survey*, Vol. 12, No. 4 (1993), pp. 423–4.
68 *Ocherki istorii kompartii Turkestana, Bukhary i Khorezma* (Tashkent: Uzbekistan, 1959), p. 9.
69 Calculations based on: Ishanov, *Rol' Kompartii i Sovetskogo pravitelstva v sozdanii natsionalnoi gosudarstvennosti uzbekskogo naroda*, p. 191.

positions in the Bukharan Republic. A similar situation prevailed in Turkestan. In 1923, the 77 Turkestani students at the Communist University of Toilers of the Orient in Moscow—the main institution to produce elite party cadres for the Soviet periphery—included not a single Tajik.[70] During 1921–22, the People's Commissariat of Nationalities of Turkestan (Turkkomnats) consisted of four national departments (Kyrgyz, Turkmen, Uzbek and National Minorities). Tajiks were under the jurisdiction of the fourth department, on a par with Armenians, Latvians and Germans. Turkkomnats published 60 newspapers and magazines in native languages, but none in Tajik.[71] Stalin, then People's Commissar of Nationalities of Russia, did not include Tajiks in the number of main Central Asian ethnic groups either: 'There are three nationalities in Bukhara: Uzbeks, Turkmens and Kyrgyzs.'[72]

Not surprisingly, there were no Tajiks in the Special Territorial Commission of the Central Asian Bureau of the Russian Communist Party, which was created in the spring of 1924 to redraw boundaries impartially according to the predominance of a particular ethnic group in a given territory. The fate of the Tajiks was decided by four Uzbeks, five Kazakhs, one Ukrainian, one Lithuanian, one Latvian, one Russian, one Turkmen and one Kyrgyz.[73] Tajikistan was to become an autonomous *oblast* within the Uzbek Soviet Socialist Republic. Uzbekistan received the most fertile, populated and developed territories of Central Asia: Ferghana, Samarkand and part of the Syr-Darya *oblasts* of Turkestan, Western Bukhara, south-eastern Khorezm and the city of Tashkent. Tajikistan was given the far less important areas of Eastern Bukhara and the Pamirs. Henceforth, in October 1924, Tajikistan was deprived of any city, and large concentrations of the Tajik population in Bukhara, Samarkand, Ferghana and Termez stayed outside its borders. While Uzbek, Kazakh, Turkmen and Kyrgyz officials bargained ferociously for every inch of land, the Uzbek national sub-commission quietly determined borders for the Tajiks. In the meantime, Uzbek newspapers published articles maintaining that the 'small number and dispersedness of Tajiks over great expanses do not allow them to create an independent political life',[74] and that, anyway, the inevitability of assimilation of the Tajiks 'is predetermined by ... social progress'.[75] It was only intervention by the Politburo of the Russian

---

70 I. M. Muminov, ed. *Istoriia Uzbekskoi SSR s drevneishikh vremen do nashikh dnei* (Tashkent: Fan, 1974), p. 330.

71 G. P. Makarova, *Narodny komissariat po delam natsionalnostei RSFSR. 1917–1923* (Moscow: Nauka, 1987), pp. 82–3.

72 Stalin, *Sochineniia*, Vol. V, p. 250.

73 Masov, *Tadzhiki*, p. 193.

74 M. S. Sadykov, *Istoricheskii opyt KPSS po stroitelstvu sotsializma v Tadzhikistane (1917–1959gg.)* (Dushanbe: Irfon, 1967), p. 115.

75 Vishnevsky, *Leninskaia natsionalnaia politika v deistvii*, p. 76.

Communist Party Central Committee on 11 October 1924 that precluded the transformation of Tajikistan into simply one of the districts of Uzbekistan: the Tajik state entity was instead elevated to the status of an autonomous republic.[76]

In December 1924, the first government of the Tajik autonomy of the Uzbek Soviet Socialist Republic was created, and in March 1925 the Tajik Autonomous Soviet Socialist Republic was officially proclaimed. The inadequate character of the national–territorial delimitation as far as the Tajiks were concerned was accentuated by the fact that the capital of the new republic, in the absence of alternatives, had to be established in the *qishloq* (village) of Dushanbe, which, with less than 1000 inhabitants, had never before served as a cultural or administrative centre.[77] The Tajik autonomy embraced only 63.1 per cent of all Central Asian Tajiks; 35.8 per cent of them remained enfolded by Uzbekistan.[78] The elevation of Tajikistan to a full Union Republic in October 1929,[79] and the acquisition of Khujand and other Tajik lands in Ferghana, rectified the situation only partially. Samarkand and Bukhara, the two paramount cultural, spiritual and economic centres of the Tajiks, remained in Uzbekistan. The Uzbek leaders used underhand tactics to achieve this: the capital of Uzbekistan was temporarily moved from Tashkent to Samarkand, where Tajik citizens were encouraged to call themselves Uzbeks, otherwise they could be sent to 'brotherly Tajikistan' to help overcome its backwardness. This policy yielded the following results: in 1917, there were 44 758 Tajiks and 3301 Uzbeks recorded amongst the Samarkandis; the corresponding figures in 1926 stood at 10 716 and 43 304.[80] In reality, however, Tajiks constituted more than 70 per cent of the population of Bukhara and Samarkand *oblasts*.[81]

---

76   *Ocherki istorii kompartii Turkestana, Bukhary i Khorezma*, p. 73. Bergne argues that part of the motivation for the creation of the autonomous Tajik republic was that '[a] strongly unified and culturally developed Tajik Autonomous Oblast could serve as a centre of attraction and target for emulation by the neighbouring Afghan Tajiks whose numbers were variously estimated to be about a million'. See: Bergne, *The Birth of Tajikistan*, p. 49.
77   V. V. Barthold, 'Zapiska po voprosy ob istoricheskikh vzaimootnosheniiakh turetskikh i iranskikh narodnostei Srednei Azii', *Vostok*, No. 5 (1991), p. 166.
78   Shirin Akiner, *Islamic Peoples of the Soviet Union* (London: Kegan Paul International, 1983), p. 306.
79   The various hypotheses given for the motivations behind the creation of a full Tajik Republic include: 'establishing a Soviet model Iranian state' to serve 'as an example to Asian neighbours'—that is, Iran and Afghanistan (Bergne, *The Birth of Tajikistan*, p. 114; also: Rakowska-Harmstone, *Russia and Nationalism in Central Asia*, pp. 71–4); an acknowledgment by Moscow of the fact that Tajikistan 'met the three criteria for union membership: it was a border area, its leading nationality formed a compact majority, and, after the Khodzhent region was transferred from Uzbekistan to the new republic, its population reached the one million mark' (Rakowska-Harmstone, *Russia and Nationalism in Central Asia*, p. 71); the creation of the Tajik SSR was 'was designed to undercut the hegemony of the Uzbeks there, and by the Communist desire to destroy the Pan-Islamic, Pan-Turkic unity of Turkestan' (ibid., pp. 71–2); the result of lobbying by Tajik and Kazakh elites, as well as by their supporters in Moscow (Anaita Khudonazar, 'The Other', Berkeley Program in Soviet and Post-Soviet Studies Working Paper Series [2004], pp. 4–5).
80   Masov, *Tadzhiki*, p. 119. See also: Valerii Tishkov, *Ethnicity, Nationalism and Conflict in and after the Soviet Union: The Mind Aflame* (London: Sage, 1997), p. 20.
81   *Grazhdanskie dvizheniia v Tadzhikistane* (Moscow: TSIMO, 1990), pp. 101, 106.

The new Tajik government had to start nation-state building from scratch. Apart from the fact that eponymous people accounted for an absolute majority (74.6 per cent) of the republic's population, there was little else to bind them together. A Tajik scholar has written that 'Tajiks who lived in the Hisor Mountains did not have knowledge about Tajiks residing in Khujand. And Tajiks of the Zarafshon Valley were not in the least cognisant of the life of Tajiks in Gorno-Badakhshan.'[82] As late as 1935, nine *raions* (districts) of Tajikistan had no telephone and telegraph installations, and seven other *raions* were devoid of any means of communication at all.[83] The level of development of constituent regions in the republic varied considerably: the north (Khujand, Isfara, Kanibodom) had relatively industrialised areas with market-oriented farming; the centre and the south (Hisor, Kulob, Qurghonteppa, Gharm) clung to subsistence agriculture, and had very little access to the benefits of a modern market economy;[84] as for the Pamirs, its people still practised outmoded methods of agriculture and constantly teetered on the edge of survival.[85] The task of bringing all Tajiks together appeared almost impossible, but the nascent Tajik elite had a very powerful instrument at its disposal: the Soviet government machine, with its vast economic potential and efficient coercive mechanisms.

In the 1920s and early 1930s, what can be called a 'territorial nation' was being feverishly constructed in Tajikistan. It was based on a sense of clear-cut boundaries, as well as on a commonality of laws and legal and governmental institutions. Between 1926 and 1929, the previously ill-assorted territorial administrative structure was unified and simplified throughout the republic: the newly created seven *okrugs* (districts) and one autonomous *oblast* were divided into *raions*, which in turn comprised several *selsovets* (primary administrative organs) each. In 1926, the process of mass Sovietisation of the Tajik Autonomous Soviet Socialist Republic began, and was successfully completed in 1929 (extraordinary dictatorial organs—revolutionary committees, *revkoms*—had previously been replaced in northern Tajikistan with elected soviets). In 1931, the Constitution of the Tajik Soviet Socialist Republic was adopted, consolidating and sanctioning the changed political system. Finally, the independent Communist Party of Tajikistan (CPT) was set up in 1929, with a membership of 1479 (48 per cent Tajiks),[86] compared with the total of 11 communists in

---

82   B. S. Asimova, *Iazykovoe stroitelstvo v Tadzhikistane, 1920–1940* (Dushanbe: Donish, 1982), p. 71.

83   *Ocherki istorii narodnogo khoziaistva Tadzhikistana* (Dushanbe: Donish, 1967), p. 233.

84   In 1925, the chairman of the Kulob *viloyat*, Abdulaziev, made this statement: 'I represent a very backward people. We don't have schools. I have a facsimile seal in my pocket and when they bring me a paper [for signature] I stamp it, but I don't know what is written there ... We drink from wooden cups. Our footwear is also made of wood. Everything we have is made of wood. We have never seen glass.' See: Sadykov, *Istoricheskii opyt KPSS po stroitelstvu sotsializma v Tadzhikistane*, p. 117.

85   I. Mukhitdinov, *Osobennosti traditsionnogo zemledelcheskogo khoziaistva pripamirskikh narodnostei v XIX – nachale XX veka* (Dushanbe: Donish, 1984), pp. 48, 144, 157.

86   Rakowska-Harmstone, *Russia and Nationalism in Central Asia*, p. 100.

Eastern Bukhara in 1924.[87] The Tajik communist elite had grown sufficiently to fill vacancies in state agencies, especially at the grassroots level; while at the beginning of 1925, 80 per cent of personnel in local executive committees were former emirate officials,[88] by 1931 they had been all but expunged.

The growth of a national elite in Tajikistan was facilitated by the general policy of nativisation (*korenizatsiia*) of cadres, conducted by Moscow during 1920–34. As Stalin pointed out in 1923:

> [I]n order to make Soviet power dear to peasants of another [non-Russian] nation, it is necessary to make it understandable to them, to have it operating in the native language, to staff schools and organs of government with people who know the tongue, traditions, customs, and everyday life of non-Russian nationalities.[89]

The Commission for Tajikisation of the State Apparatus was set up in Dushanbe in March 1926. In October 1929, the ratio of indigenous personnel in central republican organs reached 14.3 per cent, at the *okrug* level 22.2 per cent and in *raions*, 44.9 per cent (72 per cent in 1933).[90] Of course, all more or less important matters were decided in Moscow, and their solutions were supervised by centrally appointed personnel. Still, the policy of nativisation laid a solid foundation for the emergence of a viable territorial bureaucracy in Tajikistan in the 1970s.

The advancement of a common Tajik culture was potentially another important factor for fostering a sense of national cohesion; however, the loss of the tremendous cultural and intellectual resources of Samarkand and Bukhara inhibited this process. The dialect of these two regions was supposed to form the basis of a contemporary literary Tajik language, but there were not enough qualified people in Tajikistan to promote it. Nor did the introduction of Latin (1928) and then Russian (1940) alphabets instead of the old Arabic script help to preserve the great medieval tradition. On the other hand, it was not until the advent of Soviet power that the rich cultural heritage and history of the Tajiks became subject to systematic research and popularisation. In 1930, the special Committee of Tajik Studies was established in Dushanbe, and two years later it was transformed into the State Research Institute, dealing with an array of topics in Tajik history, language, literature and ethnography.[91] The Soviet authorities also sponsored national cinematography, fine arts and other forms of intellectual activity that altogether constituted 'the new motor of ethnic

87 Ishanov, *Rol' Kompartii i Sovetskogo pravitelstva v sozdanii natsionalnoi gosudarstvennosti uzbekskogo naroda*, p. 191.
88 Vishnevsky, *Leninskaia natsionalnaia politika v deistvii*, p. 85.
89 Stalin, *Sochineniia*, Vol. V, pp. 240–1.
90 Vishnevsky, *Leninskaia natsionalnaia politika v deistvii*, p. 104.
91 Sadykov, *Istoricheskii opyt KPSS po stroitelstvu sotsializma v Tadzhikistane*, p. 293.

revival'.[92] The unprecedented spread of education created an ever-growing social stratum receptive to the ethnic myths reconstructed and elaborated by the Tajik intelligentsia.

Politicisation of Ethnic Identity

After World War II there was a reversal in primary ideological emphasis in the Soviet Union from class to ethnicity. Previously nationalism was officially viewed as a stage in the evolution towards a class-based socialist society.[93] In Yuri Slezkine's words, nationalism became, with the full support of Soviet authorities, a 'sacred principle of marxism-leninism'.[94] As a result, according to Valery Tishkov's analysis of Soviet social sciences, the view of ethnicity became politicised and primordialistic (the equivalent is easily found in Western scholarship). There was heavy emphasis on ethnogenesis, with social scientists providing writings to trace a group origin as far back as the upper-Palaeolithic era, to identify cultural heroes, and to demonstrate the existence of a people with 'their "own" territories and their "own" states'.[95] Victor Shnirelman provides a very similar critique,[96] and notes that this 'invention of the past' is used to raise self-esteem, usually in relation to neighbouring groups, and to demand 'special rights and privileges with respect to others who lack their glorious past'.[97] According to Alisher Ilkhamov, in response to the perception of growing nationalism—particularly in the Uzbek Soviet Socialist Republic— the central Communist Party initiated a parallel process whereby they 'gave the green light to ethnographic investigations that would raise doubts about the homogeneous nature of the modern Uzbek nation and question the reasons for

---

92   Smith, *The Ethnic Origins of Nations*, p. 160.
93   Yuri Slezkine, 'The USSR as a Communal Apartment, or How a Socialist State Promoted Ethnic Particularism', *Slavic Review*, Vol. 53, No. 2 (Summer 1994). Slezkine writes that as part of this process 'linguists and ethnographers expected—and tried to bring about—the fusion and consequent disappearance of linguistic and ethnic communities' (ibid., p. 137). See also: Yuri Slezkine, 'The Fall of Soviet Ethnography, 1928–38', *Current Anthropology*, Vol. 32, No. 4 (1991), pp. 476–84. According to Adeeb Khalid, it was in the mid 1930s that 'official Soviet discourse came to accept—indeed, to assert—that national and ethnic identities were real and permanent, but it still did not compromise on the basic universalism of historical progress'. See: Adeeb Khalid, *Islam after Communism: Religion and Politics in Central Asia* (Berkeley: University of California Press, 2007), p. 65.
94   Slezkine, 'The USSR as a Communal Apartment', p. 414.
95   Valery A. Tishkov, 'Inventions and Manifestations of Ethno-Nationalism in and after the Soviet Union', in *Ethnicity and Conflict in a Post-Communist World: The Soviet Union, Eastern Europe and China*, eds Kumar Rupesinghe, Peter King and Olga Vorkunova (New York: St Martin's Press, 1992), p. 42.
96   Victor A. Shnirelman, *Who Gets the Past? Competition for Ancestors among Non-Russian Intellectuals in Russia* (Baltimore: The Johns Hopkins University Press, 1996), pp. 1–12, 58–61. Shnirelman notes the importance of autochthonism (that is, a certain group has always inhabited its current location) and particularism (de-emphasising common roots and stressing differences) (ibid., p. 12).
97   Shnirelman, *Who Gets the Past*, p. 2.

the inclusions of certain ethnic groups'.[98] As a result, it is possible to find clearly separate discourses on nationalism, identity and ethnic origins in the Soviet-era scholarship.

The search for a 'glorious past' is not an irrelevant, isolated intellectual pursuit. While academics may provide the basic material, those 'amateurs in the field' such as popular writers, journalists, educators and artists are the ones who play a significant role, and often in a manner that is 'less restrained' and 'highly selective'.[99] Shnirelman notes that as part of this search for a past, 'an ethnic group may encroach upon or even appropriate the past and cultural legacy of another group, leading to misunderstandings, arguments and tensions'.[100] These types of claims are not without their material logic, as the 'special rights and privileges' part of Shnirelman's explanation above demonstrates. All governments use historical symbols and historiography to cultivate patriotism, explain and justify policies, and secure the acquiescence and cooperation of the people in times of crises. Symbolic encapsulation of the themes of regime legitimacy, common identity and cultural revival through historical references is particularly crucial for emerging nations. The newly independent Central Asian countries present no exception to this pattern.[101]

The Tajik official histories, for their part, traced the completion of their 'ethnogenesis' to the Samanid era (ninth–tenth centuries).[102] Shirin Akiner claims, in an assertion that can only be safely applied to nationalist intellectuals and select politicians, that '[h]istoriography is to Tajiks an intensely emotive, fiercely contested political issue'.[103] Contemporary Tajik nationalists stress not only their Persian (Western Iranian) heritage, but also their Soghdian (Eastern Iranian) heritage in order to counteract the claim of 'their Turkic neighbours' (that is, Uzbek nationalists in Uzbekistan) that Turkic peoples are the original inhabitants of Central Asia and that the Tajiks are latecomers.[104] An excellent

---

98   A. Ilkhamov, 'Archeology of Uzbek Identity', *Anthropology & Archeology of Eurasia*, Vol. 44, No. 4 (Spring 2006), p. 27.

99   Shnirelman, *Who Gets the Past*, pp. 58–9. Similarly, as Schoeberlein-Engel notes about Central Asia, 'the debate amongst those who promote or oppose Uzbek nationalist claims … is built more on emotion than on history'. See: Schoeberlein-Engel, 'The Prospects for Uzbek National Identity', *Central Asia Monitor*, No. 2 (1996), p. 13; Schoeberlein-Engel, *Identity in Central Asia*, pp. 66, 72.

100   Shnirelman, *Who Gets the Past*, pp. 2, 60–1. Shnirelman notes that this is especially true when the encroachment involves claims on others' territory.

101   Nourzhanov, 'The Politics of History in Tajikistan', n.p.

102   Ghafurov, *Tojikon*, pp. 494–501; Nourzhanov, 'The Politics of History in Tajikistan', n.p.; *Tadzhikskaia Sovetskaia Sotsialisticheskaia Respublika* (Dushanbe: AN TadzSSR, 1974), p. 88, as cited in Subtelny, 'The Symbiosis of Turk and Tajik', p. 53; Laruelle, 'The Return of the Aryan Myth'.

103   Akiner, *Tajikistan*, p. 10. This is clearly not a new phenomenon, as demonstrated by Guissou Jahangiri in her analysis of Tajik-centric journals involved in the Tajik intellectual discourse in the 1920s. See: Guissou Jahangiri, 'The Premises for the Construction of a Tajik National Identity, 1920–1930', in *Tajikistan: The Trials of Independence*, eds Mohammad-Reza Djalili, Frederic Grare and Shirin Akiner (New York: St Martin's Press, 1997).

104   Muriel Atkin, 'Tajikistan's Relations with Iran and Afghanistan', in *The New Politics of Central Asia and its Borderlands*, eds Ali Banuazizi and Myron Weiner (Bloomington: Indiana University Press, 1994), pp. 97–8.

example of this is in a recent article by Shamsiddin Kamoliddin, a researcher at the Institute of History in Uzbekistan, wherein he makes the uncited claim that modern-day Uzbeks are descended from sedentarised 'proto-Turks' who were the indigenous population of Central Asia *before* the arrival of Indo-European peoples. He further claims (again uncited) that these Turks had inhabited the region (and specifically not as nomads) since the second millennia BC, only to be forced out by 'Aryan invaders'.[105] As a reply to these extremely dubious historical assertions, Tajik nationalists can easily point in turn to the claim made by the prominent Tajik academic Bobojon Ghafurov that the 'Iranian eastern populations did not come to Central Asia out of nowhere but constituted themselves there, on the ground'.[106]

Soviet Nationality Policies

Muriel Atkin notes that before the Soviet nation-building process in Central Asia, the 'overwhelming majority of indigenous inhabitants considered themselves part of the Muslim community but also saw that community as subdivided into groups which were different and, not infrequently, mutually hostile'.[107] Atkin lists these divisions as ethnicity, religious ties, loyalty to dynasties or local tribal chiefs, tribal or clan affiliation, economic interests, geographic locations and political ideologies.[108] Subtelny provides fewer identity categories, listing tribe, town or religion.[109] Sergei Abashin provides a more comprehensive list:

> The basic cultural frontiers in pre-Russian Central Asia were not shaped along ethnic or ethnic-national lines. The main divides used to differentiate 'one of us' from someone 'foreign' were based on position in the social hierarchy, religious separation into Sunni, Shi'ite, or Ishmaelite, membership of different Sufi brotherhoods, economic-cultural categorization between settled, mountainous, nomadic or semi-nomadic groups, family or tribal distinctions, or by regional classification.[110]

By the beginning of the Soviet era, in Abashin's words, the many 'cultural and social categories and "named groups" that existed in Central Asia was [sic] artificially and administratively reduced to an extremely limited range of

---

105   Shamsiddin Kamoliddin, 'The Notion of Ethnogenesis in the Ethnic Atlas of Uzbekistan', *Archeology & Anthropology of Eurasia*, Vol. 44, No. 4 (Spring 2006), pp. 43–4.
106   B. G. Gafurov, *Istoriia tadzhikskogo naroda v kratkom izlozhenii* (Moscow: Politizdat, 1949), p. 26, as translated and cited in Laruelle, 'The Return of the Aryan Myth', p. 56.
107   Atkin, 'Religious, National and Other Identities in Central Asia', p. 47.
108   Atkin, 'Religious, National and Other Identities in Central Asia', p. 47.
109   Subtelny, 'The Symbiosis of Turk and Tajik', p. 51.
110   Abashin, 'The Transformation of Ethnic Identity in Central Asia', p. 32. Abashin argues that these categories are 'much more important than a "functional" characteristic like language'.

"nationalities" or "national groups"'.[111] The manipulation of identity categories began at an early date. One example is from the 1920 census, in which there was, in addition to difficulty in assigning ethnic identity to those within the Tajik-Uzbek categories, 'deliberate misidentification for political purposes, particularly in the Tajik-Uzbek case'.[112] Similarly, Atkin writes that many people 'feared being forcibly relocated to ensure that a given nationality would be entirely contained within "its" own republic. Thus some of the self-designations as "Tajik" and "Uzbek" did not reflect that individual's ethnic consciousness but rather his estimate of which answer would enable him to remain in his home.'[113] The Tajik historian Rahim Masov takes the above themes to a much higher level, dedicating much of his writing to demonstrating what he perceives to be the ethnic injustices inflicted upon Tajiks by both Uzbeks and fellow Tajiks. Masov convincingly demonstrates that many Tajiks outside the present-day area of Tajikistan were forced into the 'Uzbek' category through discrimination, falsified census results, local bureaucratic subterfuge, and various other methods.[114]

Soviet social scientists' work was 'closely tied into the official ideology and politics of ethno-nationalism dominant in the Soviet state—with ethnic groups forming pseudo-federal administrative units or Republics'.[115] In Soviet Central Asia, Uzbek and Tajik cultural histories were 'redefined' on the basis of language and territory; however, many of those now determined to be Uzbeks and Tajiks had often shared the same territory, culture and languages throughout recent history, so the 'compartmentalization of individual elements from this common background into "Uzbek" and "Tajik" was bound to create confusion and overlap'.[116] Centlivres and Centlivres-Demont maintain that Soviet ethnographers took many diverse Persian-speaking and Turkic-speaking groups and gathered them into two categories, Tajiks and Uzbeks respectively, and 'treated them as homogeneous entities';[117] however, this focus on the Soviet central government's plans does not take into consideration the manipulative roles played by local allies of the Bolsheviks. As an example, Carlisle points especially to Fayzulla Khojaev, a Jadid (Muslim reformer) and Moscow's 'primary native ally'.[118] Obiya Chika focuses entirely on Khojaev's career and identity, noting that as his career

111   Abashin, 'The Transformation of Ethnic Identity in Central Asia', p. 33. An example of this wide variety of 'named groups' that were to be administratively eliminated is a census list from 1924 of Uzbek tribe and clan names in Bukhara, which, when sub-clan categories are included, has more than 100 categories. See: I. Magidovac, 'Administrativnoe delenie', *Materialy po raionirovaniiu Srednei Azii*, Vol. 2, No. 2, pp. 29–60, as cited in Schoeberlein-Engel, *Identity in Central Asia*, pp. 153–5.
112   Sengupta, 'Imperatives of National Territorial Delimitation and the Fate of Bukhara', p. 411.
113   Atkin, 'Religious, National and Other Identities in Central Asia', p. 49.
114   Masov, *Istoriia topornogo razdeleniia*, pp. 16–18, 78, 105, 113.
115   Tishkov, 'Inventions and Manifestations of Ethno-Nationalism in and after the Soviet Union', p. 42.
116   Subtelny, 'The Symbiosis of Turk and Tajik', p. 52.
117   Centlivres and Centlivres-Demont, 'Tajikistan and Afghanistan', p. 5.
118   Carlisle, 'Uzbekistan and the Uzbeks', p. 26.

progressed he 'seemed to show a drastic change of self-identity—from Bukharan to Uzbek',[119] and that ultimately he was the most active of any Central Asian leaders in the process of national delimitation.[120] Masov is particularly critical of the role played by Khojaev and other local leaders—both Uzbek and Tajik—in manipulating the process whereby the population of Central Asia was divided ethnically into nationality categories and geographically into republics.[121]

Sergei Abashin describes the process whereby an ethnic consciousness developed amongst Soviet citizens:

> Over seven decades, Soviet power was responsible for huge changes in people's self-consciousness. Moscow mobilized all of the instruments and resources necessary to achieve this: a national state, a national culture, national language and literature, national education and national media (particularly television). Among the most powerful tools for introducing ethnic self-consciousness to the masses were internal passports and the census, which, in effect, was a survey of the population's ethnic-national allegiance. Every person had to be formally registered as a specific 'nationality,' which he/she could not change later, even if he/she wished to. Education also contributed to this socialization process. Thus, in the Soviet period, a citizen's consciousness, the sense of belonging to the Uzbek or Tajik state, came increasingly to resemble ethnic self-consciousness, as in identifying with a certain culture, language and history.[122]

After demarcation the government in Tajikistan introduced a standardised Tajik language, expanded the reach of the media and formed 'national, political, cultural and educational institutions', while intellectuals 'gave shape and substance to the Tajik heritage',[123] creating a palpable sense of shared national identity, particularly when viewed in juxtaposition with other newly created Central Asian republics. Driven from above and confined to the highly visible public domain in big cities, Soviet modernisation was limited in its success in excoriating the parochial, sub-ethnic identities. These limitations were seen

---

119   Obiya Chika, 'When Faizulla Khojaev Decided to be an Uzbek', in *Islam and Politics in Russia and Central Asia (Early Eighteenth to Late Twentieth Centuries)*, eds Stéphane Dudoignon and Komatsu Hisao (London and New York: Kegan Paul, 2001), p. 100.
120   Chika, 'When Faizulla Khojaev Decided to be an Uzbek', p. 103.
121   Masov, *Istoriia topornogo razdeleniia*. In particular, the appendix of Masov's book (starting on page 115) provides a view into the internal workings of the committees presided over by local leaders.
122   Abashin, 'The Transformation of Ethnic Identity in Central Asia', pp. 33–4.
123   Shirin Akiner, 'Prospects for Civil Society in Tajikistan', in *Civil Society in the Muslim World: Contemporary Perspectives*, ed. Amyn B. Sajoo (London: I. B. Tauris, 2004), p. 153.

most acutely in rural society, as demonstrated polemically by Sergei Poliakov in his study of the 'traditional' lives of Central Asians.[124] In regards again to identity categories, the local loyalties and associations were often 'incorporated' into the larger nationality categories. As a result, these pre-existing identities continued to survive 'unofficially' below the level of nation and nationality, as will be further illustrated later in this book.

---

124   Sergei P. Poliakov, *Everyday Islam: Religion and Tradition in Rural Central Asia* (London: M. E. Sharpe, 1992), esp. pp. 53–144.

3. State Formation in the Soviet Era, 1917 to the 1960s

From the second half of the nineteenth century, Central Asia was inexorably subjected to internal developments in the Russian Empire. The hectic, often controversial process of modernisation that commenced in Russia under Alexander II, continued under Stolypin and finally took the form of socialist revolution in 1917 could not have affected this region in a more dramatic way. If modernisation is viewed as the transformation of a traditional society that commences 'once the leaders of a society have decided to adapt their existing institutions and values to modern functions'[1] then the natural questions to ask are: who were the real leaders in the Central Asian societal milieu? How resistant did traditional institutions prove to be vis-a-vis elements of modernisation, such as industrialisation, territorial unification, universal education, administration and legal principles? Why did this adaptation not take the conventional linear form of moving from an agrarian to an industrial society? This chapter, which is chronologically set in the period from 1917 to the 1960s, deals with the peculiarities of Tajikistan's movement towards the Soviet form of modernity, concentrating on the initially violent character of the process and its inherently contradictory features.

The Russian Revolution and Turkestan

While the Russian conquest, and the innovations that followed, resulted in the establishment of lasting peace and significant improvement in living standards in the region, it all came at a high price for the indigenous population. They acquired the status of second-grade people in their own land.[2] The imperial regime's administrative, legal, educational and land reforms, initiated in Turkestan under governor-general K. P. von Kaufman (1867–82), were aimed primarily at strengthening and maintaining Russian supremacy; all other goals were secondary. Once a certain degree of stability was achieved in the region and Turkestan became incorporated into the all-Russian economy, there was no compelling need for the tsarist government to press on with reforms, especially in the political field. During his tenure as chairman of the Council of Ministers

---

1 Cyril E. Black, 'Inner Asia and Modernisation: The Problem', in *The Modernisation of Inner Asia*, ed. Cyril E. Black (Armonk, NY, and London: M. E. Sharpe, 1991), p. 19.
2 For one of many examples, see the anecdotes in: A. I. Iakovlev and S. A. Panarin, 'Protivorechiia reform: Araviia i Turkestan', *Vostok*, No. 5 (1991), p. 117.

of the Russian Empire (1907–11), P. A. Stolypin delivered a clear message that the Russians were not prepared to share their monopoly on power with the native population in Central Asia.

Ultimately, however, the empire found it difficult to cope with the social forces it had inadvertently unleashed in Turkestan. First, the ever-growing class of local entrepreneurs, industrialists and intellectuals grew more and more vociferous in its demands for equal rights with Russians. Whereas in 1906 they had asked only for religious freedom, the return of expropriated lands and the creation of a Muslim religious administration in Tashkent,[3] in 1916, for the first time, an explicit demand for independence and the establishment of a sovereign state of Turkestan was made public at the Congress of Nationalities in Lausanne.[4] Second, Russian rule failed to weaken traditional institutions, such as *adat* (customary law), *shari'a* (Islamic law) or the patriarchal family; in fact, indigenous social control[5] at the grassroots level gained from the Russian Government's recognition of local men of authority as its representatives. While proclaiming allegiance to the tsar, many traditional leaders were disposed to pursue their own agenda in crisis periods and incite the masses against Russian rule, as happened in 1892 in Tashkent with *qozi* Muhitdin and *ishon* Abu-l-Qasim—'hitherto notable amongst the natives for their loyal speeches and declarations'.[6]

The imperial government did not manage to create a solid social base amongst the indigenous population. Two worlds coexisted in Turkestan: one of Russian settlers and administrators, the other of the local inhabitants; interaction between the two was minimal. By 1917, this coexistence had acquired overtones of open hostility. The tsarist regime was no longer in a position to ameliorate economic difficulties in Turkestan, nor could it resort to intimidation in order to maintain the status quo, for its army and police were in complete disarray.[7] The Russian Empire entered 1917 with its economy, armed forces and moral foundations badly shaken by the continuing war in Europe. Turkestan was no

---

3   Carrère d'Encausse, *Islam and the Russian Empire*, p. 77.

4   Hambly, *Central Asia*, p. 228.

5   In this book, 'social control' is used as a neutral term 'to cover all social processes to induce conformity ranging from infant socialisation through to public execution'. See: Stanley Cohen, *Visions of Social Control: Crime, Punishment and Classification* (Cambridge: Polity Press, 1994), p. 2.

6   Barthold, *Sochineniia*, Vol. II, Part 1, p. 374.

7   During winter–spring 1917, the number of deserters from the Russian armed forces rose almost fivefold, from 6300 a month to a staggering figure of 30 900. See: N. N. Golovin, 'Voennye usiliia Rossii v mirovoi voine', *Voenno-istoricheskii zhurnal*, No. 4 (1993), p. 29. Arrest and dismissal of officers by the rank-and-file soldiers were the order of the day and, as the military commander of the Samarkand *oblast* reported, there were evident 'tremendous decay of discipline in the regiments and general licentiousness of soldiers'. See: D. I. Soifer, 'Bolshevistskie voennye gruppy Turkestanskogo voennogo okruga v 1917g.', in *Voennye organizatsii partii bolshevikov v 1917g.*, ed. Iu. I. Korablev (Moscow: Nauka, 1986), p. 252.

exception to the generally catastrophic state of affairs in the Romanovs' realm. The political situation had become highly volatile in the general-governorship by 1917.

Both Russians and the indigenous population of Turkestan welcomed the abdication of Nicholas II and the establishment of the Provisional Government on 27 February 1917. The Russians anticipated a quick end to the war and an easing of the economic crisis; the locals hoped to achieve the right to self-determination. Arguably, the short period of spring to autumn 1917 was a time of an unheard-of level of freedom in Russia, and particularly in Turkestan. More than 70 political parties and organisations were operative throughout the former empire,[8] including a variety of reformist (*jadid*) and conservative Muslim groups, united in Shurai Islamiya (the Islamic Council) and Jamiyati Ulama (the Assembly of the Clergy) respectively. In May 1917, the First All-Russian Muslim Congress was held in Moscow. The majority of its 800 delegates, one-third of whom represented Central Asia, voted in favour of federation with Russia, with territorial self-rule for each nationality.[9]

The Russian Provisional Government, dominated by constitutional democrats, socialist revolutionaries and Mensheviks, was reluctant to share power with local elites in Turkestan. It retained the anti-native attitudes of the tsarist regime and, moreover, preserved the old administrative structures. Governor-General Kuropatkin issued a decree in March 1917 that stipulated that the proportion of Russians in local legislative bodies must not be lower than 50 per cent.[10] One month later, an official of the Executive Committee of the Provisional Government made a comment to the effect that 'the revolution has been waged by Russians; that is why the power is in our hands in Central Asia'.[11]

In 1917, only the Bolsheviks appeared to have a positive solution to the nationality question. Their Seventh All-Russian Conference in April confirmed the right of nations to self-determination, but made it conditional with the supreme interests of the proletariat's struggle for socialism,[12] thus creating a space for political manoeuvre. A sizeable part of the native intelligentsia in Turkestan found the Bolshevik doctrine attractive, since it promised equality with Russians and an accelerated pace of social progress. As Alexandre

8   *Borba kommunisticheskoi partii protiv neproletarskikh partii, grupp i techenii v posleoktiabrskii period* (Leningrad: Izdatelstvo Leningradskogo universiteta, 1982), p. 5.
9   Richard Pipes, *The Formation of the Soviet Union: Communism and Nationalism, 1917–1923* (Cambridge, Mass.: Harvard University Press, 1970), p. 77.
10   *Pobeda Oktiabrskoi revolutsii v Uzbekistane: Sbornik dokumentov*, Vol. 1 (Tashkent: Izdatelstvo AN UzSSR, 1963), p. 30.
11   Hélène Carrère d'Encausse, 'The Fall of the Czarist Empire', in *Central Asia: A Century of Russian Rule*, ed. Edward Allworth (New York: Columbia University Press, 1967), p. 218.
12   S. V. Kuleshov, *Velikii Oktiabr i torzhestvo leninskoi natsionalnoi programmy partii* (Moscow: Vysshaiia Shkola, 1987), pp. 72–4.

Bennigsen has noted, 'their Marxism was vague, if not unlearned. Their aims were twofold: reformist vis-á-vis traditional Islam and nationalist vis-á-vis the creation of independent Muslim polities free from Russian domination.'[13] The Bolsheviks, in turn, regarded Muslim socialists as a useful means of spreading the party's influence in Central Asia.

The second half of 1917 was characterised by a further decline of authority in Turkestan. Organs of the Provisional Government coexisted and competed with various self-proclaimed Soviets of Workers' and Soldiers' Deputies whilst the bulk of the indigenous population stood aloof from the political struggle.[14] In the end it was precisely Bolshevik and left-wing socialist revolutionary influence in the army that secured victory over the Provisional Government throughout Turkestan in October 1917.[15]

Nationalist elements in Turkestan were too weak and fragmented to challenge Russian supremacy, and inevitably had to decide which side to support in the Russian Civil War. The idea of preserving the old state of affairs did not appeal to them, and finally the bulk of the national intelligentsia either joined the Turkestan Communist Party (TCP) or at least remained neutral in respect to its activities. After the Red Guards quashed the short-lived Kokand Autonomy in February 1918 and the Turkestan Autonomous Soviet Socialist Republic (TASSR) was promulgated on 1 May 1918, Soviet power became the single most important force in the region.[16] All alternative political organisations, including Shurai Islamiya and Jamiyati Ulama, were disbanded, and even Muslim soviets (*Musovdepy*) were merged with district Soviets of Workers' and Soldiers' Deputies (*Raisovdepy*) because, according to the TASSR Government, there could not be 'division between Russians and Muslims in Soviet Turkestan'.[17] The adoption in October 1918 of the TASSR Constitution, which emulated Soviet Russia's basic laws, and placed its defence, foreign affairs, communications, transport, industry and finances under Moscow's jurisdiction, underlined the process of Turkestan's integration into the Soviet realm. It received further impetus with the end of fighting in mainland Russia in 1920; henceforth the vast territories of Turkestan, which included northern Tajikistan, shared all major perturbations of the communist experiment in full measure. The patterns of War Communism, wholesale nationalisation, the New Economic Policy (NEP), industrialisation and collectivisation in Khujand and Isfara did not differ much from those in Tambov or Donetsk.

---

13   Bennigsen and Wimbush, *Muslim National Communism in the Soviet Union*, p. 22.

14   *Pobeda Oktiabrskoi revolutsii v Uzbekistane*, Vol. 1, p. 266.

15   Soifer, 'Bolshevistskie voennye gruppy Turkestanskogo voennogo okruga v 1917g.', pp. 249–50.

16   As the White General Denikin noted, 'by the Summer of 1918 the whole Turkestan *okrug* had been captured by the Bolsheviks with the assistance of Hungarian and German prisoners-of-war settled there'. See: Gen. A. I. Denikin, 'Ocherki Russkoi smuty', *Voprosy Istorii*, No. 2 (1995), p. 106.

17   *Pobeda Oktiabrskoi revolutsii v Uzbekistane: Sbornik dokumentov*, Vol. 2 (Tashkent: Izdatelstvo AN UzSSR, 1972), p. 481.

The Downfall of Bukhara

The situation was quite different in the Bukharan Emirate. The two revolutions of 1917 had a very modest impact on this country. Soviets were organised exclusively in Russian settlements there, and generally kept a low profile. In November 1917, there were only three Bolsheviks in Bukhara.[18] Emir Alim Khan's main concern was the increasing activism of the *jadid* movement, which demanded liberal reforms, particularly in the sphere of education. In April 1917, the most active *jadids* were arrested and flogged, and their leaders—most notably, Fayzulla Khojaev—sought asylum in New Bukhara and Turkestan. With the triumph of the Bolsheviks in Turkestan came an opportunity for the *jadids* to implement their reformist program. In September 1918, some 200 radical *jadids* created the Bukharan Communist Party (BCP); two years later its membership exceeded five thousand.[19] Fayzulla Khojaev, though not a member of the BCP, was included in the Turkestan Commission (Turkkomissiia)—the plenipotentiary body established by the Russian Communist Party and the Russian Government in March 1919 to supervise and coordinate all party and state activities in the region.[20]

The first attempt to overthrow the emir and install *jadid* authority in Bukhara took place in February 1918 when F. I. Kolesov, chairman of the Turkestan Government and an ardent Bolshevik, arrived in Bukhara with 500 Red Guards from Tashkent only to find that Fayzulla Khojaev's promise of mass popular revolt against Alim Khan was a bluff. He had to retreat, and for more than two years, Bukhara was allowed to live in relative peace. Whenever the question of sending additional troops and resources to Turkestan was raised, Lenin invariably opposed it: 'Your demands for personnel are exorbitant. This is ridiculous or worse than ridiculous if you imagine that Turkestan is more important than the Centre or Ukraine ... In my opinion, Frunze asks for too much. We should capture Ukraine first, let Turkestan wait and get by somehow.'[21] In the summer of 1920 the wait was over. On 28 August, forces of the Turkestan Front under the command of Mikhail Frunze attacked the Bukharan Emirate, and by 2 September had taken control of its capital city and northern and central districts. An easy victory was guaranteed not only by the technical superiority of the Red Army;[22] as had happened many times before, the constituent principalities showed little desire to fight side-by-side with the emir. Only the city of Bukhara offered

---

18   Vladimir Medvedev, 'Nechaiannaia revolutsiia', *Druzhba Narodov*, No. 1 (1992), p. 145.

19   *Istoriia Tadzhikskogo naroda*, Vol. III, kn. 1 (Moscow: Nauka, 1964), p. 90.

20   Ishanov, *Rol' kompartii i Sovetskogo pravitelstva v sozdanii natsionalnoi gosudarstvennosti uzbekskogo naroda*, pp. 91–2.

21   V. I. Lenin, *Sochineniia*, Izd. 4, Vol. 51 (Moscow: Izdatelstvo politicheskoi literatury, 1965), pp. 89–90.

22   The taskforce of the Turkestan Front comprised 7000 infantry, 2500 cavalry, 40 cannons, 230 machine guns, 10 armoured vehicles, five armoured trains and 11 planes, and was opposed by the emir's 8300 infantry, 7600 cavalry, 23 cannons and 16 machine guns. See: Khudoiberdyev, *Boevaia druzhba, rozhdennaia Oktiabrem*, p. 79.

fierce resistance. Alim Khan fled to Dushanbe. On 6 October 1920, the Bukharan People's Soviet Republic was proclaimed, and Fayzulla Khojaev became the head of its *jadid*-dominated government.

The deposed emir failed to gather any considerable forces around him in Dushanbe. His position was thoroughly weakened by intermittent clashes between local warlords; in December 1920, the strongmen of Qarotegin rebelled against him. Consequently, the Soviet Hisor Expeditionary Corps, formed in November 1920 to gain control over Eastern Bukhara, managed to resolve this task by the spring of 1921. Alim Khan fled to Afghanistan, and the Extraordinary Dictatorial Commission was set up in Eastern Bukhara to act as a supreme administrative organ on behalf of the Bukhara People's Republic. Similarly, the Military-Political Trio was empowered by the TASSR to rule in the Pamirs.

The Tajiks of Eastern Bukhara initially welcomed the Red Army soldiers. They knew nothing about communism, and the majority of them had not even heard about the dramatic events of 1917; what they understood and cared about was that the oppressive rule of the emir and his Uzbek warlords was over. The isolated, self-sufficient peasant communities in Eastern Bukhara strove for autonomous existence according to ancient traditions in a peaceful environment, with as little state interference as possible. Of course, these hopes could not eventuate under the new regime. The Dictatorial Commission appointed revolutionary committees (*revkoms*) to each of the five *vilayets* of Eastern Bukhara, and these began to requisition food, confiscate private and *vaqf* (belonging to the mosques) lands and mobilise people for public works. In European Russia, the 'arrogant, often abutting on malversation activities of *revkoms*, indulgence in bribery, drinking and other excesses'[23] caused a large-scale peasant revolt led by A. S. Antonov between autumn 1920 and summer 1921. In Central Asia the defensive reaction of the indigenous population took the form of the so-called *basmachi* movement.

The Resistance in Central Asia

The interpretation of the *basmachi* as mere gangs of 'counter-revolutionary feudal elements' who favoured 'political banditism in combination with criminal activities'[24] cannot hold, for the movement at its height had an undoubtedly mass character and pursued definite political goals, centred mainly on the preservation of the old economic and social orders. It even managed to form a provisional government in Ferghana in August 1919. It is equally hard to corroborate the

23   P. A. Aptekar, 'Krestianskaia voina', *Voenno-istoricheskii zhurnal*, No. 1 (1993), p. 50.
24   V. I. Abylgaziev, 'Iz istorii borby narodov Turkestana za vlast Sovetov', in *Boevoe sodruzhestvo sovetskikh respublik. 1919–1922* (Moscow: Nauka, 1982), pp. 175–6.

notion that 'the struggle between the Basmachi and the Soviet Russian troops was not between Communists and anti-Communists, as in Russia, but between Russians and Moslems'.[25] The Ferghana Provisional Government was formed as a result of an alliance between an eminent *basmachi* leader, Madamin Bek, and a former tsarist officer, Monstrov, commander of the Russian Peasant Army—an alliance that 'enjoyed support from merchants and townspeople of both nationalities' and survived 'both Monstrov's death in January 1920 and Madamin's surrender in March of the same year'.[26] On the other hand, in late 1920 indigenous conscripts made up almost 33 per cent of the regiments of the Turkestan Front that fought the *basmachi*.[27] At the risk of oversimplifying, it seems that the main conflict stemmed from protests by the predominantly peasant society of Turkestan against any attempts at radically reforming existing economic patterns and concomitant rules of social behaviour. Ideological, religious and nationalist considerations were of secondary importance in this context. The successes and defeats of Soviet power in its struggle with the *basmachi* were directly linked to its agrarian policies.

During 1918–19, *basmachi* forces in the Ferghana Valley, including northern Tajikistan, numbered 7000 fighters, but by the spring of 1920 their ranks had swollen fourfold.[28] The Soviet authorities began to realise that they could not succeed by purely military methods, and opted for some social and economic concessions. The Sixth Congress of the Turkestan Communist Party (in August 1921) stressed that the abolition of mandatory food requisitions, cessation of looting by the Red Army, a broad propaganda campaign, nativisation of the local administrative bodies, and the especially cautious implementation of land reform, which 'absolutely did not affect peasants of average wealth [*seredniaki*]', had been instrumental in undermining the *basmachi* movement.[29] The arrival of reinforcements from Russia and the endorsement of a general amnesty enabled the Soviet authorities to deal a final blow to the *basmachi* in Turkestan in 1922, when from February to October, 119 of 200 *basmachi* groups dissolved or surrendered,[30] and the rest were annihilated or moved elsewhere.

The situation in Eastern Bukhara (modern-day southern Tajikistan) had distinctive features. The euphoria caused by the collapse of the emirate quickly gave way to popular resentment of marauding Red Army units and the new dictatorial organs that they supported. In the summer of 1921, the local population began to create paramilitary formations and demand the withdrawal

---

25   Michael Rywkin, *Russia in Central Asia* (New York: Collier Books, 1963), p. 57.

26   Martha B. Olcott, 'The Basmachi or Freemen's Revolt in Turkestan 1918–24', *Soviet Studies*, Vol. XXXIII, No. 3 (July 1981), p. 356.

27   Khudoiberdyev, *Boevaia druzhba, rozhdennaia Oktiabrem*, p. 37.

28   *Grazhdanskaia voina v SSSR* (Moscow: Voennoe izdatelstvo, 1986), pp. 128, 357.

29   *Inostrannaia voennaia interventsiia i grazhdanskaia voina v Srednei Azii i Kazakhstane*, Vol. 2 (Alma-Ata: Nauka, 1964), pp. 686–9.

30   A. I. Chugunov, *Borba na granitse. 1917–1928* (Moscow: Mysl, 1980), p. 118.

of the Red Army. Unlike in Ferghana, these formations acted exclusively as self-defence forces, and very seldom operated outside their parochial territories. Each of them was headed by a local strongman: a former *bek*, mullah, tribal chief or village elder. They offered resistance both to the Soviet authorities and to Alim Khan's guerrilla units. In Turkestan in 1922, the Soviet state had been able to enforce social control through established agencies, such as the ramified communist organisation, numerous garrisons linked by railroad and the hierarchy of elected soviets that began to replace *revkoms* in 1919; but Eastern Bukhara was completely devoid of those attributes. The nominal incorporation of some strongmen into the Soviet structures[31] by no means meant the strengthening of Soviet power in Eastern Bukhara. By the end of 1921, in the absence of an overarching state authority, the whole country had slipped into anarchy and violence.

In Eastern Bukhara, Ibrahim Bek and other *basmachi* leaders relied upon the remnants of the Bukharan Government as well as local kinship and patronage networks.[32] During the anti-*basmachi* campaign here the influx of civil authorities, and the use of village self-defence units and irregular troops, some of whom were former *basmachi*, resulted in the disruption of local power networks.[33] Another factor disrupting local power structures was the Soviet and *basmachi* use of famine relief as a tool in their respective struggles, with the Soviets distributing food 'according to political criteria' and the *basmachi* also using the redistribution of food as a reward for communities that were loyal to them.[34] In the struggle between the *basmachi* and the Soviets in Eastern Bukhara, 'the population's allegiance depended on the ability of different actors in satisfying its most basic needs'.[35]

The Red Army was also fighting against Enver Pasha's guerrillas, who were operating from Afghanistan with the emir's blessing and with British money and supplies. Ibrahim Bek, a chief of the Uzbek Loqay tribe, raided adjacent Tajik districts,[36] and periodically assaulted both Soviet and Enver Pasha's troops.

---

31   In July 1921, Davlatmin-bek (formerly *bek* of Kulob) and *ishan* Sultan (a noble from Gharm) were appointed to head *revkoms* in their respective territories.

32   Beatrice Penati, 'The Reconquest of East Bukhara: The Struggle against the Basmachi as a Prelude to Sovietization', *Central Asian Survey*, Vol. 26, No. 4 (2007), pp. 522, 533. Penati notes: 'The presence of Bukharan Emirate government personnel in Soviet power structures complicated the fight against the *Basmachi* as some bureaucrats were collaborating with the *Basmachi* or passively resisting engaging in activities directed against the *Basmachi*' (see: ibid., p. 527).

33   Penati, 'The Reconquest of East Bukhara', pp. 521–2, 532–4.

34   Penati, 'The Reconquest of East Bukhara', p. 532.

35   Penati, 'The Reconquest of East Bukhara', pp. 521–2, 532–4. This pragmatism of the common people, as described by Penati, is echoed by Nourzhanov's description of the *Basmachi* leadership: 'the Basmachi were *excellent* politicians, and changed allegiances and ideological platforms to offer their communities the best chance of survival.' See: Nourzhanov, 'Reassessing the Basmachi', p. 61.

36   Even before 1917 the Loqay terrorised and plundered their Tajik neighbours and pushed them out of the Yovon Valley. Some 25 000 Loqay nomads enjoyed the emir's favour and were a kind of bête noire for the rest of the population in Eastern Bukhara. See: Karmysheva, *Ocherki etnicheskoi istorii iuzhnykh raionov*

In mountainous districts, such as Mastchoh, Darvoz and Qarotegin, villagers blocked and fortified narrow roads, and ambushed all strangers, irrespective of their origin or party affiliation. In lowlands where people could not effectively resist more or less large armed units, they either met the stronger party's demands for supplies and booty or joined its ranks to avenge their relatives. Most commonly, they migrated abroad: 206 800 people, one-fourth of Eastern Bukhara's population, left their homes, predominantly in south-western and western districts, during 1920–26.[37] All in all, the situation in Eastern Bukhara in that period bears a striking resemblance to that in Tajikistan in 1992. In both cases it was not the state (the Soviet or the emir's) that offered the populace a viable strategy for survival, but rather an assortment of local strongmen who were in a position to guarantee (or deny) livelihoods, and to organise defence.

Red Army commanders indiscriminately labelled all their adversaries *basmachi*; Enver Pasha's soldiers called themselves *mujahideen*; but the local population itself employed neither of these terms in reference to their militias. Instead of ideological, political or religious markers, they used the name of a specific warlord for identification purposes: Fuzail Makhsum in Gharm, Dilovarsho in Darvoz, Yuldosh Sohibnazar in Hisor, Asror Khan in Mastchoh, and so on.[38] In late 1922, there were 250 self-defence paramilitary groups in Eastern Bukhara. They comprised 5000 people,[39] recognised no supreme authority, and fought ferociously against any intruder.[40] The thoroughly reinforced Red Army regiments had destroyed the emir's forces in Eastern Bukhara by the summer of 1923, but the task of subduing local strongmen proved far more difficult.

In February 1922, the Politburo of the Central Committee of the Russian Communist Party decreed that in order to cope with the *basmachi* in Bukhara it was imperative 'to make concessions to the local population, particularly to return the confiscated *vaqf* lands, restore traditional courts and pardon moderate elements of the *basmachi*'.[41] In 1923, Eastern Bukhara became exempt from land tax and received substantial credits and shipments of consumer goods from Russia. In November 1923, selective land and water reform was carried out in the Loqay district, which benefited the majority of the local inhabitants at the expense of the late emir's estate. Soon after, a conference of Loqay *ulama*

Tadzhikistana i Uzbekistana, pp. 97–8, 154–6.

37   Kamol Abdoullaev, 'Central Asian Emigres in Afghanistan: First Wave 1920–1931', *Central Asia Monitor*, No. 5 (1994), p. 19.

38   Sadykov, *Istoricheskii opyt KPSS po stroitelstvu sotsializma v Tadzhikistane*, p. 92; *Istoriia Tadzhikskogo naroda*, Vol. III, kn. 1, pp. 122–3.

39   Khudoiberdyev, *Boevaia druzhba, rozhdennaia Oktiabrem*, p. 94.

40   It is estimated that between 1922 and 1924 in Kulob and Gharm alone 5528 people perished and 2912 were wounded at the hands of fellow Muslims Ibrahim-bek and Enver-pasha. See: A. I. Zevelev, Iu. A. Poliakov and L. V. Shishkina, *Basmachestvo: Pravda istorii i vymysel falsifikatorov* (Moscow: Mysl, 1986), p. 179.

41   Muminov, *Istoriia Uzbekskoi SSR s drevneishikh vremen do nashikh dnei*, p. 323.

issued a judgment to the effect that, on the one hand, Soviet power was not in contradiction with Islamic norms, and on the other hand the *basmachi* could not be regarded as defenders of the faith.[42]

Two well-organised campaigns that combined military, political and economic measures brought Eastern Bukhara under Soviet control during 1925 and 1926. This region was spared the horrible excesses that accompanied the strengthening of communist rule in Ukraine and Kazakhstan. Still, any serious crisis, such as the bad harvest in 1925 or the attempt at mass collectivisation in 1929, would cause the resurgence of armed resistance.[43] In Eastern Bukhara, 'although Soviet in name, the local authority structure remained unchanged from the pre-revolutionary period, traditional leaders merely assuming the new Soviet titles'.[44] This situation precluded the implementation of socialist reforms in southern Tajikistan, but at the same time negated any possibility of an all-out anti-Soviet uprising. Fuzail Makhsum in 1929 and Ibrahim Bek in 1931 managed to assemble only 150 to 200 warriors in what are considered the two last outbursts of the *basmachi* movement in Tajikistan.[45] A certain Sufi dignitary summed up the hopelessness of their enterprise when he appealed to Makhsum: 'Fuzail, don't fight against the Red Army, because you have neither a state, nor arms. How can you possibly fight such a big and strong power … If you die in this war you will die an ass. You are not going to become a *shahid*.'[46] The pacification of Eastern Bukhara was nearing its end, and the period of Soviet transformation and adjustment was about to commence.

Governance

The Soviet authorities in Eastern Bukhara, due to the absence of educated locals to recruit as cadres, had to exercise central rule through a small number of 'poorly-supervised local agents'.[47] And some of the 'new' local Soviet officials were in fact the same old local authority figures. Certain local leaders joined the Bolshevik side as they saw an opportunity to use the Soviet 'power structures' as

---

42 Vladimir Medvedev writes that '[i]t was one of the first sentences passed on the resistance movement. Shortly, a similar kurultai took place in Bukhara, and 113 religious authorities signed and sealed a proclamation which denounced the insurgents and called upon the populace to render assistance to the Red Army.' See: Vladimir Medvedev, 'Basmachi—obrechennoe voinstvo', *Druzhba narodov*, No. 8 (1992), p. 156.

43 Not surprisingly, in 1932 only 38.5 per cent of all peasant homesteads were collectivised in Tajikistan, compared with 60 per cent throughout Central Asia. See: Sadykov, *Istoricheskii opyt KPSS po stroitelstvu sotsializma v Tadzhikistane*, p. 263. In remote mountain areas collective farms were not established until 1936.

44 Olcott, 'The Basmachi or Freemen's Revolt in Turkestan 1918–24', p. 363.

45 *Istoriia Tadzhikskogo naroda*, Vol. III, kn. 1, pp. 212, 260.

46 Medvedev, 'Basmachi', p. 156.

47 Barnett R. Rubin, 'Russian Hegemony and State Breakdown in the Periphery: Causes and Consequences of the Civil War in Tajikistan', in *Post-Soviet Political Order: Conflict and State Building*, eds Barnett R. Rubin and Jack Snyder (London: Routledge, 1998), p. 149.

a vehicle to promote their own interests.[48] The Central Commission for Struggle against the *basmachi* complained that as of the late 1920s the local power structures were mostly untouched and that the local Soviet bureaucracy was 'colonised' by former bureaucrats of the Bukharan Emirate.[49] Another aspect of 'colonisation' concerned not former bureaucrats of the Bukharan Emirate, but powerful local figures. In Tajikistan, wealthy local elites were able—assisted by their local patronage networks—to be elected to serve in Soviet institutions, especially at the rural district level. This even led to factional fighting, power struggles and abuse of power by those in positions of authority. The Soviets noticed this problem and worried that 'clans' would successfully integrate themselves within the Soviet bureaucracy.[50] In the former Bukharan Emirate the Kremlin encountered particular difficulty transforming the local power structures into Soviet institutions, unlike elsewhere, where the transformation was from tsarist to Soviet.[51] As for Tajikistan, Moscow finally found the educated class needed as bureaucrats with the 1929 addition of the northern urban centre of Khujand to the Tajik SSR.[52]

Patterns of Economic Development

Overcoming the 'economic inequality' of the peoples of Central Asia was always regarded in Moscow as an important element of its nationality policy in the region. Theoretically, the aim was to achieve similar levels of socioeconomic development throughout the Soviet Union by eliminating what was referred to as the grim legacy of tsarist rule in non-Russian regions[53]

---

48   Schoeberlein-Engel, *Identity in Central Asia*, p. 23.

49   Penati, 'The Reconquest of East Bukhara', p. 526. See also: Bergne, *The Birth of Tajikistan*, pp. 60, 66.

50   Penati, 'The Reconquest of East Bukhara', pp. 526–7. A contemporary traveller to the region, E. E. Kisch, quoted a Soviet official regarding local authority figures: 'In many districts the clergy and the *kulaks* have taken the Soviet apparatus into their own hands. Some of them have even joined the Party and exercise their corrupt reign of terror in the name of the Soviet, extorting registration fees, levying taxes, and coolly pocketing the money.' See Egon Erwin Kisch, *Changing Asia* (New York: Alfred A. Knopf, 1935), pp. 36–7, as quoted in Navruz R. Nekbakhtshoev, *Clan Politics: Explaining the Persistence of Subethnic Divisions in Tajikistan: Comparative Approach* (Master of Arts Thesis: Duquesne University, 2006), p. 50.

51   Penati, 'The Reconquest of East Bukhara', p. 526. For example, public works projects required the cooperation of a traditional authority figure in order to mobilise the labour.

52   Rubin, 'Russian Hegemony and State Breakdown in the Periphery', p. 149. As for the highest levels of leadership, during the first years of the Tajik SSR (from 1929) Pamiris and Gharmis dominated the top positions of power. During the purges of 1937 an ethnic Russian was appointed as first secretary; and then, from 1946, with the appointment of Bobojon Ghafurov, all the first secretaries were from Khujand. See: Idil Tuncer Kilavuz, *Understanding Violent Conflict: A Comparative Study of Tajikistan and Uzbekistan* (PhD Thesis: Indiana University, 2007), pp. 101–2. Rubin provides a less subtle analysis, characterising the 1930s as a period of 'Russification' in Tajikistan, with an ethnic Russian first secretary and large-scale purges of cadres. See: Rubin, 'Russian Hegemony and State Breakdown in the Periphery', p. 149.

53   Adapted from: P. M. Alampiev, *Likvidatsiia ekonomicheskogo neravenstva narodov Sovetskogo Vostoka i sotsialisticheskoe razmeshenie promyshlennosti* (Moscow: Izdatelstvo AN SSSR, 1958), pp. 22–6.

- narrow specialisation of the economy in producing food and raw materials
- absence of heavy industry
- one-sided and primitive structure of industry
- extreme technological backwardness of industry and agriculture
- lack of infrastructure and transport networks
- absence of a native working class
- general cultural 'backwardness' of the population.

In practice, however, considerations of pragmatism and expediency determined the course of economic modernisation in Central Asia. As Geoffrey Jukes has pointed out:

> [I]ndustrialisation is not merely an act of social policy; for it may make little *economic* sense to establish industry in a border area, remote from central markets, perhaps vulnerable to invasion, possibly poorly endowed with raw materials, or with a labour force which is difficult to train because of backwardness, language difficulties, or the lack of an industrial tradition.[54]

Other experts often put special emphasis on geostrategic factors, such as the proximity of China, as a reason the Soviets sought to support economic modernisation in Central Asia.[55]

It appears, however, that it was the internal logic of the Soviet Union's economic development that affected the course of modernisation in Central Asia most profoundly. Tajikistan apparently was in the category of territories less suitable for rapid industrialisation. In 1926, Moscow set up the Permanent Expedition for Exploring Productive Forces of Tajikistan (PEEPFT), which almost immediately arrived at the conclusion that 'we cannot talk about modernisation of industry in Tajikistan, because there isn't any, it is an agricultural country'.[56] The expedition implemented an impressive amount of work and finally came up with a set of guidelines as to how exactly the republic's economy should be developed in the future. Its main recommendations included[57]

- establishing mining industry, hydro-power generation and cotton-growing as priorities

---

54   Geoffrey Jukes, *The Soviet Union in Asia* (Sydney: Angus & Robertson, 1973), pp. 39–40.

55   Hélène Carrère d'Encausse, *Decline of an Empire: The Soviet Socialist Republic in Revolt* (New York: Newsweek Books, 1982), p. 112.

56   A. G. Ananiev, 'Promyshlennye vozmozhnosti TASSR', in *Narodnoe khoziaistvo Tadzhikistana* (Dushanbe: Izdatelstvo Gosplana TASSR, 1926), p. 179.

57   *Problemy Tadzhikistana. Trudy i Konferentsii po izucheniiu proizvoditelnykh sil Tadzhikskoi SSR*, Vol. 1 (Leningrad: Izdatelstvo AN SSSR, 1933), pp. 11, 21, 23–6, 130.

- setting up basic industry and infrastructure with the help of a workforce and materials imported from the European Soviet Union
- dividing Tajikistan into several economic zones with particular production specialisation
- rapid restoration and expansion of the irrigation network.

This blueprint was in compliance with the All-Union economic strategy promulgated at the Sixteenth Congress of the Communist Party of the Soviet Union in 1930[58] and remained valid well into the postwar period. The Kremlin invested generously in the development of Tajikistan,[59] and in 1932 the share of industry in the republic's economy reached 22 per cent, compared with 6.6 per cent four years earlier.[60]

The Soviet modernisation of Tajikistan, which was conceived and implemented as a process of forced industrialisation *par excellence*, brought about two fateful developments as early as the mid 1930s. First, it destroyed a local economic mechanism that organically combined handcrafts and cottage industries on the one hand and modern factory production on the other. In the 1920s, the traditional sector of the economy, based on private and cooperative ownership, was growing at an impressive rate in Turkestan, registering a 42–45 per cent increase in the number of those employed annually, and accounting for 34–37 per cent of industrial output in the region.[61] In the early 1930s, all private and family-owned enterprises in Tajikistan were closed or nationalised; the share of cooperatives in industrial production had decreased to 15.3 per cent by 1940 and stabilised at 3 per cent in the postwar period.[62] Large state-owned factories emerged as the backbone of the republic's economy (Table 3.1).

Table 3.1 Dynamics of Industrial Output in Tajikistan, 1913–40 (1913 = 1)

Year	All industry	Large industry*
1913	1.0	1.0
1928	0.98	8.2
1932	1.4	43.7

---

58   The congress's resolution stated in particular that 'industrialisation of the country can no longer rest solely on the Southern coal-metallurgical base [that is, Donbass]', hence 'the Congress deems it necessary to begin accelerated development in eastern territories (the Urals, Siberia, Kazakhstan, Central Asia) of industries based on local sources of raw materials (non-ferrous metallurgy, textile industry, etc.)'. See: *KPSS v rezoliutsiiakh i resheniiakh s'ezdov, konferentsii i plenumov TsK*, Vol. 4 (Moscow: Izdatelstvo politicheskoi literatury, 1970), pp. 441–2.

59   Centralised financial transfers in Tajikistan's budget (1926–30), measured by subvention as a percentage of the republican budget: 1926 (84.4 per cent); 1927 (92.2 per cent); 1928 (79.9 per cent); 1929 (72.6 per cent); 1930 (78.5 per cent). Source: M. N. Nazarshoev and M. A. Solomonov, *Sotsialno-ekonomicheskoe razvitie Tadzhikistana* (Dushanbe: Izdatelstvo TGU, 1989), p. 10.

60   A. Rahmatulloev and S. Mukhtorov, *Ocherkhoi ta'rikhi Tojikistoni Soveti* (Dushanbe: Maorif, 1989), p. 93.

61   V. N. Uliakhin, 'Mnogoukladnost v sovetskoi i zarubezhnoi Azii', *Vostok*, No. 5 (1991), pp. 132, 134.

62   *Narodnoe khoziaistvo Tadzhikskoi SSR v 1979g*(Dushanbe: Irfon, 1981), p. 72.

| 1937 | 5.1 | 183 |
| 1940 | 8.8 | 324 |

* For the year 1913, large industry includes enterprises with 30 or more workers; for later years, it comprises factories subordinated to All-Union and republican industrial ministries.

Source: *Narodnoe khoziaistvo Tadzhikskoi SSR* (Stalinabad: Gosstatizdat, 1957), p. 16.

According to Sergei Poliakov, in Tajikistan

> city-based industrial production was completely dependent on drawing settlers from the ... industrially developed regions of the country, whereas development of rural areas was based on local human resources. But in terms of qualitative characteristics the latter were not prepared enough to guarantee smoothness and efficiency of the process of industrialisation.[63]

In 1938, migrants from the European part of the Soviet Union accounted for 46 per cent of the entire workforce in industry, construction and transport in Tajikistan.[64] Despite constant attempts on the part of Soviet authorities to increase indigenous representation in these areas, the problem was never satisfactorily resolved.[65] The main reasons for such a state of affairs were not the absence of vocational training facilities, poor command of the Russian language or limited supplies of food and housing in the cities; it was rather caused by the persistence of traditional values and attitudes in Tajik society, whereby industrial labour was not regarded as a very respectable occupation. A sociological study conducted at a number of industrial enterprises in Tashkent revealed that as late as 1985 there were dramatic differences between Russians and Central Asians in terms of work ethics and preferences (Table 3.2).

---

63 S. P. Poliakov, 'Sovremennaia sredneaziatskaia derevnia: traditsionnye formy sobstvennosti v kvaziindustrialnoi sisteme', in *Krestianstvo i industrialnaia tsivilizatsiia*, eds Iu. G. Aleksandrov and S. A. Panarin (Moscow: Nauka, 1993), p. 183.

64 M. I. Irkaev, ed. *Kommunisticheskaia partiia v bor'be za formirovanie i razvitie rabochego klassa v Tadzhikistane* (Dushanbe: Irfon, 1967), pp. 75, 82.

65 For instance, in 1979 ethnic Tajiks still constituted a mere 10.9 per cent of industrial workers—almost three times less than the figure for Russians. See: *Naselenie Tadzhikskoi SSR. Po dannym Vsesoiuznoi perepisi naseleniia 1979g* (Dushanbe: TsSU TSSR, 1980), p. 47.

Table 3.2 Comparative Behavioural Parameters of Workers in Central Asia

	Russians	Central Asians
1.	Prefer to be employed in industry or construction.	Prefer to be engaged in the non-productive sphere of activities (retail trade, public catering, health, education, culture) and agriculture.
2.	Amongst industrial specialisations, prefer machine-building, metallurgy and metal-working.	Amongst industrial specialisations, prefer textiles, tanning, footwear manufacturing and food processing.
3.	In terms of contents of labour, prefer industrial-type professions with the use of machinery.	In terms of contents of labour, prefer handcraft-type professions where individual manual skills are important.
4.	Professional roles of men and women differ insignificantly. Women are more attracted than men by professions that require higher education.	Professional roles of men and women differ considerably. Women are less prone to work in public sector and prefer labour-intensive jobs that do not require higher education.
5.	When selecting profession or employment, are guided by their own inclinations, mass media and conspicuous advantages of a given enterprise (convenient location, high salary, and so on).	In similar situations, take into consideration opinion, or follow example, of elders, relatives, or generally pursue established lifetime patterns; pay great attention to value attributes of a job (prestige, perceived usefulness to the community, status conferred, and so on).
6.	Are less interested in socialisation at work. Prefer to carry responsibility and be paid for individual performance.	Attach great importance to socialisation at work. Prefer collective forms of labour, value mutual assistance and support. Are sensitive to interpersonal relations in a team.
7.	Do not pay attention to the national affiliation of colleagues.	Prefer to work and socialise in a mono-ethnic environment.
8.	Prefer democratic forms of management. The authority of leadership is related to its businesslike qualities. As a rule, assess its performance critically.	Accept authoritarian style of leadership. Managers and higher-ups enjoy greater authority. Strive for dominance in a team.
9.	Are demanding in terms of conditions and contents of labour.	Are less demanding in terms of conditions and contents of labour.

Source: O. I. Shkaratan and L. S. Perepelkin, 'Ekonomicheskii rost i natsionalnoe razvitie', *EKO*, No. 10 (1988), pp. 18–19.

The Soviet system offered no substantial incentives to technical personnel and skilled workers employed in more sophisticated branches of industry. Additionally, it strongly encouraged the influx of indigenous cadres into bureaucracy, academia, arts communities and other non-productive spheres. It has been observed that such a skewed arrangement in Tajikistan was made possible due to the fact that practically all national income produced in the region is utilised in the non-productive sphere, and expenditure on national economy is footed by the Centre. This 'benevolent' economic regime provides for the level of life comparable with that of the population of the industrialised regions. Henceforth, as a rule, indigenous people choose agriculture or the services sector to work in.[66]

Consequently, not only were opportunities for inter-ethnic socialisation 'below the expected level for an otherwise "integrated international work force"',[67] but eventually a binary pattern of settling began to evolve in Tajikistan, whereby the two largest distinctive groups of the populace—industrial and white-collar workers living in some 70 cities and towns, and peasants inhabiting 3500 villages—differed from one another quite substantially in a whole range of parameters: ethnic composition, culture, religious observance, level of education, and even language.

The salient ethnic division of labour quickly became a characteristic feature of Tajikistan's economy. Its dualism also found reflection in the fact that right from the start the economy was geared to meet the needs of the All-Union markets. From the 1940s to the 1980s, republican authorities controlled only one-tenth of the volume of industrial output in their territory;[68] generally, it was up to central ministries in Moscow to determine what and how much should be produced in Tajikistan. As one Tajik scholar cautiously remarked in the early 1970s, industry in that republic 'is characterised by the lack of correspondence between production profiles of a significant number of enterprises and the structure of demands of the republic and adjacent districts'.[69] The level of economic integration amongst regions in Tajikistan remained low. Soviet planning practices resulted in paradoxical situations—for example, in the 1960s, three-quarters of the republic's light industry was located in the northern Leninobod *oblast* and the bulk of its output, primarily textiles, was exported to other Soviet republics; at the same time, the southern regions had to import fabrics from European Russia, more than 4000 km away.[70] Similarly,

---

66   Rustam Narzikulov, 'Dvulikii Ianus v serdtse Azii: nekotorye itogi 70-letnego razvitiia sredneaziatskikh respublik v sostave SSSR', *Vostok*, No. 5 (1991), p. 125.

67   Michael Rywkin, 'The Impact of Socio-Economic Change and Demographic Growth on National Identity and Socialisation', *Central Asian Survey*, Vol. 3, No. 3 (1985), p. 87.

68   *Narodnoe khoziaistvo Tadzhikskoi SSR*, p. 13; *Narodnoe khoziaistvo Tadzhikskoi SSR v 1988 godu* (Dushanbe: Irfon, 1990), p. 163.

69   R. K. Rahimov, ed. *Tadzhikistan: ekonomicheskii rost i effektivnost* (Dushanbe: Irfon, 1972), p. 38.

70   H. M. Saidmuradov, ed. *Narodnoe khoziaistvo Tadzhikistana v period formirovaniia ekonomicheskikh predposylok razvitogo sotsializma* (Dushanbe: Donish, 1985), pp. 95–7.

the textile combine at Uroteppa had to import 95 per cent of raw materials from Uzbekistan, although nearby districts could have provided an almost unlimited supply of cotton.[71]

The 'predilection in Soviet planning towards overconcentration and monopoly production (i.e., localising all of the USSR's output of a particular product at one or a few production sites)'[72] is a well-known phenomenon. The pronounced emphasis on cotton-growing in Tajikistan was caused by two major factors: a) optimal climatic conditions,[73] and b) Moscow's relentless efforts to achieve self-sufficiency in this strategic commodity.[74] Generally, this task had been accomplished by about 1950, when the Soviet Union gathered five times more raw cotton than imperial Russia had in 1913.[75] The 'cottonisation' of Tajikistan resulted in a dramatic decline of staple crops and a growing dependence on food imports from other parts of the USSR.[76] Until 1958, cotton enjoyed very favourable terms of trade compared with other agricultural products. In the early 1950s, for instance, grain and meat producers in the USSR would receive less than one-seventh of the world price, whereas the government purchased cotton at a rate that was 30 per cent above the international price.[77] As a result, Tajikistan's agricultural income grew impressively. The fixed capital of the republic's *kolkhozes* (collective farms), which included houses, cinemas, hospitals, kindergartens and other institutions of social infrastructure on top of the productive base, increased fifteen-fold between 1940 and 1958.[78] Between 1954 and 1955, the state budget allocated funds for the construction of 38 schools in Tajikistan; at the same time, 119 schools were built using money from local collective farms.[79] The labour-intensive character of cotton cultivation[80]

71   Abdulqodir Holiqzoda, *Ta'rikhi siyosii Tojikon az istiloi Rusiya to imruz* (Dushanbe: Self-published, 1994), p. 96.

72   Andrew R. Bond, 'Russia Coping with "Cotton Crisis"', *Post-Soviet Geography*, Vol. 35, No. 5 (1993), p. 330.

73   In terms of soil characteristics and temperature regime, Tajikistan, especially the Vakhsh Valley in the south, 'is unparalleled by any other cotton-growing locality in the USSR'. See: R. Dilovarov, *Istifodai oqilonai zamin* (Dushanbe: Irfon, 1991), p. 15.

74   The importance attached to this problem by the Bolshevik regime, even at times when its very existence was threatened by civil war, can be illustrated by the fact that of 600 decrees issued by the Soviet Government from November 1917 to August 1918, 42 dealt directly or indirectly with matters pertaining to cotton production in Turkestan. See: M. Khamraev, *Deiatelnost Kommunisticheskoi partii po razvitiiu irrigatsii v Tadzhikistane* (Dushanbe: Donish, 1972), p. 95.

75   V. Ahmedov, *KPSS v borbe za intensifikatsiiu khlopkovodstva* (Dushanbe: Irfon, 1976), p. 319.

76   For example, in 1928 Tajikistan produced 4.391 million centners of cereals and 371 000 centners of cotton (one centner equals 100 kg). Thirty years later, cereal production had dropped to 1.871 million centners, while cotton had surged to 4.212 million centers. See: *Tadzhikistan za gody Sovetskoi vlasti* (Dushanbe: Statistika, 1967), p. 79.

77   Azizur Rahman Khan and Dharam Ghai, *Collective Agriculture and Rural Development in Soviet Central Asia* (London: Macmillan, 1979), p. 25.

78   M. Irkaev and P. Safarov, *Rol' Kommunisticheskoi partii v prevraschenii dehkan v aktivnykh stroitelei sotsializma* (Dushanbe: Irfon, 1968), p. 176.

79   *Rezoliutsiia X s'ezda Kommunisticheskoi partii Tadzhikistana*(Stalinabad: Tadzhikgosizdat, 1956), pp. 5–6.

80   The first combine harvesters appeared on cotton plantations in Tajikistan in 1961 and accounted for a meagre 2 per cent of that year's yield. See: *Kommunist Tadzhikistana*, 26 January 1962. An anonymous expert referred to agricultural methods and techniques practised in Tajikistan as being those of the eighteenth

helped to absorb the consequences of high population growth. During the first three decades of its existence as a Soviet state, Tajikistan offered plentiful corroboration to the following conclusion made for the entire region:

> The attainment of prosperity in the Central Asian republics has not come through the classical path of industrialisation. The industrial progress of the region has no doubt been very substantial, but rapid growth in agriculture has been a key element in their progress. A distinctive and related feature of their experience has been the continued predominance of the rural sector … What the Central Asian republics experienced was rapid agricultural growth leading to a rising standard of living in the rural areas and the consequent absence of pressure to move out of the rural society.[81]

The specialisation in cotton was complemented by a spectacular increase in yield per hectare due to the introduction of new long-stapled varieties, implementation of massive irrigation schemes and use of chemical fertilisers.[82] Even in the late 1980s the republic continued to have the best yields in the USSR and was not far behind the main world cotton producers.[83] While it is true that cotton production in Tajikistan became 'the focus for the development of a large economic complex embracing many industrial sectors: irrigation; production of agricultural machinery; production of mineral fertilisers and toxic chemicals; the cotton refining, oil producing, paper manufacturing and—to a lesser extent— sewing and knitting industries',[84] it is important to remember that this complex never presented a viable manufacturing entity capable of guaranteeing the republic's balanced independent development. It was meant, first and foremost, to provide 'USSR, Inc.' with deficit materials—a design 'logically stemming from and imposed by the strategy of the [Soviet] command-administrative system that favoured creation of agricultural and raw-material enclaves in the national economy'.[85] Throughout the Soviet period only 4 to 5 per cent of Central Asia's cotton was processed locally; the rest was dispatched to the European part of the USSR, where more than 70 per cent of the country's output of cotton textiles was generated.[86] Apart from raw cotton and cotton fibre, Tajikistan exported a variety of ores and ore concentrates—most notably, rare earths, zinc, lead,

---

century. See: *Problems of the Peoples of the USSR*, No. 11 (1961), p. 66.

81   Khan and Ghai, *Collective Agriculture and Rural Development in Soviet Central Asia*, pp. 102–3.

82   *Tadzhikistan* (Moscow: Mysl, 1968), p. 81.

83   *Kommunist Tadzhikistana*, 25 May 1991.

84   Igor Lipovsky, 'The Central Asian Cotton Epic', *Central Asian Survey*, Vol. 14, No. 4 (1995), p. 534.

85   Ia. T. Bronshtein, '"Soizmeriat" vklad respubliki i ee vozmozhnosti', *EKO*, No. 11 (1989), p. 29.

86   Boris Z. Rumer, 'Central Asia's Cotton Economy', in *Soviet Central Asia: The Failed Transformation*, ed. William Fierman (Boulder, Colo.: Westview Press, 1991), p. 83. Although starting in the second half of the 1960s Tajikistan's economy showed a perceptible tendency towards diversification based on the growth of the processing industry, even in 1989 the share of finished goods in the republic's net material product (NMP) did not exceed 46 per cent. See: M. R. Boboev, *Ekonomicheskoe razvitie respubliki v usloviiakh rynka* (Dushanbe: TadzhikNIINTI, 1991), p. 2.

mercury, silver and gold. In the 1940s, rich uranium deposits in the Leninobod *oblast* began to be exploited. Production of fissile materials at the mammoth VOSTOKREDMET plant situated in the town of Chkalovsk played a crucial role in the success of the Soviet nuclear program.[87]

One cannot but agree with Aziz Niyazi's statement that 'the Soviet regime, though established by force, nevertheless greatly stimulated the economic development of Central Asia'.[88] In the prewar period, Tajikistan registered an average annual industrial growth of 9 per cent, and progress in the production of basic commodities continued.[89] The initial great surge in the industrialisation of Tajikistan slowed markedly, however, in the 1950s.[90] As a result, in 1960 it remained the second least-industrialised republic in the Soviet Union (after Moldova) as far as the structure of employment was concerned: only 18.2 per cent of those employed worked in industry compared with the USSR's mean of 35 per cent.[91] All the same, the suggestion that comparatively low levels of urbanisation and industrial participation could serve as indicators of inappropriate economic development and inadequate standards of living[92] should be treated with a degree of caution. The peculiar economic system that had emerged in Tajikistan was the result of Moscow's deliberate policy of the All-Union division of labour, and for quite a few decades this worked satisfactorily, considering that 'the nationalities of Soviet Central Asia had achieved living standards, insofar as these may be expressed by wages, health and educational opportunity, somewhat lower than those of the European USSR, but a great deal higher than those of their independent neighbours'.[93] Its continuous functioning, however, depended on two crucial factors: a) the centre's ability to transfer the amount of resources necessary to meet the demands of the growing population of the republic in exchange for raw materials, and b) the availability of natural conditions, especially fertile land and water, to sustain extensive growth of the cotton-based economy.

---

87   *Izvestiia*, 13 August 1993.

88   Aziz Niyazi, 'Tajikistan', in *Central Asia and the Caucasus after the Soviet Union: Domestic and International Dynamics*, ed. Mohiaddin Mesbahi (Gainesville: University Press of Florida, 1994), p. 168.

89   *Tadzhikistan za gody Sovetskoi vlasti*, pp. 40–1, 48–9.

90   Boris Z. Rumer, *Soviet Central Asia: A Tragic Experiment* (Boston: Unwin Hyman, 1989), p. 54; *Narodnoe khoziaistvo Tadzhikskoi SSR*, p. 17.

91   Narzikulov, 'Dvulikii Ianus v serdtse Azii', p. 122.

92   Alastair McAuley, 'The Central Asian Economy in Comparative Perspective', in *The Disintegration of the Soviet Economic System*, eds Michael Ellman and Vladimir Kontorovich (London and New York: Routledge, 1992), pp. 138–42.

93   Jukes, *The Soviet Union in Asia*, p. 48.

The Transformation of Society

In 1897, only 0.5 per cent of the Tajiks in Eastern Bukhara were literate,[94] but after the creation of a national republic Tajikistan registered spectacular progress in literacy, even in comparison with its richer Central Asian neighbours.[95] Compared with a literacy rate of about 20 per cent in Iran, Turkey and the Indian subcontinent, in Tajikistan complete literacy was claimed by the late 1950s.[96] In 1940, in Tajikistan there were six tertiary education institutions and 30 colleges, with 8262 students, 74 per cent of whom were being trained to become teachers.[97] That year allocations to education programs accounted for 39.5 per cent of all outlays from the republic's budget.[98] In the early 1960s, the number of tertiary students per 10 000 of population was 131 in Tajikistan, 71 in France, 24 in Turkey, 18 in Pakistan and two in Afghanistan.[99]

The unprecedented social mobilisation achieved in the course of the communist experiment throughout the USSR was instrumental in turning the latent and degenerating Tajik *ethnie* into a proto-nation. It hardly mattered that the whole mobilisation process had been conceived to serve the ultimate goal of building a communist society devoid of class, national or state distinctions. What mattered in the 1920s and 1930s was that the Tajiks acquired a common and concrete political goal—that is, the establishment of the Tajik socialist nation. The populace may not have cared about socialism per se, but large sections were forced to take up political activism, and consequently considered themselves members of a great Tajik community that transcended traditional local affiliations—previously the privilege of a handful of intellectuals.

The usual triad of Bolshevik mobilisation and penetration methods (industrialisation, collectivisation, cultural revolution) was augmented by women's emancipation and mass resettlement in Tajikistan. It was a cold, pragmatic consideration that

> to provide women with unconditional access to suffrage, and to all elective or appointive, as well as legislative and administrative, offices in the land, would not just challenge the traditional male monopoly of

---

94 Asimova, *Iazykovoe stroitelstvo v Tadzhikistane*, p. 14.

95 From 1926 to 1939, the rate of literacy among Tajiks increased from 3 per cent to 67 per cent. See: Iu. A. Poliakov, 'Vozdeistvie gosudarstva na demograficheskie protsessy v SSSR (1920–1930e gg.)', *Voprosy istorii*, No. 3 (1995), p. 127.

96 Khan and Ghai, *Collective Agriculture and Rural Development in Soviet Central Asia*, pp. 18–19.

97 Calculations based on: *Narodnoe khoziaistvo Tadzhikskoi SSR v 1965g* (Dushanbe: Statistika, 1966), pp. 227–8.

98 *Ocherki istorii narodnogo khoziaistva Tadzhikistana* (Dushanbe: Donish, 1967), p. 309.

99 *Tadzhikistan za gody Sovetskoi vlasti*, p. 177.

the political arena; it would immediately and decisively undermine the position of traditional political elites—tribal chieftains, village elders, and notables.[100]

The emancipation campaign (*hujum*) launched in 1926 envisaged the abolition of women's seclusion, their promotion to party and state structures, and generally the creation of a climate of equal opportunities for both sexes. In Tajikistan in 1925, 99.4 per cent of women were illiterate; 10 years later 35.7 per cent of all students in primary and secondary schools were girls.[101] Indigenous women, erstwhile confined to the family hearth, made up almost 80 per cent of the labour force in Tajikistan's light industry by 1937.[102] Numbers of female members of the CPT grew from three in 1925 to 1016 in 1932.[103] In 1928, 957 women worked in *selsovets*—22 times more than during 1925–26.[104]

Following incorporation into Russia, Central Asia experienced a demographic explosion at the turn of the twentieth century, when the natural population growth rate rocketed from 0.3 to 2.5 per cent every year.[105] In Tajikistan rural overpopulation began to be felt in the late 1920s, especially in northern Tajikistan and Gharm. Two waves of resettlement took place between 1926–29 and 1933–37 whereby some 30 000 peasant families from Gharm, Uroteppa (Istaravshon), Panjakent, Gorno-Badakhshan, Hisor, Kulob and Ferghana, as well as those returning from Afghanistan, were forcibly moved to develop virgin lands in the Qurghonteppa *okrug*, only sparsely populated by Uzbek nomadic tribes.[106] This major demographic undertaking was presented by the Soviet authorities as 'rectifying the historical injustice emanating from the Emirate's feudal policy towards the Tajik people, which had been pushed into the mountains'.[107] In reality the forcible resettlement of people to the south of Tajikistan was primarily to facilitate the construction of irrigation works and the production of cotton. The Soviet resettlement policies in the Qurghonteppa Province (including the Vakhsh Valley) were clearly part of its strategy to boost agriculture, particularly cotton. The result in the Qurghonteppa region was the construction of thousands of kilometres of irrigation canals as part of the Vakhsh Valley irrigation system that started in 1931. After this time numerous groups and individuals arrived in the region to work on the construction of the canals

---

100   Gregory J. Massell, *The Surrogate Proletariat: Moslem Women and Revolutionary Strategies in Soviet Central Asia* (Princeton, NJ: Princeton University Press, 1974), p. 142.

101   *Velikii Oktiabr i raskreposhchenie zhenshin Srednei Azii i Kazakhstana (1917–1936)*(Moscow: Mysl, 1971), pp. 177, 440.

102   *Istoriia Tadzhikskogo naroda*, Vol. III, kn. 1, p. 286.

103   Rakowska-Harmstone, *Russia and Nationalism in Central Asia*, p. 100.

104   *Velikii Oktiabr i raskreposhchenie zhenshin Srednei Azii i Kazakhstana*, p. 235.

105   V. I. Bushkov, 'Tadzhikskii *avlod* tysiacheletiia spustia', *Vostok*, No. 5 (1991), p. 76.

106   *Istoriia Tadzhikskogo naroda*, Vol. III, kn. 1, pp. 191, 308.

107   Ibron Sharipov, *Zakonomernosti formirovaniia sotsialisticheskikh obshestvennykh otnoshenii v Tadzhikistane* (Dushanbe: Donish, 1983), p. 79.

and in the cultivation of cotton.[108] Border issues also played a role in population transfers, as, starting in the early 1930s, tens of thousands of households in southern Tajikistan were moved by the state to southern frontier regions to assist in securing the Afghan–Soviet border regions.[109] The policies of resettlement into the valleys, which make up only 7 per cent of the territory of Tajikistan, resulted in the density of the population exceeding the capacity of the land to support that population. Niyazi notes that in the 1920s approximately 70 per cent of the population of Tajikistan was living in the foothills and mountains. The contemporary situation has been reversed and now 70 per cent of the population lives in the lowlands.[110]

✱ ✱ ✱

In the 1920s and 1930s, the Tajik *ethnie* was revitalised and underwent processes of mobilisation, territorialisation and politicisation. At the beginning of this century it seemed that the Tajik ethnic community was close to losing its demographic and cultural continuity. The communist leadership in Moscow deemed it necessary to preclude such a development and created the Tajik Soviet Socialist Republic. Its sovereignty may have been ephemeral, its boundaries artificial, but it did provide the Tajik *ethnie* with an institutional basis for transformation into a modern nation.

The socioeconomic development of Tajikistan in the first half of the twentieth century was an extremely uneven and controversial process. Over a surprisingly short time, Tajikistan achieved remarkable progress in improving standards of living, literacy, culture and emancipation for women. In a sense, however, it was a Pyrrhic victory, for these successes did not reflect the real growth of productive forces in Tajik society. Stalin's leadership was of the opinion that 'the triumph of socialist construction in Turkestan is completely dependent on the *rapid* solution of the literacy problem of the indigenous population',[111] and it allotted huge resources to the development of non-productive spheres in the region. Consequently, the upkeep of the relatively overinflated stratum of intellectuals, doctors, teachers and other professionals in Tajikistan was entirely up to the Kremlin's discretion. The depth of cultural changes across Tajik society also remained rather equivocal.

---

108   Christian Bleuer, 'State-building, Migration and Economic Development on the Frontiers of Northern Afghanistan and Southern Tajikistan', *Journal of Eurasian Studies*, Vol. 3 (2012).

109   Botakoz Kassymbekova, 'Humans as Territory: Forced Resettlement and the Making of Soviet Tajikistan, 1920–38', *Central Asian Survey*, Vol. 30, Nos 3–4 (2011).

110   Aziz Niyazi, 'Migration, Demography and Socio-Ecological Processes in Tajikistan', *JCAS Symposium Series*, Vol. 9 (2002), pp. 169–71.

111   Andrei Vydrin, 'Fitrat, Polivanov, Stalin i drugie', *Zvezda Vostoka*, Nos 5–6 (1994), p. 156.

By the same token, economic development of the republic was regulated by the current needs of the centre, and not by considerations for the long-term prosperity of the Tajik people. Investment occurred primarily in those branches that promised quick returns and provided the All-Union industrial complex with raw materials: cotton-growing and mining. Although a number of sophisticated machine-building, electro-technical and chemical enterprises had been set up in Tajikistan, modern industry remained largely alien to it, because they employed primarily non-indigenous workers and their profile had nothing to do with the requirements of the republic. Such a grotesque economic mechanism could exist and be reasonably efficient only when state socialism in the USSR was in its prime and the Kremlin was able to carry out its role as a universal planner, provider and distributor. The relationship between the Soviet state on the one hand and the institutions of Tajik society on the other, which forms the centrepiece of Tajikistan's modern history, will be discussed in detail in the chapters that follow.

4. Traditional Society and Regionalism in Soviet Tajikistan

The Soviet system was characterised by the incessant attempts of the state to establish overwhelming control over society. The belief that it had succeeded in penetrating all other social units, regulating social relationships down to the grassroots level, while appropriating and distributing resources at its discretion gave rise to the totalitarian concept of Soviet politics in the 1960s. This theoretical construction has, however, been criticised as far from perfect ever since (though it still appears in the literature on Tajikistan).[1] Many others have, in their work on Tajikistan, presented an analysis of qualified Soviet state effectiveness.[2] After World War II, with the fight against the *basmachi* long finished and the worst of the purges over, a picture emerges of a Soviet and a Tajik state with mixed effectiveness. For example, the local branches of the KGB were staffed by high-ranking ethnic European officers who could not speak local languages and were often rotated to new areas, and by local officers who were enmeshed in the local community and 'tended to keep troubles "inside the family"'.[3] Other factors show a Soviet state that is far from totalitarian. For example, the Loqay Uzbeks were at times confrontational with the state as late as the 1960s. While the government did defeat the last large Loqay 'uprising' in the 1960s by the use of force, the government—uncharacteristically for an effective totalitarian state—also offered concessions to the Loqay community.[4]

The main argument of the opponents of the totalitarian concept appears to be that 'the continuous process of social mobilisation, the expansion of education, and the growth of numerous professional groups and organisations created in Soviet Russia a much greater range of nuclei, the kernels of civil society'.[5]

---

1   For example, Shirin Akiner characterises 'Soviet modernisation' as being 'highly authoritarian' and implemented within a 'totalitarian system', while Olivier Roy seems to go even further, stating that 'the Soviet Union constituted a totalitarian system in which the state was the alpha, beta and omega of all socio-political existence'. See: Akiner, 'Prospects for Civil Society in Tajikistan', pp. 154–6; Olivier Roy, 'Soviet Legacies and Western Aid Imperatives in the New Central Asia', in *Civil Society in the Muslim World: Contemporary Perspectives*, ed. Amyn Sajoo (New York: I. B. Tauris, 2004), p. 126. Akiner and Roy, however, both of whom have written extensively on Tajikistan, contradict and/or qualify these statements throughout their writing.
2   As one of many examples, Menon and Spruyt argue that in Central Asia 'rival forms of rule such as clan membership, Islam, and ethnic and regional affinities have not been displaced by centralizing high-capacity states'. See: Rajan Menon and Hendrik Spruyt, 'Possibilities for Conflict Resolution in Post-Soviet Central Asia', in *Post-Soviet Political Order: Conflict and State Building*, eds Barnett R. Rubin and Jack Snyder (London: Routledge, 1998), p. 109.
3   Roy, 'Soviet Legacies and Western Aid Imperatives in the New Central Asia', p. 129.
4   Olimov and Olimova, 'Ethnic Factors and Local Self-Government in Tajikistan', p. 257.
5   S. N. Eisenstadt, 'The Breakdown of Communist Regimes', *Daedalus*, Vol. 121, No. 2 (1992), p. 30.

This notion was applicable to Tajikistan as well; however, here the Soviet state faced the toughest competition not from the offspring of its own development, but from the social institutions of tradition.[6]

The policy of Sovietisation in Central Asia envisaged the establishment of a 'modern industrial-type society devoid of social antagonisms, where social interests would be uniform and national distinctions would be erased'.[7] In the specific conditions of this region the implementation of this policy would supposedly invoke: a) accelerated economic growth, urbanisation and cultural development—'catching up' with the European part of the USSR; b) the liquidation of traditional patterns of socialisation—most notably, secularisation and dismantling of local ties and parochial loyalties; c) the installation of a new mode of socialisation based on uniform communist values; and d) the creation of viable Soviet nations on the basis of *existing* ethnic groups.

Answering the question of why the Soviet experiment in grandiose social transformation ultimately failed lies beyond the scope of this book. It is imperative, however, to try to understand why people in Tajikistan could not be 'successfully assimilated as "new Soviet men"'[8] over almost seven decades. It appears that the following social actors had the ability to challenge the monopoly of state agencies in making and enforcing rules in Soviet Tajikistan

- family
- religious community
- sub-ethnic regionalism.

Exploring their dynamic relationship with the state is likely to corroborate the notion that even in the age of modernity 'the Central Asian social system is oriented to the past in its value system as well as in its social structure'.[9]

---

6   There is an ongoing debate on the exact meaning of the words 'tradition', 'traditional' and 'traditionalism' in contemporary sociological literature. For the purposes of this study, it is assumed that 'tradition' comprises 'the statements, beliefs, legends, customs, understandings, terms, and categories of experience and social relationship that are handed down from one generation to another. Tradition, used alone, can never explain a people's behaviour, since behaviour is always situational, contextual, and circumstantial. But there are frames of meaning, biases, and entrenched understandings that people have received from their past, which are already intact when they are confronted with exigencies, and these affect how people understand their problems, how they perceive what is of immediate or of prior importance, and thus how they will be prone to act.' See: Robert L. Canfield, 'Ethnic, Regional, and Sectarian Alignments in Afghanistan', in *The State, Religion, and Ethnic Politics. Afghanistan, Iran, and Pakistan*, eds Ali Banuazizi and Myron Weiner (Syracuse, NY: Syracuse University Press, 1986), p. 88.
7   Andrei Sud'in, 'Kirgizskoe selo: akkulturatsiia i priverzhennost natsionalnoi kulturnoi traditsii', in *Etnosotsialnye protsessy v Kyrgyzstane* (Moscow: Institut Vostokovedeniia RAN, 1994), p. 17.
8   Francis Fukuyama, 'The Modernising Imperative: The USSR as an Ordinary Country', *The National Interest*, No. 31 (Spring 1993), p. 11.
9   Lawrence Krader, *Peoples of Central Asia* (The Hague: Mouton & Co., 1963), p. 166.

The Family and Traditional Patriarchy

In Tajikistan, where the transition to a modern small family is yet to be completed, the importance of the family was and is greatly enhanced by its function as a primary unit of economic, ideological and cultural activity. The traditional Tajik family has survived almost intact seven decades of ruthless pressure towards a Soviet-type modernity, retaining its main values and its adaptive role vis-a-vis society at large. The sources of such vitality are concealed in the demographic, structural and behavioural parameters of the kinship groups in Tajikistan.

There are three types of patriarchal undivided families in Tajikistan: 1) parents living with married sons; 2) families of married brothers who run one household; 3) uncles with married nephews.[10] In the early 1990s, these types constituted more than 21 per cent of all families in Tajikistan,[11] but, given the fact that their size was much bigger than the average nuclear family, they embraced more than half of the population in the republic. Table 4.1 shows that in rural areas families with seven or more members (the national average family size being 6.1) dominated the demographic landscape in Tajikistan, accounting for 51.1 per cent of all families.

Table 4.1 Number and Size of Families in Tajikistan, 1993

	Number of families	Families with the membership of:								
		2	3	4	5	6	7	8	9	> 10
Total	798 914	11.1%	11.4%	14.4%	12.9%	11.9%	10.0%	8.1%	6.1%	14.1%
Urban	319 684	19.5%	18.2%	20.6%	13.5%	9.0%	6.1%	4.1%	2.7%	6.3%
Rural	479 230	5.5%	6.8%	10.3%	12.5%	13.8%	12.6%	10.8%	8.4%	19.3%

Source: *Sem'ia v respublike Tadzhikistan* (Dushanbe: Glavnoe upravlenie natsionalnoi statistiki, 1994), p. 12.

Avlod, a word of Arabic origins,[12] is a term used in Tajikistan to describe an extended patriarchal family that serves as an informal mutual support structure.[13] Kamoludin Abdullaev refers to the *avlod* as 'the basic unit of sedentary Tajik

---

10 L. F. Monogarova, 'Struktura sovremennoi gorodskoi sem'i tadzhikov', *Sovetskaia etnografiia*, No. 3 (1982), p. 22.

11 V. I. Bushkov and D. V. Mikulskii, 'Obschestvenno-politicheskaia situatsiia v Tadzhikistane: ianvar 1992g.', in *Issledovaniia po prikladnoi i neotlozhnoi etnologii*, Series A, Document No. 26 (Moscow: Institute of Ethnology and Anthropology, 1992), p. 42.

12 In Arabic, *avlod* means 'sons'.

13 Olimov and Olimova, 'Ethnic Factors and Local Self-Government in Tajikistan', p. 249; Akiner, *Tajikistan*, pp. 24, 42. Olimova provides a short definition: 'an avlod is a patriarchal community of blood relatives who have a common ancestor and common interests, and in many cases shared property and means of production and consolidated or coordinated household budgets.' See: Saodat Olimova and Igor Bosc, *Labor Migration in Tajikistan* (Dushanbe: IOM, 2003), p. 56. Collins characterises rural *avlods* as the 'nonelite level of clans'. See: Kathleen Collins, *Clan Politics and Regime Transition in Central Asia* (Cambridge: Cambridge University Press, 2006), p. 73.

society and dominant institution of power', while noting that the 'avlod system provided survival, autonomy, and adaptability to its members, serving traditionalism and sustainability of the society'.[14] In a big patriarchal family in Tajikistan, the oldest *active*[15] male member concentrates power in his hands; he controls all major expenditures, he determines the division of labour within the family, and he decides upon the future of junior members—who should continue education and who should go to work in the fields, and so on. Even if grown-up sons separate from the parental household, they cannot claim absolute economic independence, for they continue to belong to the kinship group of a higher order—the so-called *avlod*, which ideally embodies all males descending from the common ancestor seven generations before. *Avlod*, in its ideal form, is based on: a) commonality of property (*mulkiavlodi*) in land; b) tight spiritual bonds, vested in common sacred places (*mazors*), an assortment of the spirits of the dead (*arvoh*), and traditions of blood feuds; c) compact settlement of its units, usually around one big yard—*havili*; and d) a uniformity of action in relations with the outer world. Under Soviet rule *mulki avlod* was craftily adapted to the realities of collectivisation; collective farms in Tajikistan were often created on the basis of pre-existent communal landownership, and, like their ancestors, members of an *avlod* continued to work jointly on the same allotment, disguised as a *kolkhoz* brigade.[16]

Of course, these characteristics belong to the *avlod* in its idealised form. Numerous exceptions and variations exist. For example, one anthropologist noticed that the elite families she met in Dushanbe, the Hisor Valley and Samarkand traced their prestigious lineages quite far back to a notable ancestor. Meanwhile, amongst the villagers she studied in Varzob, no-one was able to trace their lineage further back than four generations. Instead of patrilineal lineages, they stressed (often horizontal and occasionally matrilineal) networks of kin in the present, as these networks had—in their daily struggles to survive and get ahead—a high level social and economic significance.[17] Exceptions may

---

14   Kamoludin Abdullaev, 'Current Local Government Policy in Tajikistan', in *Tajikistan at a Crossroads: The Politics of Decentralization*, ed. Luigi de Martino (Geneva: Cimera, 2004), p. 8.

15   Elderly men of advanced age often transition into a role that is akin to retirement and their influence decreases.

16   N. N. Ershov, N. A. Kisliakov, E. M. Peshchereva and S. P. Rusiaikina, *Kultura i byt tadzhikskogo kolkhoznogo krestianstva* (Moscow and Leningrad: Izdatelstvo AN SSSR, 1954), p. 62; Valentin I. Bushkov, 'The Population of Northern Tajikistan between 1870 and 1990', in *State, Religion and Society in Central Asia: A Post-Soviet Critique*, ed. Vitaly Naumkin (Reading, UK: Ithaca Press, 1993), pp. 227–8.

17   Gillian Tett, *Ambiguous Alliances: Marriage and Identity in a Muslim Village in Soviet Tajikistan* (PhD Thesis: University of Cambridge, 1996), pp. 67, 69–71. For example, Tett notes (p. 66): 'Since no one workplace could provide access to all resources, the ideal network to have was a varied one, with some contacts in the town, some in the mines, some in shops and some at the farm. Very few villagers ever achieved this. However most households attempted, in however limited a way, to set up channels of contacts in a range of economic niches. There were several ways of doing this. However, one of the most basic was to have different members of a household, or a recently divided household, work in a range of economic niches.'

exist also in regards to terminology. In labelling a descent lineage or a kinship group or network in Tajikistan one will find local and contextual variations such as: *avlod, qaum, elkheshi, khesh, toyfa, kynda, tup*, and so on.[18]

Subsidiary smallholdings also constituted part of the *avlod* property and played an increasingly important role in maintaining the economic viability of kin structures in circumstances where collective farms were constantly reorganised, enlarged, combined or transformed into state farms. During the 1980s, the number of people who worked exclusively on private family plots in Tajikistan increased sixfold and reached 7 per cent of all those employed, and in some areas, such as the Gharm district, such people accounted for almost one-third of the entire rural workforce.[19] Even employees of collective farms tended to spend a substantial amount of their time on private allotments: in 1985 an average *kolkhoznik* would work only 187 days at the farm, devoting the rest to his or her personal garden, orchard or vegetable patch.[20]

As Sergei Poliakov, the most prominent scholar of 'traditionalism' in Central Asian societies, has written, 'the second part of rural economy—what is referred to as private small-holdings of *kolkhozniks* and workers of state farms … is not regulated, controlled and explored by the state'.[21] In Qarotegin (now known as Rasht) in the 1980s, it was the order of the day for a family to earn 30–50 000 roubles a year simply by selling apples from the *avlod* orchard—a sum equivalent to the annual salaries of 18 to 30 people working at the farm.[22] All revenues from wages and commercial activities went to the family fund and all spending was controlled by the head of the *avlod*, even in cases where junior members of the family lived separately.[23] The head's authority was unquestionable and he effectively prescribed the rules of behaviour to the members of the family.

Abdullaev notes that while the Soviet system 'eroded' the *avlod* to a certain extent, it continued to exist as a 'parallel system of power'.[24] Navruz Nekbakhtshoev also argues that the Soviet structures and programs indirectly altered the *avlod*, as well as pushing it out of the 'legitimate public space'; however, he notes that

18   Hafiz Kholiqovich Boboyorov, *Kinship and Islam: The Role of Collective Identities in Shaping the Institutional Order of Patronage in Southern Tajikistan* (PhD Dissertation: Rheinischen Friedrich-Wilhelms-Universität zu Bonn, 2011), pp. 91, 195, 242–3; Tett, *Ambiguous Alliances*, p. 68; Bushkov and Mikulskii, *Anatomiia Grazhdanskaia Voyny v Tadzhikistane*, pp. 11–13.

19   *Itogi vsesoiuznoi perepisi naseleniia 1989 goda po Tadzhikskoi SSR*, Vol. II, pp. 10, 40, 76.

20   N. Khonaliev, *Trudovye resursy Tadzhikistana: Problemy, perspektivy* (Dushanbe: Irfon, 1988), p. 85.

21   S. P. Poliakov, *Traditsionalizm v sovremennom sredneaziatskom obschestve* (Moscow: Znanie, 1989), p. 18.

22   Avo Suzi, 'Tadzhikskaia svadba', *Pamir*, No. 5 (1988), p. 132.

23   The family of Tanchi Kholmurodov, a typical patriarchal family in the Qurghonteppa region, consisted of 12 people; two of his elder sons were formally independent, but still brought all their money to their father. The family worked as a single brigade in a state farm, with an aggregate annual wage of 12 000 roubles. Tanchi Kholmurodov used the money as he saw fit (for example, he had bought a car and a motorcycle), and 'nobody felt hurt about it'. See: *Kommunist Tadzhikistana*, 20 March 1975.

24   Abdullaev, 'Current Local Government Policy Situation in Tajikistan', p. 8.

despite these changes the *avlod* is still an important concept in Tajikistan today, as noted by the use of 'which *avlod* are you from?' as a common question.[25] The answer to this question would include a recitation of ancestry because of the importance of the exchange of 'genealogical information' in determining 'identity' and 'difference', as kinship differences are not visible.[26] For the Uzbeks in Tajikistan who no longer have 'tribal divisions', the social structure is also based on the *avlod*, though significantly less than for Tajiks. The *avlod* structure 'encompasses' approximately 46 per cent of the detribalised Uzbeks compared with 82 per cent of certain Tajik 'subgroups'[27]—the Kulobis being at the highest range.[28] Meanwhile, Shirin Akiner argues that the *avlod* is most prevalent among the resettled groups from Darvoz and Qarotegin (Gharm), who resisted assimilation most noticeably.[29]

The *avlod's* main distinction from the undivided patriarchal family is the fact that it presents, in its ideal form, the entity of *all* relatives over seven generations, both dead and alive, and as such can incorporate more than one family.[30] Both types are derivatives of the primordial agnate clan, which means that they are essentially kinship systems. The concept of *avlod* is related to the phenomenon of *mahalla*—the neighbourhood community in a city block or village. Residents in a given territory often form a cohesive and exclusive entity that has its own organs of self-administration (*mahalla* committees, sanctioned and recognised by the civil authorities), gathering place (usually a mosque) and an array of ritual events. The *mahalla* committees are rarely elected but rather are formed by people of influence—be they local elders, spiritual leaders, wealthy merchants or, in the civil war era, armed gangs' commanders. They carry out a wide range of duties: they

- form public opinion
- monitor observation of *shari'a*, *adat* and localistic patterns of behaviour

---

25 Nekbakhtshoev, *Clan Politics*, p. 29. Navruz Nekbakhtshoev provides an example of the use of *mahallas* for interaction between Tajiks, noting the typical question between Tajiks who have just met each other: '*Shumo az kadom mahalla?*' (Which *mahalla* are you from). Nekbakhtshoev notes that it is a general 'where are you from?' question that may require further inquiry once place of origin is determined. The next, even more localised identity question, if locality is insufficient for the interaction, is given as '*shumo az kadom awlod?*' (literally, 'which *avlod* are you from?').

26 Nekbakhtshoev, *Clan Politics*, pp. 22, 29.

27 Olimov and Olimova, 'Ethnic Factors and Local Self-Government in Tajikistan', p. 249. Gillian Tett found that less than half of the households in the village she studied in Varzob fit within the *avlod* system. See: Tett, *Ambiguous Alliances*, pp. 59–61.

28 Olimova and Bosc, *Labor Migration in Tajikistan*, p. 56.

29 Akiner, *Tajikistan*, pp. 24, 42.

30 An example of the classic *avlod* is a group of families who reside in the village of Qulbai Poyon: a certain Tohirbay, who died in the 1910s, had 10 children—four of them married offspring of uncles on the father's side, four married children of uncles on the mother's side, and two remaining sons took wives from amongst distant relatives. Three generations later, Tohirbay's *avlod* consisted of more than 200 people, who cherished his memory and maintained a strong family cohesion. See: O. A. Sukhareva, 'Traditsiia semeino-rodstvennykh brakov u narodov Srednei Azii', in *Sem'ia i semeinye obriady u narodov Srednei Azii i Kazakhstana*, ed. G. P. Snesarev (Moscow: Nauka, 1978), p. 122.

- impose penalties on violators, including money payouts and ostracisation
- sanction real estate transactions
- collect municipal taxes
- organise ceremonial affairs—for example, weddings and funerals.

It is, however, the *mahalla's* role as a means of transmission of socially significant information and of regeneration of the traditional ways of life that appears to be paramount for understanding political processes in contemporary Tajikistan. Poliakov, describing the situation in the late 1980s, has written that

> the mahalla ... has ideological life entirely and firmly in its hands. The committee and its active members, the elders, use very refined techniques to direct the education of the youth. The channelling and, even more important, the interpretation of information is extremely simple: the forty-year-old father passes it from the mosque to his twenty-year-old son and his year-old grandson ... In rural areas the mahalla controls all aspects of life for people ... even more completely than it does in the city.[31]

One more recent study notes that in villages in Tajikistan the *mahalla* takes on an extra meaning. Here the *mahalla* can be used to refer to the entire community, and even to the community leader, the *rais*.[32] Many have noted the longevity of the *mahalla* as a relevant social institution. Other scholars write that the *guzors*[33] and *mahallas* that pre-existed the Soviet Union in Central Asia were integrated into Soviet power structures and functioned as a unit of the state.[34] Olivier Roy cites the *mahalla* as a relevant entity before, during and after the Soviet era in Tajikistan. He argues, in line with his analysis of other identity categories and institutions, that the *mahalla* survived collectivisation and population transfers and was 'reincarnated' in the collective farm.[35] Similarly, in an urban context, Soviet-era population transfers often involved people from the same *mahalla* being resettled in the same apartment building.[36]

---

31 Poliakov, *Everyday Islam*, pp. 78–9. Similarly, in a contemporary study on both Uzbekistan and Tajikistan, Sabine Freizer notes that *mahallas*, which 'formed' in the pre-Soviet era, regulated and assisted many aspects of a person's life. Certain elders within the community mediated disputes, helped organise communal life-cycle celebrations, and facilitated (mutual) assistance. The *mahalla* was essentially a 'forum where local values, rules of behaviour and common needs were defined'. See: Sabine Freizer, 'Central Asian Fragmented Civil Society: Communal and Neoliberal Forms in Tajikistan and Uzbekistan', in *Exploring Civil Society: Political and Cultural Contexts*, eds Marlies Glasius, David Lewis and Hakan Seckinelgin (London: Routledge, 2004), p. 116.

32 John Heathershaw, 'Peacebuilding as Practice: Discourses from Post-Conflict Tajikistan', *International Peacekeeping*, Vol. 14, No. 2 (2007), p. 230.

33 A small neighbourhood community, sometimes a single street.

34 Schoeberlein-Engel, *Identity in Central Asia*, pp. 266–7; Poliakov, *Everyday Islam*, p. 77; Freizer, 'Central Asian Fragmented Civil Society', p. 116. Freizer writes that the *mahallas* 'often functioned in symbiosis with communist institutions'.

35 Roy, *The New Central Asia*, pp. 86–7. For a more focused analysis of the *mahalla* in Tajikistan, see Sabine Freizer, 'Neo-Liberal and Communal Civil Society in Tajikistan: Merging or Dividing in the Post War Period?' *Central Asian Survey*, Vol. 24, No. 3 (2005), pp. 224–43.

36 Poliakov, *Everyday Islam*, p. 77.

It is appropriate to note in this context that the *mahalla* mosque in Tajikistan is not necessarily a centre of purely religious activities. In fact, its function as a communicative hub of the community—*gapkhona* or *mehmonkhona*—is at least equally meaningful and certainly dates to pre-Islamic times. Unlike the Friday mosque, the *mahalla* prayer space is primarily perceived as 'the public gathering point of the male population of the *mahalla*; kitchen utensils are kept there and hearths are set up in its yard'.[37] In the mountainous areas east of Dushanbe the meeting place of a *mahalla* mosque is often referred to as *alovkhona*, or 'the house of fire'—clearly a survivor of Zoroastrian rites.[38]

Male unions, widely known throughout the ancient world from Greece to China, remain very much a reality in today's Tajikistan. Their regular assemblies, known as *gashtak, gapkhuri, gap, ziyofat, osh, tukma, jura* or *maslihat* in various localities of the country, share several common features

- taboo against women's presence
- initiation procedures for newcomers
- absolute authority of the leader—*bobo*, or 'grandfather' (hence the nickname of Sangak Safarov, the infamous Tajik warlord in 1992–93: *bobo* Sangak)
- obedience and even servility of younger members to the older ones, but *only* within the limits of a given *gashtak*.

The late 1980s saw a rapid revival of the tradition of male unions in Tajikistan. It was especially evident in the cities, where they operated under the mask of newly allowed public associations and sports clubs. It has been noted, however, that in modern *gashtaks* vertical ties between generations are giving way to horizontal links, according to professional, criminal or other common interests.[39] It is noteworthy that youngsters in such formations are encouraged to go in for combat sports, such as sambo, judo and karate. Yaqubjon Salimov, a racketeer and minister of interior of Tajikistan from late 1992 to 1995, acquired some of the necessary skills for his career in the 1970s fighting for his *gashtak* based in the Dushanbe suburb of Obdoron against rivals from Shomansur.[40]

In rural districts of Tajikistan, *mahalla* and *gashtak* are almost invariably mere extensions of *avlod*. The last is, first of all, a kinship structure and as such performs primarily controlling and regulatory functions. The term *mahalla* has a territorial connotation and is essentially an organisational system. *Gashtak*, originally a subunit of *avlod*, has been acquiring a new universal function: the

---

37   Poliakov, *Traditsionalizm v sovremennom sredneaziatskom obschestve*, p. 71.

38   G. P. Snesarev, 'O reliktakh muzhskikh soiuzov v istorii narodov Srednei Azii', in *VII Mezhdunarodnyi kongress antropologicheskikh i etnograficheskikh nauk* (Moscow: Nauka, 1964), p. 2.

39   V. I. Bushkov, 'Tadzhikistan: traditsionnoe obshchestvo v postindustrialnom mire', *Etnograficheskoe obozrenie*, No. 4 (1995), p. 91. On the non-kin characteristics of these groupings, see also: Kilavuz, *Understanding Violent Conflict*, pp. 122–3.

40   Confidential source in Dushanbe, January 1996.

establishment and maintenance of viable ties amongst members of a certain occupation in the community vis-a-vis external forces, including the state. In the cities the distinction between the three is blurred, but what really matters in this case is the fact that, for the bulk of the Tajiks, the collective form of self-consciousness is yet to be replaced with the individualistic one. For many, their lives are still determined to a great extent by long-established codes and the will of various kinship and communal structures, even if those structures have undergone alteration and adaptation in the Soviet era. A representative sociological survey conducted in 11 republics and regions of the USSR between 1988 and 1990 showed that 49 per cent of the population of Tajikistan was guided in their behaviour primarily by the rules prescribed by the family, compared with 26 per cent in Moscow; the rules set by the state and society at large proved to be nowhere near as authoritative as in this Central Asian republic.[41]

Patriarchy, interpreted as a 'kinship-ordered social structure with strictly defined sex roles in which women are subordinated to men',[42] serves as a fair indication of the persistence of traditional patterns in Tajik society. The entry of women into public life, sponsored and encouraged by Soviet authorities, had weakened patriarchy to a substantial extent, but the socialisation of women, especially in rural areas of Tajikistan, remains centred on the patrilineal family and focuses on childrearing, limiting their mobility and access to employment and education (Table 4.2). It has been estimated that in Tajikistan a woman with a family of five spends an average of 45 hours a week running the household,[43] which effectively precludes her from pursuing alternative life options.

Table 4.2 Comparative Social Indicators in Tajikistan and the Soviet Union as a Whole, 1988

Social indicators	USSR	Tajikistan
Gender ratio: females per 100 males	112	101
Labour force: % female	50.6	39
Higher education: % of college population that is female	54	41
Fertility rate	2.67	5.68

Source: *Sotsialnoe razvitie SSSR* (Moscow: Finansy i statistika, 1990), pp. 27, 38, 47, 235; *Narodnoe khoziaistvo Tadzhikskoi SSR v 1988 godu* (Dushanbe: Irfon, 1990), pp. 21, 24, 31, 108.

41   Sh. Shoismatulloev, 'Stanovlenie molodoi sem'i', *Izvestiia Akademii nauk Respubliki Tadzhikistan: Seriia: filosofiia i pravovedenie*, No. 3 (1992), p. 27.
42   Valentine M. Moghadam, 'Patriarchy and the Politics of Gender in Modernizing Societies: Iran, Pakistan and Afghanistan', *South Asia Bulletin*, Vol. XIII, Nos 1–2 (1993), p. 122.
43   T. Fedorova, 'Planirovanie sem'i v regionakh rasshirennogo vosproizvodstva naseleniia', in *Sovetologi o problemakh sotsialno-ekonomicheskogo razvitiia SSSR i soiuznykh respublik* (Moscow: Institut ekonomiki AN SSSR, 1990), p. 111.

The legal status of women in Tajikistan is not different from that of men, but in practice patriarchal forms of control over women, such as the senior male's domination in the *avlod*,[44] restrictive codes of behaviour and a specific public opinion that holds female virtue the *sine qua non* of family honour, cast strong doubt on the universal effectiveness of emancipatory measures implemented in Soviet Central Asia. In private life especially, a significant proportion of Tajik women has not achieved freedom from traditional patriarchal structures. A study conducted in 1990 amongst female students of Dushanbe tertiary institutions— arguably one of the most fully socialised and mobile strata of the populace—has yielded quite revealing results (Table 4.3).

Table 4.3 Motivation for Marriage amongst College Students, 1990

Motives	National composition of the family		
	Russian	Tajik	Mixed
Mutual love	100%	64.7%	80.9%
Commonality of spiritual interests	22.2%	9.8%	28.6%
Desire to have a family	11.1%	17.6%	19.0%
Parents' will	0%	21.6%	0%

Source: *Vuzovskaia molodezh: mirovozzrencheskie i tsennostnye orientatsii* (Vypusk I. Dushanbe: Ministerstvo narodnogo obrazovaniia TSSR, 1990), p. 108.

In rural areas, the role of the family in determining the future for a girl is near absolute. Parents would more often than not give a daughter away without asking for her consent, on the basis of economic considerations and the interests of the *avlod*. The importance of dynastic marriages for *nomenklatura* clans in Tajikistan will be illustrated in a subsequent chapter; for now it is appropriate to stress the general point made for the traditional society: 'family leaders, government elites, and religious officials may promote marriages between different families as a means of enhancing or defending their political and social status, of gaining property and other wealth, or of extending business contacts and networks … The same can be said for nonelite families.'[45] There are 'still many matrimonial arrangements between cousins amongst Tajiks, such as marrying [a] mother's brother's daughter and marriages between two brothers' children. In fact, mountain Tajiks disapprove of marriages between non-relatives.'[46] Betrothal at the age of nine or even two is not infrequent in Yaghnob, for example. Of course, the actual marriage is usually postponed until the age of consent, but the

---

44   Gillian Tett did find a few powerful grandmother figures running an extended household. See: Tett, *Ambiguous Alliances*, pp. 59–60.
45   Dale F. Eickelman and James Piscatori, *Muslim Politics* (Princeton, NJ: Princeton University Press, 1996), p. 85.
46   N. A. Kisliakov, *Nasledovanie i razdel imushchestva u narodov Srednei Azii i Kazakhstana* (Leningrad: Nauka, 1977), p. 99.

bride-to-be constantly remains 'the subject of attention and speculation, not in terms of beauty and physique, but the emerging aptness as a house-keeper and worker. These qualities are valued most of all.'[47] The feeling of being trapped between traditional and modern ways of life often results in tragedy: Tajikistan was the only republic in the USSR where women constituted the majority (52 per cent) of those who committed suicide; self-immolation was an especially gruesome method of settling scores with life amongst women 'confined to the family circle'.[48] A lengthy quotation from a Tajik academic probably gives the best account of the state of affairs in the republic at the end of the Soviet era:[49]

> The Tajik woman, who has experienced fear of derision, punishment, and solitude for centuries, has been trying to fulfil all whims and demands of the husband and his family with obedience and has been enduring injustice, cruelty and abasement. They have penetrated her flesh and blood and have been transmitted from generation to generation, to daughters and grand-daughters. This situation, fortified by public opinion and learned through experience, traditions and family and marriage customs, has oriented the Tajik girl towards married life and the role of the mother of a large family at a very early age. The same experience has cultivated in her such features as indecisiveness, servility, reticence, unquestionable subordination to the husband and parents' will, modesty and high regard to a woman's virtue and a mother's duty.

For 70 years traditional family structures and values in Tajikistan continued to exist parallel to and independently of official ideology, concealed from the eyes of strangers and proving to be 'something difficult to control even for a Soviet-style state'.[50] With the weakening of the communist monolith in the late 1980s, they began to play a more salient role in local politics. When alternative political organisations and social movements, such as Rastokhez and the Democratic Party, emerged in Tajikistan, their rank-and-file membership consisted more so of *avlods*, *mahalla* committees and men's unions related to the political leaders by blood or otherwise, rather than individuals sharing their programmatic ideals.[51] The Islamic Revival Party, despite its stated ideology, employed the same tactics.[52]

---

47   E. M. Peshchereva, *Yagnobskie etnograficheskie materialy* (Dushanbe: AN TSSR, 1976), p. 35.

48   Saodat Safarova, 'Vyzov, broshennyi zhizni', *Pamir*, No. 8 (1988), pp. 140, 142. In 1987, 57 cases of female suicide were registered in the Leninobod *oblast*. None of them was properly investigated.

49   Khurram Rahimov, *Traditsii tadzhikskogo naroda i ikh rol' v podgotovke starsheklassnikov k semeinoi zhizni* (Dushanbe: NII pedagogicheskikh nauk RT, 1992), pp. 52–3.

50   Michael Rywkin, 'National Symbiosis: Vitality, Religion, Identity, Allegiance', in *The USSR and the Muslim World: Issues in Domestic and Foreign Policy*, ed. Yaacov Ro'i (London: George Allen & Unwin, 1984), p. 4.

51   V. I. Bushkov and D. V. Mikulskii, *"Tadzhikskaia revoliutsiia" i grazhdanskaia voina (1989–1994gg.)* (Moscow: TSIMO, 1995), pp. 52–3.

52   This is discussed later in a dedicated section on the Islamic Revival Party.

In times of political instability, traditional institutions tend to play an ever-growing part in providing security and welfare to the populace in Central Asia. It has been revealed that even in the period of Soviet stagnation, and even in such a cosmopolitan and heavily industrialised city as Tashkent, at least 30 per cent of indigenous males were actively involved in the *gap* and *tukma* activities.[53] In Tajikistan, where the process of urbanisation was far less advanced and a high percentage of city-dwellers were still employed in agriculture, this figure must have been much higher. Moreover, beginning in the late 1980s, quasi-traditional structures began to evolve in hitherto unaffected areas. In the Dushanbe suburb of Bofanda, for example, residents of four nine-storey apartment buildings decided in 1989 to pool their efforts to cope with day-to-day problems, such as frequent power failures and garbage disposal. They furnished a gathering place in the yard (which also served as a mosque), and elected a *mahalla* committee, comprising a vocational schoolteacher, a cinema director and the supplies manager of a tannery cum self-taught mullah. This *mahalla* would not be different from thousands others around the country, but for the fact that 80 per cent of Bofanda residents at the time were workers at the Tajik textile combine and thus mostly non-Tajiks. As a result, only 10–15 people attend purely religious events in that community, while the rest are more interested in maintenance and leisure activities. During outbreaks of civil disorder in 1990 and 1992, all the grown men of the *mahalla* formed a self-defence unit, regardless of their nationality or political and religious affiliation.[54]

In summary, the kinship-familial setting of Tajik society has coped well with the realities of Soviet rule. The seemingly omnipresent and omnipotent party-state machine failed to alter significantly the major attitudes to the problems of human existence and cultural order amongst the Tajiks. The communist regime, although it was the only sanctioned political system in the society, could not transform what Shmuel Eisenstadt has called the second level of organisational activities—that is, the traditional collectivities and communities 'whose systemic boundaries are organised or patterned around symbols or likeness of common attributes and of participation in them, but which are not necessarily structured as systems with clear organisational boundaries'.[55] The interaction of the state and traditional society did limit the effectiveness of the state, but the way in which the two operated helped, in certain situations, to gain people's acceptance of communist rule. For example, in one village an observer noted that by the late Soviet era most of the government officials were from the village itself. These officials, being tied by traditional bonds, used the state to assist

---

53   L. A. Tultseva, 'O nekotorykh sotsialno-etnicheskikh aspektakh razvitiia obriadovo-prazdnichnoi kultury v Uzbekistane', *Sovetskaia etnografiia*, No. 5 (1984), p. 22.
54   Information gathered during fieldwork in Tajikistan in February 1995.
55   S. N. Eisenstadt, *Traditional Patrimonialism and Modern Neopatrimonialism* (Beverly Hills and London: Sage, 1973), p. 63.

those in their family and patronage networks. The result was an acceptance of Soviet rule and then, with the collapse of the Soviet Union, 'deep shock, confusion, and disbelief', followed a year later by yearning for a return to the 'former Communist status quo'.[56]

Traditional Social Institutions in the Collective Farm

During the communist era the Soviets maintained control at the national level over the distribution of resources and the promotion of cadres; however, in the rural areas the Soviet security apparatus and central government representatives had much less of a presence than in the cities. In the rural areas during the early Soviet era the government allowed already established local leaders to be the middlemen between the people and the state. This allowed some local leaders to maintain their own power bases.[57] The government did not destroy the pre-existing solidarity groups (such as *qaum*, *avlod*, *mahalla*). Instead it often formed collective farms (*kolkhozes*) from some of these groups, allowing their structure to remain intact throughout the Soviet era. Within the *kolkhoz*, the *qaum* and *mahalla* were often duplicated/transported wholesale into the work brigades and housing estates (*uchatska*). In Olivier Roy's words, the *kolkhozes* 'became the new tribes of Central Asia'.[58] The phenomenon of the creation of collective farms on the basis of pre-exiting *avlods*, as described by researchers in the 1950s, was noted above.[59] Sergei Poliakov makes a similar argument based on later research. He describes land administration in rural Central Asia as having been changed 'in name, but not in substance'[60] by collectivisation, with local patterns of authority transferred into the collective farms and the 'customary way of life unaffected'.[61] And, like Roy, Poliakov also notes that collective farms and work brigades in rural Central Asia were formed on the basis of traditional communal solidarity groups. He provides as an example 13 *avlods* in a town in northern Tajikistan being established as 13 *kolkhozes*. And after these 13 farms were united into a single *kolkhoz*, these *avlods* became discrete work brigades.[62]

---

56   Tett, *Ambiguous Alliances*, pp. 76, 78, 191, 196.

57   Roy, *The New Central Asia*, pp. 85–6. Roy calls these leaders the 'new beys and khans'.

58   Roy, *The New Central Asia*, pp. 85–9, 102–6; Roy, 'Soviet Legacies and Western Aid Imperatives in the New Central Asia', p. 128.

59   Ershov et al., *Kultura i byt tadzhikskogo kolkhoznogo krestianstva*, p. 62.

60   Sergei P. Poliakov, 'Modern Soviet Central Asian Countryside: Traditional Forms of Property in a Quasi-Industrial System', in *State, Religion and Society in Central Asia: A Post Soviet Critique*, ed. Vitaly Naumkin (Reading, UK: Ithaca Press, 1993), p. 139. Poliakov elaborates further on this subject. See: Poliakov, *Everyday Islam*, pp. 16–17.

61   Poliakov, 'Modern Soviet Central Asian Countryside', p. 137.

62   Poliakov, *Everyday Islam*, pp. 17, 140. Furthermore, he notes that 'in distributing personal-use plots to collective farm workers … the boundaries of the old "tribal" and "avlod" holdings were strictly observed'. Ibid., p. 17.

There was an attempt by the Soviets to break apart these traditional solidarity groupings, starting in the mid 1950s, when the state restructured the *kolkhoz*. At this time the government (at a higher level) started to appoint the head of the *kolkhoz* and to consolidate multiple *kolkhozes* into one state farm (*sovkhoz*).[63] These changes, however, did not destroy the solidarity groups, which often remained intact. Sometimes, the *kolkhoz* itself became a new solidarity group. In either case, relatively autonomous communities persisted.[64] Collectivisation placed considerable resources under the control of collective farm bosses; however, the patterns of farm-boss strength and patronage varied considerably throughout the Soviet Union, and within Central Asia, though generally speaking the Soviet state relied on farm bosses for mobilisation of rural labour, resource distribution, effective use of technical resources, and fulfilment of agricultural plans. The collective farms soon became 'critical instruments of social control'.[65] The *kolkhoz* leadership, thanks to its monopoly on the distribution of resources within the community, as well as the option of physical force, was able to control the inhabitants of the *kolkhoz*. The *kolkhoz* was also able to assist members who had left the community. *Kolkhozniks* who moved to cities were able to rely on a network of former members of their *kolkhoz* as well as the collective farm leadership's connections in the Communist Party bureaucracy.[66]

State control over collective farms was inadvertently weakened during Khrushchev's time in office and even further during Brezhnev's tenure. By this time collective farm chairs 'emerged as Soviet style local strongmen'.[67] Farm chairmen and factory bosses were engaged with regional politicians in patronage networks in which the exchange was protection and access to resources for the bosses in return for illicit income for the politicians. For example, in Qurghonteppa the Leninobodi elite had endeavoured to install their own people

---

63   Roy, *The New Central Asia*, pp. 85–9, 102–6; Roy, 'Soviet Legacies and Western Aid Imperatives in the New Central Asia', p. 128. Bliss describes the process of creating larger units: 'The originally small cooperative farms (kolkhoz) were first amalgamated into larger units and then, sometime in the early 1970s, the majority of these were turned into purely state-run farms. This created a strong economic unit with a mandate extending far beyond the actual work of a farm. The sovkhoz organised and maintained the entire infrastructure, ranging from water and energy supplies to running the nursery and primary schools. Democratically elected members of each Soviet were not able to make real decisions or carry out any administrative functions, because everything depended de facto on the leader of the sovkhoz and his budget.' See: Frank Bliss, *Social and Economic Change in the Pamirs (Gorno-Badakhshan, Tajikistan)* (New York: Routledge, 2006), p. 246.

64   Roy, *The New Central Asia*, pp. 85–9, 102–6; Roy, 'Soviet Legacies and Western Aid Imperatives in the New Central Asia', p. 128. Eventually, according to Roy, the Communist Party settled on a policy of manipulating existing regional factions against each other instead of trying to reconfigure them.

65   Lawrence Markowitz, *Collapsed and Prebendal States in Post-Soviet Eurasia: Cross-Regional Determinants of State Formation in Tajikistan and Uzbekistan* (PhD Thesis: University of Wisconsin-Madison, 2005), pp. 32–3, 35.

66   Kilavuz, *Understanding Violent Conflict*, p. 88. Kilavuz writes further: 'The kolkhoz was the main source of its members' work, social welfare and social services, income, irrigation and housing. The Soviet system gave the *brigadirs* (kolkhoz brigade leaders) immense power within the kolkhoz they directed. The *brigadirs* had control over the economic resources in the kolkhoz, and the power to distribute these resources as they wished.'

67   Markowitz, *Collapsed and Prebendal States in Post-Soviet Eurasia*, pp. 38–9, 54, in regards to Tajikistan.

(Leninobodis, those of Leninobodi descent or ethnic Uzbeks) as collective farm chairs and district *raikom* secretaries in order to control the region's wealth-producing bases, while Kulob, with its relatively modest economic base, was of much less interest to the Leninobodi elite. In Kulob, local authority figures embezzled agricultural profits while taking over local law enforcement and judicial agencies as a way to protect their scheme. By the end of the Soviet period, farm bosses and regional politicians in Kulob exercised 'significant influence' over law enforcement agencies and the courts while increasingly relying on illegal income.[68] As for the Gharmi Tajiks in Qurghonteppa, they were, towards the end of the Soviet era, more focused on 'free enterprise' and positioned themselves in opposition to the collective farm directors, who were often Uzbeks or Kulobis.[69]

Regionalism: The Ultimate Cause of Social Polarisation

Apart from familial and religious affiliations, which overlap and complement one another, there is another important source of identity that arguably matters most for Tajiks in the context of political processes. Much of the population of Tajikistan self-identifies not by ethnicity, but by locale. Amongst Tajiks, individuals identify themselves by town or region of origin. The use of 'Tajik' is, of course, only for identifying oneself to outsiders.[70] French scholar Olivier Roy was one of the first in the West to attempt an analysis of 'the influence of political loyalties based on geographic origin' in shaping conflict in Tajikistan, defining this phenomenon as 'localism'.[71] He also drew a very important distinction between 'localism' and the social fragmentation along clan and ethnic lines, thus contrasting with so many authors who are tempted to mix together 'the long-suppressed clan, regional and ethnic rivalries' in Tajikistan.[72] Roy's early work, however, is somewhat sketchy, and its other major postulate, that 'the present fragmentation is largely a product of the Soviet period',[73] could be misleading. Regional identities were not created during the Soviet era, but had in fact already been important at both the elite and the non-elite levels. Soviet policies, however, gave these identities the 'meaning and structure' that

---

68   Markowitz, *Collapsed and Prebendal States in Post-Soviet Eurasia*, pp. 40–3, 56, 88–90, 95, 101.

69   Rubin, 'Russian Hegemony and State Breakdown in the Periphery', p. 152.

70   Olimov and Olimova, 'Ethnic Factors and Local Self-Government in Tajikistan', p. 237; Irina Zviagelskaya, *The Tajik Conflict* (Reading, UK: Ithaca Press, 1997), n.p. Accessed online: <http://www.ca-c.org/dataeng/st_09_zvjag.shtml>

71   Olivier Roy, *The Civil War in Tajikistan: Causes and Implications* (Washington, DC: United States Institute of Peace, 1993), p. 16.

72   For example: Ahmed Rashid, *The Resurgence of Central Asia: Islam or Nationalism* (Karachi: Oxford University Press, 1994), p. 159.

73   Roy, *The Civil War in Tajikistan*, p. 16.

they currently have by politicising regional identities, giving them relevance at both the elite and the non-elite levels. 'Which region are you from?' is a standard inquiry in both Uzbekistan and Tajikistan, although in Tajikistan the question became more sensitive after the civil war. Individuals may cite the wider region of their origin or a town within it, depending on the situation. Nevertheless, many here identify with their region of origin, even after being three generations removed. People identify with their paternal grandfather's place of birth, and in order to identify with that region, according to popular belief, an individual's ancestors must have been there for a minimum of three generations.[74]

In Tajikistan, regional identity can be seen as a factor in not just group conflict and competition, but also in many types of other social behaviour such as marriage preferences for co-regionals and university socialisation patterns, where there are reports of students from the same region eating, drinking and living together, with the occasional fights between groups of youths from different regions.[75] Locally based identities, whether at the regional, village or *mahalla* level, can be significant when a person leaves their home. In their new location their origin is frequently employed to seek assistance from co-regionals.[76] 'Regionalism', according to presidential candidate Davlat Khudonazarov, 'manifested itself even in the spatial distribution of Dushanbe, where people of the same region often lived clustered together.'[77]

It has been shown in the preceding chapters that the entire course of Tajik history, both before and after the 1917 revolution, has been conducive to the emergence and survival of distinctive sub-ethnic communities that could never merge effectively into a modern nation. Called *mahallagaroyi* or *mantaqagaroyi* in the Tajik language, this phenomenon will hereinafter be referred to as 'regionalism', which appears to be a more precise term than 'localism', both linguistically and in view of the realities in today's Tajikistan. In this study, the region is understood to be an area with a recognisable community that has[78]

---

74 Kilavuz, *Understanding Violent Conflict*, pp. 80–1, 88.
75 Kilavuz, *Understanding Violent Conflict*, p. 82; 'Speech by First Secretary K. M. Makhkamov to the 24th Congress of the Tajikistan Lenin Communist Youth League', *Kommunist Tadzhikistana* (22 February 1987), pp. 2, 5; and *Kommunist Tadzhikistana* (21 February 1987), pp. 3–4, in *The Current Digest of the Post-Soviet Press*, Vol. 39, No. 9 (1 April 1987), p. 9.
76 Kilavuz, *Understanding Violent Conflict*, pp. 114–15.
77 Davlat Khudonazar, 'The Conflict in Tajikistan: Questions of Regionalism', in *Central Asia: Conflict, Resolution, and Change*, eds Roald Z. Sagdeev and Susan Eisenhower (Chevy Chase, Md: CPSS Press, 1995), p. 256. Khudonazar describes the areas where Gharmis, Kulobis and Pamiris lived as dilapidated and neglected. Kilavuz notes that region of origin for Tajiks and Uzbeks is even important outside Tajikistan. She cites Soviet-era Uzbek workers in Siberia and contemporary Tajik workers in Russia self-identifying by region of origin and forming 'mutual-support networks' with co-regionals. Kilavuz, *Understanding Violent Conflict*, p. 82.
78 Adapted from: Louis Wirth, 'The Limitations of Regionalism', in *Regionalism in America*, ed. Merrill Jensen (Madison and Milwaukee: University of Wisconsin Press, 1965), pp. 382–4.

- distinctive physical traits, such as weather, length of growing season, vegetation, and similar features
- a distinctive history
- special cultural characteristics such as dialect, costume, architecture, use of given tools, rituals—what is referred to in anthropology as a 'culture area'
- natural and artificial barriers—for example, mountain ranges and administrative borders
- a focus of gravitation, such as a trade centre and/or political or historical capital
- an ad-hoc problem: environmental pollution, crime, ethnic tension, and so on.

Akiner lists the cultural 'markers' of the various sub-Tajik regional identities as including 'group histories, social structures, customs, music, folklore, and material culture (e.g., traditional styles of clothing and ornamental designs)'.[79] Kilavuz provides a very similar list of markers when she writes that significant differences, especially cultural, are given for those from the different regions of Uzbekistan and Tajikistan. The people themselves cite regional differences amongst the same ethnic group that manifest in 'dialect, physical appearance, traditions and customs'.[80] In regards to language, Muriel Atkin notes that while members of the Tajik elite can speak literary Tajik (and Russian), most people speak various Tajik dialects, divided most broadly between northern and southern dialects, with 'several further subdivisions'.[81] Kilavuz cautions that while the regions may have their own characteristic dialects, with differences even within the region, many people have the ability to speak in different dialects, including the standard literary form promoted by the government.[82] Akiner adds 'psychological stereotyping' as a significant factor in marking group boundaries amongst Tajiks. The examples of stereotypes she provides are that: Qaroteginis (Gharmis) are 'flexible and adaptable'; Kulobis are 'conservative and obstinate, reluctant to compromise'; and 'northerners like consensus and continuity, [and] are good at manipulating people'.[83]

Akiner also argues for the importance of geographical influences, particularly the mountain–plains dichotomy, on the distinct sub-Tajik identities, citing these regions of Tajikistan—having distinct 'economic, political and cultural environments'—traditionally having a low level of interaction with each other

---

79   Akiner, *Tajikistan*, p. 7.
80   Kilavuz, *Understanding Violent Conflict*, p. 80.
81   I. M. Oranskii, *Tadzhikoiazychnye etnograficheskie gruppy Gissarskoi doliny (Sredniaia Aziia)* (Moscow: Nauka, 1983), pp. 29–30; L. F. Monogarova, 'Evolutsiia natsional'nogo samosoznaniia pripamirskikh narodnostei', in *Etnicheskie protsessy u natsional'nykh grupp Srednei Azii i Kazakhstana* (Moscow: Nauka, 1980), p. 130. Both cited in Atkin, 'Religious, National and Other Identities in Central Asia', p. 60.
82   Kilavuz, *Understanding Violent Conflict*, pp. 80–1. She then goes on to cite the primacy of ancestry over dialect in determining identity.
83   Akiner, *Tajikistan*, p. 7, n. 3.

in the Soviet era.[84] The small size and relative isolation of mountain settlements created 'tight-knit communities with strong local identities'.[85] By the end of the Soviet era, the majority of Tajiks lived in rural areas and more than 80 per cent of the rural population still lived in their place of birth, in one of more than 3000 villages. Rural social life in Tajikistan, the least urbanised of the Soviet republics, was still 'comparatively isolated and inward focused'.[86] At this time many villages in Tajikistan were mono-ethnic, and where they were multi-ethnic they may in fact be divided into mono-ethnic neighbourhoods. In addition, Tajik villagers are, according to several Soviet-era researchers, 'highly endogamous'.[87] Atkin, however, warns that these conclusions should be viewed with caution due to the 'imprecision' of the Uzbek and Tajik nationality categories.[88]

Aziz Niyazi sets a contrast when describing Tajiks in southern Tajikistan, noting that they are more isolated and 'self-contained'. He posits that they (Kulobi and Gharmi Tajiks) are, in comparison with valley Tajiks (for example, Ferghana Valley Tajiks), subjected to more fragmented local subcultures.[89] The term 'Gharmi Tajiks' (hereinafter 'Gharmis') refers to Tajiks from the now defunct Province of Gharm—a usage that began after the large-scale transfer of Tajiks from Gharm Province to the lowlands of the Vakhsh Valley; however, the term 'Qaroteginis' is also used, as Gharm Province included the Qarotegin Valley, as well as the smaller Darvoz and Vakhyo valleys. Qarotegin and Darvoz, as well as provinces such as Kulob, roughly match pre-Soviet areas that were ruled as semi-independent *beks* in the Bukharan Emirate. The name for Gharm Province is taken from the small city of Gharm, which was the pre-Soviet capital of the Qarotegin *bek*.[90]

---

84   Akiner, *Tajikistan*, pp. 7–8.
85   Akiner, *Tajikistan*, pp. 7–8. Davlat Khudonazar also writes that in mountainous areas the Tajiks were isolated from outside cultural influences. See Khudonazar, 'The Conflict in Tajikistan', p. 250.
86   Atkin, 'Religious, National and Other Identities in Central Asia', pp. 59–60.
87   T. S. Saidbaev, *Islam i Obshchestvo* (Moscow: Nauka, 1984), p. 222; A. Islomov, 'Az ki madad juem?' *Tojikiston soveti*, No. 25 (March 1986), p. 3; Ia. R. Vinnikov, 'Natsional'nye I etnograficheskie gruppy Srednei Azii po dannym atnicheskoi statistiki', in *Etnicheskie protsessy u natsional'nykh grupp Srednei Azii i Kazakhstana* (Moscow: Nauka, 1980), p. 36; *Sotsial'no-kul'turnyi oblik sovetskikh natsii* (Moscow: Nauka, 1986), pp. 153, 167. All as cited in Atkin, 'Religious, National and Other Identities in Central Asia', p. 60.
88   Atkin, 'Religious, National and Other Identities in Central Asia', p. 60.
89   Aziz Niyazi, 'Tajikistan I: The Regional Dimension of Conflict', in *Conflicting Loyalties and the State in Post-Soviet Russia and Eurasia*, eds Michael Waller, Bruno Coppieters and Alexei Malashenko (London: Frank Cass, 1998), p. 147. Akiner notes that Kulobis, thanks to their historical independence and regional domination, developed a 'clearly defined identity', as perceived by both themselves and outsiders. See Akiner, *Tajikistan*, p. 8.
90   Bushkov and Mikulskii, *Anatomiia grazhdanskoi voiny v Tadzhikistane*, p. 9; Roy, *The New Central Asia*, p. 96; Rubin, 'Russian Hegemony and State Breakdown in the Periphery', pp. 143–4.

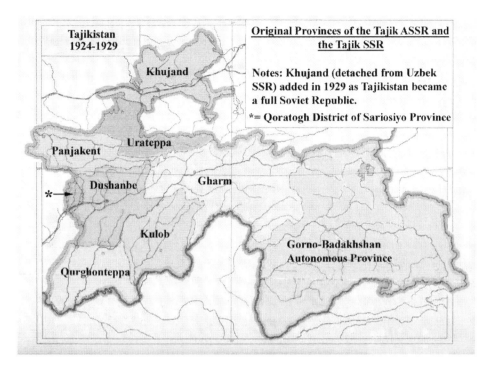

Map 3 Original Provinces of Tajikistan, 1924–29

Source: Map adapted and modified under the Creative Commons Attribution-Share Alike 3.0 Unported licence, <http://commons.wikimedia.org/wiki/File:Provinces_of_Tajikistan_1924-1929.jpg>. 'Qoratogh' (transliterated from Uzbek) is more commonly rendered via Russian as 'Karatag'.

In the following analysis, regions and regionalism are treated as predominantly cultural categories; many issues pertaining to regional sub-ethnic identities in Tajikistan in historical perspective have already been discussed. The crucial point about regionalism in contemporary Tajikistan is that, unlike in America or Europe, it does not denote the interrelationship between the several areas in the *total nation*, and, therefore, has a pronounced divisive meaning. Economic factors and institutional variables (such as regional representation in decision-making bodies) play a subordinate role in shaping self-awareness in a given region compared with the fundamental 'givens' of communal affect; still, they warrant a thorough examination, for they do influence the *intensity* of this self-awareness and the ways it transforms into political action.

The Regions

The administrative demarcation in the Tajik Soviet Socialist Republic was largely implemented along pre-existent boundaries. The constituent regions were incorporated into the All-Union division of labour, but the level of economic integration inside the republic remained low—the potential for productive cooperation between *oblasts* and *raions* of the republic in the late 1980s was 12–18 per cent.[91] The specific Soviet economic policy, however, was only one element in the intricate mosaic of inter-regional interests and contradictions in the republic, which in recent years have acquired the following configuration.

I. Leninobod

Now renamed Sughd, the Leninobod *oblast* (or *viloyat* in Tajik) in the north with its centre in Khujand has always been the most developed and populated part of Tajikistan (Table 4.4). Its economy is based on grain, cotton-growing and modern industry: in 1992, 616 of the republic's 733 factories were located there.[92] In 1994, this region accounted for 62 per cent of the state budget's revenues.[93] The spirit of entrepreneurship has never been extinguished amongst the Khujandis; even at the height of Stalin's rule they continued with private productive activities, mainly on family allotments, and with trade, which allowed for higher living standards than elsewhere in Tajikistan.[94] Consequently, the cooperative movement initiated in the USSR in the late 1980s, and the process of small privatisation that followed, has yielded impressive results. The variety of privatised, semi-privatised and de facto-privatised enterprises operational in Khujand (usually headed by government officials of some kind) in the immediate post-independence period was astounding.[95]

Inside Tajikistan, the Khujandis have a reputation of being pragmatic people obsessed with making a profit and prone to striking dubious deals and gambling.[96] It is also believed that

---

91   O. K. Bobokalonov and L. L. Savello, *Promyshlennye uzly: formirovanie, razvitie, effektivnost'* (Dushanbe: Donish, 1992), p. 34.
92   *Promyshlennost Respubliki Tajikistan za 1993 god* (Dushanbe: GVTs GU Natsionalnoi statistiki, 1994), pp. 14, 29.
93   The authors are indebted to Dr Azizullo Avezov, director of the Khujand Branch of the Institute of World Economy and International Relations of the Tajik Academy of Sciences, for the data related to the economic performance of the regions supplied during a series of interviews in March 1995 in Khujand.
94   N. A. Kisliakov, ed. *Kultura i byt tadzhikskogo kolkhoznogo krestianstva* (Moscow and Leningrad: Izd-vo Akademii Nauk SSSR, 1954), p. 110. Also: *Osnovnye pokazateli ekonomicheskogo i sotsialnogo razvitiia oblastei, gorodov i raionov Tadzhikskoi SSR za gody XII piatiletki* (Dushanbe: Goskomstat TSSR, 1991), pp. 10–13, 18–19, 26–7.
95   For example, the government has a 40 per cent stake in the Khujand-based 'Sham' Joint-Stock Company, which was established in 1988 on the basis of several cotton-processing plants; another 40 per cent belongs to the employees and the remaining 20 per cent to private investors. In 1994, however, all profits of the company were utilised single-handedly by Sham's president, Fattoh Azizov, a close of the then Prime-Minister Jamshed Karimov, and the state's participation in running the enterprise was reduced to supplying raw materials and energy at heavily subsidised prices. (Taped interview with a confidential source in Khujand, 7 March 1995).
96   Their collective nickname, *budanaboz* ('quail fight fan'), testifies to this stereotype. At present, *budik* is heard more often, and carries with it the connotation of someone lacking the characteristics of an honest, straight-talking man with manly habits.

the political ideal of the Leninobodis is a combination of rigid authoritarian central power and freedom of private entrepreneurship and initiative … The freedom of entrepreneurship by no means is associated with freedom *per se*, it is realised through communal mechanisms with their authoritarian character, paternalism and negation of individualism.[97]

The Leninobod/Sughd *oblast* is an organic part of the multi-ethnic Ferghana Valley and, in terms of infrastructure and even ethnic composition, it is closer to Uzbekistan than rump Tajikistan; suffice to mention that Uzbeks make up 43 per cent of the population in the northernmost Asht *raion*.[98] This region was connected with Dushanbe by one narrow mountain road, which was out of operation several months a year; there is no direct railway link, and the only reliable means of transportation for many years was airplane. The sense of isolation from the rest of Tajikistan is so entrenched that Khujandi businessmen flying from their hometown to Dushanbe would routinely say that they were going 'to Tajikistan'.[99] Valley Tajiks who live in the north have been traditionally viewed as half-Turkicised by mountain Tajiks in the south and south-east of the republic. In their turn, some Khujandis go to great lengths to assert their purity and cultural superiority, claiming, for example, that they are direct descendants of the Aryans, Cyrus the Great and Ismoil Somoni, and that only ignorant people would say their capital city is 2500 years old, because in reality it has a 8400-year history.[100]

Table 4.4 Urban and Rural Populations of Tajikistan, 1989

	Tajikistan	Leninobod *oblast*	Kulob *oblast*	Qurghonteppa *oblast*	GBAO^	Gharm group of raions	Hisor *raion**
Population	5 092 603	1 554 145	619 066	1 044 920	160 887	224 615	259 258
Urban	1 655 105 (32.5%)	522 384 (33.7%)	156 130 (25.2%)	182 009 (17.4%)	20 154 (12.5%)	9 510 (4.2%)	65 948 (25.4%)
Rural	3 437 498 (67.5%)	1 031 761 (66.3%)	462 936 (74.8%)	862 911 (82.6%)	140 733 (87.5%)	215 105 (95.8%)	193 310 (74.6%)

^ GBAO = Gorno-Badakhshan Autonomous Oblast

* Including the city of Tursunzoda

Source: *Itogi Vsesoiuznoi perepisi naseleniia 1989 goda po Tadzhikskoi SSR*, Vol. II (Dushanbe: Goskomstat TSSR, 1991), pp. 10–23.

---

97 M. Olimov, 'Ob etnopoliticheskoi i konfessionalnoi situatsii v Tadzhikistane i veroiatnosti mezhetnicheskikh konfliktov', *Vostok*, No. 2 (1994), pp. 80–1.
98 'Leninabod Business and Politics: Touring the Economic Engine of Tajikistan: Beyond Khujand', *The US Embassy Report*, Publication of the Business Information Service for the Newly Independent States (1 May 1996).
99 Personal observations in Khujand, March–April 1995. See also: Rakowska-Harmstone, *Russia and Nationalism in Central Asia*, p. 8.
100 *Tirozi jahon* (5 March 1994).

Between 1946 and 1991, the top leadership of Tajikistan was invariably recruited from Leninobod (Table 4.5). In addition to the position of first secretary of the republican Party Central Committee, people from the north were traditionally in charge of industry and trade, and, generally, dominated the top party organs. Moreover, the *oblast* enjoyed the privilege of trading abroad directly, bypassing Dushanbe. Beginning with Jabbor Rasulov, the CPT Central Committee (CC) first secretary in 1961–82, the Leninobodi ruling elite adopted a truly Machiavellian tactic in preserving their control: representatives of other regions did gain access to positions of authority, however, they were selected 'not as people who cherished [the] interests of their compatriots, but spineless individuals, or, even worse, "marginals" (those who had a Russian or Leninobodi wife, or had been brought up somewhere "far away"), or complete nincompoops, in order to discredit the southern nomenklatura clans in the eyes of Moscow'.[101] Hikmatullo Nasriddinov, a Kulobi who was appointed minister for irrigation in 1980, remembers with a degree of bitterness that one condition of his promotion was he could never employ fellow-townsmen in the ministry:

> Of course, these incantations of Jabbor Rasulov about inadmissibility of nepotism and favouritism were correct. But I saw that Rasulov himself, as well as his high-placed co-regionalists, did not uphold them. Their words were one thing, and their deeds—quite another. They tried in every imaginable way to plant cadres from the North in positions of influence and income in the mountainous regions.[102]

Table 4.5 Regional and Ethnic Composition of the CPT Central Committee

Total membership	Place of origin						
	Leninobod	Khatlon	Hisor	Gharm	GBAO*	Europeans	Unidentified locals
123 (1960)	42 (34.1%)	22 (17.8%)	9 (7.3%)	4 (3.5%)	9 (7.3%)	28 (22.7%)	9 (7.3%)
140 (1981)	48 (34.2%)	24 (17.1%)	7 (5%)	8 (5.7%)	11 (7.9%)	30 (21.4%)	12 (8.6%)

* GBAO = Gorno-Badakhshan Autonomous Oblast

Notes: Khatlon includes Kulob and Qurghonteppa; Gharm includes adjacent mountain districts; 'unidentified locals' are mostly people born in Dushanbe or Tajiks of Samarkand or Bukhara origin and Asians whose affiliation to regions in Tajikistan could not be traced.

Source: Printed materials of the eleventh, twelfth, thirteenth, fourteenth and fifteenth congresses of the CPT and party telephone directories.

It would be wrong to depict the Leninobodi regional clique as a cohesive entity with a clear-cut political agenda. After all, it is an area where traditional ties and

101   Akbar Tursunov, 'Politicheskie improvizatsii vozrozhdaiushegosia natsionalnogo dukha: o destruktsiiakh kulturogennykh', *Bibliotechka 'Charogi ruz'* [Supplement brochure of the *Charoghi ruz* newspaper] (1995), p. 7.
102   Hikmatullo Nasriddinov, *Tarkish* (Dushanbe: Afsona, 1995), pp. 23–4.

allegiances have been most weakened both by communist efforts at modernisation and by the rekindled taste for a market economy. There is an assortment of rival kinship and solidarity networks, which came into existence in the Soviet period and continued to play a pivotal role in contemporary Tajik politics in the immediate post-independence era. The Uroteppa (Istaravshon) 'clan' headed by Salohiddin Hasanov, the Panjakent grouping centred on Isomitdin Salohiddinov, the Qayraqqum-Yaghnob cluster represented by Safarali Kenjaev, and the Osimov-Olimov family agglomeration in Khujand, which had viable ties in the religious establishment throughout Central Asia, were only a few of these groups. All of them competed for greater autonomy and larger allocations for their patrimonies, or for political influence on the republican level, in defiance of the more powerful and well-established structures, such as the Leninobod-Kanibodom group of families (the Arabovs-Karimovs), Abdumalik Abdullojonov's shadowy empire, or ex-premier Samadov's patronage web. In times of peril, however, the feeling of regional loyalty invariably proves stronger than the resentments of more localised ambitions. This was the case when a Leninobodi, Rahmon Nabiev, was removed from the leadership of Tajikistan in 1985 and the Kremlin was looking for a replacement from amongst mountain Tajiks. This situation continued into the early post-independence era—all strongmen in the region united in order to defend the privileged status of their homeland.

II. Kulob

The Kulob region in the south is a predominantly agricultural zone—in 1989, only 16.5 per cent of those employed worked in industry.[103] Cotton was and still is the single most important crop, and foodstuffs have had to be imported from adjacent districts and Uzbekistan. Rural overpopulation and hidden unemployment became perceivable as early as the mid 1960s, and a decision was made in Moscow to create the South Tajik Territorial Manufacturing Complex (STTMC) to tackle this problem. The project envisaged the accelerated industrial development of the region as well as the continuing increase of cotton production in the newly irrigated lands.[104] Its practical implementation was to be supervised by the republican authorities—that is, people from the north. Naturally, there has emerged an understanding between elite groups from Khujand and Kulob, which reached symbolic heights in 1990 when the two cities became twins.

---

103 *Itogi Vsesoiuznoi perepisi naseleniia 1989 goda po Tadzhikskoi SSR*, Vol. II, p. 348.
104 The Tenth Five-Year Plan (1976–80) stipulated that 65 per cent of growth in industrial and agricultural output in Tajikistan was to be achieved through developing the STTMC. See: 'Iuzhno-Tadzhikskii kompleks—iz piatiletki deviatoi—v desiatuiu', *Druzhba narodov*, No. 2 (1976), p. 188.

Kulob featured prominently in the medieval history of Central Asia. Its lancers were famous for their bravery and recklessness. The Kulobis are stereotyped as hardworking people, short-tempered and not particularly bright.[105] Before the creation of the Tajik Soviet Socialist Republic, the Kulobis made up 60 per cent of the population of Eastern Bukhara,[106] and, as has been mentioned, were viewed as real 'mountain' Tajiks, in opposition to the Turkicised 'valley' Tajiks in the north. In the 1980s, the feeling of past greatness was still alive. A certain Berdyeva, a Supreme Soviet deputy from Kulob, once stirred a sensation when she said in public: 'I wonder why everyone thinks that a Kulobi woman cannot give birth to a leader.'[107] Since independence, a concerted program has been initiated by local intellectuals to revise the annals of history and portray Kulob as the cradle of Zoroastrian civilisation, blessed with a great urban culture that reached its zenith 2700 years ago.[108]

Patriarchy and kinship bonds are much stronger in Kulob than in the Leninobod region. Although prior to 1992 local solidarity groups had never played an important role in the republic's politics, their positions inside the *oblast* were extremely strong. It was especially evident at the level of separate collective farms—the backbone of Kulob's economy. The *kolkhoz* chairman—respectfully referred to by peasants as *rais* or *bobo*—usually combined the features of an 'oriental despot'[109] and the head of a big patriarchal family. Mirsaid Mahmadaliev, twice Hero of Socialist Labour, headed the Lenin *kolkhoz* for more than three decades. By the mid 1970s, his *kolkhoz* had evolved into an impressive enterprise, with 350 tractors, 57 combine harvesters, 35 cotton-growing brigades, six dairy farms, 13 retail shops, seven schools and an assortment of other facilities, which made it entirely self-sufficient and profitable at the same time.[110] *Bobo* Mirsaid managed the *kolkhoz* as his own fiefdom without any interference from outside, for he had taken the precaution of becoming a deputy of the Supreme Soviet of the USSR and had served as a CPT CC member for quite some time. He was also in the habit of inviting influential guests from Moscow and entertaining them in a princely way. Mirsaidov patronised a few young aspiring graduates from

---

105   The stereotype of the unsophisticated rural hick manifests itself in 'Kulobi jokes' whereby a Kulobi is usually the butt of a joke in which he fails to comprehend some modern technology or practice that is common in the city (Personal observations in Tajikistan and amongst Tajiks overseas, 2007–12). Their nickname, *govsvor* ('cow-rider'), also speaks for itself, though some Kulobi locals prefer to interpret it as 'a person who can mount a wild bull'.

106   Karmysheva, *Ocherki etnicheskoi istorii iuznykh raionov Tadzhikistana i Uzbekistana*, p. 45.

107   Interview with Iskandar Asadulloev, former official of the Communist Party of Tajikistan, Dushanbe, 25 March 1995.

108   Muzaffar Azizi, 'Chun sabza umedi bardamidan budi', *Daryo*, No. 2 (1994), p. 14. See also: Gholib Ghoibov, *Ta'rikhi Khatlon as Oghoz to Imruz* (Dushanbe: Donish, 2006).

109   'Oriental despotism' is used here in the classical and Marxist sense of the term, not in any popular sense, to describe leadership.

110   *Kommunist Tadzhikistana*, 7 January 1975.

Kulob; one of them, Qurbon Mirzoaliev, eventually became chairman of the executive committee of the Kulob *oblast* and continued to feature prominently in the Tajik political arena.

III. Hisor

The Hisor Valley, which includes Tajikistan's capital, Dushanbe, is another industrialised zone. The aluminium plant at Tursunzoda near the Uzbek border is one of the largest in Asia and, immediately after independence, generated 50 per cent of Tajikistan's hard-currency earnings.[111] By the early 1990s, an unofficial alliance had emerged between the industrial and financial captains of Leninobod and Hisor; the latter had been allowed to occupy high positions in the state bureaucracy as a sign of recognition of Hisor's industrial and agricultural potential (Table 4.6). The geographical proximity of the two regions as well as close cultural ties complemented the political rapprochement.

Table 4.6 Indices of Regional Economic Development, 1990

Economic zone	Capital investment	Industrial output	Agricultural production
Leninobod	17.2%	36.4%	24.8%
Hisor	45.0%	42.9%	16.7%
Qurghonteppa	10.0%	15.4%	39.5%
Kulob	7.3%	4.9%	13.7%
Gharm	19.1%* (< 2%)	-	3.3%
GBAO^	1.4%	0.4%	2.0%
Tajikistan	100%	100%	100%

* Mostly investment in the construction of the Roghun hydro–electric power station

^ GBAO = Gorno-Badakhshan Autonomous Oblast

Source: M. Nurnazarov and M. Rahimov, *Khojagii khalqi Tojikiston* (Dushanbe: Vazorati maorifi Jumhurii Tojikiston, 1994), pp. 148–65.

Hisor was a major princedom from the fifteenth to the nineteenth centuries. It was subjugated by the Emirate of Bukhara only in 1868, in the wake of the 15-day battle of Dehnav. Local activists have always believed it is unfair that Hisor should be just one of the *raions* under Dushanbe's direct jurisdiction; they have demanded its elevation to *oblast* status and mooted the idea of a 'reacquisition' of territories in Qurghonteppa, Qubodiyon, Boisun, Sherobod and even Darvoz and Qarotegin, for 'they belonged to the realm of the *bek* of Hisor, or sent him annual metayage and were accountable to him'.[112] But its relatively small

---

111   *EIU Country Report* (4th Quarter 1993), p. 54.
112   Marhabo Zabarova and Zafar Dustov, 'Tajlili Navruz dar Hisori Shodmon', in *Dar justujui farhangi vodii Hisor*, ed. N. N. Ne'matov (Dushanbe: Mamnu'gohi ta'rikhi-madanii Hisor, 1992), p. 65.

population and its sheer heterogeneity (45 per cent of the population is Uzbek)[113] effectively precluded a dramatic rise in Hisor's influence in the republic until the civil war.

The region's location at a trade crossroads of Central Asia, the presence of hard-currency-earning industries in its territory, the relatively high degree of mobility of the population and the folklore tradition of Hisori *polvons*—the outlawed fighters against the Manghit authorities—were instrumental in the emergence of organised crime groupings as a potent unofficial institution in the region by the early 1990s. At that time the four main gangs specialised mostly in extortion, smuggling and car theft.[114] They also maintained close contacts with colleagues in Uzbekistan and enjoyed protection in high places in Tashkent.[115]

IV. Gharm

The mountainous region of Gharm, east of Dushanbe, is the granary of Tajikistan, due to its mild climate and abundance of water. In addition to the Gharm *raion* proper, it includes the districts of Komsomolobod (historical Qarotegin), Tavildara, Fayzobod and Jerghatol (the Qarotegin Valley has since been renamed Rasht). The Gharmis, 95 per cent of whom in this region live in villages, have traditionally been engaged in growing fruit and vegetables rather than cotton. An average Gharmi farmer would gain up to 80 times more profit from one acre of citrus trees than his Kulobi colleague growing cotton, spending much less effort.[116] Gradually, the Gharmis accumulated substantial capital through trading agricultural produce on local markets and began to penetrate the republican trade structures, both legal and shadowy, that had been previously dominated by the Leninobodis and Uzbeks. Yet their growing wealth and sprawling commercial activities failed to bring about any rise in the political status of the region. On the contrary, it was downgraded from *oblast* status to just 'a group of *raions*' in 1955. In the late 1970s, the regional elite's aspirations were rekindled—this time it was connected with the name of Mirzo Rahmatov, the USSR's ambassador in Ghana and a personal friend of Brezhnev. Brezhnev's untimely death in 1982, however, put an end to these hopes.

The principalities of Gharm, Qarotegin and Darvoz were always hard to conquer and administer. They were the last to fall into the fold of Bukhara with the help of Russian armed forces during 1869 and 1870. These areas formed a stronghold

---

113   Barnett R. Rubin, 'Tajikistan: From Soviet Republic to Russian-Uzbek Protectorate', in *Central Asia and the World*, ed. Michael Mandelbaum (New York: Council on Foreign Relations, 1994), p. 211.

114   *Narodnaia gazeta*, 18 February 1993.

115   For a more detailed account, see: Kirill Nourzhanov, 'Alternative Social Institutions and the Politics of Neo-Patrimonialism in Tajikistan', *Russian and Euro-Asian Economics Bulletin*, Vol. 5, No. 8 (August 1996), pp. 4–6.

116   A. V. Vorobiova, 'Vinovat li rost naseleniia?' *Vostok*, No. 5 (1991), p. 157.

of the *basmachi* movement until the late 1930s. The highlanders of Gharm cling staunchly to their traditional institutions, such as the non-divided agnate family, *adat* and *shari'a*. They often called themselves *oqab* (eagle) or *Tojiki toza* (pure Tajik), and are noted for their religious piety and traditional values. In 1974, a certain *sovkhoz* in Gharm had no less than 30 *mazors* (shrines), and in 1977 there was only one girl from Komsomolobod who studied in a tertiary institution.[117]

The Gharmis arguably suffered more than other Tajiks from Soviet demographic exercises. Tens of thousands of people from this region were resettled to the Vakhsh Valley in the south-west between 1928 and 1931 in order to develop new cotton plantations. The whole project was based on forced labour and scores perished from the drastic change of climate, a 'lack of the most elementary facilities ... and an epidemic of typhoid'.[118] In 1934, the CPT CC passed a special resolution that aimed 'to carry out, in the shortest possible time, the special investigation amongst the settlers in the Vakhsh Valley, with the aim of getting rid of them'.[119] As a result of this purge, many Gharmi peasants ended up in the Gulag. After World War II the authorities continued to press the Gharmis to migrate from their homeland—which registered the highest birth rate in the republic (over the period 1979–89 the population in the region grew by 36 per cent, compared with the republic's figure of 26 per cent).[120] In the mid 1970s, the construction of a gigantic hydro-power station began at Roghun, which would have required the evacuation of 62 villages and could have led to massive social and ecological changes in the Gharm region.[121] Approximately 30 000 Gharmis were scheduled to be removed from the flooded area and resettled in Kulob and in the Vakhsh Valley.[122] Not surprisingly, the population of Gharm felt aggrieved by the government's plans. The sentiments of internal protest and subdued opposition were widely spread amongst Gharmi settlers (*muhajirs*) throughout the republic as well. The then Dushanbe-based poet Gulrukhsor Safieva was especially active in voicing the grievances of fellow Gharmis.[123]

V. Badakhshan

The Gorno-Badakhshan Autonomous Oblast (GBAO) in the Pamirs occupies almost half of Tajikistan's territory but accounts for only 2.5 per cent of the country's population. It is the least-developed part of the country, totally

---

117   Iuri Smirnov, 'Strannyi islam', *Pamir*, No. 2 (1988), pp. 118, 122.
118   Rakowska-Harmstone, *Russia and Nationalism in Central Asia*, pp. 118–19.
119   Sh. I. Kurbanova, *Pereselenie: kak eto bylo* (Dushanbe: Irfon, 1993), p. 72.
120   *Itogi Vsesoiuznoi perepisi naseleniia 1989 goda po Tadzhikskoi SSR*, Vol. II, p. 30.
121   *Sogdiana*, No. 1 (February 1990), pp. 1–2.
122   *Adabiyot va san'at*, 17 August 1989.
123   The Cultural Foundation for the Spiritual Wealth of the Tajik Nation, which she came to head in 1990, saw that its important duty was to expose 'the Communist terror which devoured the best sons and the spiritual treasures of the Tajik nation'. See: Shams, 'Nist bod Gulrukhsor!' *Haft ganj*, No. 19 (31) (1992), p. 7.

dependent on external supplies delivered via two seasonal roads. Badakhshan is characterised by appalling unemployment rates and the lowest standard of living. Amazingly, such basic foods as potato and cabbage were only introduced to the Pamirs in 1938, and 10 years later people still wore homespun clothes.[124] On the other hand, the ratio of people with a college education amongst the Pamiris was the highest in Tajikistan at the end of the Soviet era: 124 per 1000 employed, compared with 100 in Leninobod and 66 in Qurghonteppa.[125] In the postwar period these graduates could not find jobs according to their specialisation in their place of birth and moved to major urban centres of the republic. Progressively, the Pamiris formed a sizeable stratum of Tajikistan's 'prestige elite'—that is, writers, artists, scholars, and so on.[126] By 1991, 180 000 Pamiris lived and worked outside the GBAO—more than that *oblast's* actual population.[127]

The Pamiris have always differed from other Tajiks in important cultural characteristics, such as language, religion and stronger familial affiliation. Their languages and dialects belong to the Eastern Iranian language group as opposed to the Western Iranian Tajik. The majority of Pamiris adhere to the Ismaili sect of Shiism whilst the bulk of valley and mountain Tajiks are Sunnis. All eight Pamiri sub-ethnic groups retain potent self-consciousness and can identify themselves on at least three levels: by their primary cultural name—for example, *rykhen*, *zgamik*, *khik* and so on—when dealing with one another; by their collective name, *pomiri* (Pamiri), when interacting with other groups in Tajikistan; and, finally, as Tajiks when outside the republic. In the 1980s, the official line of the Tajik leadership denied the Pamiris their cultural uniqueness: 'the Pamiris are Tajiks by descent and their languages are nothing more than dialects of Tajik.'[128]

The ancient consanguinal commune with its patrilineal and patrilocal characteristics—natural economy, cult of ancestors, even blood feuds—has survived in the Pamirs. There used to be a joke in Tajikistan to the effect that if communism were ever to be built in the USSR, it would happen in Badakhshan as commodity-market relations were virtually unknown there. Trade was a rather disfavoured occupation there, and when in the 1970s a market was finally opened in Khorog, there was not a single local amongst the vendors.[129] Family solidarity amongst Pamiris, and the stereotype it spawned, is exceptional

---

124 L. F. Monogarova, 'Iazgulemtsy Zapadnogo Pamira', *Sovetskaia etnografiia*, No. 3 (1949), pp. 93, 99.

125 *Itogi Vsesoiuznoi perepisi naseleniia 1989 goda po Tadzhikskoi SSR*, Vol. II, pp. 480, 492, 496, 500.

126 In 1990, 20 poets of Pamiri extraction were members of the prestigious Writers' Union of Tajikistan. Over 30 years, the GBAO produced in excess of 300 scholars with the qualification of doctor or candidate of sciences—more than all other regions of Tajikistan put together. See: Dodkhudo Karamshoev, 'Polemika o Pamire', *Pamir*, No. 6 (1991), p. 111.

127 R. K. Mirzoev, ed. *Problemy razvitiia i razmesheniia proizvoditelnykh sil Tadzhikistana* (Dushanbe: SOPS AN TSSR, 1988), p. 213.

128 *Kommunist Tadzhikistana*, 24 June 1988.

129 Aleksei Ganelin, 'Na kryshe mira', *Ogonek*, No. 40 (1989), p. 8.

even in the context of Tajikistan; for them, there is nothing inherently bad in nepotism. As an example, there was a case in 1975 when a certain Mahmadakov had managed to plant all 16 of his children in various scientific institutions throughout the republic.[130]

Although the republican authorities paid lip-service to the necessity of the accelerated development of the GBAO, in reality nothing was being done and the region, with 0.03 per cent of Tajikistan's total material production, was constantly on the brink of survival.[131] Since the early 1970s, the Pamiri elite strove to upgrade the region to the status of an autonomous republic in an attempt to change the situation, but to no avail. Even worse, by 1980 all leading positions in the region had been occupied by people from the north—a situation that made an important visitor from Moscow exclaim: 'What is this invasion of Leninobodis during the Tenth five-year plan all about?'[132]

VI. Qurghonteppa

The Qurghonteppa region in the south-west, which includes the Vakhsh Valley, is the melting pot of Tajikistan. Only sparsely populated before 1917, it became, under Soviet rule, subject to an enormous influx of Tajiks from Gharm and Kulob as well as Uzbeks, Russians, Germans and representatives of other nationalities, who mixed with local Tajiks, Turkmens, Arabs and Baluchi. Between 1926 and 1929 alone, 160 000 new settlers arrived there.[133] All of them participated in 'great construction projects of communism', such as the Vakhsh Irrigation Complex. In 1990, more than one-fifth of the republic's population lived in the Qurghonteppa *oblast*; its share in Tajikistan's industrial output exceeded 15 per cent and 39 per cent in cotton production.[134]

Qurghonteppa in the early 1990s was where 'the complex of national inferiority was the strongest and most transparent. It was exacerbated by the emergence of a dual economy, whereby "giants" of industry were not oriented towards local labour resources and traditions, had no links with [the] local industrial complex and formed enclaves of alien "big industry".'[135] In rural areas, *kolkhoz* bossism similar to that in Kulob flourished,[136] with the difference that local collective farms were even richer, particularly in the Kolkhozobod *raion*, renowned for

---

130   *Kommunist Tadzhikistana*, 10 October 1975.

131   Gavhar Juraeva, 'Tragic Visions in Tajikistan', *Pacific Research*, Vol. 7, No. 2 (May 1994), p. 15.

132   Bronislav Kholopov, 'Pamir vstupaet v dialog', *Druzhba narodov*, No. 1 (1981), p. 187.

133   Sharipov, *Zakonomernosti formirovaniia sotsialisticheskikh obshestvennykh otnoshenii v Tadzhikistane*, p. 80.

134   Nurnazarov and Rahimov, *Khojagii khalqi Tojikiston*, pp. 148–65.

135   Olimov, 'Ob etnopoliticheskoi i konfessionalnoi situatsii v Tadzhikistane', p. 85.

136   The Hero of Socialist Labour Ishbek Sattarov, an ethnic Uzbek, came to the Vakhsh Valley in 1929 and later rose to head the 'Yangiabad' *kolkhoz*—a position he held for 33 years. See: *Kommunist Tadzhikistana*, 24 July 1975. His name has been immortalised in a series of literary works and a village has been named after him.

its long-staple cotton. The struggle for dominance in Qurghonteppa involved Kulobis, Gharmis and Uzbeks (the last made up almost one-third of the population).[137] In the 1980s, power in Qurghonteppa was divided between an *obkom* first secretary from Kulob, the chairman of the executive committee from Gharm and the head of the local cooperative society (*Tojikmatlubot*)—an ethnic Uzbek. Needless to say, newly established settlements in the Vakhsh Valley were organised on ethnic and regionalistic lines, and, for example, 'if there happened to be a wedding in an Urghut *kolkhoz*, their Gharmi neighbours were not likely to be invited'.[138]

Regionalism in Practice

The statements of Soviet authorities to the effect that 'the spread of literacy, general rise of culture caused by industrialisation and reconstruction of agriculture have made the groups of Tajiks closer to each other'[139] are not particularly convincing. Certainly, it would have required the concerted efforts of several generations to achieve any positive shifts at the popular cultural level. An immensely thorough study of Tajik folktales completed in 1971 linked most of their moralities and plot lines to Iranian, Sanskrit, Arabic and even Chinese influences, which was not surprising; however, experts noted the unusually high level of localised variation in motifs, functions and language forms of the 419 analysed texts coming from different regions of Tajikistan.[140] Shodmon Yusuf, an eminent Tajik political opposition figure, commented on one occasion that 'the so-called Tajik people do not have a single song that would satisfy all regions [of Tajikistan]'.[141]

Tensions among six historical-geographical regions of Tajikistan failed to diminish as the grotesquely uneven development patterns lingered. They could be checked temporarily either by coercive methods (such as campaigns against *mestnichestvo*, or localism, under Stalin and Khrushchev) or by channelling more resources from the centre (as was the case under Brezhnev), but they were always present. Interaction amongst regional elites has formed the core of all symbolic processes and practical endeavours in Tajikistan. During the Brezhnev era, the Tajik party-state structure demonstrated an almost infinite capacity to control regional ambitions in the republic. Moscow's *stabilnost kadrov* (stability of cadres) policy allowed the web of informal 'understandings' and exchanges

---

137 Rubin, 'Tajikistan', p. 211.

138 Taped interview with A. Abdurazikov, school inspector of Kolkhozabad *raion*, 27 March 1995.

139 I. S. Gurvich, 'Obshee i osobennoe v etnicheskikh protsessakh u razlichnykh narodov SSSR', in *Sovremennye etnicheskie protsessy v SSSR*, ed. Iu. V. Bromlei (Moscow: Nauka, 1977), p. 518.

140 *Kulliyoti folklori Tojik*, Vol. I (Moscow: Nauka, 1981), p. 63.

141 Quoted in: I. Rotar, 'Sredniaia Aziia: etnosotsialnaia perspektiva', in *Islam v Rossii i Srednei Azii*, eds Igor Ermakov and Dmitrii Mikulskii (Moscow: Lotus Foundation, 1993), p. 208.

amongst the regional elites in Tajikistan to become institutionalised. In the 1980s, it was the order of the day for the authorities to issue quotas for regional representation in the republican legislature, industrial management and law enforcement agencies, or to decree how many doctorate degrees should be given to each region.[142] These practices found reflection at the popular level in a common saying that 'in our republic nobody sits idle: Leninobod rules, Kulob guards, Qurghonteppa ploughs and Pamir dances'. As long as Tajikistan fulfilled its economic obligations to the Union and complied with the general line prescribed by the Communist Party of the Soviet Union (CPSU), Moscow did not seem to object to the peculiarities of local personnel policy.

In the Soviet period bargaining for resources on behalf of the regions was an essential part of political activism in Tajikistan. It was also an arcane process, hidden from public view. In September 1961, during the CPT congress, Saidali Jumaev, first secretary of the Gharm *raikom*, must have stirred quite a commotion when he criticised the republican leadership for its lack of interest in the development of his region.[143] After the congress Jumaev was sacked. Twenty-five years later, people in Tojikobod staged a protest against neglect of their needs on the part of Dushanbe; 60 or 70 of their delegates came to the capital and marched to the building of the CPT Central Committee. The next day all editors of republican, regional and district newspapers received an order to refrain from mentioning Tojikobod forthwith, in any context, in order 'to expunge this word from people's memory altogether'.[144]

Competition and overt animosity amongst people from different regions can have various manifestations. The most obvious of them is the wedding taboo[145]—for example, representatives of the Tajik sub-ethnic group of *suguti*, who live in Varzob to the north of Dushanbe and are anthropologically close to the Hisoris, would never marry Kulobis, though technically both of them are mountain Tajiks.[146] The division between mountain and valley, or between northern and southern Tajiks, where the Hisor mountain range serves as a geographical marker, certainly remains intact. As a well-known Tajik poet, Saidali Mamur, has put it:

---

142   Narzikulov, 'Dvulikii Ianus v serdtse Azii', p. 128. See also: Rafis Abazov, 'Central Asia's Conflicting Legacy and Ethnic Policies: Revisiting a Crisis Zone of the Former USSR', *Nationalism & Ethnic Politics*, Vol. 5, No. 2 (1999), pp. 67–9.

143   *XIV s'ezd Kommunisticheskoi partii Tadzhikistana: Stenograficheskii otchet* (Dushanbe: Tadzhikskoe gosudarstvennoe izdatelstvo, 1962), pp. 260–1.

144   Narzullo Dustov, *Zakhm bar jismi vatan* (Dushanbe: Irfon, 1994), p. 28.

145   The most comprehensive study of the social, political and economic aspects of marriage alliances (including an analysis of ethnic, regional and local restrictions in coupling) is by a British anthropologist. See: Tett, *Ambiguous Alliances*.

146   R. L. Nemenova, 'Slozhenie tadzhikskogo naseleniia Varzoba', *Sovetskaia etnografiia*, No. 5 (1969), p. 37.

> 'Where do you come from?' is the first thing you ask,
> Then you check all my ancestry—that's a difficult task.
> North or South—should it really matter that much?
> Put this discord away, and in peace shall we bask.
>
> Why don't you ask what I keep in my hand?
> Your only query is about my homeland.
> Alas, you have never offered me help,
> There's stone in your heart, all good feelings are banned.[147]

It is the division amongst six main regions, however, that presented the major cleavage in Tajik society, especially in the immediate post-independence era. Indeed, anthropologically, the Kulobis and the inhabitants of Gharm and the Western Pamirs are very similar, but there is little love lost between them. With this in mind, it is hard to disagree with a Tajik journalist's opinion that

> the most tragic absurdity in the history of Tajikistan is a hostility that lasted for many years between the people of the Pamirs and the people of Kulob. No one was able to explain clearly the reason for this confrontation which in the past had been confined to hooligan tricks, and from the beginning of the political struggle it has led to the heavy and bloody conflict.[148]

As a hypothesis, it can be argued that contemporary political struggles are reinforced by the historical memory of the populace: Kulobis formed a part of the Afghan army when it ravaged the Pamiri principalities in the late nineteenth century. The narrative of the Afghan army's massive atrocities (and the role played by the Kulobis) has been passed on from generation to generation.[149]

Stereotypes and prejudices of a similar kind are widely spread throughout Tajikistan. In the words of academician Tursunov: 'regionalism has firmly settled in the consciousness of our people, and not its backward section at that; the regionalistic self-awareness manifests itself at all levels of social stratification, especially, to our shame, amidst the intelligentsia.'[150] Within the rigid framework of the Soviet system it could never acquire the form of violent political action. Moreover, it had been de facto institutionalised and, henceforth, could be controlled and manipulated to a certain extent. The ruling regional elite from Leninobod did not need to invoke traditional institutions of power

---

147   Translation from the Tajik text quoted in: Buri Karimov, *Qurboni du Zakhma* (Dushanbe: Oryono, 1992), p. 129.
148   Anvar Shakhov, 'Why Tadzhiks Kill Tadzhiks? Regional and Ethnic Background of the Conflict', *Russia and the Moslem World*, No. 10 (1994), p. 37.
149   Some elders in Badakhshan may still believe that 'Afghans [and Kulobis with them] are from the confounded kin of Satan. Their place is in hell, in the eternal flames and inferno.' See: M. S. Andreev, *Tadzhiki doliny Khuf* (Stalinabad: Izdatelstvo AN TSSR, 1953), p. 23.
150   Tursunov, 'Politicheskie improvizatsii vozrozhdaiushegosia natsionalnogo dukha', p. 8.

to maintain its privileged position; its legitimacy was guaranteed by Moscow. Generally, in the Soviet period traditional social structures and popular Islam on the one hand, and regionalism on the other, operated on different planes: private and public. These phenomena were closely linked, however, and there always remained a possibility that informal networks would be activated as the primary mechanism for establishing the authority of a clique with roots in a particular region.

* * *

The Soviet drive towards modernisation of Tajikistan yielded ambiguous results. Accelerated economic development, growth of education, secularisation of culture and political mobilisation of the masses altered the fabric of Tajik society considerably. The profundity and irreversibility of these changes, however, were questionable. After all, 70 years of the communist experiment and millennia of continuous cultural tradition in this country are incomparable in historical perspective. Modernity presumes that

> local ties and parochial perspectives give way to universal commitments and cosmopolitan attitudes; that the truths of utility, calculation, and science take precedence over those of the emotions, the sacred, and the non-rational; that the individual rather than the group be the primary unit of society and politics ... that the identity be chosen and achieved, not ascribed and affirmed.[151]

The most important failure of Soviet rule in Tajikistan was that it could not reform the world view of the Tajiks, based on traditional allegiances and the omnipresent spirit of collectivism, which made an individual completely dependent on institutions such as the family, neighbourhood, solidarity network and, at a higher level, on a coterie of fellow-regionalists. A prominent Soviet anthropologist, Lyudmila Chvyr', produced a scathing verdict on the state of affairs in the republic at the end of the communist period: 'Inhabitants of each of these regions considered only themselves to be the real, "pure", "genuine" representatives of their people, regarding others as Tajiks of sorts, surely, but not quite conforming to the ideal of "Tajikness".'[152]

In a handful of cities, in industrial enterprises, scholarly institutions and government agencies, activities were ostensibly no different from patterns of mono-organisational socialism elsewhere in the USSR. At the same time,

---

151 Cyril E. Black, ed. *The Modernisation of Inner Asia* (Armonk, NY: M. E. Sharpe, 1991), p. 18.
152 L. A. Chvyr', 'O strukture tadzhikskogo etnosa (nauchnaia i narodnaia tochka zreniia)', in *Rasy i narody. Sovremennye etnicheskie i rasovye problem*, ed. G. P. Vasilieva (Moscow: Nauka, 2001), p. 12.

in rural areas that were of little interest to Moscow-based industrialisers and where 'even the People's Commissariat of Internal Affairs (NKVD) proved to be incapable of setting up a network of informers',[153] an ethno-cultural mentality based on traditional patrimonialism, popular Islam and regionalism had survived unscathed, and any breakdown in the mechanisms of social control would inexorably transpose it into the realm of political action.

---

153 A. V. Malashenko, 'The Eighties: A New Political Start for Islam', *Russian Politics and Law*, Vol. 31, No. 4 (1993), p. 25.

5. Formal and Informal Political Institutions in Soviet Tajikistan

The state has traditionally been an important venue of political analysis in any society. True, 'the state ... merely provides one framework for political interaction ... To proceed from here to the subordination of all other units to the state level is not only uncalled for, but probably misses the point as well'.[1] Still, it is imperative to understand the functioning of government mechanisms in order to investigate their dynamic relationship with other social actors. It has been argued that 'the emergence of a strong, capable state can occur only with a tremendous concentration of social control. And such a redistribution of social control cannot occur without exogenous factors first creating catastrophic conditions that rapidly and deeply undermine existing ... bases of social control.'[2] This chapter investigates the instalment of Soviet political order in Tajikistan and its subsequent evolution. The role of coercive methods in administration, the centre–periphery relationship and especially the terms of contract between 'rule-applying bureaucracies' in Moscow and 'task-achieving bureaucracies' in the republic[3] will be major points of discussion.

Restructuring of Political Authority

In 1959 Nazarsho Dodkhudoyev, the chairman of the Council of Ministers of the Tajik SSR, claimed, in a book intended for external audiences:

> The Tajik people decide all their internal affairs themselves. Our government directs the entire economic and cultural development of the country. The Council of Ministers of the U.S.S.R. cannot annul decisions or revoke orders of the Tajik government. Finally, the sovereignty of our Republic is guaranteed by the right to secede from the Federation, granted to us by the Constitution of the U.S.S.R.[4]

Obviously, the reality was somewhat different. After all major spots of armed resistance in the territory of Tajikistan were quashed by the early 1930s, the

---

1 Naomi Chazan, *An Anatomy of Ghanaian Politics: Managing Political Recession, 1969–1982* (Boulder, Colo.: Westview Press, 1983), p. 7.
2 Joel S. Migdal, *Strong Societies and Weak States: State–Society Relations and State Capabilities in the Third World* (Princeton, NJ: Princeton University Press, 1988), p. 262.
3 Terminology used by Harry Rigby. See: T. H. Rigby, 'Introduction: Political Legitimacy, Weber and Communist Mono-Organisational Systems', in *Political Legitimation in Communist States*, eds T. H. Rigby and Ferenc Feher (London: Macmillan, 1982), p. 11.
4 Nazarsho Dodkhudoyev, *Tajikistan: Land of Sunshine* (London: Soviet Booklets, 1959), p. 7.

Soviet authorities continued to erect, at an accelerated pace, a new social order there that reflected the pattern implemented elsewhere in the USSR. It was based on

- a single universalistic ideology, which proclaimed the building of communism as the supreme goal of the country's development
- a single economic system, heavily centralised and planned
- the principles of 'Soviet federalism', whereby the borderlands were gradually deprived of their autonomy in favour of Moscow, behind the ostensibly federal structure of the state.

The year 1928 was a turning point in the history of the Soviet Union. Stalin's 'Revolution from Above' meant that the All-Union Communist Party (Bolsheviks) (VKP[b]), or, more precisely, its administrative apparatus, had evolved as the sole centre of power in Soviet society. The period of relative political and economic liberalism of the early 1920s was over. The party now sanctioned and supervised the activities of all other social institutions.[5] Tajikistan presented no exception to the emerging Soviet mono-organisational order. At the time of the creation of the Tajik Soviet Socialist Republic in October 1929, the Communist Party of Tajikistan (CPT) was a formidable and well-organised force, with its 146 primary cells and 3848 members (up from 17 cells and 435 members five years before).[6]

Moscow, however, had its doubts in regards to the loyalty of local cadres, many of whom were National Communists—carryovers from the *jadid* movement, such as Abduqodir Muhiddinov, head of the Tajik Government between 1926 and 1928. Until 1934, the effective management of Tajikistan remained in the hands of the Central Asian Bureau of the VKP(b) Central Committee and its proxies, such as the Central Asian Economic Council, the Central Asian Planning Committee, or plenipotentiary representatives of the All-Union Commissariats.[7] Statements of Soviet historians to the effect that 'this measure in no sense limited the sovereignty of the republics of Central Asia and did not infringe upon the rights of autonomous republics and regions'[8] are hardly credible, if

---

5   As one contemporary Russian scholar observed, '[c]ommunism in its "purest", utmost form implies the liquidation of the state. However, this very liquidation is viewed as the process of the absorption of all functions of the state ... by the VKP [All-Union Communist Party], which would incorporate everything that is not yet the VKP ... The Party's monopoly in the state has been complicated by the state's monopoly in all major spheres of social, economic and cultural life of the country. The state has substituted the people, and the Party has replaced the state. The Party's monopolism has been squared.' See: St. Ivanovich, *VKP: Desiat Let Kommunisticheskoi Monopolii* (Paris: Biblioteka Demokraticheskogo Sotsializma, 1928), pp. 5, 27.

6   *Kommunisticheskaia partiia Tadzhikistana v tsifrakh za 60 let* (Dushanbe: Irfon, 1984), pp. 3, 22.

7   For a number of years, Ivan Fedko, the commander of the XIII Rifle Corps stationed in the republic, carried out the duties of Tajikistan's People's Commissar of Agriculture.

8   *K sotsializmu, minuia kapitalizm: Istoricheskii opyt KPSS po sotsialisticheskomu stroitelstvu v Srednei Azii i Kazakhstane v 1917–1937gg.* (Moscow: Politizdat, 1974), p. 128.

only for economic considerations: in 1931, 80 per cent of capital investments in Tajikistan were planned and implemented by the centre, bypassing local authorities.[9]

Stalin's strategy of creating government structures in Tajikistan that would be unquestionably faithful to him and to the Central Committee's Secretariat did not differ from the design applied elsewhere in the USSR and envisaged three measures: a) elimination of old cadres; b) large-scale posting of reliable officials from the centre; and c) quick promotion of suitably indoctrinated locals. The Central Asian Bureau of the VKP(b) Central Committee passed a resolution 'About the Work of the Tajik Party Organisation' in 1931, which stressed in particular that 'alongside … the purification of Soviet, economic, cooperative and other apparatuses from class-antagonistic and bureaucratic elements, it is necessary to carry out mass promotion of cadres from amidst workers, *kolkhoz* members … tested during struggle against the *bai*'.[10] Purges of party members and other elites in Tajikistan commenced in 1933 with the removal of the first secretary of the CPT Central Committee, M. Huseinov; the chairman of the Central Executive Committee, N. Makhsum; and the chairman of the Council of People's Commissariat, A. Hojibaev. Their arrests were made with the standard accusations of being 'bourgeois nationalists', 'enemy agents', 'counter-revolutionary elements' and 'saboteurs'.[11] In May 1934, a group of 79 high-ranking officials including A. Muhiddinov, then the chairman of the State Planning Committee of Tajikistan, was executed. It was reported that Muhiddinov had objected to the renaming of Dushanbe as Stalinobod.[12] In the months that followed, dozens of Tajik intellectuals, amongst them renowned poets Ikromi, Hakim Karim, Ghani Abdullo, Zehni, Fitrat, Alikhush, Hamdi and Munzim, were imprisoned, exiled or put to death. Even Sadriddin Aini, the founding father of contemporary Tajik literature, invariably loyal to the Soviet regime, was labelled 'pan-Turkist', 'pan-Islamist', a 'Bukharan adventurist' and a 'homeless Baha'i', and only the intercession of Russian colleagues saved him from arrest in 1937.[13]

The number of victims of Stalin's reprisals is still to be revealed;[14] however, the fact that 7883 people sentenced in Tajikistan from the 1930s to the 1950s

---

9   *Ocherki istorii narodnogo khoziaistva Tadzhikistana*, p. 193.

10   M. Shukurov, *Istoriia kulturnoi zhizni sovetskogo Tadzhikistana (1917–1941)*, Part I (Dushanbe: Irfon, 1970), p. 317.

11   M. Nazarshoev, *Muborezi Rohi haqiqat* (Dushanbe: Irfon, 1993), p. 90.

12   Holiqzoda, *Ta'rikhi siyosii Tojikon az istiloi Rusiya to imruz*, p. 75.

13   K. Aini, 'Didori vopasin', *Sadoi Sharq*, No. 4 (1980), pp. 83–4.

14   According to the NKVD Order No. 00447, 'On the Operation to Repress Former Kulaks, Criminals, and Other Anti-Soviet Elements', dated 30 July 1937, 500 people were to be arrested and executed in Tajikistan, and 1300 more were to be sent to labour camps. There are reasons to believe that in its first two months alone the operation affected three times more people than originally planned. See: Y. Albats, *The State within a State: The KGB and its Hold on Russia—Past, Present, and Future* (New York: Farrar, Straus & Giroux, 1994), pp. 80–2, and flyleaf.

have been rehabilitated (half of them posthumously)[15] may be a fair indication of the scale of terror in the republic. The new leadership in Tajikistan was subservient and tolerably literate; it feared and readily obeyed directives from Moscow, if only to survive. The case of Munavvar Shogadoev, the chairman of the Central Executive Committee (later Presidium of the Supreme Soviet) of Tajikistan between 1937 and 1950, provides an excellent example of the Stalinist appointee.[16] He had an impeccable social background (son of peasants, day-labourer at a cotton mill) and scant education (three years of *rabfak*—crash educational courses—in Tashkent). Shogadoev joined the party in the late 1920s and was appointed head of a district party committee in his native mountainous region of Gharm in 1930, where he showed himself to be an exemplary executant, having managed to recruit hundreds of fellow highlanders to take part in irrigation projects in south-west Tajikistan. He had a poor command of Russian, but the establishment of Russian schools in Gharm was amongst his main priorities. Shogadoev fully demonstrated his organisational skills and dedication in the 1940s, when, as head of the republic's legislative body, he sanctioned and supervised the forced resettlement of tens of thousands of people from his native Gharm to the Vakhsh Valley—a project that cost scores of human lives.

The CPT, thoroughly purged and restaffed, became an organisation that could be entrusted with day-to-day management of the republic. The policy of nativisation was abandoned. Moreover, from 1930 to 1932 alone, 217 party officials were posted to Tajikistan from the centre.[17] Table 5.1 illustrates the process of the 'adjustment' of the republic's party structures to the demands of Stalin's era.

Table 5.1 Changes in the Membership and Ethnic Composition of the CPT, 1933–38

	Total membership	Tajiks	Uzbeks	Russians	Others
1933	14 329	52.9%	22.2%	17.3%	7.6%
1938	4 715	41.8%	16.4%	25.4%	16.4%

Source: *Kommunisticheskaia partiia Tadzhikistana v tsifrakh za 60 let* (Dushanbe: Irfon, 1984), pp. 27, 33.

Members of traditional elite groups, even those who had hailed the advent of Soviet power, were singled out for extermination. The wave of terror affected not only the representatives of institutionalised Islam and the old status hierarchies (such as *sayids*—descendants of the prophet Mohammad; *khojas*—descendants

---

15   Alimov and Saidov, *Natsionalnyi vopros*, p. 34.
16   *Kommunist Tadzhikistana*, 12 April 1991.
17   E. S. Postovoi, A. I. Polskaia and N. T. Bezrukova, *Ocherki istorii Kommunisticheskoi partii Tadzhikistana* (Dushanbe: Irfon, 1964), pp. 82, 101.

of the first four caliphs; *turas*—progenies of the Timurid rulers; *pirs* and *ishons*—dynastic leaders of Ismaili and Sunni communities; and *mirs*—chieftains and old landed aristocracy), it also destroyed the whole stratum of the Bukharan literati, who had carefully preserved and propagated old cultural values. This campaign swept Tajikistan in 1937—much later than in other Central Asian republics[18]—but was waged with the same ferocity and yielded similar results. Contemporaries testified that in the city of Uroteppa (Istaravshon) the public baths were heated for a month by burning confiscated books and manuscripts of ecclesiastical works and classical poetry.[19] Naturally,

> the subsequent formation of the Tajik intelligentsia largely rejected the old cultural tradition. It consisted mainly of newcomers from the peasantry, often the products of children's homes and boarding schools to whom Soviet rule had given everything and for whom a totalitarian regime was a familiar and accustomed reality. The new intelligentsia was not only formed by the authorities, it was also tied to representatives of the structures of power by close, almost literally kinship bonds.[20]

The Structure and Performance of Government

The institutional foundations of the Soviet state in Tajikistan were laid in the Constitution of 1931[21] and were further elaborated in the Constitution of 1937, which was a carbon copy of the All-Union Constitution adopted in 1936. The republic acquired a ramified set of governmental organs that was characterised by a relatively clear-cut separation of powers and a stable structure. The official legislature of the Tajik SSR was the Supreme Soviet, elected every four years on the basis of universal suffrage by citizens over eighteen years of age. Articles 15, 22, 23 and 28 of the Constitution of 1937 conferred upon the Supreme Soviet the status of the sole authoritative law-making body of Tajikistan. Yet in reality it had little power to elaborate or endorse independent policies and acted primarily to furnish the party's directives with a veil of legitimacy. During 1946 and 1953, in the heyday of Stalin's command-administrative system of government, the Supreme Soviet of Tajikistan was not even approached for a formal approbation of the annual plan for economic development of the republic, in direct violation of Article 15 of the Constitution.[22]

---

18   An eminent Soviet scholar dates the mass anti-religious drive in Uzbekistan from 1928. See: Saidbaev, *Islam i obschestvo*, p. 165.

19   Holiqzoda, *Ta'rikhi siyosii Tojikon az istiloi Rusiya to imruz*, p. 78.

20   S. Olimova and M. Olimov, 'The Educated Class of Tajikistan in the Upheavals of the Twentieth Century', *Russian Politics and Law*, Vol. 31, No. 4 (1993), p. 44.

21   In fact, the first comprehensive body of laws was ready in 1929, at the moment of the formation of the Tajik Soviet Socialist Republic, but its provisions could not be fully implemented at the time when large parts of Tajikistan were yet to be pacified.

22   V. S. Iavich, *Verkhovny Sovet TSSR* (Moscow: Gosudarstvennoe izdatelstvo iuridicheskoi literatury, 1958), p. 40.

The composition of the Supreme Soviet was carefully regulated and remained stable for decades (Table 5.2), despite an impressive turnover rate of more than 50 per cent.[23] It was meant to emphasise the representative nature of the republican legislature, on the one hand, and its inseparable links with the party, on the other. The chairman of the Presidium of the Supreme Soviet was always a member of the CPT Central Committee's Bureau, and for many party functionaries, work in the organs of the national parliament provided a necessary step for their future career. Additionally, the Supreme Soviet served as a symbol of statehood of the Tajik nation: it usually had a distinct Tajik majority, inconsistent with the actual ethnic mosaic in the republic.[24]

Table 5.2 Composition of the Supreme Soviet of Tajikistan

Convocation	Number of deputies	Women	Workers and peasants	Party members
IV (1955)	300	33.0%	47.8%	71.8%
VI (1963)	300	33.0%	48.0%	69.3%
VIII (1971)	315	34.0%	50.4%	68.9%
X (1980)	350	35.1%	50.6%	68.3%

Source: Calculations are based on data provided in the *Great Soviet Encyclopaedia Annuals*: 1958 (p. 160); 1966 (p. 173); 1970 (p. 171); 1971 (p. 178); 1983 (p. 162).

Elections to the Supreme Soviet and local legislative bodies (regional, district, city and village soviets) were not contested; sometimes all 100 per cent of eligible voters turned up at polling stations and unanimously supported the candidate of the 'bloc of communists and non-party people'. Plenary sessions of the Supreme Soviet conducted twice a year were formal and tedious affairs, where hardly any deputy would dare vote against a decision or abstain. Even during Gorbachev's *perestroika*, important bills would be put to the vote and approved without discussion due to the apparent lack of interest on the part of the Tajik MPs.[25]

At the inception of the USSR in 1922, the constituent republics were given a high degree of autonomy in handling domestic matters. Maintenance of law and order, public health, education, social welfare and agriculture was within the competence of the republics' executive institutions; the formation of dominant federal organisations was not envisaged.[26] The republics also enjoyed broad

---

23   J. Hough and M. Fainsod, *How the Soviet Union is Governed* (Cambridge, Mass.: Harvard University Press, 1979), p. 367.

24   Rakowska-Harmstone, *Russia and Nationalism in Central Asia*, p. 112.

25   *Sessiyai hashtumi Soveti Olii RSS Tojikiston, da'vati yozdahum: Hisoboti stenografi* (Dushanbe: Izdaniie Verkhovnogo Soveta Tadzhikskoi SSR, 1988), p. 99.

26   'Postanovlenie Plenuma TsK RKP(b) o vzaimootnosheniiakh s nezavisimymi Sovetskimi Sotsialisticheskimi respublikami. 6 oktiabria 1922g.', in *KPSS v rezoliutsiiakh i resheniiakh s'ezdov, konferentsii i plenumov TsK*, Vol. 2 (Moscow: Gospolitizdat, 1970), pp. 401–2.

financial independence within their share of the All-Union budget. In the late 1920s and early 1930s, however, as the country was preparing for rapid industrialisation and forced collectivisation, the republics' autonomy was dramatically reduced, and federal and local executive bodies were transformed to fit a super-centralised chain of command based on the branch rather than the territorial principle.

Article 39 of the 1937 Constitution identified the Council of Ministers of Tajikistan as the highest executive and administrative organ in the republic. At the same time, its status and prerogatives were not clearly defined—for example, technically it did not have the right to initiate legislation, though in reality draft bills were often prepared in ministries and state committees. Article 41 stipulated that Tajikistan's Council of Ministers act to implement decrees and orders given by the USSR's Council of Ministers. The latter also had the right to suspend the execution of the former's directives, but in more than 50 years such a contingency never arose.

As elsewhere in the USSR, in Tajikistan the ministerial structure consisted of two tiers: republican ministries, answerable exclusively to the Council of Ministers of Tajikistan, and union-republican ministries of dual subordination that took orders from the central institutions (and ultimately from the Council of Ministers of the USSR) but simultaneously were under the jurisdiction of the republic's Council of Ministers (Table 5.3). Gregory Gleason has rightfully observed that 'this overlapping authority frequently has resulted in an awkward pattern in the distribution of responsibilities', often leading to disputes over competence.[27] In practice, however, the centre always had the upper hand. Its dominant positions in Tajikistan were reinforced by the fact that more than half of the republic's gross industrial output was produced by enterprises under direct control of All-Union ministries, which are beyond even nominal control by Tajikistan's government.[28] Such vital industries as mining, machine-building, metallurgy, chemicals and electricity generation in Tajikistan were developed exclusively under the auspices of central institutions that did not necessarily take the republic's demands into consideration. In the 1980s only 7–10 per cent of all industrial enterprises in Tajikistan were subordinate to the republic;[29] the rest operated in the interests of various All-Union branches rather than those of the local economy.

---

27   Gregory Gleason, *Federalism and Nationalism: The Struggle for Republican Rights in the USSR* (Boulder, Colo.: Westview Press, 1990), p. 64.

28   I. Sh. Muksinov, *Sovet ministrov soiuznoi respubliki* (Moscow: Iuridicheskaia literatura, 1969), p. 51.

29   Narzikulov, 'Dvulikii Ianus v serdtse Azii', p. 124.

Table 5.3 Ministries in Tajikistan, 1976

Union-republic organs		Republic organs	
Ministries	State committees and main administrations	Ministries	State committees and main administrations
Foreign Affairs	State Security (KGB)	Local Industry	Labour Resources
Justice	Geology	Public Services	
Interior	People's Control	Municipal Services	
Culture	Statistics	Motor Transport and Main Roads	
Education	Cinematography	Social Security	
Agriculture	Prices Policies		
Milk and Meat Industry	Vocational Technical Education		
Land Reclamation and Irrigation	Agricultural Equipment		
Light Industry	Radio and TV		
Food Industry	Planning		
Procurement	Supplies		
Health	Publishing		
Finance	Fruit and Vegetables		
Trade			
Construction			
Rural Construction			
Building Materials			
Communications			
Total: 18	Total: 13	Total: 5	Total: 1

Source: Val Ogareff, *Leaders of the Soviet Republics, 1971–1980* (Canberra: The ANU Press, 1980), pp. 268–83; *Konstitutsii soiuznykh sovetskikh sotsialisticheskikh respublik* (Moscow: Izdatelstvo Izvestiia sovetov deputatov trudiaschikhsia SSSR, 1972), pp. 392–4.

In a situation in which the Supreme Soviet of Tajikistan was little more than a ceremonial institution and the republic's executive organs acted as mere extensions of central ministries, it was the party apparatus that carried out decision-making and served as the vehicle to articulate the republic's needs at the federal level. The party institutions permeated the entire society and were well geared to implement social control, political indoctrination and economic management. Party organs at lower levels—regional, district and city committees—had a similar configuration, with a ramified network of specialised departments that covered every aspect of life of the populace in a given territory. In the USSR, the Communist Party ceased to be just a major centre of power *primus inter pares* in the late 1920s. Under Stalin it not only became the core of the government, it also eventually subjugated or liquidated all other formal social institutions, thus putting in place the Soviet mono-organisational order where the party 'is entrusted with integrating all the others into a single organisational whole, and does so primarily by appropriating and exercising on their behalf the key prerogatives of any autonomous organisation, namely determination of their goals, structures and leadership'.[30]

The party performed its integrative role through: a) prescribing the innumerable rules of behaviour in the society based on its unchallenged political legitimacy; b) empowering its organs at all levels with control and coordination functions; and c) placing its cadres at the head of non-party hierarchies. Soviet legitimation— that is, 'an acceptance, even approbation, of the state's rules of the game, its social control, as true and right'[31]—was based on the supreme goal of building communism, the validity of which was never allowed to be questioned. The leadership deduced intermediate tasks and objectives from this ultimate goal. Accordingly, as T. H. Rigby has noted, 'the central role in the [Soviet] political system is played by institutions concerned with formulating the goals and tasks of the constituent units of society and supervising their execution'.[32] This state of affairs found formal reflection in the USSR Constitution of 1977 (Article 6) and the 1978 Constitution of Tajikistan (Article 6). Of course, it would be incorrect to assume that before this time party directives had not been legally binding for all Soviet citizens, as they most certainly were.[33]

Officials in the legislature, government institutions, judiciary and law enforcement agencies, industrial and agricultural managers as well as the party

---

30   T. H. Rigby, *The Changing Soviet System: Mono-Organisational Socialism from its Origins to Gorbachev's Restructuring* (Aldershot, UK: Edward Elgar, 1990), p. 6.
31   Migdal, *Strong Societies and Weak States*, p. 33.
32   Rigby, *The Changing Soviet System*, p. 166.
33   The most obvious illustration is myriad decrees issued jointly by All-Union and republican central committees and councils of ministers on almost every matter of any importance, including staff structure, programs and budgets of public associations, theatre repertoire, erection of monuments, and so on. See: Muksinov, *Sovet ministrov soiuznoi respubliki*, pp. 28, 131, 136–7.

membership were subordinated to the party apparatus through an effective system of personnel appointments, the so-called *nomenklatura* system that was characterised by

> first, the concentration of important positions in all official and 'voluntary' organisations in the *nomenklatury* of *party* committees; second, the inclusion of *elective* positions (and most of the more important ones are in form elective); and third, the *comprehensiveness* of the system, which omits no position of any significance in the society, and thereby incidentally converts the occupants of nomenklatura positions into a distinct *social* category.[34]

Party organisations exercised the power of personnel selection and placement according to the administrative level on which they operated. Their spheres of jurisdiction changed frequently, but in the postwar period the general trend was for the republic and regional party committees to acquire more independence in staffing official structures.

In the 1930s, almost all positions of authority in Tajikistan, including secretaries of district and city party committees, were in the sphere of duty of the VKP(b) Central Committee.[35] After Stalin's death the situation changed dramatically. In 1960, there were more than 7000 officials of authority (*otvetstvennye rabotniki*) in the republic who were answerable to local party committees,[36] 1779 of whom were in the *nomenklatura* of the CPT Central Committee.[37]

As Rolf Theen has astutely observed:

> [W]e must be aware that the appointment, advancement, transfer, and dismissal of key personnel in the apparatuses of the trade unions, the Komsomol, the central and local soviets, the administrative organs (police, courts, procuracy), the vast ministerial structure, as well as all economic and cultural organisations, are subject to a *nomenklatura* process controlled by the leading officials in those institutions, that is, almost invariably by members of the CPSU or non-party individuals who are considered politically trustworthy.[38]

---

34 T. H. Rigby, *Political Elites in the USSR: Central Leaders and Local Cadres from Lenin to Gorbachev* (Aldershot, UK: Edward Elgar, 1990), p. 74.
35 'Materialy fevralsko-martovskogo plenuma TsK VKP(b) 1937g.', *Voprosy Istorii*, No. 10 (1995), p. 7.
36 *XIII s'ezd Kommunisticheskoi partii Tadzhikistana. Stenograficheskii otchet* (Stalinabad: Tadzhikskoe gosudarstvennoe izdatelstvo, 1960), p. 80.
37 *XIII s'ezd Kommunisticheskoi partii Tadzhikistana*, p. 173.
38 Rolf H. W. Theen, 'Party and Bureaucracy', in *Public Policy and Administration in the Soviet Union*, ed. Gordon B. Smith (New York: Praeger, 1980), p. 44.

Table 5.4 Examples from *Nomenklatura* Lists of Party Organisations

Party organ	Powers of appointment
CPSU Central Committee	a) First secretary of the CPT CC, heads of departments and party control of the CPT CC, first secretaries of regional party committees
	b) Members of government, the KGB chairman, members of the Presidium of the Supreme Soviet, chairman of the Supreme Court
	c) Chairman of the council of trade unions, first secretary of the Komsomol, editor of the republican newspaper *Kommunist Tadzhikistanad*) Directors of crucial industrial enterprises (for example, VOSTOKREDMET uranium complex in Chkalovsk)
CPT Central Committee	a) Regional and city party secretaries and heads of departments, secretaries of district party committees in the districts of republican subordination
	b) Chairmen of the executive committees of the regional soviets and cities, judges at all levels
	c) Heads of public associations such as Society for Nature Protection, regional Komsomol leaders, editors of newspapers and magazines
	d) Directors of industrial enterprises, research and cultural institutions
Regional Party Committee (*obkom*)*	a) Party functionaries at the district and city levels, secretaries of primary party organisations of large factories and farms
	b) Chairmen of the executive committees of districts
	c) Secretaries of the district Komsomol committees, trade union leaders of districts
	d) Chairmen of collective farms (kolkhozy) and directors of state farms (sovkhozy), engineers and managerial personnel of industrial enterprises, directors of vocational training colleges, university professors
District and City Party Committee (*raikom, gorkom*)	a) Raikom and gorkom instructors, heads of primary party cells
	b) Chairmen of local representative organs (mahalla soviets)
	c) Heads of primary Komsomol cells, functionaries of primary trade union organisations (mestkoms)
	d) Brigade leaders at factories and farms, schoolteachers, librarians

* The administrative division of Tajikistan provided for the existence of districts subordinated directly to Dushanbe. In their cases, the prerogative of staffing the most important positions belonged to the CPT CC, which thus fulfilled the role of an *obkom*.

Source: Newspapers and statutes of the Communist Party of Tajikistan; *Rol' selskikh raikomov partii v osuschestvlenii agrarnoi politiki KPSS v sovremennykh usloviiakh* (Moscow: Izdatelstvo politicheskoi literatury, 1987), pp. 17, 45, 116–17.

Nomenklatura lists of various bodies often overlapped and contradicted one another, but party organs always had the final say in matters involving movement of cadres. For example, the Ministry of Culture of Tajikistan would appoint graduates of its training institutions as directors of provincial clubs, libraries and museums, but district party committees would not let them work, nominating their own candidates, who sometimes 'could not carry out their duties on the grounds of not knowing the job'.[39]

It was general practice that the party committees, on top of providing universal coordination and staffing for all other agencies, were directly involved in executing local and specialised measures, especially in the economic sphere. Setting tasks for the economic development of national republics always featured prominently on the agenda of the CPSU Central Committee; suffice to say that of the 56 cases between 1931 and 1980 when Tajikistan was mentioned in resolutions passed by the highest party bodies, 49 (or 88 per cent) were of a purely economic nature and only three dealt with political issues.[40] The lower the level of a party committee, the more it focused on the running of the economy. The CPT Central Committee issued one-year and five-year guidelines for economic development of the republic wherein, within the limits set by the centre, all major economic indicators and the ways to attain them were specified in a very detailed manner. At the district level, the *raikoms* eventually ran industrial enterprises and collective farms. As a Soviet source has stated, the district party committees

> often had to bear the economic-distributional functions uncharacteristic of them: to allocate funds for supply of agricultural machinery and other materials, to be thoroughly immersed into the questions of growing various crops, to coordinate the activities of economic partners, to arbitrate, etc. All this placed an excessive burden on the Party apparatus and did not allow it to indulge fully into organisational and political work.[41]

Failure to fulfil the directives of the party organs usually meant sacking for the manager in question. The turnover amongst agricultural administrators was especially high: in 1956, more than 50 per cent of *kolkhoz* chairmen were replaced.[42] In 1984, the first secretary of the Qurghonteppa *obkom*, F. Karimov, assembled more than 400 *kolkhoz* chairmen, brigade leaders, agronomists and other specialists from the region in a conference hall and in the course of five

---

39 A. Kuvatov, 'Podgotovka, rasstanovka i vospitanie kadrov kulturno-prosvetitelnykh uchrezhdenii (1956–1965gg.)', in *Materialy k istorii Kommunisticheskoi partii Tadzhikistana*, Vypusk 4, chast II, ed. K. N. Gavrilkin (Dushanbe: Izdatelstvo TGU, 1972), p. 334. A certain Akhunov was appointed by the Kolkhozabad *raikom* as director of the library at Uzun only because he was an old party member, had a big family and suffered from some disability. He was barely literate at that, so this position became a genuine sinecure for him (ibid., p. 333).

40 Calculations are based on: *KPSS v rezoliutsiiakh i resheniiakh s'ezdov, konferentsii i plenumov TsK*, Vols 5–13 (Moscow: Izdatelstvo politicheskoi literatury, 1970–81).

41 *Rol' selskikh raikomov partii v osuschestvlenii agrarnoi politiki KPSS v sovremennykh usloviiakh* (Moscow: Izdatelstvo politicheskoi literatury, 1987), p. 81.

42 *XI s'ezd Kommunisticheskoi partii Tadzhikistana: Stenograficheskii otchet* (Stalinabad: Tadzhikskoe gosudarstvennoe izdatelstvo, 1958), p. 55.

hours a special commission questioned every single one of them about his/her performance during an extraordinarily bad harvest campaign; those who could not come up with a plausible account of their work were dismissed or demoted on the spot.[43]

Generally, the structure of the political system in Tajikistan conformed ideally to the common Soviet model, which remained stable from the 1930s; it consisted of a core organisation, the Communist Party of Tajikistan, and a number of specialised agencies with varying degrees of autonomy. The entire decision-making process was concentrated almost exclusively in the CPT Central Committee, which: a) initiated projects and settled conflicting interests vested in them; b) mobilised support for their implementation by launching public campaigns, coercion or otherwise; and c) put them into effect. Consequently, in Tajikistan until the late 1980s political activism was confined to covert struggle amongst units *within* the CPT hierarchy or to bargaining with the superior organs of the CPSU for more resources and the freedom to use them.

The Political Elite in Tajikistan: Composition, Mobility and Patronage-Building

Being on the *nomenklatura* list of the CPT Central Committee was a fair indication of belonging to the elite in Tajikistan; however, the governing elite (that is, according to S. F. Nadel, the group of political rulers who had decisive pre-eminence over other social and specialised elites)[44] was somewhat smaller. Its membership 'was synonymous for all practical purposes with the membership of the Central Committee of the Tadzhik Communist Party'.[45] As Table 5.5 shows, ethnic Tajiks dominated the governing elite in Tajikistan in the postwar period. Prior to 1946, except for a short period in 1937, the republic's party organisation was headed by people dispatched from Moscow,[46] but after the removal of Dmitry Protopopov—a career CheKa and OGPU (both secret police organisations) and People's Commissariat of Internal Affairs (NKVD) officer who bore personal responsibility for the purges amongst local cadres and intelligentsia—this position remained invariably in the hands of a Tajik.

---

43 *Kommunist Tadzhikistana*, 19 February 1985.

44 Adapted from: Geraint Parry, *Political Elites* (London: George Allen & Unwin, 1969), pp. 70–2.

45 Rakowska-Harmstone, *Russia and Nationalism in Central Asia*, p. 146.

46 The list of the CPT CC first secretaries is as follows: M. Huseinov (Azeri), 1929–33; G. I. Broido (Jew), 1933–34; S. K. Shadunts (Armenian), 1934–36; U. Ashurov (Tajik), 1937; D. Z. Protopopov (Russian), 1937–46; B. Ghafurov (Tajik), 1946–56; T. Uljaboev (Tajik), 1956–61; J. Rasulov (Tajik), 1961–82; R. Nabiev (Tajik), 1982–85; Q. Mahkamov (Tajik), 1985–91.

Table 5.5 Ethnic Composition of the CPT Leadership

Year	CC members		CC candidate members		Members of the CPT Revision Commission	
	Locals	Russians and other non-locals	Locals	Russians and other non-locals	Locals	Russians and other non-locals
1958	95 (79.8%)	24 (20.2%)	51 (86.4%)	8 (13.6%)	32 (82.1%)	7 (17.9%)
1960	96 (78.0%)	27 (22.0%)	53 (79.1%)	14 (20.9%)	38 (84.4%)	7 (15.6%)
1976	108 (78.3%)	30 (21.7%)	45 (76.3%)	14 (23.7%)	33 (71.7%)	13 (28.3%)
1981	108 (78.3%)	30 (21.7%)	45 (73.8%)	16 (26.2%)	40 (85.1%)	7 (14.9%)

Source: Documents of the eleventh, thirteenth, eighteenth and nineteenth congresses of the CPT.

With the end of Stalin's era of uncontrolled despotism and terror and the emergence of more stable, institutionalised and reciprocal patterns of exchange amongst various units of the Soviet leadership (the process that T. H. Rigby has referred to as the emergence of a 'self-stabilising oligarchy'),[47] the indigenous elites in the national republics gradually increased their participation in the administration of their respective territories. The impressive economic growth and diversification, the continuous process of social mobilisation, and the expansion of education and culture necessitated and made possible the rise of ethno-territorial bureaucracies that 'often sought to use feelings of local "ethnofidelity" to promote government policies, and, often enough, their personal political agendas'.[48]

The recruitment and movement of elite cadres in Tajikistan, as in any other republic of the USSR, were based on, a) objective-rational, and b) personality, factors. If under Stalin and, to a lesser degree, Khrushchev, elite careers were made and ruined primarily at the discretion of higher officials in the party hierarchy, in later years knowledge, technical and administrative skills and 'life experience' played an ever-growing part in the elite's upward mobility. To advance rapidly through the party/state ranks, a person was required

- to be a Tajik
- to have a lengthy record of party membership (minimum of five years for *obkom* secretaries, three years for *raikom* secretaries and one year for primary cell secretaries)
- to have a good education (Table 5.6)
- to possess practical experience as a government official or an industrial or agricultural manager[49]
- to show commendable administrative performance.

---

47   Rigby, *Political Elites in the USSR*, p. 217.
48   Gregory Gleason, 'On the Bureaucratic Reinforcement of Nationalism in the USSR', *Canadian Review of Studies in Nationalism*, Vol. XIX, Nos 1–2 (1992), p. 51.
49   In the postwar period, all first secretaries of the CPT CC, except Bobojon Ghafurov, were promoted from the position of chairman of the republic's Council of Ministers.

Table 5.6 Educational Levels of Secretaries of Regional, City and District Committees of the CPT

	1947	1957	1967	1971	1974
Higher	4.9%	14.6%	87.8%	92.7%	96.9%
Incomplete higher	4.5%	63.4%	9.9%	4.9%	1.9%
Secondary	32.4%	14.7%	2.2%	1.4%	1.2%
Incomplete secondary	25.0%	7.3%	-	-	-
Primary	33.2%	-	-	-	-

Source: *Kommunisticheskaia partiia Tadzhikistana v tsifrakh* (Dushanbe: Irfon, 1974), p. 48.

Grey Hodnett has put Tajikistan into the 'partly self-administering' category of the Soviet republics in his exhaustive study of personnel movement in the USSR,[50] using the criterion of native occupancy of all leading positions in a given republic. Indeed, certain crucial jobs (second secretaries of the CPT CC and regional and district party committees responsible for personnel matters, heads of industrial departments of the CPT CC and the Council of Ministers, the KGB chairman, and so on) were reserved for non-natives, usually Russians. It should be kept in mind, though, that these officials arrived in Tajikistan for a tour of duty and after its completion were transferred to other regions of the USSR. At the same time, native cadres in Tajikistan had the lowest age thresholds for positions of authority of all Soviet republics; they also faced less competition for primary leadership jobs than aspirants elsewhere in the USSR.[51] All these favourable conditions for the Tajik elite existed only within the boundaries of the republic; it was almost impossible for a Tajik party or state official of high standing to be transferred to a higher or equal position in the All-Union hierarchy. Unlike their colleagues from Kazakhstan and Uzbekistan, Tajik party leaders never made it to the Politburo or Secretariat of the CPSU Central Committee. Secretaryship of the CPT CC appeared to be the limit in terms of upward mobility for local cadres; upon reaching the level of a regional party secretary or deputy minister (usually, stepping-stone posts in the Soviet personnel system), a Tajik would find it extremely difficult to make further merit-based advancement. This may explain why *obkom* functionaries in Tajikistan had the most protracted initial tenures in office in the entire Soviet Union: 191 months, 2.5 and three times longer than those of their Uzbek and Kazakh peers respectively.[52]

---

50 Grey Hodnett, *Leadership in the Soviet National Republics: A Quantitative Study of Recruitment Policy* (Ontario: Mosaic Press, 1978), p. 104.

51 Hodnett, *Leadership in the Soviet National Republics*, p. 80. See also: Rakowska-Harmstone, *Russia and Nationalism in Central Asia*, pp. 96–7.

52 William A. Clark, *Soviet Regional Mobility after Khrushchev* (New York: Praeger, 1989), p. 87.

The tendency to let officials occupy one position in a particular region for a substantial period, especially salient under Brezhnev's policy of 'stability of cadres' (1964–82), was conducive, alongside other factors, to the creation of well-established networks of informal exchange amongst elite groups in Tajikistan. As S. N. Eisenstadt has shown, the monolithic Soviet political system

> gives rise to areas of uncertainty which ... create conditions under which patron–client relations thrive. Such conditions are also fostered by the monopolistic character of the ruling groups, which seemingly reinforces the possibility of control by various 'stronger' groups over access to markets and to public goods. The combination of these factors allows a very far-reaching spread of patron–client relations, their continuous reappearance, and their concentration into somewhat more enduring patterns among the central elites.[53]

Practices of favouritism, cronyism, protection, overt and covert sponsorship not only flourished in the context of bureaucratic contacts but also pervaded the daily life of the populace under the circumstances of scarcity of the most basic commodities (food, clothes, housing) in the USSR. In Tajikistan, the viability of patronage networks was reinforced by the existence of particular patrimonial, family and sub-ethnic social institutions.

Due to a number of systemic determinants (small population, low level of industrial development, and remoteness from the centre), Tajik political leaders constantly failed to establish strong personalised cliental relationships with top bureaucrats in Moscow. Perhaps Tursun Uljaboev, the CPT CC first secretary from 1956 to 1961, came close to acquiring status as Khrushchev's protégé: he had been selected for promotion to the position of secretary of the CPSU CC, but anti-Khrushchev opposition in the Central Committee (F. R. Kozlov, G. I. Voronov and L. F. Ilichev) effectively removed Uljaboev from the political scene.[54] Tajikistan retained only token representation in the Central Committee, the Supreme Soviet and the Council of Ministers of the USSR, and henceforth its elite had limited opportunities to lobby for resources. The importance of direct access to the All-Union top leadership in terms of distribution of funds to national republics can be illustrated by the following fact: over the period 1971–85, per capita investment in Uzbekistan was 1.75 times higher than in Tajikistan, Turkmenistan or Kyrgyzstan; irrigation works in Uzbekistan consumed 20.4 billion roubles of capital investments compared with the figure of 7.9 billion roubles for the three other republics combined, although the return from those investments in Uzbekistan was two to five times lower.[55] Obviously, Sharaf

---

53   S. N. Eisenstadt and L. Roniger, *Patrons, Clients and Friends: Interpersonal Relations and the Structure of Trust in Society* (Cambridge: Cambridge University Press, 1984), p. 190.
54   Mazhabsho Muhabbatsho, 'Fojiai Uljaboev', *Daryo*, Nos 1–2 (1995), p. 28.
55   Vasily Seliunin, 'Bremia deistvii', *Perestroika*, Vol. 5 (Moscow: Sovetskii pisatel, 1990), p. 173.

Rashidov, the first secretary of the Communist Party of Uzbekistan (CPUz) CC, a candidate member of the Politburo and a crony of Leonid Brezhnev, was in a good position to persuade the centre to allocate additional funds to his republic.

At the level of the republic, the creation of potent patron–client dyads was a natural product of the peculiar nature of the centre–periphery relationship in the Soviet polity. Moscow assigned local authorities specific economic tasks, which were to be met at any cost. If in the course of their implementation the prescribed standard operation modes were violated or altered, the centre, more likely than not, would turn a blind eye, provided that the plans were (or appeared to be) fulfilled. In Gregory Gleason's words:

> [F]or local leaders to succeed in their charges, they must develop and steward the resources necessary to inspire, enthuse, mobilise, and promote within their republics. That is, they must develop political resources. To the extent that they succeed at this, they concentrate in their hands the ability to conduct politics in the traditional sense of the word, namely, to help friends and hurt enemies.[56]

Informal Political Exchange

The concept of goal rationality as the source of the legitimation of authority in the USSR, put forward by T. H. Rigby, implied, amongst other things, that at all levels of the Soviet polity 'the dominant rationale for evaluating social action is the achievement of prescribed tasks'.[57] And while command mechanisms predominated in Soviet society, exchange continued to play a substantial role in coordinating social activity due to the sheer magnitude of the problems the country faced, and the physical inability of controlling institutions to offer quick and plausible solutions. Under circumstances in which the main mode of institutionalised exchange—contractual relations based on private property rights—was anathema, 'grey' and 'black' markets, corruption and other forms of informal exchange inevitably came to the fore. These phenomena were not necessarily detrimental to the Soviet system; in fact, some sociologists agree that they may have served as 'a stabilising or conservative force in systems experiencing rapid change and institutional decay', and they may have had 'positive functions that were not adequately performed by formal institutions and legally devised arrangements'.[58] The black market 'was allowed to flourish precisely *because* much of the time it distributed goods and services more

56   Gleason, *Federalism and Nationalism*, p. 96.
57   Rigby, 'Introduction', p. 13.
58   Charles A. Schwartz, 'Corruption and Political Development in the USSR', *Comparative Politics*, Vol. II, No. 4 (July 1979), p. 425.

efficiently than the formal institutions of the state'.[59] According to official statistics, in 1991 the black market accounted for 8 per cent of the USSR's gross national product (GNP).[60] There are reasons to believe that the figure for Central Asia, the region with strong traditions of entrepreneurial activity, was even higher. The fact that in the late 1970s an underground congress of criminal leaders adopted a resolution to charge illegal shops producing unregistered products a 15 per cent commission[61] could be regarded as an indicator of the steady growth in the shadow economy.

Olivier Roy argues that solidarity networks based on kinship and/or patronage allow a population to resist the interference of an authoritarian state, or to 'compensate for the weakness or corruption of the state'.[62] Schoeberlein-Engel notes, however, the role of patronage/kin networks in 'corruption':

> Since virtually all property and resources are state-controlled, connections are essential in order to negotiate the extra-legal and unofficial mechanisms that regulate access to the resources necessary for any kind of economic activity: permission to sell goods on the market, provision of raw materials, access to vehicles or buildings— even simply freedom from the legal or illegal interference of 'law enforcement' authorities. All this requires an elaborate and effective network of mutual back-scratching relationships, which most readily develop within the family framework ... However, as each person seeks to maximize the breadth and effectiveness of her network, it is often expedient to draw on criteria of connections that extend beyond the family to a larger community.[63]

This creates a tautological problem of 'circular cause and consequence': did state corruption force people into what is often termed 'clan behaviour'? Or did pre-existing 'clan behaviour' create the corruption and the weakness of the state? It can be at least argued that the two are mutually reinforcing. Navruz Nekbakhtshoev points out the mutually reinforcing nature of the cycle,

---

59 William A. Clark, 'Crime and Punishment in Soviet Officialdom, 1965–1990', *Europe–Asia Studies*, Vol. 45, No. 2 (1993), p. 278.

60 Peter Rutland, 'Economic Crisis and Reform', in *Developments in Soviet and Post-Soviet Politics*, eds Stephen White, Alex Pravda and Zvi Gitelman (London: Macmillan, 1992), p. 220.

61 Dmitri Likhanov, 'Organised Crime in Central Asia', *Telos*, Vol. 75 (Spring 1988), p. 95.

62 Roy, 'Soviet Legacies and Western Aid Imperatives in the New Central Asia', pp. 124, 127.

63 Schoeberlein-Engel, *Identity in Central Asia*, pp. 268–9. Navruz Nekbakhtshoev makes a similar argument: 'No longer the comprehensive source of social and cultural identity that it had been in the past, clans in the Soviet period served a narrow purpose as an underground means through which Central Asians navigated everyday life. The contours of clans were subject to change as [the] shortage economy compelled clan members to seek allegiance with non-members through marriages and client–patron relationships in order to create networks of access to economic and politic[al] resources. And since its advantages [were] predicated on goods/ power distribution, it had become a centrally political phenomenon.' See Nekbakhtshoev, *Clan Politics*, p. 95.

blaming it for the proliferation of 'clan behaviours'.[64] He argues that the corrupt behaviour by 'members of clan networks' creates shortages in the economy for others and therefore creates a situation in which those outside the dominant network replicate the behaviour of that dominant group and engage in the same 'clan behaviours' to compensate for the shortages that were created.[65] Rafis Abazov, for his part, sees the patronage networks of the Soviet era in Tajikistan as not a completely new phenomenon, but rather as a continuation of 'tribal and communal (i.e., *mahallagaroyi*) affiliations'.[66] As an example of such behaviour, one woman from a village in Varzob attended university in Dushanbe in the 1960s and rose through the ranks of the party. Once in a position of some power, she used her position to favour her village in the allocation of state resources, much to the resentment of people in neighbouring villages.[67]

The 'stability of the cadres' during the Brezhnev era—when local officials remained in their regional positions for lengthy tenures—allowed patronage networks to thrive. Regional elites, serving long careers in the same locality, were able to strengthen their power bases and further strengthen personal allegiances and 'localism' (in Russian: *mestnichestvo*, in Tajik: *mahallagaroyi*).[68] At the height of Soviet rule in the Tajik SSR, patronage networks, as well as other forms of 'semi-legal and illegal exchange', were commonplace.[69] The characteristics of the centre–periphery relations in the Soviet Union allowed patronage to flourish. If local authorities could meet, or appear to meet, the goals of the prescribed economic plans, the violations on the ground would be ignored.[70] Political patronage networks thus 'diverted, undermined and used state power for their own end—facilitating benefits for the group'.[71]

Regional affiliations were an important aspect of this patronage. During the Soviet era these affiliations became a source of economic and political power for the elites and a source of political and economic resources for the masses. At the republic level this patronage relationship united the elites and their regional constituencies in the competition for the resources controlled by the state.[72]

---

64   Nekbakhtshoev, *Clan Politics*, p. 92.

65   Nekbakhtshoev, *Clan Politics*, p. 92.

66   Abazov, 'Central Asia's Conflicting Legacy and Ethnic Policies', p. 66. Nekbakhtshoev also portrays the clan behaviour of the Soviet era as an adaptation by pre-existing clans. See the previous note.

67   Tett, *Ambiguous Alliances*, pp. 75–6.

68   Kilavuz, *Understanding Violent Conflict*, p. 93. Kilavuz also argues that the increased ratio of the titular nationality in positions of power resulted in the expansion of local patronage networks (ibid., p. 94). See also: Akiner, 'Prospects for Civil Society in Tajikistan', p. 156. Bobojon Ghafurov, the first secretary of the Tajik Communist Party (1946–56), wrote in 1959 that he 'deplored "localism and friendship ties" which led to the selection of ignorant, inexperienced people who lacked "political faith"'. B. G. Gafurov, *Nekotorye voprosy national'noi politiki KPSS* (Moscow: Gospolitizdat, 1959), p. 2, as cited in Nekbakhtshoev, *Clan Politics*, p. 53.

69   Nourzhanov, 'Alternative Social Institutions and the Politics of Neo-Patrimonialism in Tajikistan', n.p.

70   Nourzhanov, 'Alternative Social Institutions and the Politics of Neo-Patrimonialism in Tajikistan', n.p.

71   Roy, 'Soviet Legacies and Western Aid Imperatives in the New Central Asia', p. 128.

72   Pauline Jones Luong, *Institutional Change and Political Continuity in Post-Soviet Central Asia: Power, Perceptions, and Pacts* (Cambridge: Cambridge University Press, 2002), pp. 62–3.

And at the *oblast* level the first secretaries of the local party committees (*obkoms*) formed local patronage networks with the help of their power to distribute resources and appoint people to official positions within the province.[73] Beyond enriching themselves, regional leaders used their powers of economic distribution and appointment to benefit their families, friends or persons who could provide some 'reciprocal benefit'.[74] This system ensured that the people and the elites both had strong incentives to be loyal to their 'regions'.[75]

Despite the importance of regional identity, it should obviously not be mistaken as an all-determining factor for social and political behaviour. At the elite level, there are divergent interests and divisions within the 'regionally based elite networks' and links between elites from different regions with mutual interests. The various 'regional identities and loyalties, while important, are not the only factor in the formation of elite networks'.[76] Regional identities, despite their importance, should not be overstated. They are often 'crosscut' by other considerations.[77] Regional identity is just one factor in the formation of high-level political power networks. Factors of 'education, career and work experiences, self-interest, and personal relationships' are also important in the formation of these 'political networks with regional bases'.[78] Kilavuz argues that these networks, while they may have a regional base, should not be considered 'unitary actors', as '[p]eople from the same region can be rivals, while people from different regions can be allies'.[79] There are 'sub-factions' within a region that can both 'ally with each other against a common competitor' and 'clash' with each other.[80] Matteo Fumagalli makes a similar point about the internal competition within the 'regions', a concept that he considers reification.[81]

73   Roland Dannreuther, *Creating New States in Central Asia: The Strategic Implications of the Collapse of Soviet Power in Central Asia*, Adelphi Paper No. 288 (London: Brassey's, for the IISS, 1994), p. 13, as cited in Kilavuz, *Understanding Violent Conflict*, p. 92.

74   T. H. Rigby and Bohdan Harasymiw, eds *Leadership Selection and Patron–Client Relations in the USSR and Yugoslavia* (London: George Allen & Unwin, 1983), p. 6, as cited in Kilavuz, *Understanding Violent Conflict*, p. 92. Antoine Buisson describes a similar process: 'Political factions work in accordance with the rule of "localism" (or mahallgerayi in Tajik, mestnichestvo in Russian), which consists in relying on people from one's region of origin to make a career of oneself, and to promote them in return once a position has been obtained in state structures or elsewhere. This involves practices of cronyism, nepotism and patronage. Another specificity is that these solidarity networks are articulated with the state production sector. As well as with the informal and criminal sectors that were already vibrant at the end of the Soviet period. Apparatchiki and technocrats got used to diverting state economic resources and channelling them to their solidarity networks. This involved the mobilization of illegal groupings and activities that could prosper under the protection these influential political figures could ensure by working in the Party-State apparatus.' See: Antoine Buisson, 'State-Building, Power-Building and Political Legitimacy: The Case of Post-Conflict Tajikistan', *China and Eurasia Forum Quarterly*, Vol. 5, No. 4 (2007), p. 136.

75   Luong, *Institutional Change and Political Continuity in Post-Soviet Central Asia*, pp. 62–3.

76   Kilavuz, *Understanding Violent Conflict*, pp. 13, 80.

77   Akiner, *Tajikistan*, p. 41.

78   Kilavuz, *Understanding Violent Conflict*, pp. 14, 113.

79   Kilavuz, *Understanding Violent Conflict*, p. 14.

80   Kilavuz, *Understanding Violent Conflict*, p. 119.

81   Matteo Fumagalli, 'Framing Ethnic Minority Mobilisation in Central Asia: The Cases of the Uzbeks in Kyrgyzstan and Tajikistan', *Europe-Asia Studies*, Vol. 59, No. 4 (2007), p. 575, n. 18.

The elites in a single region may have divergent interests, making it difficult to accurately predict political behaviour based on region of origin. And as the political environment changes, the nature of these regional bases may also change.[82] Regional loyalty is not a 'definite or reliable criterion' as some politicians will cooperate with whomever has the strongest network and switch their allegiance when it is in their own private interest to do so. A client will be loyal to his patron (for example, a *kolkhoz* boss or an *obkom* secretary) as long as the patron continually provides the benefits and resources ('providing employment, promotions, assistance, welfare, permits, access to important goods and services, land, etc').[83] Lawrence Markowitz also rejects the notion of unitary regional political blocs in Tajikistan. He instead stresses the political contestations within these 'blocs' as well as the individual crosscutting ties between the blocs.[84]

'Clans', Elite Families and Patronage Networks: Corruption in Action

In a situation in which lawfulness of means of achieving state goals was of secondary importance, those 'who played by the informal rules could be assured of protection … The corrupt system was widely understood, and, for many years, quite stable'.[85] In Tajikistan, informal political, parochial, kinship and criminal networks often overlapped and were inseparable from one another. The life and career of Abdumalik Abdullojonov, the prime minister of independent Tajikistan from 1992 to 1993, is especially illustrative in this sense.[86] His rise began in 1983, when he divorced his Ossetian wife and married the daughter of the chief KGB officer responsible for the Nov district (now Spitamen). The bride's mother happened to head the procurement authority of the same district. Almost immediately, the hitherto inconspicuous engineer was appointed director of the Nov bakery. Connections within the KGB helped Abdullojonov shortly afterwards: acts of embezzlement were uncovered at the bakery, but he avoided jail and was even promoted to deputy minister of grain products of Tajikistan. At this juncture he started to build his own entourage. Abdullojonov pulled some of his former subordinates out of prison and placed

---

82   Kilavuz, *Understanding Violent Conflict*, p. 14. Kilavuz notes that the regionally based power networks are not 'permanent and fixed categories'.

83   Kilavuz, *Understanding Violent Conflict*, pp. 121, 123.

84   Markowitz, *Collapsed and Prebendal States in Post-Soviet Eurasia*, p. 4.

85   Jim Leitzel, Clifford Gaddy and Michael Alexeev, 'Mafiosi and Matrioshki: Organised Crime and Russian Reform', *The Brookings Review*, Vol. 13, No. 1 (Winter 1995), p. 27.

86   Details of Abdullojonov's biography were collected during a number of interviews in Dushanbe and Khujand in February–April 1995 and also derive from an extensive article in *Sadoi Mardum* (11 June 1994) as well as from a book by a well-known Tajik politician (Nasriddinov, *Tarkish*, pp. 236–86).

them throughout the republic. More than one furtive director of a bakery found protection from deputy minister, later minister, Abdullojonov, in return for particular services. The most spectacular case involved Partov Davlatov—head of the grain procurement authority in the city of Tursunzoda. The Inspectorate of the Ministry of Finances produced a 946-page report in early 1991 in which Davlatov was accused of stealing thousands of tonnes of grain. Abdullojonov sacked Davlatov, only to appoint him to a similar position in the capital city of Dushanbe a few months later, after destroying all evidence of malfeasance. Davlatov instantaneously turned the Dushanbe baking combine into his personal enterprise, where all 400 employees were either his relatives or originated from his native village. Abdullojonov's positions in the republic grew even stronger after the collapse of the Soviet Union when grain, which constitutes the basic (and sometimes the only) element of people's rations in Tajikistan, became a scarce commodity and selling stolen grain on the black market became an exceptionally profitable occupation. With the absence of superior independent control authorities, it also became, in Partov Davlatov's words, 'a very easy occupation, since all leading officials in the Ministries of Grain Production and Finance and other agencies involved are actually our people'.[87]

At the beginning of 1992, Abdumalik Abdullojonov's personal wealth was widely rumoured to exceed 2 billion roubles. He had loyal protégés in every corner of Tajikistan, and after becoming prime minister in September 1992, he worked feverishly to promote them to higher positions. Thus, Abdujalil Homidov, formerly director of the Nov bakery, was made chairman of the executive committee of the Leninobod region; Timur Mirzoev, a distant relation of Abdullojonov, received the post of mayor of Dushanbe; Farhod Mirpochoev, Abdullojonov's nephew, became adviser to the Cabinet of Ministers, and so on. Much in line with the changing times, Abdullojonov was behind the creation of several private firms (Edland, Somoniyon, Tojikbonkbiznes, Timur-malik) that easily received export licences and lavish credits from the state. Even three years after Abdullojonov's dismissal, so many people owed their positions and influence to him that he was seldom criticised for his deeds and still remained in the public service of his country, as Tajikistan's ambassador to Turkmenistan. He eventually fell too far from grace, however, and fled into a comfortable exile in California.[88]

The example of Abdumalik Abdullojonov's patronage network is not typical for Tajikistan, in the sense that it was constructed primarily along professional linkages and encompassed people of different nationalities and from different regions of Tajikistan who could relatively easily break away after their patron's

---

87   Nasriddinov, *Tarkish*, p. 247.
88   In early 2013, Abdullojonov narrowly escaped extradition to Tajikistan from Ukraine, his former location of university studies, which he was visiting on business.

dismissal. This is exactly what happened to Abdujalil Homidov, who was in hostile opposition to Abdullojonov when the latter was running for president in 1994. In their ideal state, patron–client webs in Tajikistan bear an imprint of kinship solidarity and are characterised by: a) less pronounced inequality and asymmetry in interaction amongst those involved; b) lifelong endurance; c) more diffused spheres of penetration—far beyond strictly professional activities; and d) relative closeness. These hierarchal structures could be, with some qualifications, referred to as clans, for they have some consonance with the attributes of a classic agnate clan

- common ancestry of the nucleus of the entity
- territorial unity (the clan coincides with the local group)
- social integration inside the clan—in particular, the coopting of new members through marriage.[89]

The importance and authority of the patriarchal authority figure within the 'clans', or rather extended families, are reflected in the fact that many of the 'clan divisions' are named after them.[90] And far from being a new phenomenon, some of the elite families have been prominent since before the Soviet era,[91] an example being the Arabovs of northern Tajikistan.[92] Rural elites, in particular, engage in strategically sending younger members to urban areas to expand their network and its ability to access resources. The urban Tajik is often not an 'isolated entity', but rather in fact still a part of the rural networks. He/she has many connections to the 'extended family or clan' that is based in the village or region of origin. Family elders push an individual member towards a certain profession and expect that the city-dweller will provide benefits and resources to family members back in the village. And reciprocally, the city-dweller often seeks resources such as agricultural products from the extended rural family.[93] Schoeberlein-Engel gives the same description of the urban family member providing resources from the city to rural relatives; however, he specifically names the 'rural elite' as engaging in this strategic behaviour of sending their children to the city for a university or technical education. He notes that many of them will return, but others will remain in the city in order for the extended family to access 'scarce' resources.[94]

---

89   Adapted from: N. A. Butinov, 'Obschina, sem'ia, rod', *Sovetskaia Etnografiia*, No. 2 (1968), p. 91.

90   Mikulskii, *The History of Civil War in Tajikistan*, p. 12, as cited in Nekbakhtshoev, *Clan Politics*, p. 32. The example of several extended families (*tup*) in a village in northern Tajikistan is given by Mikulskii: tup-i Niyozi, tup-i Hofizi, tup-i Qozigi, and tup-I Mullotolibi.

91   Schoeberlein-Engel, *Identity in Central Asia*, p. 276.

92   Nourzhanov, 'Alternative Social Institutions and the Politics of Neo-Patrimonialism in Tajikistan', n.p.

93   Mikulskii, *The History of Civil War in Tajikistan*, p. 14, as cited in Nekbakhtshoev, *Clan Politics*, p. 55. See also: Poliakov, *Everyday Islam*, p. 130; Tett, *Ambiguous Alliances*, pp. 66–7.

94   Schoeberlein-Engel, *Identity in Central Asia*, p. 277.

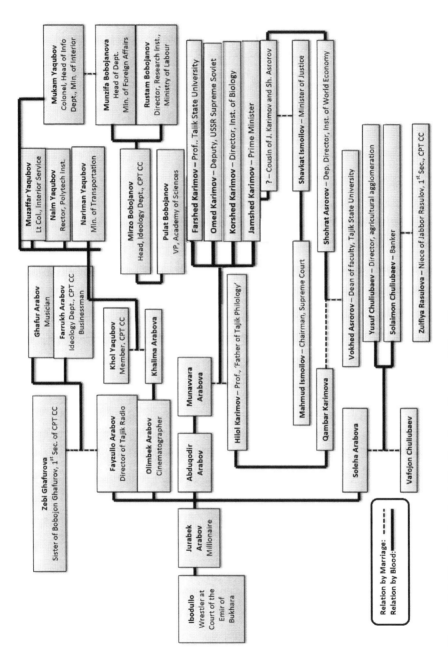

Figure 5.1 The Leninobod-Kanibodom Group of Families

Source: Author's research.

Two 'clans' from different parts of Tajikistan featured prominently in the republic's life in the postwar period.[95] The Leninobod-Kanibodom clan (Figure 5.1) had its base in the north of the republic and consisted of six major families: the Arabovs (Bukhara-Leninobod), the Yaqubovs (Leninobod), the Karimovs (Kanibodom), the Asrorovs (Leninobod), the Chuliubaevs (Leninobod) and the Bobojanovs (Leninobod-Dushanbe). The Arabov family, the stem of the clan, migrated to Khujand from Bukhara in the late nineteenth century. While not belonging to the prestigious status groups of *sayids*, its members traced their roots to the times of Arab rule, of which their family name was an indication. Jurabek Arabov was a successful entrepreneur and land developer under the tsarist regime and in 1917 managed to transfer all his capital to Germany. In 1925, he was executed by the OGPU, but legends about his unclaimed treasures linger in Tajikistan.

The Asrorovs, as an old family from Bukhara, enjoyed great respect and bestowed additional lustre on people connected with them. From the 1940s to the 1960s, Khol Yaqubov and Hilol Karimov joined them and subsequently played a significant role in expanding the power of the clan. Yaqubov was responsible for agricultural matters, sheep-breeding in particular, in the central committee, and Karimov was an influential member of the Tajik intelligentsia. He was the creator of the first textbooks of contemporary Tajik, and he and his relatives for decades dominated academia in Tajikistan. In a situation in which education remained a relatively rare commodity but presented a crucial element to social mobility, the ability to control admission to tertiary institutions inevitably gave certain groups within Tajikistan's prestigious elite a valuable resource to offer in exchange for favours. A sociological poll conducted amongst school-leavers in the republic in May–June 1989 yielded results that generally confirm this postulate (Table 5.7).

Table 5.7 Main Criteria for Admission to Higher Education Institutions

Knowledge	Well-connected relatives	Bribes	Relatives in educational institutions	Regionalism and patrimonialism
35.2%	34.4%	32.2%	22.5%	19.2%

Note: Each respondent could give two preferences.

Source: R. Alimov and M. Saidov, *Natsionalnyi vopros: raschety i proschety* (Dushanbe: Irfon, 1991), p. 93.

In later years, Hilol Karimov's son, Jamshed Karimov, became the pivotal member of the clan. He was born in 1940, educated in Moscow and for a long time

---

95   Data for the genealogical schemes were collected during fieldwork in Tajikistan in 1994–95. The authors would like to express gratitude to M. A. Arabov—the oldest surviving son of Abduqodir Arabov, who made invaluable comments and alterations to them.

worked in the Tajik State University, where he acquired the degree of Doctor of Economics. In 1983, he was appointed the deputy chairman of the State Planning Committee of Tajikistan and in 1988 was promoted to head it, with the concomitant rank of deputy chairman of the Council of Ministers. During 1989–91, Jamshed Karimov held the important position of first secretary of Dushanbe *gorkom*. In 1992, he returned to the government as first deputy prime minister; in December 1994 he became prime minister and served in that position until February 1996. Several cabinet members owed their posts directly to Karimov—Shavkat Ismoilov, minister of justice, for one. It was Karimov's support that allowed Ismoilov to retain his portfolio during the tumultuous period in early 1995 when President Rahmon was extremely dissatisfied with his performance. Entrepreneur Solaimon Chuliubaev and the commercial bank Sharq with which he was closely connected increased their operations dramatically thanks to the benevolent attitude of the prime minister's office.

According to information supplied by a member, the clan's families met regularly to discuss household and business matters. There is no longer strict subordination to elders, but the oldest surviving Arabov—Mamadqul, son of Abduqodir—always presided over ceremonial gatherings despite his modest position as a director of documentary films. Junior members of the clan were encouraged to pursue careers in such relatively new fields as business and the diplomatic service. In the immediate post-independence era, some members had already found employment with the Ministry of Foreign Affairs and foreign missions in Dushanbe—the Organisation for Security and Cooperation in Europe (OSCE) in particular.

The second clan (Figure 5.2) is of special interest because it has been developing in strict coordination with the sociopolitical processes in Tajikistan. Aqasharif Juraev, whose centenary was widely marked in 1995, was born in Darvoz (Qalai Khumb) and throughout his life remained an ardent propagandist of its traditional music and folklore culture. As an extraordinarily talented musician, he was amongst five or six Tajiks who were allowed to travel abroad from the 1940s to the 1960s. His tours of Iran in 1957 and of Afghanistan in 1959 attracted tens of thousands of admirers. Juraev was a friend of first secretary Tursun Uljaboev, who helped him and his big family to settle comfortably in Dushanbe. His son Qandil, a member of the Presidium of the Supreme Soviet of Tajikistan, was also an outspoken advocate of interests of the southern mountainous districts—for example, he vehemently opposed the abolition of the Gharm *oblast* in 1955.

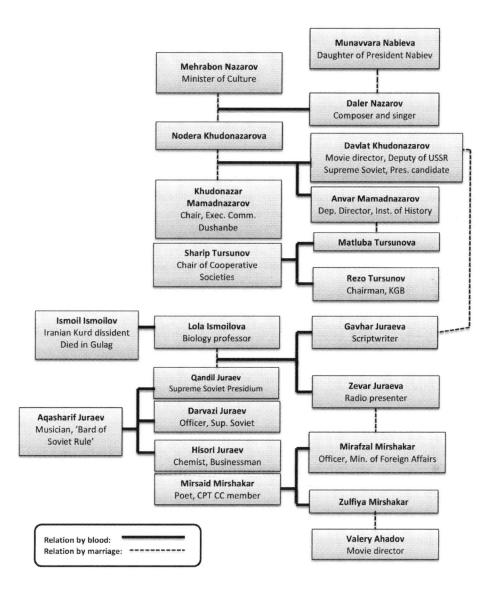

Figure 5.2 The Gharm-Pamirs Group of Families

Source: Author's research.

Mirsaid Mirshakar, the author of the gigantic poem 'Lenin at the Pamirs', stayed on good terms with all postwar party leaders in Tajikistan. He was richly decorated for his literary works glorifying Soviet rule, ascended to the CPT CC membership and finally was elected chairman of the Supreme Soviet of Tajikistan in 1966. He patronised scores of young Pamiri poets and writers and made a substantial contribution to the establishment of a thriving community of intellectuals from Badakhshan in Dushanbe. This was a significant accomplishment, since in the 1950s and 1960s people from Gharm and the Pamirs were rapidly losing ground in Tajikistan's political structures. The appointment of Mehrabon Nazarov as minister of culture in 1966 should be regarded as an exception. The younger generation of the clan in question realised itself mostly in creative and artistic capacities. Davlat Khudonazarov, arguably the brightest of them all, became a symbol of the Pamiri cultural renaissance in the late 1980s. He was elected as a deputy to the last Supreme Soviet of the USSR and made numerous contacts amidst political figures in Moscow in the late Gorbachev period. His relation, colleague and close friend Valery Ahadov became famous throughout the USSR as the director of popular comedy movies. Links with the Moscow intelligentsia established by Khudonazarov and Ahadov proved to be useful for Khudonazarov's political career—during the 1991 presidential campaign in Tajikistan, he managed to use Moscow's TV channels to canvass the electorate. Needless to say, Khudonazarov's clan did a good job mobilising the masses to vote for him, too: he received an almost 100 per cent result in the Pamirs.

Almost every locality in Tajikistan can boast one or more patronage networks. They may take the form of a purely cliental dyad, as in Abdumalik Abdullojonov's case, or that of 'clans'—kinship structures with primarily horizontal links and tacit obligations. They can run to the national level and beyond, but they can also be confined to a certain village or district. The point is that all these informal organisations have always played an important role in regulating life and channelling resources within the community in Tajikistan. S. N. Eisenstadt has made a general observation for the USSR that patron–client relations there, 'just as in most modern democratic societies', constituted 'above all an addendum to the institutional centre of the society'.[96] This notion was only partly true for Tajikistan with its still potent traditional society; the formalised exchange prevailed there so long as uniform institutionalised organisations executed effective social control, through coercion and meeting the basic needs of the majority of the populace.

Informal exchange and its most obvious form—corruption—were tacitly recognised parts of political life in Tajikistan. In 1975, A. Schelochinin, procurator-general of Tajikistan, disclosed the details of a major fraud in the

---

96   Eisenstadt and Roniger, *Patrons, Clients and Friends*, p. 50.

republic's system of consumer goods retailers, which ostensibly ran 'for decades' and implicated Tajikistan's minister of the food industry, a deputy minister of trade and 28 directors of shops and warehouses who 'had developed their own standards of behaviour, their own morale and office ethics'.[97] Those exposed usually received relatively mild penalties, unless Moscow directly ordered otherwise.[98] Belonging to the *nomenklatura* on the one hand and to a patronage network on the other was the best guarantee against imprisonment. Over the period 1965–90 only nine officials were punished for official crimes in Tajikistan (two were removed from their posts and seven were incarcerated)—the lowest figure in all five Central Asian republics.[99]

Bribery was instrumental in fulfilling economic plans. The *Kommunist* deplored the methods of a certain district party committee secretary, who 'intercepted fertilisers and fodder designated for others. He acquired them using bribes collected from the *kolkhozes* of his district.'[100] There existed a fairly rational system of bribes along the following chain: director of a collective farm or industrial enterprise, *raikom* secretary, *obkom* secretary, minister or the CPT CC secretary. Eventually, it came to resemble a taxation system, since the accrued funds were spent mostly on economic development and social welfare.[101] Promotions, mentions in the awards list or honorary titles were to be paid for separately. Another ingenious way of amassing shady money was based on manipulation of cotton procurement. Unlike their colleagues in Uzbekistan, officials in Tajikistan did not indulge in upward quantitative distortion. They preferred instead to decrease the fibre content in raw cotton (from the average of 34.4 per cent in 1962 to 29.4 and even 18 per cent in 1984), which gave them a robust additional revenue of 140 roubles per tonne gathered.[102] Given the fact that in the 1980s the annual cotton crop in Tajikistan was in the vicinity of 900 000 t, there could be as much as 126 million roubles in unregistered profits from cotton sales a year (of which collective farms retained 50 per cent), amounting to approximately 8 per cent of the entire republican budget.[103]

---

97   *Kommunist Tadzhikistana*, 5 April 1975.

98   Another interesting case occurred in 1961, when a group of high-ranking officials in Dushanbe was caught red-handed embezzling public funds to build private homes (one of the accused was Mahmud Ismoilov, then chairman of the Juridical Commission of the Council of Ministers). It took one year, three articles in the central *Izvestiia* newspaper and intervention on the part of the CPSU CC to induce the Tajik leadership to take any serious action in this regard. See: *The Current Digest of the Post-Soviet Press*, Vol. 14, No. 16 (1962), p. 28; Vol. 14, No. 24 (1962), p. 24.

99   Clark, 'Crime and Punishment in Soviet Officialdom, 1965–1990', p. 269.

100   G. Zimanas, 'Mestnichestvo—vredny perezhitok', *Kommunist*, No. 2 (1963), p. 78.

101   In the Kolkhozobod district a *raikom* secretary used to require chairmen of 13 collective farms to contribute 5000 roubles a year to the 'slush fund' in order to organise summer camps for children, build kindergartens, and so on (Taped interview with Moazza Osmanova, deputy head of Kolkhozabad *hukumat* [district administration], 27 March 1995).

102   Seliunin, 'Bremia deistvii', p. 186.

103   Calculations are based on: *Kommunist Tadzhikistana*, 6 December 1985.

It is worth noting that long career association with Tajikistan made non-indigenous officials equally susceptible to local models of exchange and behaviour. For example, P. S. Obnosov, a Russian second secretary of the CPT CC, posted to Tajikistan in order to monitor the activities of first secretary T. Uljaboev, formed a sort of *entente cordiale* with him. Together they even managed for some time to block the work of the special investigative commission sent in 1961 to Tajikistan by the CPSU Central Committee. The CPSU CC Presidium member F. R. Kozlov, who came to Dushanbe in order to rectify the affair, accused Obnosov of 'having been Tajikicised' and of concealing facts of corruption and mismanagement.[104] As it became clear from Obnosov's speech at the thirteenth congress of the CPT (in February 1960), he had created his personal clique of protégés in the republic, which included native first secretaries of the Gharm, Komsomolobod and Jerghatol district committees and Uroteppa city committee.[105]

It may be appropriate to outline the major attributes, or role expectations, of a member of Tajikistan's governing elite under Soviet rule

- conformity with the set of rules and directives prescribed by Moscow
- commitment to the cause of the development of the republic
- development of personal political resources inside and outside Tajikistan
- conflict avoidance, settlement of disputes with peers as unobtrusively as possible.

As long as a national leader could strike the right balance between contradictory loyalties to the centre and to the republic, as long as he managed to build up and maintain networks of informal exchange without attracting too much attention from the centre's control organs, and as long as he could successfully lobby for centralised allocations, his job would be secure and he would be in a position to make policies, especially in the cultural sphere, that stuck. After Uljaboev's dismissal, the leaders of Tajikistan more or less succeeded in these endeavours, and the conclusion made by Gregory Gleason that 'by the early 1980s, with the end of Brezhnev's *zastoi* period, the bureaucratic structures within the fifteen national republics of the USSR had developed an unprecedented basis of internal political resourcefulness'[106] was fully applicable.

Regional Elite Competition

As the ratio of the titular nationality serving in positions of power within the governments of the Uzbek and Tajik SSRs increased, it lessened the importance

---

104 Muhabbatsho, 'Fojiai Uljaboev', p. 28.
105 *XIII s'ezd kommunisticheskoi partii Tadzhikistana*, p. 172.
106 Gleason, *Federalism and Nationalism*, p. 131.

of cleavages between the titular nationality and non-titular groups such as the Russians and increased the importance of cleavages within the titular nationalities, therefore increasing the social and political significance of 'regionalism'.[107] Khujandis from Leninobod dominated the Tajik Communist Party and the government, but they did not hold positions of power exclusively, as the central Soviet government attempted to maintain a balance between the regions in regards to elite appointments.[108] According to Davlat Khudonazarov, from 1956 to 1961, first secretary Tursunboy Uljaboev 'balance[d] the representation of the regions' and distributed resources equally before being removed on the pretext of falsifying cotton production figures, a very common practice at the time.[109] The argument that Leninobod politically dominated Tajikistan is qualified by Shirin Akiner. She notes the much larger population, higher levels of education and political awareness, as well as the industrialised economy of Leninobod and argues that it would be natural that this area would produce the elite of the state.[110] Matteo Fumagalli makes a similar argument, crediting the Leninobodi elite's dominance in the Tajik SSR to 'economic, socio-cultural and geographic factors'.[111]

At the republic level, the Soviet government divided the state apparatus among the various factions, which produced competition for power and resources among the different region-based factions.[112] The Leninobod/Khujand-based 'faction' came to dominate the Tajik government after World War II.[113] The Khujandi elite maintained their dominant position by constantly changing the administrative status of the other regions. The elite from other regions were not able to develop a region-wide patronage network as they lost their province (*oblast*, *viloyat*) status and found their networks disrupted.[114] There was, however, a level of power-sharing involving the Kulobi elites in a patronage relationship starting in the 1970s.[115] Of course, the Kulobis were in the junior position. The various reasons given for the relationship are that it was a response

---

107   Kilavuz, *Understanding Violent Conflict*, p. 94. Kilavuz notes that in Tajikistan the Tajiks, between the 1940s and the 1960s, held 45 per cent of the positions in the Communist Party. By 1980 it was 61 per cent.

108   Kilavuz, *Understanding Violent Conflict*, pp. 97, 102–4.

109   Khudonazar, 'The Conflict in Tajikistan', pp. 254–5. Khudonazarov categorises Uljaboev as an ethnic Uzbek. All other sources list him as Tajik.

110   Akiner, *Tajikistan*, pp. 19–20.

111   Fumagalli, 'Framing Ethnic Minority Mobilisation in Central Asia', p. 575, n. 18.

112   Roy, 'Is the Conflict in Tajikistan a Model for Conflicts throughout Central Asia?', p. 146; Saodat Olimova, 'Opposition in Tajikistan: Pro et Contra', in *Democracy and Pluralism in Muslim Eurasia*, ed. Yaacov Ro'i (London and New York: Frank Cass, 2004), p. 250.

113   Shahram Akbarzadeh, 'Why Did Nationalism Fail in Tajikistan?' *Europe-Asia Studies*, Vol. 48, No. 7 (1996), p. 1108; Barnett R. Rubin, 'Central Asian Wars and Ethnic Conflicts—Rebuilding Failed States', *United Nations Human Development Report Office Occasional Paper* (2004), p. 10; Rubin, 'Russian Hegemony and State Breakdown in the Periphery', p. 151; Foroughi, 'Tajikistan', p. 46.

114   Kilavuz, *Understanding Violent Conflict*, pp. 108–12.

115   Akbarzadeh, 'Why Did Nationalism Fail in Tajikistan', p. 1108; Rubin, 'Central Asian Wars and Ethnic Conflicts', p. 10; Rubin, 'Russian Hegemony and State Breakdown in the Periphery', p. 151; Foroughi, 'Tajikistan', p. 46.

to the Leninobodi elite being challenged by local competitors or even, as argued by Stephane Dudoignon, that is was a result of economic exchanges between the two involving cotton.[116] Indeed, the creation of the South Tajik Territorial Manufacturing Complex resulted in the creation of stronger ties between Khujand and Kulob (see the earlier section on Kulob). As for the other groups, Akiner stresses that the power held by Leninobodis (mostly from Khujand) was not exclusive. She argues that positions in the higher levels of the Tajik government were often held by Russians, Pamiris and Gharmis as part of the power balancing of the elite;[117] however, the positions held by Gharmis and Pamiris were generally not portfolios that held significant power, an example being the chairmanship of the Supreme Soviet (see further below). And during this time the Tajik SSR's large Uzbek minority in the north had an informally protected status thanks to the Tajik Communist Party's close links to Uzbekistan and the political domination of the Leninobodi faction that secured benefits for the north's population, including the Uzbeks.[118] The exceptions, according to Akiner, were the Kulobis, who, despite holding many high-ranking positions in the security forces and having started a patronage-network relationship with the Leninobodis in the 1970s, were generally marginalised at the national level. Akiner offers an alternative explanation for the exclusion of Kulobi elites from the national level: lack of interest in pursuing positions outside Kulob. Within Kulob the local elites had autonomy and development projects that were directly funded by the central Soviet government, as well as enjoying 'status, wealth (often illegally acquired) and a social environment in which they were at ease'.[119] As a result, there was not a need to pursue appointment at the Tajik SSR level. Still, some secondary positions below Khujandis in the bureaucracy in Dushanbe were given to Kulobis.[120]

Concerning the Gharmi elite, the position of chairman of the Supreme Soviet of Tajikistan was 'reserved' for Gharmis; however, for almost the entire Soviet era it was a position of little power and influence that held no significant economic or

---

116   Rubin, 'Russian Hegemony and State Breakdown in the Periphery', p. 151. Another possible factor is the incident in which, in the early 1970s, a Khujandi sent to Kulob to head the regional government was found dead, possibly assassinated, in his Kulob hotel room one day after arriving. See: John Anderson, *The International Politics of Central Asia* (Manchester: Manchester University Press, 1997), p. 176; Igor Rotar, 'Voina bez pobeditelei', *Nezavisimaia Gazeta* (13 September 1992), p. 6; Gavhar Juraeva, 'Ethnic Conflict in Tajikistan', in *Ethnic Conflict in the Post-Soviet World: Case Studies and Analysis*, eds Leokadia Drobizheva, R. Gottemoeller, C. McArdle Kelleher and L. Walker (London: M. E. Sharpe, 1996), p. 260.

117   Akiner, *Tajikistan*, pp. 19–20.

118   Matteo Fumagalli, *The Dynamics of Uzbek Ethno-Political Mobilization in Kyrgyzstan and Tajikistan: 1991–2003* (PhD Thesis: University of Edinburgh, 2005), p. 217; Shale Horowitz, 'Explaining Post-Soviet Ethnic Conflicts: Using Regime Type to Discern the Impact and Relative Importance of Objective Antecedents', *Nationalities Papers*, Vol. 29, No. 4 (2001), p. 650. The close relationship between the Leninobodis and Uzbekistan was partly owing to Tajikistan's status as part of Uzbekistan from 1924 to 1929, when Tajikistan was an autonomous republic within the Uzbek SSR. Also, until 1929 Khujand was part of the Uzbek SSR.

119   Akiner, *Tajikistan*, pp. 19–21.

120   Collins, *Clan Politics and Regime Transition in Central Asia*, pp. 163, 199.

bureaucratic decision-making authority.[121] As a result, Gharmis had 'relatively little stake' in national-level power structures and a greater one in the 'emergent market economy' and in the national academy of sciences, which Barnett Rubin calls the 'principle institution of national cultural identity'.[122] The exclusion from government and economic institutions meant that Gharmis could not create any patronage networks on the scale that the Leninobodis and Kulobis could,[123] at the national and provincial levels, respectively.

Markowitz notes that the party positions at district (*raikom*) and province (*obkom*) levels became the focus of local power struggles. From these positions one could access resources from the centre and even work towards higher-level postings. As these positions were 'aggressively sought after', local political manoeuvring became 'perhaps the most fluid and uncertain venue of political contestation within the Soviet state structure'.[124] In Qurghonteppa the Leninobodi elite installed their own people (Leninobodis, those of Leninobodi descent or ethnic Uzbeks) as collective farm chairs and district *raikom* secretaries in order to control the region's wealth-producing bases, while Kulob, with its relatively modest economic base, was of much less interest to the Leninobodi elite. The stability of the cadres under Brezhnev took away a tool for the Leninobodis to control southern Tajikistan: the regular turnover of local officials. As a result the Leninobodis used their national-level positions to distribute patronage and manage networks based on resources distributed from the national level. Using resources derived from their patronage relationships with the centre, local elites in Kulob and Qurghonteppa were able to maintain local patronage networks. By the late Soviet era the local elites in Qurghonteppa and Kulob were using the 'informal economy' as a power base, but still needed their relationships with the Leninobodi-dominated centre to protect this base from scrutiny.[125] By the late 1980s Gharmi Tajiks, Kulobi Tajiks and Uzbeks were fighting over administrative positions in Qurghonteppa;[126] however, this was a time when state capacity was steadily weakening—resulting in the inability of the government to effectively manage this competition.

∗ ∗ ∗

The political system in Tajikistan under Soviet rule was formed according to the basic principles of Moscow's nationality policy, which in its turn was yet

---

121   Rubin, 'Russian Hegemony and State Breakdown in the Periphery', p. 160, n. 64.
122   Rubin, 'Russian Hegemony and State Breakdown in the Periphery', pp. 151–2.
123   Rubin, 'Russian Hegemony and State Breakdown in the Periphery', pp. 151–2.
124   Markowitz, *Collapsed and Prebendal States in Post-Soviet Eurasia*, pp. 47–8.
125   Markowitz, *Collapsed and Prebendal States in Post-Soviet Eurasia*, pp. 34, 56, 59–60.
126   Niyazi, 'Tajikistan I', p. 154.

'another aspect of the all-out mobilisation of the population for state building and extensive economic growth. And, with the aid of repression ... this worked about as well as the rest of the system during its decades of expansion under Stalin and Khrushchev.'[127] The Kremlin managed to create the administration in Tajikistan, which was largely nativised, reasonably efficient and thoroughly dependent on centralised decision-making. The bureaucratic structures of the Communist Party of Tajikistan constituted its centrepiece, and, from the republic level downwards, in the power triangle made by party committees, coercive organs and legislative bodies, the last played the least important role.

The notion of 'Russian hegemony' in the Soviet multinational state[128] could be misleading; there never was a deliberate policy of Russification in the political realm in the USSR. It is much more appropriate to speak about the policy of complete subjugation of national interests to the 'hegemonistic strength of the sole true *minority*'[129] in the country—that is, the CPSU leadership. As a result, the Tajik political elite was afflicted by a dichotomy between allegiance to the central party institutions, to which it owed its privileged position in the first place, and its native cast and the specific cultural environment in which it had to operate. The particulars of compromise reached between these two opposing tendencies varied, but until the mid 1980s the general trend was towards the emergence of a cohesive self-regulated state bureaucracy in Tajikistan that was in a position to implement directives and redistribute resources sent from Moscow in a rather flexible manner, operating beyond the prescribed rules of administration. In Martha Brill Olcott's characterisation: 'the conditions of *zastoi* ... were well suited to Central Asia's party elite. They ruled like feudal overlords, free to steal and spend as they wished, once they had dispatched the required tribute to Moscow.'[130] Patterns of informal understandings, semi-legal and illegal exchanges, and patronage networks were widespread; in the Brezhnev era, 'the system of social relations based on the combination of the feeling of impunity, mafia-type solidarity and security from the so-called "common people" embraced the not so narrow circle of persons. It included not only *obkom* secretaries but academics, journalists and other intellectuals as well.'[131]

In Tajikistan, perhaps more than elsewhere in the USSR, the process of decision-making was concealed from public view; it was essentially crypto-politics,

---

127 Martin Malia, *The Soviet Tragedy: A History of Socialism in Russia, 1917–1991* (New York: The Free Press, 1994), p. 439.
128 Gail Lapidus, Victor Zaslavsky and Philip Goldman, eds *From Union to Commonwealth: Nationalism and Separatism in the Soviet Republics* (Cambridge: Cambridge University Press, 1992), p. 5.
129 Guy G. Imart, 'A Unique Empire', *Central Asian Survey*, Vol. 6, No. 4 (1987), p. 16.
130 Martha Brill Olcott, 'Central Asia's Political Crisis', in *Russia's Muslim Frontiers*, ed. Dale F. Eickelman (Bloomington: Indiana University Press, 1993), p. 51.
131 A. Bystritsky and D. Shusharin, '"Ten" Brezhneva menia usynovila', *Literaturnaia Gazeta*, 30 March 1994, p. 11.

concentrated largely within the limits of the CPT Central Committee and its apparatus. Under Brezhnev the governing elite in Tajikistan transformed itself into a self-stabilising oligarchy that could retain its status even without resorting to blatant coercion. The overall sum of authority enjoyed by the communist state was impressive; it effectively coped with the problems of legitimation, compliance and distribution in Tajikistan. At the same time, as this chapter and the previous one showed, its success in penetrating a number of social institutions and containing rival identities and loyalties within society was much more modest; this was fraught with potential for political upheavals. This opportunity would arise along with the reforms implemented by Gorbachev.

6. Experimentation, Turmoil and Fragmentation under Gorbachev, 1985–1991

On 24 May 1979, the US Embassy in Moscow sent a cable (in reply to an assessment by the US diplomatic mission in Kabul arguing that the Soviets were worried about stability in Central Asia) that said:

> All information that we have been able to gather on this region [Soviet Central Asia] testifies that Moscow controls the situation completely. During frequent visits of Embassy officers to Soviet Central Asia few signs of discontent were discovered. Central Asian republics under Soviet leadership have achieved considerable social and economic progress and have a higher standard of living than neighbouring districts of Iran and Afghanistan.[1]

The same year, 81 per cent of Uzbeks living in cities and 85 per cent of those living in rural areas said that they were satisfied with the fulfilment of the prime values of their lives.[2] Yet, just more than a decade later, much of the region witnessed ethnic conflict, fratricide and civil violence, or, at a minimum, tremendous deprivation. What allowed this to occur?

The answer is linked with the name of Mikhail Sergeevich Gorbachev, the last general secretary of the CPSU CC and the president of the USSR, and the policies implemented by him and a coterie of his associates known under the aggregate name of *perestroika*. This chapter attempts to analyse the impact of *perestroika* on patterns of modernisation, nation gestation and political authority in Tajikistan, and to explain why Tajiks in the immediate post-Soviet era, when asked whom they regarded as the biggest villain in world history, named Gorbachev, who took an impressive 13.5 per cent lead over the next contender—Adolf Hitler.[3]

---

1   Quoted in: V. Spolnikov and L. Mironov, 'Islamskie fundamentalisty v borbe za vlast'', *Aziia i Afrika segodnia*, No. 4 (1992), p. 26. The cable is available through the Cold War International History Project. The exact cable is titled: 'Afghanistan: Prospects for Soviet Intervention', AMEMBASSY Moscow to SECSTATE, Moscow 13083 (24 May 1979).

2   Iu. V. Arutiunian and Iu. V. Bromlei, 'A Sociological Profile of Soviet Nationalities: Ethnosociology Research Results', *Soviet Anthropology and Archeology*, Vol. 27, No. 1 (Summer 1988), p. 58.

3   *Vechernii Dushanbe*, 10 June 1994. Attitudes to Gorbachev remain very negative in Tajikistan. He is still the Soviet figure perceived most negatively. See: Evraziiskii monitor, 'Vospriyatie naseleniem novykh nezavisimykh gosudarstv istorii sovetskogo postsovetskogo periodov 11-ya volna, Aprel'–Mai 2009 g.', *Osnovnye rezul'taty Al'bom diagram* (30 June 2009), online: <http://www.eurasiamonitor.org/rus/research/event-158.html>

The Controversy of Centrally Planned Development

Stalin's strategy of forced industrialisation, which had transformed the USSR into the world's second-largest economy and allowed it to compete with a varying degree of success with the United States for global domination, was based primarily on the extensive means of growth: expansion of production was achieved through channelling natural and human resources to certain sectors of the economy, heavy industry in particular, at the expense of others. By 1960, however, 'it was clear to the Soviet leadership that the scope for further extensive growth was exhausted. Capital accumulation was at maximum levels and the labour resources of the country were fully mobilised.'[4] In-depth analyses of the state of the Soviet economy under Brezhnev and of his successors' attempts at reforming it can be found elsewhere;[5] however, the authors share Myron Rush's view that in 1985, when Gorbachev came to power, the USSR

> was not poised for a collapse, nor was it even in acute crisis ... The economy was stagnant and falling farther behind the West, but inflation was not a serious problem; agriculture ... fed the Soviet people adequately, perhaps better than in the past; and industry provided them with their basic needs. The economy had been in worse shape, arguably, in Khrushchev's last years, 1963 and 1964. There was no compelling need for the Soviet Union to enter on the dangerous path of systemic reform.[6]

The system had enough internal resources to stay afloat for decades, tackling the symptoms, if not the causes, of its numerous maladies.

In the case of Tajikistan, the most acute problems of the time were

- the continuing demographic explosion
- the inability of the centralised planned economy to sustain steady growth
- the declining living standards of the population
- the decaying environment.

As mentioned earlier, following incorporation into the Russian empire, Tajikistan experienced a demographic explosion: its annual growth between 1870 and 1917 was estimated at 1.2 to 1.5 per cent, compared with a meagre 0.2

---

4   Rutland, 'Economic Crisis and Reform', p. 202.
5   See, for instance: Alec Nove, *An Economic History of the USSR* (London: Penguin Books, 1990), pp. 362–79; Robert F. Miller, 'The Soviet Economy: Problems and Solutions in the Gorbachev View', in *Gorbachev at the Helm: A New Era in Soviet Politics?* eds R. F. Miller and T. H. Rigby (New York: Croom Helm, 1987), pp. 109–35.
6   Myron Rush, 'Fortune and Fate', *The National Interest*, No. 31 (Spring 1993), pp. 19, 21.

per cent in the first half of the nineteenth century.[7] This tendency gained further momentum under Soviet rule. By the mid 1970s, Tajikistan had overtaken all other republics of the USSR in terms of birth rate, which, coupled with its low mortality rate, gave it the highest natural growth in the Soviet Union (Table 6.1).

Table 6.1 Birth and Mortality Rates and Natural Population Growth in the USSR and Soviet Republics (per 1000 of population)

	Number of births			Number of deaths			Natural growth of population		
	1940	1960	1986	1940	1960	1986	1940	1960	1986
USSR	31.2	24.9	20.0	18.0	7.1	9.8	13.2	17.8	10.2
Russia	33.0	23.2	17.2	20.6	7.4	10.4	12.4	15.8	6.8
Uzbekistan	33.8	39.8	37.8	13.2	6.0	7.0	20.6	33.8	30.8
Tajikistan	30.6	33.5	42.0	14.1	5.1	6.8	16.5	28.4	35.2

Source: *Narodnoe khoziaistvo SSSR za 70 let* (Moscow: Finansy i statistika, 1987), pp. 406–9.

With its population doubling every 20 years, and reserves of cultivable land all but exhausted,[8] the demographic pressure[9] came to be felt in Tajikistan in no uncertain way. It has been estimated that in the predominantly peasant Central Asian society, an allotment of 0.28 ha of arable land per person is required to guarantee reproduction on a simple scale.[10] The corresponding figure for Tajikistan was considerably lower,[11] and, generally, it was incapable of producing enough food to meet domestic demand.[12] The south-western Qurghonteppa region was particularly inauspicious demographically: by 1989 its population density had reached 91.7 people per square kilometre—2.5 times the average for Tajikistan and far ahead of the second-most densely populated area, Leninobod (59.5).[13]

Even at the height of Soviet rule, regulation of land allotments at the local level (village or *kolkhoz*) tended to generate tension. An account of the 1983 gathering

---

7   Vladimir Bushkov, 'Tadzhikistan na ostrie demograficheskogo supervzryva', *Rossiia i musulmanskii mir*, Vol. 37, No. 7 (1995), p. 46.

8   In 1951–60, 341 000 ha of new agricultural lands were put into circulation; in 1961–70, 231 000 ha; in 1971–80, 144 000 ha; and in 1980–90 only 89 000 ha. See: *Narodnoe khoziaistvo Tadzhikskoi SSRv 1965g.* (Dushanbe: Statistika, 1966), p. 83; *Narodnoe khoziaistvo Tadzhikskoi SSR v 1988 godu* (Dushanbe: Irfon, 1990), p. 212; *Narodnoe khoziaistvo Tadzhikskoi SSR v 1990g.* (Dushanbe: Goskomstat TSSR, 1991), p. 163.

9   See: R. Turner, 'Tajiks Have the Highest Fertility Rates in Newly Independent Central Asia', *Family Planning Perspectives*, Vol. 25, No. 3 (May–June 1993), pp. 141–2.

10   V. Medvedev, 'Prazdnik obshchei bedy', *Druzhba narodov*, No. 8 (1990), p. 208.

11   For land and food provision figures for 1940–80, see: *Narodnoe khoziaistvo Tadzhikskoi SSR v 1979g.*, pp. 94, 104, 108; *Narodnoe khoziaistvo SSSR v 1979g.* (Moscow: Finansy i statistika, 1979), pp. 242, 253, 275; *Narodnoe khoziaistvo SSSR v 1989g.* (Moscow: Finansy i statistika, 1990), pp. 442, 467; *Narodnoe khoziaistvo SSSR za 70 let*, pp. 226–7, 259, 274–5.

12   In the 1980s, Tajikistan harvested 5–7 per cent of the quantity of grain it needed. See: *Komsomolets Tadzhikistana*, 11 October 1991.

13   Calculations are based on: *Itogi Vsesoiuznoi perepisi naseleniia 1989 goda po Tadzhikskoi SSR*, Vol. II, pp. 10–18.

of some 6000 inhabitants of the village of Surkh in northern Tajikistan, who had assembled to decide upon redistribution of parcels of privately held land, stated that, despite the presence of district party and soviet officials, 'there were moments when the discussion seemed to have become unmanageable. The strain began to tell, and nerves gave way.'[14] Six years later the same village and three other settlements of the Isfara *raion* found themselves in the epicentre of land disputes with adjacent districts of Kyrgyzstan. In July 1989 thousands of Tajiks and Kyrgyzs clashed, one person was killed and 27 were injured or wounded;[15] it took the leaders of the two republics and their superiors in Moscow more than one month to quell the 'Isfara–Batken incident'.[16]

The policy of economic development based primarily on rapid agricultural growth that had been imposed on Tajikistan by planning authorities in Moscow was not conducive to the migration of people from the countryside. In fact, in the postwar period the movement to urban centres was constantly declining: in 1960, 1 per cent of Tajikistan's rural population chose to settle in cities; in 1970, 0.8 per cent; and in 1976, 0.7 per cent.[17] In later years a process of real de-urbanisation became evident in the republic—an unprecedented phenomenon in the USSR. The share of city-dwellers dropped from 35 per cent in 1979 to 32 in 1990; in 1991 for the first time there was an absolute decline in the urban population.[18] Tajik experts have offered the following explanations for the weak migratory mobility of the agricultural population[19]

- skill levels are too low for industrial employment
- large family size and high birth rates create problems in finding adequate housing and childcare facilities in cities
- inadequate knowledge of Russian complicates the acquisition of 'city professions'
- strong urban–rural ties are a disincentive to move.

---

14   Anastasia Gelischanow, 'The Employment Situation in Tajikistan', *Radio Liberty Research Bulletin*, No. 26 (3231) (28 December 1983), RL 482/83.

15   *Ezhegodnik Bolshoi sovetskoi entsiklopedii* (Moscow: Sovetskaia entsiklopediia, 1990), p. 167.

16   The history of the conflict is as follows. In 1958, the Tajik *kolkhoz* named after Kalinin ceded 144 ha of its fallow lands to the namesake *kolkhoz* in the Batken *raion* of Kyrgyzstan. Thirty years later, the Kyrgyzs decided to build a huge irrigation canal in that area, thus allegedly depriving their Tajik neighbours of water. Additionally, due to imprecise mapping, the issue of ownership of a land parcel of 95 ha remained moot. By the late 1980s, the population on both sides of the administrative borders had grown to an extent where even this exiguous patch appeared a coveted prize. The inquiry instituted by the USSR Supreme Soviet commission concluded that 'outwardly the conflict looks like one between nationalities. In fact, however, it is based on socio-economic problems which have built up over years … The tension in the region is created by "land" issues: the shortage of farmland, the scarcity of water, the surplus manpower.' See: *BBC Summary of World Broadcasts*, Part I USSR (18 July 1989), SU/0511 B/2. See also the brief commentary in: Tishkov, *Ethnicity, Nationalism and Conflict in and after the Soviet Union*, p. 74.

17   R. K. Rahimov, *Sotsialno-ekonomicheskie problemy razvitiia Tadzhikskoi SSR* (Dushanbe: Donish, 1984), p. 43.

18   *Narodnoe khoziaistvo Tadzhikskoi SSR v 1990g.*, p. 7.

19   Khonaliev, *Trudovye resursy Tadzhikistana*, p. 15.

While accepting the validity of these arguments, it appears that at least two other fundamental factors are responsible for the laggard country-to-town migration. First, the Soviet system did not provide sufficient remuneration to industrial workers or skilled managers. Indeed, it would be very hard for a Tajik family with half a dozen children to survive on a bare salary. The story of a qualified builder who left Dushanbe, where he earned a decent wage of 350 roubles a month, for a remote village where he would get 70 roubles and still 'feel happy',[20] was a typical one. In the countryside a private plot generated the bulk of family income. A certain agronomist in 1981 received 2280 roubles in wages; his 50 apple trees fetched him another 15 000, and his two cows and some sheep saved him the trouble of buying meat and dairy in state shops.[21] The second factor is rooted in the traditionalism of Tajik society. As Aziz Niyazi has observed, 'young people are not at all enthusiastic about moving to towns, notwithstanding the fact that incomes in the rural areas are low. Many of the young people are bound by family ties, as it is not easy to get parental consent for moving away.'[22] In a patriarchal family every pair of working hands means additional output from its privately owned strip of land, even more so in a situation where tractors and other means of mechanisation are not readily available. Additionally, industrial employment is not a prestigious occupation for the eponymous population, who prefer to work in agriculture, trade and services.

Not surprisingly, a survey conducted in the early 1980s in Tajikistan revealed that 65 per cent of rural young people wanted to stay in the countryside, only 15 per cent wanted to move to the capital city, and 8 per cent to other towns.[23] In 1986, as many as 25.7 per cent of the working-age population may have been unemployed;[24] the figure for rural areas was higher—probably in the region of 35 per cent.[25] An estimate made in 1985 suggested that 7.1 million people would have to leave Central Asia before 2000 simply to maintain its existing level of national income per able-bodied inhabitant.[26] Admittedly, Tajikistan fared badly even compared with its neighbours: 'an absolute majority of the republic's

---

20   *Kommunist Tadzhikistana*, 31 May 1975.

21   'Why Do Central Asians Stay on Farms?' *The Current Digest of the Post-Soviet Press*, Vol. XXXV, No. 8 (March 1983), p. 2.

22   Niyazi, 'Tajikistan', p. 169.

23   'Why Do Central Asians Stay on Farms', p. 1.

24   McAuley, 'The Central Asian Economy in Comparative Perspective', p. 141.

25   The number of able-bodied people of working age not studying or working at state/cooperative enterprises. See: V. V. Vybornova and E. A. Dunaeva, 'Nereshennye protivorechiia kak istochnik mezhnatsionalnykh konfliktov', *Izvestiia AN TSSR. Seriia: Filosofiia i pravovedenie*, No. 3 (1992), p. 37.

26   William Fierman, 'Central Asian Youth and Migration', in *Soviet Central Asia: The Failed Transformation*, ed. William Fierman (Boulder, Colo.: Westview Press, 1991), p. 258.

population does not accept even modest attempts aimed at the reduction of population growth … The demographic situation in Tajikistan has passed the critical level and is no longer under control.'[27]

The leadership of Tajikistan was reluctant to acknowledge even the existence of such a problem. Not until 1985 did Rahmon Nabiev, first secretary of the CPT CC, publicly express concern at the fact that the growth of agricultural production in the republic lagged hopelessly behind population growth.[28] The first comprehensive set of legislation dealing with family planning was passed only in June 1988.[29] The centre remained equally incapable of dealing with the growing demographic pressure in the republic. A low-key program to move 15 000 Tajiks to sparsely populated areas of the USSR, the Khabarovsk *krai* in particular, was aborted soon after its inception in 1983 due to the unwillingness of the would-be settlers to leave their birthplaces.[30]

From the 1960s to the 1980s Tajikistan, like any other republic of the USSR, succumbed to two tendencies in the autarkic Soviet economy. On the one hand, the planning centre gradually lost its ability to control all the links in the economic mechanism due to its sheer expansion and complexity. On the other hand, branch ministries, most importantly 'base supermonopolies',[31] became ever more powerful in strategic decision-making. The ideals of the comprehensive, integrated development of Central Asia, if they ever existed at all, were eventually sacrificed to the interests of ministerial lobbyists in Moscow who craved unlimited government allocations for grandiose but hardly feasible projects in the region.

In order to cope with the burgeoning population growth it would have been natural to build low-cost and labour-intensive production enterprises in Tajikistan to utilise local resources. In the 1970s, investment of 1 million roubles could create more than 600 seamstress posts, 380–450 in the leather, textile or footwear industries, or 165 in food or cotton-processing, versus only 35–40 in

27 S. Poliakov, 'Politicheskii krizis v Tadzhikistane', *Rossiia i musulmanskii mir*, No. 5 (1992), p. 46.

28 *The Current Digest of the Post-Soviet Press*, Vol. XXXVII, No. 20 (1985), p. 21.

29 'Qarori Soveti Olii RSS Tojikiston dar borai tadbirhoi ta'mini muhofizati manfiathoi modar va kudak, behtar namudani sharoiti mehnatu maishati zanon va vus'at dodani fa'oliyyati onho dar hayyoti istehsoli va jam'iyyati', in *Sessiyyai hashtumi Soveti Olii RSS Tojikiston: Da'vati yozdahum; Hisoboti stenografi* (Dushanbe: Soveti Olii RSST, 1988), pp. 167–72. Still, contraception and other means of family planning have not been embraced by traditional society, and even 'urban Tajik women, students, factory workers and activists, have to plan the number of children in secret from their husbands'. See: Monogarova, 'Struktura sovremennoi gorodskoi sem'i tadzhikov', p. 24.

30 'Recruitment and Resettlement of Workers from Tajikistan', *Radio Liberty Research Bulletin*, No. 26 (3231) (29 June 1983), RL 247/83.

31 Ministries of energy, oil and gas, irrigation, ferrous and non-ferrous metallurgy, and fertilisers—a powerful agglomeration whose capital assets in 1987 exceeded those of the entire light industry fifty-six-fold. See: Iu. G. Alexandrov, 'Sredniaia Aziia: spetsificheskii sluchai ekonomicheskoi slaborazvitosti', *Vostok*, No. 5 (1991), p. 143.

the aluminium or chemical industries.[32] Yet it was precisely the last two that received rising capital allocations from Moscow. Tajik economists cautiously expressed their astonishment:

> In recent years in the republic, as compared to the rest of the USSR, more capital-intensive and less labour-intensive industrial development has been in evidence. Generally speaking, this contradicts the strategy of industrial development of the republic which is based on the necessity to put emphasis on labour-intensive and capital-saving manufacturing.[33]

Central planners and ministerial heavyweights in Moscow continued to pursue the fetish of physical economic growth at all costs, primarily through inflating the capital stock. The creation of the South Tajik Territorial Production Complex (STTPC) is probably the best illustration of the inefficient planning and investment and total disregard of local agendas that were inherent in the Soviet command-administrative system of economic management. The STTPC, conceived in the early 1960s, was to become the new industrial centre of Tajikistan. It embraced 37 per cent of Tajikistan's territory with 64 per cent of its population. Utilisation of the area's enormous hydro-power potential[34] formed the centrepiece of the design. In the initial stage, covering the period until 1985, the gigantic Norak hydro-electric power station was the major element of the STTPC, with an aluminium smelter in the city of Tursunzoda, an electrochemical plant in Yovon and a fertiliser combine in Vakhsh, as well as 46 other enterprises reliant on its electricity. Poor interdepartmental communication and lack of a clear-cut construction program plagued the project from the start.[35]

It took the Ministry of Energy of the USSR 22 years instead of 10, and 2.5 times the originally allocated money, to build the Norak station, with a capacity of 2.7 million kW.[36] In 1981, however, the ministry started work on an even more powerful (3.2 million kW) hydro power station at Roghun. Three years later the construction manager exclaimed in frustration that it might take up to a hundred years, rather than the planned 12, to complete the project,[37] but it did

---

32 H. M. Usmanov, *Tekhnicheskaia rekonstruktsiia industrii Tadzhikistana v usloviiakh perestroiki* (Dushanbe: Irfon, 1989), p. 20.

33 R. K. Mirzoev, *Tempy, proportsii i effektivnost obschestvennogo proizvodstva v Tadzhikskoi SSR* (Dushanbe: Donish, 1983), p. 39.

34 Tajikistan's rivers have the potential of generating 283 billion kWh of energy annually, with the Vakhsh and Panj in southern Tajikistan accounting for more than 100 billion kWh. See: M. S. Osimov, ed. *Tadzhikskaia SSR* (Dushanbe: AN TSSR, 1974), pp. 175–6.

35 'Lack of coordination amongst various ministries and institutions was evident, in that they strove to decide, and consequently to finance the measures that stemmed primarily from their own, albeit important, but still narrowly selfish interests.' See: G. B. Poliak and B. I. Annenkov, 'Sovershenstvovanie finansirovaniia', in *Territorialno-proizvodstvennye kompleksy: planirovanie i upravlenie*, ed. A. G. Aganbegian (Novosibirsk: Nauka, 1984), p. 120.

36 Pavel Gorbachev, 'Uroki Nureka', *Druzhba narodov*, No. 3 (1983), p. 209.

37 N. Savchenkov, 'Vremia ne zhdet', *Druzhba narodov*, No. 3 (1984), p. 166.

not really matter; it would be impossible anyway to use surplus electricity, as projects implemented by other ministries were in even worse shape. The smelter in Tursunzoda, with a capacity of 517 000 t of primary aluminium a year, was built between 1965 and 1984, and proved to be, at the time, a disaster: 'People at the plant say that their aluminium costs more than the gold extracted from the bottom of the Zeravshan river … just two years after start-up, the plant is already in urgent need of major overhaul and reconstruction.'[38] The factory in Yovon, commissioned in 1981 instead of 1974, was operating at 37 per cent of its nominal capacity, and in 1983 its production costs were twice its revenues.[39] Despite all this waste and inefficiency, money continued to flow freely from Moscow: from 1965 through to 1980, annual investment in all industries in Tajikistan rose from 155 to 320 million roubles, 'with two-thirds of fixed assets, output, and labour force represented by the South Tajik Complex'.[40]

The Spiral of Economic Decay

Even in better years, returns on capital in Tajikistan were 10 per cent below the USSR's average.[41] Since 1968, the volume of incomplete construction constantly exceeded that of absorbed capital investment. Insufficient attention to infrastructure development and reliance on an expensive imported workforce[42] also impeded Tajikistan's economic performance. In 1985, 15 per cent of all industrial enterprises and 31 per cent of all collective and state-owned farms were loss-making.[43] Gorbachev's ill-conceived reforms exacerbated the situation even further. In line with the Kremlin's new *idée fixe* of accelerated development of high-technology sectors, Tajikistan was issued with a program that envisaged[44]

- increases in the volume of capital investment and its share of national income
- emphasis on re-equipping and reconstructing operating factories
- expansion of the share of new equipment in the overall sum of investments

---

38   Rumer, *Soviet Central Asia*, p. 52.

39   Sh. Dustbaev, *Problemy khimizatsii otraslei narodnogo khoziaistva Tadzhikistana* (Dushanbe: Donish, 1989), p. 34.

40   Leslie Dienes, *Soviet Asia: Economic Development and National Policy Choices* (Boulder, Colo., and London: Westview Press, 1987), p. 126.

41   I. A. Lenshin, 'Proizvodstvennyi apparat Tadzhikistana: sostoianie i vozmozhnosti sovershenstvovaniia', *Izvestiia AN TSSR. Seriia: filosofiia, ekonomika, pravovedenie*, Vol. 23, No. 3 (July–September 1991), p. 38.

42   In the 1960s, 80 per cent of all those employed in the STTPC were recent immigrants from other republics of the Soviet Union. See: *Vestnik statistiki*, No. 8 (1991), p. 80. One of the many absurdities in the recent history of Tajikistan was a steady influx of European settlers, mainly skilled workers, to already overpopulated areas. They accounted for 17.5 per cent of the population growth in the republic over the period 1960–70, which was much higher than the corresponding figure for the rest of Central Asia. See: I. K. Narzikulov and A. G. Khajibaev, 'Tadzhikskaia Sovetskaia Sotsialisticheskaia respublika', in *Naselenie soiuznykh respublik* (Moscow: Statistika, 1977), p. 252.

43   Kh. Umarov, *Khoziaistvenno-upravlencheskie aspekty perestroiki* (Dushanbe: Irfon, 1988), p. 102.

44   Usmanov, *Tekhnicheskaia rekonstruktsiia industrii Tadzhikistana v usloviiakh perestroiki*, p. 23.

- more allocations to the machine-building and construction industries.

Once again, planners in Moscow ignored light industry and agriculture. Millions of dollars were spent on purchasing hardware and technology abroad, but state-of-the-art machinery rusted quietly in factory backyards because there were no personnel to install and operate it. The stockpile of imported equipment standing idle rose almost elevenfold from 1988 to 1991 in Tajikistan.[45] Growth in industrial labour productivity was the slowest amongst Soviet republics, and in 1990 actually declined by 1.2 per cent,[46] while in agriculture labour productivity sank by 1991 to 75.6 per cent of its 1980 level.[47] On average, construction workers in Tajikistan took three times as long to build a house as their counterparts in Russia.[48] Tajikistan's agriculture was especially badly hit by Gorbachev's reforms, particularly by his obsession with gigantic and amazingly inefficient agro-industrial complexes. Over the period 1988–91, the republic's agricultural output decreased by 17 per cent.[49] The disruption of old All-Union food-supply mechanisms in 1990 brought about the spectre of hunger in Tajikistan.

It appears that Tajikistan's economy, especially its industry, could exist and produce so long as it remained an integral part of the Soviet economic mechanism.[50] In 1988, Tajikistan exported 21 per cent of its produce to other republics, and imported 29 per cent of what it consumed from them—more than any other entity in the USSR.[51] Throughout the Soviet period, Tajikistan had a negative trade balance with other republics.[52] Additionally, Tajikistan received substantial cash infusions from Moscow. Critics of the command economy cited Tajikistan as evidence that 'administrative redistribution and non-equivalent exchange, "brotherly help", have created conditions in which it is economically more feasible to be backward and ask for assistance, than to work better'.[53]

---

45 *Narodnoe khoziaistvo Tadzhikskoi SSR v 1990g.*, p. 123.

46 *Khojagii khalqi jumhurii Tojikiston omori soli 1992* (Dushanbe: Kumitai davlatii omori jumhurii Tojikiston, 1993), p. 127.

47 *Selskoe khoziaistvo Respubliki Tadzhikistan* (Dushanbe: GSA pri pravitelstve RT, 1994), p. 49.

48 *Vestnik statistiki*, No. 6 (1991), p. 51.

49 Production of cotton dropped by 14 per cent, cereals by 12 per cent, fruit by 15 per cent, grapes by 36 per cent, meat by 19 per cent and eggs by 21 per cent. See: *Dehkanskoe khoziaistvo: Voprosy organizatsii i zakonodatelnye osnovy ego sozdaniia* (Dushanbe: AN RT, 1993), p. 72.

50 It has been argued that 'the level of integration amongst regions and branches in the USSR is much higher than in the European Economic Community'. See: M. N. Rutkevich, 'Obostrenie natsionalnykh otnoshenii v SSSR', *Sotsiologicheskie issledovaniia*, No. 1 (1991), p. 29.

51 *Vestnik statistiki*, No. 3 (1990), pp. 36–7.

52 And, as Lucjan Orlowski has convincingly demonstrated, 'inter-republican trade flows in which prices for goods were set by the authorities independently from the market became … [a] powerful channel of income transfers'. See: Lucjan T. Orlowski, 'Indirect Transfers in Trade among Former Soviet Union Republics: Sources, Patterns and Policy Responses in the Post-Soviet Period', *Europe-Asia Studies*, Vol. 45, No. 6 (1993), p. 1001.

53 V. Terliatskas and V. Baldishis, 'Tak nuzhny li respublikanskie dengi?' *EKO*, No. 3 (1990), p. 136.

A Western author, analysing budgetary practices in the centre–periphery relationship in both Soviet and post-Soviet times, has judged that the fiscal system in the former Soviet Union was 'not truly a "system", but rather a series of ad hoc bargained agreements, non-transparent at best, whose effects and incentives are not well understood'.[54] It is safe to assume, however, that tax-sharing schemes and direct, centralised subsidies constituted two major elements in Soviet fiscal federalism. In the second half of the 1980s, Tajikistan was one of the few republics allowed to retain 100 per cent of turnover tax collected,[55] and 14–21 per cent of its budget revenues comprised direct subventions from Moscow.[56]

Not surprisingly, when in September 1987 the Baltic republics, Belarus, Ukraine, Georgia, Moldova, and a number of Russia's *oblasts* floated the idea of regional self-financing (*regionalnyi khozraschet*), the most vehement opposition arose from the Central Asian republics, Tajikistan in particular.[57] Similarly, Gorbachev's legislation introduced in June 1987, which granted individual enterprises managerial freedom, did not work well in Tajikistan: local factories simply could not survive without the patronage of a branch ministry.[58] A sociological survey conducted that year revealed that people in Tajikistan were resolutely against Gorbachev's economic reforms.[59]

It would be incorrect to say that Tajikistan lived off the more developed regions of the Soviet Union. After all, indicators such as the volume and structure of net material production and national income, labour productivity, and resource and investment efficiency simply reflected the sectoral composition of republican economic complexes that had been moulded according to directives from Moscow. As long as the All-Union economic mechanism was intact, it made little sense to speculate who was the donor and who was the recipient inside USSR, Inc. A senior Russian diplomat based in Dushanbe, who had previously served with the Soviet State Planning Authority (GOSPLAN), recollected that 'while Tajikistan produced one million tonnes of cotton a year, we could provide it

---

54   Daniel Treisman, 'The Politics of Intergovernmental Transfers in Post-Soviet Russia', *British Journal of Political Science*, Vol. 26, Part 3 (July 1996), p. 307.

55   Usmanov, *Tekhnicheskaia rekonstruktsiia industrii Tadzhikistana v usloviiakh perestroiki*, p. 56; *Gosudarstvennyi biudzhet SSSR* (Moscow: Finansy i statistika, 1989), p. 131; *Kommunist Tadzhikistana*, 6 December 1985.

56   A. G. Granberg, 'Ekonomicheskii mekhanizm mezhrespublikanskikh i mezhregionalnykh otnoshenii', *EKO*, No. 9 (1989), p. 43.

57   V. Koroteeva, L. Perepelkin and O. Shkaratan, 'Ot biurokraticheskogo tsentralizma k ekonomicheskoi integratsii suverennykh respublik', *Kommunist*, No. 15 (October 1988), p. 29.

58   *Osnovnye pokazateli ekonomicheskogo i sotsialnogo razvitiia oblastei*, p. 34.

59   In another poll, the responses in Tajikistan were far more negative when the survey was in regards to 'Public Attitude towards Transition to a Market Economy', in June 1990: 4.9 per cent positive; 19.3 per cent ambivalent; 56.9 per cent negative; 2.7 per cent indifferent; 15.8 per cent 'hard to answer'. Meanwhile, the Soviet average for 'positive' in this poll was 9.9 per cent and in Estonia it was 34.4 per cent. See: *Vestnik statistiki*, No. 2 (1991), p. 61.

with all the goods it needed and even some extras, without incurring losses'.[60] The leaders of Tajikistan were happy with such an arrangement and could not, or did not want to, respond to the crisis resulting from Gorbachev's economic endeavours.[61] At a time when the political cohesion of the USSR was in tatters, when the breakdown of central planning and severe monetary and fiscal crises signalled the end of the Soviet socialist economy, such inaction betrayed either extreme naivety or, at the very least, an astonishing level of complacency.

The Mounting Social Problems

The downward spiralling economy inevitably led to a deteriorating quality of life in the USSR. It has been suggested that in 1987 'simply to maintain the current standard of living in Tajikistan, which was already the poorest republic, would demand a 250 per cent increase in investment or another 6 to 7 billion roubles more. Considering that the entire budget in 1988 was only 2.1 billion roubles, no such investment was possible'.[62] According to official figures and considering revenues from the formal sector only, in 1988, 12.6 per cent of the Soviet population lived below the poverty line; the corresponding figure for Central Asia was 45 per cent, and for Tajikistan a staggering 58.6 per cent.[63] By 1991 this figure had increased to 87.3 per cent.[64] It can be argued that the actual state of affairs may have been better in Central Asia due to undeclared incomes and produce-in-kind from private plots, but statistical evidence shows that Tajikistan was the worst off amongst all Soviet republics on a variety of socioeconomic parameters.[65] Even the food pyramid of an average Tajik family did not meet nutritional norms—as in centuries before, bread remained its major element.[66]

---

60 Recorded interview at the Russian Embassy, Dushanbe, 3 March 1995.

61 For example, as late as May 1991, Dr Rustam Mirzoev, then director of Tajikistan's Productive Forces Research Council, wrote that 'in the next 50 years there will be no alternatives to the existing production-technological integrity of this country's economy … It is impossible to act against the laws of the established production-technological system and violate its manageability … The coordinating and regulating role of the Centre in strategic spheres of public production constitutes the inalienable element of management of the republics' economies.' See: R. K. Mirzoev, 'Tanzimi inkishofi mintaqavi dar sharoiti iqtisodi bozargoni', *Akhboroti Akademiyyai fanhoi RSS Tojikiston. Seriyyai falsafa, iqtisodiyyot, huquqshinosi*, No. 3 (1991), pp. 21–2.

62 Rashid, *The Resurgence of Central Asia*, p. 171.

63 McAuley, 'The Central Asian Economy in Comparative Perspective', p. 146.

64 *Vestnik statistiki*, No. 12 (1991), p. 10.

65 *Sotsialnoe razvitie SSSR*, pp. 40, 126, 197. These include consumption of goods and services, housing, availability of communal services, infant mortality, and preschool facilities. See also: Leonid A. Fridman, 'Economic Crisis as a Factor of Building Up Socio-Political and Ethnonational Tensions in the Countries of Central Asia and Transcaucasia', in *Central Asia and Transcaucasia: Ethnicity and Conflict*, ed. Vitaly V. Naumkin (Westport, Conn.: Greenwood Press, 1994).

66 *Vestnik statistiki*, No. 9 (1991), pp. 54–6.

In another serious development that was detrimental to the social order, towards the end of the 1980s crime increased dramatically in Leninobod, Kulob and Qurghonteppa.[67] In Qurghonteppa, local mafias operated in the black market with some official protection during the 1980s.[68] Fraud, theft of state property, falsification of cotton production and other forms of organised crime and embezzlement all contributed to weakening state capacity. In response, first secretary, Qahhor Mahkamov—forced by a second secretary appointed by Moscow[69]—implemented a campaign against corruption between 1986 and 1991, resulting in a large turnover of political and economic elites.[70] At a lower level in society, youth problems were becoming increasingly violent in nature by the mid 1980s. Instances of mass violence, 'hooliganism', binge drinking and violent assaults were all cited as serious problems in Dushanbe. In two of the more notorious events, foreign students at the Agricultural Institute were attacked in 1987, and two years later, just down the street, a mass riot involving students from the Pedagogical Institute, the riot police and a third unidentified group spilled over into attacks on uninvolved pedestrians and theatre patrons, who were assaulted with sticks and iron bars.[71]

Environmental problems also seriously affected the quality of life in Tajikistan. Until the mid 1980s, the Soviet government's efforts to solve them 'were still at least partially effective … This situation changed in 1985 and 1986 … One contributing factor was certainly the erosion of technological discipline in industry that took place under *perestroika*'.[72] Soil degradation, deforestation, air and water pollution and loss of biodiversity emerged as major ecological hazards. Overuse of agricultural lands resulted in appalling soil degradation.[73] According to agronomic norms, plantations in Tajikistan should have produced 700 000 t of raw cotton a year in the 1980s.[74] In reality, annual yields approximated 1 million tonnes. This was achieved primarily through massive use of chemicals. Every hectare of arable land in Tajikistan received 31.6 kg of pesticides in

---

67 Markowitz, *Collapsed and Prebendal States in Post-Soviet Eurasia*, pp. 83–4.

68 Akiner, *Tajikistan*, p. 26.

69 The role of second secretary Petr Luchinsky will be discussed later in this chapter.

70 Markowitz, *Collapsed and Prebendal States in Post-Soviet Eurasia*, pp. 83–6. Markowitz argues that Roy (*The New Central Asia*) and Kathleen Collins (*Clan Politics and Regime Transition in Central Asia*) have 'erroneously suggested that perestroika-era purges were not implemented fully in the republic'.

71 'Student Teachers in Dushanbe Violence', *Komsomolskaya Pravda* (22 February 1990), *Summary of World Broadcasts—Soviet Union* (BBC) [hereinafter *SWB SU*], 0393 (24 February 1989), i; 'Speech by First Secretary K. M. Makhkamov to the 24th Congress of the Tajikistan Lenin Communist Youth League', *Kommunist Tadzhikistana* (22 February 1987), pp. 2, 5, in *The Current Digest of the Post-Soviet Press*, Vol. XXXIX, No. 9 (1 April 1987), p. 9.

72 Georgii S. Golitsyn, 'Ecological Problems in the CIS During the Transitional Period', *RFE/RL Research Report*, Vol. 2, No. 2 (8 January 1993), p. 34.

73 In 1989, the humus content in land under cultivation was barely 30 per cent of the 1940 level. See: Kh. Umarov, 'Sovremennye sotsialno-ekonomicheskie protsessy i problemy razvitiia sovetskoi Srednei Azii', in *Sovetologi o problemakh sotsialno-ekonomicheskogo razvitiia SSSR i soiuznykh respublik* (Moscow: Institut ekonomiki AN SSSR, 1990), p. 13.

74 *Kommunist Tadzhikistana*, 25 May 1991.

1986—10 times the average for the USSR.[75] It was normal for farmers to use mineral fertilisers at twice and even six times the recommended rate 'in the false belief that the more fertilisers you put in, the more cotton you harvest'.[76] Given the omnipresence of cotton plantations in Tajikistan, which pervaded even suburban areas and traditional zones of fruit and vegetable growing, there was little exaggeration in the assessment that 'the employment of the so-called high technologies of cotton production had led to such catastrophic chemicalisation of agriculture, that local ancient fertile oases became poisoned for long years to come'.[77]

In 1989, 82.3 per cent of all pregnant women residing in cotton-sowing areas suffered from anaemia, due to exposure to harmful substances, poor diet and backbreaking labour in plantations.[78] Great quantities of chemical residues returned to surface streams and aquifers with drainage water. The result was not unexpected: 'The analysis of the high rate of infant mortality has shown that its main cause consists of acute digestive diseases, and especially of the fact that 45 percent of the rural population procured drinking water from open reservoirs.'[79] To make the situation even worse, industrial sewage escapes in Tajikistan more than doubled over the period 1985–89.[80] In 1990, 15 per cent of drinking water samples showed chemical pollution and 21 per cent of samples had bacteria infestation.[81]

Newly built factories were often put into operation without any recycling or rectification facilities. Several types of vegetation died within a 10-km zone around the smelter in Tursunzoda because the fluorine content of the soil rose tenfold between 1979 and 1986, and an environmental disaster eventually turned into a problem of human ecology: it became dangerous to live in the region where 'the air basin is saturated with compounds of aluminium, fluorine, lead, zinc, cadmium, copper, mercury, arsenic, sulphur and nitrogen oxides, and mineral acids'.[82] Emissions of toxic chemicals by the Yovon electrochemical plant increased from 451 t in 1985 to 853 t in 1987; the concomitant rise in fines—from 300 to 1110 roubles[83]—indicated not punishment but criminal indifference of the authorities to environmental protection. A study conducted

75   *Tojikistoni Soveti*, 28 August 1988.
76   Ahmedov, *KPSS v borbe za intensifikatsiiu khlopkovodstva*, p. 278.
77   Shamil Sultanov, 'Dukh evraziitsa', *Nash sovremennik*, No. 7 (1992), p. 146.
78   *Zdravookhranenie Tadzhikistana*, No. 2 (1990), p. 21.
79   S. E. Karimova, 'Meditsinskoe obsluzhivanie trudiashikhsia Tadzhikistana (60–80-e gody)', *Izvestiia AN RT. Seriia: vostokovedenie, istorii, filologiia*, No. 2 (26) (1992), p. 43.
80   *Narodnoe khoziaistvo Tadzhikskoi SSR v 1990g.*, p. 100.
81   *Vestnik statistiki*, No. 12 (1991), p. 61.
82   Dustbaev, *Problemy khimizatsii otraslei narodnogo khoziaistva Tadzhikistana*, p. 75.
83   M. N. Nurnazarov, *Agropromyshlennye kompleksy Tadzhikistana* (Dushanbe: Donish, 1990), p. 72.

in 1991 revealed that residents of Dushanbe, once regarded as the greenest and cleanest capital city in the USSR, were seriously concerned about looming ecological problems.[84]

In the post–World War II period, the acreage of forests in Tajikistan decreased almost fourfold.[85] Still, the Soviet-era powers had enough commonsense to set up a number of nature reserves. The most famous reserve, 'Tiger Gorge', was established in 1938 in the southern segment of the Vakhsh Valley.[86] A special permit from the republican State Committee for Forestry was required simply to visit it. In the 1960s, however, following the construction of dams on the Vakhsh River, the marshes and bogs in Tiger Gorge began to dry up. In the early 1990s, with the weakening of the political centre, unauthorised agricultural development and logging commenced in the reserve.

Scarce financing of conservation and protection measures, irresponsible behaviour by industrial and agricultural managers, and demographic pressures had undermined the unique ecological potential of Tajikistan. Environmental degradation was beginning to affect the health of the population in a gruesome way, similar to that in Turkmenistan.[87] In one cotton-growing *kolkhoz*, only three of 368 children who underwent medical examination were pronounced healthy.[88] In 1990, Dr Sofia Hakimova, director of the Institute for Reproductive Health in Dushanbe, assessed the situation as follows: 'The health of the nation has been sacrificed for cotton. Our genetic fund has been completely destroyed. It must be [considered] a case of genocide.'[89] In the early 1990s Tajikistan had the worst ratings amongst all republics of the Soviet Union on a number of indicators pertaining to quality of life, sanitation and medical provision, and the situation was likely to deteriorate.[90] Furthermore, the ability of local authorities to deal with the fallout of the health crisis was unsatisfactory. In one appalling example, an inspection of Clinical Hospital No. 1 of Dushanbe in 1990 revealed that *all* the diagnoses made by its specialists were wrong.[91]

---

84   Some 82.5 per cent complained about dust and gas pollution, 77.8 per cent noted the increasing presence of vermin and 99.9 per cent deplored high noise levels. See: *Zdravookhranenie Tadzhikistana*, No. 2 (1993), pp. 37–8.

85   Umarov, 'Sovremennye sotsialno-ekonomicheskie protsessy i problemy razvitiia sovetskoi Srednei Azii', p. 13.

86   It offered sanctuary to 30 species of mammals, 140 species of birds and 150 species of plants; many of them were extremely rare and endemic to Tajikistan. See: F. G. Patrunov, *Po Tadzhikistanu* (Moscow: Profizdat, 1987), pp. 187–9.

87   For example, in 1991 only 12.2 per cent of children in the age cohort three to twelve months born in the countryside were without developmental abnormalities. See: V. A. Purdenko, M. D. Amanekov and O. N. Kulberdyeva, 'Problemy ekologii narodonaseleniia Turkmenistana', *Vostok*, No. 6 (1992), p. 93.

88   *Sogdiana*, No. 1 (February 1990), p. 2.

89   Interview in: *Mesiats ushcherbnoi luny*, [Documentary film] (Dushanbe: Tadzhikfilm, 1990).

90   Christopher M. Davis, 'Health Care Crisis: The Former USSR', *RFE/RL Research Report*, Vol. 2, No. 40 (8 October 1993), pp. 36–41.

91   A. A. Ahmedov, 'Sovremennoe sostoianie zdravookhraneniia v respublike i zadachi kollektiva TGMU im. Abuali Ibn Sino v dele podgotovki vrachebnykh kadrov i razvitiia meditsinskoi nauki', *Zdravookhranenie Tadzhikistana*, No. 3 (246) (1993), p. 11.

By the late 1980s, it had become obvious that Tajikistan was in the middle of a 'systemic structural crisis that economically hinged on absolute land and water starvation, and socially—on the exceptionally high birthrate and the loss by the grassroots social structures of their self-sustainability functions'.[92] Its symptoms used to be ameliorated by the centre's redistributive policies—the share of aggregate external transfers in the national income used in Tajikistan rose from 6.7 per cent in 1970 to 12 per cent in 1988.[93] Obviously, this situation could not last forever in the conditions of economic collapse during the late Gorbachev period. Tajikistan was living on borrowed time, trying desperately to maintain production and welfare provision at the levels of the more fortunate years of 'developed socialism'. The crunch in the economic sphere came in 1991. The republic's budget for that year envisaged a deficit of 23.8 per cent, even though Moscow had promised to contribute 35.8 per cent of all budgetary revenues in subsidies.[94] When the centre failed to deliver, it was only a matter of time before economic catastrophe would become a major factor in the coming political turmoil.

The Politics of Centralisation and Increased Regionalism

As discussed earlier, the Brezhnev era was characterised by a high degree of stability in the ruling establishment in the union republics. In the 1970s in particular, the tacit compromise between the Kremlin and regional elites 'allowed strong, extensive political machines to develop *sub rosa* in the Central Asian union republics'.[95] Territorial bureaucracies had acquired virtual autonomy in handling domestic affairs. The long-serving communist leaders of Central Asia were regarded by the indigenous population as the fathers of their respective nations, who governed not according to some obscure laws imposed by Moscow but in line with traditional sets of values and practices. Donald Carlisle has coined the following metaphoric description while writing about Uzbekistan's first secretary from 1959 to 1983, Sharaf Rashidov:

> There surfaced a variant of communist feudalism, or, to put it another way, an Uzbek version of Oriental Despotism, with Rashidov ruling as khan or emir and the CPSU bureau serving as a council of viziers.

---

92 Bushkov and Mikulskii, *'Tadzhikskaia revoliutsiia' i grazhdanskaia voina*, p. 14.

93 Misha V. Belkindas and M. J. Sagers, 'A Preliminary Analysis of Economic Relations among Union Republics of the USSR: 1970–1988', *Soviet Geography*, Vol. XXXI, No. 8 (October 1990), p. 640.

94 Boboev, *Ekonomicheskoe razvitie respubliki v usloviiakh rynka*, p. 33.

95 Edward Allworth, 'The New Central Asians', in *Central Asia: 130 Years of Russian Dominance, A Historical Overview*, ed. Edward Allworth (Durham, NC: Duke University Press, 1994), p. 556.

A great deal of power was also delegated to the party secretaries of the various provinces, who administered them much in the way begs (or beks) had ruled their dominions before the Russian conquest.[96]

The situation changed dramatically in 1985 with Gorbachev's appointment as general secretary of the CPSU Central Committee. Curtailing the independence of regional apparatuses was crucial for consolidating his position at the apex of the Soviet power pyramid. Gorbachev had far greater powers than did Brezhnev and Khrushchev at the beginning of their tenures; still, he worked feverishly to expand his power base, and by the time of the CPSU's twenty-seventh congress, held in February–March 1987, 'Gorbachev supporters occupied the key positions in the strategically important fields of foreign affairs, agriculture and personnel, a situation which none of his predecessors had contrived in anything like such a short time (if at all)'.[97] It has been argued that Gorbachev may have needed to strengthen his primacy within the party before he could embark upon systemic reform,[98] but people who worked closely with him, such as his chief of staff, Valery Boldin, have suggested that unlimited power was a goal in its own right for the new Soviet leader.[99]

Gorbachev's methods of re-establishing Moscow's firm hand in Central Asia included wholesale purges, unfair trials and a massive influx of 'trusted cadres' from the centre. First secretary of the CPT CC, Rahmon Nabiev, vehemently objected to the Politburo's plans to place 78 'outsiders' in positions of authority in Tajikistan,[100] and was dismissed in December 1985.[101] His replacement, Qahhor Mahkamov,[102] was expected to be more amenable to Gorbachev's plans. From early 1987 to the end of 1989, Mahkamov—using what Markowitz terms

---

96   Donald S. Carlisle, 'Islam Karimov and Uzbekistan: Back to the Future?' in *Patterns in Post-Soviet Leadership*, eds Timothy J. Colton and Robert C. Tucker (Boulder, Colo.: Westview Press, 1995), p. 195.

97   T. H. Rigby, 'Old Style Congress—New Style Leadership?' in *Gorbachev at the Helm: A New Era in Soviet Politics?* eds R. Miller, J. Miller and T. H. Rigby (New York: Croom Helm, 1987), p. 33.

98   Graeme Gill, *The Collapse of a Single-Party System: The Disintegration of the Communist Party of the Soviet Union* (Cambridge: Cambridge University Press, 1994), p. 32.

99   Valery Boldin, *Ten Years that Shook the World: The Gorbachev Era As Witnessed by His Chief of Staff* (New York: Basic Books, 1994), p. 112.

100   *Nomzad ba raisi jumhuri Tojikiston Rahmon Nabievich Nabiev* (Dushanbe: [No publisher], 1991), p. 5.

101   The Resolution No. 157 of the Bureau of the CPT CC of 14 December 1985 did not specify the pretext for Nabiev's dismissal; however, well-informed sources within the CPT maintained that he had been set up on order from Moscow. Allegedly, Rahmon Nabiev was secretly filmed while participating in a drunken binge during a business trip to Badakhshan; the compromising videotape was shown to the Politburo members, and in the paranoid atmosphere of Gorbachev's anti-alcohol campaign his fate was sealed. The CPSU CC secretary responsible for personnel matters, G. P. Razumovsky, was dispatched to Dushanbe, and Nabiev was out of office in a matter of days. (Interviews in Dushanbe, December 1994 – January 1995.)

102   Mahkamov, an ethnic Tajik, was born in Leninobod in 1932. He was a graduate of the Leningrad Mining Institute. In 1961 he was appointed 'Chairman of the Leninabad City Soviet Executive Committee, then Chairman of the Tadzhik SSR State Planning Committee and at the same time, beginning in 1965, Vice-Chairman of the Tadzhik SSR Council of Ministers. In 1982 he was appointed Chairman of the Tadzhik SSR Council of Ministers.' See: 'Party Congress Finishes Up; Biographies of the 24 Politburo Members', *The Current Digest of the Post-Soviet Press*, Vol. XLII, No. 36 (10 October 1990), p. 20.

'attacks', 'reforms' and an 'anti-corruption campaign'—attempted to dismantle the patronage networks within the Communist Party.[103] These included actions against the elites of patronage networks in Kulob, Qurghonteppa and Mahkamov's home province of Leninobod. Mahkamov removed many regional elites from their administrative positions and appointed 'reformist politicians'— often Pamiris and Gharmis/Qaroteginis—in their place.[104]

This portrayal of Mahkamov as a motivated reformer needs to be qualified. In particular, the reforms he carried out need to be placed in the context of the Soviet Union, in particular Moscow's relationship with and control over the republics. Mahkamov was widely regarded as a mere puppet of the Kremlin. Although he had spent many years in high government positions and served as the chairman of the Council of Ministers of Tajikistan between 1982 and 1986, Mahkamov did not have a wide-ranging power base built on parochial and solidarity ties. On top of that, Mahkamov obviously lacked features necessary for an authoritative national leader in Tajikistan. Unlike Nabiev, he did not belong to a traditional noble family; in fact, he was orphaned at age fourteen. Nor did he use marriage to create any alliances: his wife was a Tatar; his elder son married a Korean, and his daughter a Lithuanian.[105] He owed his position exclusively to good relations with higher-ups in Moscow; the real power in Tajikistan became concentrated in the hands of the second secretary of the CPT CC, a close associate of Gorbachev. Karim Abdulov, the chief of staff for President Nabiev (1991–92), writes disparagingly of Mahkamov as an 'inept' and 'slow-witted' leader who was dictated to by Moscow *desantniks* (literally, 'paratroopers'; figuratively, aggressive and arrogant outsiders who arrive suddenly and without invitation). Chief among these outsiders, in Abdulov's opinion, was the second secretary (1986–89) and true power in Tajikistan, the Moldovan Petr K. Luchinsky—better known nowadays as Petru Lucinschi, president of Moldova from 1997 to 2001. Abdulov is quite open in his feelings towards the 'chauvinist' Luchinsky, whom he blames for using and exacerbating regionalism (*mahallagaroyi*) in his placement and removal of cadres in Tajikistan.[106] Abdulov maintains that Luchinsky's tactics worsened the regional divides in Tajikistan and pushed the country towards war.[107] Abdulov is adamant about the effect of the Mahkamov–Luchinsky reforms, especially the increased level of regionalism. He points to the period from 1985 to 1990

---

103 Markowitz, *Collapsed and Prebendal States in Post-Soviet Eurasia*, pp. 5, 102–3.

104 Markowitz, *Collapsed and Prebendal States in Post-Soviet Eurasia*, pp. 5, 102–3, 118–21.

105 *Kommunist Tadzhikistana*, 2 April 1991.

106 Karim Abdulov, 'Tojikiston va Chin', n.d., online: <http://www.abdulov.tj/bk19_1.php>; '100 Solagii Rakhim Jalil: Ohanraboi Millat', n.d., online: <http://www.abdulov.tj/bk15_1.php>

107 Abdulov writes: 'I am confident of what I have concluded and I can emphatically say this: Luchinsky's contribution to the tragedies of my people and nation today is quite large. Many times he separated my people to the north and south, to the east and west. With dozens of lies and deceitful acts he took away stability and made Tajik children homeless through war.' See: Karim Abdulov, *Rohi Behbud* (Dushanbe: [Self-published], 1995), p. 16.

as a time when the people of Tajikistan 'became slaves of the centre', and when '[e]veryone became concerned with only themselves, their own families, and their own relatives'.[108] While other analysts are less concerned with assigning blame, they do agree on the increased importance of region of origin as a result of how the reforms of the late 1980s were implemented.[109] Initially, in the mid 1980s, the dividing lines for struggles among the *nomenklatura* were between the 'northerners' (Leninobod) on one side and the 'southerners' (Gharmis, Kulobis and Pamiris) on the other. The southern apparatchiks were optimistic about their chances of gaining positions of power as the hold of the Soviet centre over the Tajik SSR's mechanisms of power weakened. This process quickened considerably as Gorbachev's *perestroika* reforms took effect. Soon Makhamov was attempting to defuse the situation by appointing representatives of Kulob, the Gorno-Badakhshan Autonomous Oblast (GBAO) and Gharm to high positions in the state apparatus. By the late 1980s, thanks to *perestroika*, non-Leninobodis from the south (Pamiris, Kulobis and Garmis) were brought into high government positions, resulting in 'ambitious hopes among southerners'.[110]

None of the CPT CC secretaries of the 1985 vintage remained in office in 1987. By the end of 1986, all *oblast* leaders had been replaced in Tajikistan, and so had more than 80 per cent of party officials at *raion* (town) level.[111] There are reasons to believe that Moscow was preparing a frontal assault on the Tajik political elite along the lines of the 'Uzbek affair'.[112] In 1986, a special group of investigators was seconded to the republic from the USSR's General Procurator's Office with unlimited powers to investigate and uproot corruption. The Kulob *oblast* had been singled out, and in 1987 the *obkom* first secretary, Salohiddin Hasanov, and the head of the Regional Procurement Authority, Halil Karimov, were arrested on charges of bribery and abuse of office.[113] As in Uzbekistan,

---

108   Abdulov, *Rohi Behbud*, p. 19.

109   For example, see Markowitz's points on the appointments of Pamiris and Gharmis to the newly vacated positions.

110   Niyazi, 'Tajikistan I', p. 155. For example, Goibnazar Pallaev (Pamiri) became chairman of the Supreme Soviet; Izatullo Khayoev (Kulobi) was appointed chairman of the Council of Ministers; Shodi Shabdolov (Pamiri) was appointed Communist Party secretary for industry and ideology; Mamadayoz Navjuvonov (Pamiri) was appointed minister of the interior; and Buri Karimov (Gharmi) was appointed head of GOSPLAN, while also serving as deputy chairman of the Council of Ministers.

111   Assessment is based on the analysis of name entries in the CPT confidential telephone directories.

112   The total purge of Brezhnev-era cadres in Uzbekistan from 1983 to 1989 came to be known as the 'Uzbek' or 'Cotton affair'. Under Gorbachev, it was accompanied by a massive propaganda campaign in Soviet media conveying the message that 'bound up in the general criminal conspiracy were not nearly all but absolutely all the party, state, Komsomol, trade union and economic managers of the republic and of its regions'. See: Arkady Vaksberg, *The Soviet Mafia* (New York: St Martin's Press, 1991), p. 116. From 1985 to 1988, 58 000 senior officials in Uzbekistan were replaced. See: Carlisle, 'Geopolitics and Ethnic Problems of Uzbekistan and Its Neighbours', p. 79.

113   Hasanov wrote later: 'The investigative group was busy not establishing the truth, but incessantly collecting dubious documents that "confirmed" this or that version that would satisfy the powers that be. I was pressed to give false testimony against First Secretary of the CC, Q. Mahkamov, Chairman of the Council of Ministers, I. Khayyoev, Chairman of the republic's Supplies Agency [GOSSNAB], S. Ashurov, Chairman of the Supreme Court, I. Khojaev, Party and Soviet leaders of the Kulob *oblast* … Defamatory materials were

in Tajikistan prosecutorial attacks and judicial arbitrariness were hallmarks of Gorbachev's centralisation drive. Moreover, General S. M. Gromov, who headed the inquisition team in Tajikistan in the late 1980s, later confessed that 'violations of legality committed by investigative officers in Tajikistan were incomparably greater than in any other republic of the former Soviet Union'.[114] In 1991, Hasanov, Karimov and dozens of other high-ranking Tajik officials were fully acquitted. Lieutenant Colonel V. A. Shushakov from the USSR Ministry of Interior, who had initiated a number of illegal criminal cases in the Kulob *oblast*, went into hiding in 1990 after he became a subject of investigation himself.[115]

Gorbachev's frontal attack on the old *nomenklatura* in Tajikistan was successful in the sense that it did excoriate the elaborate system of patronage networks in Tajikistan. For the time being the Kremlin regained full control over all recruitment there; between 1986 and 1990, 'no *kolkhoz* chairman, no workshop director, no university lecturer could be appointed without Moscow's permission'.[116] The Tajik elite surrendered its positions without much resistance due to internal friction based primarily on regional rivalry. Henceforth, there was no need for a mass campaign similar to the 'cotton affair' in Uzbekistan—which had made the words 'crook' and 'Uzbek' synonyms in the Soviet media. Gorbachev's victory, however, quickly backfired. As James Critchlow has noted, the old Soviet elites in Central Asia,

> whatever their shortcomings, helped the Party to maintain political stability while promoting economic development and a degree of social change in the face of challenges of many kinds. These elites evolved over many decades in response to the Party's needs for an apparatus that could deal with a largely Islamic-traditionalist, nationalistic, elder-venerating, agrarian, male-dominated society with inherent hostility to change. Now the equilibrium of many years has changed.[117]

Gorbachev, Luchinsky and their lieutenants brought in from the European Soviet Union[118] could not and did not pay any attention to the intricacies of

---

being gathered that implicated the Minister of Interior Pulatov, deputy Procurator of the republic Emomov and many others who were destined to experience the gloom and darkness of prison cells ... Several goals were pursued in the process: those who were wholly subordinate to Moscow but still had the audacity to have personal opinion were removed, and soulless marionettes replaced them. Thus, the influence of Moscow was becoming infinite and the republic was being deprived even of the trappings of autonomy.' See: *Biznes i politika*, 8 January 1994.

114   *Biznes i politika*, 31 July 1993.
115   *Kommunist Tadzhikistana*, 3 July 1991.
116   Abdulov, *Rohi behbud*, p. 10.
117   James Critchlow, 'Prelude to "Independence": How the Uzbek Party Apparatus Broke Moscow's Grip On Elite Recruitment', in *Soviet Central Asia: The Failed Transformation*, ed. William Fierman (Boulder, Colo.: Westview Press, 1991), p. 153.
118   Their collective nickname in Tajikistan was 'paratroopers'; indeed, they appeared out of the blue sky, without the slightest idea about local culture and traditions, but with an enormous sense of superiority. A certain Vladimir V. Ruzanov presents a typical case in this respect. A Russian, who had spent all his life

Tajik domestic policies. Jabbor Rasulov and Rahmon Nabiev were very skilled operators who managed to maintain a *modus vivendi* amongst regional cliques. Between 1986 and 1989, the balance of parochial interests in Tajikistan was irreparably damaged. The fragmentation of the national power elite reached new heights. At republic level, four major competing groups emerged.

1. The group of Qahhor Mahkamov, first secretary of the CPT CC, which embraced representatives of relatively minor clans from the north, such as the CPT CC secretary, Guljahon Bobosadykova, and deputy chairman of the Council of Ministers, Habibullo Saidmurodov, from Uroteppa (Istaravshon). It also included some prominent politicians from Leninobod who were in personal opposition to Rahmon Nabiev—the charismatic regional first secretary, Rifat Khojiev, and another CPT CC secretary, Temurboy Mirkholiqov. Since Mahkamov's status was not rooted primarily in the local community, he had to rely heavily on the 'paratroopers' from Moscow and a rather limited circle of people who owed him favours.[119]

2. The group of Rahmon Nabiev. Though ousted from the top leadership, Nabiev continued to command wide respect in his patrimony, Leninobod. Old-time *nomenklatura* cadres sacked or demoted after 1985 tended to coalesce around him; they were not only northerners but influential Kulobis as well—most notably, former minister of education Talbak Nazarov. Rahmon Nabiev was chairman of the Society for Environmental Protection of Tajikistan in 1986–90, a post that allowed him to travel widely on official business and maintain personal contacts with leaders in Moscow and Central Asian capitals.

3. The group of Kulobis headed by Hikmatullo Nasriddinov, minister of irrigation and the CPT CC secretary under Nabiev. Technically, Izatullo Khayoev, the chairman of the Council of Ministers of Tajikistan, was the most senior representative of the Kulob region in the government, but he was regarded as a weak leader loyal to Mahkamov rather than to his patrimony.

4. The group of Ghoibnazar Pallaev, the chairman of the Presidium of the Supreme Soviet of Tajikistan, comprised officials of Gharmi and Pamiri extraction including the first deputy chairman of the Council of Ministers, Akbar Makhsumov—son of the widely respected first *Revkom* chairman of Tajikistan from 1924 to 1933, Nusratullo Makhsum—and Dushanbe's mayor, Maqsud Ikromov.

---

in Ukraine, he was transferred in 1986 from the humble position of a *raikom* instructor to head a sector in the Ideological Department of the CPT CC, and in 1988 became first deputy head of this department. He was notorious for his indiscriminately denigrating attitude toward all his native subordinates and peers, for he believed them to be clandestine Muslims and hence anti-communists. (Taped interview with Iskandar Asadulloev, former head of sector in the CPT CC, Dushanbe, 6 January 1995.)

119 A *Pravda* correspondent once observed that he 'is too lenient to his coterie; perhaps, he has not been selective enough while forming his "team". Indeed, he is surrounded by a fair number of quite strange persons whose presence by his side is hard to explain.' See: *Tadzhikistan v ogne* (Dushanbe: Irfon, 1993), p. 144.

Kulobis and Gharmis became primary targets of restructuring and reorganisation campaigns launched by Mahkamov and Luchinsky. Luchinsky, for his part, was a leader who wanted to completely dismantle certain regional groupings, Kulobis in particular;[120] however, the Gharmis sustained the most humiliating losses (at the national level), especially when Akbar Makhsumov was sacked from the government and made head of the republic's botanic garden. The program of accelerated industrial development of the south had been abandoned; in 1989, the Leninobod *oblast* received 60 per cent of the funds earmarked by Moscow for Tajikistan, whereas Kulob received a mere 6 per cent.[121] Thus, the main line of confrontation in the late 1980s appeared to be between the north and the south (that is, valley Tajiks and mountain Tajiks). Toshmat Nozirov, then chairman of the Executive Committee of the Farkhor *raion* in the Kulob *oblast*, reminisced that 'the conflict was brewing on the regionalistic grounds then … A group of unsavoury politicians based their intrigues on this dichotomy to play for power'.[122]

In 1989 it became clear that Gorbachev's experimentation had led to 'a diminishing of the regime's power over society, even as he sought to increase his own power over the regime'.[123] Having failed to extract the obedience of the party *apparat*, he attempted to downgrade it and use other institutions, such as the legislature, the army and security establishment, as his power base, but with little or no success. The 'mature' Gorbachev practised what Joel Migdal has called the 'politics of survival'—a 'pathological style at the apex of the state', which incorporated 'a mechanism of deliberately weakening arms of the state and allied organisations in order to assure the tenure of the top state leadership'.[124] Creation of the presidency, *glasnost*, an invitation of the masses to politics through popular referenda and contested elections, also contributed to the atmosphere of legal and political uncertainty in Central Asia.

As for the populace of Tajikistan, they held very strong, negative views on Gorbachev's reforms.[125] A sociological study conducted in the Tajik State University in 1989 revealed that students and staff members

---

120 Luchinsky once remarked: 'these churlish Kulobis should be completely and utterly destroyed.' See: Nasriddinov, *Tarkish*, p. 32.

121 Vadim Lifshits, 'Politicheskaia situatsiia v Tadzhikistane (leto 1993)', *Rossiia i musulmanskii mir*, No. 10 (1993), p. 36.

122 *Biznes i politika*, 8 March 1994.

123 W. J. Tompson, 'Khrushchev and Gorbachev as Reformers: A Comparison', *British Journal of Political Science*, Vol. 23, Part 1 (1993), p. 89.

124 Migdal, *Strong Societies and Weak States*, pp. 217, 264.

125 For example, the 'Public Views on Perestroika in Tajikistan' in one 1990 survey found: 13 per cent positive, 35 per cent ambivalent, 32 per cent negative and 'hard to say' 20 per cent. See: Alimov and Saidov, *Natsionalnyi vopros*, p. 87. In another poll the responses in Tajikistan were far more negative when the survey was in regards to 'Public Attitude towards Transition to A Market Economy' in June 1990: 4.9 per cent

> link *perestroika* with the emergence of negative phenomena in the life of modern society, such as: organised crime, economic chaos, absence of concrete deeds … aggravation of ethnic relations, inertia and reversals in social development, growth of alcoholism and its consequences, profiteering, lawlessness … absence of social protection, evanescence of public consumption goods.[126]

A year later it was disclosed that

> while seven Balts and Georgians out of every ten say there is too little freedom and very few people claim there is too much, Central Asians are quite different; only 28 percent of the Turkmen and Tadjiks and 36 percent of the Uzbeks complained of restriction on freedom, and 20 percent of the Tadjiks say there is too much freedom.[127]

Confronted with increasing dissatisfaction with his line in the union republics, Gorbachev failed to amend it: 'Given his complete lack of understanding, Gorbachev was simply dumbfounded when one nationality after another demanded attention.'[128] Gradually, the incumbent ruling elite in Tajikistan came to realise that reliance on the decaying centre could not guarantee its stay in power. It might have embarked upon the path of adapting the political machine to the new conditions, mobilising the masses under the slogans of nation-state building, as was done in the neighbouring Central Asian republics; instead, Mahkamov's clique deployed its own version of the 'politics of survival', which pursued the sole objective of pre-empting the emergence of competing power centres in Tajikistan. Coalition-building along regional lines and pitting sub-ethnic groupings against each other were two important elements of this strategy.

Mahkamov's northerners found an unlikely ally in the face of the Pamiris, who were promised greater political and economic autonomy. During the fifteenth plenum of the CPT CC in December 1989, Mahkamov declared that

> there are already shifts in this field. For example, the Chairman of the [Badakhshan] *oblast* Soviet of People's Deputies will have the status of Deputy Chairman of the Supreme Soviet of the republic. The right of

---

positive; 19.3 per cent ambivalent; 56.9 per cent negative; 2.7 per cent indifferent; 15.8 per cent 'hard to answer'. Meanwhile, the Soviet average for 'positive' in this poll was 9.9 per cent and in Estonia 34.4 per cent. See: *Vestnik statistiki*, No. 2 (1991), p. 61.

126   *Vuzovskaia molodezh*, Vypusk 1, pp. 61–2.

127   Roy D. Laird, *The Soviet Legacy* (Westport, Conn.: Praeger, 1993), pp. 171–2.

128   Anders Åslund, 'Russia's Road from Communism', *Daedalus*, Vol. 121, No. 2 (Spring 1992), p. 78.

legislative initiative has been granted to the *oblast*. A certain quota for the GBAO representatives in the Supreme Soviet should be envisaged in the future.[129]

The appointment of Mamadayoz Navjuvonov, a Pamiri army colonel with no police experience, to the position of minister of interior in March 1989 signalled a major departure from established personnel practices—previously this crucial post had been occupied exclusively by Kulobis (or by someone who allowed Kulobis to dominate in the ranks). In the words of one prominent opponent, Navjuvonov 'elevated regionalism to its repulsive heights. He placed his relatives and friends in important positions in regions, districts and towns of the republic, and especially within the Ministry of Interior.'[130] The significance of this change in the Ministry of Interior for regionally based grievances is clear.

Competition in Qurghonteppa and Kulob

The struggle for dominance in Qurghonteppa involved Kulobis, Gharmis and Uzbeks (the last made up almost one-third of the population).[131] Aziz Niyazi describes the situation in the Qurghonteppa *oblast*:[132]

> In the second half of the 1980s and at the beginning of the 1990s local conflicts constantly erupted in the region, both between Tajiks and non-Tajiks and among Tajiks themselves originating from different regions of the republic. Sharp nomenklatura infighting broke out, mostly between Uzbeks, Garm and Kuliabi Tajiks over administrative and managerial posts at all levels. It was there, in a region being industrialized at full speed, with its ethnic and subethnic mosaic, that the sores that would later affect the body of the republic first came to a head. Regional contradictions and interests were spreading over into parochial struggles involving the district and regional authorities. The localist threads of intraregional nomenklatura games were reaching out into the central power apparatus.

In the 1980s, the pattern of sharing power in Qurghonteppa was as follows: *obkom* first secretary from Kulob, chairman of the executive committee from Gharm and head of the local cooperative society (*Tojikmatlubot*) an ethnic Uzbek. In 1988 there was a restructuring of the administrative status of southern Tajikistan when Kulob and Qurghonteppa lost their *oblast* status. There are several conflicting versions for the motivations behind the merging

129   *Kommunist Tadzhikistana*, 8 December 1989.
130   Dustov, *Zakhm bar jismi vatan*, p. 24.
131   Rubin, 'Tajikistan', p. 211.
132   Niyazi, 'Tajikistan I', p. 154.

of the Kulob and Qurghonteppa *oblasts* into the united Khatlon *oblast* in April 1988: a) the leadership of Kulob had secured the merger on their initiative; b) the consolidation of Kulob and Qurghonteppa was aimed at reducing the power of Kulobi elites;[133] and c) the merger was an attempt on the part of the ruling elites to create fragmentation amongst the southerners, who were at this time starting to agitate against northern domination.[134] The Kulobis had received most of the top administrative jobs in the newly established Khatlon *oblast*, much to the annoyance of Gharmi settlers in the Vakhsh Valley, who had by that time 'gained control of transport and trade, the spheres that had always brought much profit'.[135] Nevertheless, Mahkamov's bureaucratic changes had also allowed Gharmis to secure some important positions in the Qurghonteppa regional government.[136] According to Rahmon Nabiev, the merger was a purely political exercise, costly, unnecessary and not warranted by any economic considerations.[137] Kulob and Qurghonteppa would eventually regain *oblast* status in January 1990 with the dismantling of Khatlon. At this time the locals in Kulob were able to take back control over the local government apparatuses. But while the attacks on local elites had now ended, the Kulobis were still excluded from national-level positions while Pamiris and Qarotegini (Gharmi) Tajiks were now increasingly being appointed to national-level positions. This led to an even further disaffection between the Kulobi elite and the centre as the Kulobi elite no longer saw any beneficial relationship to be had with the centre.[138]

Additionally, in 1988 a series of clashes between Gharmis and Uzbeks erupted in the Qurghonteppa region, especially in its southern Kolkhozobod *raion*. Uzbeks, who were the indigenous population, demanded fairer distribution of scarce arable lands and the break-up of collective farms into smaller units on an ethnic basis. The CPT leadership showed remarkable inability to cope with the problem. The crisis lasted a whole month and ended only when local elders took the initiative into their hands and demarcated fields and living quarters, bypassing the civic authorities. Trespassing was strictly prohibited, and ethnic militias armed with clubs and hunting guns were formed, for the first time in the Soviet period.[139] At one point the Kolkhozobod district party committee was ransacked during a mass rally:

> It was the first political gathering that claimed blood ... People driven to the edge had realised that the leader of the Tajik state, Mahkamov, was incapable and his government was in a state of paralysis. Preparations

133 Markowitz, *Collapsed and Prebendal States in Post-Soviet Eurasia*, pp. 97–100.
134 G. Khaidarov and M. Inomov, *Tajikistan: Tragedy and Anguish of the Nation* (St Petersburg: LINKO, 1993), p. 22.
135 Khaidarov and Inomov, *Tajikistan*, p. 22. See also: Niyazi, 'Tajikistan I', p. 151.
136 Markowitz, *Collapsed and Prebendal States in Post-Soviet Eurasia*, pp. 118, 121.
137 *Tojikistoni Soveti*, 23 February 1990.
138 Markowitz, *Collapsed and Prebendal States in Post-Soviet Eurasia*, pp. 97–100.
139 *Haqiqati Kolkhozobod*, 3 October 1991.

for overthrowing Q. Mahkamov's regime were underway amongst the Gharmis, Qaroteginis and Pamiris residing in the Qurghonteppa region.[140]

The stalemated pattern of leadership at the top was about to be challenged by civil violence, focusing on political issues but rooted in much deeper cultural cleavages.

While Roy pointed to the relative personal wealth of Gharmis in Qurghonteppa,[141] it was control of collective farms that was the most contentious issue in the competition between local Gharmi and Kulobi elites, as well as between the memberships of their respective networks. The collective and state farms of Qurghonteppa's Vakhsh River Valley accounted for 40 per cent of the value of Tajikistan's agricultural production, resulting in the competition for influence and control here being 'one of the greatest sources of inter-regional tension in the republic'.[142] As elsewhere in Central Asia, in Qurghonteppa Province administrators traditionally had very long tenures, the powerful chairmen of collective farms in particular. For example, in a sampling of 15 Qurghonteppa farm bosses from the late 1930s to the mid 1980s, Markowitz finds that the mean number of years in office was more than 23; however, starting in the early 1980s there was significant turnover of political and economic leaders in Qurghonteppa. The purges of the second half of the 1980s included the replacement of the purged leaders with Russians, Pamiris and Gharmis. The very brief tenure of district first secretaries in Qurghonteppa Province, as opposed to the long tenure of their predecessors, illustrated this trend. Despite these actions, the reforms in Qurghonteppa were not successful in asserting control over the local power structures, even as the old elites' patronage networks were dismantled. Established patterns of political and economic power were not easy to displace.[143] Markowitz describes the situation in Qurghonteppa leading up to independence:

> [T]he provincial elite was divided from 1988 onwards, splitting districts and even collective farms with some tied to reformist cadres

---

140   Nasriddinov, *Tarkish*, p. 44.
141   Roy, 'Is the Conflict in Tajikistan a Model for Conflicts throughout Central Asia', p. 139. Roy writes: 'For reasons that have yet to be elucidated, the Gharmis rapidly acquired a dominant position locally [in Qurghonteppa]: their wealth is apparent from their houses (often multi-storied) … [They are w]ell off, but excluded from Communist power.' Colette Harris studied Gharmi communities in Khatlon (Qurghonteppa) and offered this assessment of their income levels before the war: 'the Gharmis increased their incomes substantially by selling fruit from their private plots in Russia at high prices. Before the civil war many Gharmi families in this area possessed several cars as well as at least one television set, radio, sewing machine, and refrigerator—that is, most of the larger consumer goods available in the former Soviet Union.' See: Colette Harris, 'Coping with Daily Life in Post-Soviet Tajikistan: The Gharmi Villages of Khatlon Province', *Central Asian Survey*, Vol. 17, No. 4 (1998), pp. 657–8.
142   Markowitz, *Collapsed and Prebendal States in Post-Soviet Eurasia*, p. 52.
143   Markowitz, *Collapsed and Prebendal States in Post-Soviet Eurasia*, pp. 114–15, 119–21.

(who primarily originated from the Karategin Valley [Gharmis] and GBAO [Pamiris]) and others tied to the old guard (who had close ties to Leninabad and Kuliab) being appointed to posts in the region following Makhkamov's resignation in August 1991.[144]

Mahkamov's campaign included law enforcement investigations into areas that were previously under the protection of local party officials. Of course, the turnover was implemented in a manner that would keep Leninobodis/ Khujandis in a dominant position. But still, Pamiris and Tajiks from Qarotegin were appointed to significant national-level positions for the first time since the 1940s. In reaction to Mahkamov's policies, the elites in Kulob no longer saw a mutually beneficial patronage relationship with the central government. They soon started embezzling agricultural profits while taking over local law enforcement and judicial agencies as a way to protect their scheme. By the end of the Soviet period, farm bosses and regional politicians in Kulob exercised 'significant influence' over law enforcement agencies and the courts while increasingly relying on illegal income.[145]

Stephane Dudoignon describes an intensified competition during 1990–91 at the elite level in Qurghonteppa between the Brezhnev-era elite on one side and Gharmi and Pamiri elites on the other. The Pamiri and Gharmi elites continued to push for political and economic reforms that would bolster their decreasing power and influence.[146] In competition with the Gharmi and Pamiri elites were many apparatchiks from Kulob who were—since autumn 1991 during the lead-up to elections—working as part of an alliance with Nabiev.[147] Mahkamov's bureaucratic changes had allowed Gharmis to secure important positions in the Qurghonteppa regional government. But the situation changed by late 1991 when President Nabiev's counter-reforms allowed Kulobis to gain 'unprecedented access' to powerful positions in Qurghonteppa.[148] This was part of an effort by

---

144   Markowitz, *Collapsed and Prebendal States in Post-Soviet Eurasia*, p. 121.

145   Markowitz, *Collapsed and Prebendal States in Post-Soviet Eurasia*, pp. 84–90, 95, 99, 101.

146   Markowitz, *Collapsed and Prebendal States in Post-Soviet Eurasia*, p. 122.

147   Parviz Mullojonov, 'The Islamic Clergy in Tajikistan Since the End of the Soviet Period', in *Islam and Politics in Russia and Central Asia (Early Eighteenth to Late Twentieth Centuries)*, eds Stéphane Dudoignon and Komatsu Hisao (London: Kegan Paul, 2001), p. 248. Matveeva, however, notes that there was an earlier relationship. As early as the 1970s more personnel from Hisor and Kulob were brought into the 'ruling establishment'. This is as opposed to Gharmis, who 'had little standing' at the time. See: Anna Matveeva, 'The Perils of Emerging Statehood: Civil War and State Reconstruction in Tajikistan', *Crisis States Working Papers*, Series No. 2, Paper No. 46 (March 2009), p. 7.

148   Markowitz, *Collapsed and Prebendal States in Post-Soviet Eurasia*, pp. 118, 121.

Kulobi elites that Schoeberlein-Engel terms an attempt to 'dominate and even annex' Qurghonteppa;[149] however, not as many old elites were able to retake their positions as those in Kulob had done.[150]

By early 1992 in Qurghonteppa the competing Gharmi elites—some tied to 'patrons in the Karategin valley'—on one side and elites tied to Kulob and Leninobod on the other 'increasingly viewed their interests as under attack from the other' as each side made 'repeated efforts [to] gain ground over the other' in the competition for control over state-controlled resources.[151] Markowitz argues that '[t]ension and barely concealed hostility within the provincial elite left the region primed for the outbreak of conflict'.[152] The situation worsened once President Nabiev agreed to form a 'Government of National Reconciliation' in May 1992. The emboldened opposition leaders then attempted to remove selected leaders in the Qurghonteppa regional administration, many of whom had been appointed in late 1991 when Nabiev returned to the top leadership position. Markowitz argues that the administrators appointed by Nabiev 'had come to represent a foreign occupying force among those with patronage ties to the Karategin Valley [that is, Gharmis]'.[153] Under pressure, Nabiev allowed his new appointee to the top administrative position in Qurghonteppa to remove several politicians and attempt to remove others with ties to Kulob; however, the new appointee, Nurali Qurbonov, did not have the power to remove the strongest local politicians and economic actors. The action further polarised the two sides in Qurghonteppa.[154]

The Failure of Nationalism

During the period 1988–91, Gorbachev destroyed the mechanisms of legitimacy for state socialism and eviscerated the party's monopoly on political socialisation. Various alternative forms of social and political aggregation came into being to fill the void left by the shrinking CPSU. Analysing Gorbachev's political reforms, T. H. Rigby has observed that 'whereas in Russia proper the most influential unofficial organisations were concerned with general issues of political and social reform, in the non-Russian republics those focusing on national causes quickly came to the fore'.[155] Ostensibly, Tajikistan was no

---

149   John Schoeberlein-Engel, 'Bones of Contention: Conflicts over Resources', in *Searching for Peace in Central and South Asia: An Overview of Conflict Prevention and Peacebuilding Activities*, eds Monique Mekenkamp, Paul van Tongeren and Hans van de Veen (Boulder, Colo., and London: Lynne Rienner Publishers, 2002), p. 89.
150   Markowitz, *Collapsed and Prebendal States in Post-Soviet Eurasia*, p. 118, 121.
151   Markowitz, *Collapsed and Prebendal States in Post-Soviet Eurasia*, pp. 118–19, 122–3.
152   Markowitz, *Collapsed and Prebendal States in Post-Soviet Eurasia*, pp. 122–3.
153   Markowitz, *Collapsed and Prebendal States in Post-Soviet Eurasia*, p. 123.
154   Markowitz, *Collapsed and Prebendal States in Post-Soviet Eurasia*, pp. 123–4.
155   Rigby, *The Changing Soviet System*, p. 218.

exception to the rule—institutional processes in the republic had a distinctly nationalist imprint; however, ethnic mobilisation ultimately failed there (as did Islamist mobilisation), and political activism took the form of regional factionalism. Why did this happen?

Michael Rywkin, hardly one of Brezhnev's admirers, has assessed his era as 'the culmination of what Soviet nationality policy and the socialist economy were capable of delivering'.[156] In 1982, Rahmon Nabiev, then first secretary of the CPT CC, wrote:

> From the heights of the present day we can clearly see the heroic path covered by the Tajik people, toilers of the republic, during the years of Soviet power, the path from feudalism to developed socialism, from a state of possessing no rights to freedom, from poverty and ignorance to a peak of economic and spiritual prosperity.[157]

However bombastic and preposterous this statement may appear, the Great Socialist Myth did indeed take root in Tajik society, at least in its upper strata. And 'once a myth has been propounded in a closed society, it can be nurtured and developed through the almost unlimited controls at the disposal of the regime'.[158]

Intellectuals have always been the bearers of national consciousness in developing societies. In Tajikistan 'an impressive quota of Tajik novelists, essayists, historians, and poets from all classes and regions converged within the unerring guidelines of the writers' unions in Moscow and Dushanbe to define the republic's literary personality. As compensation for political subordination, the Tajiks ... had developed a cultural superiority complex.'[159] The Tajik intelligentsia was characterised by spiritual dualism: its commitment to traditional cultural values and forms had to coexist with the aesthetic and ideological imperatives of the Soviet era.[160] Beginning in the late 1960s, in the general context of Brezhnev's politics of 'normalcy', the moral dilemma of intellectuals lost its acuteness to an extent; the new generation of poets, writers and artists was able to express a plurality of views, albeit in camouflaged form.

---

156   Michael Rywkin, *Moscow's Lost Empire* (Armonk, NY: M. E. Sharpe, 1994), p. 181.

157   R. N. Nabiev, *Sovetskii Tadzhikistan* (Moscow: Izdatelstvo politicheskoi literatury, 1982), p. 106.

158   Lowell Tillett, *The Great Friendship: Soviet Historians on the Non-Russian Nationalities* (Chapel Hill: University of North Carolina Press, 1969), p. 5.

159   John B. Perry, 'Tajik Literature: Seventy Years Is Longer Than the Millenium', *World Literature Today*, Vol. 70, No. 3 (Summer 1996), p. 572.

160   A Tajik writer reminisced in 1994 that 'if we go back to the socialist epoch, poets then were on the top of social influence, unlike Islamists, and were making a substantial contribution to the Weltanschauung [world view] of the people ... The poet in the Orient is more than a poet. This formula ... has always been supported by the Bolsheviks in our country ... Many politicians in Tajikistan took pride in friendship with *literati* ... It was not simply a matter of prestige, but also the recognition of poetry as the main cultural component of the Oriental mentality.' See: *Literaturnaiia gazeta*, No. 41 (12 October 1994), p. 7.

Professor Rahimi Musulmoniyon, a renowned Tajik anti-communist, has written that it was a time when a lot of young, talented people not afraid of telling the truth came to the fore.[161] Eventually a number of discursive fields emerged in Tajik culture where national and Soviet themes organically merged—the unprecedented heroism of Tajiks during the Great Patriotic War for one.[162]

Gradually the denigrating Khrushchev-era image of Tajiks as primitive Asians led out of a historical backwater by progressive forces from European Russia[163] gave way to a much different appraisal of reality, based on praising the glorious past and creative present of the Tajik people. Publication in 1970 of Bobojon Ghafurov's monumental work *The Tajiks: Archaic, Ancient and Mediaeval History*,[164] which laid claim to most of the classical Persian canon, was a milestone in the process of reinventing Tajik history. It quickly became the bible of every Tajik intellectual: in 1989, 62 per cent of tertiary students of the titular nationality had this book in their possession.[165] Ghafurov gave rise to a whole school of academics who propagated the notion of the uniqueness of the Tajiks and their mission to transmit knowledge of the past in Central Asia. The prominent Tajik historian Rahim Masov has insisted that 'without the knowledge of the Tajik language, study of the cultural heritage of Turkic peoples is impossible … All pre-revolutionary spiritual culture of the peoples of Central Asia can be comprehended only with the assistance of the Tajik language.'[166]

The alleged outright Russification of non-Slavic ethnic groups used to be one of the favourite themes of Western experts on Soviet nationality policy; some of them propounded truly apocalyptic views such as 'the languages of the non-Russian peoples of the USSR seem doomed to eventual extinction'.[167] In reality, the 1970s

161   *Adolat*, No. 2 (November 1990), p. 7.
162   During the war, 13 997 Tajiks received orders and medals of the USSR; 14 of them became Heroes of the Soviet Union. See: *Natsionalnaia politika KPSS v deistvii* (Tashkent: Uzbekistan, 1979), p. 257.
163   See, for instance, the sycophantic statement made by the CPT CC first secretary, Tursun Uljaboev, in February 1960: 'Who helped us to gain freedom, to become consolidated as a nation … to build up an industry and the kolkhoz system, to liquidate illiteracy once and for all, to create a culture national in form and socialist in content—The Communist Party, the great Russian people.' See: V. Borysenko, 'The 1959 Purges in the Communist Parties of the Soviet National Republics', *Problems of the Peoples of the USSR*, No. 5 (1960), p. 13.
164   B. G. Ghafurov, *Tadzhiki: drevneishaia, drevniaia i srednevekovaia istoriia*, 2nd edn (Dushanbe: Irfon, 1989). According to Ghafurov, works by Omar Khayyam, Abdurrahman Jami and even Hafiz were classics of Tajik literature. Ibid., Vol. 2, pp. 163, 250, 255.
165   *Vuzovskaia molodezh*, Vypusk 1, p. 29.
166   Masov, *Istoriia topornogo razdeleniia*, pp. 16–17. Generally, one has to agree with Teresa Rakowska-Harmstone that 'the massive effort to adapt the traditional modes of cultural expression to the reality of the new Soviet system has been impressive, and has produced some interesting results on the part of the new Tadzhik Soviet intellectuals and artists … The dominant theme … has been the desire to preserve the traditional and Persian classical characteristics in as unadulterated a form as possible. This does not mean that the Soviet content has been wholly rejected; some of its features—especially those touching on the improvement in the economic and social conditions—appear to have been fully absorbed.' See: Rakowska-Harmstone, *Russia and Nationalism in Central Asia*, p. 267.
167   Michael Bruchis, 'The Effect of the USSR's Language Policy on the National Languages of Its Turkic Population', in *The USSR and the Muslim World: Issues in Domestic and Foreign Policy*, ed. Yaacov Ro'i (London: George Allen & Unwin, 1984), p. 146.

saw more extensive use of indigenous languages in public communication in Central Asia, at the expense of Russian.[168] In 1971, the Terminology Committee of the Academy of Sciences of the Tajik SSR published an instruction that provided for greater usage of Tajik words and grammatical constructions in state affairs and science; this was 'an important step in the direction of strengthening and formalising the national basis of the Tajik semantics'.[169] The percentage of Tajiks who claimed fluency in Russian did not increase after the 1970s and was only 30 per cent at the time of the 1989 census.[170]

A combination of factors, such as the autonomy of the nativised bureaucracy, the existence of a stratum of indigenous intellectuals, and a growing ability to express national identity through artistic means, had contributed to the phenomenon of 'Soviet-encouraged cultural nationalism'[171] in Central Asia. It remained confined, however, by and large, to specialised and governing elites in Tajikistan. In Donald Carlisle's words, 'the intelligentsia and middle class, and urban settings as opposed to rural locales, are the initial incubators for nationalism. But unless such restive elites have mass backing and their urban base expands into rural support, no powerful national amalgam emerges and no successful national movement can be born'.[172] Modernist city-based intellectuals were as alien to their traditionalist compatriots in the countryside as hi-tech factories were to the agricultural economy of Tajikistan. Moreover, the competence and breadth of outlook of writers, artists, scholars and other professionals who were trained inside and outside the republic in quite sufficient numbers[173] were often inadequate. In the 1980s, only one-quarter of all research projects pursued under the aegis of the Academy of Sciences of Tajikistan corresponded to the All-Union level.[174]

In the national republics 'the reproduction of intellectual and governing elites had acquired unprecedented proportions ... For the sake of maintaining the symbols of national statehood enormous resources were pumped into the structures of local academies of science, professional creative unions, cinematography, theatre, elite sports, etc.'[175] The new indigenous middle class in Tajikistan was reared for one purpose only: to serve USSR, Inc.; it was part of the *nomenklatura*. There was little danger that 'Soviet cultural nationalism' in

168 James Critchlow, *Nationalism in Uzbekistan: A Soviet Republic's Road to Independence* (Boulder, Colo.: Westview Press, 1991), p. 26.

169 Muhammadjon Shukurov, 'Nazare ba tahavvoli prinsiphoi istilohsozii Tojiki', *Akhboroti Akademiiai Fanhoi RSS Tojikiston: Seriyai sharqshinosi, tarikh, zabonshinosi*, No. 4 (24) (1991), p. 6.

170 *Vestnik statistiki*, No. 5 (1991), p. 74.

171 Bryant Leroy Larson, *The Moslems of Soviet Central Asia: Soviet and Western Perceptions of a Growing Political Problem* (PhD Thesis: University of Minnesota, 1983), p. 207.

172 D. S. Carlisle, 'Power and Politics in Soviet Uzbekistan: From Stalin to Gorbachev', in *Soviet Central Asia: The Failed Transformation*, ed. William Fierman (Boulder, Colo.: Westview Press, 1991), p. 120.

173 L. I. Kalandarova, 'Podgotovka kadrov khudozhestvennoi intelligentsii v Tadzhikistane (1976–1985gg.)', *Izvestiia AN TSSR. Seriia: vostokovedenie, istoriia, filologiia*, No. 2 (26) (1992), pp. 45–50.

174 Usmanov, *Tekhnicheskaia rekonstruktsiia industrii Tadzhikistana v usloviiakh perestroiki*, p. 54.

175 V. Tishkov, 'O prirode etnicheskogo konflikta', *Svobodnaia mysl*, No. 4 (1993), p. 12.

the republic would become political nationalism. Asliddin Sohibnazarov, one of the genuine proponents of Tajik nationalism, has remarked bitterly that at the beginning of *perestroika* there were just 'one–two dozen … Tajik intellectuals who had accepted progressive [that is, nationalist] ideas'.[176]

The socialist type of modernity created serious identification problems, of which national identification was just a part. Figure 6.1 depicts a hierarchy of identities in Soviet Tajikistan in ascending order. Traditional forms of spatial organisation were supplemented by affiliation with the Soviet Union and Tajikistan; in fact, as far as this affiliation was concerned, it was quite possible to speak about the 'fusion of national and imperial identities under both the Tsarist Russia and, in a different way, the Soviet regime'.[177] The fact that socialism was mapped onto the heterogeneous Tajik community by external forces need not have undermined the viability of new identities.[178] Soviet authorities created the national republic of Tajikistan; it was associated with communist rule in people's minds, and remained a potent source of identity so long as the regime's coercive and redistributive functions remained intact.

Figure 6.1 Spatial Hierarchy of Identities in Soviet Tajikistan

Soviet Union

Central Asia (Turkestan)

Tajikistan

Region

Group of villages River valley City

Village *Mahalla*

Family

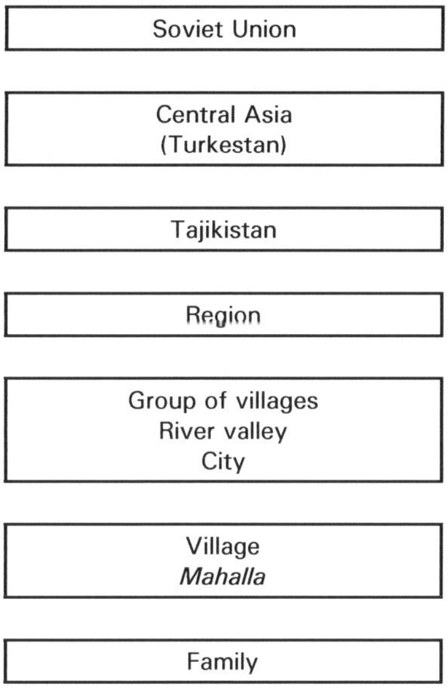

Source: Author's research.

---

176   *Tajik-Press*, No. 3 (20–27 May 1992), p. 2.

177   Veljko Vujacic, 'Historical Legacies, Nationalist Mobilisation, and Political Outcomes in Russia and Serbia: A Weberian View', *Theory and Society*, Vol. 25, No. 6 (December 1996), p. 769.

178   'A sense of identity may be consistent with inauthenticity and great impoverishment of character. In malign environments, a sense of identity may even depend upon inauthenticity of character or personality except in the most philosophically wise individuals.' See: Morton A. Kaplan, *Alienation and Identification* (New York: The Free Press, 1976), p. 164.

Alexandre Bennigsen wrote in 1979 that 'sub-national and supra-national loyalties remain strong in Central Asia and actively compete with national ones';[179] however, his thesis that this supra-national identity ought to be based on anti-Russian 'pan-Turkestanism' with the Uzbeks as its directing element is difficult to accept, at least as far as Tajikistan is involved. To begin with, in the years before *perestroika*, publically expressed anti-Russian feelings were practically unknown in Tajikistan.[180] Ethnic Tajiks dominated in all spheres of human activities in the republic, except for industry, construction and science.[181] There was practically no occupational competition between Tajiks on the one hand, and Russians and other Europeans on the other. In contrast, Uzbeks, who lived predominantly in rural areas of Tajikistan and were involved mostly in agriculture, presented a potential target for ethnic antagonism. Additionally, discriminatory policies pursued by Uzbek leaders throughout the Soviet era towards Tajiks living in Uzbekistan had led to a situation in which 'language, culture, national feelings and interests of Tajiks in these cities [Samarkand and Bukhara] were deeply harmed. Negative developments in the field of Uzbek–Tajik interlingual and interethnic relations have created perceptible social strain.'[182] Still, sociological data gathered in 1989 demonstrated that while throughout the USSR 29 per cent of the population characterised the state of interethnic relations in the country as 'very tense and prone to further exacerbation', only 14 per cent of those surveyed in Tajikistan shared this pessimistic view.[183]

Thus, it appears that affiliation with the Soviet Union was the dominant supranational identity for the Tajiks; it also served as a major source of modern political and cultural values on the national level. Old values derived vitality from traditional identities, of which regionalism was the highest form.[184] For decades the communist authorities suppressed and, to an extent, utilised regionalism in Tajikistan, but ultimately failed to overcome it. The native elite in the republic was uniform in the sense that 'it was poisoned by conformism, duplicity, cowardice and selfishness … Being its sole employer, the state had

---

179   Alexandre Bennigsen, 'Several Nations or One People? Ethnic Consciousness among Soviet Central Asian Muslims', *Survey*, Vol. 24, No. 3 (108) (Summer 1979), p. 62.

180   As Ben Fowkes has noted, corporatist compromise under Brezhnev allowed the titular nation 'to lord it over the non-titular nationalities'. See: Ben Fowkes, *The Disintegration of the Soviet Union: A Study in the Rise and Triumph of Nationalism* (New York: St Martin's Press, 1997), p. 103.

181   The share of employees of the titular nationality (that is, Tajiks) by branch in 1987 was: industry (48 per cent); agriculture (63 per cent); transport and communication (57 per cent); construction (48 per cent); trade and public catering (61 per cent); public health (56 per cent); arts and culture (56 per cent); sciences (31 per cent); government apparatus (51 per cent); communal services (56 per cent). See: V. Maltsev, 'Territorialnyi khozraschet: ot raspredeleniia k obmenu', *Vestnik statistiki*, No. 1 (1991), p. 8.

182   R. R. Rahimov, 'K voprosu o sovremennykh tadzhiksko-uzbekskikh mezhnatsionalnykh otnosheniiakh', *Sovetskaia etnografiia*, No. 1 (January–February 1991), p. 22.

183   Alimov and Saidov, *Natsionalnyi vopros*, p. 72.

184   David Harvey has commented that 'territorial place-based identity, particularly when conflated with race, gender, religious and class differentiation, is one of the most pervasive bases for both progressive political mobilisation and reactionary exclusionary politics'. See: David Harvey, 'From Space to Place and Back Again', in *Mapping the Futures: Local Culture, Global Change*, ed. Jon Bird (London: Routledge, 1993), p. 4.

secured its material and spiritual dependency'.[185] At the same time, the elite was highly compartmentalised along regional lines. According to Otakhon Saifulloev, secretary of the Writers' Union of Tajikistan between 1968 and 1973 and chairman of the State Broadcasting Committee of Tajikistan between 1991 and 1992, in the early 1970s there were 94 Tajik writers in the republic, who formed six rival groups; Saifulloev headed the largest faction of 25 Leninobodis, who dominated the Tajik literary landscape and had the lion's share of books published.[186]

The 'imaginary community' of the Tajiks in the greater part of the twentieth century was a symbiosis construed through the political actions and poetics of Soviet nationalism and the Great Tradition of Central Asian Iranians. The importance of the Soviet component, with its specific political culture, forced indoctrination and modernisation drive, should not be underestimated. However contradictory, artificial and cruel, it constituted 'the thin film of modern notions over the formidable layer of values, motivations, role expectations and behavioural stereotypes inherent in each region's traditional culture'.[187] Once the institutional core of Soviet cultural overlay began to erode under Gorbachev, political activism in Tajikistan inevitably assumed the form of regional factionalism.

Institutional Changes and the Crisis of Social Control

Radicalisation of reforms ultimately reduced Gorbachev's power base and alienated all major elites in Soviet society. The second and final stage of *perestroika* included the following measures in the political realm

- liberalisation of formal political institutions
- democratisation of public expression and public association
- withdrawal of the party's key regulatory functions
- weakening of the state's coercive mechanisms.

The communist *apparat* eventually began to realise that its very existence was under threat, but it was too late: the dismantling of the mono-organisational order was out of control.[188] In January 1987, secret ballot and multi-candidate

---

185   *Kazakhstanskaia pravda*, 31 March 1994.

186   Taped interview, Khujand, 9 March 1995.

187   Olimov, 'Ob etnopoliticheskoi i konfessionalnoi situatsii v Tadzhikistane i veroiatnosti mezhetnicheskikh konfliktov', p. 86.

188   As Charles Fairbanks views it, 'the enormous power of Gorbachev goes far to explain why the elite gave up power, contrary to our expectations. They gave up power because of their own reformism and because of fear of the public, but most of all because Gorbachev forced them to.' See: Charles H. Fairbanks, jr, 'The Nature of the Beast', *The National Interest*, No. 31 (Spring 1993), p. 55.

elections were introduced in all party organisations. Following the nineteenth CPSU conference in June 1988, party committees at all levels were stripped of the ability to oversee economic agencies, the bulk of administrative powers was transferred to the Soviets and contested elections to a new legislature were announced. In October 1988, Gorbachev was elected chairman of the USSR Supreme Soviet, signifying a shift of the loci of power from party structures. In spring 1989, the new Soviet parliament was convened, which elected Gorbachev president of the USSR. In February 1990, the CPSU formally renounced its monopoly on power. The role of the military in national decision-making decreased; withdrawal from Afghanistan, unilateral concessions to the West and usage of troops in police operations contributed to the decay of the armed forces. The KGB, an erstwhile tool of social control, was exposed to public criticism and lost, to an extent, its coercive edge.

Similar processes unfolded in Tajikistan, which remained 'the quietest and the most obedient of all the republics. Whatever the centre ordered, was accepted, with a thousand thanks.'[189] By 1989, the CPT CC apparatus had shrunk by one-third compared with 1986.[190] Party structures at lower levels were weakened to the point where they did not have the organisational capacity to implement social control: the committee of the Hisor *raion*, with a population of 230 000, had 12 staff, whereas, in comparison, four registered mosques in the district had 24 official mullahs alone.[191] In spring 1988, 25 ministries and 17 state committees that operated in Tajikistan were reorganised into 12 new agencies.[192] The Tajik KGB was especially badly crippled in the late Gorbachev period: its staff cuts were three times the All-Union ratio.[193] One major deviation from the Moscow pattern was that freedom of speech and freedom of association never really took off in Tajikistan. While in 1989 in Moscow alone there existed 500 unofficial organisations which 'strove to some degree or other to influence the domestic or foreign policy of the state',[194] Qahhor Mahkamov had the following to say on the subject of the proliferation of alternative associations:[195]

> And, really, let us think—is it appropriate today to put forward suggestions about creating this or that new public organisation, when we already have more than enough of them? Those who have a sincere desire to help *perestroika* can apply their energy, initiative and craving

---

189 Holiqzoda, *Ta'rikhi siyyosii Tojikon az istiloi Rusiyya to imruz*, p. 113.
190 Calculations based on the CPT CC telephone directories.
191 *Kommunist Tadzhikistana*, 27 February 1991.
192 *Izvestiia*, 5 April 1988.
193 *Biznes i politika*, No. 14 (120) (April 1995), p. 1.
194 Rigby, *The Changing Soviet System*, p. 217.
195 *Payyomi Dushanbe*, 8 December 1989.

to serve their people, and transform them into practical deeds, through Party, trade-union and Komsomol organisations, newly elected Soviets and our numerous existing public associations and creative unions.

At the beginning of 1990, the overall impression was that throughout Central Asia popular acceptance of the republican leaderships remained high; the participation of the population in political life was nowhere near 'as advanced or as widespread as was public involvement elsewhere in the country'.[196] The communist elite was still in charge in Tajikistan, and the major menace to its dominance emanated not from disgruntled masses of people, but from the internecine struggle inside the *apparat*.

February 1990 Demonstrations and Riots

On 25 February 1990, elections to the new Supreme Soviet of Tajikistan were to be held. In light of the latest developments in the USSR, positions in the republican legislature had acquired special attractiveness to members of the power elite. For the first time, at least some constituencies had a choice of candidates. In the absence of institutionalised forms of interest aggregation such as political parties and organisations, only belonging to the communist establishment could guarantee electoral success for would-be parliamentarians. It was clear that Mahkamov's coterie would dominate the Supreme Soviet unless something dramatic happened to change the alignment of forces in the CPT leadership. In February 1990, a desperate attempt was made by elements in the ruling oligarchy, heretofore alienated from supreme power, to oust Mahkamov. Intrigues and mini-coups were not uncommon in the Byzantine world of communist crypto-politics, but this time the attempt to redistribute power entailed mass civil disobedience that, intentionally or not, quickly turned to violence.

In early 1990, the southerners in Tajikistan understood quite well that Mahkamov's hold on power would receive further legitimation through parliamentary elections. It was also evident to them that the incumbent regime had been weakened by Moscow-inspired reorganisations and, as the clashes in Isfara and Kolkhozobod had demonstrated, it enjoyed limited abilities to deal with public strife. They also remembered that militant manifestations and consequent interference by the centre in Tbilisi in April 1989 had resulted in the leadership change in Georgia.[197] A group of prominent southern elite leaders

---

196   Bess Brown, 'The Role of Public Groups in *Perestroika* in Central Asia', *RL Report on the USSR* (26 January 1990), p. 25.
197   On 8 April 1989, mass demonstrations took place in Tbilisi. Organised by Georgia's Popular Front, they put forward slogans demanding the solution of the Abkhaz problem. The Soviet Army units deployed in the

decided to trigger—or, at a minimum, take advantage of—collective action in the capital city of Tajikistan in order to challenge, and possibly destroy, the positions of incumbent power-holders from the north.

Shahidon ('Martyrs') Square—which was to become an important location for the 1992 opposition rallies—was renamed (and later unnamed)[198] in memory of the demonstrators and rioters killed there and elsewhere in the city during the events of February 1990. On 10–11 February, up to 300 young demonstrators gathered in front of the Communist Party Central Committee building in Dushanbe and demanded an explanation from the government—and from Qahhor Mahkamov in particular—about the rumours that Armenian refugees from Azerbaijan would be given priority housing in Dushanbe amidst a housing crisis (in fact, only 29 Armenians had arrived and were being hosted by relatives in Dushanbe). As the government evaded answering, demands expanded— along with the size of the crowd—to include the resignation of Mahkamov and the purging of government officials. Mahkamov was taken by surprise and failed to react adequately. The crowd grew in size until as many as 3000 to 5000 people were in the streets when violence started. Martial law and a curfew were declared as the first detachments of Interior Ministry troops from Uzbekistan and Kazakhstan arrived to restore order amidst looting, vandalism and attacks on civilian bystanders, including ethnic Russians and other non-Tajiks.[199] In one account, at 3 pm on 12 February, the size of the protest crowd increased dramatically and no further demands were heard at this time. Instead, an attack on the CPT building commenced, with stone-throwing and even armed

---

city to protect government buildings clashed with the protestors: 16 civilians were killed and 75 servicemen were wounded. On 14 April 1989, first secretary of the Georgian Communist Party Central Committee, Jumber Patiashvili, was relieved of his duties, ostensibly for exceeding his powers by having ordered the troops to open fire. See: *BBC Summary of World Broadcasts*, Part I USSR (18 April 1989), SU/0437 A1/2. See also: Ronald Grigor Suny, *The Making of the Georgian Nation* (Bloomington and Indianapolis: Indiana University Press, 1994), pp. 322–3.

198   What was Shahidon Square is now cut in half by a large security fence protecting the Presidential Palace. It now appears to be just a large T-intersection where Rudaki Avenue (formerly Lenin Avenue) and Somoni Street (Putovskii Street) meet. A memorial placard at this location was quietly removed several years ago and very few young people or recent migrants know this placename.

199   Schoeberlein-Engel, 'Conflicts in Tajikistan and Central Asia', pp. 22–5; Jonathan K. Zartman, *Political Transition in Central Asian Republics: Authoritarianism versus Power-Sharing* (PhD Thesis: University of Denver, 2004), pp. 97–101; Kilavuz, *Understanding Violent Conflict*, pp. 131–2; Aziz Niyazi, 'The Year of Tumult: Tajikistan after February 1990', in *State, Religion and Society in Central Asia: A Post Soviet Critique*, ed. Vitaly Naumkin (Reading, UK: Ithaca Press, 1993), p. 264; Aleksandr Karpov, 'Dushanbe: Rumors Spark Riots, Deaths', *Izvestia* (13 February 1990), p. 8, in *The Current Digest of the Post-Soviet Press*, Vol. XLII, No. 7 (1990), p. 12; *Kommunist Tadzhikistana*, 16 January 1991. Atkin stresses that the February 1990 demonstrations were anti-government, not anti-Armenian. See: Muriel Atkin, 'Tajikistan: Reform, Reaction, and Civil War', in *New States, New Politics: Building the Post-Soviet Nations*, eds Ian Bremmer and Ray Taras (Cambridge: Cambridge University Press, 1997), p. 610. Some 41 200 citizens of Dushanbe, or 7 per cent of the entire population, were on the waiting list for housing. See: *Osnovnye pokazateli ekonomicheskogo i sotsialnogo razvitiia oblastei*, p. 14.

rioters.[200] While it is unclear which side fired the first shot (or attacked first),[201] what is clear is that the rioters, some carrying only pistols, were outgunned by the security forces.[202] Hastily, the 29 Armenians, plus about a hundred other Armenians who were long-time residents of Dushanbe, were evacuated on an emergency flight.[203]

On 13 February the mass meeting in the city centre continued in defiance of martial law; bands of marauders proceeded to operate in the suburbs. Late in the day, demonstrators nominated a new group (or the group appointed itself), named the Provisional People's Committee or the Temporary Committee for Crisis Resolution (TCCR), also known as Vahdat ('Unity'), to negotiate. The TCCR, endorsed by the meeting and headed by the first deputy of the chairman of the Council of Ministers and chairman of GOSPLAN, Buri Karimov, entered negotiations with Mahkamov.[204] Niyazi describes this group:

> It comprised top state officials, leaders of the unofficial social-political organisation, *Rastokhez*, representatives of the intelligentsia, businessmen, one mullah and a worker. The Committee was headed by the Deputy Chairman of the Council of Ministers and the Chairman of the Republic's Planning Board, [Buri] Karimov … The *Vahdat* representing the demonstrators put forward a number of demands including the resignation of the government. The committee warned that if this demand were not met there would be even worse violence.[205]

The various demands of the protesters included the expulsion of Armenian refugees, the resignation of the government and the removal of the Communist Party, the closure of an aluminium smelter in western Tajikistan for environmental reasons, equitable distribution of profits from cotton production, and the release of 25 protesters taken into custody.[206]

The attempt to secure the resignation of the government of the Tajik SSR, whether planned well before the demonstration and riots or hastily planned as a response to the opportunity offered by the chaotic situation, was nearly successful. On 14 February the first secretary, the chairman of the Supreme

200 Karpov, 'Dushanbe', p. 12. For a narrative that strongly condemns the rioters and praises the security forces, see: N. Sautin, 'The City Has Become Calmer', *Pravda* (20 February 1990), p. 6, in *The Current Digest of the Post-Soviet Press* (28 March 1990), p. 25.

201 For the competing claims, see: Mariia Ianovskaia, 'Dushanbe-1990: russkii vzgliad', *Fergana News Agency* (1 March 2010), online: <http://www.fergananews.com/article.php?id=6484>; Tilav Rasul-zade and Mariia Yanovskaia, 'Ochevidtsy Dushanbe-1990: Pogromy cprovotsirovali kommunisty—KGB-shniki', *Fergana News Agency* (22 February 2010), online: <http://www.fergananews.com/articles/6478>

202 Charles M. Madigan, 'Gorbachev Seeks Quick Action against Rioting', *Chicago Tribune* (15 February 1990), p. 5.

203 Karpov, 'Dushanbe', p. 12.

204 Niyazi, 'The Year of Tumult', pp. 264–6; Karimov, *Qurboni duzakhma*, p. 77.

205 Niyazi, 'The Year of Tumult', pp. 264–6.

206 Esther B. Fein, 'Upheaval in the East', *The New York Times* (14 February 1990).

Soviet and the chairman of the Council of Ministers 'agreed to sign a protocol with the *Vahdat* on the resignation of the government'.[207] The next day, Mahkamov, Khayoev and Pallaev announced their resignations. A group of high-ranking officials, including Buri Karimov,[208] began organisational work to create a Temporary Bureau of the CPT CC;[209] however, later in the same day a meeting of 'Dushanbe party and economic functionaries including members of the Central Committee and the Bureau' declared the protocol invalid on the grounds that it contradicted the decisions of the sixteenth plenary meeting of the Central Committee.[210] At this time, Soviet Interior Ministry troops were moving into the city, and by 15 February the police and military had Dushanbe under control. On 15 and 16 February, the seventeenth plenary meeting of the Central Committee was convened, where the members voted to reject the resignation of the first secretary and gave their vote of confidence.[211] The Extraordinary Plenum of the CPT CC, which convened with the participation of the CPSU CC Politburo candidate member, B. K. Pugo, rescinded Mahkamov's resignation. Most notably, all northerners voted against the resignation, while Nasriddinov's group supported it.[212]

Sporadic acts of violence continued until 19 February, but then 'everything changed abruptly overnight'.[213] Reports on the number of deaths vary—with the official Tajik government number initially given as five and unofficial accounts listing from 16 to 25 deaths.[214] During one week, more than 850 citizens were injured and, in the highest tally, 25 people were killed (all but four by firearms): 16 Tajiks, five Russians, two Uzbeks, one Azeri and one Tatar,[215] including a journalist and an uninvolved observer killed by shots fired from the CPT building.[216]

While the demonstrations and riots did not start with anti-Russian motivations, the Russian-speaking population of Dushanbe soon came under attack. One journalist reported that he heard one crowd of Tajiks at the demonstration

---

207   Niyazi, 'The Year of Tumult', pp. 264–6.
208   These include minister of culture, N. Tabarov; deputy chairman of the Council of Ministers, O. Latifi; head of the State-Juridical Department of the CPT CC, N. Khuvaidulloev; editor-in-chief of the *Tojikistoni Soveti* official newspaper, M. Mabatshoev; deputy minister of justice, Kh. Homidov; and Dushanbe mayor, Maqsud Ikramov. See: Karimov, *Qurboni duzakhma*, p. 77.
209   Karimov, *Qurboni duzakhma*, p. 77.
210   Niyazi, 'The Year of Tumult', pp. 264–6.
211   Niyazi, 'The Year of Tumult', pp. 264–6.
212   Karimov, *Qurboni duzakhma*, p. 77.
213   Viacheslav Zenkovich, 'Dushanbe: khronika semi dnei', *Dialog*, No. 7 (1990), p. 72.
214   Schoeberlein-Engel, 'Conflicts in Tajikistan and Central Asia', pp. 22–5; Niyazi, 'The Year of Tumult', pp. 264, 272; Zartman, *Political Transition in Central Asian Republics*, pp. 97–101; Kilavuz, *Understanding Violent Conflict*, pp. 131–2; *Rastokhez*, No. 3 (August 1990), p. 4.
215   *Rastokhez*, No. 3 (August 1990), p. 4.
216   Oleg Panfilov, 'Piat' let nazad v Dushanbe byla rasstreliana demonstratsiia', *Nezavisimaia gazeta* (February 1995), online: <http://olegpanfilov.com/?p=1149>

chanting 'beat the Russians!'.[217] Hospital statistics revealed that more than 56 per cent of the injured and more than 41 per cent of the severely injured people treated at Dushanbe hospitals were Russian-speakers.[218] Later recollections by ethnic Russians and Russian-speakers[219] from Dushanbe reveal that gangs of young Tajik men specifically targeted Russians and Russian-speakers, particularly women. Russian men were attacked and lynched, while Russian and Russian-speaking women, as well as Tajik women wearing European styles of clothing, were targeted for beatings and rape.[220] After the riots subsided various rumours of impending pogroms against the Russian population circulated, instilling further fear amongst the Russian-speaking population of Dushanbe.[221] The riots of 1990 would, soon after the event, and ever since, be cited as an important factor in the high number of Russians emigrating from Tajikistan.[222]

Predictably, accounts differ, with each side blaming the other for instigating the conflict. Some Western analysts prefer to cast blame on the ruling power structures, arguing that the escalation of the conflict was caused by the government's tactics of violent suppression.[223] The opposition's talking points refer to those in positions of power as being responsible for the riots.[224] For example, Muhammadali Hait,[225] then a Rastokhez activist (who later switched

217   'Rioting Out of Control in Soviet City; 37 Killed', *St Louis Post-Dispatch* (14 February 1990), p. 1A. The journalist cited, amongst the various wires services used for the story, is Alexei Shiryakhin.

218   'Soobshchenie komissii prezidiuma Verkhovnogo Soveta Tadzhikskoi SSR po proverke sobytii 12–14 Fevralia 1990g. v Dushanbe', *Sogdiana* [Moscow], No. 3 [Special Issue] (October 1990), pp. 2–8, as cited in Muriel Atkin, 'Thwarted Democratization in Tajikistan', in *Conflict, Cleavage and Change in Central Asia and Caucasus*, eds Karen Dawisha and Bruce Parrot (Cambridge: Cambridge University Press, 1997), p. 297. One local expressed his opinion in a published appeal to the USSR Supreme Soviet: 'The overwhelming majority of those injured during the days of terror were Russians; All of those assaulted were Russian; 82% of those who have left Tajikistan since the beginning of the year are Russian.' See: A. Kruhilin, 'These Days Hundreds of Russians Are Leaving the Tajik Capital—Forever', *Literaturnaya Gazeta* (28 February 1990), in *SWB SU*, 0713 (15 March 1990), B/1.

219   Meaning those people whose first language is Russian, irrespective of ethnicity. This could include all Slavs, Germans, Jews, Tatars, various ethnicities from the Caucasus, and so on.

220   N. Ol'khovaia, R. Iskanderova, A. Balashov et al., 'Raspad imperii: Dushanbe', *Dikoe pole*, No. 6 (2004), online: <http://www.dikoepole.org/numbers_journal.php?id_txt=265>; V. Starikov, 'I khotia zhivymi do kontsa doleteli', *Vyatskii nablyudatel'*, No. 5 (5 January 1999), online: <http://www.nabludatel.ru/numers/1999/5/13. htm>; V. Starikov, 'I khotia zhivymi do kontsa doleteli [Part 2]', *Vyatskii nablyudatel'*, No. 6 (February 1999), online: <http://www.nabludatel.ru/numers/1999/6/7.htm>; Ianovskaia, 'Dushanbe-1990', n.p.

221   N. Sautin, 'Emergency Situation: Not Force but Dialogue Decides', *Pravda* (18 February 1990), p. 3, in *The Current Digest of the Post-Soviet Press*, Vol. XLII, No. 7 (21 March 1990), p. 14.

222   A. Karpov, 'Skilled Labor Leaves the Republic', *Izvestiia* (5 August 1990), p. 2, in *The Russian Press Digest* (5 August 1990); Schoeberlein-Engel, 'Conflicts in Tajikistan and Central Asia', p. 24; Rasul-zade and Yanovskaia, 'Ochevidtsy Dushanbe-1990', n.p.; Ianovskaia, 'Dushanbe-1990', n.p.

223   For example, see: Schoeberlein-Engel, 'Conflicts in Tajikistan and Central Asia', p. 23; Zartman, *Political Transition in Central Asian Republics*, p. 99.

224   Unofficial explanations also accuse anti-*perestroika* forces but identify them as those in power. They are said to have provoked the turmoil in order to reinforce their own position, establish a dictatorship and suppress all opposition. There is also the suggestion that the events were the result of the destructive activities of some sinister All-Union centre initiating national and social riots in different areas of the USSR with the same intention. In general the opposition tends to highlight social, economic and political reasons for the riots, including the intrigues and perfidy of the ruling clans. See: Niyazi, 'The Year of Tumult', pp. 265–6.

225   His name is given various spellings in the local press, including Mahmadali and Hayit.

his affiliation to the Islamic Revival Party), recently accused the KGB and Tajik government of having 'masterminded' the riots in order to discredit and oppress the opposition.[226] Another opposition member, KGB officer-turned-exile Abdullo Nazarov, better known nowadays for being stabbed to death in the Pamirs, said the same—blaming the KGB for the entire incident.[227] Opposition member Gavhar Juraeva draws on Nazi analogies ('Reichstag fire' and, possibly, the 'Armenian question') to blame the government for instigating the demonstrations, which then backfired on them.[228] Twenty years later, Qahhor Mahkamov, providing very little details, cast vague blame on forces within the KGB both in Tajikistan and in Moscow while absolving the Tajik people as blameless in the events of February 1990.[229]

Niyazi, writing the most comprehensive account of the events, portrays both sides as reckless and violent.[230] For example, he singles out opposition Rastokhez Party members and their incoherent tactics and inflammatory rhetoric.[231] The official government explanation casts blame widely. On 16 February the seventeenth plenary meeting of the Central Committee expressed its confidence in the first secretary and the chairman of the Supreme Soviet. It also issued a statement regarding the violence, which

> blamed a conspiracy of anti-*perestroika* forces aimed at destabilising the situation, seizing leading positions and redistributing portfolios. The anti-*perestroika* forces were seen as comprising a group of apparatchiks (professional party men) craving power and acting in concert with criminal groups, members of the unofficial organisation *Rastokhez* and Islamic fundamentalists.[232]

The government may have reached this conclusion partly based on the negotiating group mentioned above that formed to represent the demonstrators.

The events that occurred in Dushanbe in February 1990 had several peculiar features. First, the disturbances in Dushanbe were not spontaneous. A concerted propaganda campaign, impressive logistical support (thousands of protestors were fed, sheltered and transported from one location to another) and activities

---

226 Avaz Yuldoshev, 'Massive Riots in Dushanbe in February 1990 Masterminded by KGB, Says IRP Deputy Leader', *ASIA-Plus* (12 February 2013), online: <http://news.tj/en/news/massive-riots-dushanbe-february-1990-masterminded-kgb-says-irp-deputy-leader>

227 Rasul-zade and Yanovskaia, 'Ochevidtsy Dushanbe-1990', n.p.

228 Juraeva, 'Ethnic Conflict in Tajikistan', p. 261.

229 'Qahhor Mahkamov: KGB va havodisi bahmanmoh', *BBC Persian* (9 February 2010), online: <http://www.bbc.co.uk/tajik/news/2011/02/110209_if_mahkamov.shtml>

230 Niyazi, 'The Year of Tumult', esp. p. 264.

231 'Thus between 11 and 18 February many members of Rastokhez did their best to transform the stormy riots into a peaceful political dialogue, to dampen emotions and prevent violence. But at the same time a number of Rastokhez leaders, pursuing their personal and collective ambitions regardless of the consequences, inflamed the crowd with populist and chauvinistic slogans.' See: Niyazi, 'The Year of Tumult', pp. 276–7.

232 Niyazi, 'The Year of Tumult', pp. 265–6.

by compact combat groups suggested careful planning. The organisers were also aware of the fact that at the time there were few interior troops in the city and its military garrison had been reduced.

Second, the majority of participants were not residents of Dushanbe, but people brought in from Kulob, Qurghonteppa and districts to the south of Dushanbe. Many of them did not realise what exactly they were doing in the capital, as, for instance, the 300 schoolchildren from the 'XXII Party Congress' *kolkhoz* in the Lenin *raion* who simply obeyed the orders of their four grown-up leaders.[233] Indeed, many Dushanbe residents, both Russian and Central Asian, blamed out-of-town young men for the rioting and looting.[234] Residents claimed that unnamed persons transported young men to the city and gave them 'money, drugs, and alcohol to encourage them to riot'.[235] Yaacov Ro'i cites one rumour in which 'bearded strangers', some allegedly (and implausibly) ethnic Azeris, gave alcohol to schoolboys and paid them in order to incite the riot. At the same time the Tajik Komsomol press asked, in regards to the demonstrators/rioters: 'Who could have doped them with drugs and nationalist slogans?'[236] These conspiratorial views are completely in line with the varied narratives of blame for riots and demonstrations throughout Central Asia around this time.[237]

Third, unofficial strongmen, such as *avlod* leaders and organised crime bosses, played an important role in challenging the political authorities. The heads of four major gangs in Dushanbe were asked to spring into action by the statesmen 'who feed them, protect them from law and keep them handy for a crucial time'.[238] Targets for pilfering were selected carefully during the riots: in one street, some shops were looted, but others, under racketeer protection, remained intact.[239]

Fourth, contrary to the images disseminated by the Moscow-based media,[240] the conflict did not have anti-Russian and/or pro-Islamic roots. A closer look reveals that it was a case of struggle for power, where one of the parties 'pursued its pragmatic political objectives *camouflaging* them artfully in nationalist and religious overtones'.[241] The leader of Muslims of Tajikistan, *Qozikalon* Akbar

---

233   *Tadzhikistan v ogne*, p. 61.
234   Schoeberlein-Engel, 'Conflicts in Tajikistan and Central Asia', p. 23; Kilavuz, *Understanding Violent Conflict*, p. 131, n. 14.
235   Schoeberlein-Engel, 'Conflicts in Tajikistan and Central Asia', p. 23.
236   Yaacov Ro'i, 'Central Asia Riots and Disturbances: Causes and Context', *Central Asia Survey*, Vol. 10, No. 3 (1991), pp. 34–5.
237   Ro'i, 'Central Asia Riots and Disturbances'.
238   *Pravda*, 10 May 1990.
239   *Komsomolskaia pravda*, 28 March 1990.
240   For example: Viktor Ponomarev, '"The Bells Of Hope"', *Pravda* (10 May 1990), in *SWB SU*, 0762 (12 May 1990), B/1. Similar views were expressed in the American press. See: David Aiman and Paul Hofheinz, 'Karl Marx Makes Room for Muhammad', *Time* (12 March 1990), p. 44.
241   Spolnikov and Mironov, 'Islamskie fundamentalisty v borbe za vlast'', p. 27.

Turajonzoda, was asked by B. K. Pugo to join the mediating process between the TCCR and Mahkamov's group, and succeeded in cooling passions in the city precisely because he was viewed as a neutral figure.

Fifth, law enforcement structures proved themselves useless as a means of protecting the populace. Initially, the minister of the interior, Mamadayoz Navjuvonov, was made the military commandant of Dushanbe in charge of all armed formations. He was so grossly inefficient in this role that within hours General I. Senshov from the Central Asian Military District took over. Even then, the army and interior troops could provide security only for government institutions. On 13 February, Qahhor Mahkamov called on residents of Dushanbe to defend their lives on their own. Efficient self-defence units were instantaneously organised on the basis of *mahalla* committees and groups of apartment complex residents.[242] This was yet another lesson of *perestroika* for the people of Tajikistan: only local centres of power could offer viable strategies of survival in times of tumult.

The full truth about the events in Dushanbe has never been disclosed. Qahhor Mahkamov, at the time, limited his assessment to clichéd incantations concerning the 'human factor' so characteristic of the Gorbachev period:

> Absence of attention to the man, to his necessities and demands, the second-rate attention given to this particular factor ... have led to the growth in unemployment, especially amongst youngsters, to the increase in crime. As a result, social tension has been aggravated in the republic, in the city of Dushanbe in particular.[243]

While the blame for the violence is hard to place, the effects of the violence are clear. Atkin writes that

> this outburst of violence in the capital of the republic heightened political anxieties. Various elements of Tajikistani society, including Tajik reformers, supporters of the old Soviet order, and members of the Russian minority, saw the February events as a warning that their worst fears, ranging from the stifling of reform and perpetuation of repression to Islamic revolution and the persecution of non-Muslims.[244]

---

242 These self-defence units were 'a unique phenomenon. Nothing of this kind has existed in the short but horrid history of "hotbeds." People of different nationalities stood up shoulder-to-shoulder against pogrom-mongers.' See: *Rabochaia tribuna*, 26 October 1990. For further anecdotes illustrating the importance of self-defence groups based on place of residence, see: Rasul-zade and Yanovskaia, 'Ochevidtsy Dushanbe-1990'; Ianovskaia, 'Dushanbe-1990', n.p.; Starikov, 'I khotia zhivymi do kontsa doleteli', n.p.; Starikov, 'I khotia zhivymi do kontsa doleteli [Part 2]', n.p.; Ol'khovaia et al., 'Raspad imperii', n.p.

243 *Rasshirennyi XVIII plenum TsK KPT 3 marta 1990g. Stenograficheskii otchet* (Dushanbe: Irfon, 1990), p. 11.

244 Atkin, 'Tajikistan', p. 610.

Niyazi writes of the demonstration effect:

> The February events were the first blow against the stability of the ruling
> group. They showed its lack of competence and inability to negotiate
> with people or to act without recourse to the usual party methods. As the
> analysis of large mass movements in the non-Soviet Middle East shows,
> such blows are not necessarily recognized immediately. Their effects are
> 'stored'. The results of the riots are transferred to the political sphere
> and become really apparent only after the ruling regime considers the
> crisis to have ended. Here much depends on the personal qualities and
> political abilities of the ruling elite.[245]

Interior minister, Mamadayoz Navjuvonov, stated that he believed similar
events would happen again in Tajikistan. He stated bluntly that '[t]he force
that provoked the events is a very serious force and it must be looked for in the
higher echelons, the very high ones. And not simply be looked for but exposed
and punished—disregarding the rank and the position.'[246]

The documents of the eighteenth plenum of the CPT CC held on 3 March 1990
to investigate the whole affair were loaded with vague references to 'certain
anti-*perestroika* forces', 'several unexpected developments', 'demagogues and
political profiteers', 'some leaders who overstepped norms of Soviet legality',
and so on. No names were mentioned, except for Buri Karimov and Nur
Tabarov, who were made scapegoats and expelled from the party for breach of
party discipline, but Karimov even retained his post in the government. The
likely real organisers of the events—leaders of southern regional groupings—
remained in the shadows. Mirbobo Mirrahimov, TCCR member and one of the
founding fathers of the Tajik democratic movement, though also refraining from
mentioning names, was more frank:

> Today's regime in Tajikistan is a dual power. First, this is a purely
> nominal power of the Soviets that have no rights. Second, this is the clan-
> based, party-administrative mafia of the republic, which is wrapped
> and permeated by threads of conjugal and localistic relations ... In
> order to strengthen its position, each clan has to compromise others.
> And only one goal unites them—preservation of the present regime ...
> As a result of the bloody tragedy the Party-clan mafias have strengthened
> their positions in the system of power. Some disarray and hostility in
> the CC and the Council of Ministers are temporary, very soon the clans

---

245   Niyazi, 'The Year of Tumult', p. 273.
246   A. Kruzhilin, 'Dushanbe: The Cost of Fears', *Literaturnaya gazeta* (14 March 1990), p. 11, in *The Russian Press Digest* (14 March 1990).

> will unite again for the sake of the regime's stability. The events have shattered the leading clan and damaged its authority … Other clans were in complete control and didn't lose a single member.[247]

What happened in Dushanbe in February 1990 was an attempt at an oligarchic coup; however, neither Buri Karimov nor his associates from the 17-strong TCCR, who included mostly intellectuals of Gharmi origin devoid of political influence, were the real culprits in this gambit. According to Narzullo Dustov, vice-president of Tajikistan in 1991–92, the whole scheme was masterminded by Ghoibnazar Pallaev, whose resignation alongside those of Mahkamov and Khayoev was just a manoeuvre.[248] He was actively aided by the leaders of the Kulob faction: Kulobi youths formed the backbone of hit squads during the riots, commanded by a convicted criminal, Yaqub Salimov,[249] who less than three years later would be made interior minister. Evidence suggests that the head of the Political Department of the Ministry of Interior, General A. Habibov, a Kulobi, collaborated with the rioters.[250] Needless to say, the investigation never unmasked the real figures behind the bloodshed and violence. In January 1991, Tajikistan's procurator, G. S. Mikhailin, reported that 105 people had been sentenced (all 'small fry'—'hooligans' and arsonists), and that 'at this juncture the investigation cannot provide juridical evaluation of the deeds committed by Karimov, Tabarov and others'.[251] The groups within the ruling elite had reached an accommodation and wanted to forget the whole episode.[252]

The Kulobi faction benefited most from the new alignment of forces. A steady trickle of investments was diverted to the region again. The strategically important Kulob–Qurghonteppa railroad, a project that had been in the making for 50 years, finally received the necessary financing: the USSR Ministry of Railroad Transport agreed to foot half of the 260 million rouble bill for the construction to be completed by 1995.[253] The breaking of the north–south polarisation and rapprochement between the elites from Leninobod and Kulob received symbolic capping in July 1990 when these two regional centres became sister cities. In the long run, Gharmis proved to be the major losers in the power-

---

247 *Rastokhez*, No. 1 (May 1990), p. 4.

248 Dustov, *Zakhm bar jismi vatan*, p. 28.

249 *Tadzhikistan v ogne*, pp. 72–3; Ponomarev, '"The Bells Of Hope"'.

250 *Komsomolets Tadzhikistana*, 29 August 1990.

251 *Kommunist Tadzhikistana*, 16 January 1991. As an example of a low-level conviction, see the case of a twenty-nine-year-old imam sentenced to four years in prison for inciting the demonstrators. See: *ITAR-Tass* (10 September 1990), in *SWB SU*, 0866 (11 September 1990), i.

252 Amazingly, the former minister of culture, Nur Tabarov, who had played his part as a pawn in the coup, complained in September 1990: 'There is nothing I can blame myself for. I was, and remain loyal to the authorities … I naively believed that the CC members could be objective and not make me the scapegoat. They are in no hurry to rehabilitate me … In early March [1990], when I had a conversation with Mahkamov, he promised me to help with decent employment. I haven't heard from him since.' See: *Komsomolets Tadzhikistana*, 26 September 1990.

253 *Adabiyyot va san'at*, 24 August 1990.

sharing scheme. Ghoibnazar Pallaev was relieved of his duties as the Supreme Soviet Presidium chairman. His replacement, Qadriddin Aslonov, though also a Gharmi from Qurghonteppa, did not have Pallaev's clout and influence. In March 1991 the Gharm zone of districts underwent administrative restructuring: the Komsomolobod and Gharm *raions* were broken up into smaller units with populations below 20 000 each.[254] This measure was aimed at further reducing the organisational capabilities of local bureaucratic structures.

The elections to the new Supreme Soviet of Tajikistan went as planned; 95 per cent of those elected were communists, and only two of 225 were active members of the incipient democratic movement.[255] In the lower-level soviets the communist share was not as high: 80 per cent in the *oblast* legislatures and slightly more than 50 per cent in city and *raion* soviets.[256] The effects on elite politics are clear, as the February 1990 episode 'had the effect of strengthening the existing leadership, by enabling it to eliminate opposition within the party'.[257] Similarly, Niyazi notes the increased 'authoritarian' style of administration after February 1990, including the merging of the positions of first secretary and chairman of the Supreme Soviet. When Qahhor Mahkamov was elected president on 30 November 1990, he then held executive and legislative powers. His legislative authority was certainly helped by the outcome of the 'closely supervised' Supreme Soviet elections of late February 1990 in which the Communist Party won 94 per cent of the seats.[258] Outside the Communist Party, the government blamed opposition movements of the nationalist or Islamist persuasion for the violence and restricted their freedom to operate even further. In particular, the Islamic Revival Party was not able to gain official recognition until the end of 1991.[259] Between February 1990 and August 1991, the incumbents in the government strengthened their hold on power by introducing emergency measures that included 'curfews and harassment of the opposition, as well as the usual censorship of the media and Communist party supervision of enterprises, universities and institutes'.[260]

Gorbachev's emissary Boris Pugo was instrumental in keeping Mahkamov's clique in power; however, the fact that he had to *negotiate* with the opposing sides rather than simply deliver Moscow's verdict, the failure to avert violence in advance and the sheer sluggishness with which law and order were restored in Dushanbe indicated that the Kremlin was again losing its grip on Central Asia. By 1990, bureaucrats in central government agencies, especially from industrial

---

254   *Kommunist Tadzhikistana*, 1 March 1991.
255   *Komsomolets Tadzhikistana*, 22 March 1990.
256   *Kommunist Tadzhikistana*, 6 August 1991.
257   Kilavuz, *Understanding Violent Conflict*, p. 9, see also p. 132.
258   Niyazi, 'The Year of Tumult', pp. 272–3.
259   Kilavuz, *Understanding Violent Conflict*, p. 145; Schoeberlein-Engel, 'Conflicts in Tajikistan and Central Asia', pp. 24–5.
260   Schoeberlein-Engel, 'Conflicts in Tajikistan and Central Asia', p. 25.

ministries, had become Gorbachev's main adversaries. Not only was he forced to give up centralisation efforts in the periphery, he also had to seek the support of territorial bureaucracies against the recalcitrant *apparat* in Moscow. In a very short period, ruling elites in national republics regained their autonomy and legitimised it during what was referred to as the 'parade of sovereignties'. The Supreme Soviet of Tajikistan adopted the 'Declaration on State Sovereignty' on 24 August 1990. This document stated, in particular, that

> the Tajik Soviet Socialist Republic is a sovereign multinational state. The state sovereignty manifests itself in the unity and supremacy of the state power on all territory of the Tajik SSR and independence in external relations … The Tajik SSR decides independently all questions related to political, economic, socio-cultural construction on its territory, except those which will be voluntarily delegated by it to the Union of Soviet Socialist Republics.[261]

This was everything the incumbent elite could hope for. It did not long for complete independence, it simply wanted to have a free hand in commandeering and distributing its share of the Soviet budget, and to be backed up by the centre's security apparatus, if need be.

∗ ∗ ∗

Political developments in Tajikistan from 1985 to 1991 were characterised by three main features. The first was economic decay. Tajikistan lived on an inherited endowment, gradually depleting its material and demographic resources. While the bulk of the people were still quiescent, deteriorating quality of life was about to result in a frustration-aggression reaction amongst the most deprived strata of the population. The second was the atmosphere of instability and uncertainty wrought by Gorbachev's reforms. Ideological cohesion, sets of specific values and identities, and modes of social behaviour were undermined and destroyed. The third feature was the deflation of the state, both in the sense of contraction of its agencies and in the loss of moral authority, especially after the bloody events of February 1990 in Dushanbe.

The central political authority of Tajikistan failed to adopt the national idea as a means of mass mobilisation, relying on Moscow to deal with all its problems. Consensual tasks were fulfilled more successfully on the subnational level through traditional components of the polity, primarily regional solidarity networks. Mono-organisational socialism gave the Tajik people a historical chance to emerge as a modern nation. With the demise of the Soviet order,

---

261   *Novye zakony Respubliki Tadzhikistan. Sbornik (Chast' I)* (Dushanbe: [No publisher], 1991), p. 35.

this opportunity was gone. It is not beyond the imagination, however, that the people of Tajikistan might reconstruct a viable political organism and a cohesive national community along the lines suggested by their Central Asian neighbours and based on authoritarianism and relative isolationism.

7. The Rise of Opposition, the Contraction of the State and the Road to Independence

The Gorbachev era freed Soviet society politically; however, democratic consolidation occurred only in a handful of the former Soviet republics; in many of them the transition from authoritarian rule did not take place. Economic factors in the 1990s undoubtedly contributed to the sluggishness of post-communist transformation, but *perestroika* had equally devastating effects on all Central Asian republics, yet only Tajikistan succumbed to acute civil conflict, virtual dissolution of the state and fragmentation of the country. A hypothesis deserving of proper consideration in this sense is that 'the consolidation of democratic rule depends not only on economic growth and a broad distribution of benefits; it also depends on the development of political institutions that can effectively mediate policy debates and coordinate the relations among contending social and economic interests'.[1] Additionally, a strong argument can be put in favour of the high degree of indeterminacy in the process of transition from Soviet authoritarian rule, whereby 'unexpected events (*fortuna*), insufficient information, hurried and audacious choices, confusion about motives and interests, plasticity and even indefinition of political identities, as well as the talents of specific individuals (*virtù*) are frequently decisive in determining outcomes'.[2]

As Jonathan Steele has observed, 'the Communist system was not democratic, but it was an effective administrative machine, which worked and where the "estates" … had a framework for presenting their interests'.[3] Gorbachev had broken this machine, and, during 1990–91, it was up to political elites in every republic to put something new in its place. Unfortunately for Tajikistan, its leaders in this crucial period proved to be incapable of the task.

---

1   Stephan Haggard and Robert R. Kaufman, *The Political Economy of Democratic Transitions* (Princeton, NJ: Princeton University Press, 1995), p. 335.
2   Guillermo O'Donnell and Phillippe C. Schmitter, 'Tentative Conclusions about Uncertain Democracies', in *Transitions from Authoritarian Rule*, eds Guillermo O'Donnell, Phillippe C. Schmitter and Laurence Whitehead (Baltimore: The Johns Hopkins University Press, 1986), p. 5.
3   Jonathan Steele, *Eternal Russia: Yeltsin, Gorbachev and the Mirage of Democracy* (London and Boston: Faber & Faber, 1995), p. 39.

Proto-Opposition: Public Movements and Localised Action Groups

In early 1991, Grzegorz Ekiert wrote that

> on the one hand, the swift disintegration of one-party states has left a dangerous political vacuum, setting in motion an often chaotic process of political change. On the other hand, the restoration of individual and collective rights, as well as [the] opening of public spaces, has triggered rapid political mobilisation. As a result, the power vacuum has been permeated by highly fragmented political forces prone to radicalisation not only around political and economic issues but also around ethnic and religious cleavages.[4]

In Tajikistan, the absence of stable class cleavages and mezzo-structures based upon them, as well as the general lack of civic culture, inhibited the formation of political parties that are characteristic of liberal-democratic systems. Their main functions—interest aggregation, constituency representation and structuring the vote during elections—were performed by other institutions that had nothing to do with the classical left–right continuum.

The events that took place in Dushanbe in February 1990 signalled the end of the monolithic social order, and served as a powerful catalyst for the emergence of a variety of public entities that were not in compliance with the regime. Outwardly, they appeared as mass public associations and political parties, but it will be argued here that essentially they were little more than facades for elite factions in disagreement with the ruling faction on policy questions. Henceforth, although institutional analysis is important in understanding formal structures in any polity, the transactional approach first developed by Dankwart A. Rustow, which implies that 'the key actors in the transition process are political elites, whether in the government or opposition, not interest groups, mass organisations, social movements, or classes',[5] remains the major theoretical tool in this chapter.

The opening of Tajik society in 1989 and early 1990 was marked by a rapid rise in various public associations—that is, partially institutionalised collectivities with some structure but no formal membership. Although quite often they protested and opposed government policies, they never explicitly sought to gain power. Instead, they strove to limit it; this distinguished their 'protest activities

---

4 Grzegorz Ekiert, 'Democratisation Processes in East Central Europe: A Theoretical Reconsideration', *British Journal of Political Science*, Vol. 21, Part 3 (July 1991), p. 312.
5 Haggard and Kaufman, 'The Political Economy of Democratic Transitions', p. 265.

and civil actions from opposition political party activities'.[6] It is possible to single out five types of such associations that came into being in this period in Tajikistan, according to their objectives, membership and methods of operation.

I.

The Ru ba Ru ('Face to Face') Political Club was set up in February 1989 at the initiative and under the aegis of the Tajik Komsomol (Lenin Communist Union of Youth) Central Committee. Its initial statute, while pledging allegiance to the CPSU and *perestroika*, contained a number of rather radical (for that time), programmatic provisions, such as[7]

- formation of national and political self-awareness of Tajik youngsters
- upholding of human rights and their primacy in the national legislation
- all-round development of the Tajik language
- endorsement of parliamentary candidates at all levels
- environmental protection and making public the true records of the ecological situation in the republic.

The club, based in Dushanbe, was run by a nine-member council, and all discussions were supposed to be held in Tajik. Its major form of work consisted of inviting senior party and state officials for round-table discussions. More often than not, these officials would demonstrate incompetence and plain illiteracy, much to the satisfaction of the approximately 400 members of Ru ba Ru. By September 1989, the Komsomol CC had grown weary of the club's independence, disbanded its elected council and removed controversial items from its agenda. From that time on, Ru ba Ru was ordered to discuss only those problems that had been approved by the Komsomol's bureau — 41 in total, including such items as the 'Psychological Culture of a Komsomol Propagandist' and 'Nationalism—A Tool of Subversive Activity of Imperialism'.[8] Very quickly, Ru ba Ru lost all its attractiveness to the public and slipped into oblivion.

According to some sources, the club was established with the blessing of the KGB, which planned to collect data on potential dissidents at its gatherings.[9] Even if this were true, Ru ba Ru objectively played an important role in diversifying the political landscape of Tajikistan: it served as a role model for similar clubs throughout the republic, and, more importantly, provided leaders of proto-opposition groups, such as Rastokhez, with a forum in which they could disseminate their views and recruit followers.

---

6 Katy Pickvance, 'Social Movements in Hungary and Russia: The Case of Environmental Movements', *European Sociological Review*, Vol. 13, No. 1 (May 1997), p. 36.

7 *Proekt polozheniia o politicheskom klube 'Ru Ba Ru'*, Typewritten document dated 14 March 1989, courtesy of Zafar Saidov, then head of the Ideological Department of the Komsomol CC.

8 *Metodicheskie rekomendatsii propagandistam komsomolskoi politicheskoi ucheby i rukovoditeliam komsomolsko-molodezhnykh politicheskikh klubov* (Dushanbe: Dom Politprosveta TsK KPT, 1990), pp. 33–4.

9 *Rastokhez*, No. 13 (April 1992), p. 3.

II.

The People's Movement of Tajikistan in Support of Perestroika (hereinafter Rastokhez)[10] held its first conference in Dushanbe on 30 December 1989,[11] but its pamphlets, mostly in handwritten form, were in circulation throughout the republic from early 1989. Rastokhez had coalesced around a group of intellectuals, including the poet Bozor Sobir, the philosopher Mirbobo Mirrahim and the economist Tohir Abdujabbor. In January 1988, Mirbobo Mirrahim published an article entitled 'Till When Shall the Water Flow Under the Ice?',[12] which called for the revision of the following aspects of Soviet policy

- national nihilism
- atheistic extremism
- unjust territorial delimitation
- the suppressed status of the Tajik language.

It should be remembered that as part of Gorbachev's drive for centralisation, many educational and research organisations in Tajikistan were stripped of their autonomy, and in 1987 Moscow ordered the switch to Russian as a universal medium of teaching in the Tajik State University and other tertiary institutions.[13] Henceforth, ideas propounded by Mirrahim found ample support amongst Tajik intellectuals. The language issue became, albeit for a short period, the most important and unifying component of their political thought, and resulted in the adoption of the Law on Language by the Supreme Soviet of Tajikistan in July 1989, which proclaimed Tajik the only state language. Article 23 of the law stipulated that 'in all vocational-training schools, specialised secondary and tertiary educational institutions of the Tajik SSR, regardless of their organisational affiliation, teaching is carried out in the state language'.[14] Russian was downgraded to the status of the language of interethnic communication, but its free circulation was guaranteed.[15] Overall, despite Rastokhez being a mono-

---

10   The word *rastokhez* has a dual meaning in Tajik: first, revival or resurgence, and second (rarely used), revolt, commotion and disorder. The Tajik government press interpreted the name as a sign of its subversive nature and linked it to its namesake organisation in Iran (*Tojikistoni soveti*, 23 February 1990). While it is true that the Rastokhez party existed in Iran between 1975 and 1979, it was set up by the Shah to enforce a 'centralised and absolute system, centering largely around his own personality' (Amin Saikal, *The Rise and Fall of the Shah: 1941–1979* [London: Angus & Robertson, 1980], p. 189), and as such could hardly be regarded as a destabilising element.

11   The first organisational assembly of Rastokhez took place on 14 September 1989, but its participants were just a handful of 'awakened and concerned representatives of the public of Dushanbe and adjacent districts' who petitioned authorities for recognition and provision of office space, as can be seen from a letter sent by the chairman of the *Rastokhez*, T. Abdujabbor, on 15 September 1989 to the chairman of the Presidium of the Supreme Soviet of the TSSR and the chairman of the Executive Committee of Dushanbe.

12   'To ba kai ob az tagi yakh meravad?' *Komsomoli Tojikiston*, 6 January 1988, pp. 1–2.

13   Abdulov, *Rohi behbud*, p. 8.

14   *Novye zakony Respubliki Tadzhikistan. Sbornik. (Chast' IV)* (Dushanbe: Kontrakt, 1992), p. 74.

15   *Novye zakony Respubliki Tadzhikistan. Sbornik. (Chast' IV)*.

ethnic nationalist political party, its platform did insert moderate language calling for democracy, human rights, and equality for all citizens of Tajikistan regardless of ethnicity or religion.[16]

Having assessed the situation in Tajikistan as political, economic, ecological, cultural and spiritual crises, the first conference of Rastokhez called on all inhabitants of the republic to think and act on five major issues.[17]

- First, all land, mineral and other natural resources, as well as all factories, should become the property of the populace of Tajikistan. The republic should attain complete 'economic and material sovereignty'.

- Second, in the process of establishing the economic sovereignty of the republic, the most urgent task was to reform prices for goods produced inside Tajikistan, cotton in particular. Central organs must be deprived of the ability to dictate prices.

- Third, relations with other republics, regions and states should be based on mutual agreements that recognise the equal rights of each, and on the sale and purchase of processed goods and raw materials according to the laws of the market.

- Fourth, Rastokhez would issue an all-embracing concept of economic sovereignty of the Tajik SSR that would realise 'all hopes and expectations of the peoples inhabiting the republic'.

- Fifth, the future of the Tajik nation depends on the success of democracy, hence it is imperative to elect a new parliament that is responsible and answerable to the people.

Documents of the Rastokhez conference were filled with references to the process of democratisation instigated by Gorbachev and a general appreciation of the leading role of the reformed Communist Party in implementing progressive changes in Tajikistan; they designated 'some individual officials in the apparatuses of the CPT CC and the Komsomol CC who distort truth, as they did in the years of personality cult and stagnation',[18] as the major impediment to *perestroika*'s triumph in the republic. The newly elected chairman of Rastokhez, Tohir Abdujabbor, sent a letter to Qahhor Mahkamov, in which, in a rather humble tone, he asked the first secretary to peruse and endorse programmatic statements of Rastokhez.[19] Niyazi assesses Rastokhez at an early point in its

---

16   Kilavuz, *Understanding Violent Conflict*, p. 139; Niyazi, 'The Year of Tumult', p. 275. The point on the mono-ethnicity of Rastokhez was made by Niyazi based on its public meetings and its publications.

17   *Painavishti Sozmoni 'Rastokhez' doyir ba vaz'i ijtimoi va siyosi dar jumhuri*, Typewritten letter dated 30 December 1989 and addressed to the CPT CC. Document MR SRT-1919.01.90, Archive of the Information Department of the Ministry of Foreign Affairs of the Republic of Tajikistan, pp. 1–3.

18   *Rezoliutsiyai konfronsi respublikavii sozmoni 'Rastokhez' dar borai qarorhoi noodilonai, ki nisbati ba'ze maqolahoi 'Komsomoli Tojikiston' (holo 'Javononi Tojikiston') dar avvali s. 1988 qabul shuda budand*, Typewritten letter dated 30 December 1989 and addressed to the CPT CC. Document MR SRT-1819.01.90, Archive of the Information Department of the Ministry of Foreign Affairs of the Republic of Tajikistan, pp. 1–2.

19   Document A/396, received by the CPT CC Secretariat on 24 January 1990, courtesy of Zafar Saidov, spokesperson of President Emomali Rahmonov.

history, noting that it had enough ambiguity in its charter that it did not specifically condemn communism, nor did it prohibit members from holding Communist Party membership or even high-level positions in the Communist Party. Niyazi stresses that Rastokhez was more like a 'coordinating centre' in that at an early point it did not openly oppose the Communist Party and preferred instead to lobby the government.[20]

In handwritten pamphlets, however, Rastokhez leaders severely criticised the ruling elite, but on somewhat different grounds:

> If we scan through periodicals and archive documents *for the past 100 years*, we shall find representatives of *the same families* as leading officials; if we acquaint ourselves, however briefly, with the lists of leading staff of Party and executive committees at various levels, we shall discover the eventual monopoly of people of *Leninobodi extraction* on controlling the upper echelons of power [italics added].[21]

Rastokhez even demanded a disproportionate redistribution in the Tajik Supreme Soviet away from population-based distribution of seats towards one that would favour the city of Dushanbe (where Rastokhez was strongest), a move that would hurt the Leninobod Province.[22] From such statements and demands, it appears that the perceived injustice in traditional power-sharing arrangements, rather than ideological oppression, was the major grievance harboured by Rastokhez's creators.

In mid 1989, Rastokhez leaders claimed to have up to 10 000 sympathisers throughout the republic,[23] leading up to the government's official recognition of Rastokhez as a legal entity on 21 June 1991;[24] however, Rastokhez remained an extremely poorly organised and fragmented entity.[25] *Rastokhez* was dominated

---

20   Niyazi, 'The Year of Tumult', p. 275.

21   *Grazhdanskie dvizheniia v Tadzhikistane*, p. 39.

22   Mavlon Makhamov, 'Islam and the Political Development of Tajikistan after 1985', in *Central Asia: Its Strategic Importance and Future Prospects*, ed. Hafeez Malik (New York: St Martin's Press, 1994), p. 199. Rastokhez 'pointed out bluntly that "higher circles of the state apparatus were controlled by natives of Leninabad," and demanded that this injustice be removed. In order to implement this demand, the Central Council of Rastokhez proposed on June 2, 1990, that the Leninabad province should be entitled to elect only 30 deputies to the new parliament. Ironically, one-fourth of the republic's population lived in Leninabad, while Rastokhez's supporters were to elect 50 deputies. In Dushanbe, where Rastokhez was expected to win the elections, 100 deputies were to be elected.' In Rastokhez's eyes, this reshuffling of electoral seats would have rectified the 'wrongs' of the past. Citing *Rastokhez*, No. 2 (July 1990).

23   *Javononi Tojikiston*, 22 September 1989.

24   Kilavuz, *Understanding Violent Conflict*, p. 139; Niyazi, 'The Year of Tumult', 275. Rastokhez soon incorporated several small groups: Vahdat ('Unity') in Istaravshon, Oshkoro ('*Glasnost*') in Kulob city and Ehyoyi Khujand ('Renaissance of Khujand'). See: Niyazi, 'The Year of Tumult'.

25   Clause 7.5 of the Rastokhez (PMR) Charter, for example, stated that '[t]he PMR Presidium and its city and district chapters do not bear responsibility for each others' activities'.

by secular urban intellectuals,[26] a group who enthusiastically joined reform movements and political parties.[27] This was a problem politically as these urban intellectuals were isolated from the broader Tajik society and their networks did not extend outside their small circles;[28] however, urban intellectuals were not the only members. Some Rastokhez supporters originated from very different social strata. On the one hand, there were highly educated urban intelligentsia, members of the Academy of Sciences, writers and journalists, who genuinely believed in reforming and modernising Tajik society. On the other hand, there were lumpenproletarians[29] in big cities, new arrivals from impoverished rural areas in the south and east, bazaar traders, and various shadowy figures involved in black and grey-market activities who treated the conditions created by *perestroika* as an opportunity to rapidly improve their social status.

The dichotomy in composition resulted in Rastokhez's failure to work out a clear-cut political platform that would enable it to become a genuine nationalist opposition on the lines of the popular fronts that emerged at the time in the Baltic republics and Transcaucasus. The 'intellectual' wing of Rastokhez promoted ideas of national revival based on rediscovery of the history and culture of ancient Tajiks, invoking rather sophisticated rhetoric and theoretical concepts. The motto of Rastokhez—'*Pindori nek, guftori nek, kirdori nek*' (Good thoughts, good words, good deeds)—was borrowed from Zoroastrian ethics. According to Bozor Sobir, Rastokhez was not unlike a sort of mystical order with its sacred 'mission'—to be the guide and staff (*aso*—a well-known Sufi symbol) of the nation—and with its very own spiritual leader:[30]

> A thousand thanks,
> A thousand bows,
> A thousand praises
> To Ulughzoda,[31] the *pir* of *Rastokhez*,
> The patron-prophet of *Rastokhez*.

---

26   Olimova, 'Opposition in Tajikistan', p. 252; Kilavuz, *Understanding Violent Conflict*, p. 139. Kilavuz describes these intellectuals as 'writers, artists, teachers, and other members of the urban intelligentsia', some of whom were former Communist Party members 'though not apparatchiks'.

27   Makhamov, 'Islam and the Political Development of Tajikistan after 1985', p. 197.

28   Grigorii G. Kosach, 'Tajikistan: Political Parties in an Inchoate National Space', in *Muslim Eurasia: Conflicting Legacies*, ed. Yaacov Ro'i (London: Frank Cass, 1995), p. 131, citing S. Olimova and M. Olimov, 'Obrazovannyi klass tadzhikistana v peripetiiakh XX v.', *Vostok*, No. 5 (1991), pp. 100–1.

29   In Marxist terminology, that segment of the working class without class consciousness which will likely not acquire that consciousness, and which is actually an obstacle to a Marxist revolution.

30   *Rastokhez*, No. 4 (October 1990), p. 1.

31   Satym Ulughzoda, born in 1911, is considered the father of modern Tajik historical drama and prose. His works on Rudaki, Abu Ali ibn Sino and Vose have been widely published in many languages. Ulughzoda represents an interesting case of an indigenous intellectual raised and recognised by Soviet power: he fought courageously during the Great Patriotic War, translated Lenin's writings into Tajik and eventually became a corresponding member of the Tajik Academy of Sciences. See: *Bolshaia sovetskaia entsiklopediia*, Vol. 26 (Moscow: Izdatelstvo BSE, 1977), p. 606. Ulughzoda, originally from around Namangan, always advocated the idea of restitution of all lands inhabited by Tajiks to Tajikistan, thus endearing himself to young radical intellectuals.

Davlat Khudonazarov, while not a member of Rastokhez, has given perhaps the best summary of the secular Tajik intelligentsia's philosophical outlook:

> Unlike Christianity, Islam cannot be conducive to moral resurgence of the people, this is an aggressive religion which consolidated stagnation and backwardness. Iranian peoples—the Tajiks' ancestors—had possessed the highest culture and beautiful religion prior to the Islamic conquest; Islamisation led to the slowing down and almost complete halting of social progress, the destruction and decay of culture, and, indirectly, served as a cause of Central Asia's backwardness as compared to Europe.[32]

Anti-Islamism, nationhood and Western-type modernisation were the ideas that drew freethinking professors, poets and artists in Tajikistan to Rastokhez.

The 'populist' wing of Rastokhez, however, held somewhat different and rather simplistic views on the past, present and future of the Tajik nation. For them, it was the preponderance of 'foreign elements' in the republic that made life unbearable. While Tohir Abdujabbor believed that 'Russians, Uzbeks and representatives of other nationalities can easily join us in solving problems we face',[33] his less-refined colleagues pushed forward their scenario of revivifying the Tajik nation: 'We shall go to the districts of the republic, organise meetings in student dormitories and raise them to struggle against the Russians and leaders of the republic. We have special scores to settle with the Uzbeks, with whom we shall deal after we expel the Russians.'[34] Many have noted the preoccupation with Uzbekistan amongst the membership of 'Dushanbe's reform movements'.[35] Grievances over the Tajik–Uzbek border delimitation, the historically ethnic Tajik cities of Samarkand and Bukhara in Uzbekistan, and the Tajik minority in Uzbekistan were prominent themes in these movements,[36] with rhetoric among certain members occasionally quite unrealistic. This included not just identifying Uzbekistan as a threat to Tajikistan, but also arguing for the formation of a 'Greater Iran' that would include Samarkand and Bukhara—a view that obviously aggravated the Government of Uzbekistan.[37] Some

---

32   Quoted in: Olimova and Olimov, 'Obrazovannyi klass Tadzhikistana v peripetiiakh XX v.', p. 101.

33   *Grazhdanskie dvizheniia v Tadzhikistane*, p. 37.

34   *Tojikistoni Soveti*, 16 September 1989. See also: Anaita Khudonazar, 'The Other', *Berkeley Program in Soviet and Post-Soviet Studies Working Paper Series* (2004).

35   Dudoignon's terminology here allows the inclusion of the DPT with Rastokhez.

36   Stephane Dudoignon, 'Political Parties and Forces in Tajikistan, 1989–1993', in *Tajikistan: The Trials of Independence*, eds Mohammad-Reza Djalili, Frederic Grare and Shirin Akiner (New York: St Martin's Press, 1997), p. 69. For a briefly stated contradictory view, see: Schoeberlein-Engel, 'Conflicts in Tajikistan and Central Asia', p. 6, in response to E. Naby, 'Tajik Political Legitimacy and Political Parties', *Central Asia Monitor*, Vol. 1, No. 5 (1992). Schoeberlein-Engel disagrees with Naby's assessment of Rastokhez as being hostile to Uzbeks, noting that most of the leadership and members of Rastokhez rejected these views.

37   Dudoignon, 'Political Parties and Forces in Tajikistan, 1989–1993', pp. 60, 69; Rubin, 'Russian Hegemony and State Breakdown in the Periphery', p. 142.

pamphlets distributed by young Rastokhez activists, despite their leadership's view on Islam, even called for a *jihad* to purify Tajikistan.[38] Safar Mastonzod, a worker at the footwear factory in Dushanbe and member of the Central Council of Rastokhez, thus outlined his political views:

> Seventy years of pro-Russian chauvinist propaganda have addled our brains … The planned pillage of the republic is taking place. They pump everything they can out of Tajikistan … We don't know what political culture is, but we need to channel the national movement into the river-bed of democracy … I am against the law based on shari'a. I would like Sweden to be the model of our social order … We do not lay claims on the Bukhara and Samarkand *oblasts* [of Uzbekistan] in their entirety, just on traditional lands of the Tajiks who undergo real genocide there. Those are the cities of Bukhara and Samarkand, a narrow corridor adjacent to Panjakent and part of the Qashqadarya *oblast*.[39]

It can be argued that it was this incoherent mixture of conflicting democratic, nationalist and populist ideas, and not persecution by communist authorities, that contributed to the weakness and ultimate demise of what had been conceived as a broad popular movement.[40]

III.

Throughout 1989, a number of public associations emulating the organisational structure and methods of work of Ru ba Ru appeared in regional and district centres. They proved to be more viable and independent than Ru ba Ru, for they articulated grievances of established local communities. Their populist notions of wellbeing and equity based on regionalism were more comprehensible for common people, especially in rural areas, than any nationalist platform.

The unofficial sociopolitical organisation Oshkoro (the Tajik term for Gorbachev's *glasnost*) operated under the very simple slogan: 'Kulob—to Kulobis!' Its membership included the USSR people's deputy, B. Safarov; the *sarkhatib* (chief preacher) of Kulob's Friday mosque—essentially, the official head of all Muslims of the region—Haydar Sharifzoda; honoured teacher of the republic, Rustam Abdurahimov; and many other dignitaries, Soviet and traditional, united by considerations of local patriotism. They raised seemingly mundane problems, such as why there was not enough meat in the city's stores, why the number

---

38 L. Pilman, 'Eshche odno postanovlenie?' *Orientiry*, No. 10 (1989), p. 4.

39 *Komsomolets Tadzhikistana*, 9 February 1990.

40 The program and charter of Rastokhez, written in September 1989, were not published until October 1990, although the movement started its own newspaper in May 1990. This reluctance was explained by the Rastokhez ideologues' fear of not being understood by 'wide urban and rural strata of the population, from which they were utterly separated'. See: *Grazhdanskie dvizheniia v Tadzhikistane*, p. 35. The first representative congress of Rastokhez was convened as late as March 1991.

of workshops in villages remained negligible, or why transport links with neighbouring Qurghonteppa were so hazardous. At times, however, up to 15 000 people would attend Oshkoro meetings—a figure Rastokhez leaders could only dream of.[41] The suggested solution to those problems was also clear—a thorough overhaul of republican and regional leadership: 'All persons of authority in the Party and state apparatus are Leninobodis. Is it fair? Kulob is quite capable of producing leaders from its own midst.'[42]

The Ehyoi Khujand ('Revival of Khujand') movement, based in Leninobod, was preoccupied with the restoration of the city as the most important economic and cultural centre of Tajikistan—a status 'it had been robbed of illegally by a partocratic oligarchy'.[43] In conjunction with its sister organisation in Uroteppa (Istaravshon) called Vahdat ('Unity'), Ehyoi Khujand advocated greater autonomy for the northern region and closer ties with Uzbekistan. Both refrained from criticism of the CPT and emphasised the importance of compromise and cooperation with the authorities. Their main political tenets included a broadening of the powers of local soviets and more transparency in the process of decision-making at the republic level.[44]

The La'li Badakhshon ('Ruby of Badakhshan') movement demanded elevation of the GBAO to an autonomous republic. It strove to preserve the distinct local culture and languages;[45] the movement's leaders believed that by no means were the Pamiris part of the Tajik nation.[46] Their economic program envisaged that Badakhshan should have the right to deal with the outside world on its own, bypassing Dushanbe, in order to take full advantage of the rich mineral deposits in its territory.[47]

On a lower level, entities like Hisori Shodmon in Tursunzoda, Zarafshon in Panjakent and Dirafshi Koviyon in Norak indulged in semi-autonomous

---

41   *Rohi Lenini*, 16 November 1989.
42   *Grazhdanskie dvizheniia v Tadzhikistane*, p. 57.
43   *Rastokhez*, No. 3 (August 1990), p. 5.
44   *Komsomolets Tadzhikistana*, 15 September 1989.
45   In 1989, a heated polemic flared amongst Soviet ethnographers in regards to the Pamirs. One group of scholars, especially those based in Dushanbe, believed that 'in the years of Soviet power the process of assimilation of Pamiri nationalities unfolded peacefully and harmoniously, along the path predetermined by history and without any abuses on the part of republican and local authorities', while their opponents maintained that 'everything that has happened and is happening to the Pamiri languages, script and folklore of the Pamiri nationalities reflects the policy of their forced assimilation, spanning several decades'. See: A. L. Grunberg and I. M. Steblin-Kamenskii, 'Neskolko zamechanii po povodu otklika A. S. Davydova na stat'iu S. V. Cheshko', *Sovetskaia etnografiia*, No. 4 (1989), p. 37.
46   B. Shokirov and A. Mahmadkarimov, *Paidoyeshi hizbu sozmonhoi nav dar Tojikiston va fa'oliyati onho (solhoi 1989–1992)* (Dushanbe: Donishgohi agrarii Tojikiston, 1994), p. 34.
47   A typical argument in favour of economic independence for the region was as follows: 'American, English, French and Japanese companies show interest in the GBAO. According to Academician Fersman, "The Pamirs is a real treasury of the world." All elements from Mendeleev's [periodical] table are present here. Those are all strategic raw materials … Even a non-specialist can understand our advantages if a direct route from Badakhshon to the Indian Ocean is laid.' See: *Nezavisimaia gazeta*, 27 August 1994.

political activity, contributing greatly to the institutionalisation of public life around local communities. The example of the Khovaling-based political club Hamroz ('Confidant') is illuminating in this respect: though it claimed affiliation with both Rastokhez and Ru ba Ru, its main concerns stood aloof from abstract struggles for democracy and nationhood, covering the immediate day-to-day needs of the town's population.[48]

At the grassroots level, local representative councils, regardless of their exact composition, rather than party committees, began to be viewed as decision-making organs. Usually they were village and town soviets, but sometimes discrete bodies of local strongmen were created to solve parochial problems. An action committee set up in the Komsomolobod *raion* in August 1989 to prevent construction of the Roghun hydro power station serves as an example of such ad-hoc organs. This committee comprised the *raion* party secretary, chairman of the local soviet, village elders, and a number of eminent people of Komsomolobod origin living elsewhere at the time: scientists and a Ru ba Ru functionary from Dushanbe, representatives of Gharmi settlers in the Vakhsh Valley, and so on. On 12 August 1989, it convened a meeting of protest attended by some 3600 residents of settlements that would be submerged if the Roghun project were to proceed.[49] This was the first public demonstration sanctioned by local authorities in Tajikistan in defiance of policies introduced by the CPT CC, and it signified the devolution of power and authority from Dushanbe to the periphery.

Unofficial societies with local agendas began to affect politics at the republic level in two ways. First, they were successful in imposing their specific, and often extremist, outlooks that contradicted official political ideas on substantial segments of the population. The program of the Union of Democratic Youth, Bokhtar ('Bactria'), garnered wide support far beyond its birthplace of Khovaling in the Kulob *oblast*, having become the manifesto of southern regionalism:[50]

> Politics in Tajikistan is all about the struggle between two varieties of Tajiks—the Northern and the mountain ones … If justice is not restored

---

48   Hamroz, in its plan of activities, seeks, through negotiations and consultations with party and state authorities of the district, to facilitate implementation of the following measures in the district: 1) compilation of a general plan of the district's development; 2) a share from the exploitation of natural resources of the district, such as oil, gas and gold, will be earmarked for the district's development; 3) the number of livestock will be limited to 30 000 on state farms and 30 000 in private hands to avert land erosion; 4) other districts will be prohibited from using local pastures; 5) mulberry and walnut orchards will be expanded; 6) distribution of meat will be strictly controlled; 7) gas supply to households will be accelerated; 8) loss-making state farms will be helped; 9) the issue of housing for young people will be dealt with; 10) drinking-water supply will be improved in the district centre and villages; 11) a sports complex will be built, using the proceeds from the oil, gas and gold fund; 12) a slaughterhouse will be built, which will fully satisfy people's demands for meat. Source: *Barnomai fa'oliyati mahfili siyosi-ijtimoii 'Hamroz'*, Typed document, c. August 1989.

49   *Adabiyot va san'at*, No. 33 (17 August 1989), p. 2.

50   *Grazhdanskie dvizheniia v Tadzhikistane*, pp. 64–5.

any time soon, that is, if the Party and government leadership is not altered in favour of the majority of Tajiks, confrontation will ensue. Skirmishes between Kulobis and Pamiris are simply friendly rehearsals before the fight against Leninobodis … They [northerners] are essentially Uzbeks in half-Tajik skins who have been planting pan-Turkism in Tajikistan for 70 years, trying to transform Tajiks into Uzbeks … Being at the helm, they have cardinally changed our native Persian language, they have bred hatred towards Iranians and Tajiks of Afghanistan, they have maintained the cult of the Uzbek tongue. But they have achieved nothing, only stirred the wrath and fury of the Mountain Tajiks. Our people has preserved its language (Persian-Dari), culture, art … In the long run, if we cannot become united with the half-Uzbek North of Tajikistan, we shall have to put forward the question of autonomy, up to the expulsion of the Leninobod *oblast* from the Tajik SSR. Let them live with their beloved brethren in Uzbekistan. To get rid of these scoundrels is the dream and hope of every Mountain Tajik. Just imagine, the dialect, songs and verses of Northern half-Uzbek Tajiks are repulsive to the Mountain Tajik; still, they have occupied radio, television, press and literature. One has to be an idiot or an animal not to feel disgust at all this. This aim is set before every informal organisation existing in the districts of the Khatlon *oblast* and mountainous Tajikistan.

Second, they created branches in the capital city to lobby for regional interests and, if necessary, exert physical pressure on the government. In 1989, residents of Dushanbe from the north, the Pamirs and Kulob were respectively united in societies called Hamdilon, Nosiri Khisrav and Mehri Khatlon. There is a strong argument that these groups played a significant role in the events of February 1990, acting as a sort of 'fifth column' for regional cliques in Dushanbe.[51]

IV.

In 1989, a number of non-governmental organisations which represented the interests of ethnic minorities were initiated in Tajikistan. The Uzbek Society of Tajikistan, the Russian and Ukrainian Communities, the Association of Soviet Koreans, the Society of Friends of Jewish Culture 'Khoverim', the Armenian Society named after Mesrop Mashtots, the Georgian Society 'Satvistomo Iberia' and several similar groups explicitly eschewed political activism of any kind, concentrating instead on cultural issues. The Uzbek Society's charter stated its main goals as[52]

---

51 *Komsomolets Tadzhikistana*, 1 April 1990.
52 *Tozhikiston Uzbek zhamiyati* (Dushanbe: Tojikiston, 1992), p. 5.

- exploration and propagation of the common history and traditions of Tajiks and Uzbeks
- securing a better understanding of the spiritual foundations of Uzbek culture
- establishment of Uzbek clubs, dance troupes and dramatic theatres in Dushanbe and provincial centres of Tajikistan
- promotion of Uzbek-language programs on radio and TV in Tajikistan
- facilitating quality teaching of Uzbek language and literature in secondary and tertiary education institutions
- improvement of Uzbek-language publications in Tajikistan
- rendering assistance to the needy through public foundations and relief committees.

At the same time, these organisations often served as venues of resource mobilisation to resolve issues of immediate practical importance to a given ethnic community. For instance, under Soviet rule Koreans had virtually monopolised production of rice, maize and onions in Tajikistan, deriving substantial profits from trade in these stocks. In the late 1980s they began to face competition from Gharmis and Uzbeks, who often resorted to unfair practices to evict Koreans from Tajikistan's bazaars. The Association of Soviet Koreans, which could rely on 7000 well-to-do compatriots in Dushanbe alone, hired qualified lawyers, bribed officials and even set up physical protection squads to rectify the situation.[53]

V.

Tajiks living outside their republic formed a number of associations whose primary tasks were the preservation and transmission of language and culture from one generation to another. Organisations of Tajiks residing in Uzbekistan, such as Ehyoi farhangi Bukhoro ('Revival of Bukhara's Culture'), Oryoni buzurg ('Great Land of Aryans'), Oftobi Soghdiyon ('The Sun of Soghdians') and 'Samarkand', were especially active and numerically strong. Before World War II there were only two Uzbek, two Armenian and a handful of Russian schools in Samarkand—the rest were Tajik; in 1989, not a single Tajik school operated in this city.[54] The group Samarkand's program proclaimed that '[w]e have the right to be indignant and to appeal directly to our people ... Without creation of a Tajik autonomy within Uzbekistan or *oblasts* of Uzbekistan, full equality and resolution of problems we raise is impossible.'[55] The leadership of Tajikistan supported the creation of Tajik cultural centres in Uzbekistan and elsewhere. The Society of Surkhandarya Tajiks in Dushanbe, Basvand ('Addition'), and

---

53   Interview with Victor Kim, vice-president of the Association of Soviet Koreans, Dushanbe, 16 March 1995.
54   Rahimov, 'K voprosu o sovremennykh tadzhiksko-uzbekskikh mezhnatsionalnykh otnosheniiakh', p. 22.
55   'Grazhdanskie dvizheniia v Uzbekistane', *Orientiry*, No. 1 (1989), p. 18.

particularly one outspoken member, historian Rahim Masov (who also was one of the founders of Rastokhez), spearheaded a rather aggressive ideological campaign of Tajik reassertiveness:

> There are some 900,000 Tajiks living in Uzbekistan ... and a considerable number of Tajiks whose ancestors had been forcibly registered as Uzbeks. It is high time the historical justice prevailed for those who have not been assimilated, who have not lost their mother tongue and national (ethnic) self-awareness ... People who reassume their genuine nationality should not be subject to any limitations and should be guaranteed against any discrimination on the part of local authorities.[56]

In 1991, dissemination of books and articles by Masov in Uzbekistan was prohibited, and members of Samarkand smuggled this literature in to satisfy the high demand.[57]

In October 1989, the Society for Relations with Compatriots Abroad, Paivand ('Family Link'), was set up in Dushanbe. It operated under the aegis of the Council of Ministers, had many eminent Tajik intellectuals in its ranks and was entrusted with the mission of spreading information about the achievements of Soviet Tajiks throughout the world, even though its primary targets were the descendants of some 900 000 emigrants who had left Central Asia, escaping from the Russian and then Soviet incursions, and who had then settled in Afghanistan, Iran and China.[58] Members of Paivand established broad connections with cultural figures in Iran and Afghanistan, and very soon the Soviet-style propaganda activities of this organisation were augmented by ideas of creating a Greater Tajikistan.[59]

In January 1989, Tajiks residing in Moscow, mostly students, professors and creative intelligentsia, founded the Society of Tajik Culture, Soghdiyon ('Soghdiana'). They organised courses in the Tajik language and Sunday schools for children of Tajik expatriates, offered counselling services to the newly arrived students, and so on. At the same time, they maintained strong ties with

---

56 Masov, *Istoriia topornogo razdeleniia*, pp. 110–11.
57 N. R. Hafizova, 'Omukhtani problemahoi hessi grazhdani dar kursi siyosatshinosi', Report at the I Conference on Teaching Political Science Disciplines in Tajikistan, Dushanbe, 25 January 1995.
58 *Komsomolets Tadzhikistana*, 9 June 1989.
59 Confidential sources in Dushanbe. Interestingly, the ill-fated Tajik ruler of Afghanistan Habibullah-khan, alias Bachai Saqaw (1928–29), was hailed by some Paivand members as the true champion of the Tajik cause; one of them proudly showed the author a copy of a book allegedly smuggled from Afghanistan in 1991 that eulogised Habibullah and praised his efforts to found a mighty Tajik state with the centre in Bukhara. See: Abdurrahman Ali Najib, *Afghanistan dar gozargahi atash wa khun* (Peshawar: Haj Nayyer Hosaini, 1991), p. 165.

Rastokhez, Ru ba Ru and influential politicians of the younger generation, such as Davlat Khudonazarov. Soghdiyon was the most vociferous critic of Mahkamov's administration.[60]

By the end of 1989, an area beyond the CPT's direct control had evolved within which limited interest articulation and interest aggregation were allowed. This phenomenon was as much the result of pressure from Moscow to 'democratise' as it was the product of the internal dynamics of Tajikistan's political system. The aforementioned informal groups did not constitute serious political opposition to Mahkamov's government; however, their very existence denoted the emergence in the republic of the classic 'Dahl dilemma of mixed regimes': if the authorities could tolerate *some* opposition, could they indefinitely enforce *any* limits to toleration short of the wide limits set in polyarchies?[61]

The Failure of Public Movements

Freizer argues that the activities of civil society organisations during the early *glasnost* period in Tajikistan 'attracted mainly the urban middle classes— scientists, professors, teachers and students—and bypassed many rural communities'.[62] Olimova describes a similar constituency for the first early social movements, noting that their support at the end of the 1980s came first from the '[W]estern-oriented national intelligentsia'.[63] Mavlon Makhamov, referring to the groups that formed in 1989 and 1990, wrote that their gestation was an urban process and that 'rural society mostly stayed out of the process of politicization of social life'.[64] Whatever the exact composition of these groups, it was clear that

---

60   Its assessment of the events in Dushanbe in February 1990 was as follows: 'The real reason for protests in Dushanbe was not the presence of innocent refugees, but the acute dissatisfaction of the Tajik people with the republic's government, which for decades had been doing whatever it wanted to do in the republic, ignoring interests of its people and bringing it to the brink. The real reasons are economic backwardness, the penury of the population, especially in rural areas, where mass unemployment and unsettled existence deprive youths of hopes for the future.' See: *Sogdiana*, No. 1 (1) (February 1990), p. 1.

61   Robert A. Dahl, 'Introduction', in *Regimes and Oppositions*, ed. Robert A. Dahl (New Haven, Conn., and London: Yale University Press, 1973), p. 13.

62   Freizer, 'Central Asian Fragmented Civil Society', p. 117. Related to the growth of civil society, Dudoignon writes that 'the 1980s had seen the resurgence of alternative social phenomena, as witnessed by the blossoming of numerous underground cultural and sports clubs'. See: Dudoignon, 'Political Parties and Forces in Tajikistan', p. 64.

63   Olimova, 'Opposition in Tajikistan', p. 246. She also notes, however, Nina Chicherina's assessment that poor, unemployed rural migrants in Dushanbe 'played a significant role in the opposition movements'. Ibid., citing N. G. Chicherina, *Grazhdanskie dvizheniia v Tadzhikistane* (Moscow: Akademia nauk, 1990), p. 18.

64   Makhamov, 'Islam and the Political Development of Tajikistan after 1985', p. 198. Olimova lists some exceptions, noting that some 'tradesmen and private farmers' also participated. See: Olimova, 'Opposition in Tajikistan', pp. 246–7.

while they were growing, they still had relatively limited numbers and their active members made up only a very small percentage of the total population of Tajikistan.[65]

In regards to the goals of these new groups, Freizer stresses that while some individuals wanted massive changes in the system of government, generally the civil society groups of the 1980s did not oppose the state and focused mostly on local issues.[66] Also, there were additional issues on the agenda in the late 1980s beyond just nationalist and religious ones, evidenced by critical newspaper articles regarding the economy, health and the environment.[67] In the opinion of Makhamov, however, most active civil society groups had a very low level of influence.[68] Dudoignon provides an explanation for why the Soviet government allowed these non-state actors to form: 'The alternative political organisations and parties in Tajikistan were initially tolerated because they were thought to provide so many necessary and convenient outlets for the frustrations of the country's urban population, and ensure that these did not escalate into inter-communal violence.'[69] Niyazi has a similar, but more cynical explanation for the emergence of certain groups in the late *glasnost* period:

> The authorities try to counteract the opposition by using 'nonformula' organisations such as social-political clubs like 'The Workers' Perestroika' of the Dushanbe Railway District Committee of the CPSU, '*Ru ba Ru*' (face to face) of the Komsomol Central Committee, and '*Tajdid*' (renewal or renaissance) of the Vakhsh Komsomol District Committee. They were all set up and continue to be controlled by the authorities. It is quite evident, however, that they are unable to give any really effective support to the regime.[70]

While Freizer's and Mahkamov's above assessments may work for a narrow definition of civil society and public movements, they do not describe the late-*glasnost* political opposition movements very well. Atkin writes that 'by the end of the 1980s and beginning of the 1990s, a growing number of people advocated more substantial change than the republic-level leadership was willing to allow'.[71] The government, however, implemented some of the changes demanded by the

---

65   Muriel Atkin, 'FAST Case Study: Tajikistan' (Bern: Swiss Peace Foundation, Institute for Conflict Resolution, 3 February 1999), p. 1.

66   Freizer, 'Central Asian Fragmented Civil Society', p. 117.

67   Kilavuz, *Understanding Violent Conflict*, p. 138.

68   Makhamov, 'Islam and the Political Development of Tajikistan after 1985', p. 199. Makhamov provides some examples of these groups: '*Ehya-i Khojent* (Revival of Khojent); the sociocultural association of Samarkand; *Oftab-i Sugdian* (the Sun of Sogdiana); *Vahdat* (Unity); a popular front of supporters of reconstruction; *Oshkoro* (Publicity); society *Maihan* (Homeland); and *Haverim* (society of the friends of Jewish culture).'

69   Dudoignon, 'Political Parties and Forces in Tajikistan', pp. 56–7.

70   Niyazi, 'The Year of Tumult', p. 285.

71   Atkin, 'FAST Case Study', p. 1. For example, in 1990, '[t]he Tajik ex-apparatus reformers proposed turning the USSR into a commonwealth of independent states, long before the term existed … They hoped to

early opposition movements—possibly with strategic motives. For example, while the communist government had previously criticised nationalism and the influence of religion, it eventually coopted some of the opposition's platform. Starting in 1989 the government started to implement elements of the nationalist agenda, including the passage of a language law favouring Tajik.[72]

The decline of Rastokhez is most fully analysed by Lawrence Markowitz. He argues that Rastokhez continued to use the themes of Tajik nationalism and cultural revival as its main mobilising frame at a time when the people and government of Tajikistan had more tangible concerns—particularly the increasingly regionalised nature of power. In response to its declining support, Rastokhez allied with the Islamic Revival Party (IRP) and the Democratic Party of Tajikistan—both of which were able to 'usurp' the Rastokhez program—leaving it redundant as early as late 1990.[73] Niyazi adds further to the discussion of Rastokhez's decline. He argues that their credibility was harmed when the group became involved in the political manoeuvring surrounding the February 1990 riots and the attempt to force the leadership of the Tajik SSR to resign. Niyazi's harsh assessment is that

> [t]he February events showed that *Rastokhez* failed when put to the democratic test. Many of its leaders were drawn into 'palace intrigues'. They became members of the *Vahdat* committee and joined forces with influential functionaries. Then they sought power on the wave of the riots and were ready to accept any top positions in the party and government that happened to become vacant. They did not threaten the pyramid power structure. Only its summit and the blocks immediately supporting it did not suit them.[74]

Niyazi stresses that the Tajik media's biased coverage of the February 1990 events further contributed to damaging Rastokhez's reputation;[75] however, even though nine members of the Temporary Committee for Crisis Resolution belonged to Rastokhez, and despite a massive media campaign to present Tohir

---

enjoy all the benefits of political independence while receiving from Moscow all the grants necessary for the maintenance of the Tajik economy which the Soviet system had so long guaranteed them.' See: Dudoignon, 'Political Parties and Forces in Tajikistan', p. 62.

72   Kilavuz, *Understanding Violent Conflict*, pp. 144–5. As well as 'the appearance of nationalist concerns in official newspapers' and 'the establishment of a cultural foundation to preserve Tajik heritage'.

73   Lawrence Markowitz, 'How Master Frames Mislead: The Division and Eclipse of Nationalist Movements in Uzbekistan and Tajikistan', *Ethnic and Racial Studies*, Vol. 32, No. 4 (2009), esp. pp. 717–18, 728–30. Dudoignon gives an earlier date, arguing that Rastokhez had been replaced with the DPT and the IRP as early as summer 1990. See: Stephane Dudoignon, 'Communal Solidarity and Social Conflicts in Late 20th Century Central Asia: The Case of the Tajik Civil War', *Islamic Area Studies Working Paper Series*, No. 7 (Tokyo: Islamic Area Studies Project, 1998), p. 10.

74   Niyazi, 'The Year of Tumult', pp. 275–6.

75   Niyazi, 'The Year of Tumult', pp. 275–6.

Abdujabbor and his colleagues as power-thirsty villains, people had little doubt in their minds about the main forces responsible for the conflict in Dushanbe (Table 7.1).

Table 7.1 Who is to Blame for the Events in February 1990 in Dushanbe? (Results of a poll conducted throughout Tajikistan in May–June 1990)

Communist leadership of Tajikistan	35.2%
Law enforcement agencies	13.9%
Informal associations	11.5%
Religious circles	10.7%
Dushanbe city authorities	9.7%
Tertiary institutions' professors	9.0%
Creative intelligentsia	8.2%

Source: R. Alimov and M. Saidov, *Natsionalnyi vopros: raschety i proschety* (Dushanbe: Irfon, 1991), p. 101.

Nevertheless, these attacks resulted in Rastokhez changing its tactic to 'tough defence' and 'open confrontation with the government', whereas previously Rastokhez had been more focused on lobbying the government and seeking cooperation.[76] Rastokhez, despite its 'tough defence', would soon be eclipsed by a splinter party founded by disgruntled members: the Democratic Party of Tajikistan (DPT).

The Emergence of Political Opposition: The Democratic Party of Tajikistan

Prior to February 1990, the communist regime successfully maintained barriers to broad public participation in the political process. There was no legislation regulating the activities of unofficial organisations—they were invariably 'attached' to some government organ (Komsomol central or district committee, the Council of Ministers, soviets and so on), or, like Rastokhez, operated without registration, on a semi-legal basis. They had no publications of their own, and their access to state-controlled media was limited. As a result, even Rastokhez was relatively unknown to the bulk of the population and had no ability to mobilise the masses.

Part of the 'deal' brokered by Boris Pugo in February 1990 included the diversification of political space in Tajikistan to create checks and balances vis-a-vis the omnipotent *apparat*, according to the formula suggested by Gorbachev for the rest of the USSR. Already on 20 February 1990, the Tajik SSR

---

76   Niyazi, 'The Year of Tumult', pp. 275–6.

Supreme Soviet Presidium adopted a resolution 'On the Temporary Procedure of Registering Charters and Programs of Public Associations of Citizens of the Tajik SSR', which was an exact copy of an All-Union document.[77] On 12 December 1990, the Supreme Soviet of Tajikistan passed a law 'On Public Associations of the Tajik SSR', providing for further institutionalisation of non-governmental organisations. Between February 1990 and November 1992, 208 requests for registration were lodged with the Ministry of Justice of Tajikistan; 143 requests, including those of Rastokhez and most regional political groups, were approved.[78]

The Democratic Party of Tajikistan was founded on 10 August 1990 as a faction led by the philosopher Shodmon Yusuf (Yusupov), who had left Rastokhez along with many others. The DPT claimed a membership of 7000, of which about 85 per cent were ethnic Tajiks. The leadership, including a few ethnic Russians, was similar to Yusuf, coming almost entirely from academia and the intelligentsia.[79] During the August 1990 DPT conference, the newly elected chairman, Shodmon Yusuf, thus summarised the objectives of his 4000-strong party:[80]

1. The most important task of the DPT is the creation in Tajikistan of a law-based, authentically democratic civil society with a free economy and genuine state sovereignty and welfare of all citizens regardless of their national, racial, language, religious and philosophical identification.

2. The USSR cannot continue to exist in its present form. It should be transformed into a confederation of sovereign and independent states.

3. Tajikistan should conduct an independent foreign policy with special emphasis on good relations with Afghanistan, Iran, India, Pakistan, China and the Arab countries.

4. The republic should become independent economically through the promotion of a free market and various forms of ownership.

5. Education at all levels should combine classical traditions and progressive achievements of world civilisation.

---

77   *Kommunist Tadzhikistana*, 21 February 1990.

78   *Narodnaia gazeta*, 27 April 1993.

79   Dudoignon, 'Communal Solidarity and Social Conflicts in Late 20th Century Central Asia', p. 10; Atkin, 'Thwarted Democratization in Tajikistan', p. 285; Niyazi, 'The Year of Tumult', pp. 276–7. Until February 1990, Yusuf worked as a senior research fellow in the Department of Philosophy of the Tajikistan Academy of Sciences. See: Makhamov, 'Islam and the Political Development of Tajikistan after 1985', p. 208, n. 3. See also: Kilavuz, *Understanding Violent Conflict*, pp. 140–1. Kilavuz points to the Academy of Sciences as a noted source of DPT leadership.

80   Sh. Yusupov, 'Neobkhodimost' sozdaniia Demokraticheskoi partii Tadzhikistana i ee blizhaishie zadachi', Transcript of Sh. Yusuf's speech at the Constituent Conference of the DPT, 10 August 1990, courtesy of Dr V. M. Zaichenko, Dushanbe.

6. The DPT is motivated by the cultural heritage of the ancient Tajiks, respects religious values and fights for the unswerving implementation of the Law on the National Language.

7. The Tajiks should maintain close ties with democratic Russia, the Baltic states, the Caucasus, and Central Asian peoples.

8. The DPT is ready to cooperate with all political parties and movements standing on positions of democracy, whose goals do not contravene truth and justice.

9. Environmental protection and public health are a major concern of the DPT.

According to one prominent leader of the Russian Social-Democratic Party, 'the DPT's program was not different from the platform of the Russian democratic movement (especially the Democratic Party of Russia), and at times it was appropriate to speak about conscientious copying of the latter'.[81] Similar to Rastokhez, the DPT advocated for the abolishment of one-party communist rule and for the promotion of democracy, sovereignty, religious freedom and civil rights while condemning the ideology of Marxism-Leninism.[82]

In practice, however, the Tajik democrats' vision of building a new society in the republic proved to be as blurred and eclectic as that of their ideological predecessors—the members of Rastokhez. Its program claimed that 'the DPT draws from such great thinkers as Marx, Engels, Plekhanov, Bakunin, Lenin, Kautsky, Bernstein and others'.[83] Elsewhere, Shodmon Yusuf opined that socialism was the right choice, if it combined elements from the teachings of the Prophet Muhammad and Jesus Christ, the ideas of Lenin 'shortly before his death' and modern European social-democratic thought.[84] The dynamic DPT chairman, who possessed the academic degree of Candidate of Philosophical Sciences, was renowned for bombastic statements based on Western liberal parlance that carried little or no meaning to the wider public.[85]

The authors of the DPT program correctly discerned the economic distortions occurring in Tajikistan, particularly in the industrial sector; however,

---

81   Lifshits, 'Politicheskaia situatsiia v Tadzhikistane', p. 37.
82   Atkin, 'Thwarted Democratization in Tajikistan', p. 285; Niyazi, 'The Year of Tumult', pp. 276–7.
83   *Adolat*, No. 1 (September 1990).
84   *Charoghi ruz*, No. 2 (June 1991).
85   For example: 'We shall form an Opposition that will induce the Communist Party to become cleaner and more humane, we shall block the path to totalitarianism. As a philosopher, I am against all parties altogether. If the CP dissolved itself, we would follow its example immediately … If our people taste real freedom, the advent of a dictator will be impossible. As it is impossible in the USA, France and England … I understand the culture of France a little, and I would like to go to that country to lead a normal life.' See: *Komsomolets Tadzhikistana*, 10 August 1990.

they had an evidently weak understanding of the reasons for these distortions and the ways and goals of reforming the economy. Most importantly, they completely failed to comprehend the real socio-economic conditions of Tajikistan, ignoring the fact that the republic had been a subsidised region for decades, and had become incapable of providing itself with vitally important produce without carrying out deep social and economic changes which were not even mentioned in this document.[86]

'Easy' solutions were sought and found by the DPT experts: 'the main role in the economy and well-being of the peoples of Tajikistan will be played by precious stones, noble, non-ferrous and rare metals … today not more than one-tenth of the profits of the mining industry remains in the republic.'[87]

The DPT became the first organised political force, apart from the CPT, that had openly declared its intention to fight for power in Tajikistan, by using parliamentary procedures, moulding public opinion and building political coalitions. Mahkamov's regime was alarmed by the emergence of a serious rival. In a confidential CPT CC memorandum circulated in October 1990, it was acknowledged that the ruling party was losing members to the DPT, and a number of countermeasures were suggested, 'taking into consideration the special menace posed by the DPT leaders … who, speaking against the totalitarianism of the Communist party, have nothing against establishing a totalitarian state system of their own under the guise of a government of national concord'.[88] As a result, the DPT faced major difficulties in establishing regional and district chapters because local soviets delayed and frustrated their registration, sometimes using preposterous excuses: in Ordzhonikidzeobod (later Kofarnihon, now Vahdat), the letterhead of the DPT committee was pronounced 'not befitting the image of a solid organisation'.[89]

The DPT structure presented a mixture of principles borrowed from communists (only 'democratic centralism' was renamed 'democratic unity') and traditional organisational forms: Clause 4.1.1 of its charter envisioned flexibility of its primary cells, which could consist of family members, *mahalla* neighbours, cultural clubs and so on. Unlike Rastokhez, the DPT had rudiments of intra-party discipline, membership cards and permanent executive bodies: the Central Coordination Committee, the Central Revision Commission and the Main Editorial Council. Nevertheless, as Eden Naby has pointed out, 'the Democratic Party remains chiefly rooted in regional politics with an agenda similar to the old Rastakhiz Party … The problem is that [this] party neither cuts across

---

86 Bushkov and Mikulskii, *'Tadzhikskaia revoliutsiia' i grazhdanskaia voina*, p. 17.
87 *Rastokhez*, No. 6 (March 1991).
88 *Rastokhez*, No. 4 (October 1990).
89 *Komsomolets Tadzhikistana*, 23 November 1990.

regions nor does it have widespread backing'.[90] In terms of election success, the DPT was only successful in securing votes from Dushanbe's 'radical youth' and 'intellectual circles'—and in a few limited cases in special circumstances outside Dushanbe in the small centres of Uroteppa (Istaravshon), Kofarnihon (Vahdat) and Fayzabad.[91]

Table 7.2 Public Support for Political Parties in Tajikistan in November 1991 and June 1992 (percentage of those polled)

	IRP	DPT	Rastokhez	Communists	No party
November 1991	6	21	6	36	31
June 1992	6	10	3	40	39

Source: Grigorii Kosach, 'Tajikistan: Political Parties in an Inchoate National Space', in *Muslim Eurasia: Conflicting Legacies*, ed. Yaacov Ro'i (Ilford, UK: Frank Cass, 1995), pp. 134–6.

In terms of its support base, close scrutiny reveals that from the start Gharmis and Pamiris dominated the DPT. Its chairman, Shodmon Yusuf, was born in Vakhyo—the most conservative part of Qarotegin—while the independent Davlat Khudonazarov, widely accepted in Moscow and the West as the envoy of the Tajik democratic movement, represented the GBAO. The DPT received financial support for its activities, especially publication of the newspaper *Adolat*, from Gharmi merchants and the Islamic establishment.[92] In the eyes of anti-Leninobodi regional cliques it was a more efficient vehicle to promote their interests than Rastokhez, and by 1991 the latter showed signs of decay, 'retaining just a few motley groupings ... and a couple of familiar faces (Tohir Abdujabbor, H. Homidov and several others)'.[93]

The reforms of the late 1980s had, in Markowitz's words, 'emboldened many of the informal groups' in the republic while the 'elites' of the Communist Party 'had not yet regrouped from the attacks on their patronage bases'.[94] Starting in September 1991 and continuing through the winter of 1991–92, the DPT was preoccupied with condemning the Communist Party elites' strategy of creating joint ventures that would be out of reach of any future election winner's attempts to take over Communist Party-controlled economic assets. In particular, DPT-aligned journalists attacked Kulobi apparatchiks in print and

90 Eden Naby, 'Tajik Political Legitimacy and Political Parties', *The Iranian Journal of International Affairs*, Vol. V, No. 1 (Spring 1993), p. 197.
91 Dudoignon, 'Communal Solidarity and Social Conflicts in Late 20th Century Central Asia', pp. 10–11. Dudoignon describes the special circumstances: 'Ura-Teppa in the north (a traditional rival of Khujand), Kafirnihan (an industrial satellite of Dushanbe) or Fayzabad (situated between Dushanbe's plain and Gharm's valley, and fatherland of the popular poet Bazar Sobir, spokesman of the radical intelligentsia against the political apparatus).'
92 Dustov, *Zakhm bar jismi vatan*, p. 143.
93 *Charoghi ruz*, No. 1 (June 1991).
94 Markowitz, *Collapsed and Prebendal States in Post-Soviet Eurasia*, pp. 102–3.

wrote about 'illegal capital transfers from Dushanbe to Khujand'.[95] During this time public approval ratings for the DPT plummeted and their support fell by half (Table 7.2).[96]

Any assessment of Tajikistan's political landscape would be deceptive if based primarily on an exploration of ideological concepts and political thoughts—the easiest and most conventional path taken by many Western scholars.[97] When it comes to the translation of programmatic statements of these groups into concretely identifiable behaviour, such an approach proves faulty; it cannot, for example, explain why secular democratic forces in the republic failed to unite in 1990–91,[98] and why in 1992 some of them deemed it possible to form a coalition with Islamic organisations. Cultural traits, particularly local identification, and not ideological considerations, played the pivotal role in these processes.[99] The glow of liberalism and nationalism of the DPT catered to international public opinion and flickered brightly: Shodmon Yusuf, despite his stated fondness for France, also claimed to aspire to emulate the experience of Kuwait, Singapore and other illiberal states in Tajikistan, depending on which country he was touring at the time.[100]

95   Dudoignon, 'Communal Solidarity and Social Conflicts in Late 20th Century Central Asia', p. 18. The DPT claimed that a 'considerable number' of journalists and media professionals were members. See: Makhamov, 'Islam and the Political Development of Tajikistan after 1985', p. 198.

96   Kosach, 'Tajikistan', pp. 134–6, citing *Ozhidaniia i nadezhdy liudei v usloviiakh stanovleniia gosudarstvennosti (Oput sotsiologicheskikh issledovanyi v Tadzhikistane, Kazakhstane, Rossii i na Ukraine)* (Moscow: Russian Academy of Management, 1992), pp. 29–43. No polling was conducted in GBAO. Polling was conducted in the Leninobod, Qurghonteppa and Kulob *oblasts*, Dushanbe and surrounding regions such as Hisor and Tursunzoda. The poll does not break down respondents into nationality/ethnicity. Industrial workers were heavily dominated by Russian speakers. Kosach remarks on the survey: 'Despite all the errors, which are unavoidable in this type of work, these surveys obtained information on the social base of the political parties which can be considered generally accurate.' See: ibid., pp. 133–4.

97   Even such an astute observer as Muriel Atkin has followed it: 'In Tajikistan, as in other countries, the fact that some political groups had pronounced regional associations did not preclude their also having political platforms. The outcome of the power struggle will determine not only who will govern but also toward what ends they will do so, whether the political clock will be turned back to the Brezhnev era or whether some form of post-Communist political system will evolve.' See: Muriel Atkin, 'The Politics of Polarisation in Tajikistan', in *Central Asia. Its Strategic Importance and Future Prospects*, ed. Hafeez Malik (New York: St Martin's Press, 1994), p. 212.

98   There were at least two attempts initiated by the DPT to form the Union Party on the lines of Russia's Movement for Democratic Reforms, but both times Rastokhez and regional blocs objected feverishly. See: Mirzoi Salimpur, 'Infarkti savvumi KPSS', *Charoghi ruz*, No. 4 (July 1991), p. 1.

99   As Honi Fern Haler has suggested, 'each coalition is made up of separate groups, and each group has an identity. Where do they get this identity if not by coming together as a community, drawn together by similar interests, needs, or in other words, by similar (partial) identities?' See: Honi Fern Haler, *Beyond Postmodern Politics: Lyotard. Rorty. Foucalt* (London: Routledge, 1994), p. 128.

100   Dustov, *Zakhm bar jismi vatan*, p. 145.

The Failure of the Intelligentsia

The people who dominated the base of support for Rastokhez and the DPT were at times a dysfunctional group. Aziz Niyazi, himself a Tajik academic and son of a prominent intellectual,[101] clearly has a high level of disdain for some of his peers:

> It was mainly among social scientists that the Soil Movement developed and continues to develop. It has a strong tendency to focus on ethnic, nostalgic and pseudo-rationalist ideas and has weak links with reality. It has a lot in common with the Russian 'patriotic bloc,' and in the same way does considerable harm to the movement for national and cultural renaissance. It prefers to use feelings of hurt national pride and ignorance. By encouraging Russophobia and Turkophobia, the ideologists of the Tajik Soil Movement transfer the evil of the system to the peoples. They seem to believe that national consciousness can be cemented by hatred towards other nations.[102]

Concerning 'Turkophobia', Uzbek-themed insults were used amongst rival intellectuals with some of the newer generation (native-born and usually from the mountains or the migrant communities in the Vakhsh Valley) accusing the older generation (intellectuals from Khujand and Samarkand) of secretly being foreign Uzbeks who arrived to Dushanbe in the late 1930s after the CheKa secret police allegedly killed off the 'true' Tajik intelligentsia.[103] These fights were even found in television production studios in the 1970s.[104] There was a marked generational difference, as older Tajik intellectuals were equally at ease in Uzbek and Tajik, plus Russian, while younger intellectuals were mostly limited to Tajik and Russian.[105] The main enemy was never clearly singled out, and intellectuals among the literary community variably attacked Russia (as the 'evil step-mother'), Uzbekistan (the 'evil step-father') and Khujand (the 'half-brother'—that is, not a full, genuine Tajik).[106]

---

101   Aziz Niyazi is currently employed as a researcher at the Russian Academy of Sciences in Moscow. His father is the Samarkandi Tajik author Shavkat Niyazi, whose family moved to Dushanbe in the early 1930s. For more on the Niyazi family, see: Iraj Bashiri, *Prominent Tajik Figures of the Twentieth Century* (Dushanbe, Tajikistan: Academy of Sciences of Tajikistan & International Borbad Foundation, 2002), pp. 213–14.

102   Niyazi, 'The Year of Tumult', p. 278.

103   Dudoignon, 'Communal Solidarity and Social Conflicts in Late 20th Century Central Asia', p. 18.

104   Moukhabbat Khodjibaeva, 'Television and the Tajik Conflict', *Central Asia Monitor*, No. 1 (1999), p. 11. Khodjibaeva writes that nationalist discussion regarding Samarkand and Bukhara took place amongst the producers of Tajik TV in an environment in which southerners expressed resentment towards those from the north and their alleged pro-Turkic/Uzbek 'intentions'. And it was in the 1970s that the first southern Tajik was appointed chair of the State TV and Radio Committee.

105   Eden Naby, 'Tajiks Reemphasize Iranian Heritage as Ethnic Pressures Mount in Central Asia', *Report on the USSR*, Vol. 2, No. 7 (16 February 1990), p. 21.

106   Khudonazar, 'The Other', pp. 3–4.

A further divide is described by Dudoignon, a specialist on the history of intellectuals in Tajikistan, who notes that the older Tajik intelligentsia changed their strategy and stopped advocating for reforms when it became clear that the reforms could threaten their careers. This led to a rift with the younger generation, which had no such privileged positions and much less to lose.[107] Additionally, Dudoignon writes of a rift between the 'young radical students' and the older intellectuals of the DPT that occurred when the urban youth supporters of the DPT became dissatisfied with the 'liberal intelligentsia's' level of verbal attacks on the CPT 'conservatives'.[108] And, as noted above by Dudoignon,[109] members of the newer generation of intellectuals were usually from the mountains or from the migrant communities of the Vakhsh Valley (that is, Gharmis). Dudoignon, using the terms 'Kuhistanian'[110] and '*muhajir*'[111] in place of Gharmi, Qarotegini or 'Mountain Tajik' below, notes how aspiring students from these areas were pushed into powerless social niches:[112]

> Kuhistanian intellectual elites were victims of the division of work created since the mid-1970s inside Tajik higher education and professional distribution system[s]. Increasing numbers of students from Kuhistan and *muhajir* communities of central and southern Tajikistan were oriented, during two decades, toward 'literary' faculties and deprived of real possibilities of acquiring 'interesting' technical abilities (in such fields as law or economics).

As mentioned above, political party networks that relied on urban intellectuals lack the means to extend into broader parts of society. And the intellectuals who were most prominent—the academics and scientists—did not hold any positions of influence in government, a fact admitted at the 1990 annual session

---

107 Dudoignon, 'Communal Solidarity and Social Conflicts in Late 20th Century Central Asia', p. 18.

108 Dudoignon, 'Communal Solidarity and Social Conflicts in Late 20th Century Central Asia', p. 11. Dudoignon points to one incident as particularly important in this process. On 8 January 1991, Gorbachev approved 'a measure which made the kolkhoz and sovkhoz presidents the true directors—and virtual beneficiaries—of any future agrarian reform. More and more unsatisfied with this economic policy, the young Tajik intellectuals began to radicalize their discourse about nationality problems inside the republic, accusing the power in place of betraying the interests of the local population at large.' Ibid., p. 9.

109 Dudoignon, 'Communal Solidarity and Social Conflicts in Late 20th Century Central Asia', p. 18.

110 An awkward translation from French that should instead be 'Kuhistani': literally a person from 'Kuhistan', or 'mountainous area'. The term is also used in Afghanistan and Pakistan.

111 In Tajikistan this term is broadly used to describe migrants of all sorts, not just the religious refugees to whom this term is usually applied. Here it is used to denote the Gharmi Tajiks who were forcibly transferred to the lowlands and valleys.

112 Dudoignon, 'Communal Solidarity and Social Conflicts in Late 20th Century Central Asia', pp. 21–2. Mullojonov makes a similar point about the rural Gharmi students who came to Dushanbe. He refers to the 'the anti-establishment organizations of young urban intelligentsia—the Tajik "second intelligentsia," which were being formed since the 1980s notably by the first waves of migrant Gharmi youth coming from Qurghonteppa's cotton farms to the suburbs of Dushanbe, where they enrolled mostly in the humanities'. See: Mullojonov, 'The Islamic Clergy in Tajikistan Since the End of the Soviet Period', p. 249.

of the Tajik Academy of Sciences.[113] The intelligentsia, deprived of influence in the politics of the republic, was quite vulnerable. Dudoignon offers a harsh assessment:[114]

> The fondness felt by many Tajik intellectuals of the apparatus for the institutions and political sphere handed down by the USSR can be explained in part by their awareness that radical political reform would fell the branch on which they were comfortably perched: the intellectual mediocrity prevalent in Dushanbe, as in all the Soviet provincial capitals, precluded any hope of the intelligentsia's survival.

The 'liberal intelligentsia', who were often 'official writers and technocrats closer to the Communist party', became worried about preserving their careers and became increasingly uncomfortable with the alliance with the 'Islamists'.[115] In Tajikistan, as elsewhere in the Soviet Union, the 'technocrats initially allied with elements of the intelligentsia to support perestroika against an entrenched party apparat'.[116] The violence of the February 1990 riots, however, and the increasingly radicalised nationalism of the DPT and the 'Islamic politics' of the IRP 'pushed the old intelligentsia and the technocrats back into an alliance with the apparat'.[117] The lack of any broad support that could be mobilised in any forceful manner was fatal in 1992 when the DPT 'apparatus would be submitted to hard pressure from the power [sic] and many of its members would more or less rapidly return to the bosom of the Communist party'.[118] One DPT leader even conceded later that the weakness of the party lay in its lack of 'armed supporters'.[119]

Characterising and Categorising the Political Organisations

Sporadic attempts at categorising major political parties and public associations in Tajikistan using the conventional arsenal of ideological criteria have so far yielded somewhat equivocal results. Two scholars from Tajikistan have offered the following typology: 1) conservatives—orthodox members of the CPT; 2) liberal reformers—Paivand, Khoverim, Oryoni buzurg, Ehyoi Khujand, Vatan,

---

113   Niyazi, 'The Year of Tumult', p. 277. Niyazi notes that in 1990 the Supreme Soviet had 'practically no lawyers, economists, ecologists, sociologists or political scientists' serving as deputies.
114   Dudoignon, 'Political Parties and Forces in Tajikistan', p. 58.
115   Dudoignon, 'Communal Solidarity and Social Conflicts in Late 20th Century Central Asia', p. 11.
116   Rubin, 'Russian Hegemony and State Breakdown in the Periphery', p. 152.
117   Rubin, 'Russian Hegemony and State Breakdown in the Periphery', p. 152.
118   Dudoignon, 'Communal Solidarity and Social Conflicts in Late 20th Century Central Asia', p. 10.
119   Abdunabi Sattorzoda, 'The Democrat Party', in *Politics of Compromise: The Tajikistan Peace Process*, eds Kamoludin Abdullaev and Catharine Barnes (London: Conciliation Resources, 2001), p. 29.

Oshkoro, Hamdilon and some others; 3) reactionary radicals—the IRP, the DPT, Rastokhez, Ru ba Ru and La'li Badakhshon.[120] Unfortunately, the authors have not gone into great detail to explain it. An equally obscure yet popularly accepted scheme portrayed the following picture: 1) quasi-communism—the Communist Party; 2) political pluralism—the DPT; 3) Islamic liberalism—Rastokhez; 4) Islamic fundamentalism—the IRP; 5) irredentism—La'li Badakhshon.[121] It appears that even such a basic dichotomy as 'programmatic parties'/'electoral parties'[122] is not fully applicable to Tajikistan, because those who participate in party activities often do so not by virtue of sharing that party's ideology or pursuing elective office, but rather by following traditional collective incentives, such as familial, local or regional solidarity. A satisfactory theoretical solution, perhaps, should be credited to Zsolt Enyedi, who has introduced the notion of the 'subcultural party': a party 'involved directly or indirectly, in non-political (i.e., cultural, recreational, educational, religious, etc.) activities and surrounded by different, strongly interlinked social organisations, though sometimes the party itself can be regarded as the satellite organisation of other subcultural bodies'.[123] In Tajikistan, as can be seen from the foregoing account, the bulk of the newly established political organisations in the late 1980s and early 1990s served to promote and defend the interests of particular regional cliques and local strongmen. The definition of the opposition as a 'coalition of democrats, nationalists, Islamists, and inhabitants of regions seldom represented in the government'[124] should have read 'a coalition of inhabitants of regions underrepresented in the ruling elite who used democratic, nationalist and Islamic slogans'.

In Tajikistan, even under mono-organisational socialism, mobilisation rooted in traditionalism, localism and regionalism ordered the social behaviour of the majority of the population. Communism, viewed not as a Marxist dogma but rather as a specific form of social organisation in which all elite groups are centralised and abide by common codes of conduct, allowed these elites to maintain a stable regime. Once it was undermined, the need for elites to find a new way to frame their mobilisation efforts arose, and was finally realised under the guises of 'liberalism', 'democracy', 'Islamism' and 'orthodox communism'. The DPT and the IRP, by and large, represented the same community: the deprived people of Gharm, Qarotegin and elsewhere. They used different political languages,

120   Shokirov and Mahmadkarimov, *Paidoyeshi hizbu sozmonhoi nav dar Tojikiston va fa'oliyati onho*, pp. 12–13.
121   Hafizullah Emadi, 'State, Ideology and Islamic Resurgence in Tadjikistan', *Central Asian Survey*, Vol. 13, No. 4 (1994), p. 567.
122   John T. Ishiyama, 'Red Phoenix? The Communist Party in Post-Soviet Russian Politics', *Party Politics*, Vol. 2, No. 2 (1996), p. 152.
123   Zsolt Enyedi, 'Organising a Subcultural Party in Eastern Europe: The Case of the Hungarian Christian Democrats', *Party Politics*, Vol. 2, No. 3 (1996), p. 379.
124   Quoted in: Mehrdad Haghayeghi, *Islam and Politics in Central Asia* (New York: St Martin's Press, 1995), p. 149.

symbols and ideas to mobilise specific segments within those sub-ethnic groups according to their educational, residential and occupational status. By the same token, organisations like Oshkoro and Vahdat employed communist rhetoric not because their leaders and rank-and-file members believed in the withering away of the state or permanent revolution, but because the communist order, especially in its Central Asian variant, provided, at least potentially, for the privileged position of their respective localities.

Regional Aspects of Political Organisations

Towards the end of 1990, Mahkamov had been unable to reconcile the 'increasingly radicalized reformist movements and a "reactionary" wing of the Communist Party'.[125] With Mahkamov becoming increasingly weak, the DPT and the IRP became the strongest supporters of further reforms. The opposition supporters placed themselves in a position of conflict with the conservative elements of the Communist Party with their demands for further reforms in Kulob, Qurghonteppa and Leninobod.[126] Markowitz writes that as part of this process the collective farm bosses began to lose the protection of the 'conservative political elites' to whom they were tied through mutual 'regional interests', resulting in 'ideological divisions in the centre [becoming] increasingly tied to regional interests'.[127] This strategy placed the opposition movement in conflict with the incumbent elites in these regions as Gharmi and Pamiri elites started to also use the new opposition movements as a tool to mobilise against their rivals.[128] Olimova argues that Pamiri and Gharmi/Qarotegini elites had accumulated some economic strength by the late Soviet period. Elements within these two groups then decided to use the new *glasnost*-era opposition movements as a vehicle to gain a greater share of the political power. As a result, 'regional origin exerted a major influence on the choice of behavioural strategy of the new elites', while support or opposition to the 'Soviet imperial centre' was 'determined by regional affiliation'.[129]

The political competition immediately after independence in 1991 pitted the opposition, which included Rastokhez, the Democratic Party, the Pamiri party

125 Markowitz, *Collapsed and Prebendal States in Post-Soviet Eurasia*, p. 103. Elsewhere, Markowitz writes: 'ideological divisions widened between political elites in the centre, juxtaposing those who sought to dismantle the political-administrative system and its ties to the republic's lucrative cotton economy against those elites who sought to preserve that system.' See: Markowitz, 'How Master Frames Mislead', p. 12.

126 Markowitz, *Collapsed and Prebendal States in Post-Soviet Eurasia*, pp. 103–4.

127 Markowitz, 'How Master Frames Mislead', p. 12.

128 Olimova, 'Opposition in Tajikistan', p. 249. On a related note, Roy stresses that Gharmis in the government apparatus were not displaced by mullahs as the only source of power in the Gharmi community, even as the IRP made gains around this time. See: Roy, 'Is the Conflict in Tajikistan a Model for Conflicts throughout Central Asia', p. 139.

129 Olimova, 'Opposition in Tajikistan', p. 249.

La'li Badakhshon, and the heavily Gharmi Tajik IRP, against the Khujandi-dominated faction in power.[130] Opposition leaders, allied with the leaders of 'solidarity networks in disenfranchised regions, appealed to regional loyalties in officials of various agencies of state control'.[131] Olimova assessed the results of this strategy: 'Gradually, the proportion of members belonging to a specific Tajik ethno-regional group grew in all these organizations, and under cover of an all-national purpose, regional interests became distinct … The regional elites turned to the parties as instruments of political mobilization and political struggle.'[132] Specifically, the Gharmi/Qarotegini and Pamiri 'regional elites, having achieved economic clout, sought to change the balance of forces in their own interest and used the newly emerging opposition movements to this end'.[133] In regards to Kulobis, Nabiev had chosen to enter into a more solid alliance with the Kulobi faction in the autumn of 1991. The reasoning for this strategy, according to Parviz Mullojonov, is that they seemed to be the weakest in the republic.[134] Other reasons could include the obvious: the Kulobi elites were not using opposition movements to rally against the incumbent government, or they were the only partners with any mobilisation capabilities available in the vicinity of the capital. Another option could be that the Kulobis were not strangers to alliances with the dominant Leninobodi elite group in power. Starting in the early 1970s there was a level of power-sharing involving the Kulobi elites in a patronage relationship with the dominant elites of the central government.[135] The creation of the South Tajik Territorial Manufacturing Complex also brought Kulobi and Khujandi elites closer in terms of mutual economic interests.[136] One example of the Khujandi/Leninobodi-Kulobi arrangement was the composition of the Interior Ministry during the 1980s. Kulobis dominated the ranks until the Pamiri Mamadayoz Navjuvonov was appointed minister of the interior. After this a process began in which Kulobis were pushed out in favour of Pamiri police officers.[137] And an even more recent tying together of Khujandi and Kulobi

---

130 Stuart Horsman, 'Uzbekistan's Involvement in the Tajik Civil War 1992–97', *Central Asian Survey*, Vol. 18, No. 1 (1999), pp. 37–8; Kirill Nourzhanov, 'Saviours of the Nation or Robber Barons?' *Central Asian Survey*, Vol. 24, No. 2 (2005), pp. 111–12.

131 Zartman, *Political Transition in Central Asian Republics*, p. 94.

132 Olimova, 'Opposition in Tajikistan', p. 252.

133 Olimova, 'Opposition in Tajikistan', p. 249.

134 Mullojonov, 'The Islamic Clergy in Tajikistan Since the End of the Soviet Period', p. 248.

135 Akbarzadeh, 'Why Did Nationalism Fail in Tajikistan', p. 1108; Rubin, 'Central Asian Wars and Ethnic Conflicts', p. 10; Rubin, 'Russian Hegemony and State Breakdown in the Periphery', p. 151; Foroughi, 'Tajikistan', p. 46.

136 See the section on Kulob.

137 Zviagelskaya, *The Tajik Conflict*, n.p., citing V. I. Bushkov and D. V. Mikulskii, *Tajikistan: chto proiskhodit v respublike?* (Moscow: Institute of Ethnology and Anthropology of the Russian Academy of Sciences, 1992–93), pp. 25–6; Collins, *Clan Politics and Regime Transition in Central Asia*, p. 200; Said Akhmedov, 'Tajikistan II: The Regional Conflict in Confessional and International Context', in *Conflicting Loyalties and the State in Post-Soviet Russia and Eurasia*, eds M. Waller, B. Coppieters and A. Malashenko (London: Frank Cass, 1998) p. 175; Niyazi, 'Tajikistan I', p. 151. On Pamiri domination in the ranks of the Ministry of the Interior, see: Schoeberlein-Engel, 'Conflict in Tajikistan and Central Asia', p. 37; Matveeva, 'The Perils of Emerging Statehood', p. 7.

interests was seen in early to mid 1990 in the wake of the February events.[138] All of these factors facilitated a more formal arrangement between the northern elites and their junior Kulobi partners. In Rubin's characterisation, the Kulobis 'thus fit the prototype of a conservative impoverished group attached to an old regime by the small share of power it gave them and resistant to a new order that might displace them'.[139]

After independence, the leaders of most Central Asian states were able to maintain the system of regional patronage networks; however, due to the weakness of the system in Tajikistan (for example, the purges of cadres), the elites of previously less privileged regions successfully challenged the dominant Leninobod faction for an increased share of power and resources.[140] Before independence, starting in 1990, the capabilities and power of the government in Tajikistan rapidly deteriorated,[141] with different parts of the state apparatus divided between the different regional factions.[142] After the collapse of the Soviet Union, the central government in Tajikistan became even weaker, deprived of the perception of control and order in the eyes of its population. Furthermore, the state was now facing political opposition from various groups.[143] Atkin argues that the Khujandi/Leninobodi elite—and their new Kulobi allies as junior partners— wished to preserve the system, not for reasons of ideology, but to keep the monopoly of power and the control of resources that they enjoyed during the Soviet era.[144] Dudoignon writes that at this time the 'two newly shaped sides' were settled: northern 'Khujand Communists' and the southern Kulobis on one side versus the Pamiri party La'li Badakhshon, the DPT, and the Gharmi-dominated IRP on the other side. Dudoignon writes further that both sides 'were almost ready for an armed conflict and would prepare themselves for it during winter 1991–92. [By] February 1992 ... everybody would have chosen his side once and for all'.[145] Despite the government's efforts, by spring 1992 the country was divided among various regional factions and the central government was completely ineffective.[146]

---

138 See the section on the February 1990 demonstration and riots.

139 Rubin, 'Russian Hegemony and State Breakdown in the Periphery', p. 151.

140 Jones Luong, *Institutional Change and Political Continuity in Post-Soviet Central Asia*, p. 100; P. Jones Luong, 'The Future of Central Asian Statehood', *Central Asia Monitor*, No. 1 (1999), pp. 4, 8.

141 Niyazi, 'Tajikistan I', p. 146.

142 Roy, 'Is the Conflict in Tajikistan a Model for Conflicts throughout Central Asia', p. 146.

143 Nourzhanov, 'Saviours of the Nation or Robber Barons', p. 111; Menon and Spruyt, 'Possibilities for Conflict Resolution in Post-Soviet Central Asia', p. 113.

144 Atkin, 'Tajikistan', pp. 614–16. Ideology was far less important. John Anderson argues that the government was 'concerned less with preserving Marxist-Leninist ideology against a new philosophy than with protecting positions and influence built up over decades'. See: John Anderson, *The International Politics of Central Asia* (Manchester: Manchester University Press, 1997), pp. 172–3.

145 Dudoignon, 'Communal Solidarity and Social Conflicts in Late 20th Century Central Asia', p. 14.

146 Niyazi, 'Tajikistan I', p. 146.

There were numerous exceptions to the rule of region of origin determining political loyalty. Atkin and Kilavuz both note prominent exceptions at the elite level, both on the opposition and the pro-government sides. Some prominent Pamiris and Gharmis supported Rahmon Nabiev[147] while certain prominent Kulobis and Khujandis/Leninododis supported the opposition parties.[148] As for pro-government politicians from regions whose elites trended towards the opposition, Atkin remarks that those who benefited personally under 'the old order' were likely to work towards preserving that system. This resulted in 'veteran politicians' from Gharm and Badakhshon who had previously benefited from the existing system of power distribution working on the pro-government side in an effort to preserve it, along with their positions of power.[149] Nevertheless, the overall trend was towards regionalisation of political loyalties.

The Disintegration of the Soviet Political System

Prior to 1985, regional elites in Tajikistan were united in a single political organisation, publicly professed the same ideology, and conducted elementary consensual activity inside the CPT Central Committee. With the commencement of *perestroika*, elite factions gained an opportunity to take opposition stances in public, and in February 1990 eventually took the risk of pushing them to violent confrontation. But even then an elite settlement could be achieved within existing institutional structures. With the rapid decay of the mono-organisational system, especially following the twenty-eighth CPSU congress in July 1990, the national elite in Tajikistan quickly reached a 'disunified' state, characterised by 'ruthless, often violent, inter-elite conflicts. Elite factions deeply distrust each other, interpersonal relations do not extend across factional lines, and factions do not cooperate to contain societal divisions or to avoid political crises.'[150]

---

147 Atkin, 'Tajikistan', p. 615; Kilavuz, *Understanding Violent Conflict*, pp. 183–4. For example: Akbarsho Iskandarov (who became speaker of the Supreme Soviet in May 1992). Nabiev even had some powerful Gharmi allies, including Sadulloh Khairulloev (vice-premier, 1991–92) and Munavar Nazriev (a leader in the Communist Party).

148 Atkin, 'Tajikistan', p. 615; Kilavuz, *Understanding Violent Conflict*, pp. 183–4. For example: Kulobi opposition members include Mullah Abdurahim (an IRP leader, one of the original founders), Said Ibrahim (IRP leadership), Odina Khoshim (folk singer), Rajab Ali Safarov (Soviet-era transport minister), Asaev (mathematician), Sharofaddin Imomov (deputy chair of Rastokhez). Opposition supporters from Khujand include: DPT members Abdunabi Sattarov, Jumaboy Niyozov, Latifi and Haluknazarov. There were also many Rastokhez members from the north, most prominently the organisation's leader, Tohir Abdujabbor.

149 Atkin, 'Tajikistan', p. 615.

150 Michael G. Burton and J. Higley, 'Elite Settlements', *American Sociological Review*, Vol. 52 (June 1987), p. 296.

In the second half of 1990 and in 1991, the CPT continued to contract and implode, following the All-Union pattern. Internal haemorrhaging of the CPSU and the CPT proceeded along different lines, however, the former was splitting on ideological grounds,[151] and the latter disintegrating according to the territorial criterion. This was especially evident during the seventh plenum of the CPT CC, held in February 1991. While the mandatory report of Qahhor Mahkamov was, as always, filled with empty phrases and commitments 'to defend staunchly positive democratic gains of *perestroika*',[152] his colleagues from regions and districts were surprisingly frank and businesslike. Representatives of Leninobod and Kulob, interested in maintaining the status quo, deplored the party's loss of its governing functions; they argued that *perestroika* was 'a succession of precocious, inconsequent, incompetent decisions and mistakes in the national economy' and that 'as a result of the Party's withdrawal from administration economic decay has become visible, negative processes in social and moral spheres have been unfolding and the Soviet people have been suffering hardships'.[153] The first secretary of the Khorog *gorkom*, Qozidavlat Qoimdodov, spoke in favour of reforms that were defined somewhat narrowly but brazenly as an increased share for Pamiris in the leadership.[154] A group of *raikom* functionaries, without going much into high politics, insisted on delegating the right to use party property from the CPT CC to district committees.[155] The demolition of central control in the CPT was in the making. In 1990 its membership contracted by 2070—a 1.6 per cent decrease[156]—whereas the CPSU shrank by 1.3 per cent.[157] It is illuminating that the greatest numbers of defectors were registered in Dushanbe (one-third of the total) and in the Gharm group of districts,[158] while the Leninobod *oblast* organisation actually grew by 804 people.[159] The party was exhibiting a tendency towards becoming a political organisation of northerners *par excellence*.

Despite its emaciation and fragmentation, and despite its inability to cope with the mounting problems in Tajikistan, the CPT was still viewed by many as the only institution guaranteeing a semblance of stability and national unity. A political observer of the opposition newspaper *Charoghi ruz* wrote in June 1991: 'Contrary to the triumphant shouts of the opposition that "Communists have lost dignity and prestige" … the Communist party remains a formidable

---

151   In March 1991 there were up to 10 platforms and factions operating in the party. See: Gill, *The Collapse of a Single-Party System*, p. 144.
152   *Kommunist Tadzhikistana*, 21 February 1991.
153   *Kommunist Tadzhikistana*, 27 February 1991.
154   *Kommunist Tadzhikistana*, 27 February 1991.
155   *Kommunist Tadzhikistana*, 22 February 1991.
156   *Nazare ba ta'rikh: Ma'lumotnomai mukhtasar* (Khujand: Komiteti viloyati Leninobodi partiyai kommunistii Tojikiston, 1994), p. 16.
157   Gill, *The Collapse of a Single-Party System*, p. 155.
158   *Kommunist Tadzhikistana*, 21 February 1991.
159   *Kommunist Tadzhikistana*, 25 May 1991.

political force in Tajikistan … the insignificant level of public protest against measures of the Communist government signifies that the CPT enjoys sufficient political respect here.'[160] Opinion polls corroborated this conclusion.[161]

The results of the referendum on the preservation of the USSR held on 17 March 1991 also indicated strong public support for the continuous Soviet corporatist compromise in Tajikistan. The CPT called on the population to vote for retaining the Soviet Union as a rejuvenated federation of sovereign republics with equal rights, while the DPT and Rastokhez urged it to boycott the poll. At the end of the day, the overwhelming majority of the people of Tajikistan participated in the referendum and said 'yes' to the union by 96.2 per cent to 3.1 per cent.[162]

The CPT still formed the centrepiece of the republic's political system; it had lost its control and implementation functions, but its role in strategic decision-making remained substantial, and all positions of authority in state structures were still staffed with communists. There were forces within the party, grouped around the deputy chairman of the Council of Ministers, Abdujalil Samadov, who favoured dialogue with opposition groups and offered balanced solutions to the socioeconomic problems that Tajikistan faced. In November 1990, they published a document entitled 'The Program of Concrete Measures of Economic Stabilisation and Transition to a Market in the Tajik SSR',[163] which envisaged

- continuing economic cooperation within the USSR
- partial price liberalisation
- gradual privatisation of state property
- encouragement of small businesses and private entrepreneurship
- creation of a market infrastructure
- land reform
- rationalisation of the government apparatus
- adoption of laws conducive to the emergence of a market economy.

Qahhor Mahkamov failed to rally the reformist elements in the CPT to secure the regime's gradual adaptation to changing conditions. He followed Gorbachev's

---

160   *Charoghi ruz*, No. 1 (June 1991), p. 3.

161   Trust in the CPSU and the CPT in 1990–91 differed strongly. In autumn 1990, the CPSU was trusted by less than 10 per cent of people union-wide, and less than 6 per cent one year later. In contrast, in Tajikistan the CPT was trusted by 40 per cent of people in autumn 1990 and by 36 per cent one year later. Sources: Matthew Wyman, *Public Opinion in Post-Communist Russia* (London: Macmillan, 1997), p. 63; *Narod i politika. (Tadzhikistan: iiun' 1992 goda)*, A confidential analytical report prepared for the Cabinet of Ministers of Tajikistan, Typewritten document dated 22 July 1992 and signed by Professor V. Boikov of the Russian Academy of Social Sciences, p. 6; *Vybory Prezidenta Respubliki Tadzhikistan: Sotsiologicheskii monitoring* (Dushanbe: Press-sluzhba KM RT, 1991), p. 16.

162   *Kommunist Tadzhikistana*, 28 March 1991.

163   *Programma konkretnykh meropriiatii po stabilizatsii ekonomiki i perekhodu k rynku v Tadzhikskoi SSR. Proekt* (Dushanbe: [No publisher], 1990).

path, neither breaking completely with the party nor using its potential. In November 1990, the Supreme Soviet elected Mahkamov president of the Tajik Soviet Socialist Republic. He faced strong opposition in the person of Rahmon Nabiev, but persuaded the deputies to vote for him by making all manner of promises and resorting to political jockeying.[164] President Mahkamov received vast executive powers—most importantly, to rule by edict, and appoint and dismiss senior public servants at his will. He used these powers not to initiate and oversee reformist policies, but to secure his position and the wellbeing of his immediate supporters.

Mahkamov's regime had to achieve accommodation at three levels: a) within the upper state leadership itself, b) with organised opposition, and c) with political actors in the regions and districts. While handling top bureaucrats, Mahkamov employed the tactics of political musical chairs, arbitrary political appointments and frequent changes to the institutional and legal frameworks of administration. As one Tajik MP lamented in July 1991: 'Is it normal that every session of the Supreme Soviet has to approve a new government structure? Top echelon cadres … are replaced every 3–4 months. As a result, for example, the republic's agriculture does not have a unified structure and lacks coordination.'[165] Still the CPT CC first secretary, Mahkamov, in February 1991, sanctioned transferral of the party's assets to an obscure holding company, EKOMPT. This firm took over the CPT's polygraphic facilities, transport pool and construction organisations, and used them in tourism, entertainment and export–import businesses, refraining, however, from channelling profits to 'material-financial support of the CPT activities'.[166] The CPT *apparatchiks*, even in the Leninobod *oblast*, began talking about the 'betrayal on the part of the leaders which has pushed the Communist Party from the political arena'.[167]

Mahkamov acted as if opposition parties and organisations did not exist. Martial law, introduced in February 1990 in Dushanbe, precluded them from holding mass rallies in the capital, and infrequent meetings of the DPT and

---

164   One of Mahkamov's arguments was that Gorbachev, who had become the Soviet Union's president five months previously, would disburse 1 billion roubles to cover Tajikistan's 30 per cent budget deficit more easily if he were elected. See: Nasriddinov, *Tarkish*, p. 133.

165   *Kommunist Tadzhikistana*, 19 July 1991. The Tajik leadership copiously reproduced Gorbachev's patterns of administration, with a time lag of four–five months. The USSR's prime minister, Nikolai Ryzhkov, came up with the following statement in November 1990: 'Control has been totally lost at all levels of the state structure. Authority has been paralysed … Universal destructiveness is basically becoming the norm. One can say with sufficient conviction and grounds that, throughout the greater part of the country's territory, a situation has been created in which no one is in charge, and that this has led to a complete or partial deterioration of all systems of administration.' Quoted in: John P. Willerton, 'Executive Power and Political Leadership', in *Developments in Soviet and Post-Soviet Politics*, eds Stephen White, Alex Pravda and Zvi Gitelman (London: Macmillan, 1992), p. 65.

166   *Kommunist Tadzhikistana*, 23 July 1991.

167   M. Hojiev, *Ta'rikh guvoh ast (Sahifaho az ta'rikhi Partiyai Kommunistii Tojikiston)* (Khujand: Omor, 1994), p. 25.

Rastokhez supporters in Leninobod and Kulob were regularly disrupted by members of local action groups with tacit police approval. The IRP kept a low profile, and the handful of vociferous opposition parliamentarians could be safely ignored. In fact, the Supreme Soviet of Tajikistan in 1990 and 1991 was an amorphous collection of communist and ex-communist officials with little or no experience of the legislative process, factionalised according to regional affiliation and rather easy to manipulate. It also resembled a glorified *gashtak*: women were all but expunged from its ranks,[168] the judgment of the *bobo*—that is, the president—was seldom questioned, and its entire modus operandi bore an imprint of patrimonialism:

> When a parliamentary commission head or a member of the government is to be appointed, they take into consideration how many seats representatives from this or that locality already have ... Sometimes an appointment can be blocked if there is an evident surplus of a particular clan's representatives amongst office-holders. Some instances of blackballing are truly laughable, when members of the parliament, forgetting their democratic image, begin to discuss openly the place of birth and clan affiliation of a vacancy-seeker. Hundreds of thousands of Tajikistan's residents witnessed such debates in the parliament on TV not long ago.[169]

In March 1991, another blow was dealt to the old system of checks and balances inside the power structure. A new law on local government suggested merging the positions of chairman of the soviet and chairman of the executive committee of the soviet. Henceforth, at the district-town level, legislative and executive powers became vested in one person, who was elected by the corresponding soviet, but who could be dismissed directly by the president. Mahkamov hoped that this move would help him in combating the *oblast* leaders, but very soon local bosses developed political resources that made their positions virtually unassailable either by the head of state or by regional authorities. Of 60 newly elected chairmen of executive committees only 10 were communist functionaries; others were local strongmen of various description, ranging from *sovkhoz* and factory directors to shadowy traders.[170]

Qahhor Mahkamov tried to create a number of executive bodies, not necessarily mentioned in the Constitution, to advise him in setting policies and to control their implementation. The most important of them was the 15-strong Presidential Council, established in February 1991. This organ had considerable potential to evolve as a forum for negotiations amongst elite factions, but the president

---

168 Women made up 36 per cent of the Supreme Soviet deputies in 1985, and only 3.9 per cent in 1990. See: *Kommunist Tadzhikistana*, 25 July 1991.

169 Narzikulov, 'Dvulikii Ianus v serdtse Azii', p. 128.

170 *Kommunist Tadzhikistana*, 9 August 1991.

appeared to have selected its members on the basis of personal loyalty rather than political influence and ability. With the exception of the vice-president, Izatullo Khayoev, and the minister of the interior, Mamadayoz Navjuvonov, the council consisted of rather nondescript characters—the Kulob region, for example, was represented by a sixty-eight-year-old pensioner, Nizoramo Zaripova, who may have commanded respect due to the fact that she was well advanced in years, but who had no influence in the decision-making process. The council sank into oblivion without leaving a trace in Tajikistan's political history.

In the meantime, the economic situation in the republic was nearing a critical point. In 1990, Tajikistan's GDP contracted by 2.2 per cent, but the national income used actually grew by 6.4 per cent due to transfers from the centre.[171] By the second half of 1991, the following grim picture had emerged[172]

- production of 56 of 77 major commodity groups lagged far behind targets
- civil construction stood at 50 per cent of the 1990 figure
- scarcity of food in cities was a pressing problem
- the budget deficit exceeded 1.7 billion roubles, and there were absolutely no internal resources to cover it.

Mahkamov's regime did nothing to reform the economy. As always, he pinned all his hopes on Moscow. The communiqué of the leaders of Central Asian republics published on 14 August 1991 stated that they wholeheartedly supported the new union treaty prepared by Gorbachev whereby this region would continue to receive 'financial resources for socio-economic development and for covering compensation pay-outs to the population'.[173] The signing of the treaty was pre-empted by the abortive coup in Moscow on 19–21 August 1991, in the wake of which any continuation of the Soviet Union, even as a loose confederation of states, was impossible. Following other Central Asian republics, Tajikistan proclaimed its independence on 9 September 1991; to borrow Martha Brill Olcott's expression, it was 'a freedom more forced on them than acquired or won'.[174]

President Mahkamov's mishandling in Tajikistan of the August 1991 attempted coup against Gorbachev led to protests that ended in his resignation. Mahkamov did not support the putsch, contrary to popular myth.[175] Mahkamov's actions

171 *Narodnoe khoziaistvo Tadzhikskoi SSR v 1990g.*, pp. 3, 6.

172 *Kommunist Tadzhikistana*, 6 August 1991.

173 *Kommunist Tadzhikistana*, 17 August 1991.

174 Martha Brill Olcott, 'Nation Building and Ethnicity in the Foreign Policies of the New Central Asian States', in *National Identity and Ethnicity in Russia and the New States of Eurasia*, ed. Roman Szporluk (Armonk, NY: M. E. Sharpe, 1994), p. 209.

175 According to Ben Fowkes, 'only Mahkamov (Tajikistan) came out directly in favour of the coup'. See: Ben Fowkes, *The Disintegration of the Soviet Union: A Study in the Rise and Triumph of Nationalism* (New York: St Martin's Press, 1997), p. 191. For additional arguments that stress that Mahkamov supported the coup, see: Markowitz, *Collapsed and Prebendal States in Post-Soviet Eurasia*, p. 104; Schoeberlein-Engel, 'Conflicts in

around the time of the coup were neither in support nor in rejection, but rather cautious non-involvement and then denial once it was clear that the coup had failed.[176] He was disoriented and confused, and did not come up with any political statements concerning the political struggle in Moscow—years of subservience to the Kremlin had obviously taken their toll.[177] The opposition used this as an opportunity to accuse the government of supporting the coup. In response, the opposition held a large rally in Dushanbe's Shahidon Square and demanded Mahkamov's resignation.[178]

On 27 August 1991, Mahkamov signed a decree disbanding the CPT structures in government agencies and sequestrating its property. On 28 August, he and the chairman of the Presidium of the Supreme Soviet, Qadriddin Aslonov, formally quit the party. The next day, under pressure from inside and outside the republic, Mahkamov resigned as president of Tajikistan. On 9 September 1991, the Government of Tajikistan declared independence. The communist era in the history of Tajikistan came to an end.

Over 70 years the Soviet political system in Tajikistan embraced and coopted elements of the traditional culture, cultivated legal, semi-legal and illegal links amongst various units of society and restrained fissures within it. This system was based on the communist mono-organisational order, and, eventually, 'the communists were better adapted to this neotraditional society than the mullahs or the "democrats"'.[179] The system was altered and ultimately destroyed in the Gorbachev period, primarily by exogenous forces. In a society in which

---

Tajikistan and Central Asia', pp. 26–7. One statement from Mahkamov offers no illumination. When asked if he had supported the coup, Mahkamov replied: 'Yes, in principle.' See: Interview by Otakhon Latifi in the weekly *Soyuz* as cited in 'Events of the Week', *Radio Dushanbe Network* (1 September 1991), ITPRS Report, FBIS-USR-91-028, 6 September 1991, pp. 76–7, as cited in John W. Parker, *Persian Dreams: Moscow and Tehran Since the Fall of the Shah* (Washington, DC: Potomac Books, 2008), p. 60.

176   Kilavuz, *Understanding Violent Conflict*, pp. 146–8.

177   When asked by the opposition whom he had sided with during the failed putsch against Gorbachev, Mahkamov claimed that he was not being informed about the unfolding events. See: Monica Whitlock, *Land Beyond the River: The Untold Story of Central Asia* (New York: St Martin's Press, 2003), pp. 150–1. Akbar Turajonzoda recollected that when he called Mahkamov on 19 August and asked about his reaction to the coup, Mahkamov simply said, 'I don't know.' See: *Nezavisimaia gazeta*, 18 September 1991. As a Tajik political expert has put it, 'the enemies of the [Tajik] state presented this silence as unconditional support for the GKChP [State Committee for the State of Emergency]. Government media did not bother to deny this categorically. Mahkamov did not have the skill, wisdom and shrewdness of Nazarbaev [President of Kazakhstan], who officially hailed the coup but two days later denounced it, having received hundreds of millions of roubles from the leaders of Russia—investment into their countries' independence.' See: Ibrohim Usmon, *Soli Nabiev* (Dushanbe: [No publisher], 1995), pp. 6–7.

178   Kilavuz, *Understanding Violent Conflict*, pp. 146–8. See also: Schoeberlein-Engel, 'Conflicts in Tajikistan and Central Asia', p. 25.

179   Roy, *The Civil War in Tajikistan*, p. 22.

political life was characterised by consensual activity and direct bargaining by local and regional groups and self-interested politicians, the institutionalisation of political opposition was premature. All opposition figures were interested in gaining access to power rather than concerned with the expression of independent attitudes. The absence of a viable economy, the reluctance of the political leaders to form broad coalitions under the banner of nationhood, the flimsiness of the constitutional framework for political process, and the breakdown of state mechanisms of social control presaged a turbulent future for the independent Republic of Tajikistan.

8. Islam in Society and Politics

Islam as a Traditional Institution

Islam was another traditional institution that proved to be extraordinarily resistant to the policies initiated by the communist state. While there is little doubt that in Soviet Central Asia 'political institutions and political processes have been completely freed from the influence of religion',[1] Islam retained its position as a source of identity, a transmitter of cultural tradition and, more generally, as a way of life. In regards to the 'survival' of Islam in the Soviet Union, scholars have remarked on the importance of the large 'network' of unsanctioned mullahs who, despite the existence of the officially endorsed clerics of the Spiritual Directorate of the Muslims of Central Asia and Kazakhstan (SADUM), 'established Qur'an schools, preserved shrines, presided at burials, weddings and other rituals and, in the urban Muslim settings at least, monitored the observation of "traditions" [that is, in the *mahalla*]' during the Soviet era.[2] Religious practice was not, however, confined to just the 'unofficial' mosques. For example, as noted in one village at the very end of the Soviet era, religious practices centred on the village mosque 'represented a small proportion of the total religious activity in the village. For alongside this mosque-based activity, there also existed a whole range of less visible religious practices which were centred either around the household and/or groups of women.'[3]

Secularisation and atheistic education were permanent components of the party line in Tajikistan. The concrete policy towards religious observance, however, fluctuated substantially. Between 1920 and 1927, the secular state had to tolerate the existence of Islamic schools (*maktabs* and *madrasas*), real estate property of mosques (*vaqf*) and *shari'a* courts. The years from 1928 to 1941 witnessed a ferocious attack on the Muslim establishment: certain religious practices were

---

1   Shams-ud-din, *Secularisation in the USSR* (New Delhi: Vikas Publishing House, 1982), p. 206.
2   Martha Brill Olcott, 'Islam and Fundamentalism in Independent Central Asia', in *Muslim Eurasia: Conflicting Legacies*, ed. Yaacov Ro'i (London: Frank Cass, 1995), p. 24.
3   Tett, *Ambiguous Alliances*, p. 81. On women, Tett further argues (p. 95) that '[d]uring most of the Soviet period, in other words, it appeared that women were carrying the main religious burden in the community … Just as a woman was able to shame a household through sexual misbehaviour, so too there was a sense in which she could shame the religious and cultural standing of a household and community through her religious misbehaviour'.

outlawed,[4] religious institutions were closed,[5] *vaqf* was abolished and the clergy was thoroughly purged. The predominantly Ismaili population of the Pamirs was prohibited from sending annual tribute to their spiritual leader, the Aga Khan in India, and his representative in Tajikistan, *ishon* Seid Yusofalisho, was arrested in 1931.[6] The Islamic courts were disbanded in November 1927, on the tenth anniversary of the Bolshevik revolution.[7] The postwar period was characterised by a somewhat more tolerant approach, with an emphasis on antireligious propaganda rather than blatant coercion.[8] The effectiveness of the seemingly relentless struggle conducted by local authorities on the ideological front, however, was often questioned by Moscow.[9] A special resolution of the CPSU Central Committee on Tajikistan (the only one of its kind throughout the Soviet period) stated in particular that '[p]arty organisations in the republic direct ideological-educational work aimed at the formation of a Marxist-Leninist outlook amidst all working people in an unsatisfactory manner … Lately atheistic propaganda has weakened and the activities of clergy and religious sects have been on the rise'.[10] Obviously, the anti-Islamic drive in Tajikistan was often maintained as a sheer formality: in 1961, for example, of 43 women's atheistic groups reported in the Panj *raion*, only one was functioning.[11] Even foreign guests to Tajikistan noted the seemingly free practice of Islam.[12]

---

4   For instance, circumcision was strongly discouraged; but the ritual operation continued to be performed at home regardless, and the number of patients admitted to hospitals with complications after circumcision remained constantly high. See: I. Ermakov and D. Mikulskii, eds *Islam v Rossii i Srednei Azii* (Moscow: Lotos, 1993), p. 105.

5   Until 1989, there was not a single officially registered *maktab* or *madrasa* in Tajikistan, in sharp contradistinction with the pre-revolutionary period: in 1903, the city of Khujand alone had 30 *maktabs* and 30 *madrasas*, where 575 students were trained to become mullahs. See: *Leninobod* (Dushanbe: Irfon, 1986), p. 166.

6   M. Nazarshoev, *Partiinaia organizatsiia Pamira v bor'be za sotsializm i kommunizm* (Dushanbe: Irfon, 1970), p. 109.

7   'This was a new Soviet tradition—to mark revolutionary holidays with labour and other accomplishments.' G. S. Azizkulova, *Tsikl lektsii po istorii gosudarstva i prava Respubliki Tadzhikistan* (Dushanbe: TGU, 1995), p. 180.

8   For example, in 1958, 2056 teams of agitators with a membership in excess of 33 000 operated in the republic, exposing the harmful and reactionary essence of Islam. See: *XI s'ezd Kommunisticheskoi partii Tadzhikistana*, p. 68.

9   See, for example, the numerous anecdotes in: Yaacov Ro'i, *Islam in the Soviet Union: From the Second World War to Gorbachev* (London: Hurst & Co., 2000).

10   'O rabote TsK Kompartii Tadzhikistana po vypolneniiu reshenii XXIII s'ezda KPSS', *Partiinaia zhizn'*, No. 1 (January 1969), p. 5.

11   *XIV s'ezd Kommunisticheskoi partii Tadzhikistana*, p. 188.

12   For example, a note was left in 1981 by visitors from India in the guestbook of the famous mosque of *mavlono* Ya'qubi Charkhi near Dushanbe: 'We are very excited about seeing the mosque. We are not Muslims ourselves, but we have become convinced that in the Soviet Union, especially in Tajikistan, the Islamic religion is fully fledged and its practice is free. We have seen it with our own eyes and have rescinded the wrong impression we had had before.' See: R. Yormuhammad, *Mavlono Ya'qubi Charkhi kist?* (Dushanbe: Tojikiston, 1992), pp. 15–16. Much earlier, an American anthropologist (and later a noted anti-Soviet activist) visited Tajikistan and noted the free operation of state-approved mosques and the presence of officially sanctioned imams; however, he added that he believed it was partially a facade meant for foreign guests and tourists. See: Louis Dupree, 'Two Weeks in Soviet Tajikistan and Uzbekistan: Observations and Trends', *American Universities Field Staff Reports Service, South Asia Series*, Vol. III, No. 4 (1959), pp. 12–14.

Sergei Poliakov's description of the rural areas shows exactly how little Soviet rhetoric and policies on religion mattered to the people here. The 'unofficial' Islamic institutions had a great deal of relevance. For example, while counting unregistered mosques in northern Tajikistan, Poliakov found that every village had at a minimum one mosque, with some villages having multiple mosques divided by *mahalla*.[13] As for the people who operated these unregistered mosques, Poliakov writes that the activities of the 'unofficial clergy are neither controlled nor administered'.[14] Olivier Roy gives nearly the same description, noting that each village and *kolkhoz* during the Soviet era had a mullah, who was usually registered as a worker.[15]

In the 1970s and 1980s, there emerged a kind of accommodation between the state and Islam in Tajikistan. It was characterised by two non-contradictory parameters: a) state-sponsored secular institutions and norms of behaviour dominated the *public* realm of social action, and b) religion was tacitly recognised as an integral element of *private* life—an element that would wither away with the progress of the communist project. As Yaacov Ro'i has observed:

> [E]ven if at first a departure from religion was imposed upon them by force, in the course of time, this population became basically secularised from conviction, education and/or force of habit. This did not mean that it renounced its Muslim identity, seeing no contradiction in declaring itself at one and the same time Muslim and atheist or non-believing.'[16]

Similarly, one anthropologist argues that the Tajik villagers she studied 'appeared to recognise a tacit division of labour' between communism and Islam:

> Communism, in the eyes of many villagers, was seen not so much as an ideological doctrine but as a *raison d'être* for a certain type of administrative system … It was not, in general, perceived as a source of personal morality. Islam, by contrast, was seen as the basis of morality and 'belief'—but not as the basis for a state administrative system.[17]

One survey conducted in 1985 showed that 55.6 per cent of Tajik communists regarded themselves as true Muslims.[18] Many people in Tajikistan were able to

---

13   Poliakov, *Everyday Islam*, p. 96, also pp. 95–112.

14   Poliakov, *Everyday Islam*, p. 106. See also: Ro'i, *Islam in the Soviet Union*, pp. 346, 351, 357–9.

15   Roy, *The New Central Asia*, p. 90. Gillian Tett notes that the village she did fieldwork in had a mullah who was officially registered as a mechanic in the *sovkhoz*. See: Tett, *Ambiguous Alliances*, p. 81.

16   Yaacov Ro'i, 'The Secularisation of Islam and the USSR's Muslim Areas', in *Muslim Eurasia: Conflicting Legacies*, ed. Yaacov Ro'i (London: Frank Cass, 1995), p. 15. Khalid remarks similarly: 'Although Muslimness distinguished locals from outsiders in the Soviet context, being Muslim was not counterpoised to being Soviet.' See: Khalid, *Islam after Communism*, p. 98.

17   Tett, *Ambiguous Alliances*, pp. 88–9.

18   A. Ignatenko, 'Islam v bor'be za politicheskoe liderstvo', in *Islam v Rossii i Srednei Azii*, eds Igor Ermakov and Dmitrii Mikulskii (Moscow: Lotus Foundation, 1993), p. 171.

reconcile Islam and communism, as neither was treated as incompatible, but rather as flexible practices. Some took the flexibility of Islam and communism even further and stressed their similarities (equality, justice, and so on). As one brigadier stated, '[e]verything Lenin said is written in the Koran'.[19] Apparently, even Bobojon Ghafurov, former first secretary of the CPT CC, made a pilgrimage to Mecca after retirement, for he was 'a son of a pious Muslim and sincerely yearned to visit the Qa'aba'.[20] Much later, in the late 1980s, first secretary Mahkamov would publicly declare that he was an atheist; but by this time there would be criticism of even those at the highest level. The *Qozikalon* of Tajikistan, Akbar Turajonzoda, in his role as the highest officially sanctioned Islamic leader in the republic, responded that Mahkamov would not be accorded Muslim burial rites upon his death.[21]

In the mid 1980s the Soviet government conducted a sociological survey of religious practices in the Muslim areas of the Soviet Union:[22]

> Its findings showed a comparatively extensive practice of [Islamic] traditions, festivals and rites among all socio-demographic groups of the population, including the young, which indicates not only a relative stabilization of the level of religiosity, but also … a mass basis for Islam's continued existence in the USSR. The results of the survey refuted the widely held opinion that Islam was becoming 'increasingly ritualistic' (*obriadovyi*) and demonstrated that the 'preservation and reproduction' (*vosproizvodstvo*) of religiosity were 'ensured by the existence of a still fairly significant number of believers characterized by a uniformity of religious consciousness and religious conduct.'

The survey revealed the importance of an Islamic-mandated morality in family life, as well as a high level of observance amongst those with high school and university education.[23]

Towards the very end of the Soviet era, the government loosened its restrictions, allowing the *Qoziyot* (the official Islamic governing body) and others to open new Islamic schools and mosques in Tajikistan, as well as to renovate *mazors*

---

19 Tett, *Ambiguous Alliances*, pp. 87–8.
20 Muteullo Najmiddinov, 'Sudi jahon dar suhbati dono shinos…', *Tojikiston*, Nos 1–2 (1995), p. 14.
21 Ludmila Polonskaya and Alexei Malashenko, *Islam in Central Asia* (Reading, UK: Ithaca Press, 1994), p. 117.
22 *Sostoianie religioznosti i ateisticheskogo vospitaniia v regionakh traditsionnogo rasprostraneniia islama* (Moscow: Akademiia obshchestvennykh nauk pri TsK KPSS, Institut nauchnogo atizma; Sovetskaia sotsiologicheskaia assotsiatsiia, 1989), pp. 5–8, as cited in Yaacov Ro'i, 'The Secularization of Islam and the USSR's Muslim Areas', pp. 13–14.
23 *Sostoianie religioznosti i ateisticheskogo vospitaniia*, pp. 5–8, 26, 32, as cited in Ro'i, 'The Secularization of Islam and the USSR's Muslim Areas', p. 13–14. See also: Muriel Atkin, *The Subtlest Battle: Islam in Soviet Tajikistan* (Philadelphia: Foreign Policy Research Institute, 1989).

and to more easily organise *hajj* to Mecca.[24] At independence the number of registered mosques surged. The great increase in the number of mosques—from 19 to more than 3000 between 1989 and 1992[25]—has sometimes been cited as an illustration of the Islamisation of Tajikistan. In reality, this surge should be attributed to simple legalisation and registration of already existing religious institutions, or, rather, traditional gathering places in villages and *mahallas*.[26]

At least two factors contributed to the reasons the Soviet regime did not treat Islam as a serious threat in Tajikistan in the postwar period. First, the so-called 'official Islam', or 'that segment of religious life revolving around the functioning mosques, registered mullahs and officially recognised religious communities',[27] was closely monitored and regulated by the authorities. All working mosques[28] and clerics were registered with the republican branch (*Qoziyot*) of SADUM, as well as with the Council for Religious Affairs—an organ of the Council of Ministers of Tajikistan. Official mullahs were on a government payroll and their appointment was subject to the authorities' approval. Second, the 'parallel', or 'popular', Islam, based on the activities of clandestine Sufi orders and popular cultural traditions and free of all interference from the state, had 'too apolitical a character and too diffuse a structure to rally believers under an anti-Soviet political banner'.[29]

Popular Islam in Tajikistan had several important characteristics that made it different from similar phenomena in the other republics of the former Soviet Union. Its ideological core—that is, the 'popular knowledge of Islam'[30]—was always more pronounced for the simple reason that the corpus of Muslim literature that embodied not only ecclesiastic texts but also classic medieval lyrics, stories and anecdotes inherited from the past, had been written mostly in Persian. On the other hand, it would be an exaggeration to say that adherence to the main tenets of Islam or understanding of its theoretical dogmas are stronger

---

24   Atkin, 'Thwarted Democratization in Tajikistan', p. 283; Makhamov, 'Islam and the Political Development of Tajikistan after 1985', p. 200. Makhamov notes the quid pro quo: 'Representatives of official Islam regularly called on their followers to remain loyal to the government and to observe state laws.'

25   Qadi Akbar Turajonzoda, 'Religion: The Pillar of Society', in *Central Asia: Conflict, Resolution, and Change*, eds Roald Z. Sagdeev and Susan Eisenhower (Chevy Chase, Md: CPSS Press, 1995), p. 268.

26   Many have made this point. For example: Rubin, 'Russian Hegemony and State Breakdown in the Periphery', p. 143. Malashenko makes this same point in regards to Central Asia in general in the early 1990s. See: Alexei V. Malashenko, 'Islam and Politics in the Southern Zone of the Former USSR', in *Central Asia and Transcaucasia: Ethnicity and Conflict*, ed. Vitaly V. Naumkin (Westport, Conn., and London: Greenwood Press, 1994), p. 111. For an exact anecdote, see Gillian Tett's description of a mosque's 'survival' in the Varzob Valley: Tett, *Ambiguous Alliances*, pp. 80–1.

27   Azade-Ayse Rorlich, 'Islam and Atheism: Dynamic Tension in Soviet Central Asia', in *Soviet Central Asia. The Failed Transformation*, ed. William Fierman (Boulder, Colo.: Westview Press, 1991), p. 188.

28   In 1963, there were only 18 officially registered mosques in Tajikistan, down from several thousand in the pre-revolutionary period. Until the late 1980s, their number remained virtually unchanged. See: Alexander Bennigsen and S. Enders Wimbush, *Muslims of the Soviet Empire: A Guide* (Bloomington: Indiana University Press, 1986), p. 90.

29   Atkin, *The Subtlest Battle*, p. 28.

30   Olivier Roy, *The Failure of Political Islam* (London: I. B. Tauris, 1994), p. 30.

among Tajiks in comparison with other Central Asian nationals. Data collected in the field in Tajikistan corroborate the general observation made for Central Asian Muslims by Nancy Lubin in the early 1990s: 'more than three-quarters of those who said they are Islamic believers do not pray at all, and three-quarters say they never fast.'[31] In regards to the private lives of Central Asians and their leaders, life-cycle rituals such as those for births, deaths and marriages continued to retain their 'Islamic' characteristics throughout the Soviet era.[32] Popular Islam in Tajikistan is centred on a seemingly endless succession of ceremonies and rituals, most of which date back to pre-Muslim times. Births, coming of age, marriages and funerals are the landmark events for every Tajik family and kinship or neighbourhood community. Their proper commemoration according to Islamic or, to be more precise, local cultural, tradition is vital for every individual, or any given social group, in terms of maintaining their social status. But even the day-to-day life of Tajiks is largely regulated by a set of beliefs that they perceive as Muslim. In reality, much of it has more to do with ancient fertility cults and various agricultural rites, to which the existence of a thriving institution of shamans testifies.

Shamans in Tajikistan, called *parikhon* and *folbin*, are omnipresent; almost every *mahalla* in a village or city can boast at least one man or woman who is believed to have a special relationship with spirits and can thus: a) diagnose and cure illnesses; b) impose or lift a curse; c) interpret omens and forecast the future; and d) find missing objects and people. People's belief in *ajina*, *chiltan*, *miros* and other supernatural creatures—hardly compatible with Orthodox Islam— has found its reflection in a Tajik saying: '*Khudo zada bosh, arvoh zada—ne*', which means 'If God strikes you—let it be, but don't let the spirits'. In rural areas there still exist whole dynasties of self-styled medics who specialise in treating infertility or pneumonia through exorcism.[33] Generally, in modern times, 'the shamans have never experienced restrictions in their practice and coexisted peacefully with the clergy. There has emerged a sort of cooperation: shamans would send the ailing to mullahs, and mullahs would advise them to go to shamans'.[34] Quite often, particularly in remote areas such as Yaghnob, one person combines the responsibilities of a mullah, hereditary Sufi leader

---

31 Nancy Lubin, 'Central Asians Take Stock: Reform, Corruption, and Identity', *Peaceworks* [United States Institute of Peace], No. 2 (February 1995). Moreover, even those who observe the fast (*ruza*) in Tajikistan, especially in the cities, would refer to health considerations for doing so, rather than treating it as a conscientious act of compliance with one of the pillars of Islam. The prevailing explanation for holding the *ruza* in Dushanbe at present is that 'it helps to purify the organism of dross' (Interviews in Dushanbe, February 1995).

32 Rainer Freitag-Wirminghaus, 'Atheistic Muslims, Soviet Legacy and Islamic Tradition in Central Asia and the Caucasus', in *The Islamic World and the West: An Introduction to Political Cultures and International Relations*, ed. Kai Hafez (Leiden: Brill, 2000), p. 222.

33 Andreev, *Tadzhiki doliny Khuf*, pp. 78–80.

34 V. N. Basilov, *Shamanstvo u narodov Srednei Azii i Kazakhstana* (Moscow: Nauka, 1992), p. 281.

and shaman.[35] Common people in Tajikistan usually do not bother themselves with the fine demarcation of these terms and tend to refer to anybody with religious charisma, obtained through position, training, inheritance, divine intervention or otherwise, as *ishon*—a word that originally carried a strictly Sufi connotation.[36]

According to Bennigsen and Wimbush:

> [P]arallel Islam is represented in Tajikistan by the adepts of some Sufi brotherhoods (mainly of the Naqshbandiya) which are more structured than in the other Central Asian republics ... The representatives of parallel Islam control numerous holy places which, in absence of working mosques, tend to become the real centres of religious life.[37]

These same authors, however, made quite a different assumption in their earlier work:

> In Tajikistan ... Sufi brotherhoods are less active and play a relatively minor role in the preservation of the religious feelings of the population. In this republic the holy places are less numerous and enjoy but a moderate prestige among the believers and the unbelievers. The religious life of the Tajiks is less dependent on parallel Islam and for this reason the role of the holy *mazors* is lesser than in Turkmenistan and Kirghizia.[38]

This issue may indeed be confusing, so long as popular Islam in Tajikistan is viewed as an extension of official Islam *par excellence*, which has become important mainly due to the atheistic onslaught of Soviet authorities. It is reasonable to adopt the approach whereby popular Islam represents a certain way of life in its wholeness, far beyond the confines of a religious creed, and as such cannot be measured quantitatively. The statement that 'there is no evidence whatsoever to suggest that Soviet Muslims have ever been less (or more) devoted to their faith than they are now'[39] then makes perfect sense.

Mazors, or holy places, in Tajikistan, in a contradistinction with the situation in other Central Asian countries, are not necessarily linked to a burial place of some real or mythical Sufi saint. The number of such shrines in the republic is

---

35   In the Zarafshon Valley, a mullah is required to spend 40 days in fast, seclusion and prayer to qualify as an exorcist. See: O. Murodov, 'Predstavleniia o devakh u tadzhikov srednei chasti doliny Zeravshana', *Sovetskaiia etnografiia*, No. 1 (1973), p. 154.

36   Abduvali Qushmatov, *Vaqf: Namudhoi zamindorii vaqf dar Shimoli Tojikiston dar solhoi 1870–1917* (Dushanbe: Irfon, 1990), p. 39.

37   Bennigsen and Wimbush, *Muslims of the Soviet Empire*, p. 91.

38   Alexandre Bennigsen and S. Enders Wimbush, *Mystics and Commissars: Sufism in the Soviet Union* (London: C. Hurst & Co., 1985), pp. 150–1.

39   Akiner, *Islamic Peoples of the Soviet Union*, p. 12.

relatively small; the two most revered are the *mazor* of *mavlono* Yaqubi Charkhi near Dushanbe, and the mausoleum of *khoja* Ishoq 'Makhdumi Azam' in Hisor (both date to the sixteenth century).[40] The bulk of the *mazors* in Tajikistan, however, are related to the primordial cult of trees, springs and stones, which are believed to harbour evil and benign spirits. It is not infrequent that the trunk of a 'sacred tree' constitutes the minaret of a village mosque.[41] In rural areas every *avlod* has at least one *mazor*, and the living members of the family pay homage to them regularly, usually on Fridays and Sundays, to placate the souls of the dead.[42]

Some *mazors* are devoted to animistic deities (for example, *bibi* Seshambe, the patroness of maternity, and *bibi* Mushkelkusho, the spirit of good fortune), or even Zoroastrian religious symbols, such as a rather popular temple of the sun, 'Shokambar Oftob', in Vakhan.[43] The pre-Islamic elements in Tajik Sufism (and wider Islamic rites)[44] form an enormous subject in themselves,[45] however, it appears that in everyday religious practice a thick layer of traditional beliefs is barely covered by Muslim rites, distorted as they are almost beyond recognition from their canonical versions.

Medieval Sufism in Central Asia had all the attributes of classical mystical Islam: several competing brotherhoods, hierarchal structure, degrees of initiation, missionary activity, and so on. In the nineteenth century, however,

> the link with the original Sufi orders was rather weak, Sufism degenerated into Ishonism—every big *ishon* virtually gave rise to a separate order, headed thereafter by his descendants. The dissociation of the Sufi brotherhoods led to the situation whereby an *ishon* became the only authority for his disciples, the sole source of spiritual authority that, according to the demands of the Sufi doctrine, was absolute.[46]

---

40   Bennigsen and Wimbush wrongfully place both sites in Hisor and identify 'Makhdumi A'zam' with a certain Molla Junayd. See: Bennigsen and Wimbush, *Muslims of the Soviet Empire*, p. 91. For an interesting discourse on the subject, see: Sherzod Abdulloev, 'Justuju dar atrofi ta'rikhi "Makhdumi A'zam"', in *Dar justujui farhangi vodii Hisor*, ed. N. N. Ne'matov (Dushanbe: Mamnu'gohi ta'rikhi-madanii Hisor, 1992), pp. 13–23.

41   Peshchereva, *Yagnobskie etnograficheskie materialy*, p. 74.

42   A typical case of the establishment of a new *mazor* was reported in 1957 in the *kolkhoz* named after Karl Marx: 'the kolkhoz worker Abdullo Umarov while being sick had made an oath that he would repair one [of his relatives'] tomb. Umarov's organism overcame illness and he convalesced. After that, Umarov mended the tomb and conveyed the whole story to his relations. In their turn, they shared the news with others. That's how the pilgrimage to this burial commenced.' See: *XI s'ezd Kommunisticheskoi partii Tadzhikistana*, p. 144.

43   A. Z. Rozenfeld, 'Materialy po etnografii i perezhitkam drevnikh verovanii tadzhikoiazychnogo naseleniia Sovetskogo Badakhshana', *Sovetskaia etnografiia*, No. 3 (1970), p. 117.

44   Niyazi notes: 'The ancient agricultural rites and festivals of the Zoroastrian and pre-Zoroastrian period are widespread amongst Sunnis and Ismailis alike; these are primarily linked with the worship of nature and the cults of fertility, fire, water and earth.' See: Aziz Niyazi, 'Islam in Tajikistan: Tradition and Modernity', *Religion, State and Society*, Vol. 26, No. 1 (1998), p. 41.

45   An excellent review of the problem can be found in: V. N. Basilov, 'Simvolika sufizma i narodnye verovaniia', *Etnograficheskoe obozrenie*, No. 6 (1994), pp. 88–91.

46   O. A. Sukhareva, *Islam v Uzbekistane* (Tashkent: Fan, 1960), p. 52.

Thus *ishons*, who originally were the middle link in the *murshed–murid* (Sufi teacher–disciple) chain, found themselves in a unique position: they wielded great power, without having proper knowledge and education.

In Tajikistan, the surviving members of traditional status groups (*sayids*, *khojas*, *mirs* and *tura*) are often treated as *ishons*. In the early 1990s, a certain police lieutenant in Mastchoh, who was also a *tura*, acted as *ishon* for a group of people living in neighbouring Uzbekistan and collected *sadaqa* (alms) from them in this capacity.[47] It is difficult to draw a dividing line between a collectivity of *murids*,[48] an extended patriarchal family and a solidarity network coalesced around representatives of a traditional elite stratum. It appears, however, that purely religious *murshed–murid* dyads are quite rare in Tajikistan. In modern times the most prominent Sufi teacher in the republic was *hazrat* Pirmuhammad Sangi Qulula, who died in 1968 in the village of Olimtoy near Kulob. His funeral was attended by thousands of people from all over Central Asia, including several dozen high-ranking party officials.[49] He was not, however, the only eminent Sufi *sheikh* in Tajikistan. Other well-known *sheikhs* were active throughout the country in the late Soviet era.[50]

In summary, there is much truth in the conclusion that for Tajikistan 'the most important dimension of Sufism is not the sophisticated mysticism practised by the Sufi adepts but the Sufi embodiment of folk Islam'.[51] Furthermore, popular Islam incorporates

> people's ancient beliefs, vestiges of magic and elements of folklore culture. Thus this is a national phenomenon and [is] perceived by many as such ... The non-conflictual co-existence of various, often directly opposite ideas, is characteristic of it ... Popular Islam is loyal to the authorities and calls for the rejection of political struggle.[52]

With this in mind, it would be easier to avoid the temptation to explain the retention of traditional customs as a manifestation of religious zeal aimed against the secular state—a theme favoured by some Western scholars from the time of Soviet rule to the present day.[53]

---

47 Bushkov and Mikulskii, 'Obschestvenno-politicheskaia situatsiia v Tadzhikistane', p. 9.

48 Every *ishon* may have from one to more than 50 disciples. See: S. M. Demidov, *Sufizm v Turkmenii* (Ashkhabad: Ylym, 1978), p. 103.

49 Muhabbatsho, 'Fojiai Uljaboev', p. 29.

50 Stephane A. Dudoignon, 'From Revival to Mutation: The Religious Personnel of Islam in Tajikistan, from De-Stalinization to Independence (1955–91)', *Central Asian Survey*, Vol. 30, No. 1 (2001).

51 Atkin, *The Subtlest Battle*, p. 23.

52 Olimova and Olimov, 'Obrazovannyi klass Tadzhikistana v peripetiiakh XX v.', pp. 99–100.

53 See, as one of many examples: Ronald Wixman, 'Ethnic Attitudes and Relations in Modern Uzbek Cities', in *Soviet Central Asia: The Failed Transformation*, ed. William Fierman (Boulder, Colo.: Westview Press, 1991), pp. 172–3.

There are few reliable data on the religious affiliation and observance of the eponymous population of Tajikistan. A survey conducted in the Qurghonteppa region in 1989 revealed that 81 per cent of those polled 'were under the influence of Islam, its traditions and rituals'.[54] Another survey showed that Islamic mores affect broad sections of Tajik society and are successfully reproduced in younger generations.[55] In 1991, the percentage of weddings conducted with the presence of a mullah was 86.5 per cent in Tajikistan.[56] Similarly, 55 to 82 per cent of polled women consider Islamic funeral ceremonies necessary, while 'in fact a much higher percentage (approximating 100 per cent of population, including atheists and non-believers) practices them'.[57] Still, such attitudes and shared understandings cannot be regarded solely as products of Islamic belief; they are part of a wider cultural order or the 'Great Tradition', and are 'so deeply rooted that they flow *almost* automatically'.[58] Moreover, Islamic mores appear to be highly particularistic, especially in the area of marital arrangements—for example, Quranic views on exogamy are strictly observed amongst Tajiks whose ancestors had migrated from Herat (Heroti), whereas mountain Tajiks by and large ignore them.[59]

In modern Tajikistan the dividing line between *adat* and *shari'a* is rather blurred. Under conditions where the society retains strong elements of patriarchy and where the stratum of carriers of orthodox Islam is thin, the job of interpreting the principles of common good and establishing codes of honour and decency— the privilege of the *ulama* in most Muslim countries—is inevitably relegated to traditional communal leaders: heads of *avlods*, elders in the *mahalla* committees, patrons of solidarity networks and members of ascribed prestigious status groups.[60] On the whole, Islam of any form or description in Tajikistan has failed to impose a set of universalistic values on the society, and thus can hardly be seen to play an overarching integrative and mobilisational role today.

---

54   S. Boronbekov, 'Religioznye verovaniia, obychai i ugolovno-pravovoe soznanie', *Izvestiia AN TSSR. Seriia: filosofiia, ekonomika, pravovedenie*, No. 4 (1991), p. 66. The methodology of the poll is not quite clear, but presumably the respondents did not include the so-called Russian-speaking population.

55   In regards to the 'Percentage of Believers amongst Tajiks' according to occupation and age, 64.8 per cent of engineers and agricultural experts, 61.3 per cent of intellectuals and professionals (doctors, teachers, and so on) and 89.1 per cent of pensioners and housewives reported being believers, while 71.3 per cent of eighteen–nineteen-year-olds, 73 per cent of twenty–twenty-four-year-olds and 77.9 per cent of twenty-five–twenty-nine-year-olds answered the same. Source: L. Bashirov, 'Islam v nashi dni', *Slovo lektora*, No. 1 (1989), p. 33.

56   F. N. Iliasov, 'Skolko stoit nevesta', *Sotsiologicheskie issledovaniia*, No. 6 (1991), p. 69. This was compared with 80.1 per cent in Turkmenistan and 32.4 per cent in Kazakhstan.

57   M. A. Tolmacheva, 'The Muslim Woman in Soviet Central Asia', *Central Asian Survey*, Vol. 12, No. 4 (1993), p. 542.

58   Dale F. Eickelman, *The Middle East: An Anthropological Approach* (Englewood Cliffs, NJ: Prentice-Hall, 1989), p. 230. It has even been argued by one author that the ratio between people who observe Muslim rituals and those who really believe in the Muslim faith is four to one. See: Saidbaev, *Islam i obschestvo*, p. 195.

59   Sukhareva, 'Traditsiia semeino-rodstvennykh brakov u narodov Srednei Azii', pp. 119–20.

60   The Tajik saying '*Avval khesh, ba'd darvesh*' ('Relatives [come] first, dervish—afterwards') connotes the primacy of the kinship allegiance over the religious one.

The Failure of Islam as a Unifying and Mobilising Force

At the beginning of the twentieth century, Barthold wrote that a Central Asian 'feels he is first a Muslim and second a resident of a specific town or location'.[61] While identifying as a Muslim may be important for some when interacting with a non-Muslim,[62] does an Islamic identity have much relevance in Central Asia when locals interact with each other? Muriel Atkin stresses that while there is some 'strength' in the Islamic identity for Central Asians, it does not mean that the identity is accompanied by some 'supranational' Islamic unity as embodied in the idea of the *umma*, the idealised concept of a unified community of all Muslims.[63] Others have argued the opposite. For example, Roland Dannreuther has pronounced that in Tajikistan

> radical Islam also has the attraction of combining radical political objectives within an outwardly traditional framework ... For people used to the all-encompassing and intrusive ideology of Marxism-Leninism, it can be reassuring to find a more authentic replacement which provides a similarly comprehensive interpretation of the world with the backing of a global internationalist brotherhood.[64]

This eloquent generalisation may be too far-reaching; it is somewhat doubtful whether members of a mosque-*gapkhona*-men's club somewhere in Qarotegin would be interested in *any* universalistic interpretation of the world—Marxist, Islamist, or otherwise. Traditional communal life is a self-sufficient microcosm for them, and it is unlikely that any ideas coming from any 'global internationalist brotherhood' could move any significant mass of them to action.

Concerning Central Asians' interactions with the broader Muslim world community, while Central Asians may see Russian models as unsuitable, they are also not interested in replicating the Muslim societies of their neighbours. Schoeberlein-Engel argues that greater exposure to the outside Muslim world since the mid 1980s has, for Central Asians, confirmed to them a 'sense of its

---

61 Barthold, *Sochineniia*, Vol. 2, Part 2, p. 528. Quoted in Abashin, 'The Transformation of Ethnic Identity in Central Asia', p. 32.
62 As noted by Nazif Shahrani: 'It is in relation to Barthold, a Russian Christian, that the Turkistanis define themselves, first as Muslim, then as residents of a particular town or village and finally, if nomads, as members of specific, named kinship categories or groups. One cannot doubt that had the same questions been posed by a non-Turkistani Muslim rather than a Russian Christian, the order and types of self identity expressed would have been significantly different.' See: M. Nazif Shahrani, '"From Tribe to Umma": Comments on the Dynamics of Identity in Muslim Soviet Central Asia', *Central Asian Survey*, Vol. 3, No. 3 (1984), p. 29.
63 Atkin, 'Religious, National and Other Identities in Central Asia', p. 47.
64 Dannreuther, *Creating New States in Central Asia*, p. 18.

being alien to them'.[65] This viewpoint is echoed by Nazif Shahrani, an Afghan-American anthropologist; however, instead of blaming increased awareness, he points to ignorance. He found during his fieldwork in Central Asia that:

> In general the peoples of former Soviet Central Asia are very poorly informed, especially about the Muslim countries to the south and west. What the post-Soviet Central Asians say about these areas is often negative and demeaning and always accompanied by an exaggerated sense of their own progress and modernity.[66]

According to these views, Central Asians do not feel any strong sense of unity with the outside Muslim world. For a quantitative example, a survey of Uzbeks and Kazakhs in 1993 asked respondents to name the countries that Uzbekistan and Kazakhstan should keep the greatest distance from. While Israel was listed at number four, the top three answers were Afghanistan, Iran and Pakistan.[67]

Additionally, there is no Islamic unity between Central Asians themselves (even discounting sectarian divides such as Sunni versus Ismaili) when measured against other categories of identity. Nancy Lubin, remarking on the results of the abovementioned survey, concluded that there are 'schisms as much within Central Asian and Muslim communities as between them and others' and that 'divisions among nationality groups in Central Asia run deep'.[68] Talib Saidbaev argues that secular social categories often prevail over religious categories. He stresses that economic interests are a more important factor than religious ones. Issues of agricultural resource access, employment and other material interests are assigned more importance than the ideal of Islamic unity. A sign of the primacy of non-religious factors is the fact that it is common for the different ethnic groups in the towns of Central Asia to have their own Muslim clergy and their own mosque.[69] Sergei Poliakov gave a similar description of separate communities within a larger rural community having their separate

---

65 Schoeberlein-Engel, *Identity in Central Asia*, p. 251. The opposite view can be found at the pinnacle of official Muslim leadership. Writing about the then *Qozikalon* of Tajikistan, Akbar Turajonzoda, Mavlon Makhamov says that Turajonzoda 'and his adherents emphasized the advantage of the Islamic way of life, maintaining that Saudi Arabia and the United Arab Emirates had achieved great success in economic development and secured high living standards for their population only through their devotion to Islam'. See: Makhamov, 'Islam and the Political Development of Tajikistan after 1985', pp. 200–1.

66 M. Nazif Shahrani, 'Islam and the Political Culture of "Scientific Atheism" in Post-Soviet Central Asia: Future Predicaments', in *The Politics of Religion in Russia and the New States of Eurasia*, ed. Michael Bourdeaux (London: M. E. Sharpe, 1995), p. 291, n. 24. Shahrani goes on to say that attitudes are beginning to change as Central Asians visit other Muslim countries. This is essentially the opposite of what Schoeberlein-Engel states: more contacts with other Muslim countries bring a more favourable opinion.

67 Nancy Lubin, 'Islam and Ethnic Identity in Central Asia: A View from Below', in *Muslim Eurasia: Conflicting Legacies*, ed. Yaacov Ro'i (London: Frank Cass, 1995), p. 67.

68 Lubin, 'Islam and Ethnic Identity in Central Asia', pp. 63–5.

69 Talib Saidbaev, 'Inter-Ethnic Conflicts in Central Asia: Social and Religious Perspectives', in *Ethnicity and Conflict in a Post-Communist World: The Soviet Union, Eastern Europe and China*, eds Kumar Rupesinghe, Peter King and Olga Vorkunova (New York: St Martin's Press, 1992), p. 168.

mosques; however, he notes that it was the *mahalla* that had its own mosque, rather than ethnic groups (this would also be a de facto ethnic segregation if the *mahalla* is mono-ethnic).[70] Roy also noted the primacy of kinship over Islam in the collective farms where kinship groups who feel marginalised start a secondary, 'oppositional' mosque. These marginalised kin-based groups 'thus tend to identify with Islam as one way of consolidating their opposition to others—although of course everyone would claim to be Muslim'.[71] In a case study undertaken in an Uzbek village in Tajikistan, Sergei Abashin found that the contestation between competing religious authorities was referred to by the locals in 'terms of kinship'.[72] This is just one anecdote Abashin provides in his article, wherein he argues that at the local (rural) level 'religious conflicts are often submerged within the dynamics of local political, kinship and economic relations, with each Muslim community containing its own interest groups and means of legitimacy'.[73]

At a higher level, Abdujabar Abduvakhitov expressed his doubts in late 1991 about the possibility of Islam as a politically unifying factor:[74]

> [During *perestroika*] Islamic activists in the Muslim community began their social activity with an appeal to the Muslim *umma*. Their appeal excluded the growing sense of nationalism. Pan-Islam, as practised in the Muslim world, was not a power that could unite millions … In the Central Asia republics, where people have for many years been united by the Muslim community, the national identity of the different peoples has limited this factor of pan-Islam. The activist movement, which includes Uzbeks, Tajiks, Turkmen, Kyrghyz, and others, must preserve itself from a growing nationalism. Tribalism and regionalism also remain strong in Central Asia. Thus it is difficult to see how pan-Islam can be a uniting factor in the political life of Central Asia.

Similarly, Aziz Niyazi noted the splits along regional and political lines amongst the 'Islamic clergy': 'There have never been any disputes on strictly theological questions amongst these groups; schisms have occurred chiefly as a result of political affiliation and regional allegiances. Tajik Islamic thought has thus not formulated many clear ideas about a desired state structure and social order.'[75]

70   Poliakov, *Everyday Islam*, p. 96.

71   Roy, *The New Central Asia*, p. 90.

72   Sergei Abashin, 'The Logic of Islamic Practice: A Religious Conflict in Central Asia', *Central Asian Survey*, Vol. 25, No. 3 (2006), p. 275.

73   Abashin, 'The Logic of Islamic Practice', p. 268.

74   Abdujabar Abduvakhitov, 'Islamic Revivalism in Uzbekistan', in *Russia's Muslim Frontiers: New Directions in Cross-Cultural Analysis*, ed. Dale F. Eickelman (Bloomington: Indiana University Press, 1993), p. 95.

75   Niyazi, 'Islam in Tajikistan', *Religion, State and Society*, Vol. 26, No. 1 (1998), pp. 43–4.

Islam in the 1970s and 1980s

Regarding the political significance of religiosity in Tajikistan, Grigorii Kosach maintains that the 'Soviet experience showed quite clearly that youthful dissidence more often than not gave way to career considerations and adaptation to ideological and political realities'.[76] Nevertheless, in the 1970s and 1980s, 'underground and semi-underground' Islamic groups were operating in southern Tajikistan.[77] Early Islamists[78] from the 1970s onwards were strongest in Qurghonteppa Province among those resettled from Qarotegin/Gharm.[79] One group of Islamists in Tajikistan was reported in 1978 in the Qurghonteppa region, in the areas populated by Gharmi settlers.[80] They consisted primarily of young men who, as a rule, did not have formal religious education, represented marginal strata of traditional society and criticised the Soviet and Islamic establishments from positions of 'pure Islam'.[81] Their grievances focused on

- the graft and corruption of local communist bosses
- the ignorance, licentiousness and greed of official and supernumerary mullahs
- Soviet involvement in Afghanistan.

The issue of Afghanistan was clearly also on the minds of those at the top levels of the scholarly community of *ulama*, as can be seen, for example, in videotaped debates from the early 1980s that include the top official Islamic leader in Tajikistan, *Qozikalon* Mirzo Abdullo Kalonzoda, the eminent scholar *Mavlavi* Hindustoni, and a prominent Sufi *sheikh* from the Hisor area, *Domullo* Sharif Hisori.[82]

It was argued earlier in this chapter that Islam could not play an integrative and mobilising role throughout Tajik society. That does not mean that Islamic ideology could not appeal to certain sections of the republic's population—namely, those sections that experienced a high level of deprivation as a result of

---

76   Kosach, 'Tajikistan', p. 133.

77   Olimova, 'Opposition in Tajikistan', p. 247. By 'semi-underground', Olimova means that the authorities were aware of the activities but took no action.

78   For the purposes of the present study, this term is employed to distinguish 'the activist, militant "true believer", and born-again Muslim from the run of the mill Muslim who takes his/her religion for granted, viewing Islam as a matter of *'aqaid* and *'ibadat* (a set of beliefs and specific acts of worship), plus a certain basic ethical code, inherited traditions, cultural conventions, and so on'. See: Sadik J. Al-Azm, 'Islamic Fundamentalism Reconsidered: A Critical Outline of Problems, Ideas and Approaches, Part I', *South Asia Bulletin*, Vol. XIII, Nos 1–2 (1993), p. 99.

79   Shirin Akiner and Catharine Barnes, 'The Tajik Civil War: Causes and Dynamics', in *Politics of Compromise: The Tajikistan Peace Process*, eds Kamoludin Abdullaev and Catharine Barnes (London: Conciliation Resources, 2001), p. 20.

80   *Jumhuriyat*, 17 December 1991.

81   *Grazhdanskie politicheskie dvizheniia v Tadzhikistane: 1989 – mart 1990g.* (Dushanbe: TsK LKSM Tadzhikistana, 1990), p. 46.

82   Dudoignon, 'From Revival to Mutation', p. 68.

Soviet modernisation efforts. In Tajikistan, those were residents of Mastchoh, Gharm and Qarotegin; those who were constantly resettled, whose villages were destroyed while hydro dams were erected, and who were forced to forgo their traditional occupations for the sake of building socialism. To borrow from John L. Esposito:

> [Losses] of village, town, and extended family ties and traditional values were accompanied by the shock of modern urban life and its Westernised culture and mores. Many, swept along in a sea of alienation and marginalisation, found an anchor in religion. Islam offered a sense of identity, fraternity, and cultural values that offset the psychological dislocation and cultural threat of their new environment ... Islamic organisations' workers and message offered a more familiar alternative which was consistent with their experience, identified their problems, and offered a time-honoured solution.[83]

'Underground' Islamic education started as soon as the traditional institutions of Islamic education were closed by the Soviets in the 1920s;[84] however, the use of 'underground' here needs to be qualified. Parviz Mullojonov, describing Tajikistan's 'underground Islamic circles' that gained momentum in the 1970s, argues that

> it is doubtful that, in the general conditions of the USSR, such underground religious circles could have escaped the KGB's gaze for more than 15 years. In fact the KGB's national departments, which used to employ a broad network of agents among the Muslim clergy, knew from the very beginning about the existence of these Islamist circles.[85]

Mullojonov believes that the Soviet authorities were obviously aware of the young mullahs' activities, but decided to leave them alone and let them weaken the 'authority of the conventional clergy, which in the 1970s and early 1980s was considered by the Soviet power as the main evil'.[86] In regards to the lower-level leadership (provincial, city, farm and factory officials) in the Vakhsh Valley, the leader of a network of Islamic teachers stressed that

> [a]lthough they were Communist Party members, in secret they maintained their original faith since they were the children of Muslims. Their connection to Islam was strong. As a result of this, even though

---

83   John L. Esposito, *The Islamic Threat: Myth or Reality?* (New York: Oxford University Press, 1992), p. 16.

84   Ashirbek Muminov, 'Fundamentalist Challenges to Local Islamic Traditions in Soviet and Post-Soviet Central Asia', in *Empire, Islam, and Politics in Central Eurasia*, ed. Tomohiko Uyama (Sapporo: Slavic Research Centre, Hokkaido University, 2007), pp. 249–62, esp. pp. 258–9.

85   Mullojonov, 'The Islamic Clergy in Tajikistan Since the End of the Soviet Period', p. 228.

86   Mullojonov, 'The Islamic Clergy in Tajikistan Since the End of the Soviet Period', p. 228. For a similar narrative in Uzbekistan, see: Abduvakhitov, 'Islamic Revivalism in Uzbekistan', pp. 82–5.

> they still did not help us, they deliberately overlooked and ignored our connection to this work [that is, unofficial Islamic schooling]. Through this behaviour they facilitated the dissemination of progressive ideas and the spirit of striving for freedom in the Vakhsh Valley.[87]

By the mid 1980s, however, the authorities began to see the 'unofficial' mullahs and underground Islam as a bigger threat and began to use the official clergy against the 'unofficial' mullahs.[88] If Mullojonov is right and the security services considered the official Soviet-sponsored clergy to be more of a threat then this speaks even more about the Soviet Union's inability to control society. Their tactic of using the two groups against each other—if that was actually the case—shows the further ineffectiveness of the state's repressive measures. An effectively repressive state would just simply eliminate both groups; however, by the mid 1980s the Soviet security services did begin to arrest and 'harass' Tajik Islamists.[89]

Sayid Abdullo Nuri and the Roots of the Islamic Revival Party

The origin of the Islamic Renaissance/Rebirth/Renewal/Revival Party (henceforth IRP)[90] of Tajikistan was a group led by Sayid Abdullo Nuri that formed an underground organisation or network in 1973. This group, which eventually took the name Nahzati Javononi Islomii Tojikiston (Revival of the Islamic Youth of Tajikistan), operated mainly in Qurghonteppa and the wider Vakhsh Valley.[91] Adeeb Khalid describes this group as not just an 'organisation',

---

87   Sayid Abdullohi Nuri, 'Hizbe, ki resha dar ormoni mardum dorad', Interview by Qiyomiddin Sattori (2 February 2003), in *Mujaddidi Asr: bakhshida ba 60-umin solgardi zodruzi ustod Sayid Abdullohi Nuri (r)*, ed. Qiyomiddin Sattori (Dushanbe: Devashtich, 2007), p. 158. More on this leader below.

88   Mullojonov, 'The Islamic Clergy in Tajikistan Since the End of the Soviet Period', pp. 228–9.

89   Mullojonov, 'The Islamic Clergy in Tajikistan Since the End of the Soviet Period', pp. 230–1.

90   In Tajik: *Hizbi Nahzati Islomi*. The word '*nahzat*' has roughly the same meaning as '*rastokhez*' (revival) but originates from Arabic.

91   Nuri, 'Hizbe, ki resha dar ormoni mardum dorad', pp. 155–8; Stephane A. Dudoignon, 'From Ambivalence to Ambiguity? Some Paradigms of Policy Making in Tajikistan', in *Tajikistan at a Crossroads: The Politics of Decentralization*, Situation Report No. 4, ed. Luigi Di Martino (Geneva: Cimera, 2004), p. 126, citing Qiyomiddin Sattori, ed. *HNIT, Zodai Ormoni mardum: Ba iftixori 30-solagii ta'sisi Hizbi Nahzati Islomii Tojikiston* (Dushanbe: Imperial-Grupp, 2003); Kilavuz, *Understanding Violent Conflict*, pp. 139–41; Olimova, 'Opposition in Tajikistan', p. 248; Conciliation Resources, 'Profiles: Said Abdullo Nuri', online: <http://www.c-r.org/our-work/accord/tajikistan/profiles.php> The IRP name came later with the formation of a Tajikistan branch of the federal IRP in 1990. See: Kilavuz, *Understanding Violent Conflict*, pp. 139–41; S. Olimova and M. Olimov, 'The Islamic Renaissance Party', Conciliation Resources, n.d., Accessed online March 2009: <http://www.c-r.org/our-work/accord/tajikistan/islamic-renaissance-party.php>

but also an 'underground network', which, according to Khalid, 'represented *hujra* students who rejected the political caution of their teachers and advocated a social, if not political status for a purified Islam'.[92]

Nuri was born Abdullo Saidov in 1947. His place of birth is Tavildara, in the now defunct Gharm Province.[93] In 1953 the government sent his family to the lower Vakhsh Valley as part of its agricultural resettlement programs. Specifically, Nuri's family lived in the 'Turkmeniston' *sovkhoz* (state farm), located in the Vakhsh District of Qurghonteppa Province. His father, Nureddin Saidov, was a *sovkhoz* director and a member of the Communist Party, while his older brother held a position of some importance in the local party apparatus. Nuri's education was at a technical school and he worked as a driver, equipment inventory manager and government land surveyor—occupations that allowed him extensive travel around the province and numerous opportunities to preach to a wider audience.[94] According to Roy, Nuri was given religious lessons at home by his father and by an unnamed 'unofficial cleric' before studying under Muhammadjon Hindustoni.[95] In an interview, Nuri named this 'unofficial cleric' as *domullo*[96] Siyomuddin, stressing that '89 per cent' of his studies were completed under this teacher. After studying under Siyomuddin, he moved on to become a student of *Mavlavi*[97] Hindustoni, a well-known Islamic scholar, for two to three years.[98]

Nuri commented on the activities of his group, which he mostly refers to as a *sozmon* (which can be translated as 'organisation' or 'society'), but also as a *junbish* or *harakat* (both translate to 'movement'). In his recollection, preparations for the formation of this group began in 1971. Nuri stresses that this process was quickened by a February 1973 KGB raid in the Hippodrome *mahalla* of Dushanbe that resulted in the arrest of 30 students in Nuri's network. This raid, which narrowly missed catching Hindustoni in class, gave a sense of

---

92   Khalid, *Islam after Communism*, p. 147. *Hujra* here refers to secret Islamic lessons.
93   Akiner, *Tajikistan*, p. 53; Conciliation Resources, 'Profiles: Said Abdullo Nuri'. Akiner gives his origin as Vakhyo (another name for the Tavildara Valley) in the 'Karategin-Darvaz' region, while Conciliation Resources refers to Tavildara being in Qarotegin. Qarotegin and Darvoz were both regions that were incorporated into the Gharm *oblast*. Conciliation Resources states that Tavildara was known previously as Sangvor. Note that there is currently a small settlement also named Sangvor approximately 80 km up the Khingob River from Tavildara.
94   Akiner, *Tajikistan*, p. 53. Conciliation Resources, 'Profiles: Said Abdullo Nuri'; Roy, 'Is the Conflict in Tajikistan a Model for Conflicts throughout Central Asia', p. 34; Roy, *The New Central Asia*, p. 154; Olivier Roy, 'The Impact of the Afghan War in Soviet Central Asia', in *In a Collapsing Empire: Underdevelopment, Ethnic Conflicts and Nationalisms in the Soviet Union*, ed. Marco Buttino (Milan: Fondazione Giangiacomo Feltrinelli, 1993), p. 344; A. V. Kudriavtsev and A. Sh. Niyazi, '"Politicheskii islam": nachalo 90-kh', in *Sovremennyi islam: kultura i politika* (Moscow: IVRAN, 1994) p. 124; V. Rabiyev, 'After the Trial: Going Nowhere', *Kommunist Tadzhikistana* (12 February 1987), p. 3, in *The Current Digest of the Post-Soviet Press*, Vol. 39, Issue 9 (1 April 1987), pp. 10–11.
95   Roy, *The New Central Asia*, p. 154; Conciliation Resources, 'Profiles: Said Abdullo Nuri'.
96   *Domullo* is a title used for religious teachers.
97   *Mavlavi* is a title given to well-established Islamic scholars.
98   Nuri, 'Hizbe, ki resha dar ormoni mardum dorad', p. 153. More on Hindustoni below.

urgency to Nuri and his associates. On 20 April 1973, Nuri met with four senior scholars,[99] including Hindustoni, and was selected to lead an underground Islamic movement that later gained many members from Nuri's generation (as opposed to the four senior scholars who selected Nuri), including the IRP's first official leader, Muhammadsharif Himmatzoda, and deputy leader, Davlat Usmon.[100] For the first one or two years, Nuri's group operated without a name until one was agreed upon: Nahzati Javononi Islomii Tojikiston[101]—referred to by members as Nahzat ('revival') or Jamiyat ('society'). Nuri is clear on the goals of Nahzat:[102]

> With the creation of our own organisation, we did not have any goals of anti-state activities; we only wanted to disseminate the beliefs of Islam amongst the youth. In essence, our organisation or movement in the beginning was a movement for Islamic social reforms, not a political movement. The main goal was to invite [those Muslims who had strayed] back to Islam, as well as the education of Muslim children.

Nuri's Nahzat had several departments: 1) proselytising (*davat*), 2) security (from KGB efforts to ascertain their activities),[103] 3) finances, and 4) education. Nuri argues that this structure borrows nothing that is foreign, which he uses to bolster his argument for the indigenous nature of Nahzat—an organisation that he stresses needed nothing and received no influences from outside local society.[104] The Islamists were few, they did not advocate changing the Soviet system and, generally, they kept a low profile. Kudryavtsev and Niyazi state that before the 1990s the underground Islamic activists in Tajikistan '[s]till retained a belief in the strength of the Soviet Union, within which the dream of an Islamic polity seemed absurd'.[105] Nevertheless, there were some exceptions. In 1978, a handful of them, led by Nuri, by this time a self-proclaimed spiritual leader of Gharmi settlers in the Vakhsh *raion*, held a rally in front of the Qurghonteppa CPT *obkom*; Nuri was arrested, but otherwise the authorities ignored the incident and no large-scale reprisals took place.[106] During the mid 1980s, Nuri

---

99   Muhammadjon Hindustoni, Ishoni Nematullo, Kholidi Abdusalom and Hoji Qalandar.

100   Nuri, 'Hizbe, ki resha dar ormoni mardum dorad', pp. 154–5. These later members include: *ustod* (professor) Muhammadsharif Himmatzoda, *Mavlalvi* Muhammadqosimi Rahim, Davlat Usmon, *ishon* Qiyomiddini Ghozi, Zubaydullohi Rozik, Mullah Muhammadsharifi *shahid*, Mullah Abdughaffori *shahid*, Mullah Haqnazari Sohibnazar, Mullah Ayomiddini Sattorzoda, Mullah Muhammadrasuli Salom, Mullah Abdullohi Khitobi *shahid*, Mullah Saididdini Rustam, Mullah Muhammadii Navid, *ishon* Mirzoyusuf, *ishon* Shamsiddinkhon and Mullah Ubaydulloh. Note: '*shahid*' (lit. 'martyr') indicates that they were killed.

101   Literally, 'Revival of the Islamic Youth of Tajikistan'.

102   Nuri, 'Hizbe, ki resha dar ormoni mardum dorad', pp. 155–6.

103   Nuri notes that members—concerned with potential KGB activities—generally did not take notes in their meetings. When they did, they wrote in code. See Nuri, 'Hizbe, ki resha dar ormoni mardum dorad', p. 157.

104   Nuri, 'Hizbe, ki resha dar ormoni mardum dorad', pp. 156–8.

105   Kudryavtsev and Niyazi, '"Politicheskii islam"', p. 112.

106   Safarali Kenjaev, *Tabadduloti Tojikiston*, Vol. I (Dushanbe: Fondi Kenjaev, 1993), p. 259.

was operating an underground Islamic school in Qurghonteppa.[107] His work did not go unnoticed. Soviet authorities warned Nuri to desist with his religious activities in 1983.[108] Khalid writes that Nuri, while not providing exact details of his plans for the form of the future state structure, began 'arguing in public, usually at well-attended feasts marking life-cycle events, for the establishment of an Islamic state in Tajikistan'.[109]

One oft-mentioned factor in the activities of underground Islamists is the role played by the Soviet war in neighbouring Afghanistan. Of course, at the official level of the Islamic leadership there was vocal support for the war in Afghanistan.[110] *Qozikalon* Mirzo Abdullo Kalonzoda publicly condemned the mujahideen, accusing them of 'burning mosques and killing innocent old people and children'.[111] But there was dissenting opinion away from the state-sanctioned Muslim leadership. Monica Whitlock writes of the effect of the Soviet–Afghan war on Nuri and his network:[112]

> Nuri and his circle had been critical of the war in Afghanistan from the start. 'It was an act of aggression against a fellow Muslim country. We said nothing in public, but of course we were dissidents,' said one of the study group who met at Hindustani's house. Hindustani had listened to all the news he could from Afghanistan, but made no comment except that to say that what was happening was absolutely dreadful. Some of his younger students were less reserved. Contemporaries remember that Nuri and others toured the villages, praying and giving homilies against the war in people's houses. Nuri won an audience among families who had lost their sons for reasons they did not understand in a country only a couple of hours' drive away.

In 1986, Nuri was finally arrested for producing and distributing religious materials.[113] The incident that precipitated this action was when Nuri, inspired by Gorbachev's *glasnost*, sent a letter to the twenty-seventh CPSU congress expounding his ideas on freedom of religious belief. Moscow's reaction was swift: on direct orders from the Kremlin, he was again put behind bars, and 24 of his comrades were sentenced to imprisonment for 'anti-state propaganda'.[114]

---

107 Mullojonov, 'The Islamic Clergy in Tajikistan Since the End of the Soviet Period', p. 230.

108 Conciliation Resources, 'Profiles: Said Abdullo Nuri'.

109 Khalid, *Islam after Communism*, p. 146. See also: Rabiyev, 'After the Trial', pp. 10–11.

110 SADUM was itself involved in assisting the war effort. Its members even deployed to Afghanistan. See: Eren Tasar, 'The Central Asian Muftiate in Occupied Afghanistan, 1979–87', *Central Asian Survey*, Vol. 30, No. 2 (2011), pp. 213–26.

111 Thom Shanker, 'Afghans Aren't Defeated; They're Being Remolded', *Chicago Tribune* (3 August 1986), p. 4.

112 Whitlock, *Land Beyond the River*, p. 140.

113 Mullojonov, 'The Islamic Clergy in Tajikistan Since the End of the Soviet Period', p. 230; Conciliation Resources, 'Profiles: Said Abdullo Nuri'. Olivier Roy's account (*The New Central Asia*, p. 154) of Nuri being arrested in 1987 for leading a pro-*mujahideen* demonstration is incorrect.

114 Kudriavtsev and Niyazi, '"Politicheskii islam"', p. 112.

When Nuri was arrested in the Vakhsh district in the summer of 1986 and taken into custody, his friends and kin, apparently concerned that Nuri would disappear in custody, held a demonstration in Qurghonteppa City outside the police building, demanding Nuri's release.[115] Whitlock frames the incident as an accidental boost to Nuri's profile:[116]

> The Afghan war was still going on, and a young teacher who was there said he saw the demonstration dove-tailing with other worries. 'Four coffins had just arrived from Afghanistan … All dead were local boys. Maybe a hundred or a hundred and twenty people came, mainly relatives, and held a mourning meeting. Then a thousand more people came and wrote a petition, demanding that their sons be brought home from Afghanistan. Because Nuri was against the war, it looked like a demonstration for him, and he grew stronger then because people did not trust the authorities any more.

Nuri was sentenced for his subversive activities[117] to 18 months in prison camp, the only prominent religious teacher among his contemporaries to be given this punishment. Whitlock maintains that this incident gave Nuri a higher level of popularity than other young clerics. One supporter remarked: 'The Soviet Union was getting weaker, we could feel it. People wanted a mulla to follow, they looked around, and they found Nuri.'[118] Yet, results were mixed. In the wake of this mini-purge, the Islamist movement in Tajikistan experienced a change of leadership: 'domination gradually shifted to representatives of old influential religious families, mostly those of *ishons* (i.e., heads of clans of Sufi mystical brotherhoods, such as Qadariya and Naqshbandiya).'[119] The result was further moderation of the movement's platform on the one hand, and a perceptible surge in the number of followers and material resources of Islamists, on the other.[120]

---

115   Whitlock, *Land Beyond the River*, p. 142–3; Khalid, *Islam after Communism*, p. 146; V. Rabiyev, 'Into the Classroom with a Koran?' *Kommunist Tadzhikistana* (31 January 1987), p. 2; and Rabiyev, 'After the Trial', pp. 10–11. Whitlock refers to the protest, debatably, as 'the first unsanctioned demonstration of any size held in Tajikistan'.

116   Whitlock, *Land Beyond the River*, p. 142.

117   Nuri was put on trial for subversive activities; however, Whitlock provides a version whereby, for reasons unknown, every witness against him recanted. As a result, the only charge that stuck was possession of marijuana, which Whitlock calls a 'standard Soviet charge against subversives'. Whitlock, *Land Beyond the River*, pp. 142–3. Kudryavtsev and Niyazi provide a different version in their very brief mention of Nuri's arrest. They state that Nuri's sentence was reduced after 'an impressive protest rally of his supporters in front of [the] Qurghonteppa executive committee'. See: Kudryavtsev and Niyazi, '"Politicheskii islam"', p. 124, n. 12. In regards to the content of the 'subversive material', Kudryavtsev and Niyazi write that '[t]he "Anti-government Propaganda", in fact, largely prevailed in their criticism of the arbitrariness of local authorities, the misconduct of the official clergy, and the senseless bloodshed in Afghanistan'. See: ibid., p. 112.

118   Whitlock, *Land Beyond the River*, pp. 142–3. See also: Mullojonov, 'The Islamic Clergy in Tajikistan Since the End of the Soviet Period', p. 230.

119   Bushkov and Mikulskii, 'Obschestvenno-politicheskaia situatsiia v Tadzhikistane', p. 27.

120   Bushkov and Mikulskii, 'Obschestvenno-politicheskaia situatsiia v Tadzhikistane'.

Nuri, after his release from jail in 1988, was given a job by *Qozi* Turajonzoda as editor of *Minbar-i Islom*, the official publication of the *Qoziyot*.[121] He even went on *hajj* with the official Tajikistan delegation in 1990.[122] Around the time of his release, Nuri 'became aligned' with other politically active men who would go on to form the Tajik branch of the IRP.[123] Nuri soon became a high-ranking leader in the Tajik IRP, but still behind others such as the top leader, Muhammad Sharif Himmatzoda, and his deputy, Davlat Usmon.[124] Nuri would eventually eclipse these men and become the top leader once the IRP was exiled.

Formal Beginning of the IRP of Tajikistan

The IRP of Tajikistan was officially established on 6 October 1990 as a branch of the Soviet Union-wide IRP, which was formed three months earlier in Russia.[125] Dudoignon speculates that in 1990 the Tajik IRP was given some support by the Kremlin leadership. The reason for this is that the Kremlin leadership saw the IRP as a force that could take support away from nationalists while also pushing against the recalcitrant segment of the Communist Party in Tajikistan that was giving the Kremlin problems.[126] Whatever the case at the union level, Tajik first secretary Mahkamov's government spared no efforts to suppress the Islamist movement. In November 1990, the CPT CC officially condemned the attempt to set up a branch of the union-wide IRP in Tajikistan. In December 1990, the Supreme Soviet of the Tajik SSR outlawed the IRP and ordered the republic's KGB, Ministry of Interior and the Prosecutor's Office to prevent any IRP activities. Even before this series of events, a media campaign was launched to portray Tajik Islamists as terrorists trained in Afghanistan and Pakistan,[127] or, alternatively, in Saudi Arabia and Iran with CIA money, who desired to 'found an exclusively Islamic society through physical elimination of ideological

---

121   Whitlock, *Land Beyond the River*, p. 143; Conciliation Resources, 'Profiles: Said Abdullo Nuri'. Whitlock doesn't portray Turajonzoda and Nuri as well acquainted with each other. She notes that Turajonzoda first met Nuri in 1983 or 1984 when Turajonzoda was briefly a student of Hindustani.

122   Roy, 'The Impact of the Afghan War in Soviet Central Asia', p. 344.

123   Conciliation Resources, 'Profiles: Said Abdullo Nuri'.

124   Roy, *The New Central Asia*, p. 155.

125   Kilavuz, *Understanding Violent Conflict*, pp. 139–41; Saodat Olimova and Muzaffar Olimov, 'The Islamic Renaissance Party', in *Politics of Compromise: The Tajikistan Peace Process*, eds Kamoludin Abdullaev and Catharine Barnes (London: Conciliation Resources, 2001); Khalid, *Islam after Communism*, p. 147. The leader of the IRP of Tajikistan at the time of its founding was Muhammad Sharif Himmatzoda, with Nuri one of its 'important' leaders. See: Kilavuz, *Understanding Violent Conflict*, pp. 139–41. The conference at which the Tajik IRP was established was held in the Dushanbe outskirts, in Chortut. See: Niyazi, 'The Year of Tumult', p. 281.

126   Dudoignon, 'Communal Solidarity and Social Conflicts in Late 20th Century Central Asia', pp. 15–16.

127   *Komsomolets Tadzhikistana*, 25 February 1990.

opponents and non-believers, and general genocide'.[128] The IRP was even accused of organising the riots in Dushanbe in February 1990 on behalf of 'the Wahhabis and other fundamentalist Islamic forces from abroad'.[129]

Mahkamov's government refused to enter into a dialogue with Tajik Islamists, but at the same time it failed to follow the hard line of Uzbekistan's leader, Islom Karimov, who clamped down on the nascent IRP of Uzbekistan in the summer of 1990, arresting some 400 delegates of its first conference.[130] The Tajik government confined itself to half-measures, such as imposing fines on Islamist activists; eventually, not a single person was tried in the republic for defying the anti-IRP legislation. Lacking the political will for either compromise or drastic action, the authorities tried to weaken the Islamist movement by wooing the official Muslim establishment. On 8 December 1990, the Supreme Soviet of Tajikistan passed a law 'On Freedom of Conscience and Religious Organisations', which resolutely broke with the communist tradition of atheism, allowed religious organisations and individuals to take part in political life, provided for the re-creation of the institution of *vaqf* and permitted religious education for children over seven years of age.[131] The ban on the IRP would eventually be temporarily lifted in September 1991 during the brief administration of interim president Qadriddin Aslonov, before being reinstated when Aslonov stepped down. Legal recognition finally came at the end of 1991.[132] On 26 October 1991, the IRP of Tajikistan held its first congress in a former Communist Party centre, with 657 delegates, 310 guests and 50 journalists attending. The congress, which was opened by Dushanbe mayor, Maqsud Ikromov, elected Muhammad Sharif Himmatzoda as leader and Davlat Usmon as the first deputy leader.[133]

The Tajikistan branch of the IRP soon broke relations with the wider IRP. Not only was the existence of an official clergy an obstacle to the Soviet-wide IRP, the nationalist cleavages within the organisation hurt coordination, while the ambitions of the overall leadership conflicted with those of the Tajik IRP. The IRP's federal leadership, which had supported the continuation of the Soviet Union, endorsed the communist candidate Rahmon Nabiev in October 1991 for the upcoming elections while condemning the Tajik IRP for allying with nationalists, whom the Tajik IRP had earlier criticised. This ended relations

---

128 *Tojikistoni Soveti*, 20 November 1990.

129 *Pravda*, 16 May 1991.

130 Bess Brown, 'The Islamic Renaissance Party in Central Asia', *Radio Liberty Report on the USSR*, 10 May 1990, p. 14.

131 *Novye zakony Respubliki Tadzhikistan. Sbornik. (Chast' II)* (Dushanbe: Kontrakt, 1991), pp. 26–31.

132 Kilavuz, *Understanding Violent Conflict*, p. 140, citing *Izvestia*, 22 November 1990. Kilavuz mentions the alleged IRP involvement in the February 1990 riots as a pretext for banning the organisation. See ibid., p. 145. On the banning and reinstatement of the IRP in the second half of 1991, see ibid., pp. 145, 148.

133 Kudryavtsev and Niyazi, '"Politicheskii islam"', p. 117. Sayid Ibrahim Hadoev was elected as second deputy leader.

between the Tajik IRP and the federal organisation.[134] By mid to late 1992, the IRP leadership was claiming a membership of 30 000, making it the second 'strongest' in terms of numbers behind only the Communist Party.[135]

IRP Influences and Interactions: Muhammadjon Hindustoni

Muhammadjon Rustamov (1892–1989), better known as 'Hindustoni' for his time spent in India (*Hinduston* in Tajik), studied Islam near his place of birth in Kokand (now in Uzbekistan) and then in Bukhara. During the Bolshevik revolution he went to Afghanistan and studied in Mazar-i Sharif before returning to Bukhara with his Afghan teacher. He soon accompanied his teacher, Muhammad Ghawth (also 'Ghaus'), to the eastern Afghan city of Jalalabad where Ghawth was appointed as the *Qozi*. From Jalalabad, Hindustoni went to India, where he studied at the Usmania *madrasa* in Ajmer for eight years, completing his studies. He returned home and settled in Kokand in 1929. During the anti-religious communist attacks of the 1930s, Hindustoni served two jail terms, including three years in Siberia. In 1940 he took up employment in a Kokand factory before being drafted into the military in 1943. He was badly wounded on the eastern front in Belarus and spent the next three years in hospital. After a year at home he moved to Dushanbe where SADUM officials eventually appointed him *imam-khotib* of a local mosque. After almost a year in Tajikistan, he was denounced and served more than four years in prison. In 1953, after Stalin's death, Hindustoni was rehabilitated and appointed to a post in Tajikistan's Academy of Sciences, where he spent most of his time translating Arabic texts and teaching Urdu. From the early 1960s Hindustoni developed a full Islamic curriculum that he taught in secret.[136]

---

134   Roy, *The New Central Asia*, pp. 155–6; Dudoignon, 'Political Parties and Forces in Tajikistan, 1989–1993', p. 65; Dudoignon, 'Communal Solidarity and Social Conflicts in Late 20th Century Central Asia', p. 16. As an example of nationalist cleavages in the federal IRP, Roy notes that the 'Moscow IRP was also split, between Tatars and Caucasians: the former wanted to impose Tatar as the preaching language in Moscow mosques, while the latter wanted to keep Russian. In fact, the IRP was imploding on all sides, along ethnic lines of cleavage.' See: Roy, *The New Central Asia*, pp. 155–6. In regards to the IRP's alliance with other opposition parties, Roy writes that secularists and even atheists joined an alliance with the Islamists. See: Roy, 'Is the Conflict in Tajikistan a Model for Conflicts throughout Central Asia', p. 135.

135   Henry Dunant Centre, 'Humanitarian Engagement with Armed Groups: The Central Asian Islamic Opposition Movements, *Henry Dunant Centre for Humanitarian Dialogue* [Geneva] (2003), pp. 12–13.

136   Bakhtiyar Babadjanov and Muzaffar Kamilov, 'Muhammadjan Hindustani (1892–1989) and the Beginning of the "Great Schism" among the Muslims of Uzbekistan', in *Islam in Politics in Russian and Central Asia (Early Eighteenth to Late Twentieth Centuries)*, eds Stephane A. Dudoignon and Komatsu Hisao (London: Kegan Paul, 2001), pp. 197–200. The authors mistakenly place the Usmania *madrasa* in Kashmir. Rather, it is in Rajasthan. See: Whitlock, *Land Beyond the River*, pp. 34–5, 146. For a longer discussion of Hindustoni's background, see: Vitaly V. Naumkin, *Radical Islam in Central Asia: Between Pen and Rifle* (Lanham, Md: Rowman & Littlefield, 2005) pp. 44–9.

Hindustoni went on to become a teacher of both Nuri and Himmatzoda. Hindustoni's 'clandestine' *madrasa* in Dushanbe was closed by the KGB in 1973, but students and teachers 'came out of it safely, thanks to family connections and corruption'.[137] Adeeb Khalid summarises Hindustoni's beliefs:[138]

> In his teaching and his writing, he took consistently conservative positions rooted in the local Hanafi tradition. He had little use for modernist reform ... Two aspects of his conservatism are worth noting: he defended local customs and traditions against attacks from all directions, and he took a resolutely quietist stance on questions of politics. Soviet rule was a test for believers, in which success lay in reliance on God (*tavakkul*) and patience (*sabr*) rather than in political or military struggle.

Khalid goes on to describe how some of Hindustoni's students rebelled against him and his 'conservatism and his quietism' in particular.[139] Before the disagreements expanded into a larger dispute about broader issues within the 'milieu of underground Islamic learning (hujra)',[140] the hostilities started with Hindustoni's students adopting Hanbali rituals as opposed to the dominant Hanafi forms practised in Central Asia. The students' view was that the Hanbali school was more closely associated with Arab countries and therefore purer and 'uncontaminated by local traditions'.[141] Furthermore, Hindustoni did not approve of the way some of his former students were mixing religion and politics. Whitlock hints that it was his long view of human ambitions and failings that made him conservative on this issue.[142] Hindustoni felt that some of his former students in the Ferghana Valley were advocating a confrontation with the Soviet state that would be disastrous for Muslims, especially considering the recent gains in freedoms they had made. The arguments at the time (mid 1970s to mid 1980s) became quite heated, as can be seen in excerpts—both defensive[143]

---

137 Roy, *The New Central Asia*, p. 154.

138 Khalid, *Islam after Communism*, pp. 113–14.

139 Khalid, *Islam after Communism*, p. 145.

140 Khalid makes clear that these disputes were confined to a narrow social group: 'The mere fact that such a dispute could take place is testimony to the vitality of underground Islam, although given the numbers involved, this rebellion was very much a storm in a teapot at the time.' See: Khalid, *Islam after Communism*, pp. 144–5.

141 Khalid, *Islam after Communism*, pp. 144–5. See also: Naumkin, *Radical Islam in Central Asia*, p. 54.

142 Whitlock, *Land Beyond the River*, p. 146.

143 For example: 'It is a shame that you do not know [my] biography; if you knew, you would be more discriminating and just. In my life, I have been deprived of my freedom three times on the charge that I was inciting the people against the Soviet government. The first time I was sentenced to one year in prison, the second time to three years, and the third time—to 25 years. I suffered such deprivations for this anti-government activity! And yet you call on me to take up the jihad? You admonish me, as if I were lost in ignorance.' See: Muhammadjan Hindustani, 'Answers to Those Who are Introducing Inadmissible Innovations into Religion', Appendix in Babadjanov and Kamilov, 'Muhammadjan Hindustani (1892–1989) and the Beginning of the "Great Schism" among the Muslims of Uzbekistan', pp. 210–18.

and offensive[144] in nature—from Hindustoni's open reply to those who accused him of apostasy and of being beholden to an atheist state. Nor did Hindustoni approve of the theological views of his former students.[145] Khalid writes:[146]

> The students called themselves the *mujaddidiya*, the renovators, while calling their opponents *mushriklar*, polytheists. Hindustoniy, for his part, argued that local customs were based on a long tradition of Hanafi jurisprudence, which in itself was based on the Qur'an and the example of the Prophet, and that by forswearing accepted Hanafi dogma, his critics had placed themselves beyond the bounds of the Sunni community of Central Asia and had become 'Wahhabis.' Hindustoniy's use of this term owed a lot to his time in India, where such debates over ritual purity were common and where opponents of the purists had long dubbed them Wahhabis. Thus, the term Wahhabi entered religious debate in Central Asia, from where it was to spread throughout the lands of the former Soviet Union.

Wahhabism

Mohammad Abd al-Wahhab, who lived during the eighteenth century in Najd Province of Arabia, preached a 'strictly puritanical doctrine', gaining momentum when he made an alliance with what was to become the Saudi royal lineage.[147] Khalid stresses that the term 'Wahhabism' was used mostly as a 'polemic foil in sectarian arguments among Muslims', including in British India, as both colonial authorities and locals used the label 'Wahhabism' to denounce reformists and 'troublesome Muslim opponents'.[148] Accusations of Wahhabism were also common in the late Soviet era. Surprisingly, some analysts in the West took these agitprop invectives in good faith and enthusiastically announced to the world that 'in some areas of Central Asia, particularly but not exclusively in central and southern Tajikistan, there has also been a resurgence of Wahhabism'.[149] The question of how exactly the 'puritanism and militancy

---

144 Later in the same open letter: 'What are you afraid of? You are like a dog, barking from behind a fence. Close your eyes and consider your evil inclinations. All the faults and mistakes you accuse me of actually belong to you! Alright, then! If you are a man, go into the street and call people to make holy war! But, in any case, such boldness is not characteristic of you, and you are not capable of such action.' See: Hindustani, 'Answers to Those Who are Introducing Inadmissible Innovations into Religion'.

145 Khalid, *Islam after Communism*, p. 145; Babadjanov and Kamilov, 'Muhammadjan Hindustani (1892–1989) and the Beginning of the "Great Schism" among the Muslims of Uzbekistan', pp. 200–1.

146 Khalid, *Islam after Communism*, p. 145. See also: Naumkin, *Radical Islam in Central Asia*, p. 51.

147 Khalid, *Islam after Communism*, p. 46.

148 Khalid, *Islam after Communism*, p. 46.

149 Yaacov Ro'i, 'The Islamic Influence on Nationalism in Soviet Central Asia', *Problems of Communism*, No. 4 (July–August 1990), p. 52.

of the Wahhabis'[150] might have become rooted amongst a population practising folk Islam characterised by broad humanism, tolerance and a liberal approach to other religions obviously never crossed their minds. For their part, Tajik academics have convincingly shown that the teachings of Mohammad ibn Abd al-Wahhab, as well as radical doctrines of other Islamists such as Sayyid Qutb, are inherently alien to the majority of the eponymous population of Tajikistan.[151]

Khalid further notes that in the former Soviet Union 'Wahhabism' has 'come into indiscriminate use to denote any and all expressions of nontraditional Islam'.[152] In Tajikistan, the use of the term 'Wahhabi' as a pejorative for the Islamist opposition was used even by the mullahs who supported the government. They juxtaposed the alleged Wahhabism of Saudi origin with a local Sufi-influenced 'national and traditional Islam';[153] however, a few scholars (for example, Dudoignon and Matveeva) and some local analysts have used the term as well—in a somewhat more neutral manner.[154] For an example of a more systematic treatment, Niyazi acknowledges that a 'very tiny section' of the religious community in Tajikistan and Uzbekistan started to refer to themselves as Wahhabis, in particular after leaders of these groups returned from the *hajj* in the late 1980s and early 1990s. He completely rejects, however, any possibility of Wahhabi influences amongst the Gharmi Tajiks (that is, from whom the IRP draws most of its support). He blames a 1990 article written in Tajikistan by the head of the Committee for Religious Affairs for popularising 'Wahhabi' as a term of abuse locally.[155] Niyazi also notes the use of the slang term '*Vovchik*' (diminutive for the name Vladimir, but here used for 'Wahhabi') as an epithet against the 'Islamic opposition'.[156] While Niyazi's article cited above is mainly a tract in praise of Naqshbandi Sufism, he cites the survival of pre-Islamic nature

---

150 An expression coined by Rafiq Zakaria in his book *The Struggle within Islam: The Conflict between Religion and Politics* (New York: Penguin Books, 1988), p. 160.

151 M. Hazrati and I. Saidiyon, *Islom: raviya, mazhab va firqahoi on* (Dushanbe: Oryono, 1992), pp. 67–70.

152 Khalid, *Islam after Communism*, pp. 46–7.

153 Roy, 'Is the Conflict in Tajikistan a Model for Conflicts throughout Central Asia', pp. 139–40.

154 For example, Dudoignon cites the 'wahhabite origins' of the IRP (Dudoignon, 'Political Parties and Forces in Tajikistan, 1989–1993', pp. 66–7), while Matveeva notes the claims of local analysts that foreign Wahhabi groups had been 'penetrating' Tajikistan—especially amongst Gharmis in Qurghonteppa and in the Ferghana Valley—as early as 16 years before the civil war. The local analysts (Ahad Mahmoudov and Faredun Hodizoda) also mention the influence of foreign Islamists through Tajiks participating in the *hajj* and Islamic education abroad, as well as through audio recordings and literature. Matveeva, 'The Perils of Emerging Statehood', p. 9.

155 Aziz Niyazi, 'Islam and Tajikistan's Human and Ecological Crisis', in *Civil Society in Central Asia*, eds M. Holt Ruffin and Daniel Clarke Waugh (Seattle: University of Washington Press, 1999), p. 195, n. 7. The article in question is: Sunnatullo Ibragimzoda, *Todzhikistoni Soveti*, 11 December 1990.

156 Niyazi, 'Islam and Tajikistan's Human and Ecological Crisis', p. 195, n. 7. For more recent uses of 'Wahhabi' in the discourse of academia and in the media of Russia and the West—particularly of the past 15 years—see: Alexander Knysh, 'A Clear and Present Danger: "Wahhabism" as a Rhetorical Foil', *Die Welt des Islams*, Vol. 44, No. 1 (2004).

worship and elements of Zoroastrianism (both abhorrent to 'Wahhabis') in Gharm to refute the idea that Wahhabi Islam has made inroads here, rather than stressing the presence of Sufi Islam in the region.[157]

The debate over Wahhabism in Tajikistan during the late Soviet era suffers from lack of a clear definition. Neither Dudoignon nor Matveeva makes an effort to define Wahhabism for the brief use in their articles cited above. A more well-defined discussion of Wahhabism is found in the work of Bakhtiyar Babadjanov and Muzaffar Kamilov, which focuses on Hindustoni's defence of traditional Hanafi doctrine and his arguments with certain reformist *ulama* in the Ferghana Valley (particularly in Kokand). They do note that Abd al-Wahhab's work was available—but very rarely acquired—in Central Asia as early as 1979, whether acquired on *hajj* or directly from the SADUM libraries (which held Arabic works by Wahhabi writers). Despite the similarities between the reforms that many of the *mujaddidiya ulama* were asking for and Wahhabi doctrine, they find the use of the label 'Wahhabi' to be inaccurate.[158]

Other 'Foreign' Islamic Influences

Dudoignon notes Iranian influences in the IRP, but not religious ones. Obviously, the Shia Islamist ideology of the Iranian rulers would have limited applicability to a Sunni party like the IRP;[159] but the Islamic revolution in Iran did provide a demonstration effect. Abdullo Nuri explained in 1994:[160]

> The revolution in Afghanistan was an impetus to our movement. But the basis of our movement was the victory of Islamic revolution in Iran in which all the forces in the [Islamic] movement and all the Muslims

---

157 Niyazi, 'Islam and Tajikistan's Human and Ecological Crisis', esp. pp. 183, 195, n. 7. Elsewhere, Niyazi writes: 'It is characteristic that Tajik fundamentalism is also tolerant of various manifestations of so-called popular Islam such as the worship of local saints or the worship of fire inherited from Zoroastrianism.' See: Niyazi, 'The Year of Tumult', p. 280.

158 Babadjanov and Kamilov, 'Muhammadjan Hindustani (1892–1989) and the Beginning of the "Great Schism" among the Muslims of Uzbekistan', esp. pp. 200–6. Unfortunately, Babadjanov and Kamilov's work does not include an analysis of those who would go on to form the core of the IRP in Tajikistan.

159 Dudoignon maintains, however, that there were some areas in which the IRP was influenced by Iran. He cites 'Khomeynist points of reference' such as Persian nationalism and anti-Western sentiments in the IRP's rhetoric. Furthermore, according to Dudoignon, this occurred when 'the IRP attempted to correct its internationalist "image" and dissociate itself from the Soviet chaos, seeking an alliance with the Islamic Republic [of Iran] in order to limit the influence of the *qazi kalan* Turajanzada, the favoured client of the Saudis.' Dudoignon does not elaborate on the Saudi relationship. See: Dudoignon, 'Political Parties and Forces in Tajikistan', pp. 66–7.

160 Pinar Akcali, 'Islam and Ethnicity in Central Asia: The Case of the Islamic Renaissance Party', *Mediterranean Quarterly* (Winter 1998), p. 148, citing *FBIS-SOV* (15 March 1994), p. 40. Speeches by Ayatollah Khomeini did circulate in the late 1980s in southern Tajikistan. See: A. Alimov, 'Business in Opium', *Kommunist Tadzhikistana* (13 May 1988), *SWB SU*, 0212 (25 July 1988), B/1.

trusted. After the Islamic revolution in Iran, these forces were convinced that when Islam was able to prevail in Iran, the same could happen in other countries, too. This gave the people self-confidence.

Foreign Sunni ideological influences would seem to be more likely sources. The Deobandi school of Islam that began in India gets an occasional mention as an influence on Islam in Tajikistan. Niyazi writes that some mullahs travelled to the Ferghana Valley and to Termez in Uzbekistan to visit teachers. In Termez some *sayids* kept Deobandi teachings alive during the Soviet era;[161] however, the only possible link between Deobandism and the IRP is the very weak connection between IRP leaders Himmatzoda and Nuri on one hand, and their one-time teacher Hindustoni on the other. Hindustoni's students and Turajonzoda claim that Hindustoni studied at Deoband during his time in India—even though Hindustoni makes no mention of Deoband.[162] Another South Asian influence may be the writings of Abu Ala Maududi—a Pakistani Islamist writer and founder of Jamaat-e-Islami—which circulated in the network that was to become the IRP.[163]

Ideological influences from the Muslim Brotherhood seem somewhat more likely. Like Wahhabi works, some Muslim Brotherhood writings were circulating in secret as early as 1979 in the Ferghana Valley.[164] Kudryavtsev and Niyazi note that among the literature seized from Nuri's underground circle in 1985–87 were works by Muslim Brotherhood leaders Hassan al-Banna, Sayyid Qutb and Muhammad Qutb.[165] Nuri was clearly familiar with the work of at least one Muslim Brotherhood figure, which was demonstrated when he quoted from and referred to the group's founder, Hassan al-Banna, in reverential terms at a 2003 Islamic conference in Iran.[166] Both Roy and Olimova stress the influence of the writings of the Muslim Brotherhood in the ideology of the IRP. Roy explicitly

---

161   Niyazi, 'Islam and Tajikistan's Human and Ecological Crisis', p. 185.

162   According to Whitlock, Hindustani's students and others claim that Hindustani studied in Deoband; however, Hindustani makes no mention of Deoband and instead mentions the Usmania *madrasa* in Ajmer, Rajasthan. Whitlock, *Land Beyond the River*, pp. 34–5, 146; Turajonzoda, 'Religion', p. 268. The Usmania *madrasa* is of the Chisti Sufi order. See their web site: <http://ajmersharifdargah.com/AJMER-sharif.html> See also: Khalid, *Islam after Communism*, p. 113.

163   Olimova, 'Opposition in Tajikistan', p. 248; Kudryavtsev and Niyazi, '"Politicheskii islam"', p. 112. See also: Alimov, 'Business in Opium'.

164   Babadjanov and Kamilov, 'Muhammadjan Hindustani (1892–1989) and the Beginning of the "Great Schism" among the Muslims of Uzbekistan', p. 202, n. 13. An example given is Sayyid Qutb's *Al-Aqida*. The authors note that Hindustani authored a satirical work that mocked 'one of the sources of inspiration of the Muslim Brotherhood'. Ibid., p. 205. See also: Alimov, 'Business in Opium'.

165   Kudryavtsev and Niyazi, '"Politicheskii islam"', p. 112. Similarly, Alexei Malashenko notes that writings by Muslim Brotherhood author Qutb and al-Banna were popular in 'Koranic clubs and schools' among Soviet Muslims circa 1990. See: Malashenko, 'Islam and Politics in the Southern Zone of the Former USSR', pp. 116–17. See also: Alimov, 'Business in Opium'.

166   Sayid Abdullohi Nuri, 'Biyoed, Muvaqqati Ikhtilofro Kanor Biguzorem', Conference speech in Iran (22–23 December 2003), in *Mujaddidi Asr: bakhshida ba 60-umin solgardi zodruzi ustod Sayid Abdullohi Nuri (r)*, ed. Qiyomiddin Sattori (Dushanbe: Devashtich, 2007), p. 114. The terms Nuri uses are '*hazrati ustod*' (roughly: 'most venerable scholar') and '*(r)*' for 'Rahmatullah Alaih' (added to names of respected religious figures).

classifies the ideology of the IRP and of Nuri and Himmatzoda in particular as that of the Muslim Brotherhood, while Olimova instead just notes the influence of Muslim Brotherhood writings in the IRP's platform.[167]

Academia and the Intelligentsia

When the All-Union IRP was formed in July 1990 in Astrakhan, it was heavily influenced by Islamist intellectuals rather than by the *ulama*.[168] Concerning the Tajikistan branch of the IRP and the movement for political Islam in general, Mullojonov notes the support from and membership of Tajikistan's 'university intellectuals'.[169] Niyazi notes that academics often had better levels of knowledge of Arabic and Islamic sources and thought than did mullahs and *ishons*.[170] Niyazi himself, while not explicitly endorsing the IRP in his publications, actually provides a good example of an intellectual who favourably views the role of Islam in society. He writes:[171]

> The ideals of an Islamic state concerning justice, equality, and brotherhood in our opinion are completely compatible with the commonly accepted contemporary understanding of civil society … The idea of a state ruled by law took root in the East on the basis of the universally accepted sharia law, which in theory eliminated estate, racial, and class privileges for the observers of the law, thus making the rights of the rank-and-file Muslim and the ruler equal.

Niyazi goes on to note that the 'Islamic opposition' did become radicalised right before the outbreak of conflict, but that this was as a response to the government's counter-opposition tactics. He stresses that '[b]efore the start of the bloodshed, supporters of "pure Islam" in Tajikistan were a wholly moderate movement'.[172]

---

167   Roy, *The New Central Asia*, p. 154; Roy, 'Is the Conflict in Tajikistan a Model for Conflicts throughout Central Asia', p. 141; Olimova, 'Opposition in Tajikistan', p. 248. Roy cites an interview with Nuri in the Tajik journal *Sukhan* (No. 18, 12 July 1991) wherein Nuri rejects the separation of politics and religion, endorses 'Islamic economy' versus communism and capitalism, 'discreetly criticizes' the official *ulama* and traditionalist mullahs and endorses the Algerian Islamic Salvation Front. The Muslim Brotherhood writers—whose works circulated amongst the network that would become the IRP—listed by Roy and Olimova are Sayyid and Muhammad Qutb and Sayyid Hawa.
168   Dudoignon, 'Political Parties and Forces in Tajikistan, 1989–1993', pp. 63–4.
169   Mullojonov, 'The Islamic Clergy in Tajikistan Since the End of the Soviet Period', pp. 249–50.
170   Niyazi, 'Islam and Tajikistan's Human and Ecological Crisis', p. 185.
171   Niyazi, 'Islam and Tajikistan's Human and Ecological Crisis', p. 193.
172   Niyazi, 'Islam and Tajikistan's Human and Ecological Crisis', p. 190.

Sufism

Mavlon Makhamov notes the prominent role that the Naqshbandi and Qadiri Sufi Muslim orders played during the pre-Soviet era in the religious life of the people living in the areas of what is now Tajikistan. It is his opinion, however, that the Soviet government destroyed these orders during the 1920s and 1930s—evidenced by the 'overwhelming majority' of Muslims in Tajikistan who are ignorant of these Sufi orders.[173] Makhamov does stress that while the orders—particularly the leading theologians and Sufi leaders who had an authoritative understanding of Sufism—may have been 'destroyed', Sufi *pirs* continued their work in a leaderless fashion:[174]

> [T]he institution of *pir* (spiritual and religious mentors), though somewhat transformed, has survived in Tajikistan, particularly in the rural areas. *Pirs* were not officially registered, but they directed all ceremonial rites in the rural area. *Pirs* are regarded with greater reverence than *ulama*, representing official Islam. Some *pirs* have disciples and adherents (*murids*), and this fact is not concealed. They function openly, though not very actively.

The role of Naqshbandi Sufism in society as protectors of the powerless against rapacious rulers is appraised glowingly by Niyazi: 'In spring 1992, as government authorities continued to ignore the interests of a desperate peasantry, authoritative *ishans* from the southeast of the country rose to their defense. The *naqshabandi* tradition of intervention on behalf of land-workers and craftsmen was reborn.'[175] The Sufi notables of Tajikistan, however, also rose to the defence of other interests. The result was that Sufi *pirs*, *ishons* and their *murids* supported various factions in the conflict,[176] overwhelmingly on the basis of regional affiliation.

---

173   Makhamov, 'Islam and the Political Development of Tajikistan after 1985', p. 203. A similar view on Sufi practices is conveyed by Oumar Arabov: 'If we ask passers by in the streets of Dushanbe, the capital of Tajikistan, what is Sufism, not many of them will be able to answer, and yet they sometimes carry out Sufi rituals. In other words, Sufism exists but is not easily discernible by people.' See: Oumar Arabov, 'A Note on Sufism in Tajikistan: What Does it Look Like?' *Central Asian Survey*, Vol. 23, No. 3 (2004), p. 345.
174   Makhamov, 'Islam and the Political Development of Tajikistan after 1985', p. 203.
175   Niyazi, 'Islam and Tajikistan's Human and Ecological Crisis', pp. 189–90.
176   Kamoludin Abdullaev and Shahram Akbarzadeh, *Historical Dictionary of Tajikistan*, 2nd edn (Lanham, Md: The Scarecrow Press, 2001), pp. 173–4; Arabov, 'A Note on Sufism in Tajikistan', p. 347. This view is reinforced by Roy, who argues that 'Sufi affiliations do not necessarily correspond to political affiliations'. See: Roy, *The New Central Asia*, p. 149.

Afghanistan

While it is true that following the revolution in Iran and the Soviet invasion of Afghanistan the trickle of Islamist ideas coming to Tajikistan from abroad increased, in 1984 Alexander Bennigsen urged caution in assessing their impact.[177] Even after the withdrawal of Soviet troops in February 1989, Afghan *mujahideen* failed to establish permanent channels of communication with their 'oppressed brethren' in the north (despite earlier fanciful claims).[178] As one of the Jamaat-e-Islami leaders in Peshawar complained in February 1990, 'there are absolutely no contacts between field commanders of the Resistance in the North of Afghanistan and citizens of Tajikistan'.[179] It seems, however, that Islamist propaganda from Afghanistan was doomed to fail because of the lack of any positive demonstration effect—in the late 1980s and early 1990s, when some Soviet Tajiks were finally allowed to visit their relatives in Afghanistan, they were not impressed by its social progress achieved under Islam.[180] In regards to the Soviet–Afghan war, the loyalty of Soviet Muslims was put to the test in Afghanistan, and, on average, Central Asian soldiers in the Red Army (including Tajiks) showed the same level of loyalty as any non-Muslims in the ranks.[181]

IRP Platform

The Soviet Union-wide federal IRP was formed in July 1990 in Astrakhan, Russia. The ideology of this organisation was based on adherence to the statutes of the Koran and *Sunna*. The IRP, as spelled out in its charter, saw itself up against not just certain non-Muslim forces, but also a Muslim community that was acting against 'universal morality and the *sharia*', and which was 'divided, ignorant, downtrodden, and infected with the nationalist and democratic ideas'.[182] The attack on 'democratic ideas' is likely a reference to the

---

177   Alexandre Bennigsen, 'Mullahs, Mujahidin and Soviet Muslims', *Problems of Communism*, Vol. XXXIII, No. 6 (November–December 1984), p. 44.

178   For example, one French journalist with good connections to the *mujahideen* was told that in Tajikistan there were '2,500 card-carrying Jamiat-e-Islam members'. See: Edward Girardet, 'Afghan Resistance: Familiar Pattern?' *Christian Science Monitor* (26 July 1992), p. 1.

179   *Kommunist Tadzhikistana*, 15 February 1991. As for another *mujahideen* group (Hizb-i Islami 'Hekmatyar'), Mavlon Makhamov claims that '[l]eaders of official Islam visited Saudi Arabia, Jordan, and Pakistan, where they met in May 1990 Gulbeddin Hekmatyar, with whom they made an arrangement of cooperation and mutual aid'. See: Makhamov, 'Islam and the Political Development of Tajikistan after 1985', pp. 200–1.

180   As an example, a resident of the Tajik city of Panj reminisced on his stay in Afghanistan: 'I went to visit my brother, whom I hadn't seen for 30 years. My God, how poorly they live, it is pitiful to look at them.' See: *Grazhdanskie dvizheniia v Tadzhikistane*, p. 112.

181   Christian Bleuer, 'Muslim Soldiers in Non-Muslim Militaries at War in Muslim Lands: The Soviet, American and Indian Experience', *The Journal of Muslim Minority Affairs*, Vol. 32, No. 4 (2012).

182   Igor Ermakov and Dmitrii Mikulskii, 'Islamskaia Partiia Vozrozhdeniia', in *Islam v Rossii i Srednei Azii* (Moscow: Lotos, 1993), pp. 181–5.

'Western-style' democrats of the Soviet Union/Commonwealth of Independent States (CIS) rather than to elections, as the IRP advocated for its goals to be achieved through democratic means. In its publications, the IRP attacked the official Muslim clergy, the leadership of the Muslim republics of the CIS, the 'national-democratic movements' in those republics, the use of Islam by those movements, the history of Russian and Soviet oppression of Muslims, and the 'state of ignorance, superstition, disunity and individualism prevailing among ordinary Muslims'.[183]

Tajik delegates participated actively in the first conference of the Islamic Revival Party of the USSR (IRPU), held in Astrakhan on 9 June 1990, and a close associate of Sayid Abdullo Nuri, Davlat Usmon, was elected chairman of the mandate commission of the newly established party and a member of its supreme body: the Council of *Ulama*. Shortly afterwards, the IRPU program was published in the underground bulletin of Tajik Islamists. Its main tenets could be summarised as follows:[184]

- the IRPU is a socio-political organisation which operates on lofty Islamic principles;
- the party consists of honest Muslims who fight for a revived and pure Islam by spreading the truth of the Quran and Sunna amongst the people;
- the party operates on a constitutional basis, condemns terrorism and reactionary theory and praxis, and respects all international treaties and agreements if they are not in violation of Islamic norms;
- the party respects human rights and upholds legal equality between Muslims and non-Muslims;
- the party demands cessation of state-sponsored atheistic propaganda, and contrives to establish Islamic educational centres, train qualified personnel, organise lectures, discussions and other events to spread the knowledge of Islam;
- the party strives to protect the honour and dignity of women, appreciates their active role in society and helps them to realise themselves fully in all capacities;
- the party favours modern economic development based on Islamic principles of pluralism; it supports environmental protection and health programs, and strong and durable families.

The IRPU advocated a federation of Muslim states that would include the Muslim-dominated areas of the CIS and some neighbouring Muslim regions. This federation would have elected Muslim leaders in a system that would

---

183 Ermakov and Mikulskii, 'Islamskaia Partiia Vozrozhdeniia', p. 185.
184 *Hidoyat*, No. 5 (July 1990), p. 5.

implement a new era of the 'Righteous Caliphs'.[185] The IRPU provided some specific examples of what the new political and social order would entail. These included *zakat* (Islamic tax) and *sadaqa* (Islamic charity), the introduction of *shari'a*-compliant banking, as well as *dhimmi* status[186] for Christians and Jews,[187] despite their earlier declaration of legal equality. Dudoignon notes that the IRPU was 'classically neo-fundamentalist' in its tenets such as proselytising, resisting the official clergy and advocating the Islamic taxes of *zakat* and *sadaqa*; however, he also notes the organisation's attempt to reassure the broader public of its moderate character through the use of 'fairly well-known' rhetoric (for example, Islam is 'humanist', 'pacifist' and 'progressive').[188]

The IRPU was registered in Moscow, but when its Tajik members applied for official recognition of the republican IRP, the authorities in Dushanbe turned them down. Nevertheless, the union-wide IRP illegally convened a regional conference organised by Davlat Usmon in the village of Chortut near Dushanbe in October 1990.[189] For the Tajikistan branch of the IRP in 1990 there was little coherence in organisation, platform and public message.[190] The message at the top levels of the party, however, was somewhat clearer. And once again, the IRP's *publicly* enunciated political agenda appeared to be rather moderate; according to Davlat Usmon, the party did not have the aim of establishing an Islamic state even in the remote future.[191]

What the early Tajik IRP lacked in organisation, it compensated for in enthusiasm. Niyazi, writing in late 1990,[192] assesses the IRP's motivations in a very favourable manner:[193]

> Now [IRP] fundamentalist activities are primarily aimed at strengthening religion. These people are united in their desire to free religious life from ubiquitous state supervision and to restore society's morals in accordance with Islamic ethics contained in the *fikh*. They want to restore and build new mosques, promote religious education, and urge Moslems to fulfill properly the prescribed rites and ceremonies. Many

---

185 That is, the *Rashidun*: the first four caliphs after the death of the prophet Muhammad.

186 This entails fewer rights for, and a special tax on, non-Muslims.

187 Ermakov and Mikulskii, 'Islamskaia Partiia Vozrozhdeniia', pp. 190–1.

188 Dudoignon, 'Political Parties and Forces in Tajikistan', pp. 63–4.

189 *Komsomolets Tadzhikistana*, 21 November 1990; Kudryavtsev and Niyazi, '"Politicheskii islam"', p. 115.

190 Niyazi, 'The Year of Tumult', pp. 281–2.

191 The reason for this, according to Usmon, is that 'it is impossible even in principle. We operate within the framework of international law and all-Union legislation … We represent the interests of the faithful Muslims. These interests lie not only in the sphere of religion, but also extend to the political, economic and social realm. But, I would like to stress it once more, our activities take place in strict compliance with the existing legislation … the IRP does not strive to make the political situation in the republic more acute.' See: *Komsomolets Tadzhikistana*, 21 November 1990.

192 The work cited is published in 1993, but it is clear that this is based on work written in late 1990.

193 Niyazi, 'The Year of Tumult', p. 282.

are demanding permission for women to attend sermons in mosques. They are appealing to their coreligionists to live modestly, to be humble and to refrain from wasting money on sumptuous parties at the expense of family well-being. It is having an effect. In many regions people are spending less on weddings, funerals, rituals of circumcision and so on. The consumption of alcohol in rural areas has decreased and Moslems in the towns have also become more moderate in their drinking.

In other words, the fundamentalists have succeeded where the state has failed. A specific example is important here. In the field of politics the Tajik IRP is against any party having a monopoly of power. It seeks to establish a legal state with normal parliamentary activity based on equal rights for all political forces in the republic. It is willing to cooperate with all reasonable political forces, including the communists. The leadership of the party undertakes to act in accordance with international and union laws and condemns nationalism in all its forms.

The official charter and platform of the IRP of Tajikistan were adopted at its October 1991 congress. The published IRP platform[194] included references to the importance of cultural,[195] social,[196] 'moral' and political factors in Tajikistan and advocated national independence, free elections and a multiparty democracy, a 'decent life' for all citizens regardless of religion[197] or ethnicity, and education of the people in Islamic principles. The platform reaches beyond religious and moral advocacy, and includes full sections on the economy, science and culture, ideology, health, and environmental protection. The call for democratic independence is clearly stressed:[198]

> The IRP stands for a multiparty system and free competition for the party. The IRP maintains links with all the democratic forces of the Republic and with all the democratic and Islamic movements from foreign countries.

---

194   Islamic Revival Party, 'Programma Islamskoi Partii Vozrozhdeniia Tadzhikistana' [26 October 1991], in *'Tadzhikskaia Revolyustiia' i Grazhdanskaia Voina (1989–1994 gg.)*, eds V. I. Bushkov and D. V. Mikulskii (Moscow: Rossiyskaia Akademiia Nauk, 1995), pp. 183–90.

195   In particular, the IRP program defends local/ethnic traditions, stressing that 'our national traditions did not differ from Islam nor do they contradict Islam'. See: Islamic Revival Party, 'Programma Islamskoi Partii Vozrozhdeniia Tadzhikistana', p. 187.

196   In the dedicated section on the 'social sphere', the IRP advocates for the '[p]rovision of basic needs for shelter, food, clothing, purchase of medicines, education, parenting, family formation', regardless of religion or ethnicity. See: Islamic Revival Party, 'Programma Islamskoi Partii Vozrozhdeniia Tadzhikistana', pp. 188–9.

197   Specifically, the program states that the IRP '[r]ecognises all heavenly religions and is sympathetic to their followers'. See: Islamic Revival Party, 'Programma Islamskoi Partii Vozrozhdeniia Tadzhikistana', p. 188. Also see the above footnote.

198   Islamic Revival Party, 'Programma Islamskoi Partii Vozrozhdeniia Tadzhikistana', p. 185.

The IRP calls for the unity of all parties and movements in order to cooperate for the sake of independence and national freedom in the name of liquidating all vestiges of colonial dependence.

Islam is, however, mentioned first, last and most often—even beyond the affirmations of some of the basic tenets of Islam. The program opens with these two lines:[199] 'IRP develops its program based on pure Islamic religion. Islam for us is a law and a guide for all political issues. The overriding purpose of IRP is the implementation of education of the people on the principles of Muslim religion.'

The most important point is inserted as a main point in the section on 'ideology', wherein the IRP states that it 'recognises no law that contradicts the *shari'a*';[200] however, the IRP does not publicly state in its program what exactly it believes 'contradicts the *shari'a*'. As for how the IRP would restructure the state and society, Kudryavtsev and Niyazi stress that the leaders of the Tajik IRP 'made no secret … [of] their ultimate goal—adoption of an independent Islamic republic of Tajikistan'.[201] As late as 1991–92, the IRP's goal was the creation—but not immediately—of an Islamic state. This was to be achieved, according to the IRP, through an election victory and then a referendum; however, this desired end-state was modified when the IRP realised that this goal was not supported by many people in Tajikistan.[202] During the lead-up to the civil war, representatives of the IRP, as well as *Qozi* Turajonzoda, stated to audiences both foreign and domestic (including when addressing supporters) that an Islamic state, however desirable in the long term, could not be a model for Tajikistan in the near term as the people were not ready, nor did they want it.[203] Khalid argues that at this time the focus of the IRP leadership was 'on breaking the hold of the incumbent elites on power—rather than on imposing Islamic law or Islamic norms on society'.[204] The Henry Dunant Centre notes that in official party statements the IRP stressed that it would take 50 to 60 years to accomplish their goal of educating 'the people in the Islamic spirit', but that 'many had the impression that the opposition was not going to wait that long'.[205]

---

199   Islamic Revival Party, 'Programma Islamskoi Partii Vozrozhdeniia Tadzhikistana', p. 184.
200   Islamic Revival Party, 'Programma Islamskoi Partii Vozrozhdeniia Tadzhikistana', p. 188.
201   Kudryavtsev and Niyazi, '"Politicheskii islam"', p. 116.
202   Sergei Gretsky, 'Civil War in Tajikistan: Causes, Developments, and Prospects for Peace', in *Central Asia: Conflict, Resolution, and Change*, eds Roald Z. Sagdeev and Susan Eisenhower (Chevy Chase, Md: CPSS Press, 1995), p. 237; Kilavuz, *Understanding Violent Conflict*, pp. 139–41; Roy, 'Is the Conflict in Tajikistan a Model for Conflicts throughout Central Asia', p. 134; Atkin, 'Tajikistan', p. 611; Khalid, *Islam after Communism*, p. 147.
203   Atkin, 'Tajikistan's Relations with Iran and Afghanistan', p. 100; Atkin, 'Tajikistan', p. 616; Niyazi, 'The Year of Tumult', p. 279. As Tett noted about the Tajiks she studied: 'On the one hand, most of the villagers said that they were delighted that the mosques and mullahs were operating freely. But on the other hand, they insisted that they were vehemently opposed both to the Islamic "fundamentalists" and to any suggestion of an Islamic state.' See: Tett, *Ambiguous Alliances*, p. 201.
204   Khalid, *Islam after Communism*, pp. 151–2.
205   Henry Dunant Centre, 'Humanitarian Engagement with Armed Groups', p. 9.

Atkin writes that in response to the IRP's attempt to portray itself as a moderate organisation willing to work in cooperation with other political forces, the incumbent political elites and their supporters framed the post-independence political struggle as one of 'modern, secular democracy against radical Islamicizers, who[se] secular coalition partners were mere window dressing'.[206] A decade later Davlat Usmon, the former IRP deputy leader, was still ambiguous regarding the goals of the IRP when he remarked that '[t]he mistake of the Islamic opposition was that at the beginning it expressed its opinions too clearly. It frightened Russia and neighbouring Uzbekistan.'[207] Within Tajikistan the rejection of an Islamic state is shown clearly in two polls conducted in late 1991 and mid 1992.[208] The key findings from the respondents in Tajikistan were[209]

- in 1991–92, 'Islamicisation in Tajikistan' was supported by only 5–6 per cent while 74–77 per cent of respondents wanted to 'preserve the secular state'
- in 1992, 18.6 per cent of respondents in Qurghonteppa Province and 14.7 per cent in Dushanbe 'supported the idea of establishing an Islamic republic in Tajikistan. However, this idea was almost fully rejected in Leninabad and Kulab oblasts, as well as in Gissar [Hisor] and Tursunzade.'

The increase in support for an Islamic state in Dushanbe and Qurghonteppa over the national average shown in the above statistics also corresponds with the level of support for the IRP voiced by respondents, of 17.5 per cent in Qurghonteppa Province and 18.4 per cent in Dushanbe.[210] The scepticism of the potential for an Islamic state in Tajikistan was summarised by Asliddin Sohibnazarov of the Democratic Party of Tajikistan: 'It would be easier to build communism in America than to create an Islamic republic in Tajikistan.'[211]

---

206   Atkin, 'Tajikistan', p. 616.

207   Henry Dunant Centre, 'Humanitarian Engagement with Armed Groups', p. 9.

208   Regarding these polls, Grigorii Kosach writes: 'In October–November 1991 and in June 1992, the Moscow-based Russian Academy of Management conducted sociological surveys in Tajikistan. They covered the north of the republic (Leninabad oblast) Kurgan-Tiube and Kulab Oblasts in the south, the capital, Dushanbe, and several of its neighboring towns and raions, such as Tursunzade and Gissar. Despite all the errors, which are unavoidable in this type of work, these surveys obtained information on the social base of the political parties which can be considered generally accurate.' See: Kosach, 'Tajikistan', pp. 133–4.

209   Kosach continues: 'Sixteen per cent of respondents in the technical professions, 10.9 per cent of professionals, and 9.3 per cent of the students favoured Islamicization. This was resolutely opposed by industrial workers and the government apparatus.' See: Kosach, 'Tajikistan', pp. 134–6, citing *Ozhidaniia i nadezhdy liudei v usloviiakh stanovleniia gosudarstvennosti*, pp. 29–43.

210   Kosach, 'Tajikistan'.

211   Chris Bowers and John Rettie, 'Russia Reinforces Embattled Russian Garrison', *The Guardian* (30 September 1992), p. 7.

Regional Support Base

Since the late 1970s the network of 'non-official *ulama*' that would go on to form the IRP was active mainly in the mountainous areas of Qarotegin/Gharm and the lower Vakhsh Valley,[212] with Qurghonteppa City as its original base.[213] In late 1990 Niyazi described the IRP as having a rural support base and being 'headed mostly by young unregistered spiritual teachers'.[214] Tajikistan, however, was not an easy recruiting ground for an Islamist organisation, aside from the obvious restrictions of the Soviet era on independent political and religious activity. Dudoignon argues that the rural nature of Tajikistan made it difficult for Islamists to recruit, as their successes have usually been in urban areas. He goes on to note the history of 'problematic relations' between the IRP leadership and the 'traditional religious elites' in rural Tajikistan, especially those affiliated with the official *Qoziyot* who also had a following among Gharmi Tajiks.[215] This may have hindered the IRP in its recruitment; however, the IRP did manage to create a politically significant support base. Its original support base had a significant number of teachers and students who were educated in the city, yet who had a rural background.[216] Other sources point instead to unofficial mullahs recruiting young men as being more important.[217] Nevertheless, the IRP developed a base that was heavily skewed towards one region. The IRP had a significant presence in Mastchoh in northern Tajikistan, Khovaling in the northern Kulob region, in the Gharm/Qarotegin region and among the Gharmi/Qarotegini migrants who were sent to the Vakhsh Valley.[218] The broad consensus, however, is that the IRP's strongest support came from Gharmi Tajiks, at home in the Gharm region and especially among the Gharmi migrants in the Vakhsh Valley,[219] leading the party

---

212   Dudoignon, 'Communal Solidarity and Social Conflicts in Late 20th Century Central Asia', p. 11. Dudoignon also notes the 'strong links with the non-official madrasas of the Ferghana valley, in Uzbekistan'.
213   Nuri, 'Hizbe, ki resha dar ormoni mardum dorad', p. 156.
214   Niyazi, 'The Year of Tumult', p. 281. This article was published in 1993 based on Niyazi's earlier work from late 1990.
215   Dudoignon, 'Communal Solidarity and Social Conflicts in Late 20th Century Central Asia', pp. 11–12, citing V. I. Bushkov & D. V. Mikulskii, *Anatomija grazhdanskoi voiny v Tadzhikistane*, pp. 106–14; Dudoignon, 'Political Parties and Forces in Tajikistan', pp. 66–7. Dudoignon notes that the IRP's main recruiting success in Dushanbe in the early part of the civil war was partly due to the number of rural refugees flooding into Dushanbe.
216   Matveeva, 'The Perils of Emerging Statehood', p. 9, citing Giampaolo R. Capisani, *The Handbook of Central Asia: A Comprehensive Survey of the New Republics* (London: I. B. Tauris, 2000), pp. 161–204.
217   Rubin, 'Russian Hegemony and State Breakdown in the Periphery', p. 143.
218   Dudoignon, 'From Ambivalence to Ambiguity', p. 126. Akiner and Barnes also note the IRP had some success among 'marginalized urban youth'. Akiner and Barnes, 'The Tajik Civil War', p. 20.
219   Olimova and Olimov, 'The Islamic Renaissance Party', p. 26; Akiner and Barnes, 'The Tajik Civil War', p. 20; Roy, *The New Central Asia*, p. 156; Roy, 'Is the Conflict in Tajikistan a Model for Conflicts throughout Central Asia', p. 139; Rubin, 'Russian Hegemony and State Breakdown in the Periphery', p. 143; Dudoignon, 'Communal Solidarity and Social Conflicts in Late 20th Century Central Asia', pp. 11–12, citing Bushkov and Mikulskii, *Anatomia grazhdanskoi voiny v Tadzhikistane*, pp. 106–14; Freizer, 'Central Asian Fragmented Civil Society', p. 117; Said Akhmedov, 'Konflikty v Tadzhikistane: Prichiny i Posledstviia', in *Etnicheskie i regionalnye konflikty v Yevrazii. Volume 1: Tsentralnaia Aziia i Kavkaz*, eds Alexei Malashenko, Bruno Coppieters and Dmitri Trenin (Moscow: Ves Mir, 1997) n.p., online: <http://poli.vub.ac.be/publi/etni-1/

to become a platform for the interests of Gharmis/Qaroteginis, with the majority of that community supporting the IRP.[220] The authors cited above who point to a Gharmi regional agenda in the IRP generally, with some exceptions,[221] do not provide details of how this pro-Gharmi agenda manifested during the latter half of 1991 and through late spring 1992. Since the IRP was not in any position of power until they received a share of the positions in the Government of National Reconciliation (GNR), there were few opportunities to use government structures to benefit Gharmi interests; however, the perception of the IRP as a 'vehicle' of Gharmi interests would have been sufficient to discourage most non-Gharmis from joining. The overwhelming dominance of Gharmis in the leadership[222] and in the base of support would suffice to create this perception. If there was any doubt about the IRP leadership's regional agenda, the summer 1992 cleansing of Kulobis from IRP third-in-command Nuri's home collective farm would most likely have solidified people's perceptions of the IRP as a Gharmi organisation.

The simple explanation that Gharmis were more religious than the Kulobis—leading the former community to rally to the IRP—is rejected by Roy, but with a weak supporting argument.[223] Niyazi, on the religiosity of the Gharmis, writes that 'communal patriarchal relations and ties were strong, and age-old customs were held in high esteem. The local population was marked by a particular piety.'[224] Nuri's views are far closer to Niyazi's outside assessment, demonstrated clearly by his answer to the question of why an Islamic movement appeared

---

akhmedov.htm> Mullojonov also mentions that the IRP was strongest amongst Gharmis in their home region and amongst those forcibly resettled from Gharm; but he also mentions support for the IRP in a few suburbs of Dushanbe. See: Mullojonov, 'The Islamic Clergy in Tajikistan Since the End of the Soviet Period', pp. 233–4, 250. Regarding the north, Mullojonov writes: 'Because of its anticommunist inspiration, the IRP could not seriously count on the northern regions of the republic, where the positions of the ruling Leninabodi clan were monopolistic.'

220   Mullojonov, 'The Islamic Clergy in Tajikistan Since the End of the Soviet Period', p. 250; Olimova and Olimov, 'The Islamic Renaissance Party'; Naumkin, *Radical Islam in Central Asia*, p. 213.

221   In Dushanbe, DPT and IRP activists, after joining the coalition government, attempted to nationalise the 'joint ventures' created the previous winter by Khujandi and Kulobi elites. See: Dudoignon, 'Communal Solidarity and Social Conflicts in Late 20th Century Central Asia', p. 19.

222   In regards to the second deputy leader, Sayid Ibrohim Hadoev—a Kulobi—nothing further was heard from him after his selection at the IRP conference in late 1991.

223   Roy, *The New Central Asia*, p. 156. Roy discusses the Gharmi dominance in the IRP: 'This does not necessarily mean that the Gharmis were more religious than their Kulabi adversaries: we have seen the role played by the Kulabis in the basmachi war. The Kulabis also experienced a religious revivalism: during his report to the Twentieth Congress of the Tajik Communist Party in January 1986, the secretary Mahkamov denounced the shortcomings of atheist policy, and explicitly attacked the two provinces of Kulab and Kurgan-Teppe.'

224   Niyazi, 'Tajikistan I', p. 151. Similarly, Igor Rotar remarks that 'Karategin is a very special region of Tajikistan. People here are much more religious than elsewhere in the whole of Central Asia.' See: Igor Rotar, 'View Central Asia through the Eyes of Journalist Igor Rotar', *Ferghana News Information Agency* (26 April 2011), Accessed online May 2001: <http://enews.fergananews.com/article.php?id=2708>

'solely' in the Vakhsh Valley. Nuri, as a clearly unabashedly patriotic Gharmi, mainly credits the Gharmi population's religiosity with the group's success in mobilising in the Vakhsh Valley:[225]

> This is a good question. As a matter of fact, at the time when our organisation or movement was coming into being, one is amazed as to why it originated in, or why it was established in, that place. I think that the main reason is this, that 60% of the inhabitants of the Vakhsh Valley are composed of people from the Qarotegin and Vakhyo Valleys [that is, the former Gharm Province], and from ancient times, compared with people of the other areas of *Movarounnahr* [Central Asia], they more so fell in love with Islam, were involved with Islam, and established the revealed religion of Islam—and amongst them were many scholars of *sharia* studies. On the other hand, these people had a boundless/ incomparable desire, striving and love for the religion of Islam—their children more so took to Islamic studies and education. And in this way they continued. Another reason is that these people, as a result of ability and hard work, had become very well-off and wealthy and sent their children to the city of Dushanbe and other Islamic cultural centres. As a result, these students advanced and became skilled. From Dushanbe, where a majority of the young students of the Vakhsh Valley studied Islamic science and education, they returned to their places of birth. Amongst them were very many enlightened and freedom-loving people.

Others point instead to political and economic reasons for the Gharmi dominance in the IRP. An important event occurred around mid 1990 when the government introduced export restrictions and price controls on farm products—changes that hurt the farming communities of the Vakhsh Valley. After this, 'young radical activists' of the IRP (as well as of the DPT) began to 'openly advocate' for the resettled population of the Vakhsh and for the mountain populations—both of which are predominantly Gharmi—against the 'technocrats of the planned economy'.[226] Dudoignon argues that by late 1991 '[t]he *Nahzat* [IRP] changed quickly its social status during and after the November 1991 presidential elections, transforming itself from a mass organization of urban youth in [sic] a party of sufi notables with a strong basis in the Dushanbe-Kafirnihan region and in Qarategin [Gharm]'.[227] Dudoignon does not say, however, whether this was a simple IRP strategy to gain more support in this community or if it was a reflection of the IRP leadership's region of origin.

---

225 Nuri, 'Hizbe, ki resha dar ormoni mardum dorad', p. 157. The question was prompted by Nuri's singling out of Qurghonteppa City and the Vakhsh Valley as his group's centre. See: ibid., p. 156.

226 Dudoignon, 'Communal Solidarity and Social Conflicts in Late 20th Century Central Asia', p. 12.

227 Dudoignon, 'Communal Solidarity and Social Conflicts in Late 20th Century Central Asia', pp. 16–17. Dudoignon continues: 'But in doing so, the *Nahzat* lost all interest as a political instrument for Moscow. From

Niyazi certainly is of the opinion that many religious leaders had a Gharmi regional agenda, even if it was borne of the noblest intentions: 'the political struggle of Islamic nonconformists was not conducted to establish the rule of the clergy, but in the first instance for a wider representation of the mountain-dwellers in the structures of power and against the violence being done by the industry minded elite on traditional culture.'[228] More cynical political motivations on the part of Gharmi government elites from outside the IRP are cited by authors such as Olimova, who argues that the Gharmi/Qarotegini 'regional elites, having achieved economic clout, sought to change the balance of forces in their own interest and used the newly emerging opposition movements to this end'.[229] Regional elites from the Pamirs and Gharm increasingly began to use the political parties and the Gorbachev reforms to make political gains as the government appointed mostly Pamiri and Gharmi reformists to the newly vacated positions. Soon, as argued by Olimova, 'regional origin exerted a major influence on the choice of behavioural strategy of the new elites', while support for or opposition to the 'Soviet imperial centre' was 'determined by regional affiliation'.[230] The strength of the IRP among Gharmis was matched by the dominance of Gharmis in the leadership of the IRP. For example, the three most powerful party leaders (Nuri, Himmatzoda and Usmon) were all Gharmi Tajiks.[231] There is also the possibility that the IRP's core from the very beginning was Gharmi. Nuri himself proudly described the important role played by Vakhsh Valley *muhajirs* from Qarotegin and Darvoz (that is, Gharm Province) in the initial formation of the network that would go on to be the basis for the IRP.[232] As networks of solidarity in Tajikistan so often form along lines of blood relations, the likelihood that the early precursors to the IRP did the same is high. Indeed, the IRP was especially keen to use traditional organisational structures: in 1992, 12 members of the Ulama Council of the IRP belonged to one *gashtak*, and functionaries at lower levels were habitually heads of kinship entities in their respective territories.[233] With many Gharmi elites in the IRP and the base of support being largely Gharmi, the party soon became a vehicle for the interests of Gharmis. The ideology of the IRP mixed with regional political issues, leading members from other regions to withdraw from the party.[234]

then on, Russia would deal mainly with the technocrats and the liberal intellectuals of the elder generation, who appeared to the Kremlin as the best possible advocates of continuity, in front of the now combined threats of nationalism and fundamentalism.'

228 Niyazi, 'Islam and Tajikistan's Human and Ecological Crisis', p. 190. Niyazi speaks glowingly of Gharm: 'The mullahs and ishans here have become renowned for their knowledge of Islamic sciences, and the population is notable for its piety. More than 95% of Garm Tajiks are peasants or craftsmen. Communal and patriarchal ties are strong. Traditional morals—*adab*—are honored. It was no accident that in the 1980s the crime rate in this region was the lowest in the republic.' See: ibid., p. 189.

229 Olimova, 'Opposition in Tajikistan', p. 249. Olimova also notes this strategy among Pamiri elites.

230 Olimova, 'Opposition in Tajikistan', p. 249.

231 Abdullaev and Akbarzadeh, *Historical Dictionary of Tajikistan*, pp. 158–9, 258–9, 368–9.

232 See the section above on the early roots of the IRP.

233 Bushkov and Mikulskii, 'Obschestvenno-politicheskaia situatsiia v Tadzhikistane', p. 8.

234 Olimova and Olimov, 'The Islamic Renaissance Party', p. 26; Roy, *The New Central Asia*, p. 156; Erica Marat, 'The State–Crime Nexus in Central Asia: State Weakness, Organized Crime, and Corruption in

Competition and Cooperation: *Qozi* Turajonzoda

[O]ur hopes can come true when there is a veritable democratic, rule-of-law and, however strange one may find it, secular state. As [a] Muslim leader, I certainly dream of living in a state governed by the laws of Islam, but, if one is realistic, one should realize that our society is not yet ready for this.

— *Qozi* Turajonzoda, September 1992[235]

The IRP did not and does not hold a monopoly in terms of Islamic leadership. Other leaders have been able to wield influence and attract supporters. The most prominent was and still is *Hoji* Akbar Turajonzoda. Turajonzoda was born Akbar Qaharov in 1954 near Vahdat (Kofarnihon) in the village of Turkobod, about 30 km from Dushanbe. Turajonzoda traces his prominent Sufi family lineage seven generations back to Samarkand. His grandfather, Sufi Abdukarim, was a Sufi leader exiled to Siberia in the 1930s, while his father, Ishon Turajon, was a Sufi *ishon* who possibly had as many as 1000 *murids* (committed followers). At age eighteen, Turajonzoda was sent to study at the Mir-i Arab *madrasa* in Bukhara. Afterwards he went on to study at the Islamic Institute in Tashkent before going to Jordan to study Islamic law at Amman University as one of a few officially approved students from the Soviet Union. After returning, he worked for the Department of International Relations of the Spiritual Directorate of the Muslims of Central Asia and Kazakhstan (SADUM).[236] He was appointed as the *Qozikalon* (the highest rank of Islamic judge/administrator in the *Qoziyot*)[237] of Tajikistan in 1988 at the age of only thirty-four. In 1990 he took on the additional position as a deputy in the Supreme Soviet of Tajikistan.[238] At this time the leaders of the

---

Kyrgyzstan and Tajikistan', *Silk Road Paper* (October 2006), p. 106.

235   Quote from an interview with Turajonzoda. See: *ITAR-Tass*, 1252 gmt (16 September 1992), in *SWB SU*, 1490 (19 September 1992).

236   This Russian acronym is most commonly used. SADUM was the Soviet governing body for religious affairs, literally the 'Spiritual Administration for the Muslims of Central Asia and Kazakhstan'. For a more complete description, see Khalid, *Islam after Communism*, esp. pp. 78–9, 110–14.

237   The *Qoziyot* was the official Islamic administrative body in Tajikistan.

238   Niyazi, 'Islam and Tajikistan's Human and Ecological Crisis', p. 196, n. 13; Dudoignon, 'Communal Solidarity and Social Conflicts in Late 20th Century Central Asia', pp. 11–12; Kilavuz, *Understanding Violent Conflict*, p. 169; Whitlock, *Land Beyond the River*, pp. 143–6; Conciliation Resources, 'Profiles: Khoji Akbar Turajonzoda', Accessed online March 2009: <http://www.c-r.org/our-work/accord/tajikistan/profiles.php>; Sergei Gretsky, 'Qadi Akbar Turajonzoda', *Central Asia Monitor*, No. 1 (1994), p. 16; Roy, *The New Central Asia*, p. 149. Whitlock maintains that Turajonzoda read Muslim Brotherhood literature while in Jordan. Also, Whitlock writes that he was in Jordan from 1982 to 1987 while Conciliation Resources instead gives the dates as the late 1970s to early 1980s. Kilavuz refers to Turajonzoda's Sufi lineage as being Naqshbandi while Dudoignon and Roy instead mention the Qadiri Sufi order. Turajonzoda's father, *ishon* Turajon, was a disciple of the prominent Sufi leader *mavlavi* Said Qalandarshoh from Qandahar in Afghanistan, who eventually made him a powerful Naqshbandi leader of Kofarnikhon, Gharm and Qarotegin. The IRP chairman, Mohammadsharif Himmatzoda, born in Gharm in 1951, spent his formative years in a village adjacent to Turkobod and knew

officially endorsed Islamic bodies were supportive of the government as they were dependent on it for their careers. This was reinforced in September 1990 with a *Qoziyot* decree/treaty agreement with the *imam khotibs* (top imams) of local mosques forbidding participation in politics, with a specific prohibition against membership of any political party—likely a response to the recent appeal by the union-wide IRP for the *ulama* to become involved in politics.[239]

For a short period, Turajonzoda had been a student of Muhammadjon Hindustoni[240] and had, in 1983 or 1984, met Sayid Abdullo Nuri, the eventual leader of the IRP. When Nuri was released from jail in 1988, Turajonzoda hired him as the editor for the official newspaper of the *Qoziyot*, *Minbar-i Islom* ('Tribune of Islam').[241] Despite whatever relationship Turajonzoda may have had with Nuri, he was disinclined to endorse the IRP as it 'advocated a different path to Muslim revival' and was a threat to his power as *Qozikalon* as it was a political party that advertised itself as the 'vehicle of revival' rather than the *Qoziyot*.[242] Kilavuz qualifies this competition:[243]

> A dispute emerged between the traditionalists and the IRP over the latter's status as an Islamic party, which the traditionalists saw as contrary to Islam. They did not object to existing relations between state and religion, or approve of the direct involvement of religion in politics. Accordingly, they accused the IRP of disrespecting or betraying Sunni Hanafi tradition. The Qazi had good relations both with the IRP and the traditionalists, who were composed mostly of Naqshbandi and Qadiri Ishans. Although these groups were suspicious of each other, in September 1991 Turajonzoda was able to convince them to unite against

Turajonzoda well. Himmatzoda introduced Said Abdullo Nuri to Turajonzoda, and the latter entrusted Nuri with editing the *Qoziyot*'s newspaper. According to some sources, the IRP deputy chairman, Davlat Usmon, is a distant relative of Turajonzoda.

239   Alexander Karpov, 'The Clergy is Outside [Political] Parties', *Izvestiia* (25 September 1990), p. 2, in *The Russian Press Digest* (25 September 1992); Niyazi, 'The Year of Tumult', pp. 280–1. Niyazi notes that some official religious leaders' support for the government increased as they were the target of accusations of wrongdoing by the 'fundamentalists'; however, he also notes that some were supportive of the 'fundamentalists'. In regards to the *ulama* being dependent on the state, see also: Makhamov, 'Islam and the Political Development of Tajikistan after 1985', p. 200.

240   A full discussion of Hindustani is included in the analysis on IRP influences.

241   Whitlock, *Land Beyond the River*, p. 143; Kilavuz, *Understanding Violent Conflict*, p. 170.

242   Conciliation Resources, 'Profiles: Khoji Akbar Turajonzoda'. There is some disagreement on the communities in which Turajonzoda and the IRP's popularity overlapped. Dudoignon stresses that Turajonzoda's *Qoziyot* was in competition with the IRP for the loyalty of believers, with both entities having their main base of support in Gharm and amongst the Gharmi communities in the Vakhsh Valley. See: Dudoignon, 'Communal Solidarity and Social Conflicts in Late 20th Century Central Asia', pp. 11–12, citing Bushkov and Mikulskii, *Anatomiia grazhdanskoi voiny v Tadzhikistane*, pp. 106–14; Dudoignon, 'Political Parties and Forces in Tajikistan', p. 64. On the other side, Vitaly Naumkin writes that Turajonzoda 'was especially popular in Zerafshan, Aini, and Matcha and also among a part of the population of Dushanbe; but contrary to the opinion of certain researchers, he did not command a support base in the Gharm group of regions—Karategin, Tavildara, Kofarnihon—and in the Leninabad region, nor did he fully control any sizable part of Dushanbe's population.' See: Naumkin, *Radical Islam in Central Asia*, p. 215.

243   Kilavuz, *Understanding Violent Conflict*, pp. 170–1.

the government. His intervention helped prevent a possible clash between the 'official' imams of the mosques, and the 'unofficial' mullahs and the political wing of Islam represented by the IRP. He was a figure who could be accepted by both sides, and who had relationships with all relevant groups.

Initially, Turajonzoda maintained a distance from the IRP and the opposition parties and continued instead to work from within the government as a deputy and as the *Qozikalon*.[244] In December 1990, Qahhor Mahkamov held an unprecedented conference with influential mullahs, where he said, in particular:

> [W]e treat religious sentiments and requests of the believers with great respect. Only during the past year—year and a half—in excess of 70 mosques and hundreds of meeting-houses were built, and an Islamic Institute was opened in the republic … In the nearest future we shall create a consultative group together with you and … subject to good will and mutual compromise, we shall be able to solve rather complicated issues in a humane and good-natured manner.[245]

The *Qozikalon* expressed appreciation of the government's efforts, but at the same time put forward several demands, the implementation of which, according to him, 'would be conducive to further strengthening of public confidence in the leadership of the republic'.[246] They included

- proclaiming high days of Islam public holidays
- shifting the weekly day off to Friday
- introducing the Quranic method of cattle slaughter (*halal*)
- exempting mosques and other holy places from taxation.

In the meantime, the official Islamic clergy promised not to support the IRP. Turajonzoda made the following public announcement:

> We have stressed more than once that Islam is a party in its own … The emergence of various parties in any state that call themselves 'Islamic society,' 'Islamic party,' 'Islamic renaissance' and so on, has led to the

---

244 Kilavuz, *Understanding Violent Conflict*, p. 171. Similarly, Atkin writes: 'The country's most influential religious figure, Qadi Akbar Turajonzoda, was not a member of any political party but supported political and economic reforms as well as recognition of Muslims' rights to practise their faith openly and without hindrance.' See: Atkin, 'Tajikistan', p. 611. In regards to the religious leadership in general, Makhamov writes: 'soon the *ulamas* registered their displeasure with the fact that the government allowed them only the opportunity to engage in purely religious matters. They wanted to determine state policy, insisting on transforming Tajikistan into an independent Muslim state.' See: Makhamov, 'Islam and the Political Development of Tajikistan after 1985', pp. 200–1.

245 *Kommunist Tadzhikistana*, 9 January 1991.

246 *Kommunist Tadzhikistana*, 9 January 1991.

weakening and dispersal of the Muslims. Taking this into consideration, the *Qoziyot* administration has made efforts to guarantee and preserve the Muslims' unity.[247]

Those few *imams* who explicitly denounced the activities of the IRP in Tajikistan won a reprieve from the Muslim spiritual board.[248]

The turning point was when Turajonzoda's proposals in the Supreme Soviet—regarding religious holidays, observance of Friday as a non-working day, *halal* regulations in abattoirs and land tax breaks for mosques—all failed.[249] In late 1991, Turajonzoda and the IRP had a 'rapprochement and then alliance' as the *Qozikalon* announced his support for the opposition demands.[250] As Mahkamov's administration was in no hurry to cater to the aforementioned demands of the *Qoziyot*, Turajonzoda gradually abandoned his neutrality. As Turajonzoda wrote in 1995,

> [T]here was a serious need to establish a political party for Muslims ... The IRP through its official activities intended to play a role in the spiritual self-realisation and development of the nation and to defend the rights and demands of Muslims, who constitute the majority of the country's population.[251]

Turajonzoda had, from late 1991, a moderating influence on the IRP, as argued by Dudoignon.[252]

The rapprochement between the *Qozikalon* and the Islamists was not unexpected—they had essentially the same power base. Aziz Niyazi thus characterised the IRP: 'These were mainly peasants and part of the town population from the Gharmi group of regions, or people who were originally from these regions who are now living in the Qurghonteppa *oblast*, Hissor Valley, Leninsky *raion*, and the city of Dushanbe.'[253] On the other hand, it was well known that 'the Supreme *Qozi* in his day-to-day activities relies on fellow-regionalists[254] from Gharm, which stirs resentment in other regions of Tajikistan'.[255] While one may

---

247 *Javononi Tojikiston*, 29 January 1991.
248 *Komsomolskaia pravda*, 23 March 1991.
249 Kilavuz, *Understanding Violent Conflict*, p. 171.
250 Mullojonov, 'The Islamic Clergy in Tajikistan Since the End of the Soviet Period', p. 237, n. 25.
251 Akbar Turajonzoda, 'Tajikistan—Politics, Religion, and Peace: A View from the Opposition', *Problems of Post-Communism* (July–August 1995), p. 25.
252 Dudoignon writes: 'At the same time, the increasing influence of qaziyat and its leader Hajji Akbar Turajanzada among the opposition favored the phenomenon of "deradicalization" of the Islamist party itself.' See: Dudoignon, 'Communal Solidarity and Social Conflicts in Late 20th Century Central Asia', p. 16.
253 Niyazi, 'Tajikistan', p. 183.
254 Referring to Turajonzoda as a Gharmi would require overstretching the definition of Gharm to include everything east of Dushanbe.
255 Bushkov and Mikulskii, 'Obschestvenno-politicheskaia situatsiia v Tadzhikistane', p. 24. Dudoignon also notes the dominance of 'Kuhistanians' (that is, Gharmis) in the *Qoziyot*, but rejects the idea that Turajonzoda had any regional agenda strategy. See: Dudoignon, 'Communal Solidarity and Social Conflicts in Late 20th Century Central Asia', p. 23.

question Narzullo Dustov's opinion that Turajonzoda 'organically hated the people of Kulob',[256] there is ample evidence of a strained relationship between Turajonzoda and religious figures in Kulob and Leninobod, especially in early 1991 when the *Qozikalon* attempted to replace Kulob's spiritual leader, Haydar Sharifzoda, with his own loyal appointee, Mullah Abdurrahim. Not only did Sharifzoda successfully repel this attack, he actually secured confirmation of his investiture directly from the SADUM, thus gaining autonomy from the *Qoziyot*.[257] In the Leninobod *oblast*, the congregations intensely disliked Turajonzoda's appointees, believing them (as well as their high-placed patron) to be 'spoiled' by years of study in Uzbekistan.[258]

* * *

By mid 1991, in many areas of central and southern Tajikistan, it had become difficult to distinguish between official and unofficial mullahs, the IRP functionaries and traditional strongmen. They had all coalesced into a somewhat obfuscated yet potent entity with a common background and agenda (Gharmi regionalism), ideology (Islam) and organisational principles (traditional consanguinal structures and *gashtaks*). Loosely called the 'Islamic opposition', it possessed tremendous organisational and financial resources,[259] and was preparing to play a more active part in political struggle. Once again, it is imperative to reiterate that 'the use of Islam by a political opposition, and indeed the mere emergence of an opposition, became possible only under conditions of relative democratisation, and then not so much in the Muslim provinces as at the centre'.[260]

---

256   Dustov, *Zakhm bar jismi vatan*, p. 14.

257   Nasriddinov, *Tarkish*, p. 147.

258   Interview with *hoji* Husain Musoev, *sarkhatib* of the Leninobod *viloyat*, 9 March 1995.

259   Apart from private donations, profits from commercial activities and foreign assistance, tax-deductible transfers from various institutions formed an important part of the Islamic establishment's income. In 1991, the Vakhsh chemical fertiliser plant alone transferred US$100 000 to the *Qoziyot* for 'charitable' purposes. See: Kenjaev, *Tabadduloti Tojikiston*, Vol. I, p. 116. By the end of 1991, declared cash reserves of the *Qoziyot* alone had reached an impressive 9.4 million roubles. See: V. I. Bushkov and D. V. Mikulskii, *Istoriia grazhdanskoi voiny v Tadzhikistane (etno-sotsial'nye protsessy i politicheskaya bor'ba, 1992–1995)* (Moscow: Institut etnologii i antropologii RAN, 1996), p. 103.

260   Malashenko, 'The Eighties', pp. 31–2.

9. From Political Confrontation to Civil War, 1991–1992

The immediate consequence of Gorbachev's political reforms in Tajikistan was a constant flux in the rules of the political game. The transition from a mono-organisational type of national elite to a disunified one was well advanced. Additionally, non-elite involvement in the political process showed potential for growth: in September 1991, approximately 20 per cent of Tajikistan's population felt that they had been driven to the edge by the deteriorating economic situation,[1] providing radicals from all elite factions with potential followers. The presence of deep cleavages in Tajik society, mainly of a sub-ethnic and regional nature, always suggested the possibility of an acute internal conflict; however, assuming that 'civil wars are about a crisis in national sovereignty, and thus about the ability of nation-states to control national space',[2] it can be argued that the practical realisation of this possibility was conditioned by deliberate acts of (or inaction by) elite leaders affecting the functioning of the state. It was not inevitable that Tajikistan would follow the path of destruction; like the USSR, it 'succumbed to ill-conceived reforms originating in the leadership, to poor governance, and to bad fortune'.[3]

The relatively open social and political environment during the *glasnost* era in the Tajik SSR (late 1980s to 1991) allowed for increased freedom of expression and for the emergence of many new civil society groups and political parties. At the same time that political parties and various independent social groups were forming, the state bureaucracy was being restructured. As mentioned in the previous chapter, Gorbachev's union wide efforts at *perestroika* reforms included attacks on and removals of 'conservative' apparatchiks in favour of 'reformist' cadres who would assist rather than obstruct the implementation of reforms. In Tajikistan this created an intersection of interests whereby pro-*perestroika* reformists in the state bureaucracy were supported by, and in turn supported, the anti-incumbent agendas of the newly emerging political parties and social movements. Another agenda that must be factored into this political environment is that of the regional elites and their local patronage networks. Local elites in Leninobod, Hisor, Kulob, and to a certain extent in Qurghonteppa,[4] worked to maintain their positions in the face of the *perestroika* bureaucratic

---

1 *Sotsialno-politicheskie usloviia perekhoda k rynku v Tadzhikistane (Itogi sotsiologicheskogo analiza)* (Moscow and Dushanbe: Rossiiskaia akademiia upravleniia, 1991), p. 19.

2 Michael Humphrey, 'Lebanon: The "Cellular" Society', in *Lebanon Beyond 2000*, eds Amin Saikal and Geoffrey Jukes (Canberra: Centre for Middle Eastern and Central Asian Studies, ANU, 1997), p. 37.

3 Rush, 'Fortune and Fate', p. 19.

4 In Qurghonteppa this would not include the Gharmi Tajiks, who overwhelmingly supported the opposition parties.

reforms. On the other side, regional elites from the Pamirs and Gharm (including Gharmis in Dushanbe and Qurghonteppa Province) increasingly began to use the political parties and Gorbachev's reforms as a vehicle to make political gains, as the government often appointed Pamiri and Gharmi reformists to newly vacated positions. Soon, region of origin became associated with support for, or opposition to, the *perestroika* reforms—both in the bureaucracy in Dushanbe and in the rural areas where local elites (for example, collective farm bosses and provincial/district leaders) had much to gain or lose from the reforms. In Qurghonteppa, the competition between Gharmi and Kulobi administrators for local government positions and control of collective farms was especially intense.

The competition for state resources and positions of influence continued into the post-Soviet era. At the same time, political parties mobilised in opposition to the incumbent leaders, who also sought to mobilise their own supporters. The combination of an election failure on the part of the opposition, continuing harassment of the opposition and the increased use of large street demonstrations in the capital, plus the reckless rhetoric and actions on both sides, led to an increasingly dangerous political and social atmosphere. The overwhelming belief on the part of both sides—in the face of the mutual security dilemmas—of the need to arm themselves soon turned to escalating violence and eventually open military combat, mainly along the lines of the 'deep cleavages' mentioned above.

The New Institutional Setting and Moscow-Imposed Conflict Regulation

The Extraordinary Session of the Supreme Soviet that sat in two stages from 29 August to 4 October 1991 introduced substantial changes to the political system of the Republic of Tajikistan

- the president was to be elected by popular vote forthwith
- the institution of vice-president was created
- the Cabinet of Ministers was to be formed by the president, but every member of the Cabinet was answerable to the Supreme Soviet
- presidiums of regional legislatures were abolished and, as at the district-town level, the chairman of the executive committee became head of the *oblast* soviet
- the president lost the ability to remove chairmen of executive committees at all levels.

Tajikistan's parliament also addressed the Congress of People's Deputies of the USSR and the Supreme Soviet of the Russian Federation with a passionate plea for help:

> We face a real threat of food and energy crisis, ecological catastrophe and a new escalation of social and ethnic tensions … We are convinced that alone, deprived of our cooperation of many years, we cannot overcome the present deep crisis … We cannot imagine our future outside the Union and without ancient indissoluble ties that linked it [Tajikistan] with Russia and other brotherly republics.[5]

Tajik government elites were quite prepared to cede attributes of independence and sovereignty for the sake of retention of the reformed Soviet Union.

On 31 August 1991, the Supreme Soviet of Tajikistan elected the Gharmi Tajik Qadriddin Aslonov—its current chairman—to serve as interim president until the 24 November presidential elections.[6] Opposition forces, which had insignificant representation in the national legislature, tried to find alternative ways to influence the decision-making process. Rastokhez and the DPT held one meeting after another in front of the Supreme Soviet's building, demanding dissolution of the Supreme Soviet and new elections, the government's resignation and prohibition of the Communist Party of Tajikistan (CPT). The *Qoziyot* and the IRP for the time being refrained from active political action, but, according to Narzullo Dustov, in late August to early September 1991, Akbar Turajonzoda, Tohir Abdujabbor and Dushanbe's mayor, Maqsud Ikromov, held several clandestine meetings with acting president, Qadriddin Aslonov, in his house.[7] The opposition, sensing its offensive advantage, continued to pressure the incumbents. On 21 September, the IRP brought its supporters by bus from the Vakhsh Valley and from the mountains of Gharm/Qarotegin to the city, where they camped.[8] In response (or possibly planned ahead of time), on 22 September, Aslonov 'decided to accommodate the crowds by placing a ban on the activities of the Communist Party and by seizing all its property'.[9] The same day, Mayor Ikromov authorised the removal of Lenin's statue from the central square of Dushanbe, an action that was carried out in front of cheering demonstrators.[10]

---

5   *Kommunist Tadzhikistana*, 3 September 1991.

6   Kilavuz, *Understanding Violent Conflict*, p. 148.

7   Dustov, *Zakhm bar jismi vatan*, pp. 88–9.

8   Whitlock, *Land Beyond the River*, p. 151.

9   Flemming Splidsboel-Hansen, 'The Outbreak and Settlement of Civil War: Neo-Realism and the Case of Tajikistan', *Civil Wars*, Vol. 2, No. 4 (1999), p. 7.

10   Whitlock, *Land Beyond the River*, p. 152; Kilavuz, *Understanding Violent Conflict*, p. 148. Both officials exceeded their powers: an existing political party could have been outlawed only by the Supreme Court of Tajikistan, and the removal of any monument should have been approved by the city soviet.

Instead of merely acting as a caretaker, Aslonov had implemented major reforms (including banning the Communist Party and its activities while legalising the IRP) that 'would destabilize the political situation, and polarize different forces in the republic'.[11] In attempting to ban the activities of the Communist Party, Aslonov was attacking the tool with which the Leninobodis and their junior partners distributed patronage. Previously, the removal of the interior minister and the purge of Kulobis in law enforcement and security bodies (resulting in gains for Pamiris)[12] were significant, as these actions removed the Kulobis' guarantee of law enforcement protection. Now their farm bosses and regional politicians were 'vulnerable to future reforms'.[13] Markowitz cites this vulnerability as the key in the shift from 'disaffection' to defensive mobilisation.[14]

The response of the overwhelming communist majority (94 per cent) in the Supreme Soviet to Aslonov's decrees—reforms that were reached without any consensus among communist leaders—was to force Aslonov out of office on 23 September during an emergency session of the Supreme Soviet and to appoint Rahmon Nabiev, a previous first secretary of the Tajik SSR, to the chairmanship of the Supreme Soviet and to the position of interim president. The Supreme Soviet immediately moved to reverse Aslonov's decrees—re-banning the IRP while reinstating the Communist Party. The Supreme Soviet reintroduced a state of emergency and martial law in Dushanbe and instructed the procurator-general, Nurullo Khuvaydulloev, to investigate the incident with Lenin's monument. In response, the opposition restarted their demonstrations in Dushanbe, this time for three weeks.[15]

On 24 September 1991, the IRP, the DPT and Rastokhez, in defiance of martial law, brought 10 000 people to a demonstration in the capital. This was a well-planned event: the participants had tents, medical units, a press centre and a 300-strong security force; the chairman of the permanent meeting, *imam-khotib* Qosim Rahmonov from Qurghonteppa, admitted to enjoying generous financial and material support from the southern and eastern districts as well as from City Hall.[16] The state of emergency had no effect in Dushanbe as thousands moved

---

11   Kilavuz, *Understanding Violent Conflict*, p. 148.

12   Niyazi writes: 'From 1990 [Pamiris] made a rather impressive addition to the personnel of the Interior Ministry, in the police.' See: Niyazi, 'Tajikistan I', p. 151. Similarly, Roy describes a 'massive entry' of Pamiris into the KGB and Ministry of the Interior in the 1980s. See: Roy, *The New Central Asia*, pp. 106, 114.

13   Markowitz, *Collapsed and Prebendal States in Post-Soviet Eurasia*, pp. 104–5.

14   Markowitz, *Collapsed and Prebendal States in Post-Soviet Eurasia*, pp. 104–5. In regards to the Interior Ministry, Markowitz writes: 'Prior to Makhkamov's appointment of Leninabadi K. Polatov (1986–89), a member of Kuliab's provincial elite, Ismail Kurbonov, held the office (from 1980–86).' See also: Dudoignon, 'Communal Solidarity and Social Conflicts in Late 20th Century Central Asia', pp. 17–18; Zviagelskaya, *The Tajik Conflict*, n.p.; Akhmedov, 'Tajikistan II', p. 175.

15   *Narodnaia gazeta*, 3 October 1991; Markowitz, *Collapsed and Prebendal States in Post-Soviet Eurasia*, p. 106; Kilavuz, *Understanding Violent Conflict*, pp. 125–6, 148–9, 163–4; Splidsboel-Hansen, 'The Outbreak and Settlement of Civil War', pp. 7–8.

16   *Narodnaia gazeta*, 3 October 1991.

into the city to join the protests. This failure on the part of the government is no surprise considering not only the Tajik government's lack of effective security forces, but also that the Soviet military announced that it would not enforce the state of emergency. In response, deputies in the Supreme Soviet voted to end the state of emergency on 30 September 1991.[17]

In addition to its previous demands, the opposition pressed for the resignation of Nabiev, procurator Khuvaydulloev and the chairman of the State Broadcasting Committee, Otakhon Sayfulloev, as well as for the reversal of the Supreme Soviet's decisions made on 23 September. For the first time 'democratic' and 'Islamist' oppositions openly confronted the government as a unified movement; however, some Tajik liberal intellectuals were appalled. According to *Narodnaia gazeta*, the prominent academic Rahim Masov left Rastokhez in protest against the

> chaos unleashed by the meeting frenzy [*mitingovschina*] and the conviction that political goals can be attained through pressure, which conviction is espoused by leaders of various parties who draw in people remote from politics … The meeting, its conduct, the masses of people brought from the districts—not from the city!—mainly the elderly and adolescents … created an impression of a well-directed theatrical performance. Foreign journalists who arrived in Dushanbe somehow discerned a protest of defenders of democracy in what was happening … The clergy had become the moving force, the spring of the events, though democrats and *Rastokhez* posed as its organisers.[18]

The Supreme Soviet's supporters organised parallel demonstrations in Dushanbe, using methods similar to those of the opposition: people were transported to the capital city from Kulob and Hisor on orders from local strongmen. In Leninobod, industrial managers issued warnings to the opposition that unless pressure on the parliament stopped they would go on strike. On 30 September, work in 11 of the largest factories in Khujand stopped. Political turmoil seriously affected Tajikistan's economy, especially agriculture.[19]

In the meantime, Gulrukhsor Safieva, by then a USSR people's deputy, and seven Sufi leaders from Gharm and Qarotegin went on a hunger strike. This move received sympathetic coverage in the Moscow-based media. Telegrams from opposition supporters poured into the Kremlin requesting intervention.[20]

---

17 Splidsboel-Hansen, 'The Outbreak and Settlement of Civil War', p. 8.
18 *Narodnaia gazeta*, 26 October 1991.
19 For example, by 4 October only 28.5 per cent of the cotton crop had been harvested—half of the 1990 figure. See: *Narodnaia gazeta*, 4 October 1991.
20 One of them, signed by eight members of Tajikistan's and the All-Union legislatures, including Davlat Khudonazarov, Bozor Sobir, Akbar Turajonzoda and Asliddin Sohibnazarov, read: 'On 23 September 1991 in the city of Dushanbe reactionary Communist forces set out to restore the totalitarian regime in our republic …

Gorbachev reacted by sending a conciliation team to Dushanbe. The activity of this team formed one of the stranger events in the modern history of Tajikistan and once again highlighted the ineffectual character of Gorbachev as the leader of a multinational state. The team comprised two members of his Political Consultative Committee: St Petersburg's mayor, Anatolii Sobchak, and vice-president of the USSR Academy of Sciences, academician Evgenii Velikhov. Both were ardent reformist democrats but had no experience of Central Asia, so they were accompanied by an advisor, an American citizen, Alexander Yanov, a history professor from the City University of New York. The juridical status of the Sobchak-Velikhov expedition was dubious—it had not been invited by the government of independent Tajikistan, and it had no clearly defined agenda. Velikhov disclosed in October 1991 that the president of the USSR had not bothered to determine their powers or to discuss possible actions and outcomes, and went on with a remarkable narrative of the mission:[21]

> Gorbachev did not hold any briefing with us prior to our departure … we just packed up quickly and flew to Dushanbe … We did not receive any useful information from Yanov … We did not offer any solutions … but we said sternly that we would not go back to Moscow while people starve themselves to death in the square … Though I am not a specialist in this field, I have made the following conclusions, having acquainted myself with the developments *in situ*: I believe, a union between Islam and democracy is necessary in the republic today. And if this union is durable and if its activities are open and understandable for the people, it will be the basis for consolidation of the main forces in the society.

Between 1 and 4 October 1991, Sobchak and Velikhov conducted a series of negotiations with Rahmon Nabiev, the Supreme Soviet leadership, *Qozikalon* Turajonzoda and major opposition figures, and spoke in front of the meeting in Ozodi Square. As a result, most of the opposition's demands were met

- the CPT (which changed its name to the Socialist Party of Tajikistan on 21 September) was suspended for two months pending an investigation of its activities during the coup
- the state of emergency was lifted
- the ban on the formation of religious parties was lifted

During numerous speeches Communist people's deputies befouled the honour and dignity of M. S. Gorbachev, B. N. Yeltsin and other democratic leaders of the Union and Russia, and called them traitors … We ask for your help to build democracy in the republic and request that until it happens, all economic, political and other ties [between Moscow and Dushanbe] be severed.' Quoted in: Dustov, *Zakhm bar jismi vatan*, pp. 115–16.

21   E. Velikhov, 'Nel'zia taschit' liudei na krest—eto kazhdyi reshaet sam', *Glasnost*, No. 42 (October 1991), p. 3. Sobchak said something very similar. See: 'Interview with Anatoly Sobchak, Yevgeny Velikhov and Head of Tajik Moslems Kazi Akbar Turanzhonzada in Dushanbe on October 6, 1991', *Official Kremlin International News Broadcast* (8 October 1991).

- Rahmon Nabiev stepped down as the chairman of the Supreme Soviet for the duration of the presidential race and was replaced with Akbarsho Iskandarov, a Pamiri
- representatives of the DPT, Rastokhez and the *Qoziyot* were included in the Electoral Commission of the Republic of Tajikistan
- presidential elections were postponed from 27 October to 25 November in order to allow opposition parties to campaign properly
- new parliamentary elections were promised, but without setting a specific date.

Sobchak addressed the meeting in front of the Supreme Soviet with the following words: 'Our task is to assist democratic forces and all political movements of the republic to find a common platform, something that would unite you all in order to help the republic start solving its economic and social problems.'[22] A Tajik eyewitness commented on this address as follows:[23]

> People like Sobchak fly here from Leningrad and without understanding anything make speeches in front of Islamists gathered in the square: 'Citizens of Leningrad greet in your presence true democrats. You are the future of Tajikistan. Already the great democrat Herzen said' ... Well, if you ask bearded Gharmis who watch the orator from Leningrad expressionlessly who Herzen is, you are unlikely to get a coherent answer. It is laughable.

While their attempts to rally the crowds may have fallen flat, Sobchak and Velikhov, perhaps, unbeknownst to them, tipped the balance of power in favour of the elite factions from Gharm, Qarotegin and the Pamirs. They had a strong bargaining chip in dealing with the incumbent Tajik leadership: the threat to sever financial support from Moscow. As Yanov frankly admitted, had they been sent with a similar mission to the economically strong Ukraine, they would have achieved nothing.[24] Central Asian leaders, Nazarbaev in particular, severely criticised Sobchak's 'mediation efforts' at the time.[25] Sobchak, while publicly declaring himself to be one of the 'initiators' of the unification of 'democratic forces in the center with the national-democratic movements in the republics', also acknowledged the important divides in Tajikistan: 'There are also serious difficulties in relations among different sections of the Tajik population ... Hence, when we hear today talks about various clans, existing in this or that locality, we realize the danger they create for national consolidation.'[26]

---

22 *Narodnaia gazeta*, 5 October 1991.
23 *Biznes i politika*, No. 43 (November 1993), p. 3.
24 *Narodnaia gazeta*, 24 October 1991.
25 Abdulov, *Rohi behbud*, p. 35.
26 'Interview with Anatoly Sobchak, Yevgeny Velikhov and Head of Tajik Moslems Kazi Akbar Turanzhonzada in Dushanbe on October 6, 1991'.

On 26 October 1991, the IRP held its first congress in Dushanbe. Muhammadsharif Himmatzoda was re-elected as its chairman and Davlat Usmon became his deputy. Although the congress that represented 15–20 000 members of the party reiterated the policy line aimed at building a 'law-based democratic secular state',[27] Himmatzoda put forward the thesis about moving to an Islamic state of Tajikistan by non-violent means, remarking that 'Western countries have their democracy and we shall have ours. Our democracy is incompatible with the Western one.'[28] The legalisation of the IRP and the suspension of the CPT were undoubtedly the most important political events in Tajikistan in autumn 1991. As Grigorii Kosach has noted:

> [T]he communists were not in a position to resume their legal activities until December 1991, when the ban on them was lifted. But by now this was a party that had been divorced from Tajikistan's power structures and lost not a few adherents … The absence of the centre's tutelage and the communists' loss of control over the entire ruling elite turned the confrontation between the two political camps into an open bid for power by the opposition, in which the differences in ideology and principle became ancillary to other considerations.[29]

The two camps would clash in earnest during presidential elections in November 1991.

The Clouding Horizon: Parties, Elections and Shaky Compromises

In September 1991 the number of candidates for the presidency exceeded twenty. Every region and every substantial political organisation (except the CPT) had nominated a hopeful. By 24 November, only eight remained. From the abovementioned figures, only Rahmon Nabiev and Davlat Khudonazarov were serious contenders, with other candidates such as Hikmatullo Nasriddinov (Kulob) and Akbar Makhsumov (Gharm) not strong candidates.[30] Nabiev represented the bloc of Leninobodis, Kulobis and Hisoris, and Khudonazarov was supported by elite factions from Gharm, Qarotegin, the GBAO (Pamirs) and *muhajirs* (that is, Gharmis in Qurghonteppa Province). The legitimate question is, then, why would strongmen in Kulob support Nabiev versus their recognised

---

27 *Narodnaia gazeta*, 29 October 1991.
28 *Nezavisimaia gazeta*, 18 September 1991.
29 Kosach, 'Tajikistan', pp. 124–5.
30 Others, including Tohir Abdujabbor, Shodmon Yusuf and Akbar Turajonzoda, had quit the race. The remaining contenders were: Ismoil Davlatov (Pamirs); Davlat Khudonazarov (Pamirs); Akbar Makhsumov (Gharm); Rahmon Nabiev (Khujand); Hikmatullo Nasriddinov (Kulob); Burikhon Salimov (Kulob); Bobisho Shoev (Pamirs); Saifiddin Turaev (Uroteppa).

leader, Nasriddinov, and, similarly, why would Gharmis vote for Khudonazarov rather than their own Akbar Makhsumov? The answer may be partially found in population statistics. Table 9.1 shows that no politician with a power base in only one particular region could have counted on electoral success. It is also indicative of the fact that this success would be heavily dependent on voters' behaviour in highly heterogeneous Qurghonteppa and Dushanbe, which accounted for one-third of the total vote between them.

Table 9.1 Regional Composition of Tajikistan's Electorate

Leninobod *oblast*	31%
Qurghonteppa *oblast*	21%
Gharm zone and eastern districts of republican subordination	16%
Kulob *oblast*	12%
Dushanbe	12%
Hisor	5%
GBAO (Pamirs)	3%

Source: *Itogi Vsesoiuznoi perepisi naseleniia 1989 goda po Tadzhikskoi SSR*, Vol. II (Dushanbe: Goskomstat TSSR, 1991), pp. 10–39.

For the presidential election of 24 November 1991, the incumbent candidate, Rahmon Nabiev, was not unfamiliar with top-level leadership, as he had been first secretary of the Tajik SSR from 1982 until 1985 when Gorbachev removed him due to his lack of enthusiasm for planned reforms.[31] Outside analysts offer critical appraisals of his character. Whitlock assesses the then fifty-nine-year-old unfavourably, stating that he had heart issues, a drinking problem and a poor work ethic.[32] Shahram Akbarzadeh has come up with the following characterisation of Rahmon Nabiev: 'a hardliner with no reformist pretences. As the epitome of the Soviet *"nomenklaturnyi"* [sic] he was used to top-down command with no taste for compromise. Nabiev had no experience in negotiating policies with diverse political currents or in seeking support from his opponents.'[33] This description needs some qualification. Nabiev was a master of traditional clan politics and temporary coalition-building, and by no means was he bound by any ideological commitments. In 1990, especially in the period preceding the twelfth session of the Supreme Soviet at which Mahkamov was elected president of the Tajik SSR, Nabiev became quite close to Akbar Turajonzoda, Asliddin Sohibnazarov, Tohir Abdujabbor and other influential opponents of Mahkamov. Opposition groups sponsored Nabiev's comeback to politics after five years of inactivity and separation from the summit of power and 'actively promoted his image as an advocate of the independence of Tajikistan

31 Bliss, *Social and Economic Change in the Pamirs*, p. 272.
32 Whitlock, *Land Beyond the River*, p. 153.
33 Akbarzadeh, 'Why Did Nationalism Fail in Tajikistan', pp. 1110–11.

and the well-being of its people. All their publications contained one refrain: weak-willed Mahkamov must be replaced by strong Nabiev. Undoubtedly, the *Qoziyot* and the IRP rendered Nabiev serious assistance. He suited them in the transitional period.'[34] As soon as Qahhor Mahkamov stepped down as president and the IRP was legalised, the tone of the opposition's statements changed rapidly: 'The election of Nabiev [as chairman of the Supreme Soviet] is wrong … Aren't there any other cadres in our republic apart from Mahkamov and Nabiev … How often is Nabiev sober? Whose fate is more attractive to Nabiev— Pinochet's, Mussolini's or Ceausescu's?'[35]

In the autumn of 1991, Nabiev managed to rally the majority of the northern 'clans' around him. He formed an alliance with Abdumalik Abdullojonov; the latter was offered indemnity from any inquiry into the activities of the Ministry of Grain Products, and his relative, Temur Mirzoev, was promised the position of mayor of Dushanbe.[36] A prominent politician, Safarali Kenjaev, who had a power base in the Ayni district of the Leninobod *oblast*, as well as in Hisor, became Nabiev's campaign manager.[37] Sayfiddin Turaev, representative of a powerful Uroteppa (Istaravshon) group of clans and another runner-up for the presidency, was seriously weakened when one of his associates, deputy procurator-general, Amirqul Azimov, defected to Nabiev's camp. Nabiev also had a substantial following in the Kulob *oblast*. By October 1991, the group of Hikmatullo Nasriddinov had become largely a spent force, for it had failed to use the post–February 1990 elite settlement to improve economic conditions in the Kulob region. Local groups, such as Oshkoro, and charismatic strongmen, such as the criminal authority Sangak Safarov, canvassed for Nabiev. Generally, Kulobis remembered Nabiev's tenure as the party leader in 1982–85 as a period of growth and prosperity; this perception received a further boost when in September 1991 massive shipments of food and consumer goods from Leninobod

---

34   G. Khaidarov and M. Inomov, *Tadzhikistan: tragediia i bol' naroda* (St Petersburg: LINKO, 1993), p. 15. Akbar Turajonzoda corroborated this conclusion in 1995: 'Since the Communist party had ostracised Nabiev and he was completely forgotten, it was only thanks to us that he was resurrected. I very much regret this move.' See: 'Interview with Qadi Akbar Turajonzoda', *Central Asia Monitor*, No. 2 (1995), p. 10.

35   Ibrohim Usmon, *Soli Nabiev* (Dushanbe: [No publisher], 1995), pp. 15–16.

36   Confidential sources in Dushanbe, January 1996. According to some reports, which could not be verified, Abdullojonov also handed Nabiev 3 million roubles for the election campaign in October 1991.

37   Safarali Kenjaev was born in 1942 in Ayni. He belongs to a family of traditional Yaghnobi notables, hence his influence on both sides of the Hisor mountain range. Kenjaev has known Akbar Turajonzoda since childhood and for some time lived in the same *mahalla* with him. Kenjaev is a qualified lawyer; in 1983–89 he acted as the regional Central Asian railway procurator and the transport procurator of the TSSR, and in 1990–91 headed the Control Commission under the President of Tajikistan. His solidarity web included several local administration heads (Qairoqqum, Varzob). In February 1990, he was put in charge of the Supreme Soviet commission to investigate the bloody events in Dushanbe, which helped him to become known throughout Tajikistan.

to Kulob commenced. Unsurprisingly, more than half of all telegrams and letters from labour collectives nominating Nabiev that were received by the Electoral Commission originated from Kulob.[38]

Nabiev's selection of Narzullo Dustov as vice-president was a carefully designed measure: the latter was born in Darvoz, in the Pamirs, but his paternal ancestors used to live in Baljuvon of Kulob. Dustov was a hardworking transport official devoid of any political ambitions, who had a reputation of being not particularly clever.[39] He had no patronage web behind him but enjoyed the reputation as a person sympathetic to the problems of the common people. In his election program, Nabiev announced that 'the accelerated growth of productive forces of the Kulob *oblast*, the GBAO, Qarotegin Valley and other mountainous districts should become the decisive element of our socio-economic strategy',[40] but, overall, this document was little more than an assortment of populist promises and did not touch upon the principles of state building in independent Tajikistan at all. The problem of sub-ethnic fragmentation in the country deserved one short line: 'regionalism has increased.'[41]

The IRP, the DPT, La'li Badakhshon, Rastokhez and a number of creative unions and public associations nominated the Pamiri cinematographer Davlat Khudonazarov as their presidential candidate. Khudonazarov is a unique and tragic figure in the political history of Tajikistan. At the age of sixteen, he was admitted to the All-Union Institute of Cinematography in Moscow. His work as a cameraman and later film director won accolades throughout the country and abroad. Although his father, Khudonazar Mamadnazarov, was a high-ranking CPT official, Khudonazarov himself was always at loggerheads with the Soviet establishment. He was a disciple of Andrei Sakharov, and after becoming a USSR people's deputy in 1989, he joined the reformist Interregional Group faction in the Soviet parliament. Gorbachev coopted him to the CPSU CC alongside 60 other reformers. Khudonazarov did not formally belong to any political organisation in Tajikistan, but his ties with the DPT and Rastokhez were well known.[42] Khudonazarov was one of the few Tajik politicians who openly castigated regionalism in the republic's politics.[43] Khudonazarov understood

---

38 Abdulov, *Rohi behbud*, p. 47. See also: Niyazi, 'Tajikistan I', p. 149.

39 The opposition referred to him as the 'village fool'. See: *Charoghi ruz*, No. 2 (80) (1995), p. 13.

40 *Barnomai amalii nomzad ba raisi jumhuri Tojikiston Nabiev Rahmon Nabievich* (Dushanbe: [No publisher], 1991), p. 12.

41 *Barnomai amalii nomzad ba raisi jumhuri Tojikiston Nabiev Rahmon Nabievich*, p. 8.

42 For a brief biography of Khudonazarov, see: Abdullaev and Akbarzadeh, *Historical Dictionary of Tajikistan*, pp. 204–5. His first name is also given as Davlatnazar, while his surname is also given as the de-Russified Khudonazar. Regarding his artistic accomplishments, see: Bashiri, *Prominent Tajik Figures of the Twentieth Century*, pp. 150–1.

43 Khudonazarov deplored 'the division of the nation as a result of the half-a-century-long usurpation of power by the leaders who defended only clan and localistic interests. The elevation of regionalism to a state policy over a lengthy period of time made the society accumulate enormous destructive energy.' See: Davlat Khudonazarov, 'Tadzhikskii rezhisser v dalnem zarubezh'e', *Iskusstvo kino*, No. 7 (1994), p. 41.

that, being a Pamiri, he had no chances of being elected on his own, so he accepted the endorsement of the force to which he had natural antipathy—that is, the Islamists. Even then he knew that his victory would require a major miracle. Still, Khudonazarov decided to fight to reform the system.

The opposition banked on Khudonazarov for purely pragmatic reasons: he was likely to attract the votes of the cosmopolitan intelligentsia and the Pamiris.[44] Even more importantly, Khudonazarov had exceptionally good ties in the Kremlin (as well as later in the West)[45] and could provide the opposition with the international publicity it so badly needed. Indeed, during the presidential campaign, Moscow-based journalists spared no effort to support his cause; Channels 1 and 2 aired a series of trailers in November that urged the voters in Tajikistan to make a decision in Khudonazarov's favour. Khudonazarov's colleagues had the following to say about his qualities.[46]

- Ella Pamfilova, USSR MP: 'As a presidential candidate, Davlat is marked by a truly statesmanlike way of thinking … He is one of those politicians who can introduce an element of lofty morality to politics.'

- Iurii Ryzhov, chairman of the Science Committee of the USSR Supreme Soviet: 'If we want to come to a civil society and social justice, we need people with a European mode of thinking. Davlat is one of them.'

- Vladimir Volkov, USSR MP: 'He enjoys great authority with the leaders of Russia, Boris Yeltsin in particular. Personal links between state leaders are extremely important, voters in Tajikistan should remember this.'

- Aleksandr Iakovlev, chief advisor to President Gorbachev: 'Democracy is the essence of life for him. He is a Man of Freedom of the *perestroika* epoch.'

Khudonazov's supporters even attempted to solicit endorsement from as far abroad as California, with the presumption that the president of Stanford University would have an interest in the upcoming elections in Tajikistan.[47]

During the campaign Nabiev put emphasis on stability and gradual change, while Khudonazarov and his would-be vice-president and the DPT deputy

---

44   Narzullo Dustov has reproduced a conversation he claims he had with Akbar Turajonzoda on 20 April 1992: the revered *Qozikalon*, with no little cynicism, explained to the slightly petrified vice-president of Tajikistan that 'we do not have any respect for the Pamiris at all, they are not accomplished Muslims anyway. The Pamirs [region] is necessary to us today in order to reach our goal, that is, state power; henceforth, we use them temporarily, then we shall part company and leave them to face their fate.' See: Dustov, *Zakhm bar jismi vatan*, p. 7.

45   This hagiography of Khudonazarov mentions his time, post Tajikistan, at the US Institute of Peace and at the Kennan Institute: Robin Wright, 'The Artful Exile from Dushanbe: First Davlat Khudonazarov Lost the Presidency of His Beloved Tajikistan, Then He Lost Everything Else. Forced Into Exile, the Charismatic Filmmaker and Politician May Be His Country's Great Hope for Unity', *Los Angeles Times* (15 May 1994).

46   Adopted from a collation of promotional trailers of Davlat Khudonazarov. Courtesy of deputy director of the Tajik Film Authority, Safar Haqdod.

47   Gregory Freidin, 'Coup II: Tadzhikistan's Havel Fights Back; Davlat Khudonazarov', *The New Republic*, Vol. 205, No. 16 (14 October 1991), p. 16.

chairman, Asliddin Sohibnazarov (who represented the interests of a group of districts to the east of Dushanbe bordering on Gharm), actively exploited the themes of reformism, nationalism and Islam. Sociological monitoring conducted by the Cabinet of Ministers of the Republic of Tajikistan showed that Nabiev's supporters had a much clearer idea about their candidate than those of Khudonazarov (Table 9.2). Nabiev had managed to capitalise on his image as an experienced and paternalistic leader; it is noteworthy that in both cases commitment to democratic ideals did not feature as an important criterion. Moreover, Khudonazarov's nationalist stance eventually repelled the non-Tajik voters (aside from of course the Pamiris), and Nabiev acquired a substantial lead amongst all ethnic electoral cohorts (Table 9.3).

Table 9.2 Personal Qualities Most Appreciated by Loyal Voters in Presidential Candidates, October 1991

	Rahmon Nabiev	Davlat Khudonazarov
Ability to unite different parties	48%	34%
Modesty	57%	25%
Moral purity	48%	32%
Good knowledge of Tajik literature and language	42%	44%
Knowledge of economics	63%	18%
Faithfulness to Islam	17%	70%
Attention to people's needs	64%	20%
Skills of managing the state	68%	19%

Note: The survey involved 1361 respondents in all regions and districts of Tajikistan, except the GBAO.

Source: *Vybory Prezidenta Respubliki Tadzhikistan. Sotsiologicheskii monitoring* (Dushanbe: Press-sluzhba KM RT, 1991), p. 21.

Table 9.3 Election Preferences of Ethnic Groups, October– November 1991

Ethnic cohort	For Rahmon Nabiev		For Davlat Khudonazarov	
	28–31 October	14–16 November	28–31 October	14–16 November
Tajiks	66%	58%	28%	26%
Uzbeks	89%	74%	14%	16%
Russians and Ukrainians	56%	79%	35%	15%
Other nationalities	47%	73%	41%	16%

Source: *Vybory Prezidenta Respubliki Tadzhikistan. Sotsiologicheskii monitoring* (Dushanbe: Press-sluzhba KM RT, 1991), p. 20.

The returns of the poll on 24 November 1991 were as follows: Nabiev, 56.92 per cent, and Khudonazarov, 30.07 per cent.[48] Generally, traditional factors proved to be decisive in the election's outcome. The structure of the vote corresponded to the regional affiliation of the candidates: Nabiev and Dustov scored 80–100 per cent in northern constituencies, 90 per cent in Kulob, but, for example, only 0.02 per cent in Qalai Khumb in the GBAO.[49] The vote in Dushanbe and Qurghonteppa was split fifty–fifty.

Nabiev's team had skilfully used prejudices to smear Khudonazarov: he was pronounced unworthy of becoming the leader because 'he was born illegally, for he was conceived by his real father when his mother was married to another man'.[50] Khudonazarov, an Ismaili Pamiri, endured pro-incumbent taunts during the election campaign labelling him a 'Badakhshani kafir' (that is, a non-Tajik and an infidel).[51] Mullahs in Kulob habitually referred to Khudonazarov as an unbeliever or a heretic, successfully 'fanning the fire of suspicion and hatred against the Ismaili sect'.[52]

The opposition claimed the vote was fraudulent, arguing that Khudonazarov had actually received 40 per cent of the vote;[53] however, Khudonazarov accepted defeat with bitterness but as something naturally determined;[54] the opposition chose not to challenge the results, although there were likely irregularities, 'in view of the widely regarded fairness of the election process'.[55] In other words, the opposition could only realistically claim that its losing margin was less than official figures. On 2 December 1991, Rahmon Nabiev took an oath as the first popularly elected president of the Republic of Tajikistan. Clearly, the elections and the accusations and rhetoric surrounding them 'further polarized forces in the republic'.[56]

---

48   The also-rans: S. Turaev, 5.03 per cent; H. Nasriddinov, 1.28 per cent; B. Shoev, 0.37 per cent; A. Makhsumov, 0.23 per cent. In total, 84.6 per cent of eligible citizens cast their vote. See: *Narodnaia gazeta*, 26 November 1991.

49   Dustov, *Zakhm bar jismi vatan*, p. 7.

50   Bushkov and Mikulskii, 'Obschestvenno-politicheskaia situatsiia v Tadzhikistane', p. 13.

51   Kilavuz, *Understanding Violent Conflict*, p. 198. The use of 'kafir' also appeared in IRP rhetoric: 'Unlike other parties and political organizations, the IRP had declared that any Muslim residing in Tajikistan could join the party. Those who refused to support this Islamic party were declared infidels (Kafirs).' See: Makhamov, 'Islam and the Political Development of Tajikistan after 1985', p. 201.

52   Akbarzadeh, 'Why Did Nationalism Fail in Tajikistan', p. 1111.

53   Abdullaev and Akbarzadeh, *Historical Dictionary of Tajikistan*, pp. 204–5; Kilavuz, *Understanding Violent Conflict*, pp. 149–50, 172.

54   He was quoted as saying that 'our place of birth predetermined our lot'. See: Usmon, *Soli Nabiev*, p. 109.

55   Naby, 'Tajik Political Legitimacy and Political Parties', p. 199.

56   Kilavuz, *Understanding Violent Conflict*, pp. 149–50.

Rahmon Nabiev's Presidency

Nabiev was certainly capable of maintaining the elite's consensual unity using his authority, flexibility, communication skills and personal charm in a *stable* mono-organisational political system. But in December 1991, he inherited a system that had become highly unstable, where the old rules of the elite settlement had been annulled and new ones had not yet emerged.[57] In the neighbouring republics at the time, Islom Karimov and Saparmurat Niyazov were feverishly constructing overtly authoritarian regimes, while Nursultan Nazarbaev and Askar Akaev opted for quasi-democratic coalitions dominated by a strong executive.[58] Nabiev as president remained somnolent: 'he was sure that after gaining power, he would inherit automatically absolute subordination to the will of "the First," which had existed before, when the system itself reliably guaranteed the functioning of various spheres of the Republic's life … Nabiev was not ready to work under new conditions.'[59]

In Uzbekistan, where friction amongst regional elites had also been on the rise since the beginning of *perestroika*,[60] President Islom Karimov, elected in December 1991, continued to depend confidently on the renamed and de-ideologised Communist Party, while building a political system with a de facto strong executive, despite dispersal of powers enunciated in the Constitution.[61] In contrast, Nabiev's attempt to build a strong presidency failed miserably. He could not even run his personal office properly. His chief of staff, Karim Abdulov, who had a staff of 33 people, has left a scathing description of how the office operated over the 10 months in 1991–92:[62]

> Nobody worked with us. The President did not have time. The Vice-President met with our officers once, and that was it. Every Councillor and Adviser worked on his own problems. Weekly briefings were deemed unnecessary by the President … Most meetings of the President took

57 Like any other leader in a transitional polity, Nabiev had a choice: 'rules can be imposed unilaterally by a dominant actor and the other players may obey them out of fear or respect, or they can be elaborated multilaterally by implicit agreements or by explicit pacts.' See: O'Donnell and Schmitter, 'Tentative Conclusions about Uncertain Democracies', p. 68.

58 Nazarbaev must have learned certain lessons from the 'meeting frenzy' in Tajikistan: when in June 1992 several hundred people assembled in front of the parliament building in Almaty under democratic banners, he ordered police to disperse them at once, saying that 'we shall preserve stability in the republic at any cost, even relying on tough measures'. See: *Izvestiia*, 18 June 1992. A more detailed account of the Kazakh president's policy can be found in: Kirill Nourzhanov and Amin Saikal, 'The New Kazakhstan: Has Something Gone Wrong?' *The World Today*, Vol. 50, No. 12 (1994), pp. 225–9.

59 Khaidarov and Inomov, *Tajikistan*, p. 17.

60 On regionalism in Uzbekistan, see: Donald S. Carlisle, 'The Uzbek Power Elite: Politburo and Secretariat (1938–1983)', *Central Asian Survey*, Vol. 5, Nos 3–4 (1986), pp. 91–132; and Sharaf Khoja, 'Uzbekistan: Friendship Gains Victory in Government's Struggle against Corruption', *Russia and the Moslem World*, No. 10 (1994), pp. 41–5.

61 Carlisle, 'Islam Karimov and Uzbekistan', p. 199.

62 Abdulov, *Rohi behbud*, pp. 59, 86.

place without preparation … [Eventually t]he traffic of visitors began to be controlled by the group of Anatolii Omoev [Nabiev's bodyguard of many years] … Day by day Omoev's and his friends' clients poured in to talk with the President … However, government officials who wanted to discuss issues of state importance did not have a hope of being given an audience.

The aggregation of pro–Nabiev support was implemented by a variety of vertical and horizontal structures, united temporarily by considerations of preserving the status quo. It would have taken immense institutional craftsmanship to make them stick together. Following his victory, Nabiev did nothing to create a political machine behind his regime.[63] In early 1992 it was disclosed that 'the relations between R. Nabiev and the Communist Party are rather complicated. According to sources close to the President, R. Nabiev will try to finish the Party off because he had suffered from the Party arbitrariness in the mid-1980s.'[64] The Supreme Court of Tajikistan cleared the CPT's name and on 18 January 1992 it held its twenty-third congress, but Nabiev refused to restore the bulk of its property, including the building of the Central Committee in Dushanbe. The newly elected CPT leader and Mahkamov's long-time ally, Shodi Shabdolov, was not on speaking terms with Nabiev.[65]

Nabiev rewarded his supporters by promoting them to senior positions in the civil service. Of course, he was not unique in making non-merit-based bureaucratic appointments and sinecures for loyalists the order of the day, but in a nascent independent state like Tajikistan there was a great need for skilled bureaucrats and stable government structures. Experienced personnel from Mahkamov's era faced wholesale dismissal; entire ministries were dissolved and then resuscitated, chaos prevailed, and the 'heavy burden of serving the people and dealing with the republic's problems landed on the shoulders of just 7–8 capable officials'.[66]

In late 1991, a think tank attached to the Cabinet of Ministers of the Republic of Tajikistan sent a detailed memorandum to the Presidential Office, pinpointing the main problems that the regime faced. This document concluded in particular that[67]

- under conditions of deepening economic crisis and decaying social welfare, political struggle is conducive to processes of disintegration in society

---

63   Barnett Rubin is certainly wrong when asserting that Nabiev relied on the renamed CPT. See: Rubin, 'Tajikistan', p. 213.
64   Bushkov and Mikulskii, 'Obschestvenno-politicheskaia situatsiia v Tadzhikistane', p. 35.
65   Interview with the first secretary of the CPT city organisation of Dushanbe, Isomiddin Salohiddinov, Dushanbe, 4 April 1995.
66   Abdulov, *Rohi behbud*, p. 69.
67   *Sotsialno-politicheskie usloviia perekhoda k rynku v Tadzhikistane*, pp. 12–22.

- the government's authority is weakened by the instability of legal foundations, the absence of mechanisms to carry out laws and decisions and weak control over their implementation, which leads to misuse of power by local structures

- the unceasing redistribution of political and economic powers between the centre and peripheral organs and executive and legislative institutions disorients the populace

- the structures of presidential authority are characterised by blurred functions, lack of levers of social mobilisation and inherent instability.

The experts' recommendation was clear: it was imperative to consolidate social control by all possible means through establishing a strong presidency; they also believed that it could be done quickly and painlessly.[68] Nabiev failed to heed this advice. He made mistake after mistake. He did not even try to gain control over regional administrations (as Karimov successfully did in Uzbekistan in January 1992 by introducing the institution of appointed governors who existed parallel to elected soviets). He was in no hurry to set up national armed forces. He retained General Anatolii Stroikin, invited in July 1991 from Kazakhstan, as the chairman of the Committee of State Security—the successor to Tajikistan's KGB; Stroikin 'could not orient himself properly in the intricate and complex situation, which led to a split in [Tajikistan's] security organs'.[69]

The economic situation in the country was critical. Food shortages were common in the cities.[70] In his radio address to the people on 29 January 1992, Nabiev said: 'You all know better than anyone else … that the republic has no reserves and no potential. The budget has been fixed only for the first three months of the year, unfortunately, and contains many faults.'[71] Yet, instead of cutting budget expenditure and introducing market reforms, Nabiev, in a truly populist fashion, blamed greedy merchants and the nascent strata of businessmen for the economic troubles and launched an attack on them under the new law 'On Strengthening Control over Cooperatives': 'In Dushanbe, regional centres and districts … cooperatives, small enterprises and procurement shops began to be liquidated. Tens of thousands of people were rendered jobless.'[72] Tajikistan joined the Commonwealth of Independent States (CIS) in December 1991, but relations amongst its member states desperately lacked proper institutionalisation.

---

68 The reason given was: 'the great proportion of the population is tired of political confrontation and is interested in putting key issues of economic life outside the brackets of political ambitions and passions.' *Sotsialno-politicheskie usloviia perekhoda k rynku v Tadzhikistane*, pp. 16–17.

69 Khaidarov and Inomov, *Tadzhikistan*, p. 26.

70 In some places bread was rationed at 170–240 g a day per person, compared with 600 g during the most difficult months of World War II. See: *Narodnaia gazeta*, 1 November 1991.

71 Bess Brown, 'Central Asia', *Radio Free Europe/Radio Liberty Research Report*, Vol. 1, No. 7 (14 February 1992), p. 20.

72 *Russkaia mysl'*, 3 July 1992.

Nabiev showed remarkable slackness in this respect—for instance, by June 1992, Tajikistan remained the only Central Asian republic that had not signed a cooperation agreement with the Russian Federation.[73]

After his inauguration, Nabiev appointed a new cabinet. Akbar Mirzoev, the chairman of the Executive Committee of the Kulob *oblast*, became premier. Nabiev also secured the election of Safarali Kenjaev as the chairman of the Supreme Soviet, instead of acting chairman, Akbarsho Iskandarov. Thus the prerogative of the Pamiris and Gharmis to head Tajikistan's legislature was violated. Both Mirzoev and Kenjaev had substantial political resources of their own and could act independently of the president. As an opposition observer wrote in May 1992 in an article entitled 'The Flailing King', 'in the ruling triumvirate Nabiev is just a figurehead … whose brain has shrunk due to excessive consumption of alcohol, and who, naturally, does not play any role in running the state'.[74] While this statement was an obvious exaggeration, Hikmatullo Nasriddinov, who at the time chaired one of the Supreme Soviet committees, concurred that 'Akbar Mirzoev considered some of the requests, suggestions and edicts of Rahmon Nabiev unacceptable and even rejected them or left them unattended'.[75] Clearly, the presence of regional strongmen at the top undercut state capabilities to extract and distribute resources, mobilise the masses and regulate social relations.

Following the presidential elections, there was a lull in the struggle amongst elite factions, while they regrouped and prepared for future battles. Relative tranquillity was also maintained by the personal efforts of Nabiev, who met with *Qozikalon* Turajonzoda and opposition leaders more frequently than with his own executives.[76] This provided a feeble alternative to working out an overarching intra-elite pact, which theoretically should have: a) confined the sphere of political action to rational, controllable processes, such as elections and parliamentary debates; b) precluded intervention of extraneous forces in decision-making; and c) envisaged a more equitable distribution of benefits amongst regional factions.

In regards to the president's strategy for dealing with the opposition, Nabiev and his allies, perceiving themselves as 'powerful and unchallengeable … began a crackdown against the entire opposition'.[77] Nabiev's tactic was to initiate a broad attack against both his internal competition within the Communist Party

---

73 *Diplomatiia Tadzhikistana* (Dushanbe: [No publisher], 1994), p. 58. The Treaty on Friendship, Cooperation and Mutual Assistance between Tajikistan and Russia was signed as late as 25 May 1993.
74 Mirzoi Salimpur, 'Shohi mu'allaq', *Charoghi ruz*, No. 20 (41) (1992), p. 2.
75 Nasriddinov, *Tarkish*, p. 151.
76 Abdulov recounts: 'he would tell them [opposition leaders] "Let us discuss things" and "Please, table your requests", and so on … Most of the time the President would receive them tête-à-tête and negotiate with them secretly.' See: Abdulov, *Rohi behbud*, p. 84.
77 Kilavuz, *Understanding Violent Conflict*, pp. 125–6, also 9–10, 163.

and all the opposition parties at the same time; however, his purges pushed some government figures into the opposition while his attacks on opposition figures and parties served to help unite them against the political leadership of Tajikistan. The result was a larger and more united opposition. At the beginning of 1992, the government strengthened its campaign against the opposition parties. The government began legal proceedings against members of the DPT, Rastokhez and the IRP. In addition, the government passed new laws restricting press freedom and the right to assemble in public. Freedom of expression was also curtailed, with government prosecutors charging various opposition leaders with insulting government leaders.[78] The conflictive environment persisted in Tajikistan and needed only a single impetus to erupt into violence. It came in March 1992.

The Use and Abuse of Mass Mobilisation: Spring 1992 Street Demonstrations

The government coalition struck first. On 6 March 1992, the pro-opposition mayor of Dushanbe, Maqsud Ikromov, was arrested on charges of corruption.[79] On 11 March 1992, one of the Rastokhez leaders, Mirbobo Mirrahim, was sentenced to two years of imprisonment for defamation of the chairman of the Supreme Soviet, Safarali Kenjaev.[80] On 25 March 1992, Kenjaev convened the Presidium of the Supreme Soviet and led televised investigations into the Interior Ministry, particularly its failure to act against anti-government demonstrators in September 1991. Kenjaev's efforts were focused on the head of the ministry, Mamadayoz Navjuvonov—an ethnic Pamiri. Kenjaev's investigation recommended that Nabiev dismiss Navjuvonov, 'for blatant violations in personnel policy, inept leadership, connivance in illegal privatising of state-owned vehicles and personal immodesty'.[81] The government attacks on Navjuvonov led several hundred

---

78   Kilavuz, *Understanding Violent Conflict*, pp. 125–6, 150, 163–5, 205–6. 'In particular, the law on the press adopted in spring 1992 made criticism of the government a crime. Mirbobo Mirrahim, one of the leaders of Rastokhez, was put on probation for allegedly insulting Kenjaev. Legal proceedings were brought against the leader of the DPT, Shadmon Yusuf, for insulting the honor and dignity of President Nabiev.'

79   Kilavuz writes: 'The mayor of Dushanbe, Maqsud Ikromov, was arrested on March 6, 1992 on corruption charges, but according to many, the real reason was related to the removal of the Lenin statue.' See: Kilavuz, *Understanding Violent Conflict*. His place was taken by Mirzotemur Mirzoev—a close relative of Abdumalik Abdullojonov. This move was widely interpreted in Dushanbe as Nabiev's 'repayment' for Abdullojonov's support during the presidential elections.

80   In February 1990, Mirrahim was put under investigation, conducted by a special commission headed by Kenjaev. Kenjaev tried to present Mirrahim as the culprit behind bloodshed and violence in Dushanbe. A bitter personal feud sprang up between the two of them. See: 'Ba Mirbobo chi shud?' *Adolat*, No. 8 (1991), p. 3.

81   Bess Brown, 'Whither Tajikistan', *Radio Free Europe/Radio Liberty Research Report*, Vol. 1, No. 24 (12 June 1992), p. 2; *Tadzhikistan v ogne*, p. 154. The real reason for Navjuvonov's dismissal was his reluctance to obey orders from the Supreme Soviet to enforce the state of emergency and disperse demonstrators in the autumn of 1991. Nabiev promised to remove him if he became president. See: *Sadoi mardum*, 31 October 1991. Nabiev later backed down on this promise.

Pamiri members of La'li Badakhshon—who viewed the firing of Navjuvonov as an 'intolerable insult to their nationality'[82]—to start demonstrating in Shahidon Square against the government and in support of Navjuvonov.[83] Navjuvonov himself also framed his case in regional-ethnic terms and 'accused the Government of persecution towards the Badakhshani [Pamiri] people'.[84] The mood amongst some Pamiris, at least in their home region, had already been quite confrontational earlier in the winter. In December 1991 demonstrators organised by La'li Badakhshon in Khorugh gathered and demanded that the Gorno-Badakhshan Autonomous Oblast (GBAO) declare independence and recall its deputies from the Supreme Soviet in Dushanbe. A compromise was reached with local authorities, who agreed to declare the Pamirs an autonomous republic within Tajikistan. A motion was passed by the GBAO soviet and then sent to Dushanbe for ratification (which never materialised).[85]

The opposition saw this as a good time to counterattack. The Pamiri demonstrators were soon joined by supporters of other opposition parties, including the DPT and the IRP.[86] This began the next phase of the opposition alliance, the first being for the November 1991 presidential elections.[87] As in September 1991, reinforcements from rural areas of Gharm and Qurghonteppa were brought in, and very soon the number of people in Shahidon Square reached 3000. On 27 March 1992, Shodmon Yusuf (DPT), Muhammadsharif Himmatzoda (IRP), Davlat Usmon (IRP), Tohir Abdujabbor (Rastokhez) and the chairman of La'li Badakhshon, Amirbek Atobek, on behalf of the participants of the meeting, put forward a list of demands, which included: the resignation of Kenjaev; the release of Ikromov from custody; dissolution of the Supreme Soviet; adoption of a new constitution; organisation of multi-party elections to the new legislature—the Majlisi milli; and cessation of reprisals against the opposition.[88] The leaders of the young political groups that developed in Tajikistan were, as noted by Akiner, 'inexperienced and prone to adopt extreme, uncompromising positions'.[89] These

---

82   Brown, 'Whither Tajikistan', p. 2. See also: Kilavuz, *Understanding Violent Conflict*, p. 150. Also, the firing of Navjuvonov could leave the ethnic Pamiris in the ministry vulnerable to a purge. On Pamiri domination in the ranks of the ministry, see: Schoeberlein-Engel, 'Conflicts in Tajikistan and Central Asia', p. 37; Matveeva, 'The Perils of Emerging Statehood', p. 7.

83   Juraeva, 'Ethnic Conflict in Tajikistan', p. 265; Schoeberlein-Engel, 'Conflicts in Tajikistan and Central Asia', p. 37; Roy, *The New Central Asia*, pp. 139–40. Juraeva stresses that Pamiris 'were also outraged by what they consider Kenjaev's dismissive remarks concerning their ethnic group'.

84   Mullojonov, 'The Islamic Clergy in Tajikistan Since the End of the Soviet Period', p. 240. See also: Kilavuz, *Understanding Violent Conflict*, p. 179.

85   Galina Gridneva, 'Pamir Highlanders Achieve New Status Compromise', *ITAR-Tass* (10 December 1992), *ITAR-Tass*, 0756 gmt (10 December 1991), in *SWB SU*, 1255 (14 December 1992), B/1.

86   Schoeberlein-Engel, 'Conflicts in Tajikistan and Central Asia', pp. 36–7; *Tajik Radio*, 1200 and 1700 gmt (31 March 1992), in *SWB SU* [Third Series], 1345 (2 April 1992), B/8.

87   Kilavuz, *Understanding Violent Conflict*, p. 151.

88   *Vechernii Dushanbe*, 1 April 1992.

89   Akiner, *Tajikistan*, p. 3. Akiner does not specify parties.

tactics were soon to be employed by the opposition at Shahidon Square. The opposition's initial demands escalated, and by mid April the opposition began to make increasingly radical demands, including the resignation of Nabiev.[90]

The ability of the opposition to coordinate effectively in a unified manner against the government—in addition to being a by-product of the government attacking all elements of the opposition at once[91]—was, in the opinion of Kilavuz, thanks to the mediating efforts of *Qozi* Turajonzoda, 'who established links between formerly unrelated opposition groups'.[92] The IRP, however, contributed the most to the demonstrations at Shahidon Square,[93] as this organisation had a strong network extending into many rural areas, unlike their allies. The IRP leadership was able to mobilise support through mullahs at mosques and collective farms, with the Turkmeniston farm—the home base for then IRP third-in-charge, Sayid Abdullo Nuri—mentioned most prominently.[94] While some demonstrators came to Shahidon willingly—and expressed their enthusiasm[95]—IRP-affiliated mullahs coerced those less enthusiastic with threats of religious penalties.[96]

Nabiev, Kenjaev and Dustov urgently summoned representatives of the power agencies in order to make an inventory of what forces they could count on. The results were not encouraging for them[97]

---

90   Splidsboel-Hansen, 'The Outbreak and Settlement of Civil War', pp. 10–11; Kilavuz, *Understanding Violent Conflict*, pp. 151–2; *Tajik Radio*, 1200 and 1700 gmt (31 March 1992), in *SWB SU*, 1345 (2 April 1992), B/8; *Postfactum*, 0945 gmt (30 March 1992), in *SWB SU*, 1345 (2 April 1992), B/8. Demonstrators' demands included the dissolution of parliament, the resignation of Kenjaev, 'establishment of national *majlis*', resignation of the government and formation of a coalition government, land redistribution, 'distribution' of factories and plants to workers, a 50 per cent price cut on all goods produced in Tajikistan, removal of amendments to the press freedom law, an 'end to persecution of democratic forces', and so on. *Tajik Radio*, 1700 gmt (7 April 1992), in *SWB SU*, 1352 (10 April 1992), B/1.

91   In regards to the government attacking the entire opposition, see: Kilavuz, *Understanding Violent Conflict*, pp. 125–6, also p. 163.

92   Kilavuz, *Understanding Violent Conflict*, p. 167, also p. 168. Kilavuz writes: 'Turajonzoda had relations with both "official" and "unofficial" mullahs, and was the link between the nationalist and Islamic opposition. Because of his position, he was able to mediate among the different opposition groups. Turajonzoda was not a member of any political party. He did not join any of the parties within the united opposition. Rather, he played the role of major link uniting opposition groups.' Turajonzoda had played the role of a 'uniter' as early as the November 1991 elections, when he persuaded all the opposition parties to field a single candidate—Khudonazarov—against Nabiev. See: ibid., p. 172.

93   Brown, 'Whither Tajikistan', p. 3.

94   Kilavuz, *Understanding Violent Conflict*, p. 179. See also: Anderson, *The International Politics of Central Asia*, p. 175. Kilavuz mentions the Qurghonteppa region as the primary source of IRP demonstrators, with Kulob a secondary mention.

95   See, for example: Gillian Tett, 'Poverty Brings Tajikistan's Political Tension to the Fore', *Financial Times* (28 April 1992), International p. 2; Whitlock, *Land Beyond the River*, p. 156.

96   For example, Whitlock and Kilavuz provide examples of demonstrators going to Shahidon or providing material support because mullahs had threatened to religiously annul their marriage and/or declare them a non-Muslim. See: Whitlock, *Land Beyond the River*, p. 156; Kilavuz, *Understanding Violent Conflict*, p. 193.

97   Kenjaev, *Tabadduloti Tojikiston*, Vol. 1, pp. 39–42.

- the state councillor, Major General Bahrom Rahmonov, disclosed that Nabiev's edict on the creation of a 700-strong national guard,[98] dated 22 December 1991, was never implemented, and that the National Guard servicemen who took an oath in January 1992 in front of Vice-President Dustov were in fact disguised Russian soldiers assembled to 'intimidate the opposition'

- the chairman of the Defence Committee, Major General F. Niyozov, reported that he had received 37 armoured personnel carriers (APCs) and other heavy equipment, which, however, could not be used for lack of trained personnel

- the military commissar of Tajikistan, Major General M. Mahmadjonov, said that he had prepared lists of 1000 officers and NCOs of the reserve ready to be drafted; further questioning revealed that those lists contained only names, without addresses, military qualifications and personal data, and, henceforth, were useless

- the deputy minister of interior, Major General A. Qahhorov, deplored the preponderance of Gharmis and Pamiris in the police force, who not only refrained from active action against the demonstrators but deserted to them in whole units, following Shodmon Yusuf's appeal

- the Committee for State Security (KGB) chairman, General A. Stroikin, proclaimed the neutrality of his officers in domestic strife and expressed the personal opinion that the opposition meeting was not a 'serious business' anyway

- the Border Troops commander (under CIS/Russian jurisdiction), General L. Martovitskii, said that his soldiers would not interfere in Tajikistan's domestic affairs under any circumstances

- the Dushanbe military commandant, also the commander of the Russian 201st Motorised Rifle Division (MRD), Colonel V. Zabolotny, explained that without explicit permission from the president of the Russian Federation, Boris Yeltsin, and the commander-in-chief of the CIS Armed Forces, Air Marshal E. Shaposhnikov, he could not help the government of Tajikistan in any way.

Having no desire to acquiesce to the protesters' demands and unable to resort to coercion, the government set up the Committee for Protection of Constitutional Order (CPCO) on 28 March 1992, which comprised activists from Leninobod, Kulob and Hisor. On 1 April 1992, they organised a mass meeting in support of President Nabiev and the Supreme Soviet. Thus, two permanent sit-ins came

---

98 On 24 December 1991, President Nabiev decreed the creation of the 'Tajikistan National Guard', a unit that was to number 700 men and be subordinate directly to the president. Major General Bahrom Rahmonov (aged forty-two), the 'former chairman of the defence support organisation', was appointed commander, as well as being appointed Nabiev's 'defence, national security and law enforcement adviser'. The tasks of the National Guard were to 'ensure security of state installations and officials, maintain order in society, and take part in state ceremonies'. See: *Tass World Service*, 1333 gmt (24 December 1991), in *SWB SU*, 1266 (31 December 1991), B/15.

into existence in Dushanbe: one in Shahidon Square backed the opposition, and another in Ozodi Square, in front of the Supreme Soviet, supported the government.

In Shahidon Square slogans of political pluralism, freedom of the press and human rights may have been uttered, but, as a correspondent of the Russian reformist newspaper *Nezavisimaia gazeta* observed,

> [T]he vast majority of the 'democrats'—bearded people in peasant robes and skull-caps—had a weak understanding of political intricacies and quite often did not understand the very word 'democracy,' but during confidential conversations eagerly told the correspondent that they had been instructed to come to the meeting by a mullah.[99]

The 'defenders of the constitutional order', assembled only a mile away, had been mobilised by traditional leaders in a similar fashion. In the village of Avangard in the Bokhtar *raion*, the chairman of the local soviet together with the village mullah explained to the residents in plain words that the government did not send grain to the village any longer because of 'non-Muslim mullahs', democrats and '*Rastokhezis*'; the CPT used to feed them, but once the '*Rastokhez* mullahs' came to the fore, their dinner table went empty; Turajonzoda was the 'puppet of Iranians', but, *inshallah*, Nabiev assisted by Russian soldiers would dispose of him.[100] After this fiery pep talk, enthusiastic crowds boarded buses and lorries and motored to Dushanbe to join the Ozodi Square meeting. Demonstrators were soon able to affect government business in Dushanbe. In particular, the new session of the Tajik Supreme Soviet started on 11 April 1992 but immediately voted to suspend until the demonstration ended.[101] By 12 April, Nabiev— increasingly frustrated with the negotiating tactics of the opposition—remarked on radio that their demands 'are increasing day-by-day'.[102]

On 12 April 1992, *Qozi* Akbar Turajonzoda and six Sufi leaders announced their support for the opposition. The number of protesters in Shahidon Square had swollen to 50 000 by then. The government was plunged into panic, and a split in the ruling coalition emerged. Two Kulobis who held a personal grudge against Nabiev, Davron Ashurov and Hikmatullo Nasriddinov, resigned from the Presidium of the Supreme Soviet. Akbar Mirzoev, on the pretext of illness, real or feigned, withdrew from the power struggle.[103] On 19 April, Nabiev gave demonstrators an ultimatum to leave by the next morning or security forces

---

99   *Nezavisimaia gazeta*, 21 January 1993.
100   *Charoghi ruz*, No. 17 (38) (1992), p. 1.
101   *ITAR-Tass* (11 April 1992), in *SWB SU*, 1355 (14 April 1992), i.
102   Nabiev mentions the opposition leaders whom he held direct talks with as Himmatzoda (IRP), Usmon (IRP), Yusuf (DPT), Abdujabbor (Rastokhez) and Turajonzoda (Qazi Kalon). No mention is made of La'li Badakhshon. See: *Tajik Radio*, 1300 gmt (12 April 1992), in *SWB SU*, 1358 (17 April 1992), B/1.
103   Bushkov and Mikulskii, '"Tadzhikskaia revoliutsiia"', p. 63.

would use 'more drastic measures';[104] however, no 'drastic measures' materialised, either because security forces were unwilling or because Nabiev was bluffing. Whatever the case, Nabiev would likely have appeared increasingly ineffective and weak.

On 20 April 1992, the thirteenth session of the Supreme Soviet commenced, which was supposed to find a solution to the political crisis. On 21 April the Supreme Soviet passed a vote of confidence in Kenjaev ('against his resignation'). In response, the same day, armed squads from the opposition occupied the parliament building and took some 20 people hostage, including 16 MPs and two deputy premiers. Safarali Kenjaev, either as a response to the taking of hostages or as a result of his inability to control the capital, resigned and opposition forces withdrew.[105] On the morning of 22 April, the hostages were released[106] and the opposition was granted many of their other demands,[107] besides just the resignation of Kenjaev. While these concessions ended the opposition's round of protests, they also re-initiated pro-government demonstrations, which began again on 24 April in Ozodi Square, where protesters—many of them Kulobis mobilised by the Kulobi mullah Haydar Sharifzoda and the Kulobi underworld figure Sangak Safarov—demanded Kenjaev's reinstatement, the removal of Turajonzoda as *Qozi* of Tajikistan and the rescinding of concessions granted to the opposition.[108]

As a response to, or emboldened by, the Ozodi Square demonstrations, the government appointed Kenjaev to chair the State Security Committee (the KGB successor).[109] Kenjaev replaced Anatolii Stroikin, who was blamed by

---

104   *Interfax* (20 April 1992), in *SWB SU*, 1360 (21 April 1992), i.
105   Bushkov and Mikulskii, '"Tadzhikskaia revoliutsiia"', p. 63; *ITAR-Tass* (22 April 1992), in *SWB SU*, 1362 (23 April 1992), i.
106   *ITAR-Tass* (22 April 1992), in *SWB SU*, 1362 (23 April 1992), i.
107   Tajik government and opposition leaders reached this comprehensive agreement: Kenjaev's resignation was confirmed, the law on 'rallies, meetings and gatherings' would be revoked, amendments to Article 104 of the criminal code adopted during the twelfth session would be revoked, a date for parliamentary elections would be set, five opposition members would be added to the Constitutional Commission, the president would pardon all participants at Shahidon, the arrest of Mayor Ikromov for bribery would be reviewed, the committee investigating Navjuvonov would report as soon as possible, and the Supreme Soviet would consider 'the issue of changing the Gornyy Badakhshan Autonomous Oblast into the Badakhshan Autonomous Republic'. In return the opposition would vacate Shahidon Square by 24 April and refrain from holding future rallies, except pre-election rallies, and observe the laws of the republic. See: *Tajik Radio*, 1200 gmt (22 April 1992), in *SWB SU*, 1362 (23 April 1992), B/2.
108   Mullojonov, 'The Islamic Clergy in Tajikistan Since the End of the Soviet Period', p. 241; Kilavuz, *Understanding Violent Conflict*, pp. 151–2, 179–80; *Postfactum*, 1219 gmt (25 April 1992), in *SWB SU*, 1365 (27 April 1992), B/3. *Postfactum* notes 500 people at Ozodi on the first night and several times more by the next day. Tett writes: '[Kenjaev's] well-organised supporters were brought by bus into the capital. They are bitterly opposed to the republic's powerful religious leader, Kazi Akbar Turajonzoda, and support Mullah Haidar Sharif, who is sympathetic to the government. Moreover, they believe that the opposition plans to create an Islamic government.' See: Tett, 'Poverty Brings Tajikistan's Political Tension to the Fore', p. 2. Gavhar Juraeva, an academic who was active in the opposition, accused Kenjaev of escalating the conflict by 'hiring mercenaries from Kulob' and transporting them to Ozodi Square. See: Juraeva, 'Ethnic Conflict in Tajikistan', p. 265.
109   Kilavuz, *Understanding Violent Conflict*, pp. 151–2.

vice-president, Narzullo Dustov, for not preventing the taking of deputies as hostages.[110] Kenjaev's appointment resulted in the opposition restarting its demonstrations in Shahidon Square. There were now two very large, sustained demonstrations in the capital making demands from the government in opposition to each other.[111] By 29 April, when the Supreme Soviet finally met— and postponed the session the same day due to the lack of a sufficient number of deputies[112]—as many as 100 000 people were on the streets demonstrating. At the same time, a third demonstration with about 7000 people was initiated by a group of Dushanbe residents and tertiary students at Sadriddin Ayni Square, demanding an end to the first two demonstrations.[113]

On 30 April 1992, Nabiev introduced direct presidential rule in Tajikistan, but both the opposition and Nabiev's confederates ignored it. All elite factions hastily armed themselves, and their leaders negotiated directly, bypassing the president. Kenjaev and Dustov met with Turajonzoda, Khudonazarov held talks with Haydar Sharifzoda, and, generally, the political process in Tajikistan degenerated into a squabble amongst region-based strongmen. In Davlat Khudonazarov's words, 'the political antagonism was reflected externally through inertia (a red flag with hammer or sickle for the government, a tri-colour banner for the opposition), but it was regional antagonism that was rapidly gaining strength'.[114] On 6 March 1992, Mirzo Samiev and Abdullo Ochilov, the only two Leninobodis in the DPT top leadership, left their party and joined Nabiev's camp.[115] That same month the Kulob regional organisation abandoned the DPT. *Charoghi ruz*, the de facto publication of the 'liberal' opposition that used to preach national unity of the Tajiks, suddenly admitted that in Tajikistan

> regionalism has never been a malaise, it is rather a social phenomenon that, to an extent, is a natural part of the national psyche of our people … Politicians who understand the situation in the republic well have not criticised the rise of localistic organisations, they have come to head them.[116]

---

110 *Postfactum*, 1219 gmt (25 April 1992), in *SWB SU*, 1365 (27 April 1992), B/3.

111 Kilavuz, *Understanding Violent Conflict*, pp. 151–2.

112 *RIA*, 1507 gmt (29 April 1992), in *SWB SU*, 1369 (1 May 1992), B/2. The additional reason given for the postponement was that Nabiev and Turajonzoda were 'still discussing their problems'.

113 *Radio-1* (29 April 1992), in *SWB SU*, 1368 (30 April 1992), i. This estimate is according to the Supreme Soviet's official press service: *ITAR-Tass* (30 April 1992), in *SWB SU*, 1369 (1 May 1992), i. Panfilov describes the third demonstration as being composed mainly of neutral tertiary students from Dushanbe educational institutes. See: Oleg Panfilov, 'Tajikistan', *Nezavisimaia gazeta* (30 April 1992), in *SWB SU*, 1371 (4 May 1992), B/3; and Brown, 'Whither Tajikistan', p. 3. *Postfactum* provides smaller numbers: Ozodi Square on 29 April had 10 000 people while Shahidon Square had 35 000 (including 7000 white-bandana opposition 'guard members' surrounding the presidential palace). See: *Postfactum*, 0615 gmt (1 May 1992), in *SWB SU*, 1371 (4 May 1992), B/5-6.

114 Khudonazar, 'The Conflict in Tajikistan', p. 258.

115 In a televised statement, both anathematised the DPT's 'Bolshevism' and 'extremism', and warned that if it came to power, 'the best and honest cadres [that is, northerners] will be killed'. See: Usmon, *Soli Nabiev*, p. 29.

116 *Charoghi ruz*, No. 33 (54) (1992), p. 5.

Any constructive political dialogue between the government and opposition became virtually impossible, not least because of the weakness of the central authorities. Opposition leaders realised that they could gain more by exerting direct pressure on government structures.

The most alarming development in April 1992 was the rapid militarisation of the struggle for power: most political figures of any degree of prominence, including Kenjaev, Khudonazarov, Turajonzoda, Abdullojonov and even Qahhor Mahkamov, acquired private armed units.[117] Political assassinations became a harsh reality. On 3 May 1992, the editor-in-chief of the pro-government newspaper *Sadoi mardum* and member of the Supreme Soviet, Murodullo Sheraliev, was gunned down. Four days later a popular radio journalist and DPT activist, Olim Zarobekov, was killed. Anarchy and violence were engulfing Dushanbe, and, as in February 1990, criminal structures made their entry to the political arena.

Organised Crime and Politics

In 1990, there were more than 1200 known criminal recidivists living in Tajikistan.[118] Many of them formed gangs specialising in extortion, narcotics, smuggling and gambling. The number of these mafia-type entities rose from four in 1989 to 22 in 1992.[119] The notorious gang of Rauf Soliev (a Samarkandi) that operated in Dushanbe consisted of several hundred well-armed people; it was alleged that the gang enjoyed the patronage of Tajikistan's procurator-general, Nurullo Khuvaydulloev, and had taken an active part in the events of February 1990.[120] An important feature of organised crime in Tajikistan is its rootedness in traditional social institutions. A contemporary study showed that in the country 'a criminal group is frequently organised and maintained by ties of kinship amongst its members'.[121] Quite often a criminal gang encompasses male

---

117   D. Mikulskii, 'Svidetelstvo voiny v Tadzhikistane', in *Islam v Rossii i Srednei Azii*, eds Igor Ermakov and Dmitrii Mikulskii (Moscow: Lotus Foundation, 1993), pp. 253, 256.

118   *Kommunist Tadzhikistana*, 5 April 1991.

119   Data disclosed by Dr Rahmatillo Zoirov during a seminar at the Institute of World Economy and International Relations of the Academy of Sciences of Tajikistan, Dushanbe, 14 February 1995. They also constantly tried to perfect their structure and methods of operation: in every gang 'executive' groups (up to 30) committed crimes; the leader and his immediate entourage—'the council'—did not participate in concrete crimes, confining themselves to strategic planning; and the support unit tackled financial issues, recruited personnel and took care of internal and external security. See: V. A. Alexeev, I. N. Borisov and A. S. Emelianov, '"Organizovannaia prestupnost": kriminalizatsiia funktsii uchastnikov prestupnykh formirovanii', *Sovetskoe gosudarstvo i pravo*, No. 10 (1991), pp. 67–8.

120   Mikulskii, 'Svidetelstvo voiny v Tadzhikistane', pp. 254–5. In the autumn of 1991, Soliev became one of the field commanders of Kenjaev's People's Front of Tajikistan.

121   R. Zoyirov and S. Sharopov, 'Kriminologicheskaia kharakteristika i analiz tendentsii razvitiia organizovannoi korystnoi prestupnosti', in *Vlast', upravlenie, pravoporiadok, Vypusk I* (Dushanbe: Ikbol, 1995), p. 82.

youths from one *mahalla*,[122] and, given the regionalistic patterns of settlement in Dushanbe and other cities, it is sensitive to issues of sub-ethnic rivalry. Soliev's gang was based in the capital's suburb Obdoron, inhabited primarily by Kulobis; his deputy, Yaqubjon Salimov, was a Kulobi, which may explain the gang's involvement in the anti-Mahkamov coup in 1990. On the other hand, Dushanbe's Ispechak and Shomansur quarters, populated by Gharmis, had their own mobsters.[123]

On 29 April 1992, 13 criminal groupings that had assumed the collective name of Youths of Dushanbe City (YDC), mostly of Gharmi extraction, from Shomansur, Ispechak, Ovul, Qozikhon and Qarotegin Street, held a meeting in one of Dushanbe's squares where they supported the opposition's political demands[124] and demanded Nabiev's resignation.[125] Two days later armed units from Shomansur attacked the TV centre. They encountered no resistance from the 'neutral' police and handed control of the centre to the opposition.[126] As Aziz Niyazi has described the Islamist movement in Tajikistan, 'to say the least, the IRP turned into a regionalistic, monoethnic organisation that found itself associated with mafia and other corrupt groups'.[127] The same characterisation could have been applied to practically every political organisation, pro-government or opposition: 'each side's regionalist ties solidified in response to the security threat posed by the other side',[128] and political leaders were not fastidious in using the underworld elements with whom they were linked by business, conjugal and patrimonial ties. One of the founding fathers of Oshkoro in 1989 was sixty-one-year-old Sangak Safarov, who had spent 23 years in jail on various charges, including homicide.[129] His influence in the Kulob *oblast* was hard to overestimate. According to the region's chairman of the executive

---

122   In 1991, there were some 140 *mahalla*-based youth groupings 'with aggressive orientation' in Dushanbe, which often clashed in neutral zones such as Putovskii market in the centre of the city. Interview with the deputy minister of labour of the Republic of Tajikistan, Bekmahmad Qurbonov, Dushanbe, 18 March 1995.

123   The city's law enforcement agencies had even developed psychological profiles of 'Khujandi', 'Kulobi', 'Samarkandi', 'Shomansuri' and other criminals according to their local identification. See: Kenjaev, *Tabadduloti Tojikiston*, Vol. 1, p. 285.

124   Bushkov and Mikulskii, '"Tadzhikskaia revoliutsiia"', p. 63.

125   One of the orators proclaimed that 'these days only Mountain Tajiks are in all Dushanbe squares, and the government can play them against each other. In the Ozodi Square, Kulobis support Kenjaev, Nabiev and Saifulloev. [But t]hey have no relation to Kulobis ... Nabiev must pay for pitting Mountain Tajiks against one another. We have one issue today—Nabiev's resignation. We must drive him away from Tajikistan.' See: Usmon, *Soli Nabiev*, p. 64.

126   *Jumhuriyat*, 15 June 1992.

127   Niyazi, 'Tajikistan', p. 184.

128   Barnett R. Rubin, 'The Fragmentation of Tajikistan', *Survival*, Vol. 35, No. 4 (Winter 1993–94), p. 78.

129   Contrary to some speculation, Safarov was not a 'thief-in-law'—the highest informal rank in the Soviet underworld; he was a 'cormorant'—a lower rung, which, however, ensured his authority amongst criminal figures not only in Tajikistan but also elsewhere in Central Asia. See: Arkadii Dubnov, 'Katastrofa v Tadzhikistane, o kotoroi v Rossii pochti nichego ne znaiut', *Novoe vremia*, No. 4 (1993), p. 14.

committee, Qurbon Mirzoaliev, who became acquainted with Safarov in 1980, he was honoured to be addressed as 'brother' by *bobo* Sangak—then ostensibly an obscure bar owner.[130]

Regional Nature of Political Competition and Protests

The counter-demonstrators, who set up close to the opposition demonstrators, were brought in mainly from Kulob, Hisor and Leninobod.[131] Numerous writers focus on the prominent role of Kulobis at the counter-opposition demonstrations, some in very explicit regional terms. Roy, for example, writes that the 'Leninabadis then received back-up from the Kulabis',[132] while Rubin notes that '[s]ince the Khujandis had no forces in the south to counter the mobilization of Garmis and Pamiris by the DPT and IRP, they called on the Kulabis'.[133] When, on 1 May 1992, Nabiev declared a state of emergency, he relied on men from Kulob to man his newly formed 'National Guard'.[134] Atkin focuses on one particular Kulobi—stressing that Nabiev relied on Sangak Safarov to lead the counter-demonstration at Ozodi Square.[135] Parviz Mullojonov also emphasises the presence of Kulobis, noting that earlier in April thousands of counter-demonstrators arrived in Dushanbe from Kulob with the assistance of Sangak Safarov and the Kulobi mullah Haydar Sharifzoda.[136] Kilavuz expands the geographical base of mobilisation and notes that Safarov was also able to bring demonstrators from the Qurghonteppa region,[137] presumably some of the many

130   Nozir Yodgori, *Saddi otash: Yoddosht, Khotira, Andesha* (Dushanbe: Firdavs, 1993), p. 82.

131   Markowitz, *Collapsed and Prebendal States in Post-Soviet Eurasia*, pp. 107–8. Roy portrays the regional origins of the protesters in a more comprehensive manner: 'It was enough to look at the out-of-town numberplates and the names on the placards to see that this was a localist mobilisation. Shahidan Square brought together Gharmis from Karategin and Kurgan-Teppe, people from Ramit and Kafirnehan, Darwazis, Pamiris and people from Zarafshan (who came individually). To Liberty [Ozodi] Square, on the other hand, came people from Kulab, Leninabad, Hissar, Shahrinau, Tursunzade, Lenin and Varzab.' See: Roy, *The New Central Asia*, p. 140. Kilavuz qualifies the presence of northerners at the protests: 'The Khujandi elite was not unified, and did not act as a group. Many of its members did not support Nabiev, come to the squares during the demonstrations, or become involved in the war.' See: Kilavuz, *Understanding Violent Conflict*, p. 185.

132   Roy, *The New Central Asia*, p. 140.

133   Rubin, 'Russian Hegemony and State Breakdown in the Periphery', p. 153.

134   Bess A. Brown, 'The Civil War in Tajikistan, 1992–1993', in *Tajikistan: The Trials of Independence*, eds Mohammad-Reza Djalili, Frederic Grare and Shirin Akiner (New York: St Martin's Press, 1997), p. 90; Rubin, 'Russian Hegemony and State Breakdown in the Periphery', p. 153.

135   Muriel Atkin, 'A President and His Rivals', in *Power and Change in Central Asia*, ed. Sally N. Cummings (New York: Routledge, 2002), p. 102. Markowitz also writes that during the demonstrations Safarov emerged as a prominent leader of the pro-government forces. See: Markowitz, *Collapsed and Prebendal States in Post-Soviet Eurasia*, p. 107.

136   Mullojonov, 'The Islamic Clergy in Tajikistan Since the End of the Soviet Period', p. 241. See also: Brown, 'Whither Tajikistan', p. 3.

137   Kilavuz, *Understanding Violent Conflict*, pp. 179–80. This of course does not mean that the demonstrators from Qurghonteppa were not Kulobis, as plenty of Tajiks from the Kulob region were sent to the Vakhsh Valley

Kulobis living in Qurghonteppa. While some express puzzlement at the alliance between the incumbents and these particular Kulobis,[138] this arrangement with Kulobi powerbrokers was likely a continuation of the political arrangements leading up to November 1991, when Sangak Safarov and Akbar Mirzoev[139]—a client of Nabiev's and the chairman of the Kulob Province Executive Committee—mobilised support for Nabiev's election campaign.[140]

Whitlock, among many others, mentions that the 'pro-government' side did not organise demonstrations to challenge the opposition's presence in the street until very late. In contrast, she notes the early opposition success in mobilising Pamiris and Gharmis.[141] This successful mobilisation showed resilience over time, and as late as 30 April large vehicle convoys bound for Shahidon were leaving Gharmi and Pamiri areas of eastern Tajikistan.[142] These anti-government demonstrators had one particular reason for feeling safe in Dushanbe. Schoeberlein-Engel writes that because most of the police in Dushanbe were Pamiris, 'many in the city believed that this would deter Nabiev and his predominantly Leninabadi government from staging a violent crackdown'.[143] On 2 May, however, Nabiev circumvented the security forces and formed a 'National Guard' (also known as 'Presidential Guard') by distributing weapons to the counter-demonstrators while unnamed persons also distributed weapons to the demonstrators at Shahidon.[144] Schoeberlein-Engel explicitly labels the newly formed and armed

---

during the Soviet migration schemes.

138 For example: Said Akhmedov shares Aleksandra Lugovaya's puzzlement over the Kulob-Leninobodi/Khujandi alliance. Akhmedov's best guesses are that the population of Kulob was instilled with a 'pro-Soviet mood', fear of an Islamic state and the presence of 'religious contradictions' between Gharm/Qarotegin and Kulob, or the possibility that the savvy Khujandi leaders took advantage of Kulob's 'naivety'. See: Akhmedov, 'Tajikistan II', p. 174, citing Aleksandra Lugovaya, 'Politicheskii krizis v Tadzhikistane byl neizbezhen', in *Tadzhikistan v ogne* (Dushanbe: Irfon, 1993–94).

139 For his efforts, Mirzoev was rewarded with the position of chairman of the Council of Ministers. See: Kilavuz, *Understanding Violent Conflict*, p. 178.

140 Kilavuz, *Understanding Violent Conflict*, p. 178.

141 Whitlock, *Land Beyond the River*, p. 161. Whitlock points to one factor mentioned in a Russian newspaper (*Komsomolskaya pravda*, 22 May 1992) that explains why the opposition had the early success in mobilising their demonstrations, this being the 'presence of a mighty idea in the minds of some, and its absence in that of others'. This quip may sound meaningless, but it can be elaborated upon using what is referred to in sociology and political science as 'frames'. Framing theory is defined by M. N. Zald as 'strategic framing of injustice and grievances, their causes, motivations, and associated templates for collective action'. See: M. N. Zald, 'Culture, Ideology, and Strategic Framing', in *Comparative Perspectives on Social Movements. Political Opportunities, Mobilising Structures, and Cultural Framings*, eds D. McAdam, J. McCarthy and M. N. Zald (Cambridge: Cambridge University Press, 1996), p. 261. For an application of frames to Central Asia, see: Fumagalli, 'Framing Ethnic Minority Mobilisation in Central Asia'. Alternatively, and more cynically, one could just posit an 'offensive advantage' on the part of the opposition. According to Flemming Splidsboel-Hansen, this included the fact that the opposition was initially 'more determined to change the status quo than the pro-government side was on preserving it, and thus willing to take greater risks'. See: Splidsboel-Hansen, 'The Outbreak and Settlement of Civil War', pp. 10–12.

142 Panfilov reported that on 30 April a 100-vehicle convoy left Khorugh (Pamirs) while 30 vehicles left Tojikobod (upper Qarotegin/Gharm). See: Panfilov, 'Tajikistan'.

143 Schoeberlein-Engel, 'Conflicts in Tajikistan and Central Asia', p. 37.

144 Markowitz, *Collapsed and Prebendal States in Post-Soviet Eurasia*, pp. 107–8. Markowitz does not name the source for the weapons at Shahidon.

National Guard as composed of out-of-town 'Kulobi demonstrators'.[145] After several days of clashes, with the state unable to control the violence, the counter-demonstrators retreated from Dushanbe. As a result, Nabiev wavered and entered into a power-sharing agreement with the opposition in the form of the Government of National Reconciliation (GNR), which included many Gharmis and Pamiris.[146]

Protests Transitioning to Violence in 1992

With a majority of the opposition-aligned deputies absent, the Supreme Soviet voted on 30 April 1992 to confer special presidential powers upon Nabiev for the next six months. These powers included: control over the legislative, executive and judicial branches; the right to 'suspend' any political party or organisation; and the right to end rallies and demonstrations.[147] The opposition soon publicly restated its demand for the resignation of Nabiev at a 2 May 1992 press conference.[148] On 3 May, the Supreme Soviet reappointed Kenjaev as its chair (a position he would hold in addition to remaining chair of the National Security Committee), scheduled new *Qoziyot* elections for 14 May, and recommended that Turajonzoda be arrested. At the same time Nabiev decreed the creation of a 'national guard corps' (alternately 'President's Guards' or 'National Guards within the Presidency'; hereinafter 'National Guards') within two weeks. In response, Ozodi Square demonstrators, '[i]ntoxicated with [their] first major victory', demanded the repeal of all earlier concessions given to the opposition.[149] The time line for the creation of the National Guards was shortened drastically when, on the same day, the government armed anywhere from 400 to 3000 demonstrators at Ozodi Square. This armed unit—dominated by Kulobis—was to presumably report directly to Nabiev and Kenjaev.[150]

On the night of 3–4 May, the Shahidon demonstrators attempted to enter the presidential palace, but were stopped by security forces. The Ozodi

---

145 Schoeberlein-Engel, 'Conflicts in Tajikistan and Central Asia', p. 38, citing Brown, 'Whither Tajikistan', pp. 1–6.

146 Markowitz, *Collapsed and Prebendal States in Post-Soviet Eurasia*, pp. 107–8.

147 *ITAR-Tass*, 1640 gmt (30 April 1992), and 0900 gmt (1 May 1992), in *SWB SU*, 1370 (2 May 1992), B/9.

148 *Postfactum*, 1154 gmt (2 May 1992), in *SWB SU*, 1371 (4 May 1992), B/4. Yusuf read the statement while Turajonzoda was in attendance.

149 *ITAR-Tass* (3 May 1992), in *SWB SU*, 1371 (4 May 1992), i; *Postfactum*, 1639 gmt (3 May 1992), in *SWB SU*, 1373 (6 May 1992), B/5; *Tajik Radio*, 0400 gmt (1 May 1992), in *SWB SU*, 1371 (4 May 1992), B/4-5. Procurator-general, Nurullo Khuvaydulloev, declined to press charges against Turajonzoda, saying that there 'were no grounds to initiate criminal proceedings'. See: *Postfactum*, 1639 gmt (3 May 1992), in *SWB SU*, 1373 (6 May 1992), B/5.

150 Juraeva, 'Ethnic Conflict in Tajikistan', p. 266; *Postfactum*, 1154 gmt (2 May 1992), in *SWB SU*, 1371 (4 May 1992), B/4; Brown, 'Whither Tajikistan', p. 3. Juraeva claims 1700 weapons were handed out at Ozodi, while *Postfactum* provides a wide-ranging estimate for the number of National Guards at 400–3000. Brown gives 2 May as the day on which weapons were distributed.

demonstrators then tried to move on Shahidon Square, but were also stopped by security forces and turned back.[151] On 5 May, a state of emergency signed by Nabiev was declared on radio. This included: a curfew from 9 pm to 5 am, demonstrations and strikes were prohibited, the activities of political parties, 'popular movements' and 'other social organizations' were banned, and the City of Dushanbe area of responsibility was to be put under the control of the military commissar of Tajikistan, Major General Mamadjonov.[152] In response to a question about how the government would deal with some of the more 'outrageous' demands of the opposition, an aide to President Nabiev replied, 'What measures were used in [the] Los Angeles [riots] last week?'[153]

At this time (midday on 5 May) there were 100 000 demonstrators in Dushanbe. It was on this same day that the violent conflict started, but not in the city. Several people were killed in a shooting at a blockade outside the city in the Yovon district at the Lenin (Rudaki) district crossroads. Soon after, shooting started in the city.[154] Overnight, pro-opposition forces took control of the TV building, the presidential palace, the railway station, the main roads and, briefly, the airport.[155] By the morning of 6 May, all main routes into the city were blocked by 'opposition patrols' checking incoming and outgoing cars.[156] On the same day, some members of the Supreme Soviet attempted to flee the city, while opposition supporters took four deputies hostage.[157] As for Nabiev, he took refuge in the blockaded Supreme Soviet building.[158] During the previous night, 'the power ministries—that is, those whose personnel had the right to carry arms—took sides'.[159] At 10 pm guardsmen at the Presidential Palace joined the demonstrators. At 2 am 'a large number of Interior Ministry men—the police force—came over to the opposition, bringing with them their arsenal. The Security Ministry, still generally known as the KGB, stayed with the government.'[160] According to a report by the Henry Dunant Centre, the opposition forces rapidly gained momentum and resources:

---

151 *Interfax* (4 May 1992), in *SWB SU*, 1372 (5 May 1992), i.

152 *Tajik Radio*, 1712 gmt (5 May 1992), in *SWB SU*, 1375 (8 May 1992), C1/1. The top two in the Interior Ministry (Rajabbov and Kaharov) were named his deputies.

153 Walter Ruby, 'Tajik President Creates Guard to Crush Protests; Democratic and Muslim Opposition Denounce "Leninabad Mafia"', *Christian Science Monitor* (6 May 1992).

154 This incident is further analysed in a later section in this chapter.

155 *Postfactum*, 1050 gmt (6 May 1992), in *SWB SU*, 1375 (8 May 1992), C1/3; *ITAR-Tass*, 0756 gmt (6 May 1992), in *SWB SU*, 1374 (7 May 1992), C2/1-2. The National Guards were able to quickly take back the airport. The opposition took over the TV broadcasts, but the signal was cut off outside the city and the government maintained control over radio. See: *Tajik Radio*, 1750 and 1900 gmt (5 May 1992), in *SWB SU*, 1375 (8 May 1992), C1/1.

156 *Postfactum*, 1628 gmt (6 May 1992), in *SWB SU*, 1375 (8 May 1992), C1/2. Opposition forces at roadblocks were stopping vehicles carrying food from going to Kulob.

157 *Channel 1 TV*[Moscow], 1100 gmt (6 May 1992), in *SWB SU*, 1375 (8 May 1992), C1/3.

158 *ITAR-Tass*, 0835 gmt (6 May 1992), in *SWB SU*, 1375 (8 May 1992).

159 Whitlock, *Land Beyond the River*, p. 163.

160 Whitlock, *Land Beyond the River*, p. 163. Whitlock notes that senior officers were non-Tajik, while one official told her that there were 'more Islamic Party members than communists' in the rank and file of the

If the opposition's arsenal was initially nothing more than a few hunting rifles and some Molotov cocktails, it quickly developed. For example, when they occupied the Presidential Palace, the opposition forces already had 250 automatic weapons and one tank. Also, on May 5, an entire OMON unit (Special Forces) of the Ministry of the Interior joined the opposition. This contributed 12 tanks, and 600 Kalashnikovs. Local police stations also quickly became a good source of weapon procurement.[161]

On 6 May, Major General Bahrom Rahmonov, an advisor to President Nabiev and the man picked to lead the National Guards, joined the opposition.[162] The next day, the top two men in the Interior Ministry also joined the opposition. This was especially significant in the capital as the deputy leader in the ministry was the commandant of Dushanbe.[163]

In response to the growing chaos, CIS military officers forcefully persuaded the government and opposition to compromise.[164] In particular, Colonel Viacheslav Zabolotny of the CIS 201st MRD forces—a Belorussian—demanded that the opposing sides meet, and threatened the leaders of both sides with arrest if they did not reach an agreement.[165] On the morning of 7 May, the preliminary agreement was announced on the radio. The initial protocols on the Government of National Reconciliation, which were signed by all the main government leaders—including Nabiev and Kenjaev—and opposition leaders plus Khudonazarov, included: bilateral disarmament, dissolution of the National Guards, the halting of all ongoing investigations, the removal of blockades from all buildings and facilities, no prohibitions on parties and organisations, dissolution of the Presidium and Presidential Council, the placing of the Committee for National Security and the Committee for Defence under the control of the GNR, and the banning of all further rallies, including the ending

---

KGB (Committee on National Security) in 1992. Tett also reports that forces of the Ministry of the Interior also joined the opposition. See: Gillian Tett, 'Tajikistan Opposition Militia Seizes Control of Capital', *Financial Times* (7 May 1992), p. 2.

161 Henry Dunant Centre, 'Humanitarian Engagement with Armed Groups', pp. 14–15. See also: Kathleen Collins, 'Tajikistan: Bad Peace Agreements and Prolonged Civil Conflict', in *From Promise to Practice: Strengthening UN Capacities for the Prevention of Violent Conflict*, eds Chandra Lekha Sriram and Karin Wermester (Boulder, Colo.: Lynne Rienner, 2003), p. 276.

162 *Postfactum*, 1628 gmt (6 May 1992), in *SWB SU*, 1375 (8 May 1992), C1/2-3; *ITAR-Tass*, 0835 gmt (6 May 1992), in *SWB SU*, 1375 (8 May 1992), C1/4; *ITAR-Tass*, 1808 gmt (6 May 1992), in *SWB SU*, 1375 (8 May 1992), C1/4; *Radio Free Europe/Radio Liberty Research Report*, Vol. 1, No. 21 (22 May 1992), pp. 76–7. Zartman (*Political Transition in Central Asian Republics*, pp. 108–9) portrays General Rahmonov's move favourably: 'In one of many efforts to prevent conflict escalation, Nabiev's military advisor General Bahrom Rakhmonov went over to the side of the opposition and Nabiev's government temporarily collapsed.' Zartman cites Juraeva ('Ethnic Conflict in Tajikistan', p. 266); however, she merely states that he joined the opposition.

163 *Russia's Radio*, 0100 gmt (7 May 1992), in *SWB SU*, 1375 (8 May 1992), C1/5. The head of the ministry was Navjuvonov, and Major General Kakharov was the deputy.

164 Zartman, *Political Transition in Central Asian Republics*, pp. 108–9.

165 Michael Orr, 'The Russian Army and the War in Tajikistan', in *Tajikistan: The Trials of Independence*, eds Mohammad-Reza Djalili, Frederic Grare and Shirin Akiner (London: Curzon Press, 1998), p. 152.

of both demonstrations.[166] Immediately after the signing of the GNR agreement many of the pro-government demonstrators started to leave Ozodi.[167] Later in the day Nabiev decreed the end of the state of emergency and announced a plan for the disarmament process.[168] Nabiev had clearly lost, and on 7 May 1992 he signed a protocol accepting the opposition's demands, dismissing senior government figures, disbanding the National Guards and lifting the state of emergency. For two days it was not clear who controlled the situation in Dushanbe; opposition leaders announced the creation of the Supreme Consultative Council, but at the same time an armed group that had occupied Tajikistan's radio station, presumably the Youth of Dushanbe City, broadcast a statement on behalf of the 'Revolutionary Council of the Union of Progressive Forces' claiming to have taken over the state.[169] After a short period of confusion, the opposition chose to refrain from a blatant violation of constitutional norms and on 9 May made Nabiev sign a power-sharing agreement. The president ceded most of his powers to the cabinet, including control over personnel appointments, coercive structures and mass media. Fresh parliamentary elections were slated for December 1992.

Certain individuals seemed unhappy with—or perhaps even emboldened by— the government's concessions. One DPT member stated that 'we can't say that the victory is total and final … The struggle is continuing. We have beheaded the dragon, but his poisonous tail and claws are still here.'[170] Meanwhile, many opposition demonstrators remained at Shahidon Square and demanded the resignation of Nabiev. By 10 May there were—with further negotiations ongoing—still thousands of demonstrators at Shahidon, amid a 'mood of irreconcilability'.[171] The leaders of the DPT, La'li Badakhshon and Rastokhez called for an end to the Shahidon Square demonstrations. In fact, much of the top opposition leadership rejected the demand for Nabiev's immediate

---

166   *Tajik Radio*, 1015 gmt (7 May 1992), in *SWB SU*, 1376 (9 May 1992), C1/1.
167   *Radio-1* [Moscow], 1500 gmt (7 May 1992), in *SWB SU*, 1376 (9 May 1992), C1/3. The military from a 'local garrison' searched a column leaving for Kulob and confiscated weapons.
168   *Tajik Radio*, 1345 gmt (7 May 1992), in *SWB SU*, 1376 (9 May 1992), C1/2.
169   *Izvestiia*, 8 May 1992.
170   Larry Ryckman, 'Tajik President Appeals for Peace; Opponents Control Capital', *The Associated Press* (8 May 1992).
171   *ITAR-Tass*, 0917 gmt (10 May 1992), in *SWB SU*, 1377 (11 May 1992).

resignation for reasons of stability.[172] One leader, the DPT's Shodmon Yusuf, called for Nabiev's resignation, but only once the situation had stabilised under a new government.[173]

The Islamic opposition negotiated in a somewhat different style. In Dushanbe 'radical activists'[174] of the IRP continued their protests at Shahidon, demanding the removal of Nabiev and his cabinet, the dissolution of the Supreme Soviet and trials for the government leaders—demands that were not supported by IRP leader Himmatzoda.[175] On 7 May, Mullah Qiyomuddin, going by the title 'General Sayyid Qiyomuddin *Ghozi*', had led 10 000 protesters in a chant:[176]

> 'What do you want?'
> 'Islam, Islam, Islam!'
> 'Do you want an Islamic state?'
> 'Yes, Yes, Yes!'

Qiyomuddin was one of the last hold-outs on the issue of Nabiev's continued leadership. On 12 May he bluntly announced that 'everyone responsible for the bloody events, first and foremost President Rakhmon Nabiyev, deserves a just punishment by law'.[177] Another of those who went against the top echelons of the opposition on the issue of Nabiev's potential removal was future IRP leader Abdullo Nuri. On 12 May he was quoted as saying that Nabiev 'must resign. After this bloodshed, he has no right to remain in power ... that is my last word.'[178] IRP deputy leader, Davlat Usmon, also denounced Nabiev and forcefully stated that the death of protesters who attempted to storm the

---

172 Correspondent Sergei Shatunov gave an explanation for the opposition leadership not wanting to remove Nabiev. Leaving Nabiev in office would: 1) preserve Nabiev's regional base of Leninobod as part of the republic, which is needed for its economy; 2) leave a familiar face for foreign affairs; and 3) leave a weakened and compliant leader in the presidency to the benefit of the opposition. See: *Channel 1 TV* [Moscow], 1800 gmt (10 May 1992), in *SWB SU*, 1378 (12 May 1992), C1/4. On 12 May, Turajonzoda said that Nabiev's resignation was not 'under consideration'. Turajonzoda remarked that '[h]e is behind the times, he has the old mentality, but the president is guarantor of the integrity of Tajikistan'. See: *ITAR-Tass*, 0903 gmt (12 May 1992), in *SWB SU*, 1379 (13 May 1992), C1/1. Turajonzoda stressed that it was a group decision by the opposition leadership. See: Bess Brown, 'Tajikistan: The Fall of Nabiev', *Radio Free Europe/Radio Liberty Research Report*, Vol. 1, No. 38 (25 September 1992), p. 13. See also: *Radio Free Europe/Radio Liberty Research Report*, Vol. 1, No. 21 (22 May 1992), pp. 76–7; Brown, 'Whither Tajikistan', p. 3. At a press conference, DPT leader Yusuf said that Nabiev must resign, but not until after the parliament was replaced and the new government was formed, since he guaranteed the republic's territorial integrity. See: *Interfax* (13 May 1992), in *SWB SU*, 1380 (14 May 1992), i.
173 *Interfax* (13 May 1992), in *SWB SU*, 1380 (14 May 1992), i.
174 Unnamed in the *Postfactum* citation below, but likely referring to Mullah/*Ishon* Qiyomiddin, 'an organizer of the opposition's national guard'. On 12 May, he said that Nabiev could not be part of the new government and called for him to be prosecuted. See: *ITAR-Tass*, 0903 gmt (12 May 1992), in *SWB SU*, 1379 (13 May 1992), C1/1.
175 *Postfactum*, 1545 gmt (10 May 1992), in *SWB SU*, 1378 (12 May 1992), C1/1-2.
176 Reuters, 'Tajikistan Opposition Takes Control; President Flees as City in Chaos', *The Globe and Mail* (8 May 1992).
177 *Interfax*, 0850 gmt (12 May 1992), in *SWB SU*, 1379 (13 May 1992), C1/1.
178 Reuters, 'President Keeps His Job as Tajikistan Creates Coalition', *The Globe and Mail* (12 May 1992).

KGB building 'closes the door to negotiations'.[179] Of course, Usmon was at this time negotiating privately for the position of deputy prime minister. But even after this point Usmon maintained that '[o]ur main demand is the resignation of Nabiyev'.[180]

On 11 May, after further negotiations mediated by Zabolotny, Nabiev signed another decree on the GNR coalition, with eight of 24 cabinet positions going to the opposition and Nabiev remaining in office. After the announcement an unstated number of the remaining protesters at Shahidon Square began to leave;[181] however, some demonstrators stayed. On 13 May, with negotiations ongoing, the now opposition-controlled state TV channel urged demonstrators to stay in Shahidon Square for the next few days. Finally, on 14 May, the opposition demonstrators left Shahidon.[182]

Some analysts make a note of the opposition receiving only one-third of cabinet positions, after remarking that the opposition had forcefully taken the capital. They frame the concessions as the opposition failing to make significant gains;[183] however, the GNR was in fact dominated by representatives of Gharm and Badakhshan, which is why its legitimacy was immediately rejected by Kulob and Leninobod.[184] The opposition gained more control over central decision-making than corresponded with one-third of the seats in the Cabinet. In many spheres, most importantly security, the opposition did in fact dominate, or at least make significant gains. In other cases the gains were made via the removal of pro-incumbent officials. Examples include the following.

---

179 Thomas Ginsberg, 'Tajik President, Muslim Opposition Agree on Coalition Government', *The Associated Press* (11 May 1992).

180 M. Warren, 'Coalition Hopes Raised in Tajikistan', *Herald Sun* (12 May 1992).

181 Whitlock, *Land Beyond the River*, p. 164; *ITAR-Tass*, 0600 gmt (11 May 1992), in *SWB SU*, 1378 (12 May 1992), C1/1; *Tajik Radio*, 1430 gmt (11 May 1992), in *SWB SU*, 1379 (13 May 1992), C1/1. Opposition cabinet portfolios included chair of the Defence Committee, chair of the State Radio and Television Committee, chairs of the Republican Bank, Sport and Tourism, the State Statistics Committee, and Minister of Education. According to Zabolotny, at the 11 May meeting, he said to Nabiev, Mirzoev and opposition leaders: 'Authorized as the garrison's commander I will arrest all of you, and no one will leave this study until you finally resolve all the disputable questions among yourself [sic].' He said the agreement on the GNR was then reached. He also stressed his unit's continued neutrality. Zabolotny then, according to his version, noted that talks continued on 12 May, this time without his presence. See: *Postfactum*, 1703 gmt (12 May 1992), in *SWB SU*, 1380 (14 May 1992), C1/3.

182 *Russia's Radio*, 0000 gmt (13 May 1992), in *SWB SU*, 1380 (14 May 1992), C1/2; *Interfax*, 1553 gmt (14 May 1992), in *SWB SU*, 1382 (16 May 1992), C1/1.

183 Kilavuz, *Understanding Violent Conflict*, p. 152; Zartman, *Political Transition in Central Asian Republics*, pp. 108–9. Specifically, Zartman, in regards to the opposition, writes that '[t]his small coalition participation does not justify any claim that they "seized power"'. Others give a higher proportion for the opposition in the new cabinet: eight of 20 portfolios. See: Timur Kadyr, 'Hot Spot: Powder Keg Under the Roof of the World', *Megapolis-Express* (16 September 1992), p. 20, in *The Current Digest of the Post-Soviet Press*, Vol. XLIV, No. 37 (14 October 1992).

184 Nourzhanov, 'Saviours of the Nation or Robber Barons', pp. 111–12. Similarly, Kilavuz writes: 'the local governments in Leninabad and Kulyab did not recognize Nabiev's concessions, or the legitimacy of the new government.' See: Kilavuz, *Understanding Violent Conflict*, p. 152.

- On 12 May, the government announced that elections for the head *Qozikalon* were cancelled, keeping safe the position of Turajonzoda—a man the counter-demonstrators had the most grievances with and who was arguably the most influential opposition member.[185]

- On 12 May, after negotiations, Nabiev decreed that a *Majlis* (national assembly) would be formed. This 80-person assembly, which was to be split evenly between the government and opposition, was supposed to have functioned until new elections on 6 December 1992.[186]

- On 13 May, Davlat Usmon, the deputy leader of the IRP, gained the position of deputy premier, as the deputy president position was abandoned. Usmon's duties required him to 'oversee' the National Security Committee (KGB), the Procuracy Office[187] and the Defence Committee. In addition, he 'would be responsible for the law enforcement bodies'.[188] Further areas of control included customs, archives, religious and regional policies.

- On 13 May, as part of the announcement of new cabinet positions, Navjuvonov regained the position of interior minister.[189]

- Rastokhez leader, Mirbobo Mirrahim, took over state TV and radio, allowing the opposition to control the airwaves.[190]

- Rezo Tursunov, recently appointed chair of the Committee for National Security (KGB), fled immediately after the GNR was announced.[191]

---

185 *Interfax*, 1616 gmt (12 May 1992), in *SWB SU*, 1380 (14 May 1992), C1/6. For example, see previous mentions of Turajonzoda in this section. For more extreme examples of anger against Turajonzoda, particularly a portrayal of him as the opposition mastermind, see: Khaidarov and Inomov, *Tajikistan*. For a more accessible source, see: Tett, 'Poverty Brings Tajikistan's Political Tension to the Fore'. As an example of Turajonzoda's power, by 7 May the opposition headquarters was stationed at the *Qoziyot* headquarters. See *ITAR-Tass*, 0750 gmt (7 May 1992), in *SWB SU*, 1375 (8 May 1992), C1/6.

186 *ITAR-Tass*, 1756 gmt (12 May 1992), and *Tajik Radio*, 1635 gmt (12 May 1992), in *SWB SU*, 1380 (14 May 1992), C1/1; *Interfax* (13 May 1992), in *SWB SU*, 1380 (14 May 1992), i; *Postfactum*, 2043 gmt (13 May 1992), in *SWB SU*, 1380 (14 May 1992), C1/2.

187 The Procuracy Office—or *Prokurator*—was an institution independent from local authorities that could initiate investigations and bring criminal charges against government officials. For an analysis of the procuracy in the late Soviet era, see: Gordon B. Smith, 'Procuracy, Citizens' Rights and Legal Reform', *Columbia Journal of Transnational Law*, Vol. 28 (1990); Gordon B. Smith, *The Soviet Procuracy and the Supervision of Administration* (Netherlands: Sijthoff & Noordhoff, 1978).

188 *Postfactum*, 2043 gmt (13 May 1992), in *SWB SU*, 1380 (14 May 1992), C1/2; *Interfax* (13 May 1992), in *SWB SU*, 1380 (14 May 1992), i.

189 *Tajik Radio*, 1430 gmt (11 May 1992), in *SWB SU*, 1379 (13 May 1992), C1/1. A day previously he was mentioned as the new minister. See: *Postfactum*, 1545 gmt (10 May 1992), in *SWB SU*, 1378 (12 May 1992), C1/2. The following day, Navjuvonov was not mentioned in the list of cabinet appointees; however, he was mentioned as head of the ministry later in the summer. See: *Radio Free Europe/Radio Liberty Research Report*, Vol. 1, No. 24 (28 August 1992).

190 *Tajik Radio*, 1430 gmt (11 May 1992), in *SWB SU*, 1379 (13 May 1992), C1/1.

191 *Russia's Radio*, 1900 gmt (12 May 1992), in *SWB SU*, 1380 (14 May 1992), C1/7; Aleksandr Karpov and Otakhon Latifi, 'Actions of Dushanbe Garrison Command Deemed Absolutely Correct', *Izvestiya* (13 May 1992), in *SWB SU*, 1380 (14 May 1992), C1/2-3. Specifically, Tursunov—after only a week in office—burned the documents on the February 1990 incident, when he was then deputy KGB leader. The replacement for Tursunov was A. Solibaev.

- On 13 May, the opposition announced that Kenjaev and the vice-president, Narzullo Dustov (a Kulobi), both fled the city after the GNR agreement.[192]

- The Presidium of the Supreme Soviet decided to appoint Akbarsho Iskandarov, an ethnic Pamiri (but not an opposition member), to what had been Kenjaev's position: chair of the Supreme Soviet.[193]

- Opposition members Sayfiddin Turaev, Akbar Turajonzoda and Asliddin Sohibnazarov were made members of the Supreme Soviet Presidium.

- A new constitution was to be drafted by July 1992 by a commission that included five representatives from each of the following organisations: the IRP, the DPT, Rastokhez, La'li Badakhshon and the *Qoziyot*.

- Opposition forces captured the main leaders of the counter-demonstrators, all of whom were Kulobis and at least one of whom was tortured for an extended period.[194]

- Major General Bahrom Rahmonov—as well as many in the Interior Ministry—had joined the opposition. On 11 May, Rahmonov announced at a press conference that the armed forces of Tajikistan consisted wholly of those present at Shahidon Square.[195]

- The armed (and unarmed) Kulobis at Ozodi Square had left Dushanbe defeated while opposition supporters celebrated.[196]

Incendiary Rhetoric and Security Dilemmas

Throughout the protests both sides engaged in inflammatory rhetoric and the spreading of rumours.[197] Some accusations, however, were based on leaders'

---

192 *Postfactum*, 2043 gmt (13 May 1992), in *SWB SU*, 1380 (14 May 1992), C1/2; *Channel 1 TV* [Moscow], 1400 gmt (14 May 1992), in *SWB SU*, 1382 (16 May 1992), C1/1. Kenjaev left Tajikistan for Uzbekistan and Dustov left to Kulob and then onwards to Khujand.

193 *Interfax*, 1855 gmt (13 May 1992), in *SWB SU*, 1380 (14 May 1992), C1/5. Atkin ('Tajikistan', p. 615) notes that Iskandarov, while a Pamiri, was actually an ally of Nabiev. Nevertheless, this still represents the loss of a strong pro-incumbent leader and his replacement with a weak one. 'Pro-government' forces in Kulob, Hisor and Leninobod were clearly not impressed by the fact that Nabiev and an ally retained control over the top two positions in government—evidenced by the fact that they rejected the authority of the central government and lost faith completely in Nabiev.

194 These three were Sangak Safarov, Mullah Sharifzoda and Rustam Abdurrahimov. The imprisonment lasted for five days and ended thanks to the intervention of Nabiev and/or Turajonzoda. See: Gretsky, 'Qadi Akbar Turajonzoda', p. 22; Khaidarov and Inomov, *Tajikistan*, p. 33.

195 *Tajik Radio*, 1850 gmt (11 May 1992), in *SWB SU*, 1380 (14 May 1992), C1/5.

196 For an example of early celebrations, see: *ITAR-Tass*, 0503 gmt (9 May 1992), in *SWB SU*, 1377 (11 May 1992), C1/1. Oleg Panfilov writes that the Kulobi Presidential Guards were defeated because of their shortage of weapons. See: Oleg Panfilov, 'Tajikistan: The Opposing Sides Open a Second Front', *Nezavisimaia Gazeta* (22 September 1992), p. 3, in *The Current Digest of the Post-Soviet Press*, Vol. XLIV, No. 38 (21 October 1992).

197 For example: IRP leaders blamed the United States—secretary of state, James Baker, in particular—for 'police rule and suppression of opposition'. *Postfactum*, 0945 gmt (30 March 1992), in *SWB SU*, 1345 (2 April 1992), B/9. On 7 April, DPT leader, Shodmon Yusuf, repeating a report by *Izvestia* from 3 April, claimed that 'Internal Troops of the Republic of Kazakhstan' had arrived in Dushanbe. *Kazakh Radio*, 0100 gmt (9 April 1992), and *Tajik Radio*, 1700 gmt (9 April 1992), in *SWB SU*, 1353 (11 April 1992), B/7. Abdullo Ochilov, a

actual statements, which were often hastily retracted. DPT leader Yusuf was especially guilty of this, demonstrated by his veiled threats against non-Tajik ethnicities[198] and his suggestion that Afghanistan may have a role to play in supporting the opposition.[199] Yusuf's position on Afghanistan was briefly shared by General Rahmonov, who then also retracted his statements.[200] The likely force behind the retractions and apologies of various opposition figures was Turajonzoda, who would usually contradict the more extreme positions in the opposition and attempt to reassure the public.[201] The discourse on the role of Islam was also a destabilising factor in spring 1992. Statements on the opposition side concerning the establishment of an Islamic state had to be refuted, with Turajonzoda again having to get involved in moderating IRP statements.[202] As part of the GNR, the IRP 'had to tone down its fundamentalist slogans' as it

---

'leader of the pro-government rally', in a television interview, labelled the DPT and Rastokhez as 'terrorist organisations'. *RIA* (27 April 1992), in *SWB SU*, 1366 (28 April 1992), i. Oleg Panfilov reported that rumours that 'several thousand [Loqay Uzbek] horsemen … supporters of the government, have set out for Dushanbe from Kulob are unconfirmed', and that, according to a 'reliable source', Haydar Sharifov (Sharifzoda), 'imam of the Kulyab mosque', has made a list of DPT and IRP members to be 'persecuted'—and 'one victim … had his ears cut off'. He notes further that opposition members are getting 'their children out of the way, fearing for their lives'. Panfilov, 'Tajikistan'.

198   Yusuf, speaking of 'crude [Russian] interference in our affairs', said this in Russian on *Tajik Radio*: 'I want again to warn the cold leaders of the CIS that there are a large number of Russian speakers in the town … I would absolutely and utterly not want, in the wake of events, this … to weigh on inter-ethnic relations in the town.' *Tajik Radio*, 1635 gmt (10 May 1992), in *SWB SU*, 1378 (12 May 1992), C1/3. A representative for the Russian 'Migration Society' interpreted Yusuf's comments as meaning that minorities 'could well be used as hostages'. *Interfax*, 1315 gmt (9 June 1992), and *Radio Moscow*, 0700 gmt (10 June 1992), in *SWB SU*, 1405 (12 June 1992), B/6.

199   After Nabiev declared the state of emergency and armed the National Guards, DPT leader, Shodmon Yusuf, declared in a statement that the opposition 'had the right to ask' for help from neighbours, especially Afghanistan. He later appeared on TV and apologised and tried to reassure the public that this was not the case. See: Brown, 'Whither Tajikistan', p. 5. See also: *Postfactum*, 2043 gmt (13 May 1992), in *SWB SU*, 1380 (14 May 1992), C1/2. Perceptions of Afghan involvement at this early state were likely not helped by the fact that Afghan President Rabbani sent a telegram to Turajonzoda, saying that Afghanistan's leaders would protect him (*Postfactum* [2 May 1992], in *SWB SU*, 1371 [4 May 1992], i), nor by Yusuf's statement that *mujahideen* leader, Ahmad Shah Massoud, was a 'great son of the Tajik people' (*Postfactum*, 2043 gmt [13 May 1992], in *SWB SU*, 1380 [14 May 1992], C1/2).

200   Rahmonov initially said that assistance from Afghanistan would not be ruled out. A day later he announced that assistance from Iran and Afghanistan was 'ruled out, the more so—military assistance'. *Tajik Radio* (11 May 1992), in *SWB SU*, 1379 (13 May 1992), i; *Postfactum*, 1136 gmt (12 May 1992), in *SWB SU*, 1380 (14 May 1992), C1/4.

201   For example: Turajonzoda met with representatives of Dushanbe's Russian community to reassure them that no-one in Tajikistan would be allowed to express 'anti-Russian sentiments' or 'perpetrate anti-Russian actions'. See: *Russia's Radio*, 1900 gmt (12 May 1992), in *SWB SU*, 1380 (14 May 1992), C1/7. On Turajonzoda as a mediator, see: Kilavuz, *Understanding Violent Conflict*, pp. 167–8, 172.

202   IRP leader, Muhammad Sharif Himmatzoda, said 'that he will work for the creation of an Islamic republic in Tajikistan. However, he said that the question of changing the social structure of the state must be decided by the people, not at a demonstration.' See: *Interfax*, 1553 gmt (14 May 1992), in *SWB SU*, 1382 (16 May 1992), C1/1. Turajonzoda—not a member of the IRP at this time—provided an opposing view on the establishment of an Islamic government: 'Only in a democratic society can religion develop normally in a non-violent way, by means of freedom of choice. So we do not make it our aim to create, to organize in Tajikistan a theocratic state, a religious state. We are all for a secular society.' See: *Channel 1 TV* [Moscow], 1800 gmt (10 May 1992), in *SWB SU*, 1378 (12 May 1992), C1/4. Davlat Usmon, the vice-premier and deputy leader of the IRP, said in an interview that he 'shared the view' of Turajonzoda that 'the decades of communist rule have

was now a partner with Rastokhez and the DPT.[203] The opposition also accused the pro-government demonstrators at Ozodi Square of being against Islam— accusations that the Supreme Soviet condemned as lies.[204] Furthermore, both sides made threats of violence against the other.[205]

As early as the first half of April this type of rhetoric did not escape the notice of President Nabiev, who said in a radio address:

> Today we have two alternatives. We can either listen to common sense or whip our horse of emotions … At the meetings slogans have appeared which are of a provocative nature. The more we had hindered them the louder these slogans would have sounded. Those slogans from which comes the scent of war and blood cannot under any circumstance be connected to democracy.[206]

Neither side of the increasingly rancorous political conflict in the capital heeded Nabiev's warning. For example, *RIA* reported that 'government supporters in Ozodi Square had threatened to kill [Turajonzoda] … And issued an ultimatum for the opposition to clear Shahidan square or they would empty it themselves'.[207] Eventually even Nabiev joined the chorus of angry voices.[208]

---

killed the trust of many people in God, and they would apparently take more than a year to accept the idea of an Islamic republic on their own'. His statement, however, only qualifies the time line for the establishment of an Islamic state. See: *Interfax*, 1047 gmt (5 June 1992), in *SWB SU*, 1400 (6 June 1992), B/5.

203   Dudoignon, 'Political Parties and Forces in Tajikistan', p. 67.

204   According to unnamed sources, the following slogans were heard at Ozodi: 'Down with Islam', 'Down with democracy, which split the Soviet Union' and 'Long live Safarali Kenjaev'. *Postfactum*, 0615 gmt (1 May 1992), in *SWB SU*, 1371 (4 May 1992), B/6. In response, the Supreme Soviet issued a statement thanking demonstrators at Ozodi and condemning rumours spread by the opposition that Ozodi protestors are against 'Islam and the Shari'ah'. The statement stressed that Ozodi demonstrators were 'indeed Muslim believers'. *Tajik Radio*, 0800 gmt (4 May 1992), in *SWB SU*, 1372 (5 May 1992), B/7. See also: Olimova and Olimov, 'The Islamic Renaissance Party'.

205   Davlat Usmon of the IRP said that if war broke out 'the current government of Tajikistan will be wiped out'. *Interfax* (27 April 1992), in *SWB SU*, 1367 (29 April 1992), i. Also, Whitlock reported that '[o]ne government man initially in sympathy with the Shahidan group froze in horror when someone there yelled "Burn the communists' houses and let them suffocate in the smoke!" He was not alone in feeling that things had gone too far, and that people had begun to play dangerous parts.' See: Whitlock, *Land Beyond the River*, p. 161.

206   *Tajik Radio*, 1300 gmt (12 April 1992), in *SWB SU*, 1358 (17 April 1992), B/3.

207   *RIA* (27 April 1992), in *SWB SU*, 1367 (29 April 1992), ii. Also, Whitlock reported that '[s]ome Azadi demonstrators shouted wildly that Turajanzada was a criminal, and should be put on trial'. See: Whitlock, *Land Beyond the River*, p. 161.

208   At the beginning of May, the president addressed the Supreme Soviet with this statement: 'The tolerance exhibited by the government and the lengthy talks are aimed at one goal—to avert bloodshed … I shall be frank with you. If we get away from slogans, the crux of the matter is as follows—the meeting in front of the Supreme Soviet building is a resolute protest of the people against the opposition meeting. It is a meeting in favour of a constitutional order and a law-based democratic state … The Qoziyot has overtly become the headquarters of the [opposition] meeting. The IRP and qozi have become its leaders. They have lied to such an extent that they have begun to believe their own fibs. They frighten people by saying that the government will close mosques, burn the sacred books and destroy Muslims … We have tolerated this so far. Tolerated it to a degree that astonished the world … Let me repeat: our people are a peaceful people … But we also should be aware of the fact that there are limits to any patience. We were patient when the opposition

One incident is credited as particularly reckless. This occurred when Mullah Qiyomiddin announced at Shahidon Square that opposition demonstrators were armed with 27 000 weapons,[209] a move that opposition supporter Gavhar Juraeva argues was 'an attempt to forestall officially sanctioned violence against the opposition'.[210] On 24 April, the IRP chairman denied the rumours about 27 000 armed men, saying only that 'self-defence groups' had been formed.[211] Sulton Hammad, a security adviser to the opposition, later said that '[i]t was a bold rather than a realistic number. But his declaration ignited rumours that both sides were arming their people, which forced each side to think about the need to actually arm their people.'[212] Zartman labels this a 'classic security dilemma', in that he believes the mullah was attempting to deter a potential forceful government response to the opposition demonstrators.[213] Davlat Usmon, at the time the IRP leader, later explained what happened:

> Before May 1992 we did not think of taking up arms. But, when on April 27–28 a rumour appeared that the government was preparing an armed militia we also started to act. We armed the first 40–50 people. All they had for weapons were one pistol, two grenades and 30–40 hunting rifles. We then started to prepare Molotov cocktails.[214]

On 1 May 1992, Nabiev made the last desperate attempt to create a loyal military force behind the presidency. His Decree No. 76 provided for the formation of a Special Tasks Battalion (STB), also referred to as the National Guards, from volunteers in Ozodi Square.[215] Soon after, on 2 May, the demonstrators at Ozodi Square matched the opposition rhetoric on weapons when Mullah Haydar Sharifzoda called for the Ozodi crowd to be given weapons to defend against

---

took a group of parliamentarians and two Deputy Premiers hostage. We were patient even when for two and a half days officials of the President's Office and the Cabinet were held hostage … Praised be our patience. But, perhaps, enough is enough. We respect the opposition. But it seems that we respect it too much, it has sat on our heads and continued to put forward demands. The respect must be mutual. The opposition does not respect us. This is its will. If so, we shall not respect it any longer … Let it be known that I shall undertake all necessary measures to guarantee normalisation of the situation and people's security.' Source: *Vechernii Dushanbe*, 5 May 1992.

209   Henry Dunant Centre, 'Humanitarian Engagement with Armed Groups', p. 13. Qiyomiddin was also known as *Ishon* Qiyomiddin, Qori Qiyomiddin Ghozi and Said Gaziev.

210   Juraeva, 'Ethnic Conflict in Tajikistan', p. 266.

211   *RIA*, 1229 gmt (24 April 1992), in *SWB SU*, 1365 (27 April 1992), B/4. He also denied that the IRP had relations with Afghan *mujahideen*.

212   Henry Dunant Centre, 'Humanitarian Engagement with Armed Groups', p. 13.

213   Zartman, *Political Transition in Central Asian Republics*, pp. 107–8. Zartman also conveys the opposition's talking points, writing that 'Kenjaev ordered a few public murders and violence escalated. Pamiris, a CIS officer and some journalists were shot.'

214   Henry Dunant Centre, 'Humanitarian Engagement with Armed Groups', p. 13. Usmon continues: 'Before the attack on the Presidential Palace, during the night from May 4, when two officers of the government forces came to the demonstration, I asked one of them: "Major, do you see a war?" and I asked the demonstrators to show their weapons. They showed bottles with inflammable oil. There were about 1500–2000 bottles.'

215   Dustov, *Zakhm bar jismi vatan*, p. 239.

opposition demonstrators.[216] A while later the CIS garrison commander in Dushanbe had to deny Turajonzoda's allegation that a CIS armoury in Kulob had lost its weapons.[217] On 3 May the security dilemma was in full effect as the government distributed as many as 1700 assault rifles to pro-government demonstrators at Ozodi Square.[218] In response, firearms were issued to the Shahidon Square militia, headed by 'people's General' Mullah Qiyomiddin from Qurghonteppa,[219] who, with active cooperation from the head of the State Automobile Inspectorate, Colonel Habib Sanginov, cut the roads leading from Kulob to Dushanbe. Opposition commanders reached a 'gentlemen's agreement' with police authorities in Kofarnihon whereby the latter surrendered weapons and vehicles to Qiyomiddin's forces.[220]

The Outbreak of Fighting in Dushanbe

Both the police and the military present in Dushanbe made claims of neutrality. Colonel Zabolotny, the head of the CIS 201st MRD, said that his unit would only act on orders of the top CIS commander and that his unit—in which only officers and warrant officers were armed—was 'adhering strictly to a policy of neutrality'.[221] On the police side, a Slav commander in OMON—a special police unit within the Interior Ministry—announced on 6 May that OMON units would be maintaining neutrality, only guarding their locations and patrolling the city. On the same day, however, they did repel an attempt by the opposition to take over a local radio station.[222] And, as earlier mentioned, one OMON unit had already joined the opposition.

---

216   *Interfax*, 1246 gmt (2 May 1992), in *SWB SU*, 1372 (5 May 1992), B/9.

217   *ITAR-Tass*, 0750 gmt (3 May 1992), in *SWB SU*, 1372 (5 May 1992), B/9. Commander Zabolotny said unsuccessful attempts by unknown persons had been made to bribe for or steal weapons.

218   Juraeva, 'Ethnic Conflict in Tajikistan', p. 266; Dustov, *Zakhm bar jismi vatan*, p. 239.

219   The quantity and source of this weaponry are not clear. One author has written about a truckload of submachine guns, 'not less than 5–6000', delivered from the *Qoziyot*. Usmon, *Soli Nabiev*, p. 73. This information could not be confirmed. Earlier Qiyomuddin made an interesting statement: 'We have armed groups. So far 27 thousand have signed up … We are able to arm them all. We have very strong ties with our mojahed brothers—Ahmad Shah Mas'ud, Burhonuddin Rabbani and Gulbuddin Hekmatyar.' See: *Sadoi mardum*, 25 April 1992. Qiyomuddin was renowned for his unsubstantiated albeit eloquent utterances (Turajonzoda once called him Dr Goebbels of the Tajik people).

220   Kenjaev, *Tabadduloti Tojikiston*, Vol. 1, p. 68. Kenjaev claims that 275 machine guns, 180 pistols and 10 vehicles were provided.

221   *ITAR-Tass*, 0750 gmt (3 May 1992), in *SWB SU*, 1372 (5 May 1992), B/9; *Postfactum*, 1628 gmt (6 May 1992), in *SWB SU*, 1375 (8 May 1992), C1/2.

222   *Channel 1 TV*[Moscow], 1100 gmt (6 May 1992), in *SWB SU*, 1375 (8 May 1992), C1/4; *ITAR-Tass*, 1808 gmt (6 May 1992), in *SWB SU*, 1375 (8 May 1992), C1/4; *Interfax*, 1740 gmt (6 May 1992), in *SWB SU*, 1375 (8 May 1992), C1/5. The commander's name was Sergei Vasilenko

As noted above—and aside from earlier minor incidents[223]—fighting started on 5 May in the outskirts of Dushanbe. This date can be regarded as the beginning of the civil war in Tajikistan. A shoot-out occurred between drivers delivering supplies to Ozodi Square from Kulob and opposition forces at a roadblock to the south of Dushanbe, with alternative versions of events blaming either side.[224] The fighting then spread overnight, with shooting between armed opposition forces and National Guards.[225] The violence continued throughout the next day, including deaths at Ozodi.[226] On the same day (6 May), the security forces offered no resistance as the opposition demonstrators—now in possession of Interior Ministry weapons and armoured vehicles—took over the presidential palace and airport.[227]

As mentioned above, on 5–6 May, Major General Bahrom Rahmonov joined the opposition. Rahmonov, an ethnic Uzbek who was initially appointed to head the National Guards, switched to the opposition side. Having declared himself a grandson of Sufi *sheikh* Abdurahmon from Qarotegin (Gharm), he defected to the opposition with seven APCs and 450 firearms,[228] and was appointed chief of staff of Mullah Qiyomiddin's militia, which by then had also named itself the National Guard (both sides were calling their units 'National Guards', or some variation thereof). The next day the opposition National Guards took control of Dushanbe's key facilities, including the presidential palace, the airport, bus terminals and the radio committee.[229] It soon became clear, however, that Rahmonov had brought little human resources to the opposition. Rahmonov—promoted to chair the National Defence Committee under the GNR—admitted as

---

223 For example, according to an opposition spokesman, unnamed authorities arrested two young Kulobis for an attempted arson attack at Turajonzoda's house. See: Panfilov, 'Tajikistan'. Also, the opposition displayed at a press conference a year 11 student from Kulob who admitted to being paid to attempt to throw a grenade into the Shahidon Square crowd. See: *Postfactum*, 1154 gmt (2 May 1992), in *SWB SU*, 1371 (4 May 1992), B/4.
224 These sources state that the National Guards shot at opposition supporters who were attempting to block Kulobis from entering Dushanbe: *Channel 1 TV* [Moscow], 1700 gmt (5 May 1992), in *SWB SU*, 1374 (7 May 1992), C2/1; *Postfactum*, 1818 gmt (5 May 1992), in *SWB SU*, 1374 (7 May 1992), C2/1; *ITAR-Tass*, 0765 gmt (6 May 1992), in *SWB SU*, 1374 (7 May 1992), C2/1-2; *Postfactum*, 1628 gmt (6 May 1992), in *SWB SU*, 1375 (8 May 1992), C1/2. On the other side, Whitlock writes that the first instance of violent conflict happened as a convoy of counter-demonstrators was arriving in Dushanbe from Kulob. In her version, unknown persons fired on the convoy, an incident that the opposition leaders maintain did not involve their supporters. See: Whitlock, *Land Beyond the River*, p. 161. See also: *Charoghi ruz*, No. 20 (41) (1992), p. 3.
225 *ITAR-Tass*, 1808 gmt (6 May 1992), in *SWB SU*, 1375 (8 May 1992), C1/4; *Postfactum*, 1628 gmt (6 May 1992), in *SWB SU*, 1375 (8 May 1992), C1/2.
226 On 6 May, unknown people threw a grenade into Ozodi Square from an ambulance and then shooting started. During the fighting unknown shooters killed a Supreme Soviet deputy at Ozodi Square on the stairs of the Supreme Soviet. The deputy was Nurullo Sheraliev, the editor of the *Sado-yi Mardum (Golos Naroda)* newspaper. See: *Postfactum*, 1628 gmt (6 May 1992), in *SWB SU*, 1375 (8 May 1992), C1/2; *Postfactum*, 1539 gmt (7 May 1992), in *SWB SU*, 1376 (9 May 1992), C1/4; *Russia's Radio*, 0800 gmt (7 May 1992), in *SWB SU*, 1376 (9 May 1992), C1/3.
227 *Postfactum*, 1628 gmt (6 May 1992), in *SWB SU*, 1375 (8 May 1992); Whitlock, *Land Beyond the River*, p. 163.
228 Abdulov, *Rohi behbud*, p. 57.
229 *Adolat*, No. 20 (32) (1992), p. 3.

much at a press conference on 11 May. While he spoke forcefully (for example, 'we must raise the people to fight against all the filth which surrounds us'), when asked about manpower he gave an honest answer:

> Q: [W]hat forces do the Ministry of Defence of the Republic of Tajikistan have at its disposal at present and what do you have under your command at the moment?
>
> A: I can say unambiguously that at present the armed forces of the Republic of Tajikistan consist of all the people present here in the [Shahidon] square at the moment. I can't say more than that just now.[230]

Rahmonov, while having had good relations with the opposition and local journalists,[231] unsurprisingly admitted that relations between Nabiev and himself were poor.[232]

One media outlet reported that demonstrators at Ozodi started to leave the city on 7 May immediately after the announcement of the preliminary GNR agreement was announced.[233] While a 'deal' may have been reached—in Whitlock's version—it clearly did not apply to the Kulobi leaders at Ozodi, several of whom were imprisoned and tortured by the opposition.[234] The meeting in Ozodi Square was terminated; its Kulobi participants retreated to their home region, carrying hundreds of arms received for the National Guards. At a higher level, Narzullo Dustov fled to Kulob, Safarali Kenjaev escaped to Uzbekistan, and Otakhon Saifulloev and other highly placed Leninobodis flew to Khujand.[235] By late in the day on 7 May—with the pro-government forces at Ozodi defeated and having left the square—the only 'centre of power' not controlled by the opposition was the National Security Committee (KGB) building, where Nabiev was being sheltered by the CIS 201st MRD.[236]

---

230 *Tajik Radio*, 1850 gmt (11 May 1992), in *SWB SU*, 1380 (14 May 1992), C1/5.

231 An undetermined number of journalists applauded Rahmonov at a press conference after one reporter used his/her question to thank him. A second questioner, from *TajikFilm*, then thanked him profusely. *Tajik Radio*, 1850 gmt (11 May 1992), in *SWB SU*, 1380 (14 May 1992), C1/5. In their enthusiasm, unnamed opposition leaders declared Rahmonov the 'general of the people'. *Postfactum*, 1628 gmt (6 May 1992), in *SWB SU*, 1375 (8 May 1992), C1/3.

232 *Postfactum* (12 May 1992), and *Russian TV*, 1900 gmt (12 May 1992), in *SWB SU*, 1380 (14 May 1992), C1/5-6.

233 *Radio-1* [Moscow], 1500 gmt (7 May 1992), in *SWB SU*, 1376 (9 May 1992), C1/3. Whitlock, however, describes what sounds more like a negotiated military retreat.

234 These three were Sangak Safarov, Mullah Sharifzoda and Rustam Abdurrahimov. The imprisonment lasted for five days and ended thanks to the intervention of Nabiev and/or Turajonzoda. See: Gretsky, 'Qadi Akbar Turajonzoda', p. 22; Khaidarov and Inomov, *Tajikistan*, p. 33.

235 *Adolat*, No. 20 (32) (1992), p. 3.

236 *Russia's Radio*, 0800 gmt (7 May 1992), in *SWB SU*, 1376 (9 May 1992), C1/3; Whitlock, *Land Beyond the River*, p. 163.

By the night of 8–9 May, the city was mostly calm, with APCs flying green flags driving through the city and opposition supporters celebrating.[237] Violent conflict restarted, however, on 10 May when opposition supporters surrounded the National Security Committee building—where President Nabiev was taking refuge. In the standoff and resulting violence, as many as 10 people in the opposition crowd were killed.[238] The opposing sides assigned blame in irreconcilable narratives, with each side the villain in the other's version.[239] After this incident   with as many as more than 100 deaths[240] in Dushanbe over five days—the demonstrators, in Kilavuz's words, 'returned to their hometowns, at which point fights began in these regions'.[241] By mid May the violence in the capital ceased;[242] however, this was not to last for long.

✳ ✳ ✳

In the twilight of the Soviet era, the pattern of escalating political competition in Tajikistan became increasingly based on regional affiliation. The relatively

---

237   *ITAR-Tass*, 0503 gmt (9 May 1992), in *SWB SU*, 1377 (11 May 1992), C1/1.

238   *Tajik Radio*, 0400 gmt (11 May 1992), in *SWB SU*, 1378 (12 May 1992), C1/4–5; *Radio Free Europe/Radio Liberty Research Report*, Vol. 1, No. 21 (22 May 1992), pp. 76–7; Whitlock, *Land Beyond the River*, p. 163.

239   Tajik Radio, now under opposition control, maintained that the crowds outside were unarmed, and blamed the 'barbaric and inhumane action on the part of the KGB forces'. See: *Tajik Radio*, 0400 gmt (11 May 1992), in *SWB SU*, /1378 (12 May 1992), C1/4–5. Tajik Radio makes no mention of any attempt to enter the building on the part of the crowd, which Radio Free Europe/Radio Liberty reports. See: *Radio Free Europe/ Radio Liberty Research Report*, Vol. 1, No. 21 (22 May 1992), pp. 76–7. An anonymous KGB officer provides another version, saying that three people were killed when armed IRP gunmen followed by protesters approached the building. He further claims that two APCs and armed gunmen opened fire on the building, which housed the KGB and the Interior Ministry. See: *RIA*, 1733 gmt (10 May 1992), in *SWB SU*, 1378 (12 May 1992), C1/5. Local witnesses of unknown sympathies said that a group approached the building escorted by 10 OMON troops with a white flag and a list of demands to convey, and that people inside the building opened fire. See: *RIA*, 1917 gmt (10 May 1992), in *SWB SU*, 1378 (12 May 1992), C1/5. An OMON commander said that he was tasked to stop demonstrators advancing, but that they were unarmed from his perspective; however, unknown shooters shot him in the leg. See: *Russian TV*, 1000 gmt (11 May 1992), in *SWB SU*, 1379 (13 May 1992), C1/2–3. Major General Martovitskiy, head of the local branch of the Central Asian Border District—whose headquarters was housed inside the building—said that demonstrators were asked to leave but they refused. The OMON fired warning shots and someone in the crowd fired back. He also mentions that APCs from the garrison (it's not clear if it was the 201st or the Border District garrison) then showed up. See: *Russian TV*, 1000 gmt (11 May 1992), in *SWB SU*, 1379 (13 May 1992), C1/2–3; *Interfax*, 0850 gmt (12 May 1992), in *SWB SU*, 1379 (13 May 1992), C1/3.

240   On 11 May, Tajik Radio reported a total of 74 deaths in Dushanbe. See: *Tajik Radio*, 0800 gmt (11 May 1992), in *SWB SU*, 1378 (12 May 1992), C1/4. Later, *Charoghi ruz* reported that 108 people perished, 233 were wounded and 104 were reported missing as a result of skirmishes in the capital city. See: *Charoghi ruz*, No. 20 (41) (1992), p. 3. For earlier tallies, see: *Radio-1* [Moscow], 1500 gmt (7 May 1992), in *SWB SU*, 1376 (9 May 1992), C1/3; *Radio Free Europe/Radio Liberty Research Report*, Vol. 1, No. 21 (22 May 1992), pp. 76–7. The exact count could be complicated since, as noted earlier by a police spokesman, locals might bury their deceased without informing the authorities. See: John-Thor Dahlburg, 'Dissidents Rout Tajikistan's Hard-Line Leader; Central Asia', *Los Angeles Times* (7 May 1992), p. 23.

241   Kilavuz, *Understanding Violent Conflict*, p. 152.

242   Aleksandr Karpov, 'Tajikistan: There Was Shooting in the Capital, and Now There's Shooting in the Provinces', *Izvestia* (11 June 1992), p. 2, in *The Current Digest of the Post-Soviet Press*, Vol. XLIV, No. 23 (8 July 1992).

open political and social environments allowed for groups and individuals to mobilise and demand changes to the structure of the state and society—whether through elections, bureaucratic appointments or large demonstrations in the capital. Regional elites who were Gharmi and Pamiri were especially likely to back Gorbachev's reforms and, later, the Tajik opposition parties against the northern elites—and their secondary allies from Kulob and Hisor—who dominated the central government. At stake for regional elites were not just powerful positions in the capital, but also local administrative and collective farm positions that involved the distribution of and control over local economic resources. In Qurghonteppa this resulted in competition between Gharmi Tajiks who backed the opposition and Kulobi Tajiks who backed the government and worked against the reforms.

The use of mass demonstrations in the capital, and the accompanying threats of violence, brought the political competition into the streets and increasingly into the hands of reckless individuals who were prepared for the use of force. By the time the government weakened and violent conflict started in May 1992, the only willing and able factions were the Gharmi Tajik-dominated IRP and their Pamiri allies in the security forces on one side and the Kulobi and Hisor-based actors on the other. While at this time there were still numerous exceptions to the rule of region of origin determining political loyalty, it is clear that the factions had a strong regional base and composition, especially in regards to those in leadership positions. This regional factor was to increase steadily as the level of violence increased throughout southern Tajikistan in the summer and autumn of 1992.

Epilogue: The Civil War of 1992

In May 1992 the political competition and street protests in Dushanbe transitioned into an extended period of violent conflict, with the worst of the violence occurring over the next seven to nine months.[1] The central government—now an uneasy power-sharing compromise—became largely irrelevant as killing, looting and destruction of property spread throughout southern Tajikistan, driving people to flee to any location safer than their homes, including to Afghanistan. At first much of the violence lacked broader coordination as no well-organised armed forces with acknowledged leadership existed at the outbreak of the civil war. The political leadership of the opposition and central government had very little, if any, control over the people apparently fighting in their name. As the conflict worsened, leaders of the militias emerged—very few of them familiar to those outside their home areas. Men of various backgrounds rose to prominence based on their ability to recruit, arm and lead men in the war. They would successfully use a variety of recruiting and mobilising techniques based on pre-exiting structures, networks and loyalties. This epilogue will provide a brief overview and short analysis of the most important phase of the civil war: from the outbreak of violence to the military victory of the anti-opposition[2] Popular Front forces in December 1992 and the arrival in the capital of Tajikistan's new leader, Emomali Rahmon.

At the beginning of the conflict the issue of regional identities being politicised was readily apparent, with Kulobi Tajiks dominant in pro-government demonstrations and Gharmi Tajiks heavily over-represented in the religious wing of the opposition. Region of origin (for example, Kulobi and Gharmi) would quickly become a matter of life or death as militias and even neighbours began to kill based on a person's origin. This would apply also to ethnicity in the case of Uzbeks and Pamiris, who came to be identified with the 'pro-government' and opposition sides, respectively. With the logic of mobilising for conflict based on these identities, the cleavages between Islamists, democrats and incumbent 'communists' became increasingly useless in terms of analytical value. The most concise description is the assessment of Brent Hierman that the best way to view the civil war in Tajikistan (with as few words as possible) is 'as a war fought between regional elites; specifically, following the collapse of the center, networks of elites, organized according to region, mobilized their

---

1 The only study conducted to determine the number of deaths in the civil war in Tajikistan put the number at 23 500, with 20 000 of these deaths occurring in 1992. See: Mukomel', 'Demograficheskie Posledstviia etnicheskikh i religional'nikh konfliktov v SNG', *Naselenie & Obshchestvo*, No. 27 (April 1997), Table 1; Mukomel', 'Vooruzhennie mezhnatsional'nie i regional'nie konflikti: lyudskie poteri, ekonomicheskii ushcherb i sotsial'nye posledstviia', in *Identichnost' i konflikt v postsovetskikh gosudarstvakh*.
2 The authors use 'anti-opposition' as the militias fighting against the pro-opposition forces were rejecting the incumbent leadership of Rahmon Nabiev and were seeking to install a different set of leaders in Dushanbe.

supporters against one another in an effort to gain control of the existing state institutions'.[3] In addition to the attempt to take control of state institutions, the militias would seize state assets, land and private property, a phenomenon that would help drive much of the conflict throughout 1992.

A Narrative of the War

While the most devastating phase of the civil war in Tajikistan was fought in the rural south, the capital managed to avoid the worst of the conflict (there were assassinations, kidnappings, theft, and so on, in the capital, but nothing on the scale of what was happening in the south). The Government of National Reconciliation was rejected by all of the relevant powerbrokers in Leninobod, Hisor, Kulob and in many areas of the broader Qurghonteppa region. President Nabiev became increasingly irrelevant and unable to perform his duties, rejected by both the opposition and the increasingly powerful Kulobi and Hisor-based forces. Finally, in early September he resigned and returned home to Leninobod, exiting politics permanently.[4] The opposition members of the coalition government proved equally inept, and few citizens had any confidence in whatever remained of the government and opposition in Dushanbe. In autumn 1992 the IRP—along with the DPT, Rastokhez and La'li Badakhshon—formed Najoti Vatan ('Salvation of the Homeland', aka the National Salvation Front), an effort at creating a broader unified military-political organisation. The leadership of Najoti Vatan attempted to form arrangements with government institutions,[5] but the organisation was eventually, if not immediately, a failure.[6] The exception to this failure, according to Bushkov and Mikulskii, was the Islamic Revival Party. The IRP was the only opposition entity able to survive the transition to civil war with any serious base of support.[7] Most of the IRP-affiliated field commanders in the south were mullahs. The IRP was able to reach out to its network of local mullahs, each of whom could recruit their followers

---

3   Brent Hierman, 'What Use Was the Election to Us? Clientelism and Political Trust amongst Ethnic Uzbeks in Kyrgyzstan and Tajikistan', *Nationalities Papers*, Vol. 38, No. 2 (2010), p. 256.
4   His place was taken by the Pamiri chair of the Supreme Soviet, Akbarsho Iskandarov, who served as interim president until the selection of Emomali Rahmon as chairman of the Supreme Soviet (the new top leadership position in Tajikistan after November 1992).
5   Najoti Vatan, the Dushanbe City Executive Committee, the city branch of the National Security Committee and the Interior Ministry signed a security agreement on 23 September regarding Dushanbe. The agreement stipulated that 'observation points' were to be set up at 'important points' in Dushanbe and that all signatories were to participate. See: *Tajik Radio* (23 September 1992), in *SWB SU*, 1495 (25 September 1992), i.
6   Davlat Khudonazarov blamed the failure on Kulobi officials who, unsurprisingly, declined to cooperate with Najoti Vatan. See: *Radio Free Europe/Radio Liberty Research Report*, Vol. 1, No. 42 (23 October 1992), p. 69.
7   Bushkov and Mikulskii, *Anatomiia grazhdanskoi voiny v Tadzhikistane*, pp. 69–70.

into militias;[8] however, as regional loyalties had prevailed, aside from a few individuals, the mullahs of Kulob and Hisor supported the incumbent, or rather anti-opposition, side, which was to eventually take the name Popular Front.[9]

Attempts were made by numerous interlocutors to arrange cease-fires in the summer and autumn of 1992. For example, the former opposition presidential candidate Davlat Khudonazarov and the executive chairman of the Bokhtar district, Abdulmajid Dostiev, a Kulobi, were amongst them. Throughout June and July 1992, they tried to prevent bloodshed in Qurghonteppa, risking their lives, but with very little success.[10] The true power-holders on the ground were the militia commanders, who ignored the proclamations of peace and urgings of negotiations by irrelevant entities and continued their operations. The only relevant outside power was Russia, which was appealed to by actors on both sides of the conflict. The forces of the 201st Motorised Rifle Division transitioned from a unified CIS command to a Russian command in late summer, which in theory allowed for the Russian leadership to make a unilateral decision on intervention without consulting its CIS partners. There was, however, no political will in Moscow to intervene, and Russia's military capabilities were stretched. The 201st forces in Tajikistan were depleted, with the enlisted ranks (mostly local Tajiks) deserting, leaving the predominantly Slav officers to watch over their bases, equipment and families, as well as to protect refugees (in Qurghonteppa), infrastructure (for example, the Norak hydro-electric facilities) and even some prominent figures such as Rahmon Nabiev.

In late May 1992, population cleansing commenced in Tajikistan: Gharmis were expelled from the Kulob region, and Kulobis were driven from Gharm and Qarotegin, as well as the Lenin (Rudaki) and Fayzobod *raions* to the south-east of Dushanbe. Displaced Gharmis poured into the capital (200 by June, more than 14 000 by August),[11] bolstering the ranks of Najoti Vatan. By July 1992, Kulob and the Gharmi-dominated districts of republican subordination had been 'homogenised'. The epicentre of the conflict now moved to Qurghonteppa, where neither of the sub-ethnic factions constituted a majority, and zones of influence were not clear. People in the southern Vakhsh Valley were left to fend for themselves. In late spring and early summer, pro-opposition forces had the

---

8 Kilavuz, *Understanding Violent Conflict*, p. 182; Rubin, 'Russian Hegemony and State Breakdown in the Periphery', p. 160, n. 68. Examples include: Abdullo Abdurrahim, Saidashraf Abdulahadov, Qari Qiyomiddin Muhammadjon, Mullah Amriddin and Mullah Abdughaffor. See: Akiner, *Tajikistan*, p. 42, n. 14.

9 Roy, 'Is the Conflict in Tajikistan a Model for Conflicts throughout Central Asia', pp. 134–5, 139–40. Regarding the mullahs of Kulob and Hisor, Roy argues that they justified their stance by developing 'an Islamic rationale for this, often based on the idea of a national and traditional Islam heavily imbued with Naqshbandi Sufism, as opposed to the "innovative" Islam imported by the "Wahhabis" (a generic and pejorative term used for Islamists, whether or not of Saudi allegiance).'

10 Eventually Abdulmajid Dostiev joined the Popular Front, after Najoti Vatan militiamen burned his house and the houses of 27 members of his family—'in the wake of this incident he could not look his relatives in the eye'. See: Rajabi Munki and Amirshoi Khatloni, *Nomus* (Dushanbe: Paik, 1994), p. 64.

11 *Vechernii Dushanbe*, 18 June 1992 and 18 August 1992.

momentum and were on the offensive throughout the south. During this time tens of thousands of Kulobi Tajiks and Uzbeks fled Qurghonteppa Province in the face of the increasingly confident pro-opposition forces, predominantly Gharmi Tajiks.

Attacks were directed not just against prominent anti-opposition figures, but also against communities as a whole. For example, in Qurghonteppa City, opposition forces attacked the Urghut Uzbek *mahalla*, leaving an unknown number dead.[12] During summer 1992 more than 100 000 Kulobis and Uzbeks had become refugees within their own country, or internally displaced persons. In the face of violence, expropriation of homes and intimidation, Kulobi Tajiks fled some *kolkhozes* wholesale, seeking refuge mainly in Kulob. Their homes were then looted and destroyed or taken over by their Gharmi Tajik neighbours. In June 1992, Gharmis of the Turkmeniston *kolkhoz* (home to the IRP third-in-command Nuri) expelled the Kulobis from their *mahalla*, leaving them no choice but to take up residence in the nearby Moskva *kolkhoz*, which was majority Kulobi. The two sides in the Turkmeniston and Moskva *kolkhozes*, now firmly 'homogenised' as Gharmi and Kulobi, fought each other from June until November, when the main Kulobi forces arrived and defeated the Gharmis of the Turkmeniston *kolkhoz*.[13] In the Qurghonteppa region, *kolkhozes* and villages that were mixed in a minority–majority region-of-origin pattern were more likely to be involved in the conflict and at an earlier point. In contrast, settlements that were evenly split stayed out of the conflict longer, with as few as just one or two managing to stay neutral for the entire conflict. When Gharmi forces came to a settlement with an even split, the local Gharmis would dissuade them from aggressive action. Local Kulobis would also do the same when Kulobi forces approached.[14] Another more cynical possibility here is that in an evenly split settlement both sides would perceive the cost of expelling the other side as high and the possible outcome as unsure, while in a settlement with a small minority the task of expulsion would not be costly in terms of effort and loss of life for the majority side.

In Kulob, the defeated Kulobis who had retreated from Dushanbe quickly killed or chased out the very few opposition supporters in the province, leaving Kulob completely controlled by the counter-opposition forces by early summer; however, opposition forces blockaded Kulob from all directions, leading Kulobis to renew their anti-opposition efforts with a renewed urgency as they grew increasingly desperate behind the blockade. Kulob would obviously not be able to hold out long with access to Dushanbe and Qurghonteppa blocked, and with its back to Afghanistan, the Pamirs and Gharm. In late summer and

---

12   See the comments by the Urgut *kolkhoz* chairman: *Golos Tadzhikistana*, 13 September 1992.
13   For the full narrative, see: Roy, *The New Central Asia*, p. 95.
14   Kilavuz, *Understanding Violent Conflict*, pp. 76–7.

early autumn, the Kulobi militias, with help from local Uzbeks, destroyed the blockade of Kulob and counterattacked into Qurghonteppa's Vakhsh Valley, making steady gains against IRP commanders and local self-defence forces. By late September the Kulobi militias and their Uzbek allies had turned the tide against the opposition forces in Qurghonteppa and continued their offensive throughout the Vakhsh Valley in October. The brutal offensive killed thousands (armed combatants and civilians) and drove countless more out of their homes, some even to Afghanistan.

By late October the counter-opposition forces had taken the name Popular Front, but were still under the command of various leaders who cooperated with each other, sometimes poorly. Nevertheless, forces commanded by Kulobi Tajiks Sangak Safarov, Langari Langariev and Rustam Abdurahimov steadily gained strength and soon set their sights on Dushanbe. The Hisor-based Popular Front commander Safarali Kenjaev and his Uzbekistan-supplied forces attempted the first takeover of Dushanbe, along with the police officer Langariev and the musician turned Oshkoro leader Abdurahimov. They met stiff resistance, however, from opposition Gharmi and Pamiri forces in the city and retreated, leaving Langariev seriously injured and Abdurahimov dead. This left the criminal underworld figure Safarov, who had not been invited to the battle, as the most prominent commander amongst the counter-opposition Popular Front forces. Safarov consolidated forces under his command, executed the uncooperative leaders of both the Kulob and the Qurghonteppa *oblasts*,[15] and prepared to take Dushanbe, which by now was starting to suffer serious deprivation. By late November the population of Dushanbe and the 100 000 refugees who were living in the city were experiencing serious hardship after two months of blockade.

On 10 November, acting president Iskandarov, the government and the Presidium of the Supreme Soviet submitted a joint resignation. The next session of the Supreme Soviet was held in the northern city of Khujand, far from the violence and chaos of the south. The sixteenth session, aided by the presence of 24 main field commanders from all sides,[16] worked out a new configuration of elite compromise in the country

- the Leninobodis agreed to sacrifice Rahmon Nabiev, whose resignation was confirmed by the parliament
- the institution of the presidency was abolished

---

15 Safarov said to Russian Defence Minister Grachev that '[i]n three months I have executed the leaders of two provinces'. See: Editor's note in Guljahon Sangakzoda, 'Sangak Safarov: Peshvoi fronti khalqiro chahor soat mekushtand', *SSSR*, No. 30 (27 July 2009), Accessed online September 2010: <http://asiaplus.tj/tj/articles/50/3896.html>
16 Arkadii Dubnov, '"Deputaty dogovorilis": Teper' delo za polevymi komandirami', *Novoe vremia*, No. 49 (December 1992), p. 15.

- Emomali Rahmonov, a forty-year-old people's deputy from Kulob,[17] was elected as the chairman of the Supreme Soviet
- Abdumalik Abdullojonov retained the premiership
- in the newly appointed Council of Ministers only one person represented Gharm; others were from Kulob, Leninobod and Hisor
- the Kulob and Qurghonteppa *oblasts* were merged again into the unified Khatlon *oblast*.

Emomali Rahmon (then known as Rahmonov), the leader of Kulob Province, was elected on a vote of 186 to eleven. Rahmon, who had only recently ascended to the top leadership position in Kulob after Sangak Safarov had executed the incumbent, was widely seen as being Safarov's client and as a weak leader put in place by far more powerful militia commanders in the background.

After the sixteenth session, Leninobod made tremendous infusions of money and weaponry into the Popular Front, which Sangak Safarov had come to head after Kenjaev's fiasco in Dushanbe. More importantly, Uzbekistan, with the explicit approval of Moscow, sent heavy equipment, instructors and even regular army units to aid Kulobi and Hisori militias, which in the beginning of December began to coalesce into a formidable 8000-strong force with a unified chain of command.[18] On 10 December, the Popular Front moved into Dushanbe with the backing of security forces from Uzbekistan. The Russian military did not interfere, while Pamiri militiamen had already retreated from the capital for Badakhshan, and within two days the Popular Front troops had easily secured the city. When the opposition had control of the capital, Pamiri and Gharmi-dominated forces had targeted Kulobis, Uzbeks and even Russians in Dushanbe for theft and murder.[19] Now a series of targeted killings in the other direction began to emerge: Popular Front forces were targeting and even executing Pamiris and Gharmi/Qarotegini Tajiks. This was later revealed to be a tactic from the very beginning of the offensive in Dushanbe when the Popular Front had attacked the Gharmi/Qarotegini population and houses in the opposition-dominated neighbourhoods of Ispechak, Ovul and Kazikhon.[20] By late December the sound

---

17   Rahmonov was born in Danghara and grew up in the *mahalla* of Sangak Safarov, who became his patron. In early November 1992, Rahmonov made a meteoric rise from the position of a *sovkhoz* director to the chairman of the executive committee of the Kulob *oblast*, to replace Jiyonkhon Rizoev, killed on 28 October by Safarov.

18   Christopher J. Panico, 'Uzbekistan's Southern Diplomacy', *Radio Free Europe/Radio Liberty Research Report*, Vol. 2, No. 13 (26 March 1993), p. 40.

19   For example: Mikulskii, 'Svidetelstvo voiny v Tadzhikistane', p. 250; V. I. Bushkov and D. V. Mikulskii, 'Tadzhikistan: chto proiskhodit v respublike?' *Issledovaniia po prikladnoi i neotlozhnoi etnologii*, No. 40 (1993), pp. 28–9; Schoeberlein-Engel, 'Conflicts in Tajikistan and Central Asia', pp. 40–1. See also: Lifshits, 'Politicheskaia situatsiia v Tadzhikistane', p. 44; Juraeva, 'Ethnic Conflict in Tajikistan', p. 268; Elif Kaban, 'Communal Warfare Tears Tajikistan Apart', *Reuters News* (27 October 1992).

20   For example: Roy, 'Is the Conflict in Tajikistan a Model for Conflicts throughout Central Asia', p. 136; Whitlock, *Land Beyond the River*, p. 180; Gillian Tett, 'The Night That Friends Turned into Murderers', *Financial Times* (19 February 1994), p. 13.

of occasional gunfire was still a nightly occurrence in the capital; however, by February 1993 the worst of the conflict throughout most of the country had subsided. Government forces, however, were still focused on opposition forces in the periphery of the country: the mountainous areas of Gharm and Tavildara, as well as along the Afghan border areas of Kulob and Qurghonteppa.

Islam, Ethnicity and the Regionalisation of Forces

The civil war of 1992 was mainly between Kulobis, southern Uzbeks (including Uzbek-speakers such as the Arabs, Qarluqs and Loqays) and Hisoris, organised later in the year as the Popular Front, on one side, and Gharmis/Qaroteginis and Ismaili Pamiris on the other. Those from the northern province of Leninobod, both Uzbek and Tajik, avoided participating in the military conflict.[21] Right from the start, the conflict in Tajikistan was mostly a confrontation amongst sub-ethnic groups, which developed in a progression from regional mobilisation to regional domination. The groups mentioned above, however, were not monolithic in their actions, nor were the sides to the conflict so hardened into their positions based on identity right from the beginning of the conflict.[22] As the conflict progressed, the parties went through a process of regionalisation (for example, Kulobis versus Gharmis) and ethnicisation.

Sangak Safarov saw the divide in regional terms from the very beginning. In April 1992 a meeting of all formal and informal leaders of Kulob *oblast* was held, during which he said: 'We and you shall become one ... All leaders born in the Kulob Valley must unite in these days of hardship and do whatever it takes to help the people of Kulob.'[23] At the protests, he was also framing the situation in regional terms when he spoke of Kulobis as being able to restore order to the city.[24] Kulob's leaders may have enunciated their policies in terms of defending the 'constitutional order' and the fight against 'Islamic fundamentalism' and 'Wahhabism', but beneath these slogans a clear image of the enemy crystallised— that of a vicious stranger belonging to a rival sub-ethnic group. An IRP official was absolutely correct when saying that 'these days the label "Wahhabi" is stuck indiscriminately ... on representatives of an entire region. Today people

---

21   Roy, 'Is the Conflict in Tajikistan a Model for Conflicts throughout Central Asia', pp. 133–6; Olivier Roy, 'Islamic Militancy: Religion and Conflict in Central Asia', in *Searching for Peace in Central and South Asia*, eds Monique Mekenkamp, Paul van Tongeren and Hans van de Veen (Boulder, Colo.: Lynne Rienner, 2002), p. 101; Nourzhanov, 'Saviours of the Nation or Robber Barons', pp. 112, 117; Schoeberlein-Engel, 'Conflicts in Tajikistan and Central Asia', p. 39; Rubin, 'Russian Hegemony and State Breakdown in the Periphery', pp. 143–4.

22   For example, see: Kilavuz, *Understanding Violent Conflict*, pp. 208–9.

23   Nasriddinov, *Tarkish*, pp. 288–9.

24   Whitlock, *Land Beyond the River*, p. 160.

from Rasht, Gharm, Vakhyo, Tojikobod, Darband, and so on, are meant by this term.'[25] An obscure head of an Uzbek militia in western Qurghonteppa put the essence of the civil conflict, as perceived by dozens of field commanders, in a nutshell: 'you are not even local Tajiks, you are strangers, from the mountains, we don't have enough land already, so clear off to your Pamirs and Gharm.'[26]

Many in the opposition saw the issue in terms of regional and ethnic affiliation as well, even within their loose coalition. Mirbobo Mirrahim, who had done so much to destroy the incumbent government, retained the post of chairman of the State Broadcasting Committee in the new GNR cabinet. On 24 September 1992, he made an entry into his personal diary that illuminates the internal divisions:[27]

> Several arrogant youths from *La'li Badakhshon*, *Nosiri Khisrav*, the DPT and the IRP have officially demanded my resignation. They know now that I am from Uroteppa ... I am an alien to the people of Gharm and the Pamirs. All power to the Gharmis and Pamiris ... They pray and fast, but they do this for the sake of money and cushy positions.

Earlier, during the days of the Shahidon Square meeting, the opposition newspaper *Haft ganj* published an inflammatory analysis of Nabiev's regime from an ethnic perspective:[28]

> The government, generally, relies on non-Tajiks, especially Uzbeks ... Naturally, the anti-national government could not have based itself on the authentic population. The second pillar of the government is Russian-speakers, but since the collapse of the Communist empire they have lost their influence ... Only grandchildren of the bloodsucking Chengiz Khan [that is, Uzbeks] could have been capable of spilling the Tajiks' blood twice in the past two years.

Opposition newspapers printed materials portraying Kulobis as dolts incapable of embracing progressive ideas; take the following attempt at 'humorous' dialogue, for example:[29]

> A. Congratulations! The people of Farkhor [southern Kulob] acquired consciousness, too. Their tents appeared [in the Shahidon Square].

---

25 *Najot*, No. 11 (1992), p. 4.

26 Dubnov, 'Katastrofa v Tadzhikistane, o kotoroi v Rossii pochti nichego ne znaiut', p. 15.

27 Mirrahim's papers were captured by Popular Front forces in Dushanbe in November 1992. Reproduced in: Safarali Kenjaev, *Tabadduloti Tojikiston*, Vol. 3 (Dushanbe and Tashkent: Fondi Kenjaev & Nashriyoti Uzbekiston, 1995), pp. 266–7.

28 *Haft ganj*, No. 19 (31) (1992), p. 7.

29 *Rastokhez*, No. 13 (April 1992), p. 4.

B. I also thought so. But then found out that those were Gharmis living
in Farkhor.

After the pro-government forces left Ozodi Square, the garbage-strewn area
was shown on (opposition-controlled) TV with a sign that read 'Museum of
Kulob' and accompanied with a commentator who remarked that Kulobis had
dirtied the capital. TV reporters filmed a room in the basement of the Supreme
Soviet filled with condoms and bottles while remarking that this was where
Kulobis had taken kidnapped local girls to be raped. Similar rumours circulated
in Kulob, where some speculated that Gharmis' goals were to seize power and
then take Kulobis' daughters. Later in May, some imams at Friday prayers took
to taunting Kulobis as 'losers' while also mocking Uzbeks.[30] Roy provides a
similar analysis, noting that 'from the first demonstrations, identity obtained
over ideological denomination in both camps: in the sermons of the mullahs,
"Kulabi" was equivalent to "Kafir" [infidel].'[31]

The opposition adviser Sergei Gretsky later acknowledged the opposition's
mistake of rhetorically attacking all Kulobis. He argues that in May 1992 'some
leaders of the opposition indulged in the vice of localism by stirring anti-Kulobi
emotions that deeply offended Kulob sensibilities and made them more prone
to fight the opposition to the end'.[32] Opposition leaders soon became much
more explicit in singling out Kulobis. In early July the Najoti Vatan deputy
chief of staff, Asliddin Sohibnazarov, stated: 'it is high time we declared war
on the people of Kulob, and on the Chairman of the Executive Committee of
the Kulob region, Qurbonali Mirzoaliev. All of us must take up arms.'[33] Some
officials, such as the Qurghonteppa Province Executive Committee chairman,
Nurali Qurbonov, at the end of September, were conciliatory when referring to
Kulobis as a whole.[34] By this time, however, it was too late. As noted by Rubin,
'the victorious militias chose men to kill not by indications of their ideology,
but by indications of the region where they were born'.[35] Kilavuz argues that

---

30 Whitlock, *Land Beyond the River*, pp. 160, 164.
31 Roy, 'Is the Conflict in Tajikistan a Model for Conflicts throughout Central Asia', p. 136.
32 Gretsky, 'Civil War in Tajikistan', p. 222. He frames this as a response, albeit a poor one, to the pro-
government side's tactic of 'exacerbating localism'; however, some individuals attempted to de-emphasise
regional cleavages. As an example, in early July *Moskoskiie novosti* reported that some in the government
were intentionally not naming sides to the conflict in order to not draw in 'local compatriots' by emphasising
regional aspects of the violent conflict in the Vakhsh Valley. See: Asal Azamova, 'Tajikistan: In Flames of
Internecine Wars', *Moskoskiye novosti* (5 July 1992), p. 9, in *The Current Digest of the Post-Soviet Press*, Vol.
XLIV, No. 26 (29 July 1992).
33 Kenjaev, *Tabadduloti Tojikiston*, Vol. 1, p. 337.
34 *Tajik Radio*, 1300 gmt (28 September 1992), in *SWB SU*, 1499 (30 September 1992), B/6. Qurbonov
commented on Tajik Radio: 'We do not want to blame the people of Kulyab. The population of Kulyab, at large,
support peace and want peace. However, those groups who are well known to us, their leaders being Sangak
Safarov, Langari Langariev, and others, including Rustam Abdurakhim, were all involved in the bloodshed.'
35 Rubin, 'Russian Hegemony and State Breakdown in the Periphery', p. 143.

> [w]hen the militias began to kill people according to their regional origin, the process itself made regional identity and regionalism one of the most important factors in [the] war. Just being from Garm or the Pamirs became grounds for being killed by pro-government forces, while the opposition came to treat Kulyabis similarly. In order to create loyalty, the warring parties used regional identities and allegiances to create antagonism towards those from other regions, and thereby generate support for themselves. The process forced the majority to side with people from their own region.[36]

There were, of course, some exceptions such as the Kulobi mullah Abdurahim, who stayed with the IRP even with the transition to violent conflict. Within the government in Dushanbe some leaders stayed above the regional conflict, despite their ethnicity or region of origin. The most prominent among these would be the acting president in late 1992, the Pamiri Akbarsho Iskandarov. Other leaders are difficult to classify, such as Safarali Kenjaev, who was of Yaghnobi origin but tied to power bases in the north and in Hisor, and who had a large number of ethnic Uzbeks under his command.

The New Powers in Tajikistan

At the beginning of the civil war, leaders of armed groups quickly rose to prominence—many from positions of obscurity. How they recruited and armed their forces is a subject that is vital to understanding how pre-existing social structures played a role in determining the characteristics of the armed formations. The 'regionalisation'[37] and ethnicisation of armed units and factions in Tajikistan were both a result of the structure of society in Tajikistan and a logical strategy—on the part of elites and non-elites involved in the conflict due to the mutual security dilemmas present.

At the outbreak of violent conflict there were not the solid cleavages between regional identities and ethnicities that existed half a year later. Ideological discourses of communism, Tajik nationalism, democracy and Islam proved to be insufficient in generating the required level of mobilisation, leaving regional loyalties as the soundest base for recruitment and for waging war; however, conflict entrepreneurs and political leaders in the opposition and in government still had to work towards this more fully polarised situation, ensuring benefits and power for themselves along the way. Starting with a significant level of political and economic relevance for regional and ethnic identities—with groups

---

36 Kilavuz, *Understanding Violent Conflict*, pp. 188–90.
37 For use here, 'regionalisation' is defined as the increased significance of region of origin in political and military decision-making (including selection of allies and foes based on region of origin).

like Kulobis and Gharmis over-represented on the incumbent and opposition sides, respectively—the violent conflict created security dilemmas whereby the most logical course of action was to side with your regional grouping while viewing other groups as a threat to your livelihood and/or your life. This created the logic of regional bases for conducting the war, both at the elite and the non-elite levels.

Despite the eventual high levels of violence, combat operations in Qurghonteppa did not start with large-scale killings of civilians, nor were the regional government structures a target. Rather, field commanders were focused on controlling economic assets, especially once the conflict turned into a low-intensity affair, in a bid to secure political (and economic) power. Qurghonteppa's economy, especially its agricultural sector, was a highly valued prize for the two sides to fight over.[38] Whether or not the fight for control of resources was one of the main causes of the civil war, the war quickly turned into a battle for resources that shaped the conflict from an early point and promoted its continuation.[39]

The Kulobis were the clear victors in the political and military struggles of late 1992. Accordingly, many of the most important positions in the government went to Kulobis. On 7 January 1993, Sangak Safarov travelled to Qurghonteppa to the regional legislature, where he made the following blunt remarks: 'The Kulobis are victors today. They have restored the state … Do not hope that we will allow you to restore the status quo.'[40] Safarov's men did well for themselves, especially his deputy, Yaqub Salimov, who became the interior minister. Journalists referred to Safarov as the 'power behind the throne'[41] and 'the backbone of the government'.[42] The view of Rahmon as a weak, unskilled leader who could only survive under the tutelage of Safarov was put to the test starting in April 1993 when Safarov was killed in a meeting-turned-gunfight with a disgruntled allied commander. Rahmon managed to survive without Safarov and has proved his skill at staying in power over the past two decades as he slowly marginalised or eliminated his former allies while also dealing with the opposition.

The diverse patterns of the conflict in 1992 have resulted in an inability to provide a single description that is true across time, location and individual or group. The most fitting examples of this are the emergence of armed factions and their attempts to recruit members and arm them. The leaders who emerged

---

38   Markowitz, *Collapsed and Prebendal States in Post-Soviet Eurasia*, pp. 128–9.

39   Schoeberlein-Engel, 'Bones of Contention', pp. 85–6; Schoeberlein-Engel, 'Conflicts in Tajikistan and Central Asia', p. 43.

40   *Golos Tadzhikistana*, 20 January 1993.

41   Steve LeVine, 'Communist Old Guard Turns the Tables on Moslems in Tajikistan: A Setback for Islamic Militants', *Financial Times* (26 November 1992), p. 4.

42   Nejla Sammakia, 'Tajik Government Extends Arms Deadline, Tales of Killings Mount', *The Associated Press* (28 December 1992).

were from a variety of backgrounds: civilian, military, police, government, criminal, religious, collective farm, and so on. And their methods of recruiting varied as well. Formal and informal networks and structures were employed to bring in recruits. The tactics employed in the recruitment process depended on the circumstances, as many fighters joined militias willingly while some were compelled by necessity or force. As for resources and arms to support their armed factions, militia leaders relied on a variety of sources, both foreign and domestic. The field commanders of the Tajik civil war, whether referred to as 'warlords', 'strongmen' or 'commanders', enjoyed a certain level of legitimacy. They tended to act in the interests of communities as well as for self-aggrandisement. Large segments of the population had to depend on various strongmen as far as their livelihood, security and often very existence were concerned.[43] For years afterward the power of these field commanders would be felt throughout the republic.

The Decline of Violent Conflict and the Expansion of State Authority

From early 1993 the IRP regrouped in Afghanistan with the support of former *mujahideen* forces and waged a cross-border insurgency under their new top leader, Sayid Abdullo Nuri. The Pamiri forces had retreated to the GBAO and blocked access to the region, essentially removing themselves from the battlefield. Meanwhile, much of the leadership of the less militarily inclined parts of the opposition (that is, the DPT and Rastokhez) went into exile in Russia, Iran and beyond. The insurgent opposition forces were never able to threaten the relevant parts of the country, and their operations were mainly to peripheral areas along the border, in Darvoz and what has now come to be named the Rasht Valley. Russia was now backing the government forces and assisted them in their campaigns; however, President Rahmon also had to deal with his ostensibly allied field commanders and militia leaders of the Popular Front. The most serious of these challenges was posed by Mahmud Khudoyberdiev, who reigned supreme in the Qurghonteppa area and had a contentious relationship with the government in Dushanbe. Khudoyberdiev even mobilised his troops towards the capital in order to extract concessions from Rahmon. He was eventually defeated in a skirmish with government forces and exiled to Uzbekistan, from where he led a failed invasion of the northern Sughd Province in 1998.

The opposition forces in exile held talks with each other and by late 1994 had the rough outlines of a negotiating group under the new name of the United Tajik Opposition (UTO); however, combat operations were the domain

---

43   For full analysis, see: Nourzhanov, 'Saviours of the Nation or Robber Barons', p. 109.

of the IRP-dominated Movement for the Islamic Revival of Tajikistan and junior partners such as the Islamic Movement of Uzbekistan. By 1996–97 the Russians, the Iranians and the IRP's sponsors in Afghanistan (for example, Ahmad Shah Massoud) realised that the ongoing civil war was detrimental to their efforts against the Taliban, which was rapidly gaining territory. All sides exerted pressure on the parties to the conflict, and in mid 1997 a peace agreement and power-sharing deal were signed between the opposition and the Tajik government. President Rahmon was then able to focus on marginalising and removing his less reliable or disruptive allies. The opposition itself was eventually targeted and the share of government portfolios it received as part of the peace deal was 'truncated' by Rahmon. The Government of Tajikistan has, since the official peace agreement, steadily expanded its authority throughout the country, despite facing occasional setbacks such as the violence in 2010 in the eastern Rasht Valley.

The Current Challenges of Sub-Ethnic Divisions and Islamism

A generation after independence, the trauma of the civil war continues to dominate the trajectory of nation-building in Tajikistan. The memory of bloodshed and violence in the collective psyche has inoculated the country somewhat against overt conflict, yet the problem of regional divisions, especially when exacerbated by the idiom of political Islam, has not withered away. The government of Emomali Rahmon has pursued a distinct ethno-centric approach to national consolidation since 1997, focusing on the historical exceptionalism of the Tajiks, their moderate Muslim sensibilities, and the 'othering' of Turkic neighbours. A lavish celebration of the 1100th anniversary of the Samanid Dynasty in 1999 introduced a major new myth to the state-sponsored discourse of nationalism. The era of the Samanids was proclaimed the Golden Age of Tajiks (as well as all Iranians), a high point in their political, cultural and economic achievements during the Middle Ages. A subtle move of the centre of Iranian civilisation to the east and the magnification of the specifically Tajik component therein were accompanied by a less subtle attack on the Turco-Mongol invaders who destroyed the Samanids and subjugated the Tajiks for centuries to come. 'The Tajik people who survived this terrible onslaught will never forget the tragic events of their history', wrote Rahmon, who then tried to reassure Uzbeks and other Turks who 'have all settled on the welcoming Tajik land and shared the fate of the Tajik people'.[44]

---

44   Rahmonov, *The Tajiks in the Mirror of History*, Vol. 1, p. 95.

The construction of Uzbekistan as an existential enemy forms an important part of the official nationalist discourse in Tajikistan. The neighbouring country is routinely accused of suppressing ethnic Tajiks on its territory, undermining the economic prosperity of Tajikistan, and interfering with its internal affairs. The regime of Islam Karimov is regularly criticised for its alleged pan-Turkism and its plans to rekindle the civil conflict in Tajikistan.[45] Greater domestic consolidation, strong government and national unity are touted as the conditions for Tajikistan's survival in this difficult environment. Constant appellation to history is essential to the dramaturgy of this process, and it is publicly manifested in the endless succession of festivities celebrating the heroes of Tajikistan, from Spitamenes of antiquity to the communist leader of Tajikistan during the Brezhnev period, Tursun Uljaboev, who transcended their patrimonial loyalties and self-interest in the service of all Tajiks. For example, 2009 saw large-scale commemoration of the 110th anniversary of Shirinsho Shotemur, a Pamiri and one of the founding fathers of the Tajik Soviet Socialist Republic, who stood up to Uzbek chauvinism and Stalin's arbitrariness to defend his nation and lost his life as a result.

The Government of Tajikistan, which is constitutionally a secular republic, has taken active steps to incorporate Islam into the fabric of nationhood, in contrast with other Central Asian republics. In 2008, President Rahmon announced Abu Hanifa (699–765 CE), the founder of one of the four major Sunni schools of Islamic jurisprudence, was an ethnic Tajik, and a year later initiated legislation declaring the Hanafi *madhab* practised by the majority of Tajiks the official creed of the country. The Islamic Revival Party of Tajikistan has been allowed to function legally and freely (though suffering some recent setbacks), with the ultimate result that 'Tajik Islamists abandoned Islamic state dreams and joined nation state making'.[46] In a 2010 national opinion survey, 81 per cent of those polled agreed that the government respected their freedom of religion; corresponding figures for other rights and freedoms were much lower.[47] Incorporating Islam into the official political discourse may thus be seen as a success for the government. Its progress in promoting 'Tajikness', however, has been more modest. The same survey indicated that 'nationality plus region' and 'region' continued to be the main markers of identity for people, at 50 and 25 per cent respectively, as opposed to 9 per cent of those who viewed themselves as 'citizens of the Republic of Tajikistan', and 4 per cent who selected 'nationality' as their primary association.[48]

---

45   Rahim Masov, *Tadzhiki: istoriia natsionalnoi tragedii* (Dushanbe: Irfon, 2008), pp. 441–2.

46   Kamoludin Abdullaev, 'Integrating Political Islam in Central Asia: The Tajik Experience', in *Islam, Oil, and Geopolitics. Central Asia after September 11*, eds Elizabeth van Wie Davis and Rouben Azizian (Lanham, Md: Rowman & Littlefield, 2007), p. 74.

47   International Foundation for Electoral Systems, *Public Opinion in Tajikistan 2010: Findings from an IFES Survey* (Dushanbe: IFES, 2010), p. 17.

48   International Foundation for Electoral Systems, *Public Opinion in Tajikistan 2010*, p. 38.

There are Islamic groups in Tajikistan aside from the mainstream IRP that seek to bring changes to the Tajik state and society. These groups, all of them illegal, seek to create an Islamic state ruled by shari'a law. Included amongst these are the Islamic Movement of Uzbekistan (IMU) and Hizb ut-Tahrir. Other organisations are less clear about their political goals and confine their activities to non-political missionary and education activities. Most notable here are Jamaati Tabligh and the Salafi movement. In regards to assessing their disruptive potential, Center for Strategic and International Studies (CSIS) researchers outlined the difficulties:

> Unfortunately, years of intemperate and biased assessments have muddied the waters of Central Asian jihadism to a state of near-impenetrable murkiness ... The skeptics ignore the demonstrated presence of jihadist groups and their clandestine support networks. The fearmongers exaggerate the threat that small groups of extremists pose and downplay the gains authoritarian states reap from dramatizing the militant menace.[49]

A 2012 survey by the Organisation for Security and Cooperation in Europe (OSCE) found that popular perceptions of the threat posed by radical Islamist groups varied significantly between Tajikistan's regions, peaking in the Vakhsh Valley, and were widely associated with Gharmis.[50] Meanwhile, perceptions of unfair domination by Kulobi Tajiks in the most powerful of the government structures are widespread in Tajikistan.[51] The echoes of the civil war are all too clear in these patterns.

In 1910, a Russian historian of Central Asia wrote:

> A close acquaintance with Tajiks, and a study of their mores, traditions, and way of life, involuntarily compels one to take sympathy to this hard-working people who had sustained so much hardship and suffering that

---

49 Thomas M. Sanderson, Daniel Kimmage and David A. Gordon, *From the Ferghana Valley to South Waziristan: The Evolving Threat of Central Asian Jihadists*, CSIS Transnational Threats Project (Washington, DC: Center for Strategic and International Studies, March 2010), p. 3.

50 Michael Taarnby, *Islamist Radicalisation in Tajikistan: An Assessment of Current Trends* (Dushanbe: Korshinos/OSCE, 2012), pp. 29, 59. While the small city of Isfara in the north is often associated with radical Islamist groups, popular perceptions in Tajikistan still mainly identify—fairly or not—Gharmis in the home region of the Rasht Valley (that is, Gharm/Qarotegin) and the Gharmi migrant community in the Vakhsh Valley as being supportive of radical Islamist views. Observation in Tajikistan by author, April 2012 to April 2013.

51 Observations and interviews in Tajikistan by author, April 2012 to April 2013.

one can only wonder how despite all of this it has not only failed to disappear from the face of the earth but also preserved in purity its tribal features.[52]

The condescending, orientalist tone of this statement notwithstanding, it captures well the drama of the Tajiks' long march through history. Their traditional social organisation and culture provided for resilience and survival in the pre-modern period. Conserved and reified during the colonial and Soviet periods, these very aspects militated against the emergence of a viable inclusive nationalism at the time of independence. More than 20 years later, these patterns persist. Tajikistan's future may be uncertain, but what is certain is that no-one should disregard the lessons of Tajikistan's past.

---

52   A. Shishov, *Tadzhiki: Etnograficheskoe issledovanie* [Reprint of the 1910 edition] (Almaty: ZhShS, 2006), p. 262.

Appendix I: Districts of Tajikistan

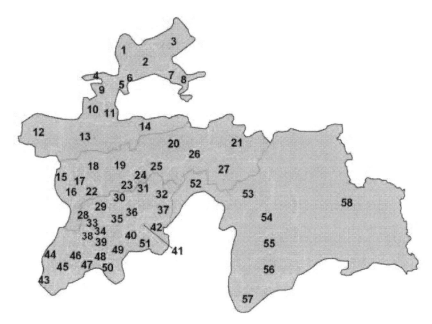

Source: Creative Commons licensed image. Credit: <http://commons.wikimedia.org/wiki/User:Ahonc> and <http://commons.wikimedia.org/wiki/User:Rarelibra>

Note: Former names in parentheses.

1. Mastchoh
2. Ghafurov
3. Asht
4. Zafarobod
5. Spitamen ('Nov' to 2003)
6. Rasulov
7. Konibodom
8. Isfara
9. Istaravshon (Uroteppa to 2000)
10. Shahriston
11. Ghonchi
12. Panjakent
13. Ayni
14. Kuhistoni Mastchoh
15. Tursunzoda (Regar to 1978)
16. Shahrinav
17. Hisor
18. Varzob
19. Vahdat (Kofarnihon to 2003)
20. Rasht (Gharm)
21. Jirgatol
22. Rudaki (Leninsky to 2003)
23. Fayzobod
24. Roghun
25. Nurobod (Darband until 2003)
26. Tojikobod
27. Tavildara
28. Khuroson (Ghozimalik to 2003)
29. Yovon
30. Norak
31. Baljuvon
32. Khovaling
33. Jomi (Khojamaston to 2004, previously Kuybyshevsk)
34. Sarband
35. Danghara
36. Temurmalik (Sovetsky to 2004)
37. Muminobod (Leningradsky)
38. Bokhtar
39. Vakhsh
40. Vose
41. Kulob
42. Shuroobod
43. Nosiri Khusrav (Beshkent)
44. Shahrituz
45. Qabodiyon
46. Jilikul
47. Qumsangir
48. Rumi (Kolkhozobod to 2007)
49. Farkhor
50. Panj
51. Hamadoni (Moskovsky to 2004)
52. Darvoz (Qalai-Khumb)
53. Vanj
54. Rushon
55. Shughnon
56. Roshtqala
57. Ishkoshim
58. Murghob

Appendix II: Major Ethnic Groups in Tajikistan

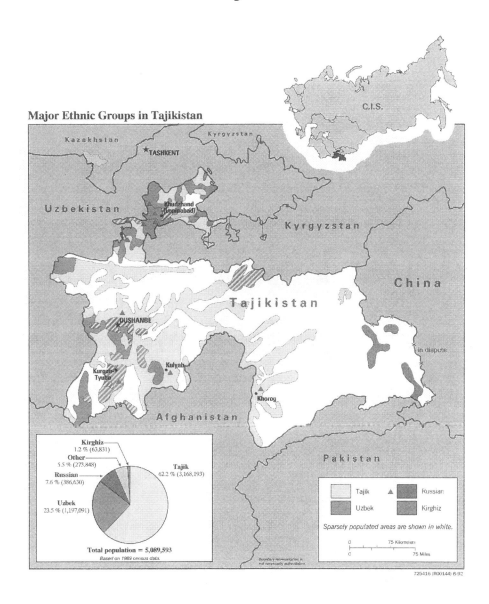

Major Ethnic Groups in Tajikistan

Kazakhstan

Kyrgyzstan

★TASHKENT

Uzbekistan

Khudzhand
(Leninabad)

Kyrgyzstan

China

Tajikistan

DUSHANBE

in dispute

Kurgan-
Tyube

Kulyab

Khorog

Afghanistan

Pakistan

Kirghiz
1.2 % (63,831)

Other
5.5 % (273,848)

Russian
7.6 % (386,630)

Uzbek
23.5 % (1,197,091)

Tajik
62.2 % (3,168,193)

Total population = 5,089,593
Based on 1989 census data.

Tajik	▲	Russian
Uzbek		Kirghiz

Sparsely populated areas are shown in white.

0   75 Kilometers

0   75 Miles

725416 (R00144) 6-92

Source: National Library of Australia.

Bibliography

1. Books, Chapters in Edited Volumes, and Pamphlets

XI s'ezd Kommunisticheskoi partii Tadzhikistana. Stenograficheskii otchet. Stalinabad: Tadzhikskoe gosudarstvennoe izdatelstvo, 1958.

XIII s'ezd Kommunisticheskoi partii Tadzhikistana. Stenograficheskii otchet. Stalinabad: Tadzhikskoe gosudarstvennoe izdatelstvo, 1960.

XIV s'ezd Kommunisticheskoi partii Tadzhikistana. Stenograficheskii otchet. Dushanbe: Tadzhikskoe gosudarstvennoe izdatelstvo, 1962.

XVIII s'ezd Kommunisticheskoi partii Tadzhikistana. Stenograficheskii otchet. Dushanbe: Irfon, 1976.

XIX s'ezd Kommunisticheskoi partii Tadzhikistana. Stenograficheskii otchet. Dushanbe: Irfon, 1983.

Abdullaev, Kamoludin. 'Current Local Government Policy Situation in Tajikistan.' In *Tajikistan at a Crossroads: The Politics of Decentralization*, edited by Luigi de Martino. Geneva: Cimera, 2004.

Abdullaev, Kamoludin. 'Integrating Political Islam in Central Asia: The Tajik Experience.' In *Islam, Oil, and Geopolitics. Central Asia after September 11*, edited by Elizabeth van Wie Davis and Rouben Azizian. Lanham, Md: Rowman & Littlefield, 2007.

Abdullaev, Kamoludin, and Shahram Akbarzadeh. *Historical Dictionary of Tajikistan*, 2nd edn. Lanham, Md: The Scarecrow Press, 2001.

Abdullo, Rashid G. 'Implementation of the 1997 General Agreement.' In *Politics of Compromise: The Tajikistan Peace Process*, edited by Kamoludin Abdullaev and Catharine Barnes. London: Conciliation Resources, 2001.

Abdulloev, Sherzod. 'Justuju dar atrofi ta'rikhi "Makhdumi A'zam".' In *Dar justujui farhangi vodii Hisor*, edited by N. N. Ne'matov, 13–23. Dushanbe: Mamnu'gohi ta'rikhi-madanii Hisor, 1992.

Abdulov, Karim. *Rohi behbud*. Dushanbe: [Self-published], 1995.

Abdulov, Karim. *Umedhoi barbodrafta yo 270 ruzi fa'oliyati prezident R. Nabiev.* Khujand: Tiroz, 1995.

Abduvakhitov, Abdujabar. 'Islamic Revivalism in Uzbekistan.' In *Russia's Muslim Frontiers: New Directions in Cross-Cultural Analysis*, edited by Dale F. Eickelman. Bloomington: Indiana University Press, 1993.

Abylgaziev, V. I. 'Iz istorii borby narodov Turkestana za vlast Sovetov.' In *Boevoe sodruzhestvo sovetskikh respublik. 1919–1922*, 166–76. Moscow: Nauka, 1982.

Adshead, S. A. M. *Central Asia in World History.* New York: St Martin's Press, 1993.

Ahmedov, B. A. *Gosudarstvo kochevykh uzbekov.* Moscow: Nauka, 1965.

Ahmedov, V. *KPSS v borbe za intensifikatsiiu khlopkovodstva.* Dushanbe: Irfon, 1976.

Aini, Sadriddin. *Vospominaniia.* Moscow and Leningrad: Izdatelstvo AN SSSR, 1960.

Akbarzadeh, Shahram. 'Abdullajanov and the "Third Force".' In *Politics of Compromise: The Tajikistan Peace Process*, edited by Kamoludin Abdullaev and Catharine Barnes. London: Conciliation Resources, 2001.

Akhmedov, Said. 'Konflikti v Tadzhikistane: Prichini i Posledstviia.' In *Etnicheskie i regionalnye konflikti v Yevrazii, Volume 1: Tsentralnaia Aziia i Kavkaz*, edited by Alexei Malashenko, Bruno Coppieters and Dmitri Trenin. Moscow: Ves Mir, 1997.

Akhmedov, Said. 'Tajikistan II: The Regional Conflict in Confessional and International Context.' In *Conflicting Loyalties and the State in Post-Soviet Russia and Eurasia*, edited by Michael Waller, Bruno Coppieters and Alexei Malashenko. London: Frank Cass, 1998.

Akiner, Shirin. *Islamic Peoples of the Soviet Union.* London: Kegan Paul International, 1983.

Akiner, Shirin. *Tajikistan: Disintegration or Reconciliation?* London: Royal Institute of International Affairs, 2001.

Akiner, Shirin. 'Prospects for Civil Society in Tajikistan.' In *Civil Society in the Muslim World: Contemporary Perspectives*, edited by Amyn B. Sajoo. London: I. B. Tauris, 2004.

Akiner, Shirin, and Catharine Barnes. 'The Tajik Civil War: Causes and Dynamics.' In *Politics of Compromise: The Tajikistan Peace Process*, edited by Kamoludin Abdullaev and Catharine Barnes. London: Conciliation Resources, 2001.

Alampiev, V. *Likvidatsiia ekonomicheskogo neravenstva narodov Sovetskogo Vostoka i sotsialisticheskoe razmeshchenie promyshlennosti.* Moscow: Izdatelstvo AN SSSR, 1958.

Albats, Yevgenia. *The State within a State. The KGB and its Hold on Russia— Past, Present, and Future.* New York: Farrar, Straus & Giroux, 1994.

Alimov, R., and M. Saidov. *Natsionalnyi vopros: raschety i proschety.* Dushanbe: Irfon, 1991.

Allworth, Edward. 'The Hunger for Modern Leadership.' In *Central Asia: 130 Years of Russian Domination: A Historical Overview*, edited by Edward Allworth. Durham, NC, and London: Duke University Press, 1994.

Allworth, Edward. 'The New Central Asians.' In *Central Asia: 130 Years of Russian Dominance, A Historical Overview*, edited by Edward Allworth, 527–52. Durham, NC, and London: Duke University Press, 1994.

Aminov, A., and A. Babakhodzhaev. *Ekonomicheskie i politicheskie posledstviia prisoedineniia Srednei Azii k Rossii.* Tashkent: Uzbekistan, 1966.

Aminov, A. M. *Ekonomicheskoe razvitie Srednei Azii (kolonialnyi period).* Tashkent: Gosudarstvennoe izdatelstvo Uzbekskoi SSR, 1959.

Amnesty International. *Tadzhikistan: Hidden Terror: Political Killings, 'Disappearances' and Torture Since December 1992.* Amnesty International Document EUR 60/04/93. London: Amnesty International, May 1993.

Ananiev, A. G. 'Promyshlennye vozmozhnosti TASSR.' In *Narodnoe khoziaistvo Tadzhikistana*, 164–86. Dushanbe: Izdatelstvo Gosplana TASSR, 1926.

Anderson, John. *The International Politics of Central Asia.* Manchester: Manchester University Press, 1997.

Andreev, M. S. *Tadzhiki doliny Khuf.* Stalinabad: Izdatelstvo AN TSSR, 1953.

Armstrong, John A. *Nations before Nationalism.* Chapel Hill, NC: University of North Carolina Press, 1982.

Asadullaev, Iskander. 'The Tajikistan Government.' In *Politics of Compromise: The Tajikistan Peace Process*, edited by Kamoludin Abdullaev and Catharine Barnes. London: Conciliation Resources, 2001.

Asimova, B. S. *Iazykovoe stroitelstvo v Tadzhikistane: 1920–1940*. Dushanbe: Donish, 1982.

Atkin, Muriel. *The Subtlest Battle: Islam in Soviet Tajikistan*. Philadelphia: Foreign Policy Research Institute, 1989.

Atkin, Muriel. 'Religious, National and Other Identities in Central Asia.' In *Muslims in Central Asia: Expressions of Identity and Change*, edited by Jo-Ann Gross. Durham, NC: Duke University Press, 1992.

Atkin, Muriel. 'Tajikistan's Relations with Iran and Afghanistan.' In *The New Politics of Central Asia and its Borderlands*, edited by Ali Banuazizi and Myron Weiner. Bloomington: Indiana University Press, 1994.

Atkin, Muriel. 'Tajiks and the Persian World.' In *Central Asia in Historical Perspective*, edited by Beatrice F. Manz. Oxford: Westview Press, 1994.

Atkin, Muriel. 'The Politics of Polarisation in Tajikistan.' In *Central Asia. Its Strategic Importance and Future Prospects*, edited by Hafeez Malik, 211–31. New York: St Martin's Press, 1994.

Atkin, Muriel. 'Tajikistan: Reform, Reaction and Civil War.' In *New States, New Politics: Building the Post-Soviet Nations*, edited by Ian Bremmer and Ray Taras. Cambridge University Press, 1997.

Atkin, Muriel. 'Thwarted Democratization in Tajikistan.' In *Conflict, Cleavage and Change in Central Asia and Caucasus*, edited by Karen Dawisha and Bruce Parrot. Cambridge: Cambridge University Press, 1997.

Atkin, Muriel. 'A President and His Rivals.' In *Power and Change in Central Asia*, edited by Sally N. Cummings. London: Routledge, 2002.

Azizkulova, G. S. *Tsikl lektsii po istorii gosudarstva i prava Respubliki Tadzhikistan*. Dushanbe: TGU, 1995.

Babadjanov, Bakhtiyar, and Muzaffar Kamilov. 'Muhammadjan Hindustani (1892–1989) and the Beginning of the "Great Schism" among the Muslims of Uzbekistan.' In *Islam in Politics in Russian and Central Asia (Early Eighteenth to Late Twentieth Centuries)*, edited by Stephane A. Dudoignon and Komatsu Hisao. London: Kegan Paul, 2001.

Baihaki, Abu al-Fazl. *Istoriia Mas'uda 1030–1041*. Tashkent: Izdatelstvo AN Uzbekskoi SSR, 1962.

Barakat, Halim. 'The Social Context.' In *Lebanon in Crisis: Participants and Issues*, edited by P. Edward Haley and Lewis W. Snider, 3–20. Syracuse, NY: Syracuse University Press, 1979.

Barnomai amalii nomzad ba raisi jumhuri Tojikiston Nabiev Rahmon Nabievich. Dushanbe: [No publisher], 1991.

Barthold, V. V. 'A Short History of Turkestan.' In *Four Studies on the History of Central Asia.* Leiden: E. J. Brill, 1956. [Essay originally published in Tashkent, 1922.]

Barthold, V. V. *Sochineniia,* Vol. II, Part 1. Moscow: Izdatelstvo vostochnoi literatury, 1963.

Barthold, V. V. *Sochineniia,* Vol. II, Part 2. Moscow: Izdatelstvo vostochnoi literatury, 1964.

Barthold, V. V. *Sochineniia,* Vol. III. Moscow: Izdatelstvo vostochnoi literatury, 1965.

Bashiri, Iraj. *Prominent Tajik Figures of the Twentieth Century.* Dushanbe: Academy of Sciences of Tajikistan and International Borbad Foundation, 2002.

Basilov, V. N. *Shamanstvo u narodov Srednei Azii i Kazakhstana.* Moscow: Nauka, 1992.

Bennigsen, Alexandre, and S. Enders Wimbush. *Mystics and Commissars. Sufism in the Soviet Union.* London: C. Hurst & Co., 1985.

Bennigsen, Alexandre, and S. Enders Wimbush. *Muslims of the Soviet Empire: A Guide.* Bloomington: Indiana University Press, 1986.

Bennigsen, Alexandre A., and S. Enders Wimbush. *Muslim National Communism in the Soviet Union. A Revolutionary Strategy for the Colonial World.* Chicago: University of Chicago Press, 1979.

Bergne, Paul. *The Birth of Tajikistan: National Identity and the Origins of the Republic.* London: I. B. Tauris, 2007.

Black, Cyril E. 'Inner Asia and Modernisation. The Problem.' In *The Modernisation of Inner Asia,* edited by Cyril E. Black, 3–22. Armonk, NY, and London: M. E. Sharpe, 1991.

Black, Cyril E., ed. *The Modernisation of Inner Asia.* Armonk, NY: M. E. Sharpe, 1991.

Bliss, Frank. *Social and Economic Change in the Pamirs (Gorno-Badakhshan, Tajikistan).* New York: Routledge, 2006.

Boboev, M. R. *Ekonomicheskoe razvitie respubliki v usloviiakh rynka.* Dushanbe: Tadzhik NIINTI, 1991.

Bobokalonov, O. K., and L. L. Savello. *Promyshlennye uzly: formirovanie, razvitie, effektivnost'*. Dushanbe: Donish, 1992.

Boldin, Valery. *Ten Years that Shook the World: The Gorbachev Era as Witnessed by His Chief of Staff*. New York: Basic Books, 1994.

Bolshaia sovetskaia entsiklopediia, Vol. 26. Moscow: Izdatelstvo BSE, 1977.

Borba kommunisticheskoi partii protiv neproletarskikh partii, grupp i techenii v posleoktiabrskii period. Leningrad: Izdatelstvo Leningradskogo universiteta, 1982.

Brower, Daniel. 'Islam and Ethnicity: Russian Colonial Policy in Turkestan.' In *Russia's Orient: Imperial Borderlands and Peoples, 1700–1917*, edited by Daniel R. Brower and Edward J. Lazzerini. Bloomington: Indiana University Press, 1997.

Brown, Bess. 'National Security and Military Issues in Central Asia.' In *State Building and Military Power in Russia and the New States of Eurasia*, edited by Bruce Parrott. London: M. E. Sharpe, 1995.

Brown, Bess A. 'The Civil War in Tajikistan, 1992–1993.' In *Tajikistan: The Trials of Independence*, edited by Mohammad-Reza Djalili, Frederic Grare and Shirin Akiner. New York: St Martin's Press, 1997.

Bruchis, Michael. 'The Effect of the USSR's Language Policy on the National Languages of its Turkic Population.' In *The USSR and the Muslim World: Issues in Domestic and Foreign Policy*, edited by Yaacov Ro'i, 129–48. London: George Allen & Unwin, 1984.

Bushkov, Valentin I. 'The Population of Northern Tajikistan between 1870 and 1990.' In *State, Religion and Society in Central Asia: A Post-Soviet Critique*, edited by Vitaly Naumkin. Reading, UK: Ithaca Press, 1993.

Bushkov, V. I., and D. V. Mikulskii. 'Obschestvenno-politicheskaia situatsiia v Tadzhikistane: ianvar 1992g.' In *Issledovaniia po prikladnoi i neotlozhnoi etnologii*, Series A, Document No. 26. Moscow: Institute of Ethnology and Anthropology, 1992.

Bushkov, V. I., and D. V. Mikulskii. *Tajikistan: chto proiskhodit v respublike?* Moscow: Institute of Ethnology and Anthropology of the Russian Academy of Sciences, 1992–93.

Bushkov, V. I., and D. V. Mikulskii. *Istoriia grazhdanskoi voiny v Tadzhikistane (etno-sotsial'nye protsessy i politicheskaya bor'ba, 1992–1995)*. Moscow: Institut etnologii i antropologii RAN, 1996.

Bushkov, V. I., and D. V. Mikulskii. *Anattomiia grazhdanskoi voiny v Tadzhikistane*. Moscow: Institut etnologii i antropologii RAN, 1996.

Bushkov, V. I., and D. V. Mikulskii. *'Tadzhikskaia revoliutsiia' i grazhdanskaia voina (1989–1994gg.)*. Moscow: TSIMO, 1995.

Canfield, Robert L. 'Ethnic, Regional, and Sectarian Alignments in Afghanistan.' In *The State, Religion, and Ethnic Politics. Afghanistan, Iran, and Pakistan*, edited by Ali Banuazizi and Myron Weiner, 75–103. Syracuse, NY: Syracuse University Press, 1986.

Capisani, Giampaolo R. *The Handbook of Central Asia: A Comprehensive Survey of the New Republics*. London: I. B. Tauris, 2000.

Carlisle, Donald S. 'Power and Politics in Soviet Uzbekistan: From Stalin to Gorbachev.' In *Soviet Central Asia: The Failed Transformation*, edited by William Fierman, 91–130. Boulder, Colo.: Westview Press, 1991.

Carlisle, Donald S. 'Uzbekistan and the Uzbeks.' *Problems of Communism*, Vol. 40, No. 5, 1991.

Carlisle, Donald S. 'Geopolitics and Ethnic Problems of Uzbekistan and its Neighbours.' In *Muslim Eurasia: Conflicting Legacies*, edited by Yaacov Ro'i, 71–104. Frank Cass: London, 1995.

Carlisle, Donald S. 'Islam Karimov and Uzbekistan: Back to the Future?' In *Patterns in Post-Soviet Leadership*, edited by Timothy Colton and Robert Tucker, 191–216. Boulder, Colo.: Westview Press, 1995.

Carrère d'Encausse, Hélène. 'Systematic Conquest, 1865 to 1884.' In *Central Asia. A Century of Russian Rule*, edited by Edward Allworth, 131–50. New York: Columbia University Press, 1967.

Carrère d'Encausse, Hélène. 'The Fall of the Czarist Empire.' In *Central Asia. A Century of Russian Rule*, edited by Edward Allworth, 207–23. New York: Columbia University Press, 1967.

Carrère d'Encausse, Hélène. *Decline of an Empire. The Soviet Socialist Republic in Revolt*. New York: Newsweek Books, 1982.

Carrère d'Encausse, Hélène. *Islam and the Russian Empire. Reform and Revolution in Central Asia*. London: I. B. Tauris & Co., 1988.

Centlivres, Pierre, and Micheline Centlivres-Demont. 'Tajikistan and Afghanistan: The Ethnic Groups on Either Side of the Border.' In *Tajikistan: The Trials of Independence*, edited by Mohammad-Reza Djalili, Frederic Grare and Shirin Akiner. New York: St Martin's Press, 1997.

Chazan, Naomi. *An Anatomy of Ghanaian Politics: Managing Political Recession, 1969–1982.* Boulder, Colo.: Westview Press, 1983.

Chicherina, N. G. *Grazhdanskie dvizheniia v Tadzhikistane.* Moscow: Akademia nauk, 1990.

Chika, Obiya. 'When Faizulla Khojaev Decided to be an Uzbek.' In *Islam and Politics in Russia and Central Asia (Early Eighteenth to Late Twentieth Centuries),* edited by Stephanc Dudoignon and Komatsu Hisao. London: Kegan Paul, 2001.

Chugunov, A. I. *Borba na granitse. 1917–1928.* Moscow: Mysl, 1980.

Chvyr', L. A. 'Ob istoricheskikh predaniiakh ashtskikh tadzhikov.' In *Kavkaz i Sredniaia Aziia v drevnosti i srednevekovie.* Moscow: Nauka, 1981.

Chvyr', L. A. 'O strukture tadzhikskogo etnosa (nauchnaia i narodnaia tochka zreniia).' In *Rasy i narody. Sovremennye etnicheskie i rasovye problem,* edited by G. P. Vasilieva. Moscow: Nauka, 2001.

Clark, William A. *Soviet Regional Mobility after Khrushchev.* New York: Praeger, 1989.

Coates, W. P., and Zelda K. Coates. *Soviets in Central Asia.* London: Lawrence & Wishart, 1951.

Cohen, Stanley. *Visions of Social Control: Crime, Punishment and Classification.* Cambridge: Polity Press, 1994.

Collins, Kathleen. 'Tajikistan: Bad Peace Agreements and Prolonged Civil Conflict.' In *From Promise to Practice: Strengthening UN Capacities for the Prevention of Violent Conflict,* edited by Chandra Lekha Sriram and Karin Wermester. Boulder, Colo.: Lynne Rienner, 2003.

Collins, Kathleen. *Clan Politics and Regime Transition in Central Asia.* Cambridge: Cambridge University Press, 2006.

Critchlow, James. *Nationalism in Uzbekistan: A Soviet Republic's Road to Independence.* Boulder, Colo.: Westview Press, 1991.

Critchlow, James. 'Prelude to "Independence": How the Uzbek Party Apparatus Broke Moscow's Grip on Elite Recruitment.' In *Soviet Central Asia: The Failed Transformation,* edited by William Fierman, 131–56. Boulder, Colo.: Westview Press, 1991.

Czaplicka, Marie. *The Turks of Central Asia in History and at the Present Day.* Amsterdam: Philo, 1973.

Dahl, Robert A. 'Introduction.' In *Regimes and Oppositions*, edited by Robert A. Dahl, 1–26. New Haven, Conn., and London: Yale University Press, 1973.

Dakhshleiger, G. F. *Sotsialno-ekonomicheskie preobrazovaniia v aule i derevne Kazakhstana (1921–1929gg.)*. Alma-Ata: Zhazushy, 1965.

Dannreuther, Roland. *Creating New States in Central Asia: The Strategic Implications of the Collapse of Soviet Power in Central Asia*. Adelphi Paper 288. London: Brassey's, for the IISS, 1994.

Dawisha, Karen, and Bruce Parrott, eds. *Russia and the New States of Eurasia: The Politics of Upheaval*. Cambridge: Cambridge University Press, 1994.

Dehkanskoe khoziaistvo: Voprosy organizatsii i zakonodatelnye osnovy ego sozdaniia. Dushanbe: AN RT, 1993.

Dekrety Sovetskoi vlasti, Vol. VI. Moscow: Izdatelstvo politicheskoi literatury, 1973.

Demidov, S. M. *Sufizm v Turkmenii*. Ashkhabad: Ylym, 1978.

Denber, Rachel, and Barnett Rubin. *Human Rights in Tajikistan: In the Wake of Civil War*. New York: Human Rights Watch, 1993.

Dienes, Leslie. *Soviet Asia: Economic Development and National Policy Choices*. Boulder, Colo., and London: Westview Press, 1987.

Dilovarov, R. *Istifodai oqilonai zamin*. Dushanbe: Irfon, 1991.

Diplomatiia Tadzhikistana. Dushanbe: [No publisher], 1994.

Dodkhudoyev, Nazarsho. *Tajikistan: Land of Sunshine*. London: Soviet Booklets, 1959.

Dubnov, Arkady Yu. 'Tadjikistan.' In *US and Russian Policymaking with Respect to the Use of Force*, edited by Jeremy R. Azrael and Emil A. Payin. Santa Monica, Calif.: RAND, 1996.

Dudoignon, Stephane. 'Political Parties and Forces in Tajikistan, 1989–1993.' In *Tajikistan: The Trials of Independence*, edited by Mohammad-Reza Djalili, Frederic Grare and Shirin Akiner. New York: St Martin's Press, 1997.

Dudoignon, Stephane A. 'From Ambivalence to Ambiguity? Some Paradigms of Policy Making in Tajikistan.' In *Tajikistan at a Crossroads: The Politics of Decentralization*, edited by Luigi di Martino. Geneva: Cimera, 2004.

Dustbaev, Sh. *Problemy khimizatsii otraslei narodnogo khoziaistva Tadzhikistana*. Dushanbe: Donish, 1989.

Dustov, Narzullo. *Zakhm bar jismi vatan*. Dushanbe: Irfon, 1994.

Ebon, Martin. *KGB: Death and Rebirth*. Westport, Conn.: Praeger, 1994.

Eickelman, Dale F. *The Middle East: An Anthropological Approach*. Englewood Cliffs, NJ: Prentice-Hall, 1989.

Eickelman, Dale F., and James Piscatori. *Muslim Politics*. Princeton, NJ: Princeton University Press, 1996.

Eisenstadt, S. N. *Modernisation: Protest and Change*. Englewood Cliffs, NJ: Prentice-Hall, 1966.

Eisenstadt, S. N. *Traditional Patrimonialism and Modern Neopatrimonialism*. Beverly Hills and London: Sage, 1973.

Eisenstadt, S. N., and L. Roniger. *Patrons, Clients and Friends: Interpersonal Relations and the Structure of Trust in Society*. Cambridge: Cambridge University Press, 1984.

Ermakov, Igor, and Dmitrii Mikulskii. 'Islamskaia Partiia Vozrozhdeniia.' In *Islam v Rossii i Srednei Azii*, edited by Igor Ermakov and Dmitrii Mikulskii. Moscow: Lotos, 1993.

Ermakov, I., and D. Mikulskii. *Islam v Rossii i Srednei Azii*. Moscow: Lotos, 1993.

Ershov, N. N., N. A. Kisliakov, E. M. Peshchereva and S. P. Rusiaikina. *Kultura i byt tadzhikskogo kolkhoznogo krestianstva*. Moscow and Leningrad: Izdatelstvo AN SSSR, 1954.

Esposito, John L. *The Islamic Threat: Myth or Reality?* Oxford: Oxford University Press, 1992.

Ezhegodnik Bolshoi sovetskoi entsiklopedii. Moscow: Sovetskaia entsiklopediia, 1990.

Fedorova, T. 'Planirovanie sem'i v regionakh rasshirennogo vosproizvodstva naseleniia.' In *Sovetologi o problemakh sotsialno-ekonomicheskogo razvitiia SSSR i soiuznykh respublik*, 106–12. Moscow: Institut ekonomiki AN SSSR, 1990.

Fierman, William. 'Central Asian Youth and Migration.' In *Soviet Central Asia: The Failed Transformation*, edited by William Fierman, 255–89. Boulder, Colo.: Westview Press, 1991.

Fowkes, Ben. *The Disintegration of the Soviet Union: A Study in the Rise and Triumph of Nationalism*. New York: St Martin's Press, 1997.

Frank, Andre Gunder. *The Centrality of Central Asia*. Amsterdam: VU University Press, 1992.

Freitag-Wirminghaus, Rainer. 'Atheistic Muslims, Soviet Legacy and Islamic Tradition in Central Asia and the Caucasus.' In *The Islamic World and the West: An Introduction to Political Cultures and International Relations*, edited by Kai Hafez. Leiden: Brill, 2000.

Freizer, Sabine. 'Central Asian Fragmented Civil Society: Communal and Neoliberal Forms in Tajikistan and Uzbekistan.' In *Exploring Civil Society: Political and Cultural Contexts*, edited by Marlies Glasius, David Lewis and Hakan Seckinelgin. London: Routledge, 2004.

Fridman, Leonid A. 'Economic Crisis as a Factor of Building Up Socio-Political and Ethnonational Tensions in the Countries of Central Asia and Transcaucasia.' In *Central Asia and Transcaucasia: Ethnicity and Conflict*, edited by Vitaly V. Naumkin. Westport, Conn.: Greenwood Press, 1994.

Frye, Richard N. *Bukhara: The Medieval Achievement*. Norman: University of Oklahoma Press, 1965.

Frye, Richard N. *Islamic Iran and Central Asia (7th–12th Centuries)*. London: Variorum Reprints, 1979.

Gafurov, B. G. *Nekotorye voprosy national'noi politiki KPSS*. Moscow: Gospolitizdat, 1959.

Gafurov, B. G. *Tadzhiki: drevneishaia, drevniaia i srednevekovaia istoriia*. Dushanbe: Irfon, 1989.

Ghafurov, B. Gh. *Tojikon. Ta'rikhi qadimtarin, qadim va asri miyona*, Vol. 1. Dushanbe: Irfon, 1983.

Ghoibov, Gholib. *Ta'rikhi Khatlon as Oghoz to Imruz*. Dushanbe: Donish, 2006.

Gibb, H. A. R. *The Arab Conquests in Central Asia*. New York: AMS Press, 1970.

Gill, Graeme. *The Collapse of a Single-Party System: The Disintegration of the Communist Party of the Soviet Union*. Cambridge: Cambridge University Press, 1994.

Gitelman, Zvi. 'Ethnopolitics and the Future of the Former Soviet Union.' In *The Politics of Nationality and the Erosion of the USSR*, edited by Zvi Gitelman, 1–25. New York: St Martin's Press, 1992.

Gleason, Gregory. *Federalism and Nationalism: The Struggle for Republican Rights in the USSR*. Boulder, Colo.: Westview Press, 1990.

Gosudarstvennyi biudzhet SSSR. Moscow: Finansy i statistika, 1989.

Grazhdanskaia voina v SSSR. Moscow: Voennoe izdatelstvo, 1986.

Grazhdanskie dvizheniia v Tadzhikistane. Moscow: TSIMO, 1990.

Grazhdanskie politicheskie dvizheniia v Tadzhikistane (1989 – mart 1990g.). Dushanbe: TsK LKSM Tadzhikistana, 1990.

Gretsky, Sergei. 'Civil War in Tajikistan: Causes, Developments, and Prospects for Peace.' In *Central Asia: Conflict, Resolution, and Change*, edited by Roald Z. Sagdeev and Susan Eisenhower. Chevy Chase, Md: CPSS Press, 1995.

Grousset, Rene. *The Empire of the Steppes*. New Brunswick, NJ: Rutgers University Press, 1970.

Gurvich, I. S. 'Obshee i osobennoe v etnicheskikh protsessakh u razlichnykh narodov SSSR.' In *Sovremennye etnicheskie protsessy v SSSR*, edited by Iu. V. Bromlei, 500–33. Moscow: Nauka, 1977.

Hafizova, N. R. 'Omukhtani problemahoi hessi grazhdani dar kursi siyosatshinosi.' Report at the I Conference on Teaching Political Science Disciplines in Tajikistan, Dushanbe, 25 January 1995.

Haggard, Stephan, and Robert R. Kaufman. *The Political Economy of Democratic Transitions*. Princeton, NJ: Princeton University Press, 1995.

Haghayeghi, Mehrdad. *Islam and Politics in Central Asia*. New York: St Martin's Press, 1995.

Haler, Honi Fern. *Beyond Postmodern Politics: Lyotard. Rorty. Foucalt*. New York and London: Routledge, 1994.

Hall, Michael. 'Tajikistan at the Crossroads of Democracy and Authoritarianism.' In *Prospects for Democracy in Central Asia*, edited by Birgit N. Schlyter. Istanbul: Swedish Research Institute in Istanbul, 2005.

Hamagoni, Azim. *Rohi rahoyi az buhron*. Dushanbe: Tojikiston, 1993.

Hambly, Gavin. *Central Asia*. London: Weidenfeld & Nicolson, 1969.

Hanf, Theodor. *Coexistence in Wartime Lebanon: Decline of a State and Rise of a Nation*. London: The Centre for Lebanese Studies in association with I. B. Tauris & Co., 1993.

Harvey, David. 'From Space to Place and Back Again.' In *Mapping the Futures: Local Culture, Global Change*, edited by Jon Bird, 3–29. London: Routledge, 1993.

Hazrati, M., and I. Saidiyon. *Islom: raviya, mazhab va firqahoi on*. Dushanbe: Oryono, 1992.

Heathershaw, John. *Post-Conflict Tajikistan: The Politics of Peacebuilding and the Emergence of Legitimate Order*. London: Routledge, 2009.

Heller, Agnes, and Ferenc Feher. 'The Gorbachev Phenomenon.' In *Gorbachev: The Debate*, edited by Ferenc Feher and Andrew Arato, 20–37. Cambridge: Polity Press, 1989.

Hindustani, Muhammadjan. 'Answers to Those Who Are Introducing Inadmissible Innovations into Religion.' Appendix in Bakhtiyar Babadjanov and Muzaffar Kamilov, 'Muhammadjan Hindustani (1892–1989) and the Beginning of the "Great Schism" among the Muslims of Uzbekistan.' In *Islam in Politics in Russian and Central Asia (Early Eighteenth to Late Twentieth Centuries)*, edited by Stephane A. Dudoignon and Komatsu Hisao. London: Kegan Paul, 2001.

Hirsch, Francine. *Empire of Nations: Ethnographic Knowledge and the Making of the Soviet Union*. Ithaca, NY: Cornell University Press, 2005.

Hodnett, Grey. *Leadership in the Soviet National Republics: A Quantitative Study of Recruitment Policy*. Ontario: Mosaic Press, 1978.

Hojiev, M. *Ta'rikh guvoh ast (Sahifaho az ta'rikhi Partiyai Kommunistii Tojikiston)*. Khujand: Omor, 1994.

Holdsworth, Mary. *Turkestan in the Nineteenth Century*. Oxford: Central Asian Research Centre, 1959.

Holıqzoda, Abdulqodır. *Ta'rıkhı sıyosıı Tojıkon az istiloi Rusiya to imruz*. Dushanbe: [Self-published], 1994.

Holt, Frank I. *Alexander the Great and Bactria: The Formation of a Greek Frontier in Central Asia*. Leiden: Brill, 1988.

Hough, Jerry, and Merle Fainsod. *How the Soviet Union is Governed*. Cambridge, Mass.: Harvard University Press, 1979.

Humphrey, Michael. 'Lebanon: The "Cellular" Society.' In *Lebanon Beyond 2000*, edited by Amin Saikal and Geoffrey Jukes, 34–56. Canberra: Centre for Middle Eastern and Central Asian Studies, ANU, 1997.

Iakubov, Iu. *Pargar v VII–VIII vekakh nashei ery*. Dushanbe: Donish, 1979.

Iavich, V. S. *Verkhovny Sovet TSSR*. Moscow: Gosudarstvennoe izdatelstvo iuridicheskoi literatury, 1958.

Ignatenko, A. 'Islam v bor'be za politicheskoe liderstvo.' In *Islam v Rossii i Srednei Azii*, edited by Igor Ermakov and Dmitrii Mikulskii, 166–74. Moscow: Lotus Foundation, 1993.

Inostrannaia voennaia interventsiia i grazhdanskaia voina v Srednei Azii i Kazakhstane, Vol. 2. Alma-Ata: Nauka, 1964.

International Foundation for Electoral Systems. *Public Opinion in Tajikistan 2010: Findings from an IFES Survey*. Dushanbe: IFES, 2010.

Irkaev, M. I., ed. *Kommunisticheskaia partiia v bor'be za formirovanie i razvitie rabochego klassa v Tadzhikistane*. Dushanbe: Irfon, 1967.

Irkaev, M., and P. Safarov. *Rol' Kommunisticheskoi partii v prevraschenii dehkan v aktivnykh stroitelei sotsializma*. Dushanbe: Irfon, 1968.

Ishanov, A. *Rol' Kompartii i Sovetskogo pravitelstva v sozdanii natsionalnoi gosudarstvennosti uzbekskogo naroda*. Tashkent: Uzbekistan, 1978.

Islamic Revival Party. 'Programma Islamskoi Partii Vozrozhdeniia Tadzhikistana.' 26 October 1991. Reproduced in *'Tadzhikskaia Revolyustiia' i Grazhdanskaia Voina (1989–1994 gg.)*, edited by V. I. Bushkov and D. V. Mikulskii. Moscow: TSIMO, 1995.

Istoriia Bukhary s drevneishykh vremen do nashikh dnei. Tashkent: Fan, 1976.

Istoriia Tadzhikskogo naroda, Vol. II. Moscow: Izdatelstvo vostochnoi literatury, 1964.

Istoriia Tadzhikskogo naroda, Vol. III, kn. 1. Moscow: Nauka, 1964.

Itogi Vsesoiuznoi perepisi naseleniia 1989 goda po Tadzhikskoi SSR, Vol. II. Dushanbe: Goskomstat TSSR, 1991.

Ivanov, P. P. *Ocherki po istorii Srednei Azii. (XVI – seredina XIXv)*. Moscow: Izdatelstvo vostochnoi literatury, 1958.

Ivanovich, St. *VKP: Desiat' Let Kommunisticheskoi Monopolii*. Paris: Biblioteka Demokraticheskogo Sotsializma, 1928.

Jahangiri, Guissou. 'The Premises for the Construction of a Tajik National Identity, 1920–1930.' In *Tajikistan: The Trials of Independence*, edited by Mohammad-Reza Djalili, Frederic Grare and Shirin Akiner. New York: St Martin's Press, 1997.

Jawad, Nassim, and Shahrbanou Tadjbakhsh. *Tajikistan: A Forgotten Civil War*. London: Minority Rights Group, 1995.

Jones Luong, Pauline. *Institutional Change and Political Continuity in Post-Soviet Central Asia: Power, Perceptions, and Pacts.* Cambridge: Cambridge University Press, 2002.

Jukes, Geoffrey. *The Soviet Union in Asia.* Sydney: Angus & Robertson, 1973.

Juraeva, Gavhar. 'Ethnic Conflict in Tajikistan.' In *Ethnic Conflict in the Post-Soviet World: Case Studies and Analysis*, edited by Leokadia Drobizheva, R. Gottemoeller, C. McArdle Kelleher and L. Walker. London: M. E. Sharpe, 1996.

K sotsializmu, minuia kapitalizm: Istoricheskii opyt KPSS po sotsialisticheskomu stroitelstvu v Srednei Azii i Kazakhstane v 1917–1937gg. Moscow: Politizdat, 1974.

Kabiri, Muhiddin. 'Tajikistan's Domestic and Regional Priorities and Challenges.' Chatham House REP Roundtable (15 October 2009).

Kaplan, Morton A. *Alienation and Identification.* New York: The Free Press, 1976.

Karimov, Buri. *Qurboni duzakhma.* Dushanbe: Oryono, 1992.

Karmysheva, B. Kh. *Ocherki etnicheskoi istorii iuzhnykh raionov Tadzhikistana i Uzbekistana.* Moscow: Nauka, 1976.

Kastelskaia, Z. D. *Iz istorii Turkestanskogo kraia.* Moscow: Nauka, 1980.

Kenjaev, Safarali. *Tabadduloti Tojikiston*, Vol. 1. Dushanbe: Fondi Kenjaev, 1993.

Kenjaev, Safarali. *Tabadduloti Tojikiston*, Vol. 2. Tashkent: Uzbekistan, 1994.

Kenjaev, Safarali. *Tabadduloti Tojikiston*, Vol. 3. Dushanbe and Tashkent: Fondi Kenjaev/Nashriyoti Uzbekiston, 1995.

Khaidarov, G., and M. Inomov. *Tadzhikistan: tragediia i bol' naroda.* St Petersburg: LINKO, 1993.

Khaidarov, G., and M. Inomov. *Tajikistan: Tragedy and Anguish of the Nation.* St Petersburg: LINKO, 1993.

Khalfin, N. A. *Politika Rossii v Srednei Azii: 1857–1868.* Moscow: Izdatelstvo vostochnoi literatury, 1960.

Khalfin, N. A. *Prisoedinenie Srednei Azii k Rossii.* Moscow: Nauka, 1965.

Khalid, Adeeb. *Islam after Communism: Religion and Politics in Central Asia.* Berkeley: University of California Press, 2007.

Khamraev, M. *Deiatelnost Kommunisticheskoi partii po razvitiiu irrigatsii v Tadzhikistane*. Dushanbe: Donish, 1972.

Khan, Azizur Rahman, and Dharam Ghai. *Collective Agriculture and Rural Development in Soviet Central Asia*. London: Macmillan, 1979.

Khojagii khalqi jumhurii Tojikiston omori soli 1992. Dushanbe: Kumitai davlatii omori jumhurii Tojikiston, 1993.

Khojaiov, T. K. *Etnicheskie protsessy v Srednei Azii v epokhu srednevekovia*. Tashkent: Fan, 1987.

Khon, A. I. *Deiatelnost Kommunisticheskoi partii po osushestvleniiu novoi ekonomicheskoi politiki v Turkestane*. Tashkent: Fan, 1986.

Khonaliev, N. *Trudovye resursy Tadzhikistana: Problemy, perspektivy*. Dushanbe: Irfon, 1988.

Khudoiberdyev, O. *Boevaia druzhba, rozhdennaia Oktiabrem*. Moscow: Nauka, 1984.

Khudonazar, Davlat. 'The Conflict in Tajikistan: Questions of Regionalism.' In *Central Asia: Conflict, Resolution, and Change*, edited by Roald Z. Sagdeev and Susan Eisenhower, 249–64. Chevy Chase, Md: CPSS Press, 1995.

Khujandi, Orifjon Yahyozodi. *Khujandnoma, yo qissaho az ta'rikhi Khujand va khujandiyon*. Khujand: Nashriyoti davlatii ba nomi R. Jalil, 1994.

Kiseleva, L. N. *Iazyk Dari Afganistana*. Moscow: Nauka, 1985.

Kisliakov, N. A., ed. *Kultura i byt tadzhikskogo kolkhoznogo krestianstva*. Moscow and Leningrad: Izd-vo Akademii Nauk SSSR, 1954.

Kisliakov, N. A. *Nasledovanie i razdel imushchestva u narodov Srednei Azii i Kazakhstana*. Leningrad: Nauka, 1977.

Kitanina, T. M. 'Iz istorii obrazovaniia kontserna Stakheeva.' In *Iz istorii imperializma v Rossii*, 100–33. Moscow and Leningrad: Izdatelstvo AN SSSR, 1959.

Kommunisticheskaia partiia Tadzhikistana v tsifrakh. Dushanbe: Irfon, 1974.

Kommunisticheskaia partiia Tadzhikistana v tsifrakh za 60 let. Dushanbe: Irfon, 1984.

Konstitutsiia SSSR: Konstitutsii soiuznykh sovetskikh sotsialisticheskikh respublik. Moscow: Izdatelstvo Izvestiia sovetov deputatov trudiaschikhsia SSSR, 1972.

Kosach, Grigorii. 'Tajikistan: Political Parties in an Inchoate National Space.' In *Muslim Eurasia: Conflicting Legacies*, edited by Yaacov Ro'i, 123–42. Ilford, UK: Frank Cass, 1995.

KPSS v rezoliutsiiakh i resheniiakh s'ezdov, konferentsii i plenumov TsK, Vol. 2. Moscow: Gospolitizdat, 1970.

KPSS v rezoliutsiiakh i resheniiakh s'ezdov, konferentsii i plenumov TsK, Vol. 4. Moscow: Izdatelstvo politicheskoi literatury, 1970.

KPSS v rezoliutsiiakh i resheniiakh s'ezdov, konferentsii i plenumov TsK, Vols 5–13. Moscow: Izdatelstvo politicheskoi literatury, 1970–81.

Krader, Lawrence. *Peoples of Central Asia*. The Hague: Mouton & Co., 1963.

Krausse, Alexis. *Russia in Asia: A Record and a Study*. London: Curzon, 1973.

Kreindler, Isabelle T. 'Soviet Muslims: Gains and Losses as a Result of Soviet Language Planning.' In *Muslim Eurasia: Conflicting Legacies*, edited by Yaacov Ro'i. London: Frank Cass, 1995.

Kudriavtsev, A. V., and A. Sh. Niyazi. '"Politicheskii islam": nachalo 90-kh.' In *Sovremennyi islam: kultura i politika*, 95–128. Moscow: IVRAN, 1994.

Kuleshov, S. V. *Velikii Oktiabr i torzhestvo leninskoi natsionalnoi programmy partii*. Moscow: Vysshaiia Shkola, 1987.

Kulliyoti folklori Tojik, Vol. I. Moscow: Nauka, 1981.

Kurbanova, Sh. I. *Pereselenie: kak eto bylo*. Dushanbe: Irfon, 1993.

Kuvatov, A. 'Podgotovka, rasstanovka i vospitanie kadrov kulturno-prosvetitelnykh uchrezhdenii (1956–1965gg.).' In *Materialy k istorii Kommunisticheskoi partii Tadzhikistana*, Vypusk 4, chast II, edited by K. N. Gavrilkin, 324–47. Dushanbe: Izdatelstvo TGU, 1972.

Laird, Roy D. *The Soviet Legacy*. Westport, Conn.: Praeger, 1993.

Lapidus, Gail, Victor Zaslavsky and Philip Goldman, eds. *From Union to Commonwealth: Nationalism and Separatism in the Soviet Republics*. Cambridge: Cambridge University Press, 1992

Lenin, V. I. *Sochineniia*, Izd. 4, Vol. 51. Moscow: Izdatelstvo politicheskoi literatury, 1965.

Leninobod. Dushanbe: Irfon, 1986.

Lubin, Nancy. 'Islam and Ethnic Identity in Central Asia: A View from Below.' In *Muslim Eurasia: Conflicting Legacies*, edited by Yaacov Ro'i. London: Frank Cass, 1995.

Lubin, Nancy. 'Leadership in Uzbekistan and Kazakhstan: The Views of the Led.' In *Patterns in Post-Soviet Leadership*, edited by Timothy J. Colton and Robert C. Tucker, 217–34. Boulder, Colo.: Westview Press, 1995.

Lugovaya, Aleksandra. 'Politicheskii krizis v Tadzhikistane byl neizbezhen.' In *Tadzhikistan v ogne*. Dushanbe: Irfon, 1993–94.

McAdam, Doug, John D. McCarthy and Mayer M. Zald. 'Introduction.' In *Comparative Perspectives on Social Movements*, edited by Doug McAdam, John D. McCarthy and Mayer M. Zald. Cambridge: Cambridge University Press, 1996.

McAuley, Alastair. 'The Central Asian Economy in Comparative Perspective.' In *The Disintegration of the Soviet Economic System*, edited by Michael Ellman and Vladimir Kontorovich, 137–56. London and New York: Routledge, 1992.

McChesney, R. D. *Waqf in Central Asia: Four Hundred Years in the History of a Muslim Shrine, 1480–1889*. Princeton, NJ: Princeton University Press, 1991.

McLean, Jennifer, and Thomas Greene. 'Turmoil in Tajikistan: Addressing the Crisis of Internal Displacement.' In *The Forsaken People: Case Studies of the Internally Displaced*, edited by Roberta Cohen and Francis M. Deng. Washington, DC: Brookings, 1998.

Makarova, G. P. *Narodnyi komissariat po delam natsionalnostei RSFSR. 1917–1923*. Moscow: Nauka, 1987.

Makhamov, Mavlon. 'Islam and the Political Development of Tajikistan after 1985.' In *Central Asia: Its Strategic Importance and Future Prospects*, edited by Hafeez Malik. New York: St Martin's Press, 1994.

Malashenko, Alexei V. 'Islam versus Communism: The Experience of Coexistence.' In *Russia's Muslim Frontiers: New Directions in Cross-Cultural Analysis*, edited by Dale F. Eickelman. Bloomington: Indiana University Press, 1993.

Malashenko, Alexei V. 'Islam and Politics in the Southern Zone of the Former USSR.' In *Central Asia and Transcaucasia: Ethnicity and Conflict*, edited by Vitaly V. Naumkin. Westport, Conn., and London: Greenwood Press, 1994.

Malia, Martin. *The Soviet Tragedy: A History of Socialism in Russia, 1917–1991*. New York: The Free Press, 1994.

Masov, Rahim. *Istoriia topornogo razdeleniia*. Dushanbe: Irfon, 1991.

Masov, Rahim. *Tadzhiki: istoriia s grifom 'Sovershenno sekretno'*. Dushanbe: Paivand, 1995.

Masov, Rahim. *Tadzhiki: istoriia natsionalnoi tragedii*. Dushanbe: Irfon, 2008.

Masov, R. M. *Istoriia istoricheskoi nauki i istoriografiia sotsialisticheskogo stroitelstva v Tadzhikistane*. Dushanbe: Irfon, 1988.

Massell, Gregory J. *The Surrogate Proletariat: Moslem Women and Revolutionary Strategies in Soviet Central Asia*. Princeton, NJ: Princeton University Press, 1974.

Masson, V. M. 'The Decline of the Bronze Age Civilization and Movements of the Tribes.' In *History of Civilizations of Central Asia*, Vol. I. Paris: UNESCO, 1992.

Menon, Rajan, and Hendrik Spruyt. 'Possibilities for Conflict Resolution in Post-Soviet Central Asia.' In *Post-Soviet Political Order: Conflict and State Building*, edited by Barnett R. Rubin and Jack Snyder. London: Routledge, 1998.

Metodicheskie rekomendatsii propagandistam komsomolskoi politicheskoi ucheby i rukovoditeliam komsomolsko-molodezhnykh politicheskikh klubov. Dushanbe: Dom Politprosveta TsK KPT, 1990.

Migdal, Joel S. *Strong Societies and Weak States: State–Society Relations and State Capabilities in the Third World*. Princeton, NJ: Princeton University Press, 1988.

Mikulskii, D. 'Svidetelstvo voiny v Tadzhikistane.' In *Islam v Rossii i Srednei Azii*, edited by Igor Ermakov and Dmitrii Mikulskii, 247–60. Moscow: Lotus Foundation, 1993

Miller, Robert F. 'The Soviet Economy: Problems and Solutions in the Gorbachev View.' In *Gorbachev at the Helm: A New Era in Soviet Politics?* edited by R. F. Miller, J. H. Miller and T. H. Rigby, 109–35. New York: Croom Helm, 1987.

Mills, Charles Wright. *The Power Elite*. Oxford: Oxford University Press, 1968.

Mirzoev, R. K. *Tempy, proportsii i effektivnost obschestvennogo proizvodstva v Tadzhikskoi SSR*. Dushanbe: Donish, 1983.

Mirzoev, R. K., ed. *Problemy razvitiia i razmesheniia proizvoditelnykh sil Tadzhikistana*. Dushanbe: SOPS AN TSSR, 1988.

Monogarova, L. F. 'Evolutsiia natsional'nogo samosoznaniia pripamirskikh narodnostei.' In *Etnicheskie protsessy u natsional'nykh grupp Srednei Azii i Kazakhstana*. Moscow: Nauka, 1980.

Mukhitdinov, I. *Osobennosti traditsionnogo zemledelcheskogo khoziaistva pripamirskikh narodnostei v XIX – nachale XX veka*. Dushanbe: Donish, 1984.

Mukhtarov, A. *Materialy po istorii Ura-Tiube*. Moscow: Izdatelstvo vostochnoi literatury, 1963.

Mukomel', Vladimir. 'Vooruzhennie mezhnatsional'nie i regional'nie konflikti: lyudskie poteri, ekonomicheskii ushcherb i sotsial'nye posledstviia.' In *Identichnost' i konflikt v postsovetskikh gosudarstvakh*.

Muksinov, I. Sh. *Sovet ministrov soiuznoi respubliki*. Moscow: Iuridicheskaia literatura, 1969.

Mullojonov, Parviz. 2001. 'The Islamic Clergy in Tajikistan Since the End of the Soviet Period.' In *Islam and Politics in Russia and Central Asia (Early Eighteenth to Late Twentieth Centuries)*, edited by Stephane Dudoignon and Komatsu Hisao. London: Kegan Paul, 2001.

Muminov, Ashirbek. 'Fundamentalist Challenges to Local Islamic Traditions in Soviet and Post-Soviet Central Asia.' In *Empire, Islam, and Politics in Central Eurasia*, edited by Tomohiko Uyama. Sapporo: Slavic Research Centre, Hokkaido University, 2007.

Muminov, I. M., ed. *Istoriia Uzbekskoi SSR s drevneishikh vremen do nashikh dnei*. Tashkent: Fan, 1974.

Munki, Rajab, and Amirsho Khatloni. *Nomus*. Dushanbe: Paik, 1994.

Nabiev, R. N. *Sovetskii Tadzhikistan*. Moscow: Izdatelstvo politicheskoi literatury, 1982.

Naby, Eden. 'The Emerging Central Asia: Ethnic and Religious Factions.' In *Central Asia and the Caucasus after the Soviet Union: Domestic and International Dynamics*, edited by Mohiadin Mesbahi. Gainesville: University Press of Florida, 1994.

Najib, Abdurrahman Ali. *Afghanistan dar gozargahi atash wa khun*. Peshawar: Haj Nayyer Hosaini, 1991.

Narodnoe khoziaistvo SSSR v 1979g. Moscow: Finansy i statistika, 1979.

Narodnoe khoziaistvo SSSR v 1989g. Moscow: Finansy i statistika, 1990.

Narodnoe khoziaistvo SSSR za 70 let. Moscow: Finansy i statistika, 1987.

Narodnoe khoziaistvo Tadzhikskoi SSR. Stalinabad: Gosstatizdat, 1957.

Narodnoe khoziaistvo Tadzhikskoi SSR v 1965g. Dushanbe: Statistika, 1966.

Narodnoe khoziaistvo Tadzhikskoi SSR v 1979g. Dushanbe: Irfon, 1981.

Narodnoe khoziaistvo Tadzhikskoi SSR v 1988 godu. Dushanbe: Irfon, 1990.

Narodnoe khoziaistvo Tadzhikskoi SSR v 1990g. Dushanbe: Goskomstat TSSR, 1991.

Narzikulov, I. K., and A. G. Khajibaev. 'Tadzhikskaia Sovetskaia Sotsialisticheskaia respublika.' In *Naselenie soiuznykh respublik*, 244–62. Moscow: Statistika, 1977.

Naselenie Tadzhikskoi SSR: Po dannym Vsesoiuznoi perepisi naseleniia 1979g. Dushanbe: TSSU TSSR, 1980.

Nasriddinov, Hikmatullo. *Tarkish*. Dushanbe: Afsona, 1995.

Natsionalnaia politika KPSS v deistvii. Tashkent: Uzbekistan, 1979.

Naumkin, Vitaly V. 'Experience and Prospects for Settlement of Ethno-National Conflicts in Central Asia and Transcaucasia.' In *Central Asia and Transcaucasia: Ethnicity and Conflict*, edited by Vitaly V. Naumkin. Westport, Conn.: Greenwood Press, 1994.

Naumkin, Vitaly V. *Radical Islam in Central Asia: Between Pen and Rifle*. Lanham, Md: Rowman & Littlefield, 2005.

Nazare ba ta'rikh (Ma'lumotnomai mukhtasar) Khujand: Komiteti viloyati Leninobodi partiyai kommunistii Tojikiston, 1994.

Nazarshoev, M. *Partiinaia organizatsiia Pamira v bor'be za sotsializm i kommunizm*. Dushanbe: Irfon, 1970.

Nazarshoev, M. *Muborezi rohi haqiqat*. Dushanbe: Irfon, 1993.

Nazarshoev, M. N., and M. A. Solomonov. *Sotsialno-ekonomicheskoe razvitie Tadzhikistana*. Dushanbe: Izdatelstvo TGU, 1989.

Negmatov, N. 'The Phenomenon of the Material Cultural of Central Asia in the Samanid's Epoch.' In *The Contribution of the Samanid Epoch to the Cultural Heritage of Central Asia*. UNESCO International Coloqium, Dushanbe 1998. Dushanbe: Adib, 1999.

Negmatov, N. N. *Gosudarstvo Samanidov*. Dushanbe: Donish, 1977.

Negmatov, N. N. 'The Samanid State.' In *The History of Civilizations of Central Asia*, Vol. IV, edited by M. S. Asimov and C. E. Bosworth. Paris: UNESCO, 1998.

Niyazi, Aziz. 'The Year of Tumult: Tajikistan after February 1990.' In *State, Religion and Society in Central Asia: A Post Soviet Critique*, edited by Vitaly Naumkin. Reading, UK: Ithaca Press, 1993.

Niyazi, Aziz. 'Tajikistan.' In *Central Asia and the Caucasus after the Soviet Union: Domestic and International Dynamics*, edited by Mohiaddin Mesbahi, 164–85. Gainesville: University Press of Florida, 1994.

Niyazi, Aziz. 'Tajikistan I: The Regional Dimension of Conflict.' In *Conflicting Loyalties and the State in Post-Soviet Russia and Eurasia*, edited by Michael Waller, Bruno Coppieters and Alexei Malashenko. London: Frank Cass, 1998.

Niyazi, Aziz. 'Islam and Tajikistan's Human and Ecological Crisis.' In *Civil Society in Central Asia*, edited by M. Holt Ruffin and Daniel Clarke Waugh. Seattle: University of Washington Press, 1999.

Nomzad ba raisi jumhuri Tojikiston Rahmon Nabievich Nabiev. Dushanbe: [No publisher], 1991.

Nove, Alec. *Stalinism and After*. London: George Allen & Unwin, 1981.

Nove, Alec. *An Economic History of the USSR*. London: Penguin Books, 1990.

Novye zakony Respubliki Tadzhikistan. Sbornik (Chast' I). Dushanbe: [No publisher], 1991.

Novye zakony Respubliki Tadzhikistan. Sbornik. (Chast' II). Dushanbe: Kontrakt, 1991.

Novye zakony Respubliki Tadzhikistan. Sbornik. (Chast' IV). Dushanbe: Kontrakt, 1992.

Nuri, Sayid Abdullohi. 'Biyoed, Muvaqqati Ikhtilofro Kanor Biguzorem.' Conference speech in Iran (22–23 December 2003) in *Mujaddidi Asr: bakhshida ba 60-umin solgardi zodruzi ustod Sayid Abdullohi Nuri (r)*, edited by Qiyomiddin Sattori. Dushanbe: Devashtich, 2007.

Nuri, Sayid Abdullohi. 'Hizbe, ki resha dar ormoni mardum dorad.' Interview by Qiyomiddin Sattori (2 February 2003) in *Mujaddidi Asr: bakhshida ba 60-umin solgardi zodruzi ustod Sayid Abdullohi Nuri (r)*, edited by Qiyomiddin Sattori. Dushanbe: Devashtich, 2007.

Nurnazarov, M. N. *Agropromyshlennye kompleksy Tadzhikistana*. Dushanbe: Donish, 1990.

Nurnazarov, M., and M. Rahimov. *Khojagii khalqi Tojikiston*. Dushanbe: Vazorati maorifi Jumhurii Tojikiston, 1994.

Ocherki istorii kompartii Turkestana, Bukhary i Khorezma. Tashkent: Uzbekistan, 1959.

Ocherki istorii narodnogo khoziaistva Tadzhikistana. Dushanbe: Donish, 1967.

O'Donnell, Guillermo, and Phillippe C. Schmitter. 'Tentative Conclusions about Uncertain Democracies.' In *Transitions from Authoritarian Rule*, edited by Guillermo O'Donnell, Phillippe C. Schmitter and Laurence Whitehead, 3–78. Baltimore: The Johns Hopkins University Press, 1986.

Ogareff, Val. *Leaders of the Soviet Republics: 1971–1980*. Canberra: ANU Press, 1980.

Olcott, Martha Brill. *The Kazakhs*. Stanford, Calif.: Hoover Institution Press, 1987.

Olcott, Martha Brill. 'Central Asia's Political Crisis.' In *Russia's Muslim Frontiers*, edited by Dale F. Eickelman, 49–63. Bloomington: Indiana University Press, 1993.

Olcott, Martha Brill. 'Nation Building and Ethnicity in the Foreign Policies of the New Central Asian States.' In *National Identity and Ethnicity in Russia and the New States of Eurasia*, edited by Roman Szporluk, 209–29. Armonk, NY: M. E. Sharpe, 1994.

Olcott, Martha Brill. 'Islam and Fundamentalism in Independent Central Asia.' In *Muslim Eurasia: Conflicting Legacies*, edited by Yaacov Ro'i. London: Frank Cass, 1995.

Olimov, M. A., and Saodat Olimova. 'Ethnic Factors and Local Self-Government in Tajikistan.' In *Local Governance and Minority Empowerment in the CIS*, edited by Valery Tishkov and Elena Filippova. Budapest: LGI Books & Open Society Institute, 2002.

Olimov, Muzaffar, ed. *Mezhtadzhikskiy konflikt: put' k miru*. Moscow: Rossiiskaia Akademiia Nauk, 1998.

Olimov, Muzaffar, and Saodat Olimova. 'Regiony Tadzhikistana: proshloe i nastoriashchee.' In *Mezhtadzhikskii konflikt: put' k miru*, edited by M. Olimov. Moscow: Rossiiskaia Akademiia Nauk, 1998.

Olimov, Muzaffar, and Saodat Olimova. 'Sotsial'naia struktura Tadzhikistana.' In *Mezhtadzhikskii konflikt: put' k miru*, edited by M. Olimov. Moscow: Rossiiskaia Akademiia Nauk, 1998.

Olimova, Saodat. 'Mezhtadzhikskii konflikt v tsentral'noaziatskom kontekste.' In *Mezhtadzhikskii konflikt: put' k miru*, edited by M. Olimov. Moscow: Rossiiskaia Akademiia Nauk, 1998.

Olimova, Saodat. 'Opposition in Tajikistan: Pro et Contra.' In *Democracy and Pluralism in Muslim Eurasia*, edited by Yaacov Ro'i. London: Frank Cass, 2004.

Olimova, Saodat. 'Regionalism and its Perception by Major Political and Social Powers of Tajikistan.' In *Tajikistan at a Crossroads: The Politics of Decentralization*, edited by Luigi di Martino. Geneva: Cimera, 2004.

Olimova, Saodat, and Igor Bosc. *Labor Migration in Tajikistan*. Dushanbe: IOM, 2003.

Olimova, Saodat, and Muzaffar Olimov. 'The Islamic Renaissance Party.' In *Politics of Compromise: The Tajikistan Peace Process*, edited by Kamoludin Abdullaev and Catharine Barnes. London: Conciliation Resources, 2001.

Oranskii, I. M. *Tadzhikoiazychnye etnograficheskie gruppy Gissarskoi doliny (Sredniaia Aziia)*. Moscow: Nauka, 1983.

Orr, Michael. 'The Russian Army and the War in Tajikistan.' In *Tajikistan: The Trials of Independence*, edited by Mohammad-Reza Djalili, Frederic Grare and Shirin Akiner. Surrey, UK: Curzon, 1998.

Osimov, M. S., ed. *Tadzhikskaia SSR*. Dushanbe: AN TSSR, 1974.

Osnovnye pokazateli ekonomicheskogo i sotsialnogo razvitiia oblastei, gorodov i raionov Tadzhikskoi SSR za gody dvenadtsatoi piatiletki. Dushanbe: Goskomstat TSSR, 1991.

Ozhidaniia i nadezhdy liudei v usloviiakh stanovleniia gosudarstvennosti (Oput sotsiologicheskikh issledovanyi v Tadzhikistane, Kazakhstane, Rossii i na Ukraine). Moscow: Russian Academy of Management, 1992.

Parker, John W. *Persian Dreams: Moscow and Tehran since the Fall of the Shah*. Washington, DC: Potomac Books, 2008.

Parry, Geraint. *Political Elites*. London: George Allen & Unwin, 1969.

Patrunov, F. G. *Po Tadzhikistanu*. Moscow: Profizdat, 1987.

Perepelitsyna, L. A. *Rol russkoi kultury v razvitii kultur narodov Srednei Azii.* Moscow: Nauka, 1976.

Peshchereva, E. M. *Yagnobskie etnograficheskie materialy.* Dushanbe: AN TSSR, 1976.

Pipes, Richard. *The Formation of the Soviet Union: Communism and Nationalism, 1917–1923.* Cambridge, Mass.: Harvard University Press, 1970.

Pobeda Oktiabrskoi revolutsii v Uzbekistane: Sbornik dokumentov, Vol. 1. Tashkent: Izdatelstvo AN UzSSR, 1963.

Pobeda Oktiabrskoi revolutsii v Uzbekistane: Sbornik dokumentov, Vol. 2. Tashkent: Izdatelstvo AN UzSSR, 1972.

Poliak, G. B., and B. I Annenkov. 'Sovershenstvovanie finansirovaniia.' In *Territorialno-proizvodstvennye kompleksy: planirovanie i upravlenie*, edited by A. G. Aganbegian, 119–26. Novosibirsk: Nauka, 1984.

Poliakov, Sergei P. *Everyday Islam: Religion and Tradition in Rural Central Asia.* Armonk, NY: M. E. Sharpe, 1992.

Poliakov, Sergei P. 'Modern Soviet Central Asian Countryside: Traditional Forms of Property in a Quasi-Industrial System.' In *State, Religion and Society in Central Asia: A Post Soviet Critique*, edited by Vitaly Naumkin. Reading, UK: Ithaca Press, 1993.

Poliakov, S. P. *Traditsionalizm v sovremennom sredneaziatskom obschestve.* Moscow: Znanie, 1989.

Poliakov, S. P. 'Sovremennaia sredneaziatskaia derevnia: traditsionnye formy sobstvennosti v kvaziindustrialnoi sisteme.' In *Krestianstvo i industrialnaia tsivilizatsiia*, edited by Iu. G. Aleksandrov and S. A. Panarin, 174–200. Moscow: Nauka, 1993.

Polonskaya, Ludmila, and Alexei Malashenko. *Islam in Central Asia.* Reading, UK: Ithaca Press, 1994.

'Postanovlenie Plenuma TsK RKP(b) o vzaimootnosheniiakh s nezavisimymi Sovetskimi Sotsialisticheskimi respublikami. 6 oktiabria 1922g.' In *KPSS v rezoliutsiiakh i resheniiakh s'ezdov, konferentsii i plenumov TsK*, Vol. 2. Moscow: Gospolitizdat, 1970.

Postovoi, E. S., A. I. Polskaia and N. T. Bezrukova. *Ocherki istorii Kommunisticheskoi partii Tadzhikistana.* Dushanbe: Irfon, 1964.

Poujol, Catherine. 'Some Reflections on Russian Involvement in the Tajik Conflict, 1992–1993.' In *Tajikistan: The Trials of Independence*, edited by Mohammad-Reza Djalili, Frederic Grare and Shirin Akiner. Surrey, UK: Curzon, 1998.

Problems of the Peoples of the USSR, No. 11 (1961).

Problemy Tadzhikistana: Trudy I Konferentsii po izucheniiu proizvoditelnykh sil Tadzhikskoi SSR, Vol. 1. Leningrad: Izdatelstvo AN SSSR, 1933.

Programma konkretnykh meropriiatii po stabilizatsii ekonomiki i perekhodu k rynku v Tadzhikskoi SSR. Proekt. Dushanbe: [No Publisher], 1990.

Promyshlennost Respubliki Tajikistan za 1993 god. Dushanbe: GVTs GU Natsionalnoi statistiki RT, 1994.

'Qarori Soveti Olii RSS Tojikiston dar borai tadbirhoi ta'mini muhofizati manfiathoi modar va kudak, behtar namudani sharoiti mehnatu maishati zanon va vus'at dodani fa'oliyyati onho dar hayyoti istehsoli va jam'iyyati.' In *Sessiyyai hashtumi Soveti Olii RSS Tojikiston: Da'vati yozdahum; Hisoboti stenografi*. Dushanbe: Soveti Olii RSST, 1988.

Qushmatov, Abduvali. *Vaqf: Namudhoi zamindorii vaqf dar Shimoli Tojikiston dar solhoi 1870–1917*. Dushanbe: Irfon, 1990.

Rahimov, Khurram. *Traditsii tadzhikskogo naroda i ikh rol' v podgotovke starsheklassnikov k semeinoi zhizni*. Dushanbe: NII pedagogicheskikh nauk RT, 1992.

Rahimov, R. K., ed. *Tadzhikistan: ekonomicheskii rost i effektivnost*. Dushanbe: Irfon, 1972.

Rahimov, R. K. *Sotsialno-ekonomicheskie problemy razvitiia Tadzhikskoi SSR*. Dushanbe: Donish, 1984.

Rahmatulloev, A., and S. Mukhtorov. *Ocherkhoi ta'rikhi Tojikistoni Soveti*. Dushanbe: Maorif, 1989.

Rahmonov, Emomali. *The Tajiks in the Mirror of History, Volume I: From the Aryans to the Samanids*. Guernsey, UK: London River Editions, [n.d.].

Rahmonov, Emomali. *Tojikiston: chahor soli istiqloliyat va khudshinosi*. Dushanbe: Irfon, 1995.

Rakhmonov, Emomali. 'Welcome Speech by Mr. E. Sh. Rakhmonov, President of the Republic of Tajikistan.' In *The Contribution of the Samanid Epoch to the Cultural Heritage of Central Asia*. UNESCO International Colloquium, Dushanbe 1998. Dushanbe: Adib, 1998.

Rakowska-Harmstone, Teresa. *Russia and Nationalism in Central Asia: The Case of Tadzhikistan*. Baltimore and London: The Johns Hopkins Press, 1970.

Rashid, Ahmed. *The Resurgence of Central Asia: Islam or Nationalism*. Karachi: Oxford University Press, 1994.

Rasshirennyi XVIII plenum TsK KPT 3 marta 1990g. Stenograficheskii otchet. Dushanbe: Irfon, 1990.

Resheniia Prezidenta i Kabineta Ministrov RT za mai 1992g. Dushanbe: UD SM RT, 1993.

Rezoliutsiia X s'ezda Kommunisticheskoi partii Tadzhikistana. Stalinabad: Tadzhikgosizdat, 1956.

Rigby, T. H. 'Introduction: Political Legitimacy, Weber and Communist Mono-organisational Systems.' In *Political Legitimation in Communist States*, edited by T. H. Rigby and Ferenc Feher, 1–26. London: Macmillan, 1982.

Rigby, T. H. 'Old Style Congress—New Style Leadership?' In *Gorbachev at the Helm: A New Era in Soviet Politics?* edited by R. F. Miller, J. H. Miller and T. H. Rigby, 6–39. New York: Croom Helm, 1987.

Rigby, T. H. *Political Elites in the USSR: Central Leaders and Local Cadres from Lenin to Gorbachev*. Aldershot, UK: Edward Elgar, 1990.

Rigby, T. H. *The Changing Soviet System: Mono-Organisational Socialism from its Origins to Gorbachev's Restructuring*. Aldershot, UK: Edward Elgar, 1990.

Rigby, T. H., and Bohdan Harasymiw, eds. *Leadership Selection and Patron–Client Relations in the USSR and Yugoslavia*. London: George Allen & Unwin, 1983.

Robinson, Neal. *Ideology and the Collapse of the Soviet System: A Critical History of Soviet Ideological Discourse*. Aldershot, UK: Edward Elgar, 1995.

Ro'i, Yaacov. 'The Secularisation of Islam and the USSR's Muslim Areas.' In *Muslim Eurasia: Conflicting Legacies*, edited by Yaacov Ro'i, 5–20. London: Frank Cass, 1995.

Ro'i, Yaacov. *Islam in the Soviet Union: From the Second World War to Gorbachev*. London: Hurst & Co., 2000.

Rol' selskikh raikomov partii v osuschestvlenii agrarnoi politiki KPSS v sovremennykh usloviiakh. Moscow: Izdatelstvo politicheskoi literatury, 1987.

Rorlich, Azade-Ayse. 'Islam and Atheism: Dynamic Tension in Soviet Central Asia.' In *Soviet Central Asia: The Failed Transformation*, edited by William Fierman, 186–218. Boulder, Colo.: Westview Press, 1991.

Rotar, I. 'Sredniaia Aziia: etnosotsialnaia perspektiva.' In *Islam v Rossii i Srednei Azii*, edited by Igor Ermakov and Dmitrii Mikulskii. Moscow: Lotus Foundation, 1993.

Roy, Olivier. *The Civil War in Tajikistan: Causes and Implications*. Washington, DC: United States Institute of Peace, 1993.

Roy, Olivier. 'The Impact of the Afghan War in Soviet Central Asia.' In *In a Collapsing Empire: Underdevelopment, Ethnic Conflicts and Nationalisms in the Soviet Union*, edited by Marco Buttino. Milan: Fondazione Giangiacomo Feltrinelli, 1993.

Roy, Olivier. *The Failure of Political Islam*. London: I. B. Tauris & Co., 1994.

Roy, Oliver. 'Is the Conflict in Tajikistan a Model for Conflicts throughout Central Asia?' In *Tajikistan: The Trials of Independence*, edited by Mohammad-Reza Djalili, Frederic Grare and Shirin Akiner. New York: St Martin's Press, 1997.

Roy, Olivier. *The New Central Asia: The Creation of Nations*. New York: NYU Press, 2000.

Roy, Olivier. 'Inter-Regional Dynamics of War.' In *Politics of Compromise: The Tajikistan Peace Process*, edited by Kamoludin Abdullaev and Catherine Barnes. London: Conciliation Resources, 2001.

Roy, Olivier. 'Islamic Militancy: Religion and Conflict in Central Asia.' In *Searching for Peace in Central and South Asia*, edited by Monique Mekenkamp, Paul van Tongeren and Hans van de Veen. Boulder, Colo.: Lynne Rienner, 2002.

Roy, Olivier. 'Soviet Legacies and Western Aid Imperatives in the New Central Asia.' In *Civil Society in the Muslim World: Contemporary Perspectives*, edited by Amyn B. Sajoo. New York: I. B. Tauris, 2004.

Rubin, Barnett R. 'Tajikistan: From Soviet Republic to Russian-Uzbek Protectorate.' In *Central Asia and the World*, edited by Michael Mandelbaum, 207–24. New York: Council on Foreign Relations Press, 1994.

Rubin, Barnett R. 'Russian Hegemony and State Breakdown in the Periphery: Causes and Consequences of the Civil War in Tajikistan.' In *Post-Soviet Political Order: Conflict and State Building*, edited by Barnett R. Rubin and Jack Snyder. London: Routledge, 1998.

Rumer, Boris Z. *Soviet Central Asia: A Tragic Experiment*. Boston: Unwin Hyman, 1989.

Rumer, Boris Z. 'Central Asia's Cotton Economy.' In *Soviet Central Asia: The Failed Transformation*, edited by William Fierman, 62–89. Boulder, Colo.: Westview Press, 1991.

Rutland, Peter. 'Economic Crisis and Reform.' In *Developments in Soviet and Post-Soviet Politics*, edited by Stephen White, Alex Pravda and Zvi Gitelman, 200–26. London: Macmillan, 1992.

Rywkin, Michael. *Russia in Central Asia*. New York: Collier Books, 1963.

Rywkin, Michael. 'National Symbiosis: Vitality, Religion, Identity, Allegiance.' In *The USSR and the Muslim World: Issues in Domestic and Foreign Policy*, edited by Yaacov Ro'i, 3–15. London: George Allen & Unwin, 1984.

Rywkin, Michael. *Moscow's Lost Empire*. Armonk, NY: M. E. Sharpe, 1994.

Sadykov, M. S. *Istoricheskii opyt KPSS po stroitelstvu sotsializma v Tadzhikistane (1917–1959gg.)*. Dushanbe: Irfon, 1967.

Saidbaev, Talib. 'Inter-Ethnic Conflicts in Central Asia: Social and Religious Perspectives.' In *Ethnicity and Conflict in a Post-Communist World: The Soviet Union, Eastern Europe and China*, edited by Kumar Rupesinghe, Peter King and Olga Vorkunova. New York: St Martin's Press, 1992.

Saidbaev, T. S. *Islam i obschestvo*. Moscow: Nauka, 1978.

Saidmuradov, H. M., ed. *Narodnoe khoziaistvo Tadzhikistana v period formirovaniia ekonomicheskikh predposylok razvitogo sotsializma*. Dushanbe: Donish, 1985.

Saikal, Amin. *The Rise and Fall of the Shah: 1941–1979*. London: Angus & Robertson, 1980.

Sami, Mirza 'Abdal 'Azim. *Tarikh-i Salatin-i Manghitiya*. Moscow: Izdatelstvo Vostochnoi Literatury, 1962.

Sandag, Sh. 'Obrazovanie edinogo mongolskogo gosudarstva i Chingiskhan.' In *Tataro-mongoly v Azii i Evrope*. Moscow: Nauka, 1977.

Sanderson, Thomas M., Daniel Kimmage and David A. Gordon. *From the Ferghana Valley to South Waziristan: The Evolving Threat of Central Asian Jihadists*. CSIS Transnational Threats Project. Washington, DC: Center for Strategic and International Studies, March 2010.

Sattori, Qiyomiddin, ed. *HNIT, Zodai Ormoni mardum: Ba iftixori 30-solagii ta'sisi Hizbi Nahzati Islomii Tojikiston*. Dushanbe: Imperial-Grupp, 2003.

Sattorzoda, Abdunabi. 'The Democrat Party.' In *Politics of Compromise: The Tajikistan Peace Process*, edited by Kamoludin Abdullaev and Catharine Barnes. London: Conciliation Resources, 2001.

Schoeberlein-Engel, John. 'Bones of Contention: Conflicts over Resources.' In *Searching for Peace in Central and South Asia: An Overview of Conflict Prevention and Peacebuilding Activities*, edited by Monique Mekenkamp, Paul van Tongeren and Hans van de Veen. Boulder, Colo.: Lynne Rienner, 2002.

Selskoe khoziaistvo Respubliki Tadzhikistan. Dushanbe: GSA pri pravitelstve RT, 1994.

Sem'ia v Respublike Tadzhikistan. Dushanbe: Glavnoe upravlenie natsionalnoi statistiki, 1994.

Sessiyai hashtumi Soveti Olii RSS Tojikiston, da'vati yozdahum: Hisoboti stenografi. Dushanbe: Izdaniie Verkhovnogo Soveta Tadzhikskoi SSR, 1988.

Shahrani, M. Nazif. 'Islam and the Political Culture of "Scientific Atheism" in Post-Soviet Central Asia: Future Predicaments.' In *The Politics of Religion in Russia and the New States of Eurasia*, edited by Michael Bourdeaux. London: M. E. Sharpe, 1995.

Shams-ud-din. *Secularisation in the USSR*. New Delhi: Vikas Publishing House, 1982.

Sharipov, Ibron. *Zakonomernosti formirovaniia sotsialisticheskikh obshestvennykh otnoshenii v Tadzhikistane*. Dushanbe: Donish, 1983.

Shishov, A. *Tadzhiki: Etnograficheskoe issledovanie*. [Reprint of the 1910 edition.] Almaty: ZhShS, 2006.

Shnirelman, Victor A. *Who Gets the Past? Competition for Ancestors among Non-Russian Intellectuals in Russia*. Baltimore: The Johns Hopkins University Press, 1996.

Shokirov, B., and A. Mahmadkarimov. *Paidoyeshi hizbu sozmonhoi nav dar Tojikiston va fa'oliyati onho (solhoi 1989–1992)*. Dushanbe: Donishgohi agrarii Tojikiston, 1994.

Shoolbraid, S. M. H. *The Oral Epic of Siberia and Central Asia*. Bloomington: Indiana University Publications, 1975.

Shukurov, M. R. *Istoriia kulturnoi zhizni sovetskogo Tadzhikistana (1917–1941)*, Part I. Dushanbe: Irfon, 1970.

Smith, Anthony D. *Nationalism in the Twentieth Century*. Canberra: The Australian National University Press, 1979.

Smith, Anthony D. *The Ethnic Revival*. Cambridge: Cambridge University Press, 1981.

Smith, Anthony D. *The Ethnic Origins of Nations*. New York: Basil Blackwell, 1987.

Smith, Gordon B. *The Soviet Procuracy and the Supervision of Administration*. Netherlands: Sijthoff & Noordhoff, 1978.

Snesarev, G. P. 'O reliktakh muzhskikh soiuzov v istorii narodov Srednei Azii.' In *Mezhdunarodnyi kongress antropologicheskikh i etnograficheskikh nauk*, Vol. II, 1–6. Moscow: Nauka, 1964.

Soifer, D. I. 'Bolshevistskie voennye gruppy Turkestanskogo voennogo okruga v 1917g.' In *Voennye organizatsii partii bolshevikov v 1917g.*, edited by Iu. I. Korablev, 245–54. Moscow: Nauka, 1986.

Sostoianie religioznosti i ateisticheskogo vospitaniia v regionakh traditsionnogo rasprostraneniia islama. Moscow: Akademiia obshchestvennykh nauk pri TsK KPSS, Institut nauchnogo atizma; Sovetskaia sotsiologicheskaia assotsiatsiia, 1989.

Sotsialnoe razvitie SSSR. Moscow. Finansy i statistika, 1990.

Sotsial'no-kul'turnyi oblik sovetskikh natsii. Moscow: Nauka, 1986.

Sotsialno-politicheskie usloviia perekhoda k rynku v Tadzhikistane. (Itogi sotsiologicheskogo analiza). Moscow and Dushanbe: Rossiiskaia akademiia upravleniia, 1991.

Stalin, I. V. *Sochineniia*, Vol. V. Moscow: Gospolitizdat, 1947.

Steele, Jonathan. *Eternal Russia: Yeltsin, Gorbachev and the Mirage of Democracy*. London and Boston: Faber & Faber, 1995.

Stephan, Manja. '"You Come to Us Like a Black Cloud": Universal versus Local Islam in Tajikistan.' In *The Postsocialist Religious Question: Faith and Power in Central Asia and East-Central Europe*, edited by C. M. Hann. Berlin: Lit., 2007.

Subtelny, Maria Eva. 'The Symbiosis of Turk and Tajik.' In *Central Asia in Historical Perspective*, edited by Beatrice F. Manz, 45–61. Boulder, Colo.: Westview Press, 1994.

Sud'in, Andrei. 'Kirgizskoe selo: akkulturatsiia i priverzhennost natsionalnoi kulturnoi traditsii.' In *Etnosotsialnye protsessy v Kyrgyzstane*, 17–30. Moscow: Institut Vostokovedeniia RAN, 1994.

Sukhareva, O. A. *Islam v Uzbekistane*. Tashkent: Fan, 1960.

Sukhareva, O. A. *Bukhara: XIX – nachalo XXv. (Pozdnefeodalnyi gorod i ego naselenie)*. Moscow: Nauka, 1966.

Sukhareva, O. A. 'Ocherki po istorii sredneaziatskikh gorodov.' In *Istoriia i kultura narodov Srednei Azii (Drevnost' i srednie veka)*, edited by B. G. Gafurov and B. A. Litvinsky, 132–47. Moscow: Nauka, 1976.

Sukhareva, O. A. 'Traditsiia semeino-rodstvennykh brakov u narodov Srednei Azii.' In *Sem'ia i semeinye obriady u narodov Srednei Azii i Kazakhstana*, edited by G. P. Snesarev, 119–20. Moscow: Nauka, 1978.

Suny, Ronald Grigor. *The Making of the Georgian Nation*. Bloomington and Indianapolis: Indiana University Press, 1994.

Taarnby, Michael. *Islamist Radicalisation in Tajikistan: An Assessment of Current Trends*. Dushanbe: Korshinos/OSCE, 2012.

Tadzhikistan. Moscow: Mysl, 1968.

Tadzhikistan v ogne. Dushanbe: Irfon, 1993.

Tadzhikistan za gody Sovetskoi vlasti. Dushanbe: Statistika, 1967.

Theen, Rolf H. W. 'Party and Bureaucracy.' In *Public Policy and Administration in the Soviet Union*, edited by Gordon B. Smith, 18–52. New York: Praeger, 1980.

Thoni, Julien. *The Tajik Conflict: The Dialectic between Internal Fragmentation and External Vulnerability 1991–1994*. Geneva: Programme for Strategic and International Security Studies, 1994.

Tillett, Lowell. *The Great Friendship: Soviet Historians on the Non-Russian Nationalities*. Chapel Hill, NC: University of North Carolina Press, 1969.

Tishkov, Valerii Aleksandrovich. *Ethnicity, Nationalism and Conflict in and after the Soviet Union: The Mind Aflame*. London: Sage, 1997.

Tishkov, Valery A. 'Inventions and Manifestations of Ethno-Nationalism in and after the Soviet Union.' In *Ethnicity and Conflict in a Post-Communist World: The Soviet Union, Eastern Europe and China*, edited by Kumar Rupesinghe, Peter King and Olga Vorkunova. New York: St Martin's Press, 1992.

Tozhikiston Uzbek zhamiyati. Dushanbe: Tojikiston, 1992.

Turajonzoda, Qadi Akbar. 'Religion: The Pillar of Society.' In *Central Asia: Conflict, Resolution, and Change*, edited by Roald Z. Sagdeev and Susan Eisenhower. Chevy Chase, Md: CPSS Press, 1995.

Tursunov, Akbar. 'Politicheskie improvizatsii vozrozhdaiushegosia natsionalnogo dukha: o destruktsiiakh kulturogennykh.' *Bibliotechka 'Charogi ruz'* [Supplement brochure of the *Charoghi ruz* newspaper], 1995.

Umarov, Kh. *Khoziaistvenno-upravlencheskie aspekty perestroiki*. Dushanbe: Irfon, 1988.

Umarov, Kh. 'Sovremennye sotsialno-ekonomicheskie protsessy i problemy razvitiia sovetskoi Srednei Azii.' In *Sovetologi o problemakh sotsialno-ekonomicheskogo razvitiia SSSR i soiuznykh respublik*, 8–21. Moscow: Institut ekonomiki AN SSSR, 1990.

US Institute of Peace. *The War in Tajikistan Three Years On*. US Institute of Peace Special Report, November 1995.

Usmanov, H. M. *Tekhnicheskaia rekonstruktsiia industrii Tadzhikistana v usloviiakh perestroiki*. Dushanbe: Irfon, 1989.

Usmon, Ibrohim. *Soli Nabiev*. Dushanbe: [No publisher], 1995.

Vaksberg, Arkady. *The Soviet Mafia*. New York: St Martin's Press, 1991.

Vambery, Arminius. *History of Bokhara*. London: Henry S. King & Co., 1873.

Velikii Oktiabr i raskreposhchenie zhenshin Srednei Azii i Kazakhstana (1917–1936). Moscow: Mysl, 1971.

Vinnikov, Ia. R. 'Natsional'nye I etnograficheskie gruppy Srednei Azii po dannym atnicheskoi statistiki.' In *Etnicheskie protsessy u natsional'nykh grupp Srednei Azii i Kazakhstana*. Moscow: Nauka, 1980.

Vishnevsky, A. Ia. *Leninskaia natsionalnaia politika v deistvii*. Dushanbe: Donish, 1982.

Vuzovskaia molodezh: mirovozzrencheskie i tsennostnye orientatsii, Vypusk 1. Dushanbe: Izdatelstvo TGU, 1990.

Vybory Prezidenta Respubliki Tadzhikistan: Sotsiologicheskii monitoring. Dushanbe: Press-sluzhba KM RT, 1991.

Whitlock, Monica. *Land Beyond the River: The Untold Story of Central Asia*. New York: St Martin's Press, 2003.

Willerton, John P. 'Executive Power and Political Leadership.' In *Developments in Soviet and Post-Soviet Politics*, edited by Stephen White, Alex Pravda and Zvi Gitelman, 44–67. London: Macmillan, 1992.

Wirth, Louis. 'The Limitations of Regionalism.' In *Regionalism in America*, edited by Merrill Jensen. Madison and Milwaukee: University of Wisconsin Press, 1965.

Wixman, Ronald. 'Ethnic Attitudes and Relations in Modern Uzbek Cities.' In *Soviet Central Asia: The Failed Transformation*, edited by William Fierman. Boulder, Colo.: Westview Press, 1991.

Wyman, Matthew. *Public Opinion in Post-Communist Russia*. London: Macmillan, 1997.

Yakubov, Iu. *Pargar v VII–VIII vekakh nashei ery*. Dushanbe: Donish, 1979.

Yodgori, Nozir. *Saddi otash: Yoddosht, Khotira, Andesha*. Dushanbe: Firdavs, 1993.

Yormuhammad, R. *Mavlono Ya'qubi Charkhi kist?* Dushanbe: Tojikiston, 1992.

Yusuf, Hasan. *Nomusu nangi millat*. Dushanbe: Irfon, 1993.

Zabarova, Marhabo, and Zafar Dustov. 'Tajlili Navruz dar Hisori shodmon.' In *Dar justujui farhangi vodii Hisor*, edited by N. N. Ne'matov, 60–70. Dushanbe: Mamnu'gohi ta'rikhi-madanii Hisor, 1992.

Zakaria, Rafiq. *The Struggle within Islam: The Conflict between Religion and Politics*. New York: Penguin Books, 1988.

Zald, M. N. 'Culture, Ideology, and Strategic Framing.' In *Comparative Perspectives on Social Movements: Political Opportunities, Mobilising Structures, and Cultural Framings*, edited by Doug McAdam, John D. McCarthy and Mayer M. Zald. Cambridge: Cambridge University Press, 1996.

Zevelev, A. I. *Iz istorii grazhdanskoi voiny v Uzbekistane*. Tashkent: Gosudarstvennoe izdatelstvo UzSSR, 1959.

Zevelev, A. I., Iu. A. Poliakov and L. V. Shishkina. *Basmachestvo: Pravda istorii i vymysel falsifikatorov*. Moscow: Mysl, 1986.

Zoyirov, R., and S. Sharopov. 'Kriminologicheskaia kharakteristika i analiz tendentsii razvitiia organizovannoi korystnoi prestupnosti.' In *Vlast', upravlenie, pravoporiadok*, Vypusk I, 77–84. Dushanbe: Ikbol, 1995.

2. Occasional Reports and Articles from Periodicals and Journals

Abashin, Sergei. 'The Transformation of Ethnic Identity in Central Asia: A Case Study of the Uzbeks and Tajiks.' *Russian Regional Perspectives Journal*, Vol. 1, No. 2 (2003).

Abashin, Sergei. 'The Logic of Islamic Practice: A Religious Conflict in Central Asia.' *Central Asian Survey*, Vol. 25, No. 3 (2006).

Abazov, Rafis. 'Central Asia's Conflicting Legacy and Ethnic Policies: Revisiting a Crisis Zone of the Former USSR.' *Nationalism & Ethnic Politics*, Vol. 5, No. 2 (1999).

Abdoullaev, Kamol. 'Central Asian Emigres in Afghanistan: First Wave 1920–1931.' *Central Asia Monitor*, No. 5 (1994): 16–27.

Ahmed, Mutahir. 'Turmoil in Tajikistan: The Role of Internal and External Powers.' *Eurasian Studies*, Vol. 2, No. 3 (Fall 1995): 69–80.

Ahmedov, A. A. 'Sovremennoe sostoianie zdravookhraneniia v respublike i zadachi kollektiva TGMU im. Abuali Ibn Sino v dele podgotovki vrachebnykh kadrov i razvitiia meditsinskoi nauki.' *Zdravookhranenie Tadzhikistana*, No. 3 (246) (1993): 7–13.

Aiman, David, and Paul Hofheinz. 'Karl Marx Makes Room for Muhammad.' *Time* (12 March 1990): 44.

Aini, K. 'Didori vopasin.' *Sadoi Sharq*, No. 4 (1980): 63–84.

Akbarzadeh, Shahram. 'Why Did Nationalism Fail in Tajikistan?' *Europe-Asia Studies*, Vol. 48, No. 7 (1996): 1105–29.

Akcali, Pinar. 'Islam and Ethnicity in Central Asia: The Case of the Islamic Renaissance Party.' *Mediterranean Quarterly*, Winter (1998).

Akiner, Shirin. 'Melting Pot, Salad Bowl—Cauldron? Manipulation and Mobilization of Ethnic and Religious Identities in Central Asia.' *Ethnic and Racial Studies*, Vol. 20, No. 2 (1997).

Al-Azm, Sadik J. 'Islamic Fundamentalism Reconsidered: A Critical Outline of Problems, Ideas and Approaches, Part I.' *South Asia Bulletin*, Vol. XIII, Nos 1–2 (1993): 93–121.

Alexandrov, Iu. G. 'Sredniaia Aziia: spetsificheskii sluchai ekonomicheskoi slaborazvitosti.' *Vostok*, No. 5 (1991): 142–54.

Alexeev, V. A., I. N. Borisov and A. S. Emelianov. '"Organizovannaia prestupnost": kriminalizatsiia funktsii uchastnikov prestupnykh formirovanii.' *Sovetskoe gosudarstvo i pravo*, No. 10 (1991): 65–70.

Alimov, A. 'Business in Opium.' *Kommunist Tadzhikistana* (13 May 1988). In *BBC Summary of World Broadcasts—Former Soviet Union*, 0212 (25 July 1988): B/1.

Alimov, Kadir. 'Are Central Asian Clans Still Playing a Political Role?' *Central Asia Monitor*, No. 4 (1994).

Aptekar, P. A. 'Krestianskaia voina.' *Voenno-istoricheskii zhurnal*, No. 1 (1993): 50–5.

Arabov, Oumar. 'A Note on Sufism in Tajikistan: What Does it Look Like?' *Central Asian Survey*, Vol. 23, No. 3 (2004).

Arutiunian, Iu. V., and Iu. V. Bromlei. 'A Sociological Profile of Soviet Nationalities: Ethnosociology Research Results.' *Soviet Anthropology and Archeology*, Vol. 27, No. 1 (Summer 1988): 7–70.

Âslund, Anders. 'Russia's Road from Communism.' *Daedalus*, Vol. 121, No. 2 (1992): 77–95.

Atkin, Muriel. 'FAST Case Study: Tajikistan.' Bern: Swiss Peace Foundation, Institute for Conflict Resolution (3 February 1999).

Atkin, Muriel. 'Tajikistan's Civil War.' *Current History*, October (1997).

Azamova, Asal. 'Tajikistan: In Flames of Internecine Wars.' *Moskoskiye novosti* (5 July 1992): 9. In *The Current Digest of the Post-Soviet Press*, Vol. XLIV, No. 26 (29 July 1992).

Azizi, Muzaffar. 'Chun sabza umedi bardamidan budi.' *Daryo*, No. 2 (1994): 14–16.

Barthold, V. V. 'Zapiska po voprosy ob istoricheskikh vzaimootnosheniiakh turetskikh i iranskikh narodnostei Srednei Azii.' *Vostok*, No. 5 (1991): 165–67.

Bashirov, L. 'Islam v nashi dni.' *Slovo lektora*, No. 1 (1989).

Basilov, V. N. 'Simvolika sufizma i narodnye verovaniia.' *Etnograficheskoe obozrenie*, No. 6 (1994): 88–91.

Belkindas, Misha V., and Matthew J. Sagers. 'A Preliminary Analysis of Economic Relations among Union Republics of the USSR: 1970–1988.' *Soviet Geography*, Vol. XXXI, No. 8 (1990): 629–56.

Benford, Robert D., and David A. Snow. 'Framing Processes and Social Movements: An Overview and Assessment.' *Annual Review of Sociology*, Vol. 20 (2000).

Bennigsen, Alexandre. 'Several Nations or One People? Ethnic Consciousness among Soviet Central Asian Muslims.' *Survey*, Vol. 24, No. 3 (108) (Summer 1979): 51–64.

Bennigsen, Alexandre. 'Mullahs, Mujahidin and Soviet Muslims.' *Problems of Communism*, Vol. XXXIII, No. 6 (1984): 28–44.

Bleuer, Christian. 'Muslim Soldiers in Non-Muslim Militaries at War in Muslim Lands: The Soviet, American and Indian Experience.' *The Journal of Muslim Minority Affairs*, Vol. 32, No. 4 (2012).

Bleuer, Christian. 'State-Building, Migration and Economic Development on the Frontiers of Northern Afghanistan and Southern Tajikistan.' *Journal of Eurasian Studies*, Vol. 3 (2012).

Bond, Andrew R. 'Russia Coping with "Cotton Crisis".' *Post-Soviet Geography*, Vol. 35, No. 5 (1993): 330–34.

Boronbekov, S. 'Religioznye verovaniia, obychai i ugolovno-pravovoe soznanie.' *Izvestiia AN TSSR. Seriia: filosofiia, ekonomika, pravovedenie*, No. 4 (1991): 66–71.

Borysenko, V. 'The 1959 Purges in the Communist Parties of the Soviet National Republics.' *Problems of the Peoples of the USSR*, No. 5 (1960): 7–15.

Bottomley, Gill. 'Identification: Ethnicity, Gender and Culture.' *Journal of International Studies*, Vol. 18, No. 1 (1997): 41–8.

Bowers, Chris, and John Rettie. 'Russia Reinforces Embattled Russian Garrison.' *The Guardian* (30 September 1992): 7.

Bronshtein, Ia. T. '"Soizmeriat" vklad respubliki i ee vozmozhnosti.' *EKO*, No. 11 (1989): 29–32.

Brown, B. 'Unrest in Tajikistan.' *Radio Free Europe/Radio LibertyReport on the USSR* (23 February 1990).

Brown, Bess. 'The Role of Public Groups in Perestroika in Central Asia.' *Radio Free Europe/Radio Liberty Report on the USSR* (26 January 1990): 20–5.

Brown, Bess. 'The Islamic Renaissance Party in Central Asia.' *Radio Free Europe/ Radio Liberty Report on the USSR* (10 May 1990): 12–14.

Brown, Bess. 'Central Asia.' *Radio Free Europe/Radio Liberty Research Report*, Vol. 1, No. 7 (14 February 1992): 17–18.

Brown, Bess. 'Whither Tajikistan.' *Radio Free Europe/Radio Liberty Research Report*, Vol. 1, No. 24 (12 June 1992).

Brown, Bess. 'Tajikistan: The Fall of Nabiev.' *Radio Free Europe/Radio Liberty Research Report*, Vol. 1, No. 38 (25 September 1992): 12–18.

Brown, Bess. 'The Conservatives Triumph.' *Radio Free Europe/Radio Liberty Research Report*, Vol. 2, No. 7 (12 February 1993).

Buisson, Antoine. 'State-Building, Power-Building and Political Legitimacy: The Case of Post-Conflict Tajikistan.' *China and Eurasia Forum Quarterly*, Vol. 5, No. 4 (2007).

Burton, Michael G., and J. Higley. 'Elite Settlements.' *American Sociological Review*, Vol. 52 (June 1987): 295–307.

Bushkov, Vladimir. 'Tadzhikistan na ostrie demograficheskogo supervzryva.' *Rossiia i musulmanskii mir*, No. 7 (37) (1995).

Bushkov, V. I. 'Tadzhikskii avlod tysiacheletiia spustia.' *Vostok*, No. 5 (1991): 72–81.

Bushkov, V. I. 'Tadzhikistan: traditsionnoe obshchestvo v postindustrialnom mire.' *Etnograficheskoe obozrenie*, No. 4 (1995): 89–95.

Bushkov, V. I. 'Population Migration in Tajikistan: Past and Present.' *JCAS Symposium Series*, No. 9 (2000).

Bushkov, V. I., and D. V. Mikulskii. 'Tadzhikistan: chto proiskhodit v respublike?' *Issledovaniia po prikladnoi i neotlozhnoi etnologii*, No. 40 (1993).

Butinov, N. A. 'Obschina, sem'ia, rod.' *Sovetskaia Etnografiia*, No. 2 (1968): 91–5.

Bystritsky, A., and D. Shusharin. '"Ten" Brezhneva menia usynovila.' *Literaturnaia gazeta* (30 March 1994): 11.

Carlisle, Donald S. 'The Uzbek Power Elite: Politburo and Secretariat (1938–1983).' *Central Asian Survey*, Vol. 5, Nos 3–4 (1986): 91–132.

Clark, William A. 'Crime and Punishment in Soviet Officialdom, 1965–1990.' *Europa-Asia Studies*, Vol. 45, No. 2 (1993): 259–79.

Cook, Linda J. 'Brezhnev's "Social Contract" and Gorbachev's Reforms.' *Soviet Studies*, Vol. 44, No. 1 (1992): 37–56.

Cornell, Svante E. 'The Devaluation of the Concept of Autonomy: National Minorities in the Former Soviet Union.' *Central Asian Survey*, Vol. 18, No. 2 (1999).

Dahlburg, John-Thor. 'Dissidents Rout Tajikistan's Hard-Line Leader: Central Asia.' *Los Angeles Times* (7 May 1992): 23.

Dailey, Erika. 'War or Peace? Human Rights and Russian Military Involvement in the "Near Abroad".' *Human Rights Watch Report*, Vol. 5, No. 22 (1993).

Davis, Christopher M. 'Health Care Crisis: The Former USSR.' *Radio Free Europe/ Radio Liberty Research Report*, Vol. 2, No. 40 (8 October 1993): 36–41.

Denikin, Gen. A. I. 'Ocherki Russkoi smuty.' *Voprosy istorii*, No. 2 (1995): 106–22.

di Maio, Micah, and Jessica Abenstein. 'Tajikistan's Peacebuilding Efforts through Promotion of Hanafi Islam.' *Journal of Peacebuilding & Development*, Vol. 6, No. 1 (2011).

Dubnov, Arkadii. 'Prodam BTR, kupliu dom v Rossii.' *Novoe vremia*, No. 43 (October 1992): 8–11.

Dubnov, Arkadii. '"Deputaty dogovorilis": Teper' delo za polevymi komandirami.' *Novoe vremia*, No. 49 (December 1992): 12–16.

Dubnov, Arkadii. 'Katastrofa v Tadzhikistane, o kotoroi v Rossii pochti nichego ne znaiut.' *Novoe vremia*, No. 4 (1993): 13–16.

Dudoignon, Stephane. 'Une segmentation peut en cacher une autre: regionalisms et clivages politico-economic au Tadjikistan.' *Cahiers d'Etudes sur la mediteranee orientale et le monde turco-iranien*, Vol. 18 (1994).

Dudoignon, Stephane. 'Communal Solidarity and Social Conflicts in Late 20th Century Central Asia: The Case of the Tajik Civil War.' *Islamic Area Studies Working Paper Series*, No. 7. Tokyo: Islamic Area Studies Project, 1998.

Dudoignon, Stephane A. 'From Revival to Mutation: The Religious Personnel of Islam in Tajikistan, from De-Stalinization to Independence (1955–91).' *Central Asian Survey*, Vol. 30, No. 1 (2011).

Dupree, Louis. 'Two Weeks in Soviet Tajikistan and Uzbekistan: Observations and Trends.' *American Universities Field Staff Reports Service, South Asia Series*, Vol. III, No. 4 (1959).

Eck, Kristine, and Lisa Hultman. 'One-Sided Violence against Civilians in War: Insights from New Fatality Data.' *Journal of Peace Research*, Vol. 44, No. 2 (2007).

Eisenstadt, S. N. 'The Breakdown of Communist Regimes.' *Daedalus*, Vol. 121, No. 2 (1992): 21–42.

Ekiert, Grzegorz. 'Democratisation Processes in East Central Europe: A Theoretical Reconsideration.' *British Journal of Political Science*, Vol. 21, Part 3 (July 1991): 285–314.

Emadi, Hafizullah. 'State, Ideology and Islamic Resurgence in Tadjikistan.' *Central Asian Survey*, Vol. 13, No. 4 (1994): 565–73.

Enyedi, Zsolt. 'Organising a Subcultural Party in Eastern Europe: The Case of the Hungarian Christian Democrats.' *Party Politics*, Vol. 2, No. 3 (1996): 377–96.

Epkenhans, Tim. 'Defining Normative Islam: Some Remarks on Contemporary Islamic Thought in Tajikistan—Hoji Akbar Turajonzoda's Sharia and Society.' *Central Asian Survey*, Vol. 30, No. 1 (2011).

Fairbanks, Charles H., jr. 'The Nature of the Beast.' *The National Interest*, No. 31 (1993): 46–56.

Fein, Esther B. 'Upheaval in the East.' *The New York Times* (14 February 1990).

Foroughi, Payam. 'Tajikistan: Nationalism, Ethnicity, Conflict, and Socio-Economic Disparities—Sources and Solutions.' *Journal of Muslim Minority Affairs*, Vol. 22, No. 1 (2002).

Foroughi, Payam. 'Nations in Transit 2004: Tajikistan.' *Freedom House Nations in Transit* (2004).

Freidin, Gregory. 'Coup II: Tadzhikistan's Havel Fights Back; Davlat Khudonazarov.' *The New Republic*, Vol. 205, No. 16 (14 October 1991): 16.

Freizer, Sabine. 'Neo-Liberal and Communal Civil Society in Tajikistan: Merging or Dividing in the Post War Period?' *Central Asian Survey*, Vol. 24, No. 3 (2005): 224–43.

Fukuyama, Francis. 'The Modernising Imperative: The USSR as an Ordinary Country.' *The National Interest*, No. 31 (Spring 1993).

Fumagalli, Matteo. 'Framing Ethnic Minority Mobilisation in Central Asia: The Cases of the Uzbeks in Kyrgyzstan and Tajikistan.' *Europe-Asia Studies*, Vol. 59, No. 4 (2007).

Ganelin, Aleksei. 'Na kryshe mira.' *Ogonek*, No. 40 (1989): 7–8.

Gelischanow, Anastasia. 'The Employment Situation in Tajikistan.' *Radio Liberty Research Bulletin*, No. 26 (3231) (28 December 1983): RL 482/83.

Ginsberg, Thomas. 'Tajik President, Muslim Opposition Agree on Coalition Government.' *The Associated Press* (11 May 1992).

Girardet, Edward. 'Afghan Resistance: Familiar Pattern?' *Christian Science Monitor* (26 July 1992): 1.

Gleason, Gregory. 'On the Bureaucratic Reinforcement of Nationalism in the USSR.' *Canadian Review of Studies in Nationalism*, Vol. XIX, Nos 1–2 (1992): 43–58.

Golitsyn, Georgii S. 'Ecological Problems in the CIS During the Transitional Period.' *Radio Free Europe/Radio Liberty Research Report*, Vol. 2, No. 2 (8 January 1993): 33–42.

Golovin, N. N. 'Voennye usiliia Rossii v mirovoi voine.' *Voenno-istoricheskii zhurnal*, No. 4 (1993): 22–30.

Gorbachev, Pavel. 'Uroki Nureka.' *Druzhba narodov*, No. 3 (1983): 201–13.

Granberg, A. G. 'Ekonomicheskii mekhanizm mezhrespublikanskikh i mezhregionalnykh otnoshenii.' *EKO*, No. 9 (1989): 29–46.

'Grazhdanskie dvizheniia v Uzbekistane.' *Orientiry*, No. 1 (1989): 18.

Gretsky, Sergei. 1994. 'Qadi Akbar Turajonzoda', *Central Asia Monitor*, No. 1 (1994).

Gridneva, Galina. 'Pamir Highlanders Achieve New Status Compromise.' *ITAR-Tass* (10 December 1992).

Grunberg, A. L., and I. M. Steblin-Kamenskii. 'Neskolko zamechanii po povodu otklika A. S. Davydova na stat'iu S. V. Cheshko.' *Sovetskaia etnografiia*, No. 5 (1989): 37.

Haggard, Stephen, and Robert R. Kaufman. 'The Political Economy of Democratic Transitions.' *Comparative Politics*, Vol. 29, No. 3 (April 1997): 263–84.

Harris, Colette. 'Coping with Daily Life in Post-Soviet Tajikistan: The Gharmi Villages of Khatlon Province.' *Central Asian Survey*, Vol. 17, No. 4 (1998).

Heathershaw, John. 'Peacebuilding as Practice: Discourses from Post-Conflict Tajikistan.' *International Peacekeeping*, Vol. 14, No. 2 (2007).

Heathershaw, John, and Sophie Roche. 'Islam and Political Violence in Tajikistan: An Ethnographic Perspective on the Causes and Consequences of the 2010 Armed Conflict in the Kamarob Gorge.' *Ethnopolitics*, No. 8 (March 2011).

Henry Dunant Centre. 'Humanitarian Engagement with Armed Groups: The Central Asian Islamic Opposition Movements.' *Henry Dunant Centre for Humanitarian Dialogue* [Geneva] (2003).

Hierman, Brent. 'What Use Was the Election to Us? Clientelism and Political Trust amongst Ethnic Uzbeks in Kyrgyzstan and Tajikistan.' *Nationalities Papers*, Vol. 38, No. 2 (2010).

Hiro, Dilip. 'Central Asia: Facing Two Ways.' *The Middle East* (May 1994): 14–15.

Horowitz, Shale. 'Explaining Post-Soviet Ethnic Conflicts: Using Regime Type to Discern the Impact and Relative Importance of Objective Antecedents.' *Nationalities Papers*, Vol. 29, No. 4 (2001).

Horsman, Stuart. 'Uzbekistan's Involvement in the Tajik Civil War 1992–97.' *Central Asian Survey*, Vol. 18, No. 1 (1999).

Human Rights Watch. 'Return to Tajikistan: Continued Regional and Ethnic Tensions.' *Human Rights Watch*, Vol. 7, No. 9 (May 1995).

Iakovlev, A. I., and S. A. Panarin. 'Protivorechiia reform: Araviia i Turkestan.' *Vostok*, No. 5 (1991): 104–20.

Iliasov, F. N. 'Skolko stoit nevesta.' *Sotsiologicheskie issledovaniia*, No. 6 (1991): 67–82.

Ilkhamov, A. 'Archeology of Uzbek Identity.' *Anthropology & Archeology of Eurasia*, Vol. 44, No. 4 (Spring 2006).

Imart, Guy G. 'A Unique Empire.' *Central Asian Survey*, Vol. 6, No. 4 (1987): 16.

Imomov, A. 'Ob obrazovanii pravitelstva natsionalnogo primireniia Respubliki Tadzhikistan.' *Izvestiia AN RT. Seriia: Filosofiia i pravovedenie*, No. 3 (1993): 65–74.

Imomov, Sharafiddin. 'Tadzhikistan. Put' k natsionalnomu soglasiiu.' *Novoe vremia*, No. 24 (July 1994): 9–11.

'Interview with Anatoly Sobchak, Yevgeny Velikhov and Head of Tajik Moslems Kazi Akbar Turanzhonzada in Dushanbe on October 6, 1991.' *Official Kremlin International News Broadcast* (8 October 1991).

'Interview with Qadi Akbar Turajonzoda.' *Central Asia Monitor*, No. 2 (1995): 9–11.

Ishiyama, John T. 'Red Phoenix? The Communist Party in Post-Soviet Russian Politics.' *Party Politics*, Vol. 2, No. 2 (1996): 147–75.

Islomov, A. 'Az ki madad juem?' *Tojikiston soveti*, No. 25 (March 1986).

Iusupov, Sh., and D. Berdiev. 'Vosstanie 1916g. v gorode Ura-Tiube i Ganchinskoi volosti.' *Izvestiia AN RT. Seriia: vostokovedenie, istoriia, filologiia*, No. 4 (28) (1992): 76–8.

'Iuzhno-Tadzhikskii kompleks—iz piatiletki deviatoi—v desiatuiu.' *Druzhba narodov*, No. 2 (1976): 186–97.

Jones Luong, P. 'The Future of Central Asian Statehood.' *Central Asia Monitor*, No. 1 (1999).

Juraeva, Gavhar. 'Tragic Visions in Tajikistan.' *Pacific Research*, Vol. 7, No. 2 (May 1994): 15–16.

Kaban, Elif. 'Communal Warfare Tears Tajikistan Apart.' *Reuters News* (27 October 1992).

Kadyr, Timur. 'Hot Spot: Powder Keg Under the Roof of the World.' *Megapolis-Express* (16 September 1992): 20. In *The Current Digest of the Post-Soviet Press*, Vol. XLIV, No. 37 (14 October 1992).

Kafouros, Wassily. 'Towards a Dynamic Two-Sector Model of Soviet Economic Decline.' *Review of Radical Political Economics*, Vol. 28, No. 3 (September 1996): pp. 35–49.

Kalandarova, L. I. 'Podgotovka kadrov khudozhestvennoi intelligentsii v Tadzhikistane (1976–1985gg.).' *Izvestiia AN TSSR. Seriia: vostokovedenie, istoriia, filologiia*, No. 2 (26) (1992): 45–50.

Kamoliddin, Shamsiddin. 'The Notion of Ethnogenesis in the Ethnic Atlas of Uzbekistan.' *Archeology & Anthropology of Eurasia*, Vol. 44, No. 4 (Spring 2006).

Karamshoev, Dodkhudo. 'Polemika o Pamire.' *Pamir*, No. 6 (1991): 100–18.

Karimova, S. E. 'Meditsinskoe obsluzhivanie trudiashikhsia Tadzhikistana (60–80-e gody).' *Izvestiia AN RT. Seriia: vostokovedenie, istorii, filologiia*, No. 2 (26) (1992): 38–44.

Karpat, Kemal. 'The Old and New Central Asia.' *Central Asian Survey*, Vol. 12, No. 4 (1993): 415–25.

Karpov, A. 'Skilled Labor Leaves the Republic.' *Izvestiia* (5 August 1990): 2. In *The Russian Press Digest* (5 August 1990).

Karpov, Aleksandr. 'Dushanbe: Rumors Spark Riots, Deaths.' *Izvestia* (13 February 1990): 8. In *The Current Digest of the Post-Soviet Press*, Vol. XLII, No. 7 (1990): 12.

Karpov, Aleksandr. 'Tajikistan: There Was Shooting in the Capital, and Now There's Shooting in the Provinces.' *Izvestia* (11 June 1992): 2. In *The Current Digest of the Post-Soviet Press*, Vol. XLIV, No. 23 (8 July 1992).

Karpov, Aleksandr, and Otakhon Latifi. 'Actions of Dushanbe Garrison Command Deemed Absolutely Correct.' *Izvestiya* (13 May 1992). In *BBC Summary of World Broadcasts—Former Soviet Union*, 1380 (14 May 1992): C1/2-3.

Karpov, Alexander. 'The Clergy is Outside [Political] Parties.' *Izvestiia* (25 September 1990): 2. In *The Russian Press Digest* (25 September 1992).

Kassymbekova, Botakoz. 'Humans as Territory: Forced Resettlement and the Making of Soviet Tajikistan, 1920–38.' *Central Asian Survey*, Vol. 30, Nos 3–4 (2011): 349–70.

Khan, M. Iqbal. 'Central Asia: Islamic Education and Culture.' *The Muslim World League Journal*, Vol. 23, No. 10 (March 1996): 43–6.

Khodjibaeva, Moukhabbat. 'Television and the Tajik Conflict.' *Central Asia Monitor*, No. 1 (1999).

Khoja, Sharaf. 'Uzbekistan: Friendship Gains Victory in Government's Struggle against Corruption.' *Russia and the Moslem World*, No. 10 (1994): 41–5.

Kholopov, Bronislav. 'Pamir vstupaet v dialog.' *Druzhba narodov*, No. 1 (1981): 176–201.

Khudonazar, Anaita. 'The Other.' *Berkeley Program in Soviet and Post-Soviet Studies Working Paper Series* (2004).

Khudonazarov, Davlat. 'Tadzhikskii rezhisser v dalnem zarubezh'e.' *Iskusstvo kino*, No. 7 (1994): 41–3.

Knysh, Alexander. 'A Clear and Present Danger: "Wahhabism" as a Rhetorical Foil.' *Die Welt des Islams*, Vol. 44, No. 1 (2004).

Korostelina, Karina. 'The System of Social Identities in Tajikistan: Early Warning and Conflict Prevention.' *Communist and Post-Communist Studies*, No. 40 (2007).

Koroteeva, V., L. Perepelkin and O. Shkaratan. 'Ot biurokraticheskogo tsentralizma k ekonomicheskoi integratsii suverennykh respublik.' *Kommunist*, No. 15 (October 1988): 22–33.

Kruhilin, A. 'These Days Hundreds of Russians are Leaving the Tajik Capital— Forever.' *Literaturnaya Gazeta* (28 February 1990). In *BBC Summary of World Broadcasts—Former Soviet Union*, 0713 (15 March 1990): B/1.

Kruzhilin, A. 'Dushanbe: The Cost of Fears.' *Literaturnaya gazeta* (14 March 1990): 11. In *The Russian Press Digest* (14 March 1990).

Laruelle, Marlene. 'The Return of the Aryan Myth: Tajikistan in Search of a Secularized National Ideology.' *Nationalities Papers*, Vol. 35, No. 1 (2007).

Lashuk, L. P. 'Opyt tipologii etnicheskikh obschnostei srednevekovykh tiurok i mongolov.' *Sovetskaia Etnografiia*, No. 1 (1968).

Leitzel, Jim, Clifford Gaddy and Michael Alexeev. 'Mafiosi and Matrioshki: Organised Crime and Russian Reform.' *The Brookings Review*, Vol. 13, No. 1 (Winter 1995): 26–9.

Lenshin, I. A. 'Proizvodstvennyi apparat Tadzhikistana: sostoianie i vozmozhnosti sovershenstvovaniia.' *Izvestiia AN TSSR. Seriia: filosofiia, ekonomika, pravovedenie*, No. 3 (23) (July–September 1991): 38–46.

LeVine, Steve. 'Communist Old Guard Turns the Tables on Moslems in Tajikistan: A Setback for Islamic Militants.' *Financial Times* (26 November 1992): 4.

Lifshits, Vadim. 'Politicheskaia situatsiia v Tadzhikistane (leto 1993).' *Rossiia i musulmanskii mir*, No. 10 (1993): 35–45.

Likhanov, Dmitri. 'Organised Crime in Central Asia.' *Telos*, Vol. 75 (Spring 1988): 90–101.

Lipovsky, Igor. 'The Central Asian Cotton Epic.' *Central Asian Survey*, Vol. 14, No. 4 (1995): 529–42.

Lubin, Nancy. 'Central Asians Take Stock. Reform, Corruption, and Identity.' *Peaceworks*, No. 2 (February 1995). United States Institute of Peace.

McKay, James, and Frank Lewins. 'Ethnicity and the Ethnic Group: A Conceptual Analysis and Reformulation.' *Ethnic and Racial Studies*, Vol. 1, No. 4 (October 1978): 412–27.

Madigan, Charles M. 'Gorbachev Seeks Quick Action Against Rioting.' *Chicago Tribune* (15 February 1990): 5.

Malashenko, A. V. 'The Eighties: A New Political Start for Islam.' *Russian Politics and Law*, Vol. 31, No. 4 (1993): 25–38.

Maltsev, V. 'Territorialnyi khozraschet: ot raspredeleniia k obmenu.' *Vestnik statistiki*, No. 1 (1991): 8.

Marat, Erica. 'The State–Crime Nexus in Central Asia: State Weakness, Organized Crime, and Corruption in Kyrgyzstan and Tajikistan.' *Silk Road Paper* (October 2006).

Markowitz, Lawrence. 'How Master Frames Mislead: The Division and Eclipse of Nationalist Movements in Uzbekistan and Tajikistan.' *Ethnic and Racial Studies*, Vol. 32, No. 4 (2009).

'Materialy fevralsko-martovskogo plenuma TsK VKP(b) 1937g.' *Voprosy istorii*, No. 10 (1995): 3–28.

Matveeva, Anna. 'The Perils of Emerging Statehood: Civil War and State Reconstruction in Tajikistan.' *Crisis States Working Papers Series*, No. 2 (46) (2009).

Medvedev, Vladimir. 'Prazdnik obshchei bedy.' *Druzhba narodov*, No. 8 (1990): 197–222.

Medvedev, Vladimir. 'Nechaiannaia revolutsiia.' *Druzhba narodov*, No. 1 (1992): 131–76.

Medvedev, Vladimir. 'Basmachi—obrechennoe voinstvo.' *Druzhba narodov*, No. 8 (1992): 122–58.

Medvedev, Vladimir. 'Saga o Bobo Sangake, voine.' *Druzhba Narodov*, No. 6 (1993).

Mirzoev, R. K. 'Tanzimi inkishofi mintaqavi dar sharoiti iqtisodi bozargoni.' *Akhboroti Akademiyai fanhoi RSS Tojikiston. Seriyai falsafa, iqtisodiyot, huquqshinosi*, No. 3 (1991): 10–22.

Moghadam, Valentine M. 'Patriarchy and the Politics of Gender in Modernizing Societies: Iran, Pakistan and Afghanistan.' *South Asia Bulletin*, Vol. XIII, Nos 1–2 (1993): 122–33.

Monogarova, L. F. 'Iazgulemtsy Zapadnogo Pamira.' *Sovetskaia etnografiia*, No. 3 (1949): 89–108.

Monogarova, L. F. 'Struktura sovremennoi gorodskoi sem'i tadzhikov.' *Sovetskaia etnografiia*, No. 3 (1982): 13–26.

Muhabbatsho, Mazhabsho. 'Fojiai Uljaboev.' *Daryo*, Nos 1–2 (1995): 24–9.

Mukomel', Vladimir. 'Demograficheskie Posledstviia etnicheskikh i religional'nykh konfliktov v SNG.' *Naselenie & Obshchestvo*, No. 27 (April 1997).

Mukomel', Vladimir. 'Demographic Consequences of Ethnic and Regional Conflicts in the CIS.' *Russian Social Science Review*, Vol. 42, No. 3 (2001).

Murodov, O. 'Predstavleniia o devakh u tadzhikov srednei chasti doliny Zeravshana.' *Sovetskaiia etnografiia*, No. 1 (1973): 148–55.

Naby, Eden. 'Tajiks Reemphasize Iranian Heritage as Ethnic Pressures Mount in Central Asia.' *Report on the USSR*, Vol. 2, No. 7 (16 February 1990).

Naby, Eden. 'Tajik Political Legitimacy and Political Parties.' *Central Asia Monitor*, Vol. 1, No. 5 (1992).

Naby, Eden. 'Tajik Political Legitimacy and Political Parties.' *The Iranian Journal of International Affairs*, Vol. V, No. 1 (Spring 1993): 195–201.

Najmiddinov, Muteullo. 'Sudi jahon dar suhbati dono shinos…' *Tojikiston*, Nos 1–2 (January–February 1995): 12–16.

Narzikulov, Rustam. 'Dvulikii Ianus v serdtse Azii: nekotorye itogi 70-letnego razvitiia sredneaziatskikh respublik v sostave SSSR.' *Vostok*, No. 5 (1991): 121–9.

Nemenova, R. L. 'Slozhenie tadzhikskogo naseleniia Varzoba.' *Sovetskaia etnografiia*, No. 5 (1969): 31 42.

Niyazi, Aziz. 'Islam in Tajikistan: Tradition and Modernity.' *Religion, State and Society*, Vol. 26, No. 1 (1998).

Niyazi, Aziz. 'Migration, Demography and Socio-Ecological Processes in Tajikistan.' *JCAS Symposium Series*, Vol. 9 (2000): pp. 169–78.

Nourzhanov, Kirill. 'Alternative Social Institutions and the Politics of Neo-Patrimonialism in Tajikistan.' *Russian and Euro-Asian Economics Bulletin*, Vol. 5, No. 8 (August 1996): 1–9.

Nourzhanov, Kirill. 'Seeking Peace in Tajikistan: Who is the Odd Man Out?' *Central Asia Monitor*, No. 6 (1998).

Nourzhanov, Kirill. 'The Politics of History in Tajikistan: Reinventing the Samanids.' *Harvard Asia Quarterly*, Vol. 5, No. 1 (2001).

Nourzhanov, Kirill. 'Saviours of the Nation or Robber Barons? Warlord Politics in Tajikistan.' *Central Asian Survey*, Vol. 24, No. 2 (2005).

Nourzhanov, Kirill. 'Reassessing the Basmachi: Warlords without Ideology?' *Journal of South Asia and Middle East Studies*, Vol. XXXI, No. 3 (2008).

Nourzhanov, Kirill, and Amin Saikal. 'The New Kazakhstan: Has Something Gone Wrong?' *The World Today*, Vol. 50, No. 12 (1994): 225–9.

Olcott, Martha B. 'The Basmachi or Freemen's Revolt in Turkestan 1918–24.' *Soviet Studies*, Vol. XXXIII, No. 3 (July 1981): 352–69.

Olimov, M. 'Ob etnopoliticheskoi i konfessionalnoi situatsii v Tadzhikistane i veroiatnosti mezhetnicheskikh konfliktov.' *Vostok*, No. 2 (1994): 79–88.

Olimova, S., and M. Olimov. 'Obrazovannyi klass Tadzhikistana v peripetiiakh XX v.' *Vostok*, No. 5 (1991): 95–103.

Olimova, S., and M. Olimov. 'The Educated Class of Tajikistan in the Upheavals of the Twentieth Century.' *Russian Politics and Law*, Vol. 31, No. 4 (1993): 39–51.

'O rabote TsK Kompartii Tadzhikistana po vypolneniiu reshenii XXIII s'ezda KPSS.' *Partiinaia zhizn'*, No. 1 (January 1969): 3–8.

Orlowski, Lucjan T. 'Indirect Transfers in Trade among Former Soviet Union Republics: Sources, Patterns and Policy Responses in the Post-Soviet Period.' *Europe-Asia Studies*, Vol. 45, No. 6 (1993): 1001–24.

Orr, Michael. 'The Civil War in Tadjikistan.' *Jane's Intelligence Review* (April 1993): 181–4.

Orr, M. J. 'The Russian Garrison in Tajikistan: 201st Gatchina Twice Red Banner Motor Rifle Division.' *Conflict Studies Research Centre, Occasional Brief*, No. 85 (18 October 2001).

Panfilov, Oleg. 'Tajikistan: The Opposing Sides Open a Second Front.' *Nezavisimaia Gazeta* (22 September 1992): 3. In *The Current Digest of the Post-Soviet Press*, Vol. XLIV, No. 38 (21 October 1992).

Panfilov, Oleg. 'Tajikistan.' *Nezavisimaia gazeta* (30 April 1992). In *BBC Summary of World Broadcasts—Former Soviet Union*, 1371 (4 May 1992): B/3.

Panfilov, Oleg. 'Piat' let nazad v Dushanbe byla rasstreliana demonstratsiia.' *Nezavisimaia gazeta* (February 1995). Accessed online: <http://olegpanfilov. com/?p=1149>

Panico, Christopher J. 'Uzbekistan's Southern Diplomacy.' *Radio Free Europe/ Radio Liberty Research Report*, Vol. 2, No. 13 (26 March 1993): 39–45.

'Party Congress Finishes Up; Biographies of the 24 Politburo Members.' *The Current Digest of the Post-Soviet Press*, Vol. XLII, No. 36 (10 October 1990): 20.

Penati, Beatrice. 'The Reconquest of East Bukhara: The Struggle against the Basmachi as a Prelude to Sovietization.' *Central Asian Survey*, Vol. 26, No. 4 (2007).

Perry, John B. 'Tajik Literature: Seventy Years is Longer Than the Millenium.' *World Literature Today*, Vol. 70, No. 3 (Summer 1996): 571–88.

Pickvance, Katy. 'Social Movements in Hungary and Russia: The Case of Environmental Movements.' *European Sociological Review*, Vol. 13, No. 1 (May 1997): 35–54.

Pilman, L. 'Eshche odno postanovlenie?' *Orientiry*, No. 10 (1989): 2–5.

Pipes, Richard. 'The Forces of Nationalism.' *Problems of Communism*, Vol. XIII, No. 1 (January–February 1964): 1–6.

Poliakov, Iu. A. 'Vozdeistvie gosudarstva na demograficheskie protsessy v SSSR (1920–1930e gg.).' *Voprosy istorii*, No. 3 (1995).

Poliakov, Sergei. 'Politicheskii krizis v Tadzhikistane.' *Rossiia i musulmanskii mir*, No. 5 (1992): 44–8.

Polikarpov, Feliks. 'Tadzhikistan. Territoriia boli.' *Ogonek*, Nos 6–7 (1993): 8–9.

Ponomarev, Viktor '"The Bells of Hope".' *Pravda* (10 May 1990). In *BBC Summary of World Broadcasts—Former Soviet Union*, 0762 (12 May 1990): B/1.

Purdenko, V. A., M. D. Amanekov and O. N. Kulberdyeva. 'Problemy ekologii narodonaseleniia Turkmenistana.' *Vostok*, No. 6 (1992): 91–3.

Rabiyev, V. 'After the Trial: Going Nowhere.' *Kommunist Tadzhikistana* (12 February 1987): 3. In *The Current Digest of the Post-Soviet Press*, Vol. 39, No. 9 (1 April 1987).

Rabiyev, V. 'Into the Classroom with a Koran?' *Kommunist Tadzhikistana* (31 January 1987): 2.

Rahimov, R. R. 'K voprosu o sovremennykh tadzhiksko-uzbekskikh mezhnatsionalnykh otnosheniiakh.' *Sovetskaia etnografiia*, No. 1 (January–February 1991): 13–24.

'Recruitment and Resettlement of Workers from Tajikistan.' *Radio Liberty Research Bulletin*, No. 26 (3231) (29 June 1983): RL 247/83.

Reuters. 'President Keeps His Job as Tajikistan Creates Coalition.' *The Globe and Mail* (12 May 1992).

Reuters. 'Tajikistan Opposition Takes Control; President Flees as City in Chaos.' *The Globe and Mail* (8 May 1992).

'Rioting Out of Control in Soviet City; 37 Killed.' *St Louis Post-Dispatch* (14 February 1990): 1A.

Ro'i, Yaacov. 'The Islamic Influence on Nationalism in Soviet Central Asia.' *Problems of Communism*, No. 4 (July–August 1990): 49–64.

Ro'i, Yaacov. 'Central Asia Riots and Disturbances: Causes and Context.' *Central Asia Survey*, Vol. 10, No. 3 (1991).

Rotar, Igor. 'Voina bez pobeditelei.' *Nezavisimaia Gazeta* (13 September 1992).

Rotar, Igor. 'Myths and Prejudice across the FSU.' *Russia and Eurasia Review*, Vol. 1, No. 14 (17 December 2002).

Rotar, Igor. 'View Central Asia through the Eyes of Journalist Igor Rotar.' *Ferghana News Information Agency* (26 April 2011). Accessed online May 2011: <http://enews.fergananews.com/article.php?id=2708>

Rozenfeld, A. Z. 'Materialy po etnografii i perezhitkam drevnikh verovanii tadzhikoiazychnogo naseleniia Sovetskogo Badakhshana.' *Sovetskaia etnografiia*, No. 3 (1970): 114–19.

Rubin, Barnett R. 'The Fragmentation of Tajikistan.' *Survival*, Vol. 35, No. 4 (1993): 71–91.

Rubin, Barnett R. 'Central Asian Wars and Ethnic Conflicts—Rebuilding Failed States.' *United Nations Human Development Report Office Occasional Paper* (2004).

Ruby, Walter. 'Tajik President Creates Guard to Crush Protests; Democratic and Muslim Opposition Denounce "Leninabad mafia".' *Christian Science Monitor* (6 May 1992).

Rush, Myron. 'Fortune and Fate.' *The National Interest*, No. 31 (Spring 1993): 19–25.

Rutkevich, M. N. 'Obostrenie natsionalnykh otnoshenii v SSSR.' *Sotsiologicheskie issledovaniia*, No. 1 (1991): 27–39.

Ryckman, Larry. 'Tajik President Appeals for Peace; Opponents Control Capital.' *The Associated Press* (8 May 1992).

Rywkin, Michael. 'The Impact of Socio-Economic Change and Demographic Growth on National Identity and Socialisation.' *Central Asian Survey*, Vol. 3, No. 3 (1985): 79–99.

Safaev, Sodyq. 'A Triumph of Gradualism.' *Transitions*, Vol. 4, No. 2 (July 1997): 98–100.

Safarova, Saodat. 'Vyzov, broshennyi zhizni.' *Pamir*, No. 8 (1988): 137–45.

Salimpur, Mirzoi. 'Infarkti savvumi KPSS.' *Charoghi ruz*, No. 4 (July 1991).

Salimpur, Mirzoi. 'Shohi mu'allaq.' *Charoghi ruz*, No. 20 (41) (1992): 2.

Sammakia, Nejla. 'Tajik Government Extends Arms Deadline, Tales of Killings Mount.' *The Associated Press* (28 December 1992).

Sautin, N. 'Emergency Situation: Not Force but Dialogue Decides.' *Pravda* (18 February 1990): 3. In *The Current Digest of the Post-Soviet Press*, Vol. XLII, No. 7 (21 March 1990): 14.

Sautin, N. 'The City Has Become Calmer.' *Pravda* (20 February 1990): 6. In *The Current Digest of the Post-Soviet Press* (28 March 1990): 25.

Savchenkov, N. 'Vremia ne zhdet.' *Druzhba narodov*, No. 3 (1984): 165–70.

Schoeberlein-Engel, John. 'Conflicts in Tajikistan and Central Asia: The Myth of Ethnic Animosity.' *Harvard Middle Eastern and Islamic Review*, Vol. 1, No. 2 (1994).

Schoeberlein-Engel, John. 'The Prospects for Uzbek National Identity.' *Central Asia Monitor*, No. 2 (1996).

Schoeberlein-Engel, John. 'Shifting Ground: How the Soviet Regime Used Resettlement to Transform Central Asian Society and the Consequences of this Policy Today.' *JCAS Symposium Series*, No. 9 (2000).

Schwartz, Charles A. 'Corruption and Political Development in the USSR.' *Comparative Politics*, Vol. II, No. 4 (July 1979): 425–43.

Seliunin, Vasily. 'Bremia deistvii.' *Perestroika*, Vol. 5 (1990): 162–217.

Sengupta, Anita. 'Imperatives of National Territorial Delimitation and the Fate of Bukhara.' *Central Asian Survey*, Vol. 19, Nos 3–4 (2000).

Shahrani, M. Nazif. '"From Tribe to Umma": Comments on the Dynamics of Identity in Muslim Soviet Central Asia.' *Central Asian Survey*, Vol. 3, No. 3 (1984).

Shakhov, Anvar. 'Why Tadzhiks Kill Tadzhiks? Regional and Ethnic Background of the Conflict.' *Russia and the Moslem World*, No. 10 (1994): 35–41.

Shams. 'Nist bod Gulrukhsor!' *Haft ganj*, No. 19 (31) (1992).

Shanker, Thom. 'Afghans Aren't Defeated; They're Being Remolded.' *Chicago Tribune* (3 August 1986): 4.

Shkaratan, O. I., and L. S. Perepelkin. 'Ekonomicheskii rost i natsionalnoe razvitie.' *EKO*, No. 10 (1988).

Shoismatulloev, Sh. 'Stanovlenie molodoi sem'i.' *Izvestiia Akademii nauk Respubliki Tadzhikistan. Seriia: filosofiia i pravovedenie*, No. 3 (1992): 27–34.

Shukurov, Muhammadjon. 'Nazare ba tahavvoli prinsiphoi istilohsozii tojiki.' *Akhboroti Akademiyai Fanhoi RSS Tojikiston. Seriyai sharqshinosi, tarikh, zabonshinosi*, No. 4 (24) (1991): 3–9.

Slezkine, Yuri. 'The Fall of Soviet Ethnography, 1928–38.' *Current Anthropology*, Vol. 32, No. 4 (1991).

Slezkine, Yuri. 'The USSR as a Communal Apartment, or How a Socialist State Promoted Ethnic Particularism.' *Slavic Review*, Vol. 53, No. 2 (1994).

Smirnov, Iuri. 'Strannyi islam.' *Pamir*, No. 2 (1988): 104–25.

Smith, Gordon B. 'Procuracy, Citizens' Rights and Legal Reform.' *Columbia Journal of Transnational Law*, Vol. 28 (1990).

Smith, Grant R. 'Tajikistan: The Rocky Road to Peace.' *Central Asian Survey*, Vol. 18, No. 2 (1999).

'Soobshchenie komissii prezidiuma Verkhovnogo Soveta Tadzhikskoi SSR po proverke sobytii 12–14 Fevralia 1990 g. v Dushanbe.' *Sogdiana* [Moscow], No. 3 (October 1990) (Special issue): 2–8.

'Speech by First Secretary K. M. Makhkamov to the 24th Congress of the Tajikistan Lenin Communist Youth League.' *Kommunist Tadzhikistana* (22 February 1987): 2, 5. In *The Current Digest of the Post-Soviet Press*, Vol. XXXIX, No. 9 (1 April 1987): 9.

Splidsboel-Hansen, Flemming. 'The Outbreak and Settlement of Civil War: Neo-Realism and the Case of Tajikistan.' *Civil Wars*, Vol. 2, No. 4 (1999).

Spolnikov, V., and L. Mironov. 'Islamskie fundamentalisty v borbe za vlast'.' *Aziia i Afrika segodnia*, No. 4 (1992): 24–31.

'Student Teachers in Dushanbe Violence.' *Komsomolskaya Pravda* (22 February 1990). In *BBC Summary of World Broadcasts—Former Soviet Union*, 0393 (24 February 1989): i.

Sultanov, Shamil. 'Dukh evraziitsa.' *Nash sovremennik*, No. 7 (1992): 143–8.

Suzi, Avo. 'Tadzhikskaia svadba.' *Pamir*, No. 5 (1988): 102–41.

Tadjbakhsh, Shahrbanou. 'National Reconciliation: The Imperfect Whim.' *Central Asian Survey*, Vol. 15, Nos 3–4 (December 1996): 325–48.

Tasar, Eren. 'The Central Asian Muftiate in Occupied Afghanistan, 1979–87.' *Central Asian Survey*, Vol. 30, No. 2 (2011).

Terliatskas, V., and V. Baldishis. 'Tak nuzhny li respublikanskie dengi?' *EKO*, No. 3 (1990): 135–9.

'Terminology and Glossary.' *Ethnic and Racial Studies*, Vol. 18, No. 4 (1986): i–iii.

Tett, Gillian. 'Poverty Brings Tajikistan's Political Tension to the Fore.' *Financial Times* (28 April 1992): International p. 2.

Tett, Gillian. 'Tajikistan Opposition Militia Seizes Control of Capital.' *Financial Times* (7 May 1992): 2.

Tett, Gillian. 'The Night that Friends Turned into Murderers.' *Financial Times* (19 February 1994): 13.

Tilley, Virginia. 'The Terms of the Debate: Untangling Language about Ethnicity and Ethnic Movements.' *Ethnic and Racial Studies*, Vol. 20, No. 3 (July 1997): 497–522.

Tishkov, Valery. '"Don't Kill Me, I'm a Kyrgyz!": An Anthropological Analysis of Violence in the Osh Ethnic Conflict.' *Journal of Peace Research*, Vol. 32, No. 2 (1995).

Tishkov, V. 'O prirode etnicheskogo konflikta.' *Svobodnaia mysl*, No. 4 (1993): 4–15.

Tolmacheva, M. A. 'The Muslim Woman in Soviet Central Asia.' *Central Asian Survey*, Vol. 12, No. 4 (1993): 531–48.

Tompson, W. J. 'Khrushchev and Gorbachev as Reformers: A Comparison.' *British Journal of Political Science*, Vol. 23, Part 1 (1993): 77–105.

Torjesen, Stina, Christina Wille and S. Neil MacFarlane. 'Tajikistan's Road to Stability: Reduction in Small Arms Proliferation and Remaining Challenges.' *An Occasional Paper of the Small Arms Survey*, No. 17 (2005).

Treisman, Daniel. 'The Politics of Intergovernmental Transfers in Post-Soviet Russia.' *British Journal of Political Science*, Vol. 26, Part 3 (July 1996): 299–335.

Tultseva, L. A. 'O nekotorykh sotsialno-etnicheskikh aspektakh razvitiia obriadovo-prazdnichnoi kultury v Uzbekistane.' *Sovetskaia etnografiia*, No. 5 (1984): 15–24.

Turajonzoda, Akbar. 'Tajikistan—Politics, Religion, and Peace: A View from the Opposition.' *Problems of Post-Communism* (July–August 1995): 24–8.

Turner, R. 'Tajiks Have the Highest Fertility Rates in Newly Independent Central Asia.' *Family Planning Perspectives*, Vol. 25, No. 3 (1993).

Tursunzod, Akbar. 'Rushdi milli: tariqati Tojikona.' *Tojikiston*, Nos 5–6 (1994): 4–5.

Uliakhin, V. N. 'Mnogoukladnost v sovetskoi i zarubezhnoi Azii.' *Vostok*, No. 5 (1991): 129–41.

Umnov, A. Iu. 'Islamskii fundamentalizm na Srednem Vostoke.' *Vestnik moskovskogo universiteta Seriia 13 'Vostokovedenie'*, No. 3 (1994): 46–51.

Velikhov, E. 'Nel'zia taschit' liudei na krest—eto kazhdyi reshaet sam.' *Glasnost*, No. 42 (October 1991): 3.

Verdery, Katherine. 'Whither "Nation" and "Nationalism"?' *Daedalus*, Vol. 122, No. 3 (Summer 1993): 37–46.

Vorobiova, A. V. 'Vinovat li rost naseleniia?' *Vostok*, No. 5 (1991): 155–61.

Vujacic, Veljko. 'Historical Legacies, Nationalist Mobilisation, and Political Outcomes in Russia and Serbia: A Weberian View.' *Theory and Society*, Vol. 25, No. 6 (December 1996): 763–801.

Vybornova, V. V., and E. A. Dunaeva. 'Nereshennye protivorechiia kak istochnik mezhnatsionalnykh konfliktov.' *Izvestiia AN TSSR. Seriia: Filosofiia i pravovedenie*, No. 3 (1992): 35–46.

Vydrin, Andrei. 'Fitrat, Polivanov, Stalin i drugie.' *Zvezda Vostoka*, Nos 5–6 (1994): 150–72.

Warren, M. 'Coalition Hopes Raised in Tajikistan.' *Herald Sun* (12 May 1992).

Wright, Robin. 'The Artful Exile from Dushanbe: First Davlat Khudonazarov Lost the Presidency of His Beloved Tajikistan, Then He Lost Everything Else. Forced into Exile, the Charismatic Filmmaker and Politician May Be His Country's Great Hope for Unity.' *Los Angeles Times* (15 May 1994).

Zaslavsky, Victor. 'Nationalism and Democratic Transition in Postcommunist Societies.' *Daedalus*, Vol. 121, No. 2 (Spring 1992): 97–121.

Zenkovich, Viacheslav. 'Dushanbe: khronika semi dnei.' *Dialog*, No. 7 (1990): 64–73.

Zimanas, G. 'Mestnichestvo—vredny perezhitok.' *Kommunist*, No. 2 (1963): 78–85.

Zulfikarov, Timur. 'Samoe bolshoe more na zemle.' *Literaturnaia gazeta* (13 March 1996): 7.

3. Dissertations and Theses

Boboyorov, Hafiz Kholiqovich. *Kinship and Islam: The Role of Collective Identities in Shaping the Institutional Order of Patronage in Southern Tajikistan.* PhD Thesis: Rheinischen Friedrich-Wilhelms-Universität zu Bonn, 2011.

Fumagalli, Matteo. *The Dynamics of Uzbek Ethno-Political Mobilization in Kyrgyzstan and Tajikistan: 1991–2003.* PhD Thesis: University of Edinburgh, 2005.

Kilavuz, Idil Tuncer. *Understanding Violent Conflict: A Comparative Study of Tajikistan and Uzbekistan.* PhD Thesis: Indiana University, 2007.

Larson, Bryant Leroy. *The Moslems of Soviet Central Asia: Soviet and Western Perceptions of a Growing Political Problem.* PhD Thesis: University of Minnesota, 1983.

Markowitz, Lawrence. *Collapsed and Prebendal States in Post-Soviet Eurasia: Cross-Regional Determinants of State Formation in Tajikistan and Uzbekistan.* PhD Thesis: University of Wisconsin–Madison, 2005.

Nekbakhtshoev, Navruz R. *Clan Politics: Explaining the Persistence of Subethnic Divisions in Tajikistan: Comparative Approach.* MA Thesis: Duquesne University, 2006.

Rowe, William Campbell, jr. *On the Edge of Empires: The Hisor Valley of Tajikistan.* PhD Thesis: University of Texas at Austin, 2002.

Schoeberlein-Engel, John. *Identity in Central Asia: Construction and Contention in the Conceptions of 'Uzbek,' 'Tajik,' 'Muslim,' 'Samarqandi' and Other Groups.* PhD Thesis: Harvard University, 1994.

Tett, Gillian. *Ambiguous Alliances: Marriage and Identity in a Muslim Village in Soviet Tajikistan.* PhD Thesis: University of Cambridge, 1996.

Zartman, Jonathan K. *Political Transition in Central Asian Republics: Authoritarianism versus Power-Sharing.* PhD Thesis: University of Denver, 2004.

4. Web Sites and Online Long-Format Articles

'100 Solagii Rakhim Jalil: Ohanraboi Millat.' (n.d.) Accessed online: <http://www.abdulov.tj/bk15_1.php>

Abdrakhmanova, Ainagul et al. 'Is Uzbek Guerrilla Force Planning Homecoming?' *IWPR Special Report* (18 November 2009). Accessed online November 2012: <http://goo.gl/7i2Fz>

Abdulov, Karim. 'Tojikiston va Chin.' (n.d.) Accessed online February 2011: <http://www.abdulov.tj/bk19_1.php>

Abdulov, Karim. '100 Solagii Rahim Jalil: Ohanraboi Millat.' (n.d.) Accessed online February 2011: <http://www.abdulov.tj/bk15_1.php>

Akhmedov, Said. 'Konflikty v Tadzhikistane: Prichiny i Posledstviia.' In *Etnicheskie i regionalnye konflikty v Yevrazii. Volume 1: Tsentralnaia Aziia i Kavkaz*, edited by Alexei Malashenko, Bruno Coppieters and Dmitri Trenin. Moscow: Ves Mir, 1997. Accessed online December 2012: <http://poli.vub.ac.be/publi/etni-1/akhmedov.htm>

Borjian, Habib. 'Kulab.' In *Encyclopedia Iranica* (July 2005). Accessed online November 2008: <http://www.iranica.com/articles/kulab>

Borjian, Habib. 'Kurgantepe.' In *Encyclopedia Iranica* (July 2005). Accessed online November 2008: <http://www.iranica.com/articles/kurgan-tepe>

Bosworth, C. E., and B. G. Fragner. 'Tādjīk.' In *Encyclopaedia of Islam*, 2nd edn, edited by P. Bearman, Th. Bianquis, C. E. Bosworth, E. van Donzel and W. P. Heinrichs. Brill Online (2009). Accessed online November 2008: <http://brillonline.nl/>

Colville, Rupert. 'Rebuilding Socialism.' *Refugees Magazine*, No. 98 (1 December 1994). Accessed online December 2010: <http://www.unhcr.org/print/3b5421984.html>

Conciliation Resources. 'Profiles: Khoji Akbar Turajonzoda.' (n.d.) Accessed online March 2009: <http://www.c-r.org/our-work/accord/tajikistan/profiles.php>

Conciliation Resources. 'Profiles: President Emomali Rakhmonov.' (n.d.) Accessed online March 2009: <http://www.c-r.org/our-work/accord/tajikistan/profiles.php>

Conciliation Resources. 'Profiles: Said Abdullo Nuri.' (n.d.) Accessed online March 2009: <http://www.c-r.org/our-work/accord/tajikistan/profiles.php>

Evraziiskii monitor. 'Vospriyatie naseleniem novykh nezavisimykh gosudarstv istorii sovetskogo postsovetskogo periodov 11-ya volna, Aprel'–Mai 2009 g.' *Osnovnye rezul'taty Al'bom diagram* (30 June 2009). Accessed online May 2013: <http://www.eurasiamonitor.org/rus/research/event-158.html>

Ianovskaia, Mariia. 'Dushanbe-1990: russkii vzgliad.' *Fergana News Agency* (1 March 2010). Accessed online May 2013: <http://www.fergananews.com/article.php?id=6484>

Kucera, Joshua. 'Why Russia Fears US Afghan Plan.' *The Diplomat* (18 October 2011). Accessed online November 2012: <http://goo.gl/IogHL>

Loy, Thomas. 'From the Mountains to the Lowlands: The Soviet Policy of "Inner-Tajik" Resettlement.' *Internet-Zeitschrift für Kulturwissenschaften*, No. 16 (August 2006), 13.2. *Issues of Internal and External Migration in Post-Soviet Central Asia*. Accessed online February 2011: <http://www.inst.at/trans/16Nr/13_2/loy16.htm>

Mirzobekova, Ramziya, and Daler Gufronov. 'Trevozhnii oktiabr 92-go.' *Asia-Plus* (30 October 2009). Accessed online September 2010: <http://www.asiaplus.tj/articles/96/4191.html>

Nourzhanov, Kirill. 'Alternative Social Institutions and the Politics of Neo-Patrimonialism in Tajikistan.' *Russian and Euro-Asian Bulletin* (August 1996). Accessed online June 2008: <http://www.cerc.unimelb.edu.au/bulletin/1996.htm>

Olimova, S., and M. Olimov. 'The Islamic Renaissance Party.' *Conciliation Resources* (n.d.). Accessed online March 2009: <http://www.c-r.org/our-work/accord/tajikistan/islamic-renaissance-party.php>

Ol'khovaia, N., R. Iskanderova, A. Balashov, et al. 'Raspad imperii: Dushanbe.' *Dikoe pole*, No. 6 (2004). Accesed online May 2013 via Archive.org: <http://www.dikoepole.org/numbers_journal.php?id_txt=265>

President.tj. 'Emomali Rahmon: Prezidenti Jumhurii Tojikiston.' Official web site of the President of Tajikistan (n.d.). Accessed online July 2010: <http://www.president.tj/tarjumai_hol.htm>

'Qahhor Mahkamov: KGB va havodisi bahmanmoh.' *BBC Persian* (9 February 2010). Accessed online: <http://www.bbc.co.uk/tajik/news/2011/02/110209_if_mahkamov.shtml>

Rasul-zade, Tilav, and Mariia Yanovskaia. 'Ochevidtsy Dushanbe-1990: Pogromy cprovotsirovali kommunisty—KGB-shniki.' *Fergana News Agency* (22 February 2010). Accessed online May 2013: <http://www.fergananews. com/articles/6478>

Sangakzoda, Guljahon. 'Sangak Safarov: Peshvoi fronti khalqiro jahor soat mekushtand.' *SSSR*, No. 30 (27 July 2009). Accessed online September 2010: <http://asiaplus.tj/tj/articles/50/3896.html>

Starikov, V. 'I khotia zhivymi do kontsa doleteli.' *Vyatskii nablyudatel'*, No. 5 (5 January 1999). Accessed online: <http://www.nabludatel.ru/ numers/1999/5/13.htm>

Starikov, V. 'I khotia zhivymi do kontsa doleteli [Part 2].' *Vyatskii nablyudatel'*, No. 6 (February 1999). Accessed online May 2013: <http://www.nabludatel. ru/numers/1999/6/7.htm>

Zviagelskaya, Irina. *The Tajik Conflict*. Reading, UK: Ithaca Press, 1997. Accessed online January 2009: <http://www.ca-c.org/dataeng/st_09_zvjag.shtml>

Yuldoshev, Avaz. 'Massive Riots in Dushanbe in February 1990 Masterminded by KGB, Says IRP Deputy Leader.' *ASIA-Plus* (12 February 2013). Accessed online: <http://news.tj/en/news/massive-riots-dushanbe-february-1990-masterminded-kgb-says-irp-deputy-leader>

5. Newspapers and Wire Services

Russian and Tajik Newspapers

Adabiyot va san'at

Adolat

Argumenty i fakty

Biznes i politika

Charoghi ruz

Glasnost

Golos Tadzhikistana

Haft ganj

Haqiqati Kolkhozobod

Hidoyat

Izvestiia

Javononi Tojikiston

Kazakhstanskaia pravda

Kommersant-Daily

Kommunist Tadzhikistana

Komsomolets Tadzhikistana

Komsomolskaia Pravda

Krasnaia zvezda

Literaturnaiia gazeta

Najot

Nezavisimaia gazeta

Payomi Dushanbe

Pravda

Pravda Vostoka

Rabochaia tribuna

Rastokhez

Rohi Lenini

Russkaia mysl

Sadoi mardum

Sogdiana

Tajik-Press

Tirozi jahon

Tojikistoni Soveti

Vechernii Dushanbe

Vek

News Agencies and Wire Services

Agence-France Press

The Associated Press

Inter Press Service

Interfax

ITAR-Tass

Postfactum

Reuters

RIA Novosti

6. Foreign-Language Broadcast, News Agency and Periodical Summaries

BBC Summary of World Broadcasts—Former Soviet Union (*BBC SWB SU*)

The Current Digest of the Post-Soviet Press

The Russian Press Digest

7. Archives, Media and Transcripts

Archive of the Information Department of the Ministry of Foreign Affairs of the Republic of Tajikistan.

Personal archive of the Spokesperson of the President of the Republic of Tajikistan, Mr Zafar Saidov.

Mesiats ushcherbnoi luny. Documentary film. Dushanbe: Tadzhikfilm, 1990.

Narod i politika. (Tadzhikistan: iiun' 1992 goda.). A confidential analytical report prepared for the Cabinet of Ministers of Tajikistan. Typewritten document dated 22 July 1992 and signed by Professor V. Boikov of the Russian Academy of Social Sciences.

Promotional trailers of Davlat Khudonazarov during the 1991 Presidential Campaign. Courtesy of the Deputy Director of the Tajik Film Authority, Mr Safar Haqdod.

Sh. Yusupov. 'Neobkhodimost' sozdaniia Demokraticheskoi partii Tadzhikistana i ee blizhaishie zadachi.' Transcript of Shodmon Yusuf's speech at the Constituent Conference of the DPT, 10 August 1990. Courtesy of Dr V. M. Zaichenko, Dushanbe.

Video recording of the XVI Session of the Supreme Soviet of Tajikistan, November 1992. Courtesy of the Chairman of the State Committee for Cinematography of the Republic of Tajikistan, Mr Sayf Rahimov.

Made in the USA
San Bernardino, CA
16 September 2016